Mutual Funds and Exchange-Traded Funds

FINANCIAL MARKETS AND INVESTMENTS SERIES
H. Kent Baker and Greg Filbeck, Series Editors

Portfolio Theory and Management
Edited by H. Kent Baker and Greg Filbeck

Public Real Estate Markets and Investments
Edited by H. Kent Baker and Peter Chinloy

Private Real Estate Markets and Investments
Edited by H. Kent Baker and Peter Chinloy

Investment Risk Management
Edited by H. Kent Baker and Greg Filbeck

Private Equity: Opportunities and Risks
Edited by H. Kent Baker, Greg Filbeck, and Halil Kiymaz

Mutual Funds and Exchange-Traded Funds: Building Blocks to Wealth
Edited by H. Kent Baker, Greg Filbeck, and Halil Kiymaz

Mutual Funds and Exchange-Traded Funds

BUILDING BLOCKS TO WEALTH

EDITED BY H. KENT BAKER

GREG FILBECK

and

HALIL KIYMAZ

OXFORD
UNIVERSITY PRESS

OXFORD
UNIVERSITY PRESS

Oxford University Press is a department of the University of Oxford.
It furthers the University's objective of excellence in research, scholarship,
and education by publishing worldwide. Oxford is a registered trade mark
of Oxford University Press in the UK and in certain other countries

Published in the United States of America by
Oxford University Press
198 Madison Avenue, New York, NY 10016,
United States of America

Cataloging-in-Publication Data is on file at the Library of Congress.

9780190207434

9 8 7 6 5 4 3 2 1

Printed in the United States of America on acid-free paper

Contents

List of Figures

List of Tables

Acknowledgments

"In the end, what makes a book valuable is not the paper it's printed on, but the thousands of hours of work by dozens of people who are dedicated to creating the best possible reading experience for you."
—John Green

Mutual Funds and Exchange-Traded Funds: Building Blocks to Wealth represents the work of many people all with the singular purpose of creating the most informative book possible on the subject. The list of contributors is long but we want to single out the following, all of whom merit special recognition. The reviewers of our initial book proposal offered useful suggestions and guidance for improving the book. The contributing authors provided multiple revisions of their work resulting in high quality and in-depth chapters. Our partners at Oxford University Press all contributed substantially to the publication of this book especially Scott Parris (Editor) and Cathryn Vaulman (Assistant Editor). Other important contributors included Cherline Daniel (Senior Project Manager), Lynn Childress (Copyeditor), and Claudie Peterfreund (Indexer). We also appreciate the support of our respective institutions—the Kogod School of Business at American University, the Black School of Business at Penn State Behrend, and the Crummer Graduate School of Business at Rollins College. Finally, our families have been highly supportive throughout the project. We dedicate this book to our families: Linda and Rory Baker; Janis, Aaron, Kyle, and Grant Filbeck; and Nilgun and Tunc Kiymaz.

About the Editors

H. Kent Baker CFA, CMA, is University Professor of Finance in the Kogod School of Business at American University. Professor Baker is an author or editor of 25 books including *Investment Risk Management, Investor Behavior: The Psychology of Financial Planning and Investing, Market Microstructure of Emerging and Developed Markets, Behavioral Finance: Investors, Corporations, and Markets, Portfolio Theory and Management*, and *Survey Research in Corporate Finance.* As one of the most prolific finance academics, he has published more than 160 refereed articles in such journals as the *Journal of Finance, Journal of Financial and Quantitative Analysis, Financial Management, Financial Analysts Journal*, and *Journal of Portfolio Management.* He has consulting and training experience with more than 100 organizations. Professor Baker holds a BSBA from Georgetown University; M.Ed., MBA, and DBA degrees from the University of Maryland; and an MA, MS, and two PhDs from American University.

Greg Filbeck CFA, FRM, and CAIA, holds the Samuel P. Black III Professor of Finance and Risk Management at Penn State Erie, the Behrend College, where he serves as the Associate Director of the Black School of Business and Department Chair for Finance and Economics. He formerly was Senior Vice-President of Kaplan Schweser and held academic appointments at Miami University (Ohio) and the University of Toledo, where he was the Associate Director of the Center for Family Business. Professor Filbeck is an author or editor of 7 books and has published more than 80 refereed academic journal articles that have appeared in journals such as *Financial Analysts Journal, Financial Review*, and *Journal of Business, Finance, and Accounting.* He conducts consulting and training worldwide for candidates for the Chartered Financial Analyst (CFA), Financial Risk Manager (FRM™), and Chartered Alternative Investment Adviser (CAIA®) designations. Professor Filbeck holds a BS from Murray State University, an MS from Penn State University, and a DBA from the University of Kentucky.

Halil Kiymaz CFA, is Bank of America Professor of Finance in the Crummer Graduate School of Business at Rollins College. He held positions at Bilkent University, University of Houston–Clear Lake, IMADEC University, East Chinese University of Science and Technology, Copenhagen Business, Ada University, and Kadir Has University. Professor Kiymaz has published more than 75 articles in scholarly and practitioner journals and co-edited 4 books. His research has appeared in the *Journal* *of Banking and Finance, Financial Review, Global Finance Journal, Journal of Applied Finance, Journal of Economics and Finance, Review of Financial Economics, Quarterly Journal of Business and Economics*, among others. He also serves on the editorial board of three journals and is the area editor of the *International Journal of Emerging Markets*. Professor Kiymaz has consulting and training experience with various governmental and public organizations such as the Central Bank of Turkey, Bankers Association, and Stalla. He received a BS from the Uludağ University and an MBA, MA, and PhD from the University of New Orleans.

About the Contributors

Rosa Adamo is Professor of Banking and Finance at the University of Calabria in Italy where she teaches ethical finance, financial intermediaries, and corporate banking. She is also Vice-Director of the School of "Dottorato" in Economic and Business Sciences and Vice-President of the Degree Course in Law at the University of Calabria. She is President of the CCT A017—Economic and Business Disciplines at the University of Calabria. Professor Adamo is member of the Italian Association of Scholars of Economics and Management of Financial Institutions and Markets (ADEIMF). In 2010, she received the Bernardino Telesio Award, Successful Calabrians. She is author of various articles and monographs on banking regulation and control, savers' protection, corporate finance and banking, financial inclusion, and ethical finance. She graduated with first-class honors in economic and social sciences from the University of Calabria. She also holds post-graduate degrees in finance from both the University of Naples and University of Florence.

Anna Agapova is an Associate Professor of Finance at Florida Atlantic University. Her primary research interests are investments, mutual funds and ETFs, financial markets, and corporate finance. Her work has been published in such journals as *Financial Management, Journal of Financial Markets, Financial Review, Journal of Portfolio Management, Journal of Applied Finance*, and *Journal of Index Investing*. She has received an outstanding paper award from the Eastern Finance Association and was a finalist in the Whitebox selected research search for the best financial research paper. She teaches graduate and undergraduate courses in investments and corporate finance. Previously, she taught at Georgia State University and Karaganda State Industrial University, Kazakhstan. She holds a BA in marketing from Karaganda State University and an MA in economics and a PhD in finance from Georgia State University.

Benjamin Aguilar CFA is a senior associate and leader of the mergers and acquisitions practice at Cathedral Consulting Group, LLC, which is a management and operational consulting firm that specializes in best business practices for small and medium private enterprises. As a senior associate, Mr. Aguilar is responsible for leading Cathedral's M&A clients in buy-side and sell-side transactions, company turnarounds, and debt/equity financings. He holds a BA in economics from the King's College.

Parvez Ahmed is a Professor of Finance at the Coggin College of Business, University of North Florida and serves as the Director of the Center for Sustainable Business Practices. He was named a U.S. Fulbright Scholar in 2009. Professor Ahmed previously taught at Penn State University–Harrisburg and the University of North Carolina at Charlotte where he was the founding faculty advisor for the student-managed investment fund. He has published in such journals as the *Journal of Portfolio Management, Financial Management, Journal of Banking and Finance, Journal of Investing, Journal of Wealth Management*, and *Financial Review*. He recently published a book titled *Mutual Funds: Fifty Years of Research Findings*. Professor Ahmed holds an MBA from Temple University and a PhD in finance from the University of Texas at Arlington.

Laura Andreu is an Associate Professor of Finance at the Economy and Business School of the University of Zaragoza and has taught courses in financial economics at that school since 2007. She was a visiting scholar at the Centre for Finance and Investment at Exeter University, Erasmus School of Economics, Finance Department at the University of Cologne, and Victoria University. Her research interests include asset management, behavioral finance, and collective investment portfolios such as mutual funds and pension funds. She has published in such journals as the *Journal of Financial Services Research, Quantitative Finance*, and *Review of Quantitative Finance and Accounting*. Professor Andreu received a degree in business administration and both an MA in accounting and finance and a PhD in finance from the University of Zaragoza.

Dimitris Andriosopoulos is a Senior Lecturer in Accounting and Finance at the University of Strathclyde. His expertise lies in the areas of corporate finance, closed-end funds, corporate governance, investments, mergers and acquisitions, and banking. He has published in such journals as the *Journal of Banking and Finance, Journal of Empirical Finance*, and *European Journal of Finance*. Professor Andriosopoulos is also a financial consultant and commodities broker. He holds an MBA and MSc in accounting from Suffolk University and a PhD in finance from Cass Business School.

Oreste Auleta is the Head of Wrapping and Product Management in Eurizon Capital SGR. After being in the economic consultancy sector in London, he entered the asset management industry where he held positions as head of third parties' fund selection and of multi-brand products' management, head of management of asset allocation global products, and head of multi-asset products' management. Mr. Oreste joined Eurizon Capital in 2010, where he was initially appointed Head of Asset Allocation and Manager Selection. He has served as Head of the Wrapping and Product Management area since 2011. He received a degree in business from La Sapienza University in Rome and an MS in quantitative economics from CORIPE Piemonte and an MS in economics from Birkbeck College in London.

Tamas Barko is a researcher and doctoral student at Tilburg University's CentER Graduate School and a research fellow at the Tilburg Sustainability Center. His research interests are corporate social responsibility, sustainable investments, investor activism, and corporate governance. He received a BA in business administration from the University of Pecs in Hungary and an MSc in finance from Tilburg University.

Tarik Bazgour is a Research Assistant and PhD candidate in finance at HEC Management School of the University of Liège. His dissertation focuses on asset allocation and performance evaluation under different market regimes. His interests include portfolio management, conditional performance evaluation, and market liquidity measurement. Mr. Bazgour has presented his research at several international conferences including the FMA European and Asian conferences and is currently working on the conditional market and liquidity timing skills of mutual fund managers during low and high volatility periods. He is an industrial engineer from the Mohammadia School of Engineering (Morocco) and holds an Advanced Master's degree in finance from the HEC Management School of the University of Liège, magna cum laude.

Michael Bianco is a finance industry professional and an investor relations consultant to publicly traded corporations. He works at NASDAQ in the firm's Corporate Solutions division as a specialist. Thomson Reuters acquired the division in 2013. Before joining Thomson Financial, Mr. Bianco was an investment advisor to high net worth individuals at a boutique brokerage firm. He has a BS in comprehensive science with minors in mathematics and business administration from Villanova University. He passed Level III of the CFA program and is awaiting the official awarding of the CFA charter.

Laurent Bodson is Affiliate Professor at HEC Management School of the University of Liège. Professor Bodson teaches courses in financial modeling and information technology as well as fixed-income securities and also presents executive seminars. He is also head of solutions of Gambit Financial Solutions S.A., a spin-off company of HEC Management School of the University of Liège that produces sophisticated software solutions for investor profiling, portfolio optimization, and risk management. His areas of expertise include portfolio and risk management. Professor Bodson has presented his research at many conferences and published in such journals as the *Journal of Empirical Finance* and *Journal of Financial Research*. He holds a PhD in finance from the University of Liège.

Alistair Byrne CFA, is Vice President and Senior Defined Contribution Strategist at State Street Global Advisors in London. Dr. Byrne previously held senior investment roles at Towers Watson and AEGON UK, as well as academic positions at the University of Strathclyde and the University of Edinburgh. He is a fellow at the Pensions Institute at Cass Business School in London and an Honorary Professor at the University of Edinburgh Business School. Dr. Byrne has published on defined contribution investment issues in the *Financial Analysts Journal* and *Journal of Portfolio Management*. He has a PhD in finance from the University of Strathclyde.

Han-Sheng Chen is an Assistant Professor at Southeastern Oklahoma State University. His research interests lie in the fields of investments and asset pricing, specifically in market efficiency and behavioral finance, volatility, and option-related issues. He has presented his research at various conferences. Professor Chen received a BS in statistics and an MBA in finance in Taiwan and has a PhD in finance from the University of Texas at Arlington.

Conrad S. Ciccotello is the Director of Wealth Management Programs in the Robinson College of Business at Georgia State University and the Executive Director of the Huebner Foundation. His research interests are in law and finance with an emphasis in financial intermediation and services. Professor Ciccotello is a Research Fellow in the TIAA-CREF Institute. He has more than 50 publications including articles in the *Journal of Financial Economics, Journal of Law and Economics, Journal of Financial and Quantitative Analysis*, and *Financial Analysts Journal*. His research has been cited in the Federal Register and entered into the record as Senate Banking Committee testimony. He has also been quoted in numerous publications including the *Wall Street Journal, New York Times*, and *Washington Post*. Professor Ciccotello serves as an independent director and audit committee chair for the Tortoise Capital Advisors Funds and for Corenergy Infrastructure Trust. He has a JD from Suffolk Law School and a PhD in finance from the Pennsylvania State University.

Sean Collins is Senior Director and Senior Economist with the Investment Company Institute (ICI), with responsibility for studying issues related to mutual fund trends, fees, and structure, and monitoring and analyzing a wide range of financial market issues that may affect registered investment companies. He began his career at the Federal Reserve Board in Washington, DC, spent five years as an economist with the Reserve Bank of New Zealand, and has been at the ICI since 2000. He received a BA in economics from Claremont McKenna College and a PhD in economics from the University of California, Santa Barbara.

Bruce A. Costa is a Professor of Finance and the Chair of the Accounting and Finance Department at the University of Montana. He served in the U.S. Navy for more than 13 years including tours as a test pilot and assistant navigator aboard the USS Saratoga during the Gulf War. His research focuses on the risk-adjusted returns of actively managed portfolios. He has published in such journals as the *Journal of Applied Finance, Journal of Multinational Financial Management, Global Finance Journal*, and *Financial Services Review*. Professor Costa has consulting experience with many businesses involving both financial and aviation-related matters. He serves on the Board of Directors for SG Long and Company, an investment advisory firm in Missoula, Montana. Professor Costa has a BS in industrial engineering/operations research from the University of Massachusetts–Amherst and a PhD in business administration with an emphasis in finance from Florida State University.

Jonathan Fletcher is a Professor of Finance at the University of Strathclyde. His research interests focus on issues in fund performance, asset pricing, and portfolio choice. He has published in a wide range of academic journals including the *Financial Analysts Journal, Journal of Banking and Finance, Journal of Empirical Finance, Journal of Financial Services Research, Journal of Financial Research, Journal of Business Finance and Accounting* among others. He is an Associate Editor of the *Financial Review*. Professor Fletcher holds an MA in accounting and economics from the University of Dundee and both an MSc and PhD in finance from the University of Strathclyde.

Mary Fletcher is a Lecturer in Accounting and Finance at the University of the West of Scotland. She has published several articles on U.K. closed-end funds and has presented her research at international conferences and symposiums. Her research interests involve closed-end funds and capital controls in financial markets. She holds an MSc and a PhD in finance from the University of Strathclyde.

Joseph A. Franco is Professor of Law at Suffolk University Law School in Boston. He teaches courses in securities regulation, investment management regulation, mergers and acquisitions, and corporations. His writing and research focus on issues affecting securities markets and investment companies. Professor Franco previously was an Assistant General Counsel with the U.S. Securities and Exchange Commission in Washington, DC, and practiced securities law in New York City. He is an independent trustee for a small series of quantitative factor-based ETFs. Professor Franco received a JD from Yale Law School, where he was a member of the *Yale Law Journal,* and also holds an MA in economics from Yale University.

Frendy is a PhD candidate at Nagoya University Graduate School of Economics where he received the Japanese Government Scholarship for Research Student (Postgraduate) Program. He previously worked as an audit associate in KPMG Indonesia. His research interests include corporate governance, audit quality, audit market competition, and financial disclosure. He has presented papers at international academic conferences and published in the *Journal of Contemporary Accounting and Economics* and *Gadjah Mada International Journal of Business.* He participated in an exchange student program in Hiroshima University of Economics and obtained a BS in economics with major in accounting from Universitas Gadjah Mada.

Robert Grohowski is a General Counsel with the Investment Adviser Association. Previously, he was Senior Counsel with the Investment Company Institute (ICI), with a primary responsibility for a wide range of issues arising under the Investment Company Act of 1940. Before joining the ICI in 1998, he was in private law practice with Kilpatrick & Cody (now Kilpatrick Townsend) in Atlanta and then with Sutherland, Asbill, & Brennan in Washington, DC. He received a BA in foreign affairs and a JD from University of Virginia, where he was a member for the editorial board for the *Virginia Journal of International Law.*

John A. Haslem is Professor Emeritus of Finance in the Robert H. Smith School of Business at the University of Maryland. He served as founding academic affairs dean and founding chair of the finance department. Professor Haslem received the Panhellenic Association's "Outstanding Teacher Award" for his first of a kind mutual funds course. He previously taught at the University of North Carolina and University of Wisconsin. His research has appeared in the *Journal of Finance, Journal of Business, Journal of Financial and Quantitative Analysis,* and *Journal of Money,* and *Credit and Banking* among others. He is an author and editor of six books including *Mutual Funds: Risk and Performance Analysis for Decision Making* and *Mutual Funds: Portfolio Structures: Analysis, Management, and Stewardship.* Professor Haslem served as consultant to the U.S. Department of Justice, NASA Goddard Space Flight Center, among others and currently serves on the board of judges of the William F. Sharpe Indexing Achievement Awards. He received an MBA and PhD from the University of North Carolina.

Sarah A. Holden is Senior Director of Retirement and Investor Research at the Investment Company Institute (ICI). Ms. Holden conducts and oversees research on the U.S. retirement market, retirement and tax policy, and investor demographics and behavior. She is responsible for analysis of 401(k) plan participant activity using data collected in a collaborative effort with the Employee Benefit Research Institute (EBRI), known as the EBRI/ICI Participant-Directed Retirement Plan Data Collection Project. She also analyzes the role of mutual funds in the retirement marketplace including defined contribution plan and IRA markets. She oversees the IRA Investor Database™, which contains data on more than 15 million IRA investors and allows analysis of IRA investors' contribution, rollover, conversion, and withdrawal activity, and asset allocation. She is also responsible for managing household survey research on a range of topics relevant to the fund industry and policy formation. Before joining the ICI, Ms. Holden worked as a staff economist in the Flow of Funds Section of the Research Division at the Federal Reserve Board. She graduated from Smith College, *cum laude*, and holds a PhD in economics from the University of Michigan.

Hunter M. Holzhauer is an Assistant Professor of Finance at the University of Tennessee–Chattanooga, where he teaches both graduate and undergraduate classes including corporate finance, investments, and behavioral finance. Professor Holzhauer has also taught at Penn State Erie, The Behrend College. His financial industry experience includes positions as a credit analyst with Colonial Bank and a financial planner and fixed-income portfolio manager with AmSouth Bank. His research interests primarily focus on new and alternative investment strategies. He received a BS in business administration and bio-psychology from Birmingham-Southern College, an MBA from Mississippi State University, and a PhD from the University of Alabama.

Keith Jakob is the Donald & Carol Jean Byrnes Professor of Finance at the University of Montana. His research interests are in dividends, market microstructure, corporate finance, initial public offerings, international finance, and investment and mutual fund performance. Professor Jakob has published in such journals as the *Journal of Financial Economics, Financial Management, Journal of Financial Research,* and *Journal of Empirical Finance.* He has consulted for and helped run various businesses, managed investment portfolios, and has acted as an expert witness on financial fraud. He has a BS in chemistry, an MA degree in civil and environmental engineering, and a PhD in finance from the University of Utah.

Eddy Junarsin is an Associate Professor of Finance at Universitas Gadjah Mada Faculty of Economics and Business, Indonesia, and also a Visiting Professor at Pforzheim University (Germany) and Arnhem Business School (Holland). His research interests cover corporate finance, corporate governance, executive compensation, and financial institutions. He has published in such journals as the *Annals of Economics and Finance* (SSCI) and *Gadjah Mada International Journal of Business* (Scopus), and is an ad hoc reviewer for *Applied Economics, Applied Financial Economics,* and *International Journal of Energy Sector Management.* He is currently the editor-in-chief of the *Journal of Indonesian Economy and Business.* Professor Junarsin received a PhD in finance from Southern Illinois University Carbondale.

Enrico Libert is a research assistant at Universitas Gadjah Mada, Indonesia, and also an entrepreneur. He previously worked in quality assurance in Gameloft Indonesia. His research interests in finance include stock exchanges, project finance, public–private partnerships, sovereign wealth funds, mutual funds, and international finance. His interests also include search engine marketing and optimization, social media marketing, business modeling, and business plans. He received both a BS in science with a concentration in electronics and computer science and an MBA with a concentration in finance from Universitas Gadjah Mada.

Ying-Chou Lin is an Assistant Professor of Finance in the John Massey School of Business at Southeastern Oklahoma State University. He previously taught at the Missouri University of Science and Technology. Professor Lin's primary research interests include corporate finance, international finance, investments, accounting information quality, and emerging market economies. He has published in such journals as the *Review of Quantitative Finance and Accounting, Review of Pacific Basin Financial Markets and Policies, Pan Pacific Journal of Business Research,* and *International Journal of Business and Finance Research.* He received an MBA from the University of Dallas and a PhD in finance from Old Dominion University.

Andrew Marshall is a Professor of Finance at the University of Strathclyde, which he joined in 1991 after leaving KPMG. He was Head of Department from 2007 to 2013. His research focuses on risk management, insider trading derivatives, and international finance. He has published more than 50 articles in such journals as the *Journal of Empirical Finance, European Financial Management, Journal of Corporate Finance,* and *Journal of Business Finance and Accounting*. He holds an MPhil in finance from the University of Strathclyde.

Christopher Milliken CFA, is an industry professional and Vice President of Hennion & Walsh Asset Management's Portfolio Management Program. Hennion & Walsh Asset Management is a Registered Investment Advisory firm that uses ETFs in constructing its investment strategies. As director, Mr. Milliken works under the chief investment officer and leads the firm's capital market research efforts and asset allocation strategy and oversees the sales and trading desk. He received a BS in business administration with a focus in finance from Marist College.

Matthew R. Morey is the New York Stock Exchange Research Scholar and Professor of Finance at the Lubin School of Business, Pace University. His research has been published in such journals as the *Journal of Empirical Finance, Journal of Banking and Finance, Journal of Financial and Quantitative Analysis, Journal of International Money and Finance, Journal of Investment Management,* and *Financial Analysts Journal.* His work has been cited in the *Wall Street Journal, New York Times, Washington Post, Chicago Tribune, Financial Times, Money Magazine,* National Public Radio, and CNBC. He received the Investment Management Consultants Association's Journalism Award. Professor Morey has also testified before Congress on mutual fund regulation. He has an undergraduate degree from the University of North Carolina–Chapel Hill and a PhD in financial economics from the University of California–Irvine.

Ehsan Nikbakht CFA, FRM, is a Professor of Finance in the Frank G. Zarb School of Business at Hofstra University and previously served as Department Chair and Associate Dean. He was on the Advisory Board of the International Association of Financial Engineers and Chair of the Derivatives Committee of the New York Society of Security Analysts. Professor Nikbakht currently serves on the editorial board of *Global Finance Journal.* He authored *Finance* published by Barron's and *Foreign Loans and Economic Performance.* Professor Nikbakht received a BA from the Tehran School of Business, an MBA from the Iran Center for Management Studies, and a DBA in finance from the George Washington University.

Trevor Oliver is Vice President and Senior Quant Analyst, State Street Global Advisors, San Francisco. Previously, he was the Vice President and Head of Defined Contribution Research at State Street Global Advisors (SSGA) in San Francisco where he was responsible for the advancement of SSGA's standard defined contribution offerings and for designing custom defined contribution solutions. Mr. Oliver cofounded Yampa Quantitative, where he developed custom allocations and asset-liability strategies for high net worth individuals and researched high frequency trading strategies. He also spent six years at Barclays Global Investors, where he held research positions in various groups including Structured Solutions, Cash Research and Analytics, and Defined Contributions. Mr. Oliver holds several financial engineering patents for dynamic retirement products. He earned a BS in physics from Harvey Mudd College.

Ojwang' George Omondi is the Banking and Finance sectional head in the Department of Business Studies at Siaya Institute of Technology in Kenya. He teaches diploma course units such as lending, financing of international trade, monetary and financial systems, and practice of banking and investment. He supervises student projects and works with various financial institutions to align student course content to industry requirements. He also teaches undergraduate courses including money and banking and financial management at Jaramogi Oginga Odinga University of Science and Technology. He has 10 research papers online as the Social Science Research Network. He received a B/ed in economics and business studies from Maseno University and an MBA in finance from the University of Nairobi.

Keith Pareti CIMA, is an industry professional and an investment consultant. He currently works at ETF Sponsor WisdomTree as a Regional Director. Mr. Pareti previously held positions at an institutional derivatives advising firm and a proprietary options trading firm. He has a BS in finance from Monmouth University.

Grady Perdue is a Professor of Finance at the University of Houston–Clear Lake. He has been active in investment research and management for many years serving both as a member of the board of a pension fund and a consultant to the investment committee of another pension system. Professor Perdue also serves on the board of directors of a large credit union. He is the author of two investments textbooks, a co-author on another text, and the author of numerous articles on investment management in such journals as the *Financial Services Review, Journal of Fixed Income,* and *Journal of Financial Planning*. Professor Perdue has served as the president of the Academy of Financial Services, an international professional association. He received a BA in political science from the University of Alabama, an MBA with a management concentration from Auburn University–Montgomery, and both an MA in finance and a PhD in economics from the University of Alabama.

Mark Potter is an Associate Professor of Finance at Babson College. He has been at Babson College since 1995 teaching more than 100 courses at the undergraduate, graduate, and executive education levels. Professor Potter has also held faculty positions at MIT's Sloan School of Management and Boston College. His areas of expertise include investments and portfolio performance, behavioral finance, and alternative investment strategies. His research has appeared in such journals as the *Journal of Portfolio Management, Journal of Business Finance and Accounting, Journal of Financial Research,* and *Journal of Alternative Investments*. His work has also been featured in the *Wall Street Journal, Kiplinger's,* and *CFA Digest*. Professor Potter received a BS in finance from Bentley College, an MBA from Boston College, and a PhD in finance from the University of Massachusetts–Amherst.

Larry J. Prather is the John Massey Endowed Chair and Professor of Finance at Southeastern Oklahoma State University. His primary research interest is in investments, specifically in mutual funds, ETFs, market efficiency, and behavioral finance.

Professor Prather has published 47 articles in such journals as the *Journal of Financial Markets, Journal of Empirical Finance, Review of Quantitative Finance and Accounting,* and *Pacific-Basin Finance Journal.* He is a past President of the Midwest Finance Association. Professor Prather is currently the Vice President of Membership of the Academy of Financial Services and an associate editor of *Financial Services Review.* He has a BS in business from Excelsior College and an MBA, MA in economics, and PhD in finance from Old Dominion University.

Luc Renneboog is Professor of Corporate Finance at Tilburg University and Director of Graduate Studies at the CentER for Economic Research. He is also a visiting Professor of Art Markets at Cambridge University. Before joining Tilburg University, Professor Renneboog was at the universities of Leuven and Oxford, and a visiting professor at the London Business School, HEC Paris, the European University Institute (Florence), and the universities of Venice, Paris-Dauphine, and Cardiff. His research interests are corporate governance, mergers and acquisitions, law and economics, socially responsible investing, and alternative investments including art and diamond markets. He has published in such journals as the *Journal of Finance, Management Science,* and *American Economic Review.* He received a BA in philosophy and an MSc in commercial engineering from the University of Leuven, an MBA from the University of Chicago, and a PhD in financial economics from the London Business School.

José Luis Sarto is an Associate Professor of Finance at the Economy and Business School of the University of Zaragoza. He was a visiting scholar at the University of Cologne. His primary research interest is in portfolio management, especially mutual funds. He has published in such journals as the *Journal of Banking and Finance, Omega: The International Journal of Management Science, Journal of Operational Research Society,* and *Journal of Behavioral Finance.* He has also supervised and participated in several projects for excellence in teaching. He received BS in in business administration and a PhD in finance from the University of Zaragoza.

Roberto Savona is Associate Professor of Financial Markets and Institutions at the Department of Economics and Management, University of Brescia (Italy). He was previously a visiting professor at the Haas School of Business at the University of California, Carroll School of Management at Boston College, and the Department of Statistics at the University of California. Professor Savona served as a member of the Board of Directors of the European Financial Management Association (EFMA) and a member of the Steering Committee of Macro-prudential Research Network–European Central Bank. He is Primary Coordinator of the "SYRTO Project" funded by the EU under FP7-SSH/2007–2013 program. He has published in *Applied Financial Economics, European Journal of Finance, European Journal of Operational Research, Oxford Bulletin of Economics and Statistics, and PLoS ONE.* He received a PhD in financial intermediation from University of Udine–Italy.

Panagiotis Schizas is a Postdoctoral Fellow at the Institute of Banking and Finance of the University of Zurich in Switzerland and Advisor at Ministry of Finance in Greece. He previously was a visiting researcher in the Zicklin School of Business of City University of New York (CUNY), and a fixed-income portfolio manager at Marfin Asset Management in Greece. His research interests focus on quantitative trading strategies for ETFs in which he created a relative pricing model that captures the asymmetric response to price volatility. Based on this model, his job market paper "Market Timing Using Asset Rotation" has been among the all-time top 10 papers in the financial market category at SSRN. He holds a BA in economics from the University of Athens, an MSc in financial management from the University of Essex, and a PhD in applied econometrics from the University of Peloponnese.

Sandeep Singh CFA, CIPM, is Professor of Finance at the College at Brockport, SUNY, where he teaches corporate finance and investment analysis. Professor Singh's research interests include retirement withdrawals, asset allocation, mutual fund performance measurement, and finance curriculum design and testing. His research has been published in the *Financial Analysts Journal, Journal of Financial Planning, Journal of Wealth Management*, and *Journal of Investing*. His research has been quoted in the national press including the *New York Times, USA Today*, and other leading publications. He consults regularly with investment management firms and not-for-profit organizations on portfolio management as well as curriculum design and exam development subjects. He received his undergraduate degree in commerce from the University of Allahabad, India, and an MBA and PhD in business administration with a major in finance and a minor in international business from Kent State University.

David M. Smith CFA, CMA, is an Associate Professor of Finance and Director of the Center for Institutional Investment Management (CIIM) at the State University of New York at Albany. He is author of more than 25 refereed articles on corporate finance and investment topics. From 2007 to 2010, he was associate editor of finance and accounting for the *Journal of Business Research*. Professor Smith received the 2006 Financial Frontiers Award for Research Excellence given by the Financial Planning Association. He was principal author of a proposal that brought $1.6 million to establish CIIM at the University at Albany. Professor Smith received the SUNY Chancellor's Award for Teaching Excellence. He is co-adviser to the University at Albany Student Investment Group, which manages part of the university's endowment. Professor Smith received a BS and PhD in finance from Virginia Tech.

Danielle Sougné is Professor of Finance at HEC Management School, University of Liège, and is the KBL Chair in Fund Industry. Professor Sougné conducts research on fund management and administration in an international context. Her current research focuses on liquidity risk and performance measures of funds. She teaches courses in the banking sector and handles various courses ranging from fundamentals to advanced levels for finance professionals. Professor Sougné is member of the board and audit committee of KBC Ancora. She holds a Master's degree in finance and a PhD in applied economics from the Catholic University of Louvain.

Andrew C. Spieler CFA, FRM, CAIA, is a Professor of Finance in the Frank G. Zarb School of Business at Hofstra University. He has published in such journals as *Real Estate Economics, Journal of Real Estate Finance and Economics*, and *Journal of Real Estate Portfolio Management*. He served as Chair of the Derivatives Committee at the New York Society of Securities Analysts. Professor Spieler also serves as Co-Director of the annual real estate conference sponsored by the Wilbur F. Breslin Center for Real Estate Studies. He received undergraduate degrees in math and economics from SUNY Binghamton, an MS in finance from Indiana University, and an MBA and PhD from SUNY Binghamton.

Filippo Stefanini is Head of Hedge Funds and Manager Selection in Eurizon Capital SGR. He was a lecturer in risk management at the University of Bergamo in Italy from 2007 to 2011 and the Deputy Chief Investment Officer and Head of Asset Allocation at Aletti Gestielle Alternative SGR from 2001 to mid-2008. He previously worked as a consultant for Accenture in the asset management and investment banking areas. Mr. Filippo authored *Investment Strategies of Hedge Funds* and *Newcits: Investing in UCITS Compliant Hedge Funds,* both published by John Wiley & Sons. He also co-authored several Italian language books published by Il Sole 24 Ore entitled *I fondi newcits, Hedge Funds: Strategie di investimento,* and *Hedge Funds: Investire per generare rendimenti assoluti.* He received a BS in management engineering from Bergamo University.

Z. Jay Wang is an Associate Professor of Finance at the Lundquist College of Business, University of Oregon. Before joining the University of Oregon, he was an Assistant Professor of Finance at the University of Illinois at Urbana-Champaign. Professor Wang's research focuses on institutional investors and the asset management industry. He has conducted empirical studies on the strategies employed by asset management companies to increase assets under management and to provide incentives to portfolio managers, the welfare implications of these strategies for fund investors, and the corporate governance mechanism alleviating agency conflicts between portfolio managers and investors. His work has been published in the *Journal of Financial Intermediation, Journal of Financial and Quantitative Analysis,* and *Review of Financial Studies.* Professor Wang received a BA in economics from Peking University, an MS in statistics and a PhD in economics from Iowa State University, and a PhD in finance from University of Michigan.

Abbreviations

ABS	asset-backed security
ACWI	All Country World Index
ADR	American depository receipt
AFI	Analistas Financieros Internacionales
AMEX	American Stock Exchange
AMLF	asset-backed commercial paper money market mutual fund liquidity facility
AP	authorized participant
APT	arbitrage pricing theory
ASRIA	Association for Sustainable and Responsible Investment in Asia
AUM	assets under management
BCG	Boston Consulting Group
BM	book-to-market
CAPM	Capital Asset Pricing Model
CAR	cumulative abnormal return
CCO	chief compliance officer
CDO	collateralized debt obligation
CDS	credit default swap
CDSL	contingent deferred sales load
CEF	closed-end fund
CFTC	Commodity Futures Trading Commission
CIU	collective investment undertaking
CNAV	constant net asset value
CS	characteristics selectivity
CSA	Credit Support Annex
CSR	corporate social responsibility
CV	coefficient of variation
D2C	direct-to-consumer
DJIA	Dow Jones Industrial Average
DJREI	Dow Jones U.S. Real Estate Index
DRIP	dividend reinvestment program
DWR	dollar-weighted return
EBRI	Employee Benefit Research Institute

ECB	European Central Bank
ECM	Error Correction Model
EGTRRA	Economic Growth and Tax Relief Reconciliation Act
EMH	efficient market hypothesis
EMMF	emerging market mutual fund
ERISA	Employee Retirement Income Security Act
ESA	Education Savings Account
ESG	environmental, social, and governance
ETF	exchange-traded fund
ETMF	exchange-traded managed fund
ETN	exchange-traded note
Eurosif	European Sustainable Investment Forum
FCA	Financial Conduct Authority
FDR	false discovery rate
FERSA	Federal Employees' Retirement System Act of 1986
FINRA	Financial Industry Regulatory Authority
FoF	funds-of-funds
FSA	Financial Services Authority
FSOC	Financial Stability Oversight Council
FTSE	Financial Times Stock Exchange
GAAP	generally accepted accounting principles
GIC	guaranteed investment contract
GICS	Global Industry Classification Standard
GLS	generalized least squares
GMM	generalized method of moments
GNMA	Government National Mortgage Association
GO	general obligation
GSE	government-sponsored enterprise
GSIA	Global Sustainable Investment Alliance
HFT	high-frequency trading
HML	high minus low
HY	high yield
IAA	Investment Advisers Act of 1940
IAPT	international arbitrage pricing theory
ICA	Investment Company Act of 1940
IETF	inverse exchange-traded fund
IFC	International Finance Corporation
IG	investment grade
IMMFA	Institutional Money Market Funds Association
IPO	initial public offering
IRS	Internal Revenue Service
ISDA	International Swaps and Derivatives Association
ISLA	International Securities Lending Association
LCR	liquidity coverage ratio
LETF	leveraged exchange-traded fund
LIBOR	London Interbank Offered Rate

LIETF	leveraged and inverse exchange-traded fund
LOP	law of one price
MBS	mortgage-backed security
MDP	managed distribution policy
MFS	Massachusetts Financial Services
MIT	Massachusetts Investors Trust
MMDA	money market deposit account
MMMF	money market mutual fund
MOM	momentum factor
MPPM	manipulation proof performance measure
MSCI	Morgan Stanley Capital International
NA	no arbitrage
NASD	National Association of Securities Dealers
NAV	net asset value
NEST	National Employment Savings Trust
NGO	nongovernmental organization
NPV	net present value
NTF	no-transaction fee
NTW	net terminal wealth
NYSE	New York Stock Exchange
OEF	open-end fund
OEIC	open-ended investment company
OTC	over-the-counter
PCAOB	Public Company Accounting Oversight Board
P/E	price/earnings
PPA	Pension Protection Act
PPP	purchasing power parity
QDIA	qualified default investment alternative
RAFI	Research Affiliates Fundamental Indexation
RBSA	return-based style analysis
RC	risk contribution
RDR	retail distribution review
REIT	real estate investment trust
RIAA	Responsible Investment Association of Australasia
RIC	registered investment company
SAA	strategic asset allocation
SAI	statement of additional information
SBJPA	Small Business Job Protection Act
SBWG	Salomon Smith Barney World Government
SCF	Survey of Consumer Finances
SDF	stochastic discount factor
SEC	Securities and Exchange Commission
SIO	social investment organization
SMB	small minus big
SPDR	Standard & Poor's Depository Receipt
SPV	special purpose vehicle

SRI	socially responsible investing
SRMF	socially responsible mutual fund
SRO	self-regulatory organization
STAR	smooth threshold auto regression
TAA	tactical asset allocation
T-bill	Treasury bill
TDF	target-date fund
TEV	tracking error variance
TGP	Temporary Guarantee Program
TIPS	Treasury Inflation Protection Securities
TNA	total net assets
TRA	Taxpayer Relief Act
TSP	Thrift Savings Plan
TVA	Tennessee Valley Authority
TWR	time-weighted rate of return
UCITS	Undertaking for Collective Investment in Transferable Securities
UIT	unit investment trust
UNGC	United Nations Global Compact
VaR	value-at-risk
VAR	vector auto regression
VNAV	variable net asset value

Mutual Funds and Exchange-Traded Funds

Part One

BACKGROUND

1

Mutual Funds and Related Investment Vehicles: An Overview

H. KENT BAKER

University Professor of Finance, Kogod School of Business, American University

GREG FILBECK

Samuel P. Black III Professor of Finance and Risk Management, Black School of Business, Penn State Behrend

HALIL KIYMAZ

Bank of America Professor of Finance, Crummer Graduate School of Business, Rollins College

The best argument for mutual funds is that they offer safety and diversification. But they don't necessarily offer safety and diversification.
Ron Chernow

Introduction

Investors face a bewildering array of choices of where to put their money from traditional investments such as stocks, bonds, and cash to various alternative investments. Some choose to build and manage their own investment portfolios. The portfolio management process of planning, execution, and feedback is a challenging undertaking especially for those investors who lack the requisite knowledge, skills, and experience. For example, these investors face such daunting tasks as determining investment objectives and constraints, integrating investment strategies with capital market expectations to select the specific assets for the portfolio, monitoring and rebalancing their investments as economic events or personal circumstances change, and evaluating portfolio performance (Maginn, Tuttle, McLeavey, and Pinto 2007).

Others choose a *separate account,* which is a plan that holds only the assets for a single individual and is managed by an investment adviser. A separate account enables the investor to customize investments based on specific criteria. Many others, however, place their funds with an *investment company,* which is a corporation, trust, or partnership that invests pooled shareholder funds in securities appropriate to the organization's objective.

In the United States, the main types of SEC-registered investment companies (RICs) are mutual funds also called open-end funds, exchange-traded funds (ETFs), closed-end funds (CEFs), and unit investment trusts (UITs). During 2014, the total U.S. net assets of mutual funds ($15.852 trillion) dwarfed those of ETFs ($1.974 trillion), closed-end funds ($289 billion), and UITs ($101 billion). The United States has the world's largest mutual fund and ETF markets (Investment Company Institute 2015).

The term "mutual fund" generally refers to the open-end type. An *open-end investment company* is the legal name for a mutual fund, indicating that it stands ready to redeem (buy back) its shares from investors at the end of every business day at the *net asset value* (NAV). *NAV* is the per-share value of a mutual fund, calculated by subtracting the fund's liabilities from the current market value of its assets and dividing by the number of shares outstanding, Open-end funds typically sell shares to the public daily at the NAV but without a legal limit on the number of shares that the fund can issue. Open-end funds are the most common type of investment company in terms of both number and combined assets.

A *mutual fund* pools money from many people and invests it on behalf of its investors according to some particular investment strategy. Each investor in the fund owns shares representing a part of the holdings in stocks, bonds, or other assets. Companies issuing these funds, such as Fidelity or Vanguard, manage the pool of money on the investors' behalf. The underlying logic of mutual funds is that they provide diverse investments without requiring investors to make separate purchases and trades. This book discusses how mutual funds and several other investment vehicles, especially ETFs, can serve as building blocks to wealth.

Mutual funds supply investment capital in securities markets around the world and play a critical role in household finances especially in retirement planning and education savings. According to the Investment Company Institute (2015), total worldwide assets invested in mutual funds in 2014 totaled almost $31.4 trillion of which about half ($ 15.852 trillion) represents U.S. mutual funds and ETFs. A total of 53.3 million U.S. households (43.3 percent) own mutual funds with a $103,000 in median mutual fund assets of fund-owning households.

ADVANTAGES AND DISADVANTAGES OF MUTUAL FUNDS

Mutual funds have both advantages and disadvantages compared to direct investing in individual assets or securities. For example, mutual funds are often the simplest and least expensive way to gain access to different markets and securities. The fund management company handles buying and selling of assets, as well as collecting any dividends and income, thus providing service and convenience to investors. When investment companies pool money from different investors, the shareholders may experience savings because they are sharing the costs and benefits from economies of scale, which allow for lower trading costs per dollar of investment. Mutual funds also enable some investors to participate in investments that may be available only to larger investors. Investing this way can potentially be less risky than directly buying shares in individual companies due to the wider spread of investments in the portfolio. Thus, mutual fund investors can benefit from increased diversification. Another benefit is professional money management in which fund managers make the decisions about when to buy and sell assets. Additional advantages include transparency due to extensive disclosure requirements, daily valuation, liquidity, regulatory oversight and accountability, and ease of comparison. In the United States, mutual funds have limits on leverage, which reduce the possibility that a fund's liabilities will exceed the value of its assets.

A broad range of mutual funds is available that invest in different assets with different strategies. Morningstar's database classifies funds into more than 65 categories. However, most mutual funds specialize in one category of the securities markets such as high-yield bonds or large cap growth stocks. Although a single fund may achieve diversification within a category, investors usually need at least several funds in a portfolio of diversified styles or asset exposures within asset classes to implement their strategies. The median number of mutual funds held by U.S. households was four (Investment Company Institute 2015). With so many choices available, determining the best vehicles to use and how to allocate among them can be difficult for any investor managing a portfolio.

In 2014, the number of mutual funds worldwide was 79,669 consisting of 22,962 funds in the Americas including 7,923 in the United States, 35,163 in Europe, 20,373 in Asia and Pacific, and 1,171 in Africa (Investment Company Institute 2015). The scope of mutual funds can be international, regional, or country-specific, whereas others are specialist funds investing in a specific type of company such as a property or technology fund. Not surprisingly, funds take different levels of risk from relatively low risk (e.g., they might invest mostly in cash) to very risky (e.g., investing in new, uncertain companies or markets) to everything in between.

Despite their appeal, mutual funds have disadvantages. Perhaps the greatest drawback involves fees and expenses. Investing in mutual funds is not free. Funds pass various costs to investors that diminish returns. These expenses fall into five categories: (1) distribution charges (sales loads and 12b-1 fees), (2) management fees, (3) other fund expenses, (4) shareholder transaction fees, and (5) securities transaction fees. Some of these expenses reduce the value of an investor's account while others are paid by the fund and reduce the NAV. Other disadvantages of investing in mutual funds include a loss of control over timing of recognizing gains, less predictable income, and no opportunity to customize.

ACTIVE VERSUS PASSIVE FUND MANAGEMENT

Most mutual funds engage in active fund management but some follow a passive approach. For actively managed funds, the fund manager is paid to research the market and to buy the assets that fit the fund's overall objective. Depending on the fund's objective, the fund manager may try to achieve better-than-average growth for the fund, to outperform certain benchmarks such as the S&P 500 index, or to get steadier returns than possible by tracking the markets. On a risk-adjusted basis, few fund managers consistently beat the market or even match it (Grinblatt, Titman, and Wermers 1995; Carhart 1997; Kosowski, Timmermann, White, and Wermers 2006; Fama and French

2010). Further, superior past performance does not guarantee continued levels of high performance in the future.

By contrast, the investment objective of an *index mutual fund* typically is to achieve approximately the same return as a particular market index. Some index funds, however, do not actually invest in the market they track but use a mixture of other investments and derivatives designed to mimic the market. These "synthetic trackers" are more risky. Because passively managed funds engage in less trading, this not only reduces costs but also limits taxable capital gains, which the fund distributes to its shareholders with the tax liability. The lower costs incurred by index funds help to explain why they tend to outperform their actively managed counterparts over the long term (Kacperczyk, Sialm, and Zheng 2005; Cremers and Petajisto 2009; Petajisto 2013). To beat index-tracking funds, fund managers must add more to returns than the cost of running the fund, which is difficult to do.

OTHER TYPES OF INVESTMENT COMPANIES

Other types of investment companies include ETFs, CEFs, and UITs. Each type offers both advantages and disadvantages.

Exchange-Traded Funds

An *exchange-traded fund* (ETF) is a type of an investment company, typically structured as an open-end fund or UIT, whose shares are traded intraday on stock exchanges at market-determined prices. Like shares of any publicly traded company, investors can buy or sell ETF shares through a broker. Most ETFs are pegged to financial indices and seek to replicate the performance of specific domestic, sector, regional, or international indexes.

In 1989, the first ETF showed up in Canada as the Toronto index Participation Fund (TIP 35). State Street Global Advisors introduced the well-known Standard & Poor's Depository Receipts (SPDRs) on the AMEX in January 1993. This ETF tracked the performance of the S&P 500 index and became the largest ETF in the world. In 1999, the first ETF introduced in Asia was the Hong Kong Tracker Fund. By the end of 2014, the U.S. ETF market with 1,411 funds with $1.974 trillion in net assets under management (AUM) was the largest in the world, accounting for 73 percent of the $2.7 trillion in ETF assets worldwide (Investment Company Institute 2015).

Various benefits explain the surge in the popularity of ETFs including coverage, costs, flexibility, leverage, tax efficiency, and transparency. First, ETFs provide easy access to broad spheres of the market. Second, they have low administrative costs compared to other investment products because the majority of them pursue a passive management investment strategy. Although ETFs are sometimes cheaper than their index-fund counterparts, investors pay a commission each time they buy or sell shares. Third, ETFs are flexible because investors can buy and sell them at current market prices throughout the trading day. Mutual funds can only be traded at the end of the day. Unlike some index funds that have high investment minimums, investors in ETFs have the flexibility of buying one or more shares. Fourth, ETFs offer leverage because investors can buy them on margin and sell them short. This feature allows investors to use ETFs in hedging. Fifth, they are tax-efficient because of low turnover resulting in fewer taxable gains. Finally, ETFs offer transparency. They are priced at frequent intervals throughout the trading day and most ETFs publish their holdings daily. By contrast, mutual funds are only priced at the end of the day.

ETFs are a hybrid. Similar to CEFs, ETFs trade on stock exchanges at prices that may be different from their NAVs but the magnitude of such differences tends to be small making the market for ETFs relatively efficient. Concerns about using ETFs as an investment vehicle often center on cash drag effects caused by small cash holdings in the ETF structure as well as dividend taxes, bid-ask spreads, and geographic distance between ETFs and the underlying assets.

Although advocates place much attention on the advantages of ETFs compared to mutual funds, mutual funds have some important advantages over ETFs that are likely to give them a net asset advantage for many years to come. Mutual funds are permitted in many retirement and pension funds while some plans do not allow ETFs. Mutual funds also offer the active management option that most ETFs lack due to being passively managed funds. Although actively managed funds are more likely to underperform passively managed funds when market frictions are considered, some actively managed funds have proven track records of outperformance over longer time intervals. In 2008, however, actively managed ETFs started operating (Hohorst 2014) and hence such ETFs do not track an index.

Closed-End Funds

A *closed-end fund* is a type of investment company whose shares are listed on a stock exchange or traded in the over-the-counter (OTC) market. CEFs issue a fixed number of shares that trade intraday at market-determined prices. After an initial public offering (IPO), CEFs can engage in additional public offerings of shares to raise more capital. A professional investment manager oversees the portfolio, buying and selling securities according to the fund's objectives and policies. Besides issuing common shares, CEFs also issue preferred shares to raise capital. Unlike common stockholders, preferred shareholders receive dividends and do not share in a fund's gains and losses.

Like investors in any publicly traded company, investors in a CEF use a broker to buy or sell shares in the open market. Unlike mutual funds, the price may differ from the NAV and is determined by supply and demand in the marketplace. Thus, the shares may sell at a premium to the NAV but more often they sell at a discount. Compared with mutual funds, CEFs often have more flexibility to invest in less liquid portfolio securities but have limited flexibility in borrowing against their assets to leverage their position.

Compared with mutual funds, the number and total net assets of CEFs in 2014 are much smaller with 568 funds and $289 billion, respectively. The number of CEFs remains below its peak of 662 at the end of 2007 as a result of the effects of mergers, liquidations, and conversions. At year-end 2014, closed-end bond funds held $170 billion or 59 percent of the total net assets with the remainder held in closed-end equity funds (Investment Company Institute 2015).

Unit Investment Trusts

A *unit investment trust* (UIT) is a type of fund that issues redeemable shares to the public when it is created and generally has a limited life span. UITs have some unique characteristics. Unlike open-end and closed-end funds, UITs do not have a professional investment manager that actively trades its investment portfolio. Instead, their portfolio of securities is established at the creation of the UIT and typically does not change. That is, UITs follow a buy-and-hold investment strategy. On a preset termination date, the dissolution of the trust occurs and the shareholders receive the proceeds from the sale of the assets.

UITs are a hybrid sharing some characteristics with mutual funds and some with CEFs. Like CEFs, UITs typically issue only a specific, fixed number of shares called *units*. Investors can redeem the units directly with the fund at any time as with an open-end fund or wait to redeem on termination of the trust. Although less common, investors can sell their shares in the open market. Unlike mutual funds, the UIT sponsor typically maintains a secondary market in the units so redemptions do not deplete the UIT's assets. At year-end 2014, there were 5,381 UITs in the United States with combined assets of $101 billion (Investment Company Institute 2015).

Purpose and Scope

The investment landscape continues to evolve and become more complex. The rapid structural, technological, and regulatory changes affecting the securities industry worldwide also affect various investment vehicles. The causes of these changes are multifaceted and thus require a level of depth and breadth that can be provided by a new book—*Mutual Funds and Exchange-Traded Funds: Building Blocks to Wealth.* This book offers a synthesis of the theoretical and empirical literature primarily on mutual funds but also discusses related investment vehicles, especially ETFs. It is not intended to be a "how to" book but takes a more scholarly and in-depth approach to these subjects. Although the book places greater attention on these different types of investments in the United States, it also examines them in a global context.

In today's financial environment, mutual funds and ETFs are dynamic areas that continue to develop at a rapid pace. Because the flow of materials on the subject is voluminous, this book, by necessity, must be selective because it cannot cover every aspect of this field. However, readers can gain important insights about each investment vehicle including its structure and uses, performance, and measurement. Beyond these core topics and issues, the book also examines the latest trends, cutting-edge developments, and real-world situations. In particular, this book should help investors make key asset allocation decisions while capturing the benefits of a highly diversified, well-constructed, lower cost portfolio of complementary strategies that enhance financial wealth.

This is a "contributed chapter" book in which noted scholars and practitioners write chapters in their areas of expertise. It interweaves the contributions of multiple authors into an authoritative synthesis of important but selective topics. Readers can learn about mutual funds and ETFs from experts from around the world. Additionally, discussion of research permeates the book.

In summary, *Mutual Funds and Exchange-Traded Funds: Building Blocks to Wealth* provides a fresh look at this intriguing but often complex subject. Its coverage spans the gamut from theoretical to practical, while attempting to offer a useful balance of detailed and user-friendly coverage. Those interested in a broad survey can benefit as well those looking for more thorough presentations of specific areas within this field of study. It is the sixth book in the Financial Markets and Investments Series by Oxford University Press.

Distinctive Features

This book has several distinguishing features.

- The book provides a detailed look at mutual funds and ETFs including the latest trends.
- It skillfully blends the contributions of scholars and practitioners into a single review of some of the most critical topics involving these investment vehicles. The varied backgrounds of the contributors assure different perspectives and a rich interplay of ideas.
- While retaining the content and perspectives of the many contributors, the book follows an internally consistent approach in format and style. Similar to a choir that contains many voices, this book has numerous chapter authors with their own separate voices. A goal of both a choir and this book is to have the many voices sing together harmoniously. Thus, the book is much more than simply a collection of chapters from an array of different authors.
- When discussing the results of empirical studies that link theory and practice, the objective is to distill them to their essential content so they are understandable to a wide range of readers with different backgrounds.
- All of the following chapters contain discussion questions that help to reinforce key concepts with guideline answers presented at the end of the book. This feature should be especially important to faculty and students using the book in classes.

Intended Audience

Given its broad scope, this practical and comprehensive book should appeal to investors, investment professionals, academics, and others interested in mutual funds and ETFs. For example, investors and investment professionals can use this book to provide guidance in helping them navigate through the key areas involving these markets and investments. For academics the book provides the basis for gaining a better understanding of the topics covered and as a springboard for future research. They can also use the book as a stand-alone or supplementary resource for advanced undergraduate or graduate courses in investments. Others including students and libraries should find this book suitable as a reference. Thus, *Mutual Funds and Exchange-Traded Funds: Building Blocks to Wealth* should be essential reading for anyone who needs a better understanding of mutual funds and related investment vehicles from seasoned professionals to those aspiring to enter the demanding world of finance.

Structure of the Book

The remaining 29 chapters are divided into six parts. A brief overview of each chapter follows.

PART ONE BACKGROUND

Besides Chapter 1, the first part has three additional chapters. These chapters examine the economics of mutual funds, role of mutual funds in retirement and education savings, and the structure and regulation of mutual funds.

Chapter 2 The Economics of Mutual Funds: Rewards and Risks (David M. Smith)

Mutual funds offer benefits over direct security investments, providing access to professionally managed, well-diversified, tax-efficient portfolios at low cost. For wealthy and sophisticated investors, these benefits make mutual funds an excellent vehicle. For less wealthy and less savvy investors, the fund landscape can be a minefield. Many benefits can be lost to brokers and fund sponsors who levy high fees upon initial investment, throughout the duration of the holding period, and also upon redemption. Thus, mutual fund investors need to be wary of various fees and loads. Relentless marketing efforts by the highest cost fund sponsors are aimed at the least sophisticated investors, ultimately producing inferior performance. Despite the fact that many rewards are available from the judicious use of funds, inherent conflicts of interest create difficulty for fund sponsors to carry out their fiduciary duty to shareholders. Partially due to scale economies, sponsors are tempted to seek investor flows in pursuit of higher profits. Although institutional investors "vote with their feet" when facing high fees and inferior risk-adjusted performance, retail investors generally do not.

Chapter 3 The Role of Mutual Funds in Retirement and Education Savings (Sarah A. Holden)

This chapter explores the role of mutual funds in U.S. households' retirement and education savings. Nearly three-quarters of mutual-fund-owning households in mid-2013 showed that saving for retirement is their household's primary financial goal. With the rise in individual account-based retirement savings, mutual funds' role in U.S. households' retirement planning has risen over the past few decades. At year-end 2013, U.S. investors had $23.3 trillion earmarked for retirement, with more than half held in individual account-based retirement savings with about half of those accounts invested in mutual funds, mainly in equity funds. One-quarter of mutual fund-owning households reported that saving for education is one of their household's financial goals. Specifically earmarked education savings totaled more than $234 billion at year-end 2013, mainly in 529 savings plans, which invest in mutual funds.

Chapter 4 The Structure and Regulation of Mutual Funds (Robert Grohowski and Sean Collins)

Mutual funds are subject to a comprehensive regulatory regime designed to protect fund shareholders. This chapter discusses the history, origins, and core principles of that regime, describing ways the structure, operation, and regulation of mutual funds protect shareholders. The chapter briefly introduces other similarly regulated pooled investment products available in the United States—CEFs, ETFs, and UITs—before returning to the legal, organizational, and operational structure of a mutual fund. The chapter summarizes the core principles of the Investment Company Act of 1940, the main federal securities law regulating mutual funds. These core principles relate to fund transparency, valuation, liquidity, leverage, diversification, custody, and conflicts of interest. While the Investment Company Act of 1940 is fundamentally about protecting fund shareholders, many of the Act's key provisions also mitigate potential systemic risk, which has become an area of heightened regulatory focus.

PART TWO MUTUAL FUNDS AND OTHER FUND TYPES

This part consists of six chapters that examine various types of funds involving pooled investments. Specifically, it examines mutual funds, target-date funds, funds-of-funds, CEFs, ETFs, leverage ETFs, and inverse ETFs.

Chapter 5 Open-End Funds (Conrad S. Ciccotello)

Mutual funds, which are open-end funds, remain the mainstay of the portfolio investment vehicles serving "mass affluent" investors in the United States. This chapter provides an overview of the key features of mutual funds such as daily liquidity at the NAV with the fund itself as the counterparty to the trade, active management, and fund family structure. The chapter then proceeds to examine the current issues facing mutual funds. These issues include the daily computation of the NAV, performance assessment in terms of time- and dollar-weighting, and the competitive environment for mutual funds both inside and outside of retirement plans. This overview chapter concludes with some predictions about the future of mutual funds and calls for research of interest to both academics and practitioners.

Chapter 6 Target-Date Funds and Other Funds-of-Funds (Alistair Byrne and Trevor Oliver)

This chapter discusses target-date funds (TDFs) and funds-of-funds (FoFs). The use of TDFs is growing rapidly in defined contribution pension plans. TDFs provide a "one-stop shop" for investing for unengaged plan participants. TDFs have grown in the United States since being included in the safe harbor provisions in the Pension Protection Act 2006. A key feature of the target date approach is *lifecycle investing*, which involves a switch in asset allocation from equities and other growth assets to bonds as the expected retirement date approaches. This glidepath can be managed to or through the retirement date in which case it keeps evolving after retirement. The glidepath can be strategic or managed dynamically. Some plan sponsors specify their own custom glidepath to suit particular plan participants. TDFs are structured as FoFs but other FoFs are also available where the asset allocation does not follow a glidepath.

Chapter 7 Closed-End Funds (Z. Jay Wang)

U.S. CEFs are publicly traded investment companies managing $279 billion total assets at year-end 2013, compared to $15 trillion assets managed by the open-end mutual funds. Despite the relatively small size, the closed-fund structure and the use of leverage make a CEF a useful vehicle for investing in less liquid asset classes. The long-standing *CEF discount puzzle*, which is the fact that fund shares can trade at a discount relative to the fund's NAV, has led to a large body of theoretical and empirical research based on both behavioral and rational explanations. The various agency conflicts between shareholders and fund managers also make the CEF industry a rich setting for corporate governance studies. In particular, the extant literature has investigated the relationship between agency problems, the effectiveness of internal and external governance mechanisms, and the CEF discount.

Chapter 8 Non-U.S. Closed-End Funds (Dimitris Andriosopoulos, Mary Fletcher, and Andrew Marshall)

This chapter reviews research into non-U.S. CEFs focusing particularly on the United Kingdom, which has a well-established and substantial CEF sector. It discusses the current structure and regulation of U.K. CEFs, usually called investment trusts in the United Kingdom, and focuses on the differences in regulation between the United Kingdom and the United States. CEFs in terms of income retention, investment areas, and ownership. The chapter also analyzes existing research evidence involving key aspects of the CEF discount puzzle in non-U.S. CEFs which refers to the initial CEF premium at the time of the IPO and the subsequent price fall leading to a discount and fluctuations in the discount. Additionally, this chapter assesses recent contributions in the areas of performance and trading strategies of non-U.S. CEFs.

Chapter 9 Exchange-Traded Funds (Ehsan Nikbakht, Keith Pareti, and Andrew C. Spieler)

This chapter discusses the origin and features of ETFs. It discusses not only the legal framework, structure, and description of available ETFs but also the past, present, and future of the ETF industry. Both similarities and differences exist between mutual funds and ETFs. The four major differences involve intraday liquidity, transparency, tax efficiency, and cost. As a result, ETFs have become a key investment vehicle for institutions, trading desks, portfolio managers, and individual investors. Wide variation exists between available ETFs spanning the spectrum from passive management (passively tracking an index) to active management. This chapter highlights the nuances of ETFs including creation/redemption, tracking error, liquidity, and arbitrage. The chapter concludes with a discussion on the trend toward actively managed ETFs.

Chapter 10 Leveraged and Inverse Exchange-Traded Funds (Benjamin Aguilar, Michael Bianco, Christopher Milliken, and Andrew C. Spieler)

Leveraged and inverse exchange-traded funds (LIETFs) combine the properties of a traditional ETF with a non-traditional return objective. The goal of the fund is to produce a daily return that is a multiple (ranging between plus and minus three times) of the underlying reference. This goal is often accomplished through using derivative strategies and partnering with another ETF provider that offers a traditional ETF tracking the same underlying reference. The attractiveness of these strategies is a function of the ease with which investors can establish a short position and the degree of leverage investors can implement without needing additional capital. LIETFs are controversial due to their complex mechanics and path-dependent returns. This chapter explores the current regulatory landscape surrounding LIETFs and their characteristics including risk and return and also discusses their potential effects on the capital markets.

PART THREE CLASSIFICATION OF FUNDS BY PRINCIPAL INVESTMENTS

This part includes five chapters that examine various types of investment funds. Specifically, it examines money market mutual funds, bond mutual funds, stock mutual funds, and socially responsible mutual funds.

Chapter 11 Money Market Mutual Funds (Anna Agapova)

Until 2011, money market mutual funds (MMMFs) represented the second largest category of the mutual fund industry in the United States. With $2.7 trillion in total net assets (TNA) as of December 2013, MMMFs account for about 18 percent of the TNA held by mutual funds in the United States. MMMFs are an important investment vehicle for individual investors and are vital liquidity providers to financial intermediaries. Investors regard MMMFs as safe money market instrument investments that provide yields above those of bank deposits. The main difference between bank deposits and MMMFs is that the Federal Deposit Insurance Corporation (FDIC) does not insure MMMFs. As evidenced by the Lehman Brothers bankruptcy in 2008 and the 2011 European banking crisis, MMMFs may threaten the stability of the financial system. This chapter offers a general overview of the history, structure, performance measures, and role of MMMFs in the financial system.

Chapter 12 Bond Mutual Funds (Sandeep Singh)

This chapter reviews open-end and closed-end bond mutual funds. It discusses the unique challenges faced by managers of bond mutual funds. The chapter presents a comprehensive literature review on performance evaluation of bond mutual funds and also discusses various segments of the bond mutual fund market. Finally, it includes guidelines that can be useful to investors and investment managers for analyzing fixed-income funds catering to a particular segment of the bond market. Most of the evidence suggests that given the largely homogeneous nature of the bond market, consistently generating risk-adjusted returns over benchmark returns (alpha) is difficult for actively managed bond mutual funds. Empirical evidence supports investment in passively managed bond mutual funds given the nature of the bond market and the challenges in consistently generating alpha. However, given liquidity and transaction inefficiencies, difficulties remain in indexing bond portfolios to broad-based fixed-income indexes.

Chapter 13 Stock Mutual Funds (Grady Perdue)

This chapter examines recent academic research concerning performance evaluation of equity mutual funds. Investors seeking to reach their financial goals should include investments that enhance the risk and return characteristics of their portfolios, and equities are often considered a viable asset allocation. However, studies show that many equity funds fail to produce a positive alpha. The chapter also discusses alternate means of assessing performance besides alpha, such as the Sharpe ratio and performance attribution, and problems associated with measuring alpha and other evaluation tools. Finally, it discusses the ability of managers to successfully engage in security selection for equity fund portfolios because this has a direct impact on their ability to generate positive risk-adjusted returns and manage risk.

Chapter 14 Socially Responsible Mutual Funds (Eddy Junarsin, Enrico Libert, and Frendy)

This chapter provides a broad overview of the development and structure of socially responsible mutual funds (SRMFs) and socially responsible investing (SRI). The chapter provides general definitions of SRMFs and SRIs, explains the investment paradigm of SRMFs and how mutual funds use environmental, social, and governance (ESG) criteria to screen assets in their portfolios. It covers ESG frameworks integration and performance measurement of SRMFs, reviews the academic literatures on SRMFs' performance and growth in North America, Europe, Australia, and Asia, and discusses future trends and development opportunities of SRMFs. The chapter also covers notable issues and challenges of SRMFs from the perspective of both investors and managers. It concludes with a discussion on the distinct challenges and future opportunities of researching and managing SRMFs in an increasingly socially conscious investing environment.

Chapter 15 Mutual Funds: Management Styles, Social Responsibility, Performance, and Efficiency (Tamas Barko and Luc Renneboog)

The mutual fund industry represents a substantial part of global financial markets with approximately 20 percent invested in mutual funds. Mutual funds offer a simple and easy-to-understand way to invest either into stocks or fixed-income products, both for retail and institutional investors. This chapter provides an overview of the literature on the performance of actively and passively managed mutual funds with special emphasis on socially responsible funds. First, the chapter offers insights into the mutual fund industry worldwide and discusses the characteristics of active and passive management. Then the chapter discusses a prominent management style—socially responsible investing. The final sections review the efficiency of the mutual fund industry, performance measurements, and sources of returns and outperformance.

PART FOUR ASSET ALLOCATION AND PERFORMANCE OF MUTUAL FUNDS

This part has six chapters that examine asset allocations and monitoring mutual funds. Specifically, it examines strategic asset allocation and rebalancing, building, analyzing, and monitoring mutual funds, predicting and evaluating mutual fund performance, and mutual fund risk.

Chapter 16 Strategic Asset Allocation and Rebalancing (Laura Andreu and José Luis Sarto)

This chapter reviews the importance of strategic asset allocations when defining a portfolio's investment policy and discusses the tactical asset allocations necessary for rebalancing portfolios. It also covers the relevance of determining an appropriate asset mix according to the risk tolerance and investment horizon of mutual fund investors and how choosing appropriate benchmarks can help managers and investors accomplish their financial goals in terms of risk and return. The chapter concludes with an empirical application of the return-based style analysis for Spanish mutual funds. This application shows a tool used to determine the strategic asset allocation of a financial instrument such as mutual funds. It also shows the value added by managing portfolios in different market scenarios by rebalancing portfolios in accordance with their investment policies.

Chapter 17 Building and Monitoring Mutual Fund Portfolios (Larry J. Prather, Han-Sheng Chen, and Ying-Chou Lin)

The process of building a mutual fund portfolio is an important topic because mutual funds are the predominant investment choice for employer-sponsored retirement plans and individual retirement accounts. This chapter discusses sources of mutual fund information, important fund characteristics, and steps in mutual fund portfolio construction such as screening funds that meet desired characteristics, determining an investor's risk tolerance, assessing historical risk and return, evaluating the benefits of diversification, and adjusting risk to optimize an investor's utility. Once the portfolio is built, it needs to be monitored and rebalanced. The chapter concludes by discussing factors that investors should consider when rebalancing such as changes in the fund's management, investor's risk tolerance, goals, and return differentials that have caused a substantial alteration in asset allocation.

Chapter 18 Analyzing Mutual Funds (Bruce A. Costa and Keith Jakob)

This chapter reviews the most widely used metrics to analyze mutual fund performance. It covers tools, risk metrics, and rating criteria popular with both academics and practitioners. Measurement of relative fund performance is tested with a set of dimensionless ratios including the coefficient of variation, Sharpe ratio, and Treynor ratio. Interpreting the precise amount of relative under- or over-performance is difficult with dimensionless ratios. In response to this drawback of using such measures, several researchers developed mutual fund performance metrics that quantify risk-adjusted performance to a greater degree. For example, the M^2 measure, Jensen's alpha, and the Carhart model are useful in quantifying risk-adjusted performance in percentage terms. The chapter presents recent extensions or enhancements to the Carhart model and also discusses the quantitative and qualitative risk metrics available from Morningstar.

Chapter 19 Predicting Mutual Fund Performance (Matthew R. Morey)

This chapter reviews the literature on factors that consistently predict mutual fund outperformance in U.S. equity funds. The factors examined include expenses, loads, turnover, past performance, mutual fund ratings, fund activeness, fund size, fund family size, fund governance, and fund manager characteristics. The research evidence suggests that for funds investing in smaller firms, smaller size mutual funds outperform larger funds. It also finds that funds with redemption and/or manager incentive fees show enhanced performance. Finally, the findings show strong past performance over the previous two quarters or less predicts future short-term performance. Along with these results, much dissonance occurs in the literature. For example, a study might find robust evidence of a certain factor predicting fund outperformance while another might report contradictory or statistically insignificant evidence for that factor.

Chapter 20 Evaluating Mutual Fund Performance within the Stochastic Discount Framework (Jonathan Fletcher)

Some view performance measures based on the stochastic discount factor approach as having a stronger theoretical basis than traditional performance measures. The stochastic discount factor approach can be used to evaluate mutual fund performance using linear factor models, nonlinear models, and measures based on weaker economic restrictions than required by a full asset pricing model. The stochastic discount factor approach can address investor heterogeneity, as investors can evaluate the value added by a fund differently from one another. This chapter provides an overview of the stochastic discount factor approach to evaluate mutual fund performance. The chapter discusses alternative approaches used to construct stochastic discount factors to evaluate fund performance and reviews empirical evidence on mutual fund performance using the stochastic discount factor approach.

Chapter 21 Mutual Fund Risk (Roberto Savona, Oreste Auleta, and Filippo Stefanini)

This chapter discusses mutual fund risk from both theoretical and operational viewpoints. It deals with the complex risk decomposition evaluation process comprising two main risk categories: (1) market risks relating to market dynamics and mutual fund exposure and (2) operational risks relating to the governance structure and the procedures of client protection assumed by the legal entity. The chapter offers an overview of the quantitative risk measurement architecture based on multifactor asset pricing modeling for which mutual funds are evaluated relative to their benchmarks. The quantitative analysis of mutual fund risks is summarized in the financial due diligence section, while the qualitative risk assessment of mutual funds is contained within the operational due diligence section. Both sections help guide managers to take the appropriate investment decision while controlling all connected risk sources.

PART FIVE FUND STRUCTURE

This section includes five chapters that focus on fund structure. Topics include the manner in which funds are organized and structured, how distributions occur, disclosure and protective features, ethical standards by which they are defined, and emerging developments within the industry.

Chapter 22 Organization, Structure, and Services of Mutual Funds (Mark Potter)

Mutual fund companies and fund families strive to perform well, control risk, and create a portfolio of complementary services and products. Funds are designed and organized around improving efficiency, creating value for customers, and improving market position in the face of increased competition from within and beyond the mutual fund world. This chapter describes the structure and set up of mutual funds and fund firms within the backdrop of industrial organization performance. It also explains the linkages between structure and performance, organization and fund services, competition and performance, and strategic advantages of the many shapes in which fund firms operate. Finally, the chapter discusses how fund structures are likely to migrate going forward. Most notably, fund companies are likely to see opportunities for growth in the areas of integrated services, analytics that involve big data, and funds that specifically match client needs in terms of their investment horizons or risk profiles.

Chapter 23 Selected Topics in Mutual Fund Distribution (John A. Haslem)

This chapter examines the channels through which mutual fund shares are distributed to investors: (1) direct, (2) advice, (3) retirement plan, (4) supermarket, and (5) institutional. The first four channels mainly serve individual investors. In the direct and institutional channels, fund distributors transact directly with investors in the sale and redemption of fund shares. In the other indirect channels, fund shareholders transact with funds through financial intermediaries. In 1980, the Securities and Exchange Commission (SEC) adopted Rule 12b-1, which emphasizes the role of independent fund directors in monitoring fund use of assets for distribution. The rule also addresses conflicts of interest between funds and fund advisers when funds pay distribution fees to grow fund assets. This chapter investigates whether introducing and adopting 12b-1 plans have benefited shareholders and fund managers.

Chapter 24 Mutual Fund Disclosure and Related Fund Investor Protection Features (Joseph A. Franco)

This chapter discusses the principal features of mutual fund disclosure regulation in the United States and the challenges faced by the SEC in designing a disclosure regime that meets the needs of retail investors and promotes investor protection. The chapter notes that, unlike conventional public companies, mutual funds are engaged in continuous offerings of securities to the public. As a result, fund disclosure, including fund advertising, is subject to ongoing regulatory requirements in terms of format and content, especially as it relates to disclosure of fund performance. The chapter then explains why regulators have been successful in making disclosure easier to understand, but face far greater challenges in designing disclosure requirements that promote rational investment decision-making given well-established behavioral biases of retail investors.

Chapter 25 New Developments in Exchange-Traded Funds (Ojwang' George Omondi)

This chapter examines ETFs since their inception and discusses their future prospects. ETFs originated in 1993 in the United States and in 1999 in Europe as passively managed index-based investment vehicles. Actively managed ETFs emerged in 2008. ETFs initially tracked established indexes such as the S&P 500 and FTSE 100. Their popularity with investors emanates from low fees, tax efficiency, and flexibility, and the ability to track specific indexes. Emerging markets are prime targets for ETFs because of their ever-expanding middle class capable of sustaining investments, especially in commodities and pharmaceuticals. Adequate legislation allows ETFs access to retirement account resources and to expand into fixed-income securities, emerging markets, commodities, and currencies. Increased competition for passive investments, growth in active ETFs, and a globalized market place with new competitive models call for coherent product designs, pricing, and distribution strategies to satisfy investors' unmet evolving needs.

Chapter 26 Ethical Standards in Mutual Funds (Rosa Adamo)

The role of ethics in finance is an issue that has begun to take on greater importance. Investors are showing increased interest in financial instruments that display ethical criteria within their structure and operation. Financial instruments incorporating ethical standards can shun short-term logic and display a tendency to be stabilizing to investors who depend on them as a long-term security. Particularly, mutual funds pursuing ethical standards represent an important sign of the restoration and reaffirmation of ethical and social values by the financial world. Some mutual funds pursue a goal of a more social nature with investments established based on the premise of transparency, trust, and social responsibility. By following ethical standards, mutual funds can reduce conflicts of interest and provide allocative efficiency within the financial markets.

PART SIX MUTUAL FUNDS WORLDWIDE

This section contains four chapters including the latest developments in emerging and developing markets, performance of global mutual funds and ETFs, and future trends within the industry.

Chapter 27 Mutual Funds in Emerging and Developing Markets (Parvez Ahmed)

This chapter outlines the market for mutual funds in emerging markets. Two types of funds to consider when describing emerging market mutual funds (EMMFs) are the funds in the United States that invest in emerging markets and funds in emerging markets that invest in their own domestic markets. This chapter provides descriptive statistics, performance evaluation, and performance persistence for funds that invest in emerging markets both domiciled in the United States and those domiciled in their home countries. The chapter also examines the factors that may explain both the persistence and determinants of performance and the performance of hedge funds. With greater public scrutiny and disclosure of hedge funds, some attention must be devoted to their performance in emerging countries. Hedge funds are increasingly popular among investors in private equity.

Chapter 28 Performance of Global Mutual Funds (Tarik Bazgour, Laurent Bodson, and Danielle Sougné)

Global and international mutual funds provide U.S. investors with an effective way to gain from international diversification. However, due to the complexity of international markets, performance evaluation of these funds is much more complex than that of U.S. domestic funds. This chapter reviews the appropriate measures for evaluating global portfolios' performance and some key properties and issues associated with each measure. It also examines the evidence these measures have produced on the stock selection and market-timing skills of global and international actively managed mutual funds. The chapter covers global and international equity funds, bond funds, and asset allocation funds. Additionally, it reviews the empirical evidence on whether global funds provide diversification benefits to U.S. investors as well as the evidence on the relationship between the performance of global mutual funds and their characteristics.

Chapter 29 Performance of Exchange-Traded Funds (Panagiotis Schizas)
This chapter documents that an ETF can provide a broadly diversified investment tool for investors that is typically designed to mimic an underlying index. Index management may appear to be a simple type of investment management but in practice its implementation is not necessarily straightforward. Such factors as tracking error, liquidity, and the difference between the closing price and the NAV may influence the choice of a performance measure. However, other factors can lead to a divergence in ETFs' performance from the underlying index. The chapter documents that international ETFs outperformed the market between 2001 and 2014 but failed to provide sufficient diversification. A single index model produces positive excess returns and risk-adjusted performance as measured by the Sortino and Omega ratios. The chapter also documents this outperformance. ETFs' outperformance becomes less pronounced after the financial crisis of 2007–2008.

Chapter 30 Issues, Trends, and Future Developments in the Mutual Fund Industry (Hunter Holzhauer)
This chapter focuses on important issues and trends in the mutual fund industry. It begins by providing an historical and global context for the current state of the industry. Next, the chapter discusses current competition from other fund types such as CEFs and ETFs. Particular attention is given to possible strategies for dealing with competition. Current trends in the overall mutual fund industry are explored including increased domestic and global demand and changes to fund sponsors. The penultimate section discusses recent trends and specific issues for a wide array of mutual fund types including bond funds, TDFs, hybrid funds, index funds, and MMMFs. The last subsection develops a case for regulatory risk as a future concern for MMMFs. The final section offers a brief conclusion focused primarily on the need for the mutual fund industry to focus on investor demand to remain relevant.

Summary and Conclusions

Mutual funds and related investment vehicles are undergoing dramatic change. The increasing popularity of ETFs has created opportunities for investors to gain exposures to a wider array of investment vehicles to broaden their opportunity set with the possibility of enhancing risk-adjusted performance. With such innovation, *Mutual Funds and Exchange-Traded Funds: Building Blocks to Wealth* provides timely information about various options for investment vehicles, classification frameworks, and structures and also explores performance and innovations occurring within the industry. The book endeavors to interweave the contributions of both scholars and practitioners into a single review of important but selective topics.

Such investment options provide an important service offering investors an opportunity to obtain diversification and professional management expertise starting at relatively low initial investment levels. This service allows individuals to achieve financial goals including retirement planning and funding for children's education costs. Many choices of investment outlets exist that require potential investors to obtain baseline knowledge to make educated choices based on their goals. As the mutual fund industry works to improve fund efficiency, reduce costs, enhance educational outreach, and increase fund options, the investing public led by aging baby boomers can find a haven for achieving their financial goals by increasing their wealth. As Ron Chernow states "mutual funds give people the sense that they're investing with the big boys and that they're really not at a disadvantage entering the stock market."

References

Carhart, Mark. 1997. "On Persistence in Mutual Fund Performance." *Journal of Finance* 52:1, 57–82.

Cremers, Martijn, and Antti Petajisto. 2009. "How Active Is Your Fund Manager? A New Measure That Predicts Performance." *Review of Financial Studies* 22:9, 3329–3365.

Fama, Eugene, and Kenneth French. 2010. "Luck Versus Skill in the Cross-Section of Mutual Fund Returns." *Journal of Finance* 65:5, 1915–1947.

Grinblatt, Mark, Sheridan Titman, and Russ Wermers. 1995. "Momentum Investment Strategies, Portfolio Performance, and Herding: A Study of Mutual Fund Behavior." *American Economic Review* 85:5, 1088–1105.

Hohorst, James. 2014. "Keeping a Secret." Markit.com. Available at http://www.markit.com.

Investment Company Institute. 2015. *2015 Investment Company Fact Book*, 55th Edition. Washington, DC: Investment Company Institute. Available at http://www.ici.org/pdf/2015_factbook.pdf.

Kacperczyk, Marcin, Clemens Sialm, and Lu Zheng. 2005. "On the Industry Concentration of Actively Managed Equity Mutual Funds." *Journal of Finance* 60:4, 1983–2011.

Kosowski, Robert, Allan Timmermann, Hal White, and Russ Wermers. 2006. "Can Mutual Fund 'Stars' Really Pick Stocks? New Evidence from a Bootstrap Analysis." *Journal of Finance* 61:6, 2551–2595.

Maginn, John L., Donald L. Tuttle, Dennis W. McLeavey, and Jerald E. Pinto. 2007. "The Portfolio Management Process and the Investment Policy Statement." In John L. Maginn, Donald L. Tuttle, Dennis W. McLeavey, and Jerald E. Pinto, eds., *Managing Investment Portfolios: A Dynamic Process*, 1–19. Hoboken, NJ: John Wiley & Sons, Inc.

Petajisto, Antti. 2013. "Active Share and Mutual Fund Performance." *Financial Analysts Journal* 69:4, 73–93.

2

The Economics of Mutual Funds: Rewards and Risks

DAVID M. SMITH
Associate Professor of Finance and Director,
Center for Institutional Investment Management, University at Albany (SUNY)

Introduction

Mutual funds offer solutions to various challenges facing investors. By investing in individual stocks and bonds, small investors often cannot diversify their holdings, face high transaction costs, and suffer the effects of a range of portfolio management errors. Mutual funds provide investors with advantages such as efficient diversification, low transaction costs, timely portfolio rebalancing, index tracking, and accurate record-keeping. Financial advisors and brokers who distribute mutual funds also offer attendant services that investors consider to be valuable, such as financial planning and portfolio monitoring. The mutual fund industry has grown as investors recognize that they cannot get the same array of advantages from other sources. As of 2013, 46 percent of all U.S. households owned mutual funds (Investment Company Institute 2014).

This chapter discusses the principal economic roles that mutual funds play, the structure and characteristics of the mutual fund industry, and economic problems associated with mutual funds. Much debate remains over the fund company, manager, and portfolio management characteristics that are most strongly associated with superior performance. The following sections present these in detail.

The Global Mutual Fund Industry

The assets managed by the mutual fund industry worldwide exceed $28 trillion. Khorana, Servaes, and Tufano (2005) investigate the determinants of the size of each country's mutual fund industry in 56 countries. Industry size is positively related to the number of years since its inception, strength of its regulations protecting investors, and education and prosperity of the country's residents. They find industry size to be negatively related to the time required to bring a mutual fund to market. Table 2.1 lists the assets under management (AUM) by open-end mutual funds, referred to in this chapter

Table 2.1 **Size of the Mutual Fund Industry and Expenses Charged Worldwide**

Country	*Mutual Funds*	*Total Assets (billions $)*	*Expense Ratio (%)*	*Management Fee (%)*
United States	7,679	13,674.47	1.00	0.66
Luxembourg	9,227	3,172.73	1.61	1.12
United Kingdom	2,715	1,478.87	1.37	1.06
Brazil	10,214	1,366.97	2.41	
Ireland	2,022	1,262.00	1.38	1.02
Canada	2,877	1,132.10	—	1.70
France	5,141	1,058.03	1.67	1.15
China	1,490	575.08	2.49	1.03
Japan	4,770	541.80	—	0.56
Australia	1,924	416.03	—	1.35
Germany	1,537	411.87	1.52	1.03
South Korea	12,386	358.07	1.18	0.36
Sweden	670	334.48	1.70	1.19
Spain	5,174	285.63	0.76	1.28
Switzerland	1,000	283.20	1.02	0.80
Italy	735	244.09	1.80	1.29
South Africa	1,047	161.72	1.66	1.05
India	822	145.11	1.80	0.85
Mexico	530	133.88	1.00	0.58
Denmark	586	126.25	1.19	1.42
Norway	352	117.97	0.98	0.91
Austria	1,224	114.84	1.46	1.08
Belgium	932	105.65	1.11	0.95
Finland	472	93.92	1.50	1.23
Thailand	1,416	89.72	1.35	1.00
Israel	1,259	69.50	—	0.99
Netherlands	279	66.62	1.77	0.83
Taiwan	626	62.31	1.61	1.42
Cayman Islands	204	46.52	1.72	1.38
Chile	508	41.86	2.68	—
Malaysia	590	41.61	1.56	1.34

continued

Table 2.1 **(continued)**

Country	*Mutual Funds*	*Total Assets (billions $)*	*Expense Ratio (%)*	*Management Fee (%)*
Hong Kong	170	41.36	1.39	1.21
Liechtenstein	513	32.79	2.25	1.24
Total 77 countries	**84,044**	**28,344.90**	**1.44**	**1.01**

Note: The table lists the number of distinct mutual funds, total AUM, and average expense ratios and management fees for countries with more than $30 billion in mutual fund assets as of November 2014. Funds are listed by country of domicile, and asset values are converted to U.S. dollars at current exchange rates. Blank cells indicate that Morningstar does not report the item for that market.

Source: Morningstar Direct 2014.

as OEFs, in the 33 countries for which assets exceed $3 billion as of November 2014. The AUM of OEFs in the United States is larger than those of the next 20 countries combined.

Khorana, Servaes, and Tufano (2008) find that management fees and expense ratios are lower in countries that offer greater investor protection. Investor protection is measured by the efficiency of the judicial system, whether regulatory approval is required to start up a fund, and whether an independent custodian is required to hold securities. The rightmost columns in Table 2.1 show average expense ratios and management fees by country. Although fees in Switzerland and Mexico are comparable to those in the United States, Canada is an outlier, with a 1.70 percent average annual management fee. Expense ratios in Brazil and China are also far above those of most other countries on the list.

Structure of the U.S. Mutual Fund Industry

Investment companies come in at least four types. Mutual funds or OEFs are the most prominent type. In the United States, these comprise over $15 trillion in assets as of December 2013. Exchange-traded funds (ETFs) are a second type of investment company with assets of about $1.7 trillion at year-end 2013. A third type is closed-end mutual funds (CEFs) with $280 billion and unit investment trusts (UITs) are the fourth type with $86 billion. Given the dominance of OEFs and the United States as the principal venue for mutual fund management and investment, the balance of this chapter covers OEFs in the U.S. market.

At the center of the mutual fund industry are investment managers who are hired annually by fund boards. Well-known companies such as Fidelity and Vanguard do not own the mutual funds that bear their names. Rather, the individual funds' boards decide each year whether these firms should be retained as advisors to manage the portfolio and provide administrative services. The incumbent manager is retained almost 100 percent of the time. Tufano and Sevick (1997) note only three cases to the contrary in 30 years.

The fund sponsor frequently hires a subadvisor to manage or help manage the fund. The *subadvisor* is a professional or firm that is not a direct employee of the fund's advisor. According to the Morningstar Direct database, 38 percent of U.S. mutual funds (2,906 of 7,679) use a subadvisor.

The Investment Company Institute (2014) reports that between 2003 and 2013, AUM of investment companies experienced a 7.3 percent annualized rate of increase. Of the $15 billion total, equity funds constitute about $8 trillion, balanced and bond funds represent $4.5 trillion, and money market funds are $2.7 trillion. The total number of distinct funds decreased from 8,125 to 7,707. Figure 2.1 shows how these series change over the years. The mix of bond, stock, and hybrid funds has also shifted over time. Figure 2.2 summarizes the changes. One of the strongest recent trends is the popularity of target-date funds. A *target-date fund* is a hybrid fund that invests in a blend of equity and fixed-income assets whose allocations change according to a predetermined schedule to achieve a specific return and risk objective.

Table 2.2 shows the market shares of the 10 largest firms. Vanguard Group is the largest, with about 15 percent market share as of November 2014. The top two firms have about a 25 percent market share, and the top nine firms have about 50 percent. Thereafter, market shares fall off dramatically and the remaining 825 companies comprise the other 50 percent of the market. The Herfindahl index for the mutual fund sector is 480. This contrasts with a minimum possible Herfindahl index of 12 if market

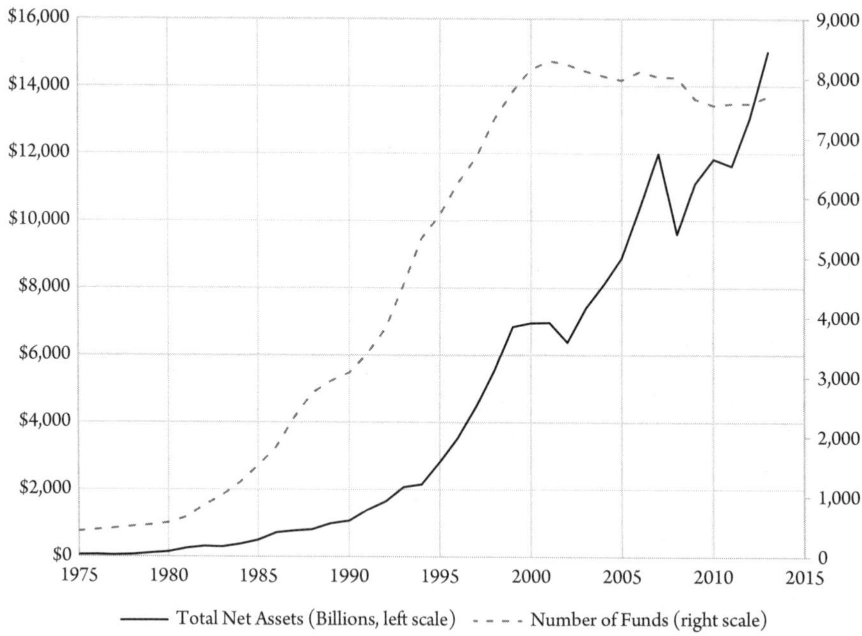

Figure 2.1 Number of U.S. Mutual Funds and Total Assets Under Management. The graph shows the total AUM by U.S. mutual funds in billions of U.S. dollars (left axis) and the total number of funds (right axis). Funds with multiple share classes are counted only once. Source: Investment Company Institute 2014.

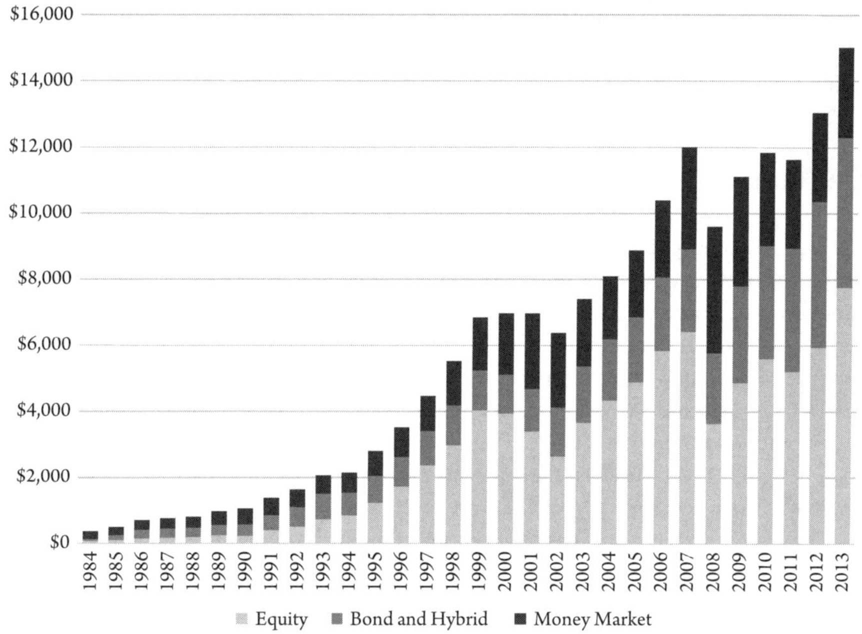

Figure 2.2 Assets Under Management for Various Types of U.S. Mutual Funds. The graph shows the total volume in billions of U.S. dollars of various types of mutual funds. Source: Investment Company Institute 2014.

Table 2.2 **Assets Under Management and Market Share of Mutual Funds for the Top 10 U.S. Advisory Firms**

Advisor Firm	*Total AUM (US$ billions)*	*Market Share (%)*	*Distinct Funds*
Vanguard Group, Inc.	1,906	15.41	83
Capital Group (American Funds)	1,131	9.15	57
Fidelity Management and Research Company	1,009	8.15	199
PIMCO	588	4.75	95
T. Rowe Price Associates, Inc.	533	4.31	125
Franklin Advisers, Inc.	310	2.51	78
Strategic Advisers, Inc.	280	2.26	99
JP Morgan Investment Management Inc.	247	2.00	119
Dimensional Fund Advisors LP	236	1.91	85
Wellington Management Company, LLP	214	1.73	7

Note: The table shows the total AUM and market share in November 2014 for the top 10 advisory firms to OEFs.

Source: Morningstar Direct 2014.

shares were uniform in this industry of 834 firms. The industry is becoming more concentrated over time, as the current Herfindahl value that is 40 times its theoretical minimum contrasts with a multiple of 38 in 2008 and 23 in 1998.

Distribution Channels

Investors obtain mutual fund shares in three major ways. Sales of funds by financial advisors and brokers represent one distribution channel. Employer-sponsored retirement programs are a second channel. Within these two channels, investment professionals serve as sales intermediaries between funds and investors. The third channel is direct purchases of mutual funds by investors. According to Investment Company Institute (2014), the first and second channels represented about 80 percent of the dollar volume of mutual fund sales in 2013. Thus, mutual funds appear to be mostly sold rather than bought. Direct purchases are about 12 percent of the total, and the distribution channel is unknown for 7 percent of fund purchases.

The distribution channel has a major impact on the profitability of fund investments. Bergstresser, Chalmers, and Tufano (2009) find that broker-sold funds underperform direct-sold funds. They conclude that brokers apparently provide services whose value is not reflected in fund returns but also that brokers have substantial conflicts of interest. Evans and Fahlenbrach (2012) provide related results in their comparison of funds that have both retail and institutional classes versus those with only retail classes. Fund sponsors serve different investors by providing access to the portfolio through different fund classes. Institutional share classes allow large investors to buy shares in high dollar amounts and pay a low expense ratio. Retail share classes provide smaller investors access to the same portfolio, but given the greater cost of servicing a retail account, the expense ratio is higher. Evans and Fahlenbrach find that institutional investors' flows are more sensitive to fees and performance than are retail investors. Retail funds with an institutional counterpart are better performers than single class funds offered to retail investors, but the launch of a new institutional class improves the performance of the associated retail class. Evans and Fahlenbrach conclude that their results are not due to institutional investors gravitating toward more successful funds but are explained by the superior monitoring of the portfolio managers provided by institutional investors.

Del Guercio and Reuter (2014) find that similar performance differences apply within the retail arena. Their results show that after-fee alphas for direct-sold actively managed funds are slightly positive. These active managers do not underperform index fund managers. In contrast, the alpha for actively managed funds sold through the broker channel is about 115 basis points a year lower than that of their direct-sold counterparts. Del Guercio and Reuter also conclude that the flows from fund shareholders who invest through the broker channel are substantially less sensitive to risk-adjusted return than are those of direct investors. But flows from the former group of investors are particularly sensitive to raw return, while flows from direct investors are not. One explanation for this result is that less sophisticated retail investors do not fully understand the concept of risk-adjusted returns. Another argument is that retail investors place a value on the financial planning and portfolio monitoring services provided by brokers that is sufficient to cause them to overlook poor risk-adjusted performance.

The Classification and Impact of Expenses, Loads, and Other Costs

Mutual fund investors bear costs that take various forms. The most universal form is the expense ratio, but substantial costs also come in other forms such as loads and trading costs.

EXPENSE RATIOS

The expense ratio contains fees paid to the fund management company for various services it provides to fund shareholders. Each fund's board annually determines the expense ratio, which is levied on shareholders daily. At the end of the trading day, each fund's net asset value (NAV) is decreased by the daily expense ratio. According to Morningstar Direct (2014), across all 29,440 U.S. mutual fund share classes (representing 7,679 unique funds), the unweighted average expense ratio is 1.27 percent and the median is 1.18 percent.

As Table 2.3 shows, actively managed funds' expense ratios are 40 to 70 basis points higher than those of funds that track a passive benchmark. Similarly, retail funds' expense ratios are also higher than those of otherwise similar institutional class funds by 40 to 70 basis points. The former comparison involves distinct funds, while the latter comparison could involve two fund classes that simply represent different routes to accessing the same underlying portfolio. As a basis for comparison, consider the average expense ratios of Vanguard funds. Even for actively managed retail funds, Vanguard's average expense ratio is 0.27 percent, and for its retail index funds the expense ratio averages 0.17 percent. The firm charges no loads or 12b-1 fees. The 27 basis points represent a rough lower bound breakeven point for the industry, suggesting that many competitors' operations are extremely profitable.

The difference between expenses for active and passive funds is consistent with French's (2008) conclusion that the pursuit of superior returns from active management costs investors 67 basis points per year in return. Related to this, Wermers (2000) finds that active equity fund managers possess stock-picking talent that allows them to beat benchmark indexes before fees. Yet, after taking account of fees and inferior returns to cash and bonds held to satisfy potential redemption requests, Wermers finds that the return advantages from superior stock-picking are more than reversed. Put differently, fund managers have the talent to outperform, but on average they fail to share those benefits with fund shareholders. Studies of active share show that the portfolios of many active managers maintain high similarity to those implied by their performance benchmarks. Miller (2007) finds that active share across the Morningstar equity universe is only about 22 percent and the implied cost of managing that active share is about 7 percent per year. This 7 percent cost of active share is strikingly similar to that reported by Smith (2014) for equity-oriented hedge funds.

Components of the Expense Ratio

Table 2.4 shows the fees that typically comprise an expense ratio, listed in descending order of prevalence. Virtually all funds report a *management fee*, which is a fee

Table 2.3 **Prevalence and Levels of Loads and Fees for Mutual Funds**

Fee or Load	*Characteristic*	*Fund Class Type*				*All (%)*
		Retail Active (%)	*Institutional Active (%)*	*Retail Passive (%)*	*Institutional Passive (%)*	
Expense ratio	Average	1.38	0.96	1.00	0.37	1.27
	Median	1.29	0.89	0.87	0.22	1.18
Front-end load	Percent of Funds with the Load	20.00	0.10	14.00	0.00	15.00
	Average Load Level	4.87	0.47	4.90	0.00	4.86
	Median Load Level	5.50	0.50	5.25	0.00	5.50
Deferred load	Percent of Funds with the Load	22.00	0.00	11.00	0.00	16.00
	Average Load Level	2.11	—	1.88	—	2.11
	Median Load Level	1.00	—	1.00	—	1.00
12b-1 fee	Percent of Funds with the Fee	78.00	3.00	62.00	7.00	61.00
	Average Fee Level	0.49	0.24	0.43	0.18	0.48
	Median Fee Level	0.25	0.25	0.25	0.15	0.25
Performance fee	Percent of Funds with the Fee	2.00	1.00	0.00	0.00	1.00
Redemption Fee	Percent of Funds with the Fee	11.00	15.00	10.00	11.00	12.00
	Average Fee Level	1.57	1.50	1.44	1.27	1.54
	Median Fee Level	2.00	2.00	1.50	1.00	2.00
Minimum Initial Investment	Percent of Funds Requiring a Minimum	77%	84%	76%	74%	78%
	Average Minimum Investment	\$9,936	\$2.68 million	\$4,444	\$7.52 million	\$0.66 million
	Median Minimum Investment	\$1,000	\$1.00 million	\$2,500	\$1.00 million	\$1,000

Note: The table shows the proportion of mutual funds (measured as 29,408 classes) that have fees and loads of various types, and the fee levels, November 2014.

Source: Morningstar Direct 2014.

Table 2.4 **Common Components of the Expense Ratio for Mutual Funds**

Fee Type	*Percent of Funds that Report Charging the Fee*	*Fee Level (% of Fund Assets)*		
		25th Percentile	*Median*	*75th Percentile*
Expense ratio	100.00	0.86	1.18	1.58
Management fee	97.35	0.43	0.65	0.85
Board of directors fee	72.31	0.00	0.00	0.01
Custodian fee	67.64	0.00	0.01	0.04
Transfer agency fee	65.45	0.06	0.13	0.23
Distribution fee	60.89	0.25	0.25	0.75
Registration fee	58.30	0.01	0.02	0.07
Shareholder reporting fee	56.82	0.01	0.01	0.03
Administrator fee	48.84	0.04	0.08	0.15
Professional fee	36.09	0.00	0.01	0.04
Auditor fee	26.31	0.00	0.01	0.04
Legal fee	23.62	0.00	0.01	0.03
Accounting fee	22.11	0.01	0.02	0.05
Insurance fee	11.28	0.00	0.00	0.01

Note: The table shows the fees that comprise the expense ratio for many U.S. mutual funds. The data include 29,408 mutual fund classes for 7,679 distinct funds as of November 2014. Cells containing 0.00 percent actually reflect nonzero costs that are below 1/100th of 1 percent of fund assets.

Source: Morningstar Direct 2014.

that the fund sponsor charges for portfolio management services. The median level is 0.65 percent. The reported level reflects the maximum management fee that the fund sponsor can charge. Table 2.5 shows that many sponsors offer discounts as the amount invested grows large, but the management fee decreases slowly. Most funds also charge a *board of directors fee*, which reflects compensation paid to the fund board for its work. This is typically a small percent of total assets. The *custodian fee* reflects payments to a bank that independently holds the portfolio's securities for safekeeping. The *transfer agency fee* is paid to the organization that the fund hires to provide services such as maintaining fund shareholder records, preparing quarterly reports, and responding to investor inquiries. This fee, which is sometimes termed an *administrator fee* (also listed near the bottom of Table 2.4), is one of the larger components of the expense ratio. *Registration fees* reflect expenses associated with meeting regulatory requirements involving registering the fund for sale in separate jurisdictions, such as in different states. The names for *auditor and legal fees* are self-explanatory, and these categories are sometimes grouped and called a *professional fee*, which appears directly above them in Table 2.4.

Table 2.5 **Breakpoints and Resulting Fees and Loads for Mutual Funds**

Fee or Load	*Basis for Breakpoint*	*Breakpoint Number*	*Breakpoint*	*Next Fee or Load (Median) (%)*
Front Load	Initial investment by investor	Initial		5.50
		First	$50,000	4.50
		Second	$100,000	3.50
		Third	$250,000	2.50
		Fourth	$500,000	2.00
		Fifth	$1,000,000	0.00
Deferred Load	Years investment held	Initial		5.00
		First	1 years	4.00
		Second	2 years	3.00
		Third	4 years	2.00
		Fourth	5 years	1.00
		Fifth	6 years	0.00
Management Fee	Total fund size	Initial		0.65
		First	$500 million	0.65
		Second	$1,000 million	0.60
		Third	$2,500 million	0.57
		Fourth	$5,000 million	0.55
		Fifth	$6,000 million	0.50
		Sixth	$10,000 million	0.45
		Seventh	$20,000 million	0.36
Redemption Fee	Days investment held	Initial		2.00
		First	30 days	0.00

Note: The table shows the median load and fee levels and their typical breakpoints as of November 2014.

Source: Morningstar Direct 2014.

12B-1 FEES

Many share classes charge a 12b-1 fee, the name of which is derived from SEC Rule 12b-1 of the Investment Company Act of 1940. The *12b-1 fee* is a fixed-percent annual fee that is paid from fund assets. It is charged to all investors of the fund and pays for marketing, compensation of brokers, printing and mailing of prospectuses and sales literature, and other shareholder services. The intent of the fee was to provide funds the ability to advertise and attract more investor flows, thus growing in AUM and reducing the percent expense ratio charged of all shareholders. The maximum that can be charged for shareholder services is 0.25 percent of the fund's assets, whereas the charge for marketing and distribution expenses cannot exceed 0.75 percent. Many funds charge the maximum 0.25 percent fee for shareholder services and are still allowed to advertise as being "no load."

Of the fund classes in existence in October 2014, 61 percent have 12b-1 fees. The average 12b-1 fee is 0.48 percent, and the median is 0.25 percent. This type of a fee is a fixture of the retail market, as 77 percent of such funds have it and only 3 percent of institutional classes do. Some contend that 12b-1 fees charged by no load mutual funds actually constitute a type of load. Just over 30 percent of funds call themselves "no load" yet they still maintain 12b-1 fees. More surprising, approximately one-sixth of all funds are both closed to new investors and maintain 12b-1 fees. Given the initial intention of helping a fund grow its assets by attracting new investors, continued existence of such fees in a competitive market remains a puzzle. Ferris and Chance (1987) conclude that 12b-1 fees are a deadweight loss to investors. They speculate that the fee's existence initially derived from investors being unfamiliar with its presence and negative impact. More than a quarter of a century later, the fee persists merely because most investors have not become better informed and demanded its cessation.

Walsh (2004) finds that although 12b-1 fees have helped to increase fund assets, expenses paid by incumbent shareholders have not decreased enough to justify their continued payment of 12b-1 fees. Increasing fund size may or may not benefit shareholders through a drop in the expense ratio. However, increases in size will unquestionably lead to an increase in revenues to the fund sponsor. Freeman (2007) notes that the application of the 12b-1 fee has produced a severe conflict in which current shareholders are forced to pay a marketing fee that the fund sponsor might normally be expected to pay. Freeman also argues that the goal of the fee, which is attracting the money of new shareholders, is a dubious one that magnifies conflicts of interest between fund managers and the shareholders to whom they owe a fiduciary duty.

TRADING COSTS

Trading costs for mutual funds can be substantial, but they do not appear in the expense ratio. Karceski, Livingston, and O'Neal (2004) estimate that explicit and implicit trading costs amount to almost 1 percent of total assets. Analyzing the individual portfolio holdings of 1,706 domestic equity funds, Edelen, Evans, and Kadlec (2007) report that average annual trading costs exceed the expense ratio (144 to 132 basis points). Thus, the sum of these two costs exceeds 2.5 percent annually. Trading costs have several components including explicit brokerage commissions, the bid-ask spread, and price-pressure effects caused by mutual funds' large trades. Although numerous studies document that trading costs are significant, mutual funds are not required to disclose the magnitude of trading costs to investors. As Mahoney (2004) notes, the estimates of brokerage commissions are well above what discount brokerage firms charged at the time. Apparently, mutual funds participated actively in soft dollar arrangements with their brokers. *Soft dollar arrangements* involve paying more than the market rate for services, but receiving a rebate from the broker in the form of research or other resources.

FUND CLASSES AND LOADS

Another traditional cost to fund shareholders is the front-end and deferred load. *Front-end loads* are charged when investors purchase mutual fund shares, and *deferred loads* are charged when investors redeem shares. The front-end load is expressed as a percent of the initial purchase amount. The deferred load is typically the lower of the initial purchase amount and the final sales amount. The identity of the fund class is an important determinant of whether a fund charges a load. Loads are far more commonly imposed on retail class funds than on institutional class funds. As Table 2.3 shows, few institutional class shares have front-end or deferred loads.

Mutual funds available to retail investors and purchased through a broker are typically available in three share classes: A, B, and C. The different share classes are usually distinguished by their loads, with A classes imposing front-end loads, B classes imposing deferred loads, and C classes imposing level loads.

To attract large investors such as 401(k) plans and pension funds, mutual fund companies have created institutional share classes that charge lower fees. Outside of 401(k) plans, the emergence of mutual fund supermarkets and discount brokers has decreased costs to investors as well. Gil-Bazo and Ruiz-Verdu (2009) show that mutual fund performance is negatively correlated to expenses even before the fees are charged. Their results reinforce that investors should avoid additional fees and expenses.

Licensed investment professionals market their ability to make suitable recommendations based on a client's needs, goals, investment time horizon, and other portfolio constraints. For many advisors, asset allocation is the main focus of suitability. Even if an investor's asset allocation is risk appropriate, multiple mutual fund fee structures must be navigated. According to O'Neal (1999), a direct conflict of interest often exists between a broker's incentives and the client's needs. This conflict results from the fact that brokers are often compensated in greater amounts for funds that cost their clients more. Houge and Wellman (2007) conjecture that this conflict of interest results from mutual fund companies directly targeting inexperienced investors with higher overall fees. If a broker suggests that a client use a "C" share class of a mutual fund rather than an "A" or "B" share class, a client should have a basic understanding of the costs of different load structures. A shareholder's allocation and fee structure should be based on his or her goals, investment constraints, and current portfolio holdings.

Front-End Loads

The maximum front-end load that the U.S. Financial Industry Regulatory Authority permits funds to charge is 8.5 percent. As Table 2.3 shows, only 15 percent of fund classes charge a front-end load. The average (median) front-end load for funds that have one is 4.86 percent (5.50 percent). Front-end loads are also sometimes referred to as *sales charges*.

According to Investment Company Institute (2014), mutual fund investors have become more cognizant of up-front fees and costs and as a result have invested much less money in front-end load funds in recent years. "A" share class mutual funds charge a front-end load, and usually also charge a small 12b-1 fee of approximately 0.25 percent throughout the life of the fund. An example of an A share class is the American Growth Fund Series One A class (ticker AMRAX). This fund charges a 5.75 percent front-end load and a 0.30 percent 12b-1 fee. The annual expense ratio is 4.96 percent. Net of the load, an investor who commits $1,000 to this fund actually ends up investing $942.50. Although the headline front-end load is 5.75 percent, it should not escape investors that relative to the $942.50 of shares acquired the $57.50 charge actually amounts to 6.10 percent.

Funds charge front-end loads almost exclusively to retail investors, although only 19 percent of retail share classes levy this fee. Of those funds that do, the mean is 4.86 percent. Fortunately for larger investors, fund sponsors specify breakpoints based on the amount invested in the fund. Firms frequently offer a front-end load discount for amounts over $50,000, and further decreases at breakpoints of $100,000, $250,000, $500,000, and $1 million. At investment amounts above $1 million the load usually drops to zero. Many funds offer a *right of accumulation,* meaning that a shareholder's prior investment in the fund counts along with the current investment toward achieving the load breakpoint.

Deferred Loads

Deferred loads are also known as back-end loads, deferred sales charges, and contingent deferred sales charges. Deferred loads are payable when the investor redeems shares. They are slightly more prevalent than front-end loads. Only rarely do funds charge both front-end and back-end loads.

A main difference between an A share class and a B share class is that a B share charges a deferred load. The purported rationale for the deferred load is to dissuade investors from selling fund shares shortly after their purchase. Usually this charge will reduce from around 5 percent to zero over a period of about six years. When investors redeem their fund shares, the fund charges the applicable deferred load that is based on the lesser of the fund's value at redemption, or the fund's value at purchase. Therefore, in a side-by-side comparison, excluding all other fees, B shares would carry a lower overall cost due to the compounding of returns if the same initial fee were taken out of the investment. However, B class shares also charge a 12b-1 fee that is usually much higher than that of an A share class. This fee typically starts at about 1 percent. After about eight years the fund converts to an A share mutual fund, and charges the lower corresponding 12b-1 fee. The American Growth Fund Series One B share class (ticker AMRBX) has a deferred load schedule as follows: 5 percent within two years, 4 percent between 2 and 4 years, 3 percent between 4 and 5 years, 2 percent between 5 and 6 years, 1 percent between 6 and 7 years, and 0 percent after 7 years. It also charges a 1 percent 12b-1 fee within an expense ratio of 5.67 percent. After a certain time period, B class shares convert to A class shares thus decreasing the expense ratio investors must pay.

C Class

C Class shares are often referred to as "level-load" funds. They usually charge no initial load, a small and temporary deferred load, and a constant 12b-1 fee that is the same as their B class counterpart. C class funds charge a relatively high annual expense ratio that stays high because they rarely convert to A class shares. The American Growth Fund Series One C share class (ticker AMRCX) has a 1 percent deferred load for investments of less than one year in duration and a 1 percent 12b-1 fee within an expense ratio of 5.63 percent.

Analyzing Loads

Comparing the multiple load structures that mutual funds charge and determining the overall cost of different share classes is a nontrivial exercise. As Morey (2003) reports, all else equal, funds with loads underperform no-load funds. Interestingly, he finds that the magnitude of the load is only a weak predictor of underperformance. The mere existence of a load is most problematic. Livingston and O'Neal (1998) present formulas to compare the costs of holding multiple share classes of mutual funds over a 20-year period. They use typical distribution arrangements to create a model for making side-by-side cost comparisons of front-end and deferred loads, and 12b-1 fees. Livingston and O'Neal's main conclusion is that investors should avoid the "C" share class unless they are investing for a time horizon of seven years or shorter. They also find that for holding periods longer than eight to nine years, front-end load mutual funds would carry slightly lower all-in costs than deferred-load funds.

Chordia (1996) provides a divergent perspective on loads. He presents a model of disparate mutual fund fees and shows that loads play the potentially useful role of discouraging investors from redeeming their stakes prematurely. Further, the investor behavior produced by imposing loads has implications for the investments that mutual funds hold. The larger the loads and fees, the less mobile are investor funds, and the more able a fund is to hold risky stocks and low cash balances. In the long run, this portfolio structure is likely to be in shareholders' interests. Chordia presents empirical results consistent with the predictions of his model.

Barber, Odean, and Zheng (2005) find that the investment and redemption decisions of mutual fund investors are insensitive to the level of the expense ratio. When splitting the expense ratio into its operating expenses and 12b-1 fee components, the authors report that investors react negatively to higher operating expenses but positively to higher 12b-1 expenditures. In this sense, some might argue that expenditures from 12b-1 fees are effective at generating new asset flows. Overall, investors are highly sensitive to front-end loads and experienced investors avoid funds with such charges.

Investment and Redemption Provisions

According to Morningstar Direct (2014), about 80 percent of mutual funds require that a minimum dollar amount be invested to establish an initial stake in the fund. This amount is lower for retail classes and higher for institutional classes. The median required investment for retail investors is $1,000 for active funds and $2,500 for passive funds. For institutional investors, the median required investment is $1 million. After the initial investment criterion is met, subsequent investments may take place in any amount. Table 2.3 shows representative values for minimum initial investment amounts.

Regarding redemption terms, funds incur costs in dealing with large investments that shareholders redeem quickly. As Edelen (1999) shows, flow-driven trades are more expensive to funds than discretionary trades. Thus, the actions of shareholders who treat funds as trading vehicles can be distracting and disruptive to portfolio managers and can produce negative externalities for other shareholders. In such situations, the "mutual" aspect of "mutual funds" is most profoundly realized. To discourage high frequency trading and recoup some costs that might occur, funds sometimes charge a redemption fee for sales taking place shortly after the investment is made. Table 2.3 shows that 11 percent of funds impose a redemption fee of some type. The average fee is 2 percent of the sales amount. Table 2.5 shows that 30 days is the median holding period required after which the redemption fee is waived.

Taxes

Mutual fund investments are not taxed at the fund level. Instead, mutual funds pass their dividends, interest, and realized capital gains and losses directly through to investors. Thus, each investor is taxed at his personal tax rate. Although mutual fund shareholders have no discretion over the timing of such distributions, funds make distributions on a designated date each year, so investors can conduct portfolio and tax planning around the cash flow. In reporting to their shareholders, funds distinguish between short-term and long-term gains, as tax rates typically give preference to the latter. Financial planners often warn their taxable clients not to buy fund shares shortly before a distribution is made to avoid paying excess taxes.

Even mutual fund portfolio managers cannot necessarily act to time the realization of their taxable gains. The fund's guarantee of immediate shareholder liquidity combined with large redemptions can require fund managers to sell portfolio holdings that the fund acquired at low prices long ago. Fund managers usually sell the highest basis portfolio holdings in response to shareholder redemption demands, but sudden large redemptions can cause liquidation of low-basis holdings as well, and trigger unusually large tax obligations. As a recent illustration, Nadig (2014) cites the Neuberger Berman Large Cap Disciplined Growth Fund, whose total distributions at year-end 2014 amount to over half the fund's NAV. In this case, new shareholders immediately receive checks for more than 50 percent of their investment amount as a taxable long-term capital gain.

Taxable investors who buy mutual fund shares need to remain aware of the degree to which their fund has a large *capital gains overhang*, which refers to the level of unrealized capital gains in the fund. Khorana and Servaes (1999) find that the propensity for new funds to be started in a particular investment objective is related to the magnitude of the capital gains overhang among extant funds pursuing that same objective. Thus, when unrealized capital gains are large, one way the industry renews itself is to start new funds in that objective.

Dickson, Shoven, and Sialm (2000) simulate the degree to which the redemption and investment decisions of other investors affect shareholder tax liabilities. They describe the possible impact of shareholder redemptions while a fund is closed to new investors as particularly devastating. Among their conclusions is that funds could consider holding a cash position as a buffer against redemptions that would otherwise trigger a tax liability for shareholders. They acknowledge that a "cash drag" on returns is a substantial cost of maintaining such a buffer, although this can be mitigated using methods of equitization, as discussed by Hill and Cheong (1996). Common methods to gain equity market exposure include using equity index futures, options, and swaps. A more recently applied technique is *income equalization* by which funds allocate to redeeming shareholders a pro rata amount of the year's gains. The purported benefit of this method is that non-redeeming shareholders are not left with a tax liability for the entire amount that the fund distributes. Only about 10 percent of funds use income equalization, which Gill and Schwarz (2011) examine in detail.

An observation about ETFs is appropriate here. The structure and redemption provisions of ETFs help investors to avoid large tax liabilities that stem from purchases made long before they became fund shareholders. A major exception occurs when the index tracked by an ETF experiences changes in its composition and is required to sell certain issues. This situation is most acute for indexes out of which firms or countries "graduate." Examples include small cap or mid-cap indexes, out of which component securities are elevated to membership in larger cap indexes. Another example is a frontier or emerging market index, out of which a country's market is elevated to membership in a developed market index.

Fund Size and Performance

An important concern for investors and fund sponsors is the relationship between fund performance and size. At least two countervailing forces determine the size-performance relationship. From an organization perspective, economies of scale are likely to be present if fixed costs comprise a large fraction of the total costs of running a mutual fund. Among the major fixed or nearly fixed costs funds face are administrative and marketing expenses and the burden of running an investment research operation.

Although costs are a promising source of scale economies, diseconomies are likely in other areas. For example, portfolio managers' security selection advantage may diminish as AUM become large. The manager's best investment ideas are not exploitable in unlimited quantities due to market liquidity constraints. This limitation is particularly acute in certain market sectors such as domestic micro-cap and emerging market equities. Despite this possible diseconomy, fund companies have some adverse incentives to let fund size grow uninhibited. For fund sponsors, the portfolio size that maximizes its total fee revenue is not necessarily the size that maximizes returns to investors. Given this potential conflict, investors must be cognizant of whether a fund has grown beyond its optimal size. Fund closings are a common response to reaching a large size, but closings bring their own potential problems.

Several studies investigate scale economies directly and indirectly. For example, Khorana and Servaes (1999) examine the conditions under which mutual funds are started. They find that other fund families mimic the recent behavior of the largest firms in the industry. Also, larger families and families that have opened the most funds in the recent past are more likely to start funds. Khorana and Servaes interpret this behavior as evidence of industry scale and scope economies.

Chen, Hong, Huang, and Kubik (2004) explore scale economies directly. They compare 37 years of mutual fund return performance to lagged fund size. For funds that invest in large capitalization stocks, they find only a weak negative relation. In contrast, they document a strong negative relation for small capitalization portfolios, an effect that appears to be driven by illiquidity in small cap names. Chen et al. also find that the performance of funds from large fund complexes is higher, all else equal. If fund complexes can spread the fixed costs of running an investment company across a large asset base, individual funds experience higher net-of-fees performance. Particularly surprising is that even gross-of-fees performance is higher for funds from larger complexes. This suggests that fund complexes enjoy scale benefits in areas such as research, trading costs, and security lending revenues.

Malhotra, Martin, and Russel (2007) report that cost increases for funds are less-than-proportional to increases in AUM. For all years and fund sizes examined, they report cost elasticities (relative to size) that are less than 1.0. Institutional class funds and funds within families that have a focused investment objective have the greatest economies of scale. In earlier work, Latzko (1999) finds that scale economies are present, but they are largely exhausted once AUM reaches about $3.5 billion. Gao and Livingston (2008) confirm that large funds do not show significant economies of scale. They find that management fees, which are another component of the expense ratio, tend to be constant as fund size changes, and that percent marketing fees actually increase as the fund size increases.

Other authors have investigated possible sources of diseconomies. Edelen et al. (2007) examine the relationship between fund performance and trading costs. As previously noted, trading costs are not a component of the mutual fund expense ratio, so they are mostly unobserved by investors. Surprisingly, Edelen et al. find that the magnitude of trading costs is actually larger than the expense ratio. They show that after controlling for trading costs, the relationship between fund performance and fund size weakens substantially.

Fund mergers are another structural matter that concerns shareholders. Khorana, Tufano, and Wedge (2007) show that mutual fund mergers usually take place when one fund has underperformed. Absorption into a better performing fund is often the only recourse to keep the weaker fund alive. Khorana et al. find that the most effective boards at enforcing performance have 100 percent independent managers. Boards with this composition tend to be the least tolerant of poor performance and the most likely to approve a merger. Jayaraman, Khorana, and Nelling (2002) find that following a merger, the target fund's performance tends to improve while the acquiring fund's performance tends to worsen.

Agency Issues, Board Structure, and Governance

Many researchers have studied agency problems in mutual funds. Mutual fund sponsors are in a challenging position as they serve the needs of two constituents. Under the Investment Company Act of 1940, mutual fund managers and boards have a fiduciary duty to act in the interests of fund shareholders. However, managers are compensated principally based on the level of AUM. In the short run, expending effort gathering investment flows from new investors is more profitable for managers than generating *alpha*, which refers to excess risk-adjusted return, on behalf of existing investors.

As noted earlier, mutual fund boards are charged with setting and approving the terms of the contract between the fund and the fund's sponsor. The Investment Company Act of 1940 required that at least 40 percent of directors be non-interested parties. In 2004, the SEC strengthened the requirement so that 75 percent of directors must be independent. Examples of interested parties include employees and directors of the fund sponsor. Tufano and Sevick (1997) report that fund board members, including those qualifying as "independent" members, are in practice selected by the fund sponsors against whom they must negotiate on behalf of fund shareholders. Birdthistle (2006) reviews many of the mutual fund-related scandals of the preceding decade and concludes that managers show signs of being highly conflicted, while boards behave as if they were powerless. He observes that believing that the industry will unilaterally improve the structure to serve shareholder interests is naïve and development of more robust regulatory measures would be the most promising way forward.

But efforts by regulators and lawmakers to increase the proportion of independent directors may not decrease the likelihood of fiduciary violations. Ferris and Yan (2007) examine whether mutual fund board structure is related to the probability of subsequent behavior that is contrary to the interests of long-term fund shareholders. They obtain data on the number of interested and independent directors from statements of additional information (SAI) filings for 448 fund families. Interestingly, more than 90 percent of all fund families as of 2002 have only one board to oversee all funds that the family sponsors. Across all the boards, 70 percent of directors were classified as "independent." Ferris and Yan find that families that were later afflicted by scandals had a larger fraction of independent directors.

A further finding by Ferris and Yan (2009) is that privately owned mutual fund families are less likely to suffer from agency problems than are publicly owned sponsors. They observe that funds run by publicly owned sponsors tend to underperform those of privately owned sponsors. Related to this, the latter also have higher fees and expenses. Khorana, Servaes, and Wedge (2007) study the relationship between portfolio performance and the degree of fund ownership by the portfolio manager. They find that subsequent performance is strongly positively related to the portfolio manager's investment in the fund. They suggest that potential fund shareholders could benefit by investigating a priori the portfolio manager's ownership status and invest accordingly.

Morningstar uses grades of A through D to evaluate fund sponsors separately according to their corporate culture and their board quality. The principal question addressed by the "corporate culture" grade is whether, in Morningstar's judgment, the fund sponsor is more interested in managing the fund than in gathering additional assets. The question addressed by the "board quality" grade is whether the fund board's interests are well aligned with those of the shareholders. One measure of this is whether the independent board members have more money invested in the fund than they receive in compensation for board service. Morningstar also provides a "stewardship" grade that is an amalgam of its grades for corporate culture and board quality, as well as its assessment of fees, management incentives, and regulatory issues. Only Dodge & Cox, T. Rowe Price, and Vanguard currently receive grades of A across all dimensions. Table 2.6 summarizes the most recent grades in three areas for major U.S. fund families.

Table 2.6 **Morningstar Grades for Stewardship, Corporate Culture, and Board Quality among Fund Families**

Fund Family	*Stewardship Grade*	*Corporate Culture Grade*	*Board Quality Grade*
American Century	C	C	B
American Funds	A	B	B
Aston	B	B	B
BlackRock	C	C	B
Columbia	C	C	B
Dimensional Fund Advisors	B	B	A
Dodge & Cox	A	A	A
Fidelity Investments	B	B	B
Franklin Templeton	B	B	B
Invesco	C	C	B
Janus	C	D	A
John Hancock	C	B	C
JP Morgan	C	C	B
Lord Abbett	C	C	B
MFS	B	B	A
Neuberger Berman	B	B	B
Oppenheimer Funds	C	C	B
PIMCO	C	C	D
Pioneer	C	C	B
T. Rowe Price	A	A	A
Vanguard	A	A	A
Wells Fargo	C	B	C

Note: The table summarizes Morningstar grades for stewardship, corporate culture and board quality among fund families as of November 2014.

Source: Morningstar Direct 2014.

The Flow and Performance Relationship

Investor flows contribute to fund size and have implications for subsequent performance. Sirri and Tufano (1998) examine the relationship between mutual fund investors' flows and fund performance from 1971 to 1990. They find that robust investor inflows follow positive excess performance by funds. However, negative performance of an equivalent magnitude does not precede investor redemptions at the same level.

This asymmetry might be due to well-performing funds receiving substantial advertising and media attention. In contrast, poor-performing funds are not advertised as such and investors are not induced to sell.

Chevalier and Ellison (1997) examine a shorter period and find evidence consistent with that of Sirri and Tufano (1998). They also account for the conflicting objectives of investors and fund managers. Investors prefer that managers use their skills to maximize risk-adjusted returns relative to a benchmark. Fund managers want to maximize AUM and thus their own personal wealth. Chevalier and Ellison hypothesize that managers who beat the market at the end of the third quarter of the year are inclined to lock in their advantage, decrease their level of active management, and track the market index through the year's final quarter. This outperformance virtually guarantees a positive flow and higher fees in the next year. In contrast, underperformance during the first nine months of the year is likely to be followed by increased portfolio risk-taking during the final quarter, in a bid to reverse losses and avoid bearing the penalty associated with shareholder redemptions. Chevalier and Ellison's empirical results bear out their predictions.

Berk and Green (2004) provide the most comprehensive model relating mutual fund flows and performance. Their framework allows for the existence of talented managers who earn positive alphas on their investments. Outperformance then attracts new fund flows, which is a trend that is likely abetted by increases in discrete quality rankings by Morningstar and others (Reuter and Zitzewitz 2013). Due to scale diseconomies in portfolio management, the portfolio managers find maintaining superior performance increasingly difficult. Berk and Green's model indicates how superior managers with growing AUM coexist persistently with investors who earn negative alpha.

Summary and Conclusions

Mutual funds provide investors with access to diversified and professionally managed portfolios. Through such funds, both institutional and retail investors can gain exposure to a wide array of industry sectors and investment styles across multiple asset classes. Many investors can participate at low cost, which has been shown to contribute meaningfully to long-horizon returns. Mutual funds are available in various forms including OEFs, CEFs, ETFs, and UITs. OEFs have, by far, the largest value of AUM.

The fund industry manages more than $60 trillion in assets worldwide, with about one-quarter in the United States. The nine largest fund sponsors have about 50 percent of the U.S. market share. Substantial evidence exists that scale economies are available in managing a fund and a fund family, but only to a certain asset size. Scale economies are most evident in small cap funds. Evidence suggests that many sponsors split the benefits of scale economies with fund shareholders. Still, taxable investors must approach OEFs with caution. Many funds carry sizable capital gains overhangs and the unpredictable redemption behavior of fellow investors can result in a torrent of involuntary taxable distributions.

Regarding fees, mutual fund investing is a "buyer beware" situation. A fee is potentially associated with whether investors are committing cash to a fund, maintaining an investment position, or redeeming shares in a fund. The all-in cost of different fee and load structures depends on the investor's holding period. The lowest cost funds in the industry involve no loads and an annual expense ratio below 30 basis points. Given that funds often charge loads and have a median expense ratio of about 118 basis points, the industry is structured to be highly profitable for fund sponsors. Marketing (12b-1) fees have become ubiquitous in the industry and are common even among funds that are closed to new investment and supposedly no longer engaging in marketing. Finally, estimates of average direct and indirect trading costs for actively managed funds show that they are more than 1 percent a year. Despite their magnitude, funds do not prominently report such costs to their shareholders.

Fund boards rehire a manager every year and negotiate the expense ratio with the fund sponsor. Evidence suggests that an all-independent board may be an ideal structure. For their part, fund managers have a high potential for agency conflicts, given their common dual role of shareholder fiduciary and marketer to attract new asset flows. Decades after its emergence, the industry is still seeking ways to manage its inherent conflicts more effectively.

Discussion Questions

1. Discuss the advantages that mutual funds provide to investors.
2. Describe the structure of the U.S. mutual fund industry.
3. Describe the various types of fees and loads that mutual fund investors must pay.
4. Explain why mutual fund managers face an inherent conflict in their roles as fiduciaries.
5. Discuss the relationship among fund performance, fees, size, and investor flows.

References

Barber, Brad, Terrance Odean, and Lu Zheng. 2005. "Out of Sight, Out of Mind: The Effects of Expenses on Mutual Fund Flows." *Journal of Business* 78:6, 2095–2119.

Bergstresser, Daniel, John M. R. Chalmers, and Peter Tufano. 2009. "Assessing the Costs and Benefits of Brokers in the Mutual Fund Industry." *Review of Financial Studies* 22:10, 4129–4156.

Berk, Jonathan B., and Richard C. Green. 2004. "Mutual Fund Flows and Performance in Rational Markets." *Journal of Political Economy* 112:6, 1269–1295.

Birdthistle, William A. 2006. "Compensating Power: An Analysis of Rents and Rewards in the Mutual Fund Industry." *Tulane Law Review* 80:4, 1401–1465.

Chen, Joseph, Harrison Hong, Ming Huang, and Jeffrey D. Kubik. 2004. "Does Fund Size Erode Mutual Fund Performance? The Role of Liquidity and Organization." *American Economic Review* 94:5, 1276–1302.

Chevalier, Judith, and Glenn Ellison. 1997. "Risk-Taking by Mutual Funds as a Response to Incentives." *Journal of Political Economy* 105:6, 1167–1200.

Chordia, Tarun. 1996. "The Structure of Mutual Fund Charges." *Journal of Financial Economics* 41:1, 3–39.

Del Guercio, Diane, and Jonathan Reuter. 2014. "Mutual Fund Performance and the Incentive to Generate Alpha." *Journal of Finance* 69:4, 1673–1704.

Dickson, Joel M., John B. Shoven, and Clemens Sialm. 2000. "Tax Externalities of Equity Mutual Funds." *National Tax Journal* 53:3, 607–628.

Edelen, Roger M. 1999. "Investor Flows and the Assessed Performance of Open-End Mutual Funds." *Journal of Financial Economics* 53:3, 439–466.

Edelen, Roger M., Richard Evans, and Gregory B. Kadlec. 2007. "Scale Effects in Mutual Fund Performance: The Role of Trading Costs." Working Paper, University of California at Davis.

Evans, Richard B., and Rüdiger Fahlenbrach. 2012. "Institutional Investors and Mutual Fund Governance: Evidence from Retail-Institutional Fund Twins." *Review of Financial Studies* 25: 12, 3530–3571.

Ferris, Stephen P., and Don M. Chance. 1987. "The Effect of 12b-1 Plans on Mutual Fund Expense Ratios: A Note." *Journal of Finance* 42:4, 1077–1082.

Ferris, Stephen P., and Xuemin (Sterling) Yan. 2007. "Do Independent Directors and Chairmen Matter? The Role of Boards of Directors in Mutual Fund Governance." *Journal of Corporate Finance* 13:2–3, 392–420.

Ferris, Stephen P., and Xuemin (Sterling) Yan. 2009. "Agency Costs, Governance, and Organizational Forms: Evidence from the Mutual Fund Industry." *Journal of Banking & Finance* 33:4, 619–626.

Freeman, John P. 2007. "The Mutual Fund Distribution Expense Mess." *Journal of Corporation Law* 32:4, 739–831.

French, Kenneth R. 2008. "The Cost of Active Investing." *Journal of Finance* 63:4, 1537–1573.

Gao, Xiaohui, and Miles Livingston. 2008. "The Components of Mutual Fund Fees." *Financial Markets, Institutions & Instruments* 17:3, 197–223.

Gil-Bazo, Javier, and Pablo Ruiz-Verdu. 2009. "The Relation between Price and Performance in the Mutual Fund Industry." *Journal of Finance* 64:5, 2153–2183.

Gill, Steven L., and Christopher Schwarz. 2011. "Tax Equalization in Mutual Funds." *Journal of the American Taxation Association* 33:2, 89–110.

Hill, Joanne M., and Rebecca K. Cheong. 1996. "Minimizing Cash Drag with S&P 500 Index Tools." Working Paper, Goldman Sachs, New York.

Houge, Todd, and Jay Wellman. 2007. "The Use and Abuse of Mutual Fund Expenses." *Journal of Business Ethics* 70:1, 23–32.

Investment Company Institute. 2014. *Investment Company Fact Book*, 54th Edition. Washington, DC: Investment Company Institute.

Jayaraman, Narayanan, Ajay Khorana, and Edward Nelling. 2002. "An Analysis of the Determinants and Shareholder Wealth Effects of Mutual Fund Mergers." *Journal of Finance* 57:3, 1521–1551.

Karceski, Jason, Miles Livingston, and Edward O'Neal. 2004. "Portfolio Transactions Costs at U.S. Equity Mutual Funds." Working Paper, University of Florida.

Khorana, Ajay, and Henri Servaes. 1999. "The Determinants of Mutual Fund Starts." *Review of Financial Studies* 12:5, 1043–1074.

Khorana, Ajay, Henri Servaes, and Peter Tufano. 2005. "Explaining the Size of the Mutual Fund Industry around the World." *Journal of Financial Economics* 78:1, 145–185.

Khorana, Ajay, Henri Servaes, and Peter Tufano. 2008. "Mutual Funds Fees around the World." *Review of Financial Studies* 22:3, 1279–1310.

Khorana, Ajay, Henri Servaes, and Lei Wedge. 2007. "Portfolio Manager Ownership and Fund Performance." *Journal of Financial Economics* 85:1, 179–204.

Khorana, Ajay, Peter Tufano, and Lei Wedge. 2007. "Board Structure, Mergers and Shareholder Wealth: A Study of the Mutual Fund Industry." *Journal of Financial Economics* 85:2, 571–598.

Latzko, David A. 1999. "Economies of Scale in Mutual Fund Administration." *Journal of Financial Research* 22:3, 331–339.

Livingston, Miles, and Edward S. O'Neal. 1998. "The Cost of Mutual Fund Distribution Fees." *Journal of Financial Research* 21:2, 205–218.

Mahoney, Paul G. 2004. "Manager-Investor Conflicts in Mutual Funds." *Journal of Economic Perspectives* 18:2, 161–182.

Malhotra, D. K., Rand Martin, and Philip Russel. 2007. "Determinants of Cost Efficiencies in the Mutual Fund Industry." *Review of Financial Economics* 16:4, 323–334.

Miller, Ross M. 2007. "Measuring the True Cost of Active Management by Mutual Funds." *Journal of Investment Management* 5:1, 29–49.

Morey, Matthew R. 2003. "Should You Carry the Load? A Comprehensive Analysis of Load and No-Load Mutual Fund Out-of-Sample Performance." *Journal of Banking and Finance* 27:7, 1245–1271.

Morningstar. 2014. Morningstar Direct database.

Nadig, Dave. 2014. "Anatomy of a Mutual Fund Tax Land Mine." ETF.com. Available at http://www.etf.com/sections/blog/23900-anatomy-of-a-mutual-fund-tax-land-mine.html.

O'Neal, Edward S. 1999. "Mutual Fund Share Classes and Broker Incentives." *Financial Analysts Journal* 55:5, 76–87.

Reuter, Jonathan, and Eric Zitzewitz. 2013. "How Much Does Size Erode Mutual Fund Performance? A Regression Discontinuity Approach." Working Paper, Boston College.

Sirri, Erik R., and Peter Tufano. 1998. "Costly Search and Mutual Fund Flows." *Journal of Finance* 53:5, 1589–1622.

Smith, David M. 2014. "Equity Hedge Fund Performance, Cross-Sectional Return Dispersion, and Active Portfolio Management." *Research in Finance* 30, 1–22.

Tufano, Peter, and Matthew Sevick. 1997. "Board Structure and Fee-Setting in the U.S. Mutual Fund Industry." *Journal of Financial Economics* 53:3, 321–355.

Walsh, Lori. 2004. "The Costs and Benefits to Fund Shareholders of 12b-1 Plans: An Examination of Fund Flows, Expenses, and Returns." Working Paper, Office of Economic Analysis, U.S. Securities and Exchange Commission.

Wermers, Russ. 2000. "Mutual Fund Performance: An Empirical Decomposition into Stock-Picking Talent, Style, Transaction Costs and Expenses." *Journal of Finance* 55:4, 1655–1695.

3

The Role of Mutual Funds in Retirement and Education Savings

SARAH A. HOLDEN

Senior Director, Retirement and Investor Research, Investment Company Institute

Introduction

In the past few decades, retirement savings have risen in importance on household balance sheets, and mutual funds' role in retirement preparation has grown, reflecting the increase in individual account-based retirement savings. Although much smaller, savings specifically earmarked for education also have grown, and mutual funds play an important role in those accounts.

This chapter aims to provide a brief history of the developments in U.S. retirement savings and education savings markets. It highlights that retirement resources can be viewed as a pyramid with five layers: (1) Social Security at the base, (2) homeownership, (3) employer-sponsored retirement plans, (4) individual retirement accounts (IRAs), and (5) other assets. Social Security forms the strong base to U.S. retirement preparation and has evolved over time essentially to be a pension for lower earning households (Brady, Burham, and Holden 2012). Complementing U.S. Social Security are U.S. retirement assets, which include employer-sponsored retirement plans and IRAs (the third and fourth layers of the resource pyramid), and within those assets specifically earmarked for retirement, individual account-based savings have grown. Over half of U.S. retirement assets are in defined contribution (DC) plan accounts or IRAs, and mutual funds manage about half of DC plan and IRA assets. Mutual funds play a key role in account-based U.S. retirement savings and nearly three-quarters of mutual-fund-owning households show that saving for retirement is their primary financial goal. Many mutual-fund-owning households also are saving for education, and mutual funds play an important role in 529 savings plan accounts and Coverdell Education Savings Accounts (ESAs).

The remainder of the chapter is organized as follows. The first section discusses U.S. retirement resources, suggesting that the components form a pyramid. Within the pyramid, households rely on assets specifically earmarked for retirement, and the next section discusses these accumulations. Within retirement accumulations, individual account-based retirement savings have grown in importance, and thus, the next section focuses on DC plans and IRAs. The discussion then focuses on mutual funds, which play an important role in DC plan and IRA investing. Finally, the chapter discusses how households save for educational expenses through 529 plans and Coverdell ESAs.

Retirement Resources

U.S. households rely on a combination of resources in retirement, and the role each type of resource plays has changed over time and varies across households. Traditionally, the analogy used to describe retirement preparation compares retirement resources to a three-legged stool, with resources divided equally among three legs—Social Security, employer-sponsored pension plans, and private savings. But this view of retirement resources does not accurately capture the full range of U.S. retirement resources. Thus, Brady et al. (2012) argue that a five-layer pyramid provides a more constructive framework.

The retirement resource pyramid has five layers, which draw from government programs, compensation deferred until retirement, and other savings: (1) Social Security; (2) homeownership; (3) employer-sponsored retirement plans, including both private sector and government employer plans, and both defined benefit (DB) and defined contribution (DC) plans; (4) IRAs including rollovers; and (5) other assets. While the importance of each layer differs by household, together they have enabled recent generations of retirees, on average, to maintain their standard of living in retirement (Brady et al. 2012).

Social Security, the base of the U.S. retirement resource pyramid, is the largest component of retiree income and the primary source of income for lower income retirees (Brady and Bogdan 2014a). Social Security benefits are funded through a payroll tax equal to 12.4 percent of earnings of covered workers (6.2 percent paid by employees and 6.2 percent paid by employers) up to a maximum taxable earnings amount, which was $113,700 in 2013 (Social Security Administration 2014). The benefit formula is highly progressive, with benefits representing a much higher percentage of earnings for workers with lower lifetime earnings (Congressional Budget Office 2013; Pang and Schieber 2014). By design, Social Security is the primary means of support for retirees with low lifetime earnings and a substantial source of income for all retired workers.

For many near-retiree households, homeownership is the second most important retirement resource after Social Security. Analysis of the Federal Reserve Board's Survey of Consumer Finances (SCF) data finds that older households are more likely to own their homes; more likely to own their homes without mortgage debt; and, if they still have mortgages, more likely to have small mortgages relative to the value of their homes (Brady et al. 2012). Housing provides shelter while households are working and for households in retirement. Retired households typically access this resource simply by living in their homes rent-free.

Employer-sponsored retirement plans and IRAs, which complement Social Security benefits and are important resources for households across all levels of income and wealth, increase in importance for households in which Social Security replaces a smaller share of earnings. Employer-sponsored DB plans typically provide a benefit based on years of tenure and average final pay, while DC plans provide an account at retirement. Both private sector and government employers offer retirement plans. In 2013, the SCF data show that about 80 percent of near-retiree households (i.e., those with a working head aged 55 to 64) had accrued benefits in employer-sponsored retirement plans—DB and DC plans sponsored by private sector and government employers—or IRAs.

Although less important on average, retirees also rely on other assets in retirement. These assets can be financial including bank deposits and stocks, bonds, and mutual funds owned outside retirement accounts. They also can be nonfinancial including business equity, investment real estate, second homes, vehicles, and consumer durables (i.e., long-lived goods such as household appliances and furniture). Higher income and higher wealth households are more likely to have larger holdings of other assets than lower income or lower wealth households.

U.S. Retirement Assets

As Figure 3.1 shows, employer-sponsored retirement plans (i.e., DB and DC plans sponsored by private sector and government employers), IRAs including rollovers, and annuities play an important role in the U.S. retirement system, with assets reaching $23.3 trillion at year-end 2013. The largest components of U.S. retirement assets were IRAs and employer-sponsored DC plans, holding $7.0 trillion and $6.3 trillion, respectively, at year-end 2013. Other employer-sponsored plans include private sector DB pension funds ($3.1 trillion), state and local government DB plans ($3.7 trillion), and federal government DB plans ($1.4 trillion). Additionally, annuity reserves outside of retirement plans were $2.0 trillion at year-end 2013.

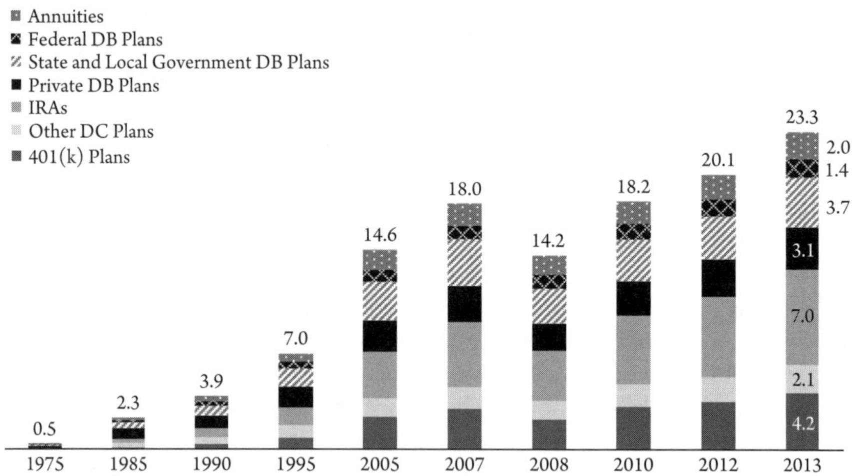

Figure 3.1 GROWTH OF U.S. RETIREMENT ASSETS. The graph shows total U.S. retirement assets in trillions of dollars at year-end for selected years and the main components. Note: For definitions of plan categories and a complete list of data sources, see Tables 1 and 5 in Investment Company Institute 2014c. Some data are estimated. Sources: Investment Company Institute, Federal Reserve Board, Department of Labor, National Association of Government Defined Contribution Administrators, American Council of Life Insurers, and Internal Revenue Service Statistics of Income Division (Investment Company Institute 2014c).

Figure 3.1 also highlights that the composition of U.S. retirement assets has shifted over time toward individual account-based approaches. DC plans and IRAs were 57 percent of retirement assets at year-end 2013, up from 43 percent in 1995, and 32 percent in 1985. This shift reflects the growing role of IRAs as a repository for rollovers (Sabelhaus and Schrass 2009; Holden and Bass 2014) and changes in the composition of private sector retirement plan offerings (U.S. Department of Labor 2014), toward a DC plan design, although the federal DC plan (i.e., the Thrift Savings Plan or TSP) also has grown to nearly $400 billion at year-end 2013, up from $35 billion at year-end 1995 (U.S. Federal Reserve Board 2014). Some are concerned that the shift to DC plan designs in the private sector may hurt retirement preparedness, but to date, more retirees are getting more retirement income from private sector plans in 2013 than in the past (Brady and Bogdan 2014a). Holden and VanDerhei (2002) and Poterba, Venti, and Wise (2007) carry out forward-looking projection analyses indicating that DC plans can be an important resource in retirement.

Engagement with formal retirement accumulation activity is prevalent across a majority of U.S. households. Holden and Schrass (2013) find that 67 percent of U.S. households of all ages (or 82 million) reported that they had employer-sponsored retirement plans, IRAs, or both in mid-2013. Sixty-one percent of U.S. households reported that they had employer-sponsored retirement plans (i.e., they had assets in DC

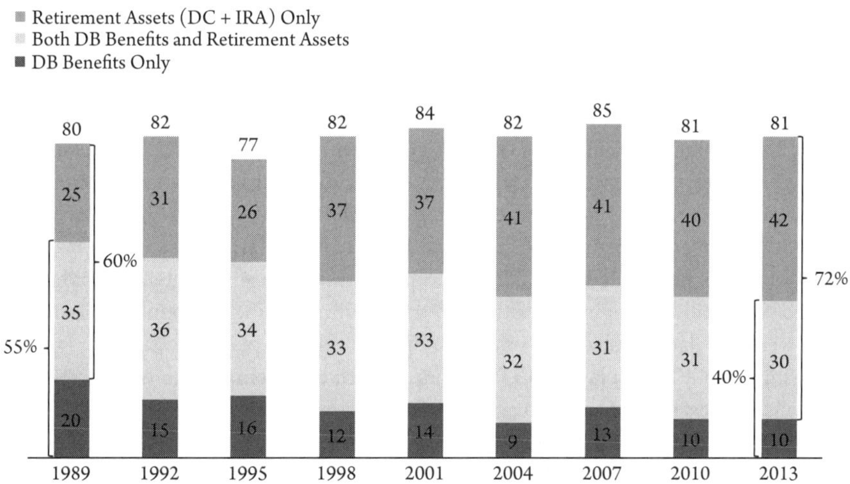

Figure 3.2 Share of Near-Retiree Households with Retirement Accumulations. The chart shows the percentage of households with working heads aged 55 to 64 who had the type of retirement accumulation indicated. It shows the share of near-retiree households with retirement accumulations is steady, but the composition has shifted. Note: Retirement assets include DC plan assets (401(k), 403(b), 457, and other DC plans) and IRAs (traditional, Roth, SEP, SAR-SEP, and SIMPLE), whether from private sector or government employers. DB benefits include households currently receiving DB benefits and households with the promise of future DB benefits, whether from private sector or government employers. Components may not add to the total because of rounding. Source: Investment Company Institute tabulations of the Survey of Consumer Finances.

plan accounts), were receiving or expecting to receive benefits from DB plans, or both. Thirty-eight percent of U.S. households reported having assets in IRAs, and 32 percent had both IRAs and employer-sponsored retirement plans. Because of the life cycle of saving, primary savings goals change as people age, moving from focusing on education and saving for a home, to retirement saving (Brady and Bogdan 2014b). The share of U.S. households with retirement accumulations tends to rise with household age. In fact, as Figure 3.2 shows, 81 percent of near-retiree households (i.e., those with a working head aged 55 to 64) had DC accounts, IRAs, and/or DB plan benefits in 2013.

Over the past two and a half decades, consistently about 8 in 10 near-retiree households have reported they have retirement accumulations, but the composition of those accumulations has changed. As Figure 3.2 shows, 80 percent of near-retiree households in 1989 had retirement assets (DC plan accounts or IRAs) or DB benefits. In 1989, 60 percent had retirement assets, 55 percent had DB benefits, and 35 percent had both. Reflecting the shift in the composition of private sector retirement plans to DC plans, the retirement accumulation pattern among near-retiree households is different in 2013, even as 81 percent have retirement accumulations. In 2013, 72 percent had retirement assets (DC plan accounts or IRAs), 40 percent had DB benefits, and 30 percent had both.

Defined Contribution Retirement Plans

DC plans provide employees with a retirement account funded with employer contributions, employee contributions, or both, plus investment earnings or losses on those contributions less withdrawals. Assets in employer-sponsored DC plans have grown faster than assets in other types of employer-sponsored retirement plans over the past quarter century, increasing from 26 percent of employer-sponsored retirement plan assets in 1985 to 44 percent at year-end 2013 (see Figure 3.1). At the end of 2013, employer-sponsored DC plans—which include 401(k) plans, 403(b) plans, 457 plans, Keoghs, the federal TSP, and other private-sector DC plans—held an estimated \$6.3 trillion in assets. With \$4.2 trillion in assets at year-end 2013, 401(k) plans were the largest share of employer-sponsored DC plan assets. Two types of plans similar to 401(k) plans—403(b) plans, which allow employees of education institutions and certain nonprofit organizations to receive deferred compensation, and 457 plans, which allow employees of state and local governments to receive deferred compensation—held another \$1.2 trillion in assets. The federal TSP, a DC plan established by the Federal Employees' Retirement System Act of 1986 (FERSA), held \$0.4 trillion in assets. Other private sector DC plans without 401(k) features held the remaining \$0.5 trillion.

401(k) PLANS

For many U.S. workers, 401(k) plan accounts have become an important part of retirement planning. Although Congress enacted legislation paving the way for 401(k) plans in 1978, the Internal Revenue Service (IRS) did not implement proposed regulations until 1981 (Holden, Brady, and Hadley 2006). Concurrent with the rising stock market in the 1990s (Fink 2011), recognition of the mobility of U.S. workers (Brady and Bogdan 2014a), increasing costs of maintaining DB plans (Brady and Bogdan 2010), and an increasing number of companies and their workers for which a DC structure made sense (Aaronson and Coronado 2005), 401(k) plans have grown rapidly among private sector employers. Investment Company Institute (2014c) estimates that 401(k) plan assets were $4.2 trillion at the end of 2013, and Holden, VanDerhei, Alonso, and Bass (2013) estimate about 52 million active 401(k) plan participants in 2012. The growth of these accounts and therefore, the income that they will provide in retirement depend, in part, on the asset allocation decisions of plan participants.

As summarized in Figure 3.3, U.S. Department of Labor (2014) reports that the vast majority (88 percent) of 401(k) plans are fully participant-directed, meaning that 90 percent of 401(k) plan participants fully determine their asset allocations, choosing from the investment menus in their plans. Plan sponsors select the investment menus for their plans, and generally do so to include a broad range of investments offering differing risk and returns, so that plan participants can find investments that are appropriate given their age, investment horizon, and appetite for risk.

On average, younger 401(k) plan participants allocate more of their portfolios to equities than older 401(k) plan participants. According to research conducted by ICI and the Employee Benefit Research Institute (EBRI) at year-end 2012, individuals in their twenties had 36 percent of their 401(k) assets in equity funds and company stock; 46 percent in target-date funds and non-target-date balanced funds; and only 11 percent in guaranteed investment contracts (GICs), stable value funds, money funds, and bond funds (see Table 3.1). All told, participants in their twenties had 73 percent of their 401(k) assets in equities, which include equity mutual funds and other pooled equity investments; the equity portion of balanced funds, including target-date funds; and company stock of their employers (Holden et al. 2013). By comparison, at

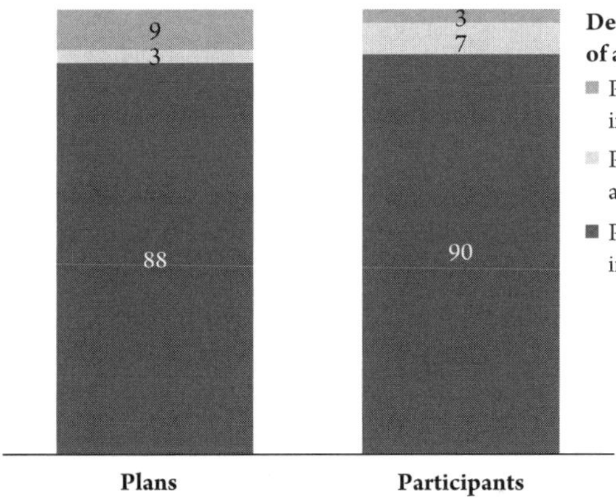

Figure 3.3 Degree of Participant Direction of 401 (k) Account Investments. The chart shows the percentage of the total by degree of participant direction of investments for plan year 2012. It shows the vast majority of 401(k) plans allow participant direction of investments. Source: Form 5500 filings for plan years ending in 2012 (U.S. Department of Labor 2014).

Table 3.1 **401(k) Asset Allocation and Participant Age**

Investment	*Participants in Their Twenties (%)*	*Participants in Their Sixties (%)*
Equity funds	30.7	32.2
Target-date funds[a, b]	34.2	12.5
Non-target-date balanced funds	11.7	6.9
Company stock[b]	5.5	6.7
Bond funds	6.4	15.2
GICs[c, b] and other stable value funds[b]	3.1	15.3
Money funds	1.9	5.6
Other funds[d]	6.4	5.5

Note: The table reports the average asset allocation of 401(k) account balances (percentage of assets) at year-end 2012 for 401(k) plan participants in their twenties or sixties. It shows 401(k) asset allocation varies with participant age. Funds include mutual funds, bank collective trusts, life insurance separate accounts, and any pooled investment product primarily invested in the security indicated. Percentages are dollar-weighted averages. Components do not add to 100 percent because of rounding.

[a]A target-date fund typically rebalances its portfolio to become less focused on growth and more focused on income as it approaches and passes the target date of the fund, which is usually included in the fund's name.

[b]Not all participants are offered this investment option.

[c]GICs are guaranteed investment contracts.

[d]Other funds include real estate funds, other investments, and assets that could not be identified.

Source: Tabulations from EBRI/ICI Participant-Directed Retirement Plan Data Collection Project (Holden et al. 2013).

year-end 2012, participants in their sixties had 48 percent of their 401(k) assets in equities (Holden et al. 2013). At year-end 2012, individuals in their sixties focused more on fixed-income investments and had 36 percent of their 401(k) account assets in GICs, stable value funds, money funds, and bond funds; only 19 percent in target-date funds and non-target-date balanced funds; and 39 percent in equity funds and company stock.

Portfolio allocation also varies widely within age groups, and younger 401(k) plan participants tend to have higher concentrations in equities in their accounts compared with older 401(k) plan participants. As Figure 3.4 shows, at year-end 2012, 64 percent of 401(k) plan participants in their twenties held more than 80 percent of their account in equities, and only 10 percent of these participants held 20 percent or less. Of 401(k) plan participants in their sixties, only 20 percent held more than 80 percent of their account in equities, and 23 percent held 20 percent or less. Some of this pattern reflects the influence of target-date fund investing, which typically puts investors in their twenties in a high allocation to equities, compared with investors in their sixties, who would be more focused on fixed-income investing.

Target-date funds, introduced in the 1990s, have grown rapidly in recent years. A *target-date fund* has a diversified portfolio that follows a predetermined reallocation of assets over time based on a specified target retirement date. The fund typically

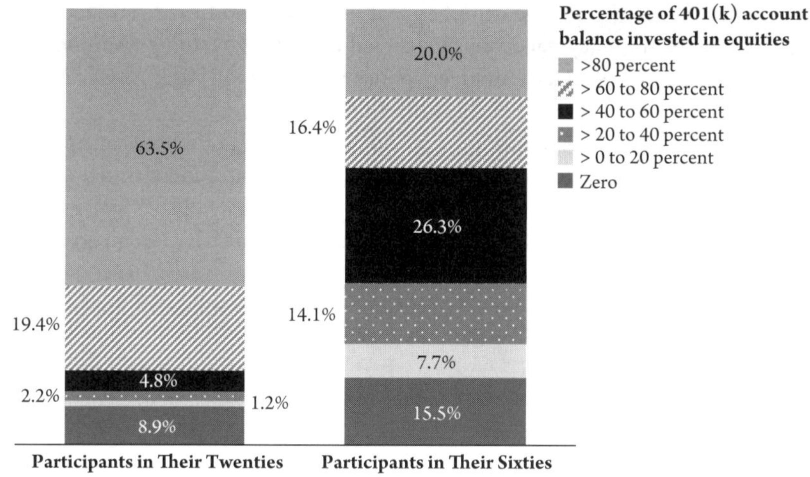

Figure 3.4 Relationship of Asset Allocation to Equities among 401(k) Plan Participants. The graph shows the percentage of 401(k) plan participants with the given asset allocation to equities at year-end 2012 for 401(k) plan participants in their twenties or sixties. It shows the asset allocation to equities varies widely among 401(k) plan participants. Note: Equities include equity funds, company stock, and the equity portion of balanced funds. Funds include mutual funds, bank collective trusts, life insurance separate accounts, and any pooled investment product invested primarily in the security indicated. Source: Tabulations from EBRI/ICI Participant-Directed Retirement Plan Data Collection Project (Holden et al. 2013).

rebalances its portfolio to become less focused on growth and more focused on income as it approaches and passes the target date, which is usually stated in the fund's name. Within 401(k) plans, target-date funds can be structured as mutual funds, collective investment trusts, and separately managed accounts. The EBRI/ICI 401(k) database has been tracking target-date funds since 2006 and has found that the share of 401(k) plan assets invested in target-date funds, the share of 401(k) plans that offer target-date funds, the share of 401(k) plan participants offered target-date funds, and the share of 401(k) plan participants holding target-date funds all have increased. Holden et al. (2013) report on target-date fund investing across all of these investment structures. At year-end 2012, the EBRI/ICI 401(k) database reveals that target-date funds accounted for 15 percent of 401(k) assets, up from 5 percent at year-end 2006. In 2012, 72 percent of 401(k) plans offered target-date funds, up from 57 percent at year-end 2006; and 41 percent of 401(k) plan participants held at least some plan assets in target-date funds, up from 19 percent at year-end 2006.

Individual Retirement Accounts

IRAs have grown to be the single largest component of U.S. retirement assets. Congress created traditional IRAs, the first type of IRA, in 1974 under the Employee Retirement Income Security Act (ERISA) (Holden, Ireland, Leonard-Chambers, and Bogdan 2005). Traditional IRAs provide all workers with a contributory retirement savings vehicle and, through rollovers, give workers leaving jobs a means to preserve the tax benefits and growth opportunities that employer-sponsored retirement plans provide. Since 1974, policymakers have changed the rules governing traditional IRAs and added more types of IRAs: employer-sponsored IRAs (SEP IRAs, SAR-SEP IRAs, and SIMPLE IRAs) and after-tax IRAs (Roth IRAs).

As Table 3.2 reports, nearly 4 out of 10, or 46 million, U.S. households owned at least one type of IRA as of mid-2013. Traditional IRAs—those introduced under ERISA—were the most common type, owned by 36 million U.S. households. Nineteen million U.S. households owned Roth IRAs, first available in 1998 under the Taxpayer Relief Act of 1997, and 9 million U.S. households owned employer-sponsored IRAs (SEP IRAs, SAR-SEP IRAs, or SIMPLE IRAs). Total IRA assets, at $7.0 trillion at year-end 2013, accounted for 30 percent of U.S. retirement assets.

TRADITIONAL IRAs

Traditional IRAs, the most common type of IRA, typically are opened with rollovers from employer-sponsored retirement plans (both DB and DC from both private sector

Table 3.2 **Types of Individual Retirement Accounts**

Type of IRA	*Year Created*	*Number of U.S. Households with Type of IRA*	*Percentage of U.S. Households with Type of IRA*	*IRA Assets by Type of IRA*
Traditional IRA	1974 (Employee Retirement Income Security Act)	36.0 million	29.4%	$6.0 trillion (86.4% of total)
SEP IRA	1978 (Revenue Act)	9.2 million	7.5%	$0.4 trillion (6.3% of total)
SAR-SEP IRA	1986 (Tax Reform Act)			
SIMPLE IRA	1996 (Small Business Job Protection Act)			
Roth IRA	1997 (Taxpayer Relief Act)	19.1 million	15.6%	$0.5 trillion (7.2% of total)
Any IRA		46.1 million	37.6%	$7.0 trillion

Note: The table shows the year that each type of IRA was created, the number and percentage of U.S. households reporting ownership of IRAs in May 2013, and IRA assets at year-end 2013. It shows traditional IRAs are the most common type of IRAs. Households may own more than one type of IRA. SEP IRAs, SAR-SEP IRAs, and SIMPLE IRAs are employer-sponsored IRAs.

Sources: Investment Company Institute and U.S. Census Bureau (Holden and Schrass 2013; Investment Company Institute 2014c).

and government employers). In 2012, investors opened 9 in 10 new traditional IRAs in The IRA Investor Database™ with rollovers (Holden and Bass 2014). Nearly half of traditional IRA-owning households in mid-2013 reported that their traditional IRAs contained rollovers (Holden and Schrass 2013).

Traditional IRA-owning households hold their traditional IRAs at a variety of financial services firms. In 2013, as Figure 3.5 shows, 76 percent of them held their traditional IRAs through investment professionals and 29 percent had opened traditional IRAs directly at a mutual fund company or discount brokerage. The most commonly used investment professionals were at full-service brokerage firms (33 percent of traditional IRA-owning households), followed by banks or savings institutions (28 percent) and independent financial advisers (26 percent). The most commonly used direct source was mutual fund companies, with 22 percent of traditional IRA-owning households indicating they held traditional IRAs directly at mutual fund companies.

Asset allocation of traditional IRAs varied with investor age. At year-end 2012, younger IRA investors tended to be more invested in equities, equity funds, and target-date funds, on average, than older investors, according to The IRA Investor Database (Holden and Bass 2014). Older investors invested more heavily in non-target-date balanced funds and fixed-income investments. For example, as Table 3.3 shows, traditional IRA investors in their thirties had, on average, more than 50 percent of their assets in equities and equity funds and another 17 percent in target-date funds. Investors in their sixties held nearly 46 percent of their traditional IRA assets in equities and equity funds, and 5 percent of their traditional IRA assets in target-date funds. Traditional IRA investors in their sixties had nearly one-quarter of their assets in bonds and bond funds, while investors in their thirties held less than one-tenth of their assets in that asset category.

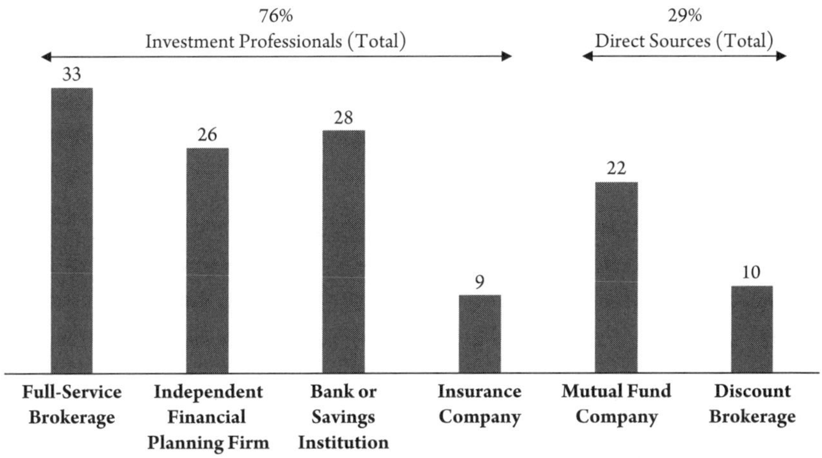

Figure 3.5 Traditional Individual Retirement Accounts Held at Financial Services Firms. The figure highlights where traditional IRA-owning households reported they held their traditional IRAs in mid-2013 (percentage of households owning traditional IRAs). It shows investors hold traditional IRAs at various financial services firms. Note: Multiple responses are included. Source: Investment Company Institute IRA Owners Survey (Holden and Schrass 2013).

Table 3.3 **Relationship between Traditional IRA Asset Allocation and Investor Age**

Assets	*Traditional IRA Investors in Their Thirties (%)*	*Traditional IRA Investors in Their Sixties (%)*
Equities and equity funds[a]	50.4	45.6
Target-date funds[b]	17.0	4.9
Non-target-date balanced funds[c]	7.9	11.3
Bonds and bond funds[d]	6.9	22.7
Money market funds	13.8	13.0
Other investments[e]	4.0	2.5

Note: The table reports the average asset allocation of traditional IRA balances (percentage of assets) at year-end 2012 for traditional IRA investors in their thirties or sixties. It shows traditional IRA asset allocation varies with investor age. Percentages are dollar-weighted averages.

[a]Equity funds include equity mutual funds, equity closed-end funds, and equity ETFs.

[b]A target-date fund, also known as lifecycle mutual fund, typically rebalances its portfolio to become less focused on growth and more focused on income as it approaches and passes the target date of the fund, which is usually included in the fund's name.

[c]Balanced funds invest in a mix of equities and fixed-income securities.

[d]Bond funds include bond mutual funds, bond closed-end funds, and bond ETFs.

[e]Other investments include certificates of deposit and unidentifiable assets.

Source: The IRA Investor Database™ (Holden and Bass 2014).

The Role of Mutual Funds in U.S. Households' Retirement Saving

Mutual funds play an important role in U.S. households' saving for retirement. The vast majority of mutual-fund-owning households report they purchased their first mutual fund through an employer-sponsored retirement plan. For example, as Table 3.4 shows, 73 percent of mutual-fund-owning households that purchased their first mutual fund in the late 1990s, 67 percent of mutual-fund-owning households that made their first mutual fund purchase between 2000 and 2004, and 63 percent of those making their first mutual fund purchase in 2005 or later, reported they did so through an employer-sponsored retirement plan. As Table 3.5 highlights, almost all mutual-fund-owning households (92 percent in mid-2013) indicate that saving for retirement is one of their financial goals for their mutual fund assets, with 72 percent indicating that saving for retirement was their primary financial goal. In mid-2013, 85 percent of mutual-fund-owning households had DC plan accounts, 63 percent had IRAs, and 95 percent had DC accounts, IRAs, or both.

Across the entire U.S. retirement market, mutual funds play a major role in IRAs and employer-sponsored DC plans, such as 401(k) plans. At year-end 2013, mutual funds held in DC plans and IRAs accounted for about $6.9 trillion, or about half of the

Table 3.4 **Source of the First Mutual Fund Purchase by Period**

	Year of Household's First Mutual Fund Purchase				
Source of First Mutual Fund Purchase	*Before 1990 (%)*	*1990 to 1994 (%)*	*1995 to 1999 (%)*	*2000 to 2004 (%)*	*2005 or Later (%)*
Inside employer-sponsored retirement plan	52	68	73	67	63
Outside employer-sponsored retirement plan	48	32	27	33	37

Note: This table shows where mutual-fund-owning households (surveyed in mid-2013) report they made their first mutual fund purchase by the year of the first purchase. It shows employer-sponsored retirement plans are increasingly the source of the first mutual fund purchase. The figures are the percentage of U.S. households owning mutual funds purchased in the time frame indicated. Employer-sponsored retirement plans include DC plans (such as 401(k), 403(b), or 457 plans) and employer-sponsored IRAs (SEP IRAs, SAR-SEP IRAs, and SIMPLE IRAs).

Source: Investment Company Institute Annual Mutual Fund Shareholder Tracking Survey (Burham et al. 2013).

Table 3.5 **Mutual-Fund-Owning Households and Their Goals**

	Percentage of Mutual-Fund-Owning Households
Financial Goals for Mutual Fund Investments	
Retirement, a goal[a]	92
Retirement, the primary goal	72
Household Ownership of Retirement Accounts[a]	
Household owned DC accounts and/or IRAs	95
Household owned employer-sponsored DC retirement plan accounts[b]	85
Household owned IRA[c]	63

Note: The table shows the percentage of U.S. households owning mutual funds (surveyed in mid-2013) with the financial goal or type of retirement savings indicated. It shows the vast majority of mutual-fund-owning households focus on retirement savings.

[a]Multiple responses are included.

[b]DC retirement plan accounts include 401(k), 403(b), 457, other DC plan accounts, and the Federal Thrift Savings Plan (TSP).

[c]IRAs include traditional, Roth, and employer-sponsored IRAs (SEP IRAs, SAR-SEP IRAs, and SIMPLE IRAs).

Source: Investment Company Institute Annual Mutual Fund Shareholder Tracking Survey (Bogdan and Schrass 2014).

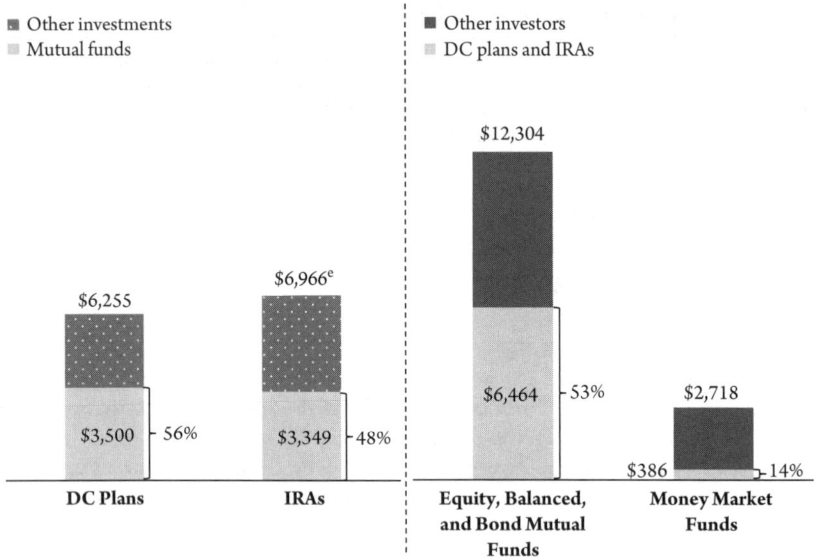

Figure 3.6 MUTUAL FUNDS AND RETIREMENT ACCOUNTS. The chart shows assets in billions of dollars at year-end 2013 for DC plans, IRAs, long-term mutual funds, and money market mutual funds. It shows substantial overlap between mutual funds and retirement accounts. e = estimated Sources: Investment Company Institute, U.S. Federal Reserve Board, U.S. Department of Labor, National Association of Government Defined Contribution Administrators, American Council of Life Insurers, and Internal Revenue Service Statistics of Income Division (Investment Company Institute 2014c).

assets in DC plans and IRAs and about 29 percent of the $23.3 trillion in total U.S. retirement assets. As Figure 3.6 reports, investors held $3.5 trillion, or 56 percent, of DC plan assets in mutual funds at year-end 2013. They invested the remaining assets in DC plans in other pooled investments (e.g., collective investment trusts, separately managed accounts, exchange-traded funds (ETFs)), guaranteed investment contracts (GICs) and other stable value funds, company stock (stock of the employer), and other investments. Mutual funds accounted for $3.3 trillion, or 48 percent, of IRA assets at year-end 2013. Investment Company Institute (2014c) reports that IRA assets also are invested in deposits (7 percent of the total), annuities (excluding variable annuity mutual funds comprising 5 percent of the total), and other investments, which include ETFs, individual stocks and bonds, and other securities held through brokerage accounts (40 percent of the total).

Substantial overlap exists between the mutual fund industry and retirement assets in the United States. As Figure 3.6 shows, the nearly $6.9 trillion in mutual fund retirement assets made up 46 percent of all mutual fund assets at year-end 2013 (Investment Company Institute 2014c). Retirement savings accounts held more than half of long-term (equity, balanced, and bond) mutual fund assets industry wide, but a much smaller share (14 percent) of money market fund assets industry-wide.

TYPES OF MUTUAL FUNDS USED BY RETIREMENT INVESTORS

Retirement investors tend to hold equity investments through the mutual funds held in their DC plans and IRAs. Table 3.6 shows that at year-end 2013, investors kept 57 percent of the $6.9 trillion in mutual fund retirement assets held in DC plans and IRAs in domestic or world equity funds. By comparison, investors held about 52 percent of overall fund industry assets—retirement and nonretirement accounts—in domestic or world equity funds. Domestic equity funds alone constituted about $3.0 trillion, or 44 percent, of mutual fund assets held in DC plans and IRAs.

Retirement investors also gain exposure to equities through balanced funds. At year-end 2013, investors had 22 percent of mutual fund assets held in DC plans and IRAs in balanced funds, which invest in a mix of equity, bond, and money market securities. Target-date (or lifecycle) and lifestyle (or target-risk) mutual funds, generally included in the balanced fund category, have grown more popular among investors and retirement plan sponsors over the past decade. A target-date fund has a diversified portfolio that follows a predetermined reallocation of assets over time based on a specified target retirement date. Typically the fund rebalances its portfolio to become less focused on growth and more focused on income as it approaches and passes the target date, which is usually indicated in the fund's name. A lifestyle fund maintains a predetermined risk level and generally uses words such as "conservative," "moderate," or "aggressive" in its name to show the fund's risk level. At year-end 2013, DC plans held $428 billion in target-date mutual fund assets, and IRAs held $129 billion, out of $618 billion in

Table 3.6 **Types of Mutual Funds Used by Retirement Investors ($ billions)**

Type of Plan	*Equity*					
	Domestic	*World*	*Balanced*[a]	*Bond*	*Money Market*	*Total*
Total in IRAs and DC plans	2,992	940	1,517	1,014	386	6,850
IRAs[b]	1,363	455	711	589	232	3,349
DC plans	1,629	485	806	425	154	3,500
401(k) plans	1,200	391	673	308	106	2,678
403(b), 457, and other DC plans[c]	429	94	133	118	48	823

Note: The table reports mutual fund assets in billions of dollars at year-end 2013 by the type of mutual fund and type of retirement account holding the mutual fund. It shows investors hold the majority of their mutual fund retirement account assets in equities. Components may not add to the total because of rounding.

[a]Balanced funds invest in a mix of equities and fixed-income securities. Most target-date and lifestyle funds are counted in this category.

[b]IRAs include traditional IRAs, Roth IRAs, and employer-sponsored IRAs (SEP IRAs, SAR-SEP IRAs, and SIMPLE IRAs).

[c]Other DC plans include Keoghs and other DC plans without 401(k) features.

Source: Investment Company Institute (Investment Company Institute 2014c).

target-date mutual fund assets. At year-end 2013, DC plans held $81 billion in lifestyle mutual fund assets, and IRAs held $71 billion out of $359 billion in lifestyle mutual fund assets (Investment Company Institute 2014c).

Table 3.6 shows that at year-end 2013, investors kept the remaining 20 percent of mutual fund assets held in DC plans and IRAs in bond funds and money market funds. Bond funds held $1,014 billion, or about 15 percent, of mutual fund assets held in DC plans and IRAs, and money market funds accounted for $386 billion, or nearly 6 percent.

With $3.5 trillion of mutual fund assets at year-end 2013, DC plans represented the largest share of retirement account assets invested in mutual funds. IRAs held $3.3 trillion in mutual fund assets at year-end 2013. Among DC plan mutual fund assets, 77 percent, or $2.7 trillion, was held in 401(k) plans, largely invested in equity mutual funds. Given the rise in 401(k) plans, much analysis of the design and costs of 401(k) plans is available.

SERVICES AND EXPENSES IN 401(k) PLANS

Employers must balance two competing economic pressures as they design their compensation packages: the need to attract and retain quality workers with competitive compensation packages and the need to keep their product offerings competitively priced. In deciding whether to offer 401(k) plans to their workers, employers must decide if the benefits of offering a plan (in attracting and retaining quality workers) outweigh the costs of providing the plan and plan services—both the compensation paid to the worker and any other costs associated with maintaining the plan and each individual plan participant account (Collins, Holden, Chism, and Duvall 2014).

To offer 401(k) plans, employers typically get a range of administrative, participant-focused, regulatory, and compliance services. Employers offering 401(k) plans typically hire service providers, who charge fees to operate these plans. The employer generally determines how the employer and employee will share the costs. Various fee structures exist: fees can be paid directly by the plan sponsor (the employer) or the plan, directly by the plan participant (the employee), indirectly by the participant through fees or other reductions in returns paid to the investment provider, or by some combination of these arrangements.

Analysis of mutual fund asset data collected by ICI and fee data collected by Lipper finds that 401(k) plan participants tend to concentrate their mutual fund assets in lower cost funds. This tendency is evident whether one looks at the asset-weighted fee on mutual funds held in 401(k) plans or the range of fees paid on mutual fund assets held in 401(k) plans.

For example, consider the case of equity mutual funds, which accounted for nearly 60 percent of 401(k) plan mutual fund assets at year-end 2013, as shown in Table 3.6. Consistent with the general industry trend, Figure 3.7 shows that average equity fund expense ratios incurred by 401(k) investors declined for the fourth straight year in 2013, falling to 0.58 percent. In 2013, 401(k) investors continued to concentrate their equity mutual fund assets in lower cost funds. The 401(k) asset-weighted average of 0.58 percent was less than half the 1.37 percent simple average for all equity mutual funds and lower than the industry-wide asset-weighted average of 0.74 percent.

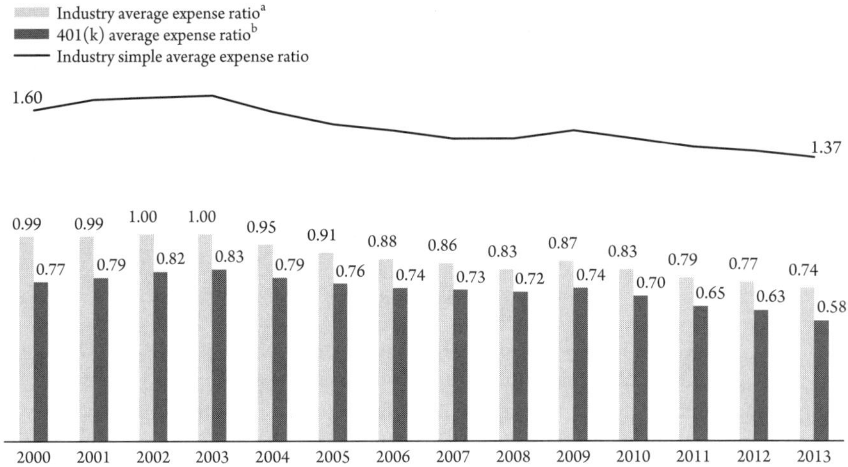

Figure 3.7 Expense Ratios over Time. This figure highlights the concentration of equity mutual fund assets in lower cost funds by plotting the asset-weighted equity mutual fund expense ratios (percent of assets) industry-wide and for 401(k) investors, as well as the industry simple average expense ratio. It shows 401(k) mutual fund investors tend to pay lower-than-average expenses. [a] The industry average expense ratio is measured as an asset-weighted average. [b] The 401(k) average expense ratio is measured as a 401(k) asset-weighted average. Note: Figures exclude mutual funds available as investment choices in variable annuities. Sources: Investment Company Institute and Lipper (Collins et al. 2014).

Expense ratios vary among the mutual funds that 401(k) plan participants hold. For example, Figure 3.8 shows that at year-end 2013, investors held 85 percent of 401(k) plan equity fund assets in mutual funds with expense ratios of less than 1.00 percent, with 38 percent invested in mutual funds with expense ratios of less than 0.50 percent.

Several factors contribute to the relatively low average expense ratios incurred by 401(k) plan participants investing in mutual funds. First, mutual funds compete among themselves and with other financial products to offer shareholders service and performance. Investment Company Institute (2014a) analyzes the Herfindahl-Hirschman Index for the mutual fund industry and finds it to be unconcentrated. Additionally, plan sponsors and shareholders are sensitive to the fees and expenses that funds charge (Collins et al. 2014).

The lower average expense ratios incurred by 401(k) plan participants also reflect other factors. Some plan sponsors choose to cover a portion of 401(k) plan costs, which allows them to select funds or share classes with lower built-in servicing costs. Further, many 401(k) plans have large average account balances, and economies of scale help reduce the fees and expenses of the funds offered in these plans. Statistical regression analysis in Deloitte Consulting LLP and Investment Company Institute (2014) finds that plan size variables—both the average account balance in the plan and number of plan participants—were negatively correlated with the comprehensive overall cost of the 401(k) plan (the "all-in" fee, reported as a percent of plan assets). Finally, unlike

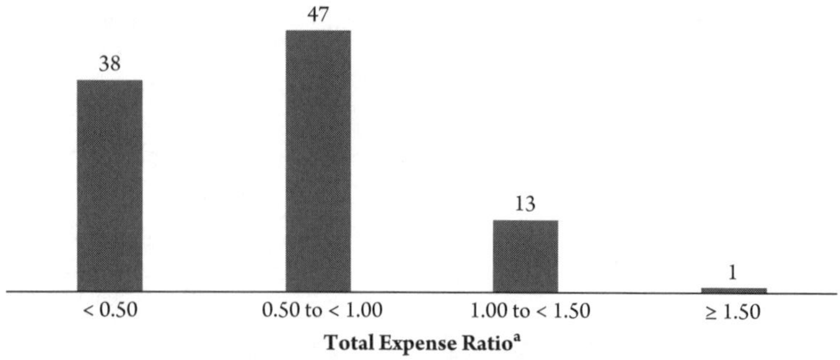

Figure 3.8 401(k) Equity Mutual Fund Assets and Expense Ratios. The figure reports the percentage of 401(k) equity mutual fund assets at year-end 2013 invested in equity mutual funds with the total expense ratios indicated. It shows that 401(k) equity mutual fund assets are concentrated in lower cost funds. [a] The total expense ratio, which is reported as a percentage of fund assets, includes fund operating expenses and 12b-1 fees. Note: The figure excludes mutual funds available as investment choices in variable annuities. Components do not add to 100 percent because of rounding. Sources: Investment Company Institute and Lipper (Collins et al. 2014).

outside 401(k) plans, where shareholders typically pay for the assistance of a financial adviser when investing in mutual funds (Burham, Bogdan, and Schrass 2013), financial adviser services have a more limited role inside these plans.

Education Resources

Households prepare for expenses for higher education for themselves, their children, or their grandchildren in various ways. Methods to cover college, professional school, and graduate school expenses range from work-study arrangements, need-based scholarships, and student loans to merit-based scholarships and household savings. Internal Revenue Service (2014) spells out different tax benefits available to help people pay educational expenses. Among tax-preferred education savings vehicles are 529 plans and Coverdell ESAs. Although a few individual states started offering prepaid and savings plans for college saving in the late 1980s and early 1990s, the Small Business Job Protection Act (SBJPA) of 1996 provided tax-exempt status to "qualified state tuition programs" and created IRC, Section 529 (Holden 2002). The Taxpayer Relief Act (TRA) of 1997 created education IRAs (IRC, Section 530) and changed the tax code to encourage education savings. Education IRAs were renamed Coverdell ESAs in July 2001. The Economic Growth and Tax Relief Reconciliation Act (EGTRRA), enacted in 2001, enhanced the attractiveness of 529 plans and Coverdell ESAs by making them more flexible and allowing greater contributions to them. Enacted in 2006, the Pension Protection Act (PPA), made the EGTRRA enhancements to 529 plans permanent. More recently, the Tax Relief, Unemployment Insurance Reauthorization, and Job Creation

Act of 2010 extended the EGTRRA enhancements to Coverdell ESAs for two years, and the American Taxpayer Relief Act of 2012 made these enhancements permanent.

Investment in 529 plans has grown over time, perhaps reflecting increased familiarity with this tax-advantaged option and perhaps responding to the improved access and flexibility in these accounts. Figure 3.9 shows that by year-end 2013, 529 plan assets had grown to $227.1 billion, with most, $205.1 billion, in 529 savings plans, and $22.0 billion in 529 prepaid plans. When structured as a 529 savings plan, the beneficiary draws funds from the accumulated account balance to pay qualified education expenses. On the other hand, 529 prepaid plans allow for the purchase of future course/semester units at current prices. All 50 states and the District of Columbia offer 529 savings plans and/or 529 prepaid plans; and a consortium of private schools participates in a private 529 prepaid plan (College Savings Plans Network 2014).

Coverdell ESAs play a much smaller role in saving for education expenses. When they were education IRAs, Coverdell ESAs were included in reporting on Form 5498 to the IRS, although tabulating comprehensive totals reflecting their uptake was extremely difficult. The IRS published total education IRA assets including those held by non-filing dependents for year-end 2000, and an estimated $1.1billion was held in education IRAs (Sailer and Nutter 2004). Investment Company Institute (2014c) reports that investors held about $1 billion in education IRAs in mutual fund assets at that time, which reflects essentially the entire education IRA total. The IRS has not produced another comprehensive estimate of education IRAs or Coverdell ESAs, but Investment Company Institute (2014c) estimates that investors held $7 billion in mutual fund assets in Coverdell ESAs at year-end 2013. An ICI household survey in mid-2013 found

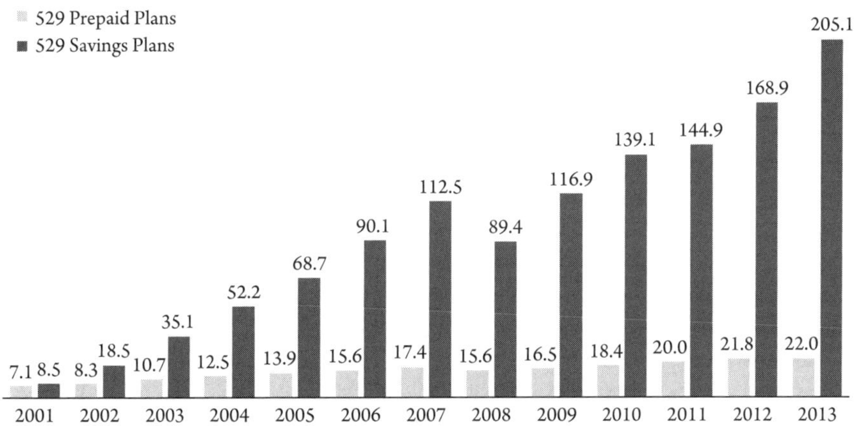

Figure 3.9 Changes in Section 529 Plan Assets over Time. The graph plots total 529 plan assets in billions of dollars by type of 529 plan (prepaid or savings) at year-end (2001–2013). It shows that Section 529 plan assets have risen over time.

Note: Data were estimated for a few individual state observations to construct a continuous time series.

Sources: Investment Company Institute and College Savings Plans Network (Investment Company Institute 2014a, b).

that more than 3 million U.S. households had Coverdell ESAs (Burham et al. 2013; Bogdan and Schrass 2014).

The Role of Mutual Funds in Households' Education Savings

Table 3.7 shows that of the U.S. households that owned mutual funds in mid-2013, 25 percent cited education as a financial goal for their fund investments and 5 percent reported it was their primary financial goal. Among mutual-fund-owning households surveyed in mid-2013, 17 percent reported that they had education-targeted savings accounts. 529 savings plans were the most commonly mentioned education savings account (9 percent of mutual-fund-owning households), followed by Coverdell ESAs (6 percent), and 529 prepaid tuition plans (1 percent).

Table 3.7 **Some Mutual-Fund-Owning Households Focus on Education Savings**

	Percentage of Mutual-Fund-Owning Households
Financial Goals for Mutual Fund Investments	
Education, a goal[a]	25
Education, the primary goal	5
Household Ownership of Education-Targeted Savings Accounts[a]	
Household owned education-targeted savings program account (total)	17
Coverdell Education Savings Account[b]	6
529 prepaid tuition or college savings plan account (total)[c]	14
529 savings plan	9
529 prepaid tuition plan	1

Note: The table shows the percentage of U.S. households owning mutual funds (surveyed in mid-2013) with the financial goal or type of education savings indicated.

[a]Multiple responses are included.

[b]Education IRAs were renamed Coverdell Education Savings Accounts (ESAs) in July 2001.

[c]529 plans are investment programs primarily offered by state governments designed to help pay future qualified higher education expenses. 529 savings plans allow contributors to create an investment account for a student, while 529 prepaid plans prepay for a number of academic periods or course units in the future at current prices.

Source: Investment Company Institute Annual Mutual Fund Shareholder Tracking Survey (Bogdan and Schrass 2014).

Summary and Conclusions

This chapter provides an overview of U.S.-based retirement resources and documents the trend toward increasing reliance on individual account-based retirement savings through DC plans and IRAs. DC plan participants and IRA investors tend to invest in equities, and younger retirement investors tend to have higher concentrations in equities than older retirement investors do. About half of DC plan and IRA assets are invested in mutual funds, and mutual fund investors tend to concentrate their assets in lower cost funds. Among mutual-fund-owning households, 92 percent report that saving for retirement is one of their financial goals and 25 percent report that saving for education is one of their financial goals. Assets specifically earmarked for education are much smaller in magnitude than those earmarked for retirement, although 529 plan assets have grown.

Discussion Questions

1. Explain how the composition of U.S. retirement assets has changed over time and identify the factors that drove that change.
2. Explain how the asset allocations of 401(k) and IRA investors vary with age.
3. Identify the role of mutual funds in the U.S. retirement market.
4. Discuss whether target-date fund investing provides diversification and rebalancing over time, and whether retirement savers are increasingly relying on these funds to manage their retirement savings.

References

Aaronson, Stephanie, and Julie Coronado. 2005. "Are Firms or Workers Behind the Shift Away from DB Pension Plans?" Federal Reserve Board Finance and Economics Discussion Series (FEDS) Working Paper No. 2005–2017.

Bogdan, Michael, and Daniel Schrass. 2014. "Profile of Mutual Fund Shareholders, 2013." *ICI Research Report* (February).

Brady, Peter, and Michael Bogdan. 2010. "A Look at Private-Sector Retirement Plan Income After ERISA." *ICI Research Perspective* 16:2, 1–40.

Brady, Peter, and Michael Bogdan. 2014a. "A Look at Private-Sector Retirement Plan Income after ERISA, 2013." *ICI Research Perspective* 20:7, 1–14.

Brady, Peter, and Michael Bogdan. 2014b. "Who Gets Retirement Plans and Why, 2013." *ICI Research Perspective* 20:6, 1–16.

Brady, Peter, Kimberly Burham, and Sarah Holden. 2012. *The Success of the U.S. Retirement System.* Washington, DC: Investment Company Institute.

Burham, Kimberly, Michael Bogdan, and Daniel Schrass. 2013. "Ownership of Mutual Funds, Shareholder Sentiment, and Use of the Internet, 2013," *ICI Research Perspective* 19: 9, 1–48.

College Savings Plans Network. 2014. "529 Plan Data." Available at http://www.collegesavings.org/529PlanData.aspx.

Collins, Sean, Sarah Holden, Elena Barone Chism, and James Duvall. 2014. "The Economics of Providing 401(k) Plans: Services, Fees, and Expenses, 2013." *ICI Research Perspective* 20: 3, 1–30.

Congressional Budget Office. 2013. *The 2013 Long-Term Projections for Social Security: Additional Information*. Washington, DC: Congressional Budget Office.

Deloitte Consulting LLP and Investment Company Institute. 2014. *Inside the Structure of Defined Contribution/401(k) Plan Fees, 2013: A Study Assessing the Mechanics of the "All-In" Fee*. Washington, DC: Investment Company Institute, and New York: Deloitte Consulting LLP.

Fink, Matthew P. 2011. *The Rise of Mutual Funds: An Insider's View*, 2d Edition. New York: Oxford University Press.

Holden, Sarah. 2002. "Saving for College with 529 Plans." *National Tax Association, Proceedings, Ninety-Fifth Conference on Taxation Conference, Orlando, Florida*, 89–98.

Holden, Sarah, and Steven Bass. 2014. "The IRA Investor Profile: Traditional IRA Investors' Activity, 2007–2012." *ICI Research Report*.

Holden, Sarah, Peter Brady, and Michael Hadley. 2006. "401(k) Plans: A 25-Year Retrospective." *Investment Company Institute Research Perspective* 12:2, 1–39.

Holden, Sarah, Kathy Ireland, Vicky Leonard-Chambers, and Michael Bogdan. 2005. "The Individual Retirement Account at Age 30: A Retrospective." *ICI Research Perspective* 11:1, 1–24.

Holden, Sarah, and Daniel Schrass. 2013. "The Role of IRAs in U.S. Households' Saving for Retirement, 2013." *ICI Research Perspective* 19:11, 1–38.

Holden, Sarah, and Jack VanDerhei. 2002. "Can 401(k) Accumulations Generate Significant Income for Future Retirees?" *Investment Company Institute Perspective* 8:3, 1–20, and *EBRI Issue Brief* 251, 1–27.

Holden, Sarah, Jack VanDerhei, Luis Alonso, and Steven Bass. 2013. "401(k) Plan Asset Allocation, Account Balances, and Loan Activity in 2012." *ICI Research Perspective* 19:12, 1–64, and *EBRI Issue Brief* 394, 1–51.

Internal Revenue Service. 2014. "Tax Benefits for Education." *Publication 970*. Washington, DC: Internal Revenue Service.

Investment Company Institute. 2014a. *2014 Investment Company Fact Book: A Review of the Trends and Activities in the U.S. Investment Company Industry*, 54th Edition. Washington, DC: Investment Company Institute.

Investment Company Institute. 2014b. "529 Plan Program Statistics, June 2014." Washington, DC: Investment Company Institute.

Investment Company Institute. 2014c. "The U.S. Retirement Market, Third Quarter 2014." Washington, DC: Investment Company Institute.

Pang, Gaobo, and Sylvester J. Schieber. 2014. "Understanding Social Security's Income Replacement Measurements." April. Available at http://ssrn.com/abstract=2433181.

Poterba, James, Steven Venti, and David A. Wise. 2007. "The Changing Landscape of Pensions in the United States." NBER Working Paper 13381. Cambridge, MA: National Bureau of Economic Research.

Sabelhaus, John, and Daniel Schrass. 2009. "The Evolving Role of IRAs in U.S. Retirement Planning." *Investment Company Institute Research Perspective* 15:3, 1–31.

Sailer, Peter J., and Sarah E. Nutter. 2004. "Accumulations and Distribution of Individual Retirement Arrangements, 2000." *Statistics of Income Bulletin*, Spring, 121–134. Washington, DC: Internal Revenue Service.

Social Security Administration. 2014. "Contribution and Benefit Base." Available at http://www.ssa.gov/oact/cola/cbb.html.

U.S. Department of Labor, Employee Benefits Security Administration. 2014. *Private Pension Plan Bulletin Abstract of 2012 Form 5500 Annual Reports* (Version 1.0). Washington, DC: U.S. Department of Labor, Employee Benefits Security Administration.

U.S. Federal Reserve Board. 2014. *Financial Accounts of the United States: Flow of Funds, Balance Sheets, and Integrated Macroeconomic Accounts, Second Quarter 2014, Z.1 Release*. Washington, DC: U.S. Federal Reserve Board.

4

The Structure and Regulation of Mutual Funds

ROBERT GROHOWSKI
General Counsel, Investment Adviser Association

SEAN COLLINS
Senior Director, Investment Company Institute

Introduction

Open-end funds, commonly called mutual funds, are subject to a comprehensive regulatory regime that addresses transparency, valuation, liquidity, leverage, diversification, custody, and conflicts of interest, among many other aspects of a mutual fund's operation. This chapter discusses the history, origins, and core principles of that regulatory regime and describes how the structure, operation, and regulation of mutual funds has protected shareholders and helped make mutual funds one of the most popular investment products in the financial marketplace.

The chapter begins by describing the history and origins of the regulatory framework for mutual funds, discussing how certain abuses and excesses led to a joint effort by regulators and industry to adopt a strong, yet flexible, regulatory structure for mutual funds. Mutual funds are one type of *registered investment company,* which is a pooled investment regulated by the Securities and Exchange Commission (SEC) under U.S. securities laws. The chapter offers a brief overview of other types of registered investment companies in the United States—closed-end funds (CEFs), exchange-traded funds (ETFs), and unit investment trusts (UITs)—before returning to the legal, organizational, and operational structure of a mutual fund. Finally, the chapter summarizes the core principles of the Investment Company Act of 1940, the main federal securities law regulating mutual funds.

The Investment Company Act of 1940 (the Investment Company Act) is based upon core principles relating to fund transparency, valuation, liquidity, leverage, diversification, custody, and conflicts of interest. The chapter describes how specific provisions of the Investment Company Act reflect these core principles and how these provisions help to protect the interests of fund shareholders. Although the Investment Company Act is fundamentally about protecting fund shareholders, this chapter also highlights ways that many of the key provisions of the Investment Company Act mitigate potential systemic risk concerns. Thus, understanding the rules and regulations governing mutual funds is valuable not only for those interested in mutual funds and securities markets but also for those interested in systemic risk, an area of study that has increased markedly in the wake of the financial crisis of 2007–2008.

Pooled Investing and the Investment Company Act

The precise origins of the concept of an investment company are unclear. According to Rouwenhorst (2004), the concept dates back to the late 1700s when a Dutch merchant and broker invited subscriptions to form a trust that would provide individuals with limited means a way to pool their investments with those of others. Fink (2008), however, credits the development of the Société Générale de Pays-Bas in 1822 by King William I of the Netherlands as being the world's first investment company.

Developments in England later in the 1800s brought "investment pooling" closer to U.S. shores when trusts, such as the Foreign and Colonial Government Trust formed in 1868, provided investors of moderate means the same advantages as the capitalists by spreading the investment over many different stocks.

The British fund model established a direct link with U.S. securities markets, helping to finance the development of the post–Civil War U.S. economy. The Scottish American Investment Trust, formed on February 1, 1873, by fund pioneer Robert Fleming, invested in the economic potential of the United States, chiefly by buying and holding bonds issued by American railroad companies. Subsequently, many other trusts targeted investments in America. Their efforts also led to introducing the fund investing concept on U.S. shores in the late 1800s and early 1900s.

The first open-end investment company (the first true mutual fund) was introduced in Boston in March 1924. This fund, the Massachusetts Investors Trust, was highly innovative. First, it was established with a simple capital structure that did not result in leverage. Second, it was an *open-end fund*, meaning that it could continuously offer newly created shares for sale to investors, allowing it to expand to meet new investor demand. While the concept of an open-end fund now seems second nature, in 1924 the concept was novel. The then-predominant form of pooled investment used by retail investors was the closed-end fund (CEF). Then, as now, the size of a CEF is typically fixed by its initial public offering (IPO) so that new shares cannot easily be created to fill excess demand. Third, the fund gave investors the ability to redeem their shares rather than hold them until the fund dissolved. This concept was in striking contrast to the closed-end structure in which investors could not sell their shares back to the fund but only to another investor through the secondary market (i.e., on the stock exchange). Finally, the Massachusetts Investors Trust set clear investment restrictions and policies.

Two other Boston groups formed funds with much the same structure. Paul C. Cabot established State Street Investment Corporation in July 1924. Edward Leffler, who had also organized the Massachusetts Investors Trust, established Incorporated Investors in November 1925, which the firm of Parker, Putnam and Nightingale managed (Fink 2008).

The stock market crash of 1929 and the ensuing Great Depression hampered the growth of pooled investments. Eventually, the passage of a series of landmark securities laws reinvigorated investor confidence in pooled investments. All four of the major securities laws passed during that time apply to funds:

- *The Securities Act of 1933* (the 1933 Act) regulates public offerings of securities, including mutual fund shares. The 1933 Act also requires that all investors receive a current prospectus describing the fund.
- *The Securities Exchange Act of 1934* (the 1934 Act) regulates the trading, purchase, and sale of securities, including mutual fund shares. The 1934 Act also regulates broker-dealers, including mutual fund principal underwriters and others selling mutual fund shares, and requires them to register with the SEC.
- *The Investment Advisers Act of 1940* (the Advisers Act) regulates investment advisers. The Advisers Act requires all advisers to mutual funds to register with the SEC. The Advisers Act contains provisions requiring fund advisers to make certain disclosures and meet record-keeping, custodial, reporting, and other regulatory responsibilities.
- *The Investment Company Act of 1940* (the Investment Company Act) regulates the structure and operations of mutual funds through a combination of disclosure requirements and restrictions on day-to-day operations. Among other matters, the Investment Company Act addresses mutual fund capital structures, custody of assets, investment activities (particularly regarding transactions with affiliates and other transactions involving potential conflicts of interest), and the duties of fund boards.

Types of Registered Investment Companies and Current Trends

Mutual funds are one type of registered investment company. The three other predominant types of registered investment companies in the United States are CEFs, ETFs, and UITs. Under the Investment Company Act, *investment companies* include any issuer that is, or holds itself out as being, engaged primarily in the business of investing, reinvesting, or trading in securities. *Registered investment companies* (RICs) are those required under federal law to register with the SEC.

Mutual funds represent the vast bulk of RIC assets in the United States. As Figure 4.1 shows, RIC assets, which totaled more than $1 trillion in 1990, had grown to over $17 trillion by year-end 2013, $15 trillion of which represented assets in mutual funds. Mutual funds issue *redeemable securities*, which means the fund issues and redeems (buys back) fund shares to and from investors daily. Most mutual fund assets ($12.3 trillion) are in long-term mutual funds (equity, bond, and hybrid funds), which invest primarily in stocks and bonds or some (perhaps varying) mix of those. Mutual funds may also use derivatives such as futures, forwards, interest rate swaps, and credit default swaps to hedge risks or manage the fund's portfolio exposure, such as by gaining exposure to certain market sectors or firms. The balance of the $15 trillion in mutual funds, about $2.7 trillion, was invested in *money market funds*, which are mutual funds that invest in very short-term, highly liquid fixed-income securities.

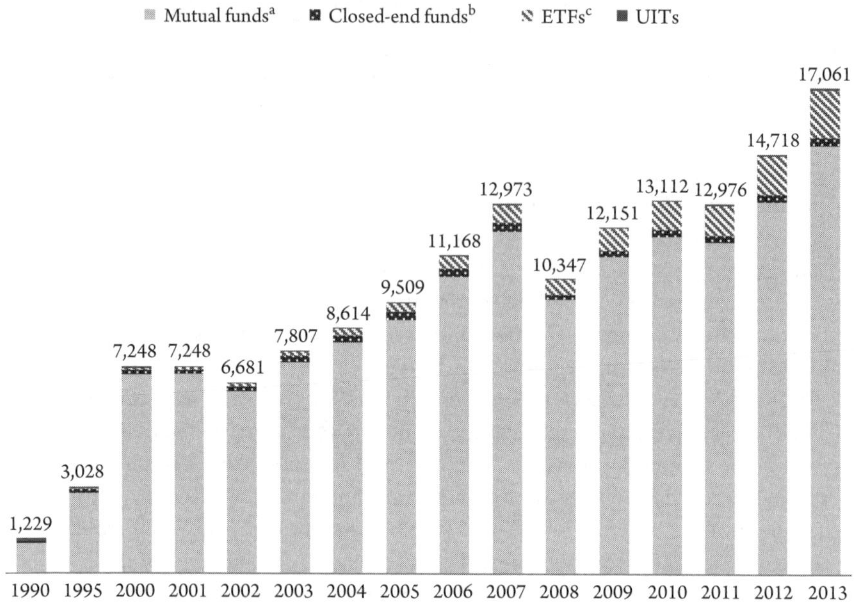

Figure 4.1 Net Assets of Registered Investment Companies, by Type. This figure shows net assets in billions of dollars of mutual funds, CEFs, ETFs, and UITs at year-end from 1990 to 2013.

[a] Mutual fund data include only mutual funds that report statistical information to the Investment Company Institute but exclude data on mutual funds that invest primarily in other mutual funds.

[b] CEF includes preferred share classes.

[c] Strategic Insight Simfund provided the ETF data before 2001. ETF data include investment companies not registered under the Investment Company Act of 1940 but exclude ETFs that primarily invest in other ETFs. Sources: Investment Company Institute 2014a.

CEFs, another type of RIC, have shares that are not redeemable. These funds issue a fixed number of shares that trade on stock exchanges. Investors sell shares of these funds just as they would trade shares of any publicly traded company, receiving the market price, which may be more or less than the net asset value (NAV) of the fund shares. The fund may periodically issue more shares or buy back outstanding shares in the market, but most CEFs rarely do so. CEFs assets totaled $279 billion at the end of 2013.

UITs have some characteristics of both mutual funds and CEFs. Like CEFs, UITs typically issue only a specific, fixed number of shares, called *units*. Like mutual funds, the units are redeemable. Unlike mutual funds, however, generally the UIT sponsor maintains a secondary market in the units so that redemptions do not deplete the UIT's assets. Also, a UIT does not actively trade its investment portfolio but instead buys and holds a set of particular investments until a set termination date, when the trust is dissolved and proceeds are paid to shareholders. Although assets in UITs are relatively small (e.g., $86.5 billion as of December 2013), their assets grew briskly from 2008 to 2013 at a 25 percent compound annual growth rate.

ETFs have features in common with mutual funds and CEFs. Most ETFs are structured as open-end funds or UITs. As such, ETFs issue redeemable shares. But like CEFs, shares of ETFs trade intraday on stock exchanges. Retail investors and most institutional investors buy or sell ETF shares on a stock exchange at a market-determined share price. This price may deviate somewhat from the fund's underlying NAV depending on market conditions. ETF shares are redeemable at the end of the day at the fund's NAV, but only by certain institutional investors called "authorized participants." *Authorized participants* are a small group of broker-dealers or market makers permitted to transact directly with the ETF.

ETFs, like mutual funds, may hold stocks, bonds, or a mix of those. Most of the assets in ETFs are held in *index ETFs,* which are ETFs that are designed to track the performance of their specified indexes. The assets in ETFs totaled $1.67 trillion as of December 2013, which includes a relatively small amount of assets in ETFs that are registered with the Commodity Futures Trading Commission (CFTC) rather than being registered with the SEC. Although this was considerably less than the assets in mutual funds, assets in ETFs have grown much more quickly over the past decade, expanding at a nearly 30 percent annual rate each year.

MUTUAL FUND TRENDS

The strong growth in mutual fund assets since 1990 in part reflects appreciation in the value of the securities that mutual funds hold. Between 1990 and 2013, the S&P 500 index has risen 423 percent and the return on bonds, as measured by the Citigroup Broad Investment Grade Bond index, has totaled 363 percent. These kinds of gains are reflected in capital appreciation of the underlying securities that long-term mutual funds hold.

The assets of long-term mutual fund assets have also increased because investors have purchased new shares. From 1990 to 2013, net new cash flow to long-term mutual funds, a measure of investors' demand for additional mutual fund shares, has totaled $3.97 trillion, relative to the $11.7 trillion dollar growth in the assets of long-term mutual funds over this period.

The increased demand for long-term mutual fund shares has generally arisen from households rather than institutional investors. Institutional investors—hedge funds, defined benefit (DB) pension plans, sovereign wealth funds, and others—generally find gaining exposure to capital markets more advantageous for tax and other reasons through either direct purchase of stock and bonds (or by taking direct positions in derivatives) or pooled vehicles other than mutual funds. Thus, in the United States, households hold most of the assets in long-term mutual funds. For example, Table 4.1 shows that as of December 2013, households held 95 percent of the $12.3 trillion in assets in long-term mutual. Households account for a smaller share of the assets of money market funds. Institutional investors such as corporations and state and local governments often find money market funds a convenient and cost-effective vehicle for managing their cash balances.

Strong demand from households for investments in mutual funds reflects a range of factors. First, despite a recession in 2000–2002 and the financial market crisis of 2007–2008, U.S. gross domestic product (GDP) has grown substantially since 1990. This growth has naturally increased the pool of dollars that households might save each year. Some evidence also suggests that mutual funds are an income elastic or "superior"

Table 4.1 **Households' Assets in Long-Term Mutual Funds and Money Market Funds**

Type of Mutual Fund	*Households ($)*	*Institutional Investors ($)*	*Total ($)*	*Household Share of Total (%)*
Long-term funds	11,685	615	12,300	95.0
Money market funds	1,791	927	2,718	65.9

Note: This figure shows the assets in billions of dollars in long-term mutual funds and money market funds held either by households or institutional investors as of December 2013.

Source: Investment Company Institute 2014a, b).

good, so that demand for mutual funds rises more than proportionally to households' incomes (Fernando, Klapper, Sulla, and Vittas 2003). For example, Figure 4.2 shows that ownership rates of mutual funds rise in the United States with the level of household income. Thus, rising U.S. household incomes may have combined with income elasticity to boost the demand for mutual funds.

Second, the demand for mutual funds in the United States has increased with the aging of the U.S. population. As the baby-boom generation has entered its peak earning years and moved closer to retirement age, new dollars have flowed into mutual funds. The evolution of employer-based retirement systems has aided this development. In the United States, as in many developed countries, employer-sponsored DB pension plans have come under pressure as these plans have proven to be more expensive than many employers anticipated. Employer-sponsored defined contribution (DC) plans, such as 401(k) plans, have provided employers with an alternative to the traditional DB plan approach. These DC plans often offer employees an array of mutual funds in which to invest.

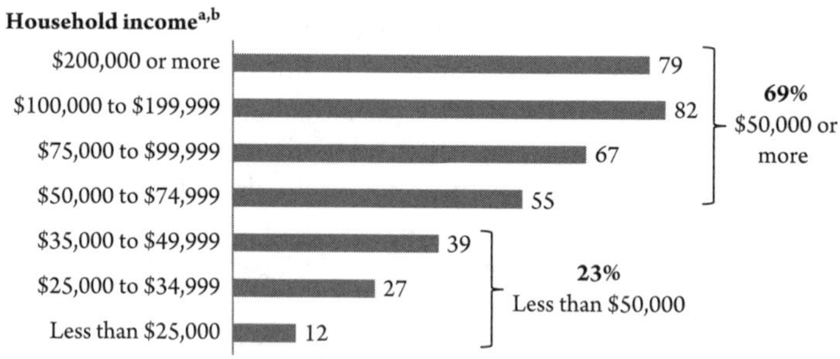

Figure 4.2 Ownership of Mutual Funds by Household Income Category. This figure shows the percentage of U.S. households owing mutual funds by income group in 2013.[a]

[a] For the complete time series of data from 1994 to 2013, see Figure A6 in the appendix of Investment Company Institute 2013.

[b] Household income before taxes in 2012. Sources: Investment Company Institute 2014a and US Census Bureau.

Table 4.2 **Stock Market Returns Compared to Yields on Liquid Bank Deposits**

	Year-End 2002–2013 in %	
Year	*Yield on Liquid Bank Deposits*[a]	*Return on Equities*[b]
2002	0.85	−18.98
2003	0.63	34.63
2004	0.73	15.75
2005	0.86	11.37
2006	1.07	21.53
2007	1.28	12.18
2008	0.83	−41.85
2009	0.41	35.41
2010	0.44	13.21
2011	0.40	−6.86
2012	0.27	16.80
2013	0.23	23.44
Average	**0.67**	**9.72**

Note: The figure shows that the return on equities is substantially higher on average than the return on liquid bank deposits worldwide.

[a] Weighted average yield on liquid bank deposits in Australia, Canada, the eurozone, Japan, Korea, the United Kingdom, and the United States, which together comprise 97 percent of worldwide equity fund assets.

[b] December to December percent change in MSCI World Index.

Sources: Various central banks and Bloomberg.

Third, the superior returns available on stocks and bonds relative to other products that compete for households' savings have supported mutual fund demand in the United States and elsewhere. For instance, Table 4.2 compares the returns on stocks worldwide with the yields on liquid bank deposit accounts between 2002 and 2013. Stock market returns varied considerably but on average returned 9.72 percent over this period, thus exceeding by a large margin the average yield of 0.67 percent on liquid bank deposit accounts. Mutual funds give investors the ability to share in the favorable returns available in capital markets through the vehicle of a diversified, professionally managed portfolio.

The Organization and Structure of a Mutual Fund

Besides the trends noted in the previous section, the strong and continuing demand for mutual funds also reflects investor confidence in the structure and regulation of mutual funds. The next section of this chapter discusses the organization of a typical mutual fund and the roles played by the fund's adviser and other principal service providers. It also discusses the important oversight role played by the fund's board.

FORM OF ORGANIZATION UNDER STATE LAW

A mutual fund typically is organized under state law either as a corporation or a business trust, sometimes called a *statutory trust*. As Figure 4.3 shows, the three most popular domiciles and forms of organization for mutual funds are Massachusetts business trusts, Maryland corporations, and Delaware statutory trusts. About 10 percent of mutual funds have other forms of organization, such as limited liability partnerships, and/or other domiciles, such as in Ohio or Minnesota.

The relative dominance of Massachusetts business trusts, Maryland corporations, and Delaware statutory trusts is largely a result of history. As discussed previously in this chapter, the first mutual fund—the Massachusetts Investors Trust—was formed as a Massachusetts business trust, which was a popular form of organization at the time for pools that invested in real estate or public utilities. That fund provided a model for other funds, leading to widespread use of Massachusetts business trusts throughout much of the industry's early history.

Developments in the late 1980s gave asset management companies other attractive choices. In 1987, Maryland amended its corporate statute to align with interpretations of the Investment Company Act concerning when funds are required to hold annual meetings, thereby making a Maryland corporation more competitive with the Massachusetts business trust as a form of organization for mutual funds. In 1988, Delaware, which was already a popular domicile for U.S. corporations, adopted new statutory provisions devoted specifically to business trusts, which have since been renamed statutory trusts. Because of these developments, many mutual funds created in the last 25 years have been organized as Maryland corporations or Delaware statutory trusts.

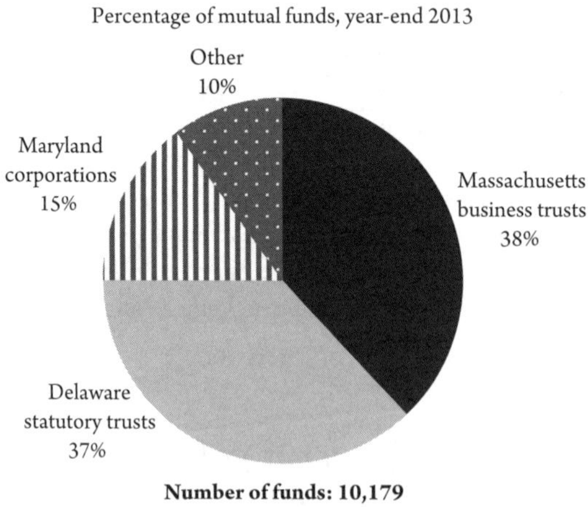

Figure 4.3 THE MOST POPULAR FORMS OF MUTUAL FUND ORGANIZATION. This figure shows that most mutual funds were organized as Massachusetts business trusts, Delaware statutory trusts, or Maryland corporations in 2013.
Source: Investment Company Institute 2014a.

OVERSIGHT BY MUTUAL FUND BOARD

Regardless of whether a mutual fund is organized as a trust or a corporation, and irrespective of the state in which it is organized, a board must oversee each mutual fund. If the fund is a corporation, it will have a board of directors. If the mutual fund is a business trust, it will have a board of trustees. For ease of reference, this chapter refers to all directors and trustees as directors and all boards as boards of directors.

The mutual fund's board plays an important role in overseeing the fund's operations. Directors typically are not involved in a fund's daily management, which is normally handled by the fund's investment adviser or administrator under a contractual arrangement with the mutual fund. Instead, directors review and approve major contracts with service providers, perhaps most notably between the fund and its investment adviser. Directors also approve policies and procedures to ensure the mutual fund's compliance with the federal securities laws, and oversee and review the performance of the fund's operations. To fulfill these duties, directors devote substantial time and consider large amounts of information, in part because they are required to perform their duties "in an informed and deliberate manner."

Mutual fund boards must maintain a particular level of independence. The Investment Company Act requires at least 40 percent of the members of a fund board to be "independent." An *independent director* is one who does not have any significant business relationship with a mutual fund's adviser or underwriter. In practice, most fund boards have far higher percentages of independent directors. As of year-end 2012, independent directors made up three-quarters of boards in approximately 85 percent of fund complexes (Independent Directors' Council 2013).

Independent fund directors play a critical role in overseeing fund operations and are entrusted with the primary responsibility for overseeing the interests of the fund's shareholders. The directors serve as watchdogs, furnishing an independent check on the management of funds. Under state law, fund directors, like directors of operating companies (e.g., non-financial companies such as Microsoft, IBM, General Electric, or financial companies such as Bank of America), owe shareholders the duties of loyalty and care. But independent fund directors also have specific statutory and regulatory responsibilities under the Investment Company Act beyond the duties required of the directors of operating companies. For example, fund directors oversee the performance of the fund, approve the fees paid to the investment adviser for its services, and oversee the fund's compliance program.

ESTABLISHING A FUND: THE ROLE OF THE FUND SPONSOR

Setting up a mutual fund is a complicated process. A fund sponsor establishes a fund and has various responsibilities. For example, it must assemble the group of third parties needed to launch the fund, including the persons or entities charged with managing and operating the fund on a daily basis. The sponsor provides officers and affiliated directors to oversee the fund and initially recruits unaffiliated persons to serve as independent directors. Once the fund is established, vacancies among the independent directors are filled by nominations put forth by the existing independent directors and then elected by the full board; sometimes, based on requirements of the Investment Company Act, new directors also must be elected by shareholders.

Some major steps in the process of starting a mutual fund include organizing the fund under state law (i.e., setting up a trust or corporation), registering the fund with the SEC pursuant to the Investment Company Act, and registering the fund shares for sale to the public pursuant to the 1933 Act. Unless otherwise exempt from doing so, the fund also must make filings and pay fees to each state, except Florida, in which the fund's shares will be offered to the public.

The Investment Company Act also requires that each new fund have at least $100,000 of seed capital before distributing its shares to the public. This capital cannot be borrowed and is usually contributed by the sponsor or adviser as an initial investment.

Unlike operating companies, a fund is typically "externally managed." Operating companies typically hire employees who work for the firm to produce goods or services. In contrast, funds rarely hire any employees. The mutual fund is established in a corporate or trust form to hold and protect the fund's assets. Beyond that, the mutual fund normally contracts for the services it needs with other firms, who hire their own employees to undertake those services. For example, the fund contracts with an investment adviser, who is also normally the fund's sponsor, to provide portfolio management of the fund's assets.

MANAGEMENT OF THE FUND: THE ROLE OF THE INVESTMENT ADVISER

Given that a fund is externally managed, it must rely on either affiliated organizations or independent contractors to invest the fund's assets and to carry out other necessary business activities the fund needs. Figure 4.4 shows the primary types of service providers with which a fund typically contracts for services.

The most important of these relationships is with the fund's investment adviser, who is also commonly the fund's sponsor. Investment advisers have overall responsibility

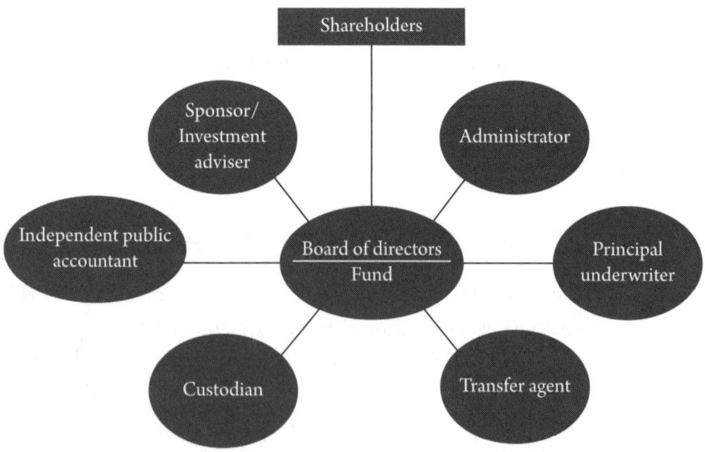

Figure 4.4 ORGANIZATION OF A MUTUAL FUND. The figure shows the primary types of service providers usually relied on by mutual funds.

Source: Investment Company Institute 2014a.

for directing the fund's investments and handling its business affairs. An investment adviser is a separate legal entity from the fund, is usually incorporated, and has its own employees. These employees typically include investment professionals who work on behalf of the fund's shareholders and determine which securities to buy, sell, or hold in the fund's portfolio, consistent with the mutual fund's investment objectives and policies.

All mutual fund advisers are required to register with the SEC and are subject to many standards and legal restrictions, including restrictions on transactions that may pose conflicts of interest, disclosure requirements, and SEC oversight. Advisers also owe a fiduciary duty to each fund they advise, meaning that they have a fundamental legal obligation to act in the best interests of the fund pursuant to a duty of undivided loyalty and utmost good faith.

Both the investment adviser and the mutual fund are required to have written compliance programs overseen by a chief compliance officer (CCO). These compliance programs establish procedures and internal controls designed to ensure compliance with all relevant laws and regulations.

OTHER SERVICE PROVIDERS: THE ADMINISTRATOR, UNDERWRITER, TRANSFER AGENT, AND AUDITOR

A fund's administrator handles the back-office functions that a fund needs to operate, such as providing office space, clerical and fund accounting services, data processing, bookkeeping and internal auditing, and preparing and filing SEC, tax, shareholder, and other reports. Fund administrators also help maintain compliance procedures and internal controls subject to oversight by the fund's board and CCO. The fund's investment adviser often also serves as the fund's administrator.

Investors buy and redeem fund shares either directly or indirectly through the principal underwriter, also known as the fund's distributor. Principal underwriters are registered under the 1934 Act as broker-dealers, and as such are subject to strict rules governing how they offer and sell securities to investors. The principal underwriter contracts with the fund to purchase and then resell fund shares to the public. A majority of both the fund's independent directors and the entire fund board must approve the fund's contract with the principal underwriter.

Transfer agents maintain records of fund shareholder accounts, calculate and distribute fund dividends and capital gains, and prepare and mail shareholder account statements, federal income tax information, and other shareholder notices. Some transfer agents also prepare and mail statements of investors' account balances and statements confirming shareholder transactions to buy or sell fund shares. A transfer agent may maintain a customer service department to respond to shareholder inquiries about shareholders' balances or other account-related questions and to explain or resolve website issues.

A mutual fund's annual reports include audited financial statements certified by a certified public accounting firm subject to oversight by the Public Company Accounting Oversight Board (PCAOB). This process ensures that the financial statements are prepared in conformity with generally accepted accounting principles (GAAP) and thus fairly represent the fund's financial position and results of its operations. Like officers of public operating companies, a mutual fund's officers are also required to make certifications and disclosures such as certifying the accuracy of the fund's financial statements.

Mutual Fund Regulation

Embedded in the structure and regulation of mutual funds are several core principles that provide important protections for shareholders: transparency, daily valuation, liquidity of fund assets, limits on leverage, diversification, custody, and the prohibition of transactions that raise conflicts of interest.

TRANSPARENCY

Mutual funds are arguably subject to the most extensive disclosure requirements of any pooled investment product. The cornerstone of the disclosure regime for funds is the "evergreen" prospectus. A mutual fund is required to maintain a current prospectus, which provides investors with information about the fund, including its investment objectives, investment strategies, risks, fees and expenses, and performance, and how to purchase, redeem, and exchange fund shares. Mutual funds may provide investors with a summary prospectus containing key information about the fund, while making more information available on the Internet and on paper upon request.

The key parts of a fund's prospectus, which are standardized to facilitate comparisons by investors, relate to fund performance and fund fees and expenses:

- *Performance information.* The prospectus depicts a fund's performance (before any sales load fee is deducted) for each of the last 10 calendar years (or the life of the fund if shorter) and also summarizes a fund's annual returns, net of sales charges, for 1-, 5- and 10-year periods compared with the returns for a representative benchmark. The prospectus must also show average annual total returns after taxes on distributions and average annual total returns after taxes on distributions and redemptions.
- *Fees.* The prospectus must provide information on sales charges and a fund's total expense ratio and selected components of expenses. The prospectus must also illustrate how much an investor would pay in fees over periods of 1, 3, 5, and 10 years, assuming an investment of $10,000 and an annual return of 5 percent. Written descriptions accompanying the fee table must be concise and easily understandable.

Mutual funds must make further disclosure through a *statement of additional information* (SAI). The SAI conveys information about the fund that, while useful to some investors, is not necessarily needed to make an informed investment decision. For example, the SAI generally includes information about the fund's history, offers detailed disclosure on certain investment policies (e.g., borrowing and concentration policies), and lists officers, directors, and other persons who control the fund.

The prospectus, SAI, and certain other required information are contained in a mutual fund's registration statement, which is filed electronically with the SEC and is publicly available on the SEC's website. As required by Section 10(a)(3) of the Securities Act of 1933, a mutual fund amends its registration statement at least once each year to ensure that financial statements and other information do not become stale. Mutual funds also amend registration statements throughout the year to reflect material changes to their disclosure.

Mutual funds provide shareholders with several other disclosure documents. Shareholders receive semiannual reports that provide current financial statements, a list of the fund's portfolio securities, management's discussion of financial performance, and other information. Rather than providing the entire list of its portfolio holdings, a fund may summarize its portfolio, provided that the fund files the complete portfolio with the SEC and provides it to shareholders upon request. The summary includes each of the fund's 50 largest holdings in unaffiliated issuers and each investment that exceeds 1 percent of the fund's net assets. Following their first and third fiscal quarters, funds must file the complete schedule of their portfolio holdings with the SEC on Form N-Q. Finally, a fund must disclose annually how it voted proxies on the portfolio companies it held; funds are the only company shareholders required to disclose each proxy vote they cast.

The breadth and volume of fund disclosure provides the public, regulators, media, and other interested parties with considerable information about funds. This information is easily and readily available from the SEC and from most funds directly. Additional information about funds is also available from private sector vendors such as Morningstar, Lipper, Strategic Insight, and others that are in the business of compiling publicly available information on funds in ways that might benefit investors.

LIMITS ON MUTUAL FUND LEVERAGE

The Investment Company Act and related guidance from the SEC and its staff strictly limit mutual funds' ability to take on leverage. These limitations stem from Section 18(f) of the Investment Company Act, which prohibits a mutual fund from issuing a class of senior security or selling any senior security of which it is the issuer, but permits borrowing from a bank provided asset coverage is at least 300 percent for all such borrowings. As a result, the maximum ratio of debt-to-assets allowed by law is 1 to 3, which translates into a maximum allowable leverage ratio of 1.5 to 1.0. These limitations greatly minimize the possibility that a fund's liabilities will exceed the value of its assets.

Generally speaking, a *senior security* is any debt such as a loan or preferred stock that takes priority over the fund's common shares (i.e., priority over the equity investments of fund shareholders). The SEC historically has interpreted the definition of senior security broadly, taking the view that selling securities short, purchasing securities on margin, and investing in many types of derivative instruments, among other practices, may create senior securities. The Securities and Exchange Commission (2014c) provides an extensive bibliography on the use and regulation of "senior securities" under the Investment Company Act.

The SEC also takes the view that the Investment Company Act prohibits a fund from creating a future obligation to pay unless it "covers" the obligation. A fund generally can cover an obligation by owning the instrument underlying that obligation. For example, a fund could "cover" a short position in a certain stock by owning an offsetting long position in that stock. The fund can also cover obligations by *earmarking* (i.e., designating certain assets on its books) or *segregating* (i.e., establishing a segregated account at its custodian) liquid securities equal in value to the fund's potential exposure arising from a leveraged transaction. For example, a fund that writes protection in a credit default swap (CDS) could cover that potential future obligation by earmarking or segregating liquid assets equal to the notional value of the written CDS. The segregated assets must be liquid, unencumbered, and marked-to-market daily. They may not be used to cover other obligations and, if disposed, must be replaced.

The Investment Company Act also limits borrowing by funds. The SEC would generally consider any promissory note or other indebtedness undertaken by the fund to be a prohibited senior security. Narrow exceptions exist such as for certain privately arranged loans and temporary loans. For example, a fund may take out a "temporary loan," so long as the loan does not exceed 5 percent of the fund's total net assets and is repaid within 60 days. Funds are also permitted to borrow from banks, but with substantial restrictions. Notably, a mutual fund may borrow from a bank only if, immediately after borrowing from the bank, the fund's total net assets are at least three times its total aggregate borrowings. As previously noted, this 300 percent test translates into a maximum allowable leverage ratio of 1.5 to 1.0.

Many funds voluntarily go beyond the prohibitions in the Investment Company Act, adopting policies that further restrict their ability to issue senior securities or borrow. For example, funds often adopt a policy stating that they will borrow only as a temporary measure for extraordinary or emergency purposes and not to finance investment in securities. Additionally, they may disclose that, in any event, borrowings will be limited to a small percentage of fund assets (e.g., 5 percent). These are meaningful voluntary measures because under the Investment Company Act, a fund's policies on borrowing money and issuing senior securities cannot be changed without the approval of fund shareholders. Thus, although funds may by law have leverage ratios of 1.5 to 1.0, very few come close to that limit and most have leverage ratios that are much

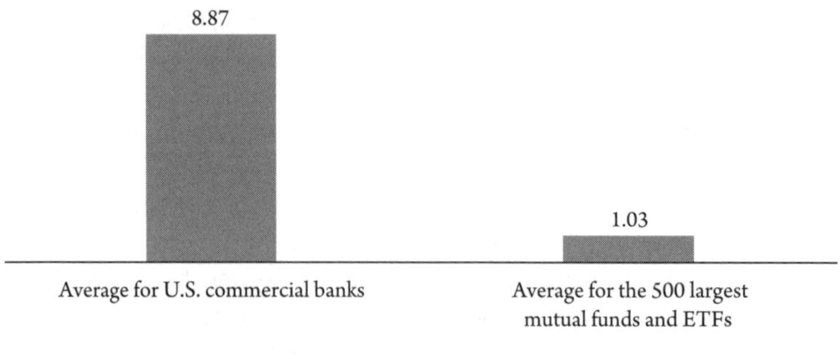

Figure 4.5 Leverage Ratios of Banks and Mutual Funds. This figure shows the leverage ratios for banks as reported by the FDIC for 2013 during the second quarter and as measured by a bank's total assets relative to its equity capital, and for mutual funds (excluding money market funds), as measured by the fund's total assets relative to its net assets.

smaller. For example, as Figure 4.5 shows, among the top 500 largest mutual funds and ETFs (excluding money market funds), which comprise 65 percent of industry assets, the (asset-weighted) average leverage ratio is 1.03. By comparison, the average leverage ratio for U.S. commercial banks is 8.87.

Limiting mutual fund borrowing is one of several factors that helps to ensure against a fund's assets ever falling short of its liabilities or, in other words, that a fund would ever go bankrupt. The limits on fund borrowing were a core component of the Investment Company Act when the Act was signed into law in 1940. Although Congress adopted the limits on borrowing to protect mutual fund investors, they also help to limit any systemic risk that might arise from long-term mutual funds. History amply shows that highly leveraged financial entities pose greater potential risk to the financial system than those firms that are not highly leveraged. Consequently, the minimal leverage of mutual funds means they are unlikely to pose the same kinds of systemic concerns as banks or other highly leveraged financial intermediaries.

DAILY REDEEMABILITY AND PRICING: UNDERSTANDING FUND NAVS

A core organizing principle of a mutual fund, which is explicit in the Investment Company Act, is the *daily redeemability* of fund shares, which enables shareholders to sell some or all of their shares back to the fund on any given day at the fund's current NAV. All new purchases of fund shares, sales of fund shares (redemptions), exchanges between shares in one fund to another fund in the same fund complex, and any distributions paid by the fund that the investor reinvests in the fund are transacted at the fund's NAV.

A mutual fund must determine its NAV at least once a day. Most but not all funds determine their NAVs as of the time the New York Stock Exchange (NYSE) closes, normally 4:00 p.m. Eastern time. On holidays or other days when the NYSE closes early, these funds would correspondingly price their shares at the earlier NYSE closing time. Funds release their daily NAVs to investors and others after they complete the pricing process, generally before 6:00 p.m. Eastern time.

To calculate an NAV, mutual funds must value all their portfolio holdings on a daily basis, based on market values if readily available. If no current market quotation for a security is available or if the market quotation is unreliable, the fund's board of directors has a statutory duty to *fair value* the security in good faith. The mutual fund uses these values to calculate its NAV each business day, pursuant to pricing policies and procedures adopted by the fund's board. Given the importance of the pricing process, these policies and procedures typically are extensive and serve several purposes: (1) define the roles of various parties involved in the valuation process; (2) describe how the fund will monitor for situations that may necessitate fair valuation of one or more securities; (3) describe board-approved valuation methodologies for particular types of securities; and (4) describe how the fund will review and test fair valuations to evaluate whether the valuation procedures are working as intended. These policies are a critical component of a mutual fund's governance process and compliance program, and accordingly are an important area of focus for the SEC during inspections and examinations. Valuation is also a critical component of the audit process.

The Investment Company Act requires mutual funds to use *forward pricing*. Under forward pricing, all orders to purchase or sell fund shares must occur at the NAV the fund next computes after it has received the order. Consider, for example, a fund that determines its NAV at 4:00 p.m., as is true for most mutual funds. If the fund receives an order at 3:30 p.m. from an investor who wants to purchase fund shares, the fund will process that order at the NAV determined 30 minutes later. If the same fund receives an order at 4:30 p.m., it will process that order at the NAV it determines at 4:00 p.m. the next business day.

As the SEC has observed, these pricing requirements are critical to ensuring that mutual fund shares are purchased and redeemed at fair prices and that shareholder interests are not diluted. They also promote market confidence and help mitigate systemic risk. Some have recently suggested that a "first-mover" advantage might prompt large-scale redemptions from mutual funds in response to an economic shock (Chen, Goldstein, and Jiang 2010; Feroli, Kashyap, Schoenholtz, and Shin 2014). According to this view, a drop in stock or bond markets will cause fund shareholders to redeem, in turn leading some fund investors to surmise that the fund will be forced to sell securities in coming days to meet those redemptions, potentially causing stock or bond prices to fall further. To avoid potential capital losses, fund investors will redeem their shares today. According to the first-mover theory, this process could set off a downward spiral between market prices and shareholder redemptions. As Stein (2014) highlights, a "first-mover" effect can arise if a fund's NAV is determined using "stale" prices for the fund's portfolio securities. As previously explained, however, a fund's NAV is determined based not on stale prices for a fund's securities but on their current market values, as reflected in readily available market quotations or fair values if no market quotations are readily available. Thus, the pricing procedures that funds must follow under the Investment Company Act, as with the restrictions on fund leverage, should mitigate concerns that shareholder redemptions could raise systemic concerns.

LIQUIDITY TO SUPPORT REDEMPTIONS

When shareholders redeem shares in a mutual fund, they can expect to be paid promptly. Section 22(e) of the Investment Company Act generally prohibits funds from suspending redemptions or delaying the payment of redemption proceeds for more than seven days. As a matter of practice, funds typically pay proceeds within one to two days of a redemption request. Funds may suspend redemptions only in extremely limited circumstances, such as if the SEC declares an emergency.

In part to ensure that a fund can meet shareholder redemptions within seven days, no more than 15 percent of a mutual fund's portfolio may be invested in "illiquid securities" (Securities and Exchange Commission 2014b). The SEC generally deems a security to be "illiquid" if it cannot be sold or disposed of in the ordinary course of business within seven days at approximately the price at which the mutual fund has valued it. Many funds adopt a specific policy regarding investments in illiquid securities; these policies are sometimes more restrictive than the SEC requirements.

Money market funds have separate liquidity and redemption rules (Securities and Exchange Commission 2014a). Rule 2a-7 under the Investment Company Act generally limits money market funds to investments with a final maturity of no more than

397 days, to hold a portfolio with a weighted average maturity of 60 days or less, and to maintain at least 30 percent of the fund's assets in securities that the SEC deems under Rule 2a-7 to be liquid within seven days.

CUSTODY OF MUTUAL FUND ASSETS

The Investment Company Act requires mutual funds to maintain strict custody of fund assets separate from the assets of the fund manager. This requirement is intended to safeguard fund assets from theft or misappropriation. Nearly all mutual funds use a bank custodian for domestic securities, and the custody agreement is typically far more elaborate than the arrangements used for other bank clients. The Investment Company Act and its rules permit other limited custodial arrangements. For example, foreign securities are required to be held in the custody of a foreign bank or securities depository. Investment Company Act Rules 17f-5 (foreign banks) and 17f-7 (foreign securities depositories) govern those arrangements.

Notably, under the Investment Company Act regulatory structure, collateral posted by a mutual fund must be placed with an eligible custodian and maintained as required under the Investment Company Act. The benefits of this approach were highlighted following the collapse of Lehman Brothers, as mutual funds with such custody arrangements could take control of both their own collateral and the collateral posted by Lehman with far less difficulty than market participants with different custody arrangements.

PROHIBITION ON TRANSACTIONS WITH AFFILIATES

The Investment Company Act contains strong and detailed prohibitions on transactions between a mutual fund and affiliated organizations such as the fund's adviser, a corporate parent of the fund's adviser, or an entity under common control with the fund's adviser. Among other things, Section 17 of the Investment Company Act prohibits transactions between a fund and an affiliate acting for its own account, such as the buying or selling of securities (other than those issued by the fund) or other property, or the lending of money or property. It also prohibits joint transactions involving a mutual fund and an affiliate. Sometimes, transactions involving an affiliate are permitted under SEC rules and exemptive orders, which impose conditions designed to protect investors. These often require the fund's board of directors, including the independent directors, to adopt and review procedures designed to ensure compliance with those conditions.

Many of these prohibitions were part of the original statutory text of the Investment Company Act, enacted in response to instances of overreaching and self-dealing by fund insiders during the 1920s in the purchase and sale of portfolio securities, loans by funds, and investments in related funds. The SEC's Division of Investment Management has said that "for more than 50 years, [the affiliated transaction prohibitions] have played a vital role in protecting the interests of shareholders and in preserving the industry's reputation for integrity; they continue to be among the most important of the Act's many protections" (Securities and Exchange Commission 1992, p. 473).

DIVERSIFICATION OF FUND ASSETS

Both tax and securities laws provide diversification standards for mutual funds. Under the tax laws, all mutual funds qualify as "regulated investment companies," which is different and separate from the laws governing "registered investment companies" as defined under the Investment Company Act, and, as such, must meet a tax diversification test every quarter. At the close of each quarter of the fund's taxable year, at least 50 percent of the value of the fund's total net assets must comprise cash, cash items, government securities, securities of other funds, and investments in other securities which, regarding any one issuer, represent neither more than 5 percent of the assets of the fund nor more than 10 percent of the voting securities of the issuer. Further, no more than 25 percent of the fund's assets may be invested in the securities of any one issuer (other than government securities or the securities of other funds), the securities (other than the securities of other funds) of two or more issuers that the fund controls and are engaged in similar trades or businesses, or the securities of one or more qualified publicly traded partnerships. The effect of these tests is that, at a minimum, a fund with a modest cash position and no government securities would hold securities from at least 12 different issuers.

The securities laws set higher standards for funds that elect to be diversified. If a fund elects to be diversified, the Investment Company Act requires that, with respect to at least 75 percent of the portfolio, no more than 5 percent may be invested in the securities of any one issuer and no investment may represent more than 10 percent of the outstanding voting securities of any issuer. Diversification is not mandatory, but all mutual funds must disclose whether they are diversified under the Investment Company Act's standards.

In practice, most funds that elect to be diversified are much more highly diversified than they need to be to meet these two tests. As of December 2013, for example, the median number of stocks held by U.S. equity funds excluding sector funds was 100.

MUTUAL FUND COMPLIANCE PROGRAMS

While compliance has always been a cornerstone for mutual funds, the adoption of the fund compliance program rule (Rule 38a-1 under the Investment Company Act) in late 2003 introduced formalized practices and new requirements for funds and their boards, and presented fund boards with new tools for overseeing compliance. Under the rule, mutual funds must adopt and implement written policies and procedures reasonably designed to prevent violations of the federal securities laws. These policies and procedures must provide for the oversight of compliance by the fund's key service providers, namely, its investment manager(s), principal underwriter(s), administrator(s), and transfer agent(s). Funds must review at least annually the adequacy of their own policies and procedures, as well as those of their service providers, and the effectiveness of their implementation.

Rule 38a-1 also requires mutual funds to designate a CCO, who administers the fund's compliance policies and procedures. The rule contains provisions designed to promote the independence of the fund CCO from the fund's investment manager. Specifically, the fund board, including a majority of the independent directors, must approve the appointment and compensation and, if necessary, the removal of the fund CCO. At least annually, the fund CCO must provide a written report to the fund board that addresses, among other things, the operation of the fund's and its service providers' policies and procedures and each material compliance matter that occurred since the date of the last report. Although the rule requires compliance reviews and reports to be undertaken at least annually, such reviews and reports may occur more frequently or on an ongoing basis throughout the year.

SEC OVERSIGHT

This chapter has been devoted to describing the history, origins, and core principles of the regulatory regime that applies to mutual funds. The role of the SEC in the regulatory regime is extremely important.

The SEC is tasked with monitoring and enforcing mutual funds' compliance with the Investment Company Act as well as all other applicable federal securities laws and regulations. The SEC staff promotes compliance with the federal securities laws through outreach, publications, and inspections of mutual funds and their managers conducted by SEC examiners, accountants, and lawyers. These inspections include a detailed review of the funds' advertisements, books and records, capital structure, fee structure, investment management contracts, corporate governance, best execution and sales practices. As part of its robust disclosure review, the SEC also reviews all mutual fund registration statements, which include the fund's prospectus, SAI, and other information. As a result, the SEC staff reviews and comments on, among other things, the funds' investment objectives and goals, capital structure, risk disclosures, fee table, financial highlights information, and financial intermediary compensation.

Summary and Conclusions

Since 1940, the regulatory regime that applies to mutual funds has helped make these funds some of the most popular and resilient investment products in the financial marketplace. The Investment Company Act has proven to be a remarkable piece of legislation, built on a foundation of core shareholder protection principles, including transparency, daily valuation, liquidity, strict limits on leverage, diversification, separate custody, and the prohibition of conflicts of interest. Such principles have helped make the law durable enough to stand the test of time, but flexible enough to foster industry growth and innovation while adapting to changing demographics and investor needs. These same attributes will continue to serve regulators, the industry, and shareholders well into the future.

Discussion Questions

1. Discuss factors contributing to the substantial growth in the assets in mutual funds since 1990.

2. Discuss the core principles of the Investment Company Act of 1940 including how these principles help protect mutual fund shareholders.
3. Discuss how the Investment Company Act of 1940 limits leverage in mutual funds.
4. Explain several reasons that mutual funds have very low leverage ratios especially compared to most commercial banks.

References

Chen, Qi, Itay Goldstein, and Wei Jiang. 2010. "Payoff Complementarities and Financial Fragility: Evidence from Mutual Fund Outflows." *Journal of Financial Economics* 97:2, 239–262.

Fernando, Deepthi, Leora Klapper, Victor Sulla, and Dimitri Vittas. 2003. "The Global Growth of Mutual Funds." World Bank Policy Research Working Paper 3055, World Bank.

Feroli, Michael, Anil Kashyap, Kermit Schoenholtz, and Hyun Song Shin. 2014. "Market Tantrums and Monetary Policy." Working Paper presented at the 2014 Monetary Policy Forum.

Fink, Matthew P. 2008. *The Rise of Mutual Funds: An Insider's View*. New York: Oxford University Press.

Independent Directors Council. 2013. *Overview of Fund Governance Practices, 1994–2012*. Available at http://www.idc.org/pdf/pub_13_fund_governance.pdf.

Investment Company Institute. 2013. "Ownership of Mutual Funds, Shareholder Sentiment, and Use of the Internet." *ICI Research Perspective* 19:9, 1–48. Available at http://www.ici.org/pdf/per19-09.pdf.

Investment Company Institute. 2014a. *2014 Investment Company Fact Book*. Washington, DC: Investment Company Institute. Available at http://www.ici.org/pdf/2014_factbook.pdf.

Investment Company Institute. 2014b. *Classification of Shareholder Assets Report: Annual Institutional Survey, 2013*. Washington, DC: Investment Company Institute.

Rouwenhorst, K. Geert. 2004. "The Origins of Mutual Funds." Working Paper, International Center for Finance, Yale School of Management, Yale University.

Securities and Exchange Commission. 1992. *Protecting Investors: A Half Century of Investment Company Regulation*. Division of Investment Management. Washington, DC: Securities and Exchange Commission. Available at http://www.sec.gov/divisions/investment/guidance/icreg50-92.pdf.

Securities and Exchange Commission. 2014a. "Money Market Fund Reform; Amendments to Form PF." Final Rule. Release No. 33-9616; IC-31166; FR-84.

Securities and Exchange Commission. 2014b. "IM Guidance Update No. 2014-01." Division of Investment Management. Available at http://www.sec.gov/divisions/investment/guidance/im-guidance-2014-2011.pdf.

Securities and Exchange Commission. 2014c. "Registered Investment Company Use of Senior Securities-Select Bibliography." Available at http://www.sec.gov/divisions/investment/seniorsecurities-bibliography.htm.

Stein, Jeremy. 2014. "Comments on 'Market Tantrums and Monetary Policy.'" Speech given at the 2014 U.S. Monetary Policy Forum, February 28, 2014. Available at http://www.federalreserve.gov/newsevents/speech/stein20140228a.htm.

Part Two

MUTUAL FUNDS AND OTHER FUND TYPES

5

Open-End Funds

CONRAD S. CICCOTELLO

Associate Professor and Director of Wealth Management Programs,
Georgia State University and Executive Director of the Huebner Foundation

Introduction

To give context to the unique features of the open-end fund (OEF), also called a mutual fund, requires returning to the time of its birth. During the Great Depression, the most common investment product was the closed-end fund (CEF). Investors could not redeem CEF shares from the fund itself but had to sell them to other investors in the marketplace. Panic wreaked havoc with the markets during the Great Depression and the thinness of the market gave CEF investors little comfort. In their panic, liquidity for shares dried up and valuations fell. The desire to be able to liquidate at "fair value" thus became important. The OEF, from its beginning, has supplied this attribute. The investor may buy or sell shares each day at the net asset value (NAV), which is established daily by the fund. Absent pre-established trading restrictions, the fund stands ready daily to buy or sell as many shares as those seeking to buy or sell demand.

Placing the OEF within the ecosystem of a widely growing array of investment vehicles requires reference to the daily liquidity at the NAV with the fund itself as the counterparty. This feature distinguishes OEFs from CEFs since investors in CEFs trade with each other on an exchange. It also distinguishes the OEF from an exchange-traded fund (ETF), whose shares trade on an exchange between investors except for a share creation and redemption mechanism for certain institutional investors. This creation/redemption mechanism is "OEF like," but exists as more of an "in-kind" exchange of securities for shares than a mechanism to provide liquidity at NAV for ordinary investors. The OEF daily liquidity can also differ from funds in separately managed accounts, which may place more restrictions on entry (e.g., higher minimum initial investment) or liquidation. Finally, the OEF daily liquidity typically differs from that of hedge funds, which permit purchases and redemptions only at certain times (e.g., quarterly).

The daily liquidity attribute of OEFs creates challenges for the structure, especially in combination with active management. While passive (index) OEFs are growing rapidly in terms of numbers and assets, active management is still the dominant OEF strategy. While active management is common in CEFs, separately managed accounts, and hedge funds, an OEF also allows daily purchases and sales of shares that add to or subtract from the fund's assets. The portfolio manager must deal with these fund flows and the daily flows can be large. In contrast, CEFs typically have no fund flows. ETFs may create and redeem shares, but most of these funds are passively managed and thus follow an index. Separately managed funds could place limits on additional investments or redemptions depending on the liquidity of the asset class of the account. Hedge funds typically permit flows in and out only on an established schedule and with certain restrictions.

Active managers attempt to buy and sell shares of funds at favorable prices based on their valuation analyses. As Edelen (1999) observed in his pioneering research, daily purchases and sales of the fund shares either bring in or remove cash from the fund itself and can affect the active management of the OEF. As will be discussed in more detail later in the chapter, the timing of daily inflows and outflows can matter to both fund and investor performance. So unlike active managers of other portfolio vehicles, active portfolio managers of OEFs must not only select securities but also manage daily cash inflows and outflows.

Another unique aspect of OEFs is the family structure. Most OEFs are part of a larger suite of offerings that share a common family name (e.g., T. Rowe Price Funds and Fidelity Investments), portfolio management team, marketing, distribution, back office, custody, and the like. The family structure is common in OEFs, creating distinctions from other types of investment vehicles. Beginning about the turn of the century, academic research such as Sirri and Tuffano (1998), Massa (2003), Nanda, Wang, and Zheng (2004), Reuter (2006), and Kempf and Ruenzi (2008) began to explore aspects of OEF family structures. Family factors such as having a "star fund" can affect cash flows to other funds in the family. Families can also influence the allocation of underpriced initial public offerings (IPOs). Thus, family structures can affect liquidity and active portfolio management, which are two attributes mentioned earlier.

Thus, combining daily liquidity at NAV, active management, and membership within a larger family of funds provides the unique setting for the OEF in the investment vehicle universe. While other vehicles may have one or two of these attributes, they are not integrated as closely as the typical OEF. Investors have found these OEF attributes to be attractive. Thus, OEFs are in a very strong position within the ecosystem of investment structures mentioned previously. The Investment Company Institute (2013) reports that the $13 trillion currently invested in OEFs is about 10 times the amount in ETFs ($1.3 trillion), five times the amount in hedge funds ($2.6 trillion), and about 20 times the amount in CEFs ($265 billion). The amount invested in separately managed accounts, however, is greater than that in OEFs, at roughly $20 trillion.

Open-End Fund Distinctions and Issues: Daily Liquidity

Providing daily liquidity at the NAV is seemingly a straightforward concept, but it has led to some of the largest problems ever faced by the OEF industry. The two main challenges are (1) computing the NAV and (2) determining when orders for fund share purchase or sale must be sent to receive that day's NAV. This section examines these two issues in detail.

The *NAV* is the fund's total assets less its liabilities divided by the number of shares outstanding. OEFs calculate the NAV each day based on the values of assets and liabilities. The common practice is to use the closing prices for the inputs as of the close of markets in the United States at 4:00 p.m. Issues arise, however, in several contexts. What if the United States domiciled OEF holds foreign stocks? If those stocks are listed on exchanges in Japan, for example, then their last trade on that exchange typically occurred around 15 hours before 4:00 p.m. Eastern Standard Time in the United States. Thus, any factors that would have affected the price of that (Japanese) stock in the last 15 hours have not been reflected in that stock's price. In the parlance of OEF pricing, this is known as a "stale price."

In their seminal paper, Greene and Hodges (2002) identify and quantify the phenomenon of "stale prices" in OEFs. They determine that U.S.-domiciled OEFs holding international stocks ("international funds") are especially prone to stale prices, and that the impact ("dilution") to the fund from stale price trading can be substantial. Dilution occurs when inflows and outflows of the fund are well-timed. So if investors add cash just before the fund's risky assets (say stocks) rise in value, then the gains are shared across a larger number of shares than if no purchase had occurred. In terms of fund redemptions, suppose that these are timed such that they occur just before declines in the values of risky assets. The negative returns are levered onto a smaller number of shares.

Normally, inflows and outflows of a fund are expected to be unassociated with daily (next day) risky asset returns. Think of the flipping of a fair coin. Half the time buy orders occur just before stocks rise so the next day return is positive. Half the time they occur before the stocks fall so the next day return is negative. But when stale pricing exists, the coin is not fair. Ciccotello, Edelen, Greene, and Hodges (2002) show that in the case of international funds, an investor can use a publicly available signal such as the current day's stock return or the return from 2:00 to 4:00 p.m. to buy or sell shares of international mutual funds. Next day success rates (i.e., buying before prices rise or selling before they fall) is achieved with a probability of about 65 percent. This finding leads to dilution of the return the fund would have earned otherwise.

Given the increasingly global nature of OEF investing, the problem of "time-zone" arbitrage is important. One of the focal points of this book on mutual funds and ETFs is that they have brought the ability to invest in securities around the globe to investors in a particular country. In the United States, the opportunities to own securities in a range of emerging market countries are many and quite valuable for building a diversified portfolio. But Chalmers, Edelen, and Kadlec (2001) show that this problem is not confined to international OEFs. OEFs holding illiquid domestic stocks such as small capitalization stocks can experience dilution if these stocks do not trade sufficiently enough to have the 4:00 p.m. price constitute a "fair value." Thus, stale prices can exist in both domestic and international funds.

Computing the NAV each day can be a challenging task. What can a fund do to prevent stale price trading? Ciccotello et al. (2002) outline two basic approaches, which they refer to as "ex ante" and "ex post." The ex ante approach is to use a pricing model to "fair value" the NAV each day, thus making short-term buying and selling to take advantage of stale prices an expected zero profit exercise. The ex post method is used to limit trading or to impose costs on trading. The former would limit "round trips" (i.e., a buy and a sell is one round trip) in the fund to a certain number over a specified period of time (e.g., four round trip trades in one year). The latter would impose costs on trades, such as redemption fees, to make taking advantage of short-term trading less or unprofitable. An example would be a 2 percent redemption fee for sales of shares held less than 90 days.

Both the ex ante and ex post methods have weaknesses. Using a model to compute fair value pricing can be considered arbitrary and may introduce bias itself. Costs or limits on trading strike at the heart of the OEFs main distinction, daily liquidity at NAV for all investors with the fund itself as the counterparty. However, failing to address the issues associated with strategic timing of flows is also dangerous.

Beginning in 2003, issues related to "market timing" and "late trading" rocked the OEF industry. In these matters, investors tried to take advantage of stale prices by exceeding trading limits and/or by submitting orders later than the deadline to receive that day's NAV. Consider what would happen if investors could trade at 7:00 p.m. using the 4:00 p.m. NAV. Those investors would have the advantage of observing after-market-close information revelation such as an earnings release. They could also watch the aftermarket futures returns and use them as a signal. In either case, these investors could use the opportunity to trade favorably, given the fund's stale pricing. They would have a coin loaded in their favor.

Distinctions and Issues: Active Management

The chapter now turns to examining the issues associated with another distinctive characteristic of OEFs—active management. Ciccotello, Greene, Ling, and Rakowski (2011, p. 277) examine capacity constraints in active management and argue that "to generate alpha in a portfolio is to exploit a mispricing through the lens of theoretical equilibrium models." *Alpha* refers to positive excess risk-adjusted returns. Is the ability to generate alpha constrained by factors related to the asset class or fund? The authors contend that OEFs provide a laboratory to study this issue due to flows into and out of the fund.

The analysis begins by examining the notion of performance itself. Funds disclose returns that are time-weighted. A *time-weighted rate of return* (TWR) reflects the compound rate of growth over a stated evaluation period of one unit of money initially invested in the account. Thus, TRWs are the returns that the fund itself experiences. But assume that a fund earns a 100 percent holding period return in year one on an asset base of $50 million, then experiences $1 billion in new cash inflows (assume at the end of the year for simplicity). Then in year two, the fund experiences a 75 percent negative holding period return. What is the two-year average TWR? It is arithmetic average of 100 percent and negative 75 percent, or 12.5 percent per year. This calculation seems like a very dissatisfying answer given the fund size differences in the two periods.

Dollar weighting attempts to address the challenge the example illustrates by considering inflows and outflows from the fund. Beginning with the work of Edelen (1999), researchers have examined how OEF flows affect fund and investor performance. Several studies find that investors time their trades poorly (Friesen and Sapp 2007; Ciccotello et al. 2011). Investors tend to add money before the fund has negative returns and redeem shares for cash before the fund has positive returns. This tendency is borne out in the estimate of lower dollar-weighted returns relative to TWRs.

Notice the contrast to the discussion in the previous section on daily liquidity at the NAV. In that case, the concern was that investors strategically take advantage of stale NAVs to dilute the fund's performance. So these investors, who are often holding the fund for one or two days as they go in and out, obtain superior performance and hurt the fund's returns, especially the fund's long-term shareholders.

Now the discussion of flow timing has taken a different turn. What happens if investors have really poor timing when entering and exiting the fund? The intuition is that those investors who enter and exit before (negative) and (positive) risky asset returns would tend to do poorly relative to the fund, the opposite of the strategic market timing case.

As previously mentioned, the TWR is the holding period return earned by the fund itself. The fund discloses this return. In the case where no inflows and outflows exist in a given period such as a year, the fund's TWR and the dollar-weighted return (DWR) are the same. Inflows and outflows, however, change this identity between time and dollar weighting.

So why is dollar weighting such a big issue with OEFs? Ciccotello et al. (2011) find that DWRs are often significantly lower than TRWs. As the former can be thought of as the return investors earn while the latter is the fund's return, the finding has serious implications for OEFs. Perhaps the biggest issue is assessing performance itself. Since TWRs drive ranking funds in comparison to peers and rankings lead to new inflows or outflows, the disconnect between dollar- and time-weighted performance can have a profoundly self-reinforcing effect. Moreover, the findings have implications for the debate about active versus passive management.

To shed light on that issue, Ciccotello et al. (2011) parse the difference in DWRs and TWRs into timing and scale components. Timing components are the extent to which flows are correlated with the fund's underlying benchmark factor returns. Scale measures the degree to which alpha is related to the size of the fund's asset base. The findings show that passively managed funds have only timing effects while actively managed funds have both timing and scale effects. So in an index fund, for example, flows tend to arrive at the "wrong time," but the portfolio strategy is not capacity constrained. This is logical because investing in an index such as the S&P 500 index, which consists of highly liquid stocks, is not a search for mispricing that becomes more difficult as assets under management (AUM) grow. The strategy is to mimic the index return in the index mentioned (i.e., the S&P 500 index). Actively managed funds, however, tend to have not only timing effects but also scale effects. Scale constraints are more severe in some asset classes than others. For example, small capitalization stock funds face more scale constraints than large capitalization stocks do. The empirical findings are also consistent with Friesen and Sapp (2007) and the foundational theoretical research by Berk and Green (2004), who model decreasing returns to scale for active management.

Flows into OEFs, and thus the dollar-weighting challenge, also confound the simple comparisons between the performance of active and passive funds. For example, the timing effect of flows in a passive fund might be larger than the sum of the timing and scale effects in an actively managed fund in the same investment category. Thus, the TRW of the passive fund might be greater than that for the active fund, but the reverse could be true for DWRs. Given the magnitude of the research debate about passive versus active management such as Wermers (2000) and French (2008), this topic calls for additional research.

Returning to the context of active management of OEFs, the challenges are thus related to both the timing and the scale effects of fund flows. Dubofsky (2010) and Rakowski (2010) provide excellent insights into fund flows and portfolio management. Since roughly three-quarters of OEFs are actively managed, comparing their situation to the investment structures discussed previously is worthwhile.

At one end of the spectrum are CEFs, which typically have no flows. CEFs thus face neither the negative timing nor the scale constraint effects that OEFs do. CEFs typically initiate an IPO, however. As Ritter (1991) notes, IPOs tend to occur after good performance in a particular sector. Thus, CEFs may launch with a negative timing effect. The portfolio manager must purchase assets to gain market exposure, and the values in the particular sector may have already experienced substantial appreciation. But as to scale effects, the CEF should be relatively immune since it does not normally accept new money. If the CEF borrows funds to invest more money and/or conducts a secondary offering, then scale may become an issue. The fund, however, decides to raise additional funds. Investors who can buy and redeem shares at will do not make this decision.

Separately managed accounts may accept new investments or honor redemption requests on a daily basis, although they may also impose restrictions based on the liquidity of the underlying assets. To the extent that separate account investors' flow timing is as poor as OEF investors' timing, the impact on active management may be similar to the typical OEF. However, since the typical OEF and separately managed account clienteles are different, a reason exists to speculate that separately managed account flows would differ in their timing compared to OEFs. This is an important area for future research, assuming data are available. Similarly, managers and investors of separately managed accounts may be more aware of capacity constraints in the fund's asset class and thus make additions more strategically. To the extent that a separately managed account is not a pooled investment vehicle, like an OEF, investors have more incentive to consider both the timing and scale effects of flows. Any negative impacts are not shared with other investors.

Hedge funds are a highly actively managed vehicle and hedge fund managers are acutely aware of the issues of fund flows. Compared to OEFs, hedge funds are much more likely to restrict both new investments and redemptions. Since hedge funds often invest in illiquid asset classes, these restrictions are even more strongly warranted.

Finally, active management is relatively new to ETFs. As certain investors have the ability to create and redeem shares in large blocks, the issue of timing of such creation and redemption in an active management context is certainly interesting. How active management will work in this vehicle should be a topic for future research.

In summary, OEFs face major challenges on the active management front relative to other structures where active management is prominent. These challenges are mainly due to the differences in investor clientele.

PASSIVE MANAGEMENT

While on the topic of comparison investment structures, the passive investment landscape is worthwhile to consider. The OEF is known as an actively managed investment product, but it also birthed the passive (index) structure. Popularized by Vanguard and its iconic leader, John Bogle, passive OEFs have grown tremendously over time. The Vanguard S&P 500 Index OEF is an example with current assets of approximately $185 billion.

In recent years, passive funds have done well relative to actively managed funds in the same investment objective. Roughly 25 percent of OEFs are passively managed, and based on recent trends, they are well positioned for growth. Among the competing investment structures, only ETFs focus on passive management. In percentage terms, passive ETFs are growing much more rapidly than passive OEFs.

Why are ETFs growing so rapidly in popularity? Some investors like the intraday trading opportunity that ETFs offer. Also, some ETFs offer extremely low expense ratios relative to OEFs. Haslem, Baker, and Smith (2006) find wide dispersion in the expense ratios of passive OEFs and link some of the differences to marketing and distribution (12b-1) fees. Some passive OEFs have expenses in the 50–60 basis point range, which is almost 10 times the ratio in the lowest cost ETFs.

Another reason is fund flows, as discussed earlier. Ciccotello et al. (2011) find flow timing effects in passive funds help to explain the difference between TWRs and DWRs. This finding means that investors in a passive OEF tend to earn less than the fund's disclosed TWR. In an ETF, retail investors trade with each other and not with the fund. So, unlike OEF investors, ETF investors do not add cash to the fund before negative risky asset (e.g., stocks in the case of a stock index fund) returns and vice versa.

An interesting issue in ETFs relates to the creation-redemption mechanism that certain investors can exploit. In theory, this is a like-kind exchange of fund shares for a basket of securities and vice versa. In this case, no DWR affects should occur because it is a like-kind exchange of the risky assets themselves for the share that proxies for the value of the risky assets. Apparently, cash is part of the creation and redemption process in some cases. Cash in the exchange raises issues similar to those in OEFs.

An area for future research would be the comparison of DWRs in OEFs versus ETFs. However, this research would require detailed data into share creations and redemptions, which may be difficult to obtain.

Because investors can purchase and redeem shares from OEFs on a daily basis, the passive OEFs have tended to benchmark relatively liquid indexes. ETFs started out tracking highly liquid indexes, but the product class has pushed toward tracking less liquid benchmarks. Attempts have been made to mimic exotic indexes where the liquidity of the securities comprising that index is quite low. So the issue may arise about whether the fund is providing liquidity to the index sector or vice versa. Additional research on the relative time- and dollar-weighted performance of passive investments in the OEF versus ETF structure would be welcome.

Institutional Issues: Fund Family

Another distinctive feature of the OEF is its place within a family structure. Families offer a suite of funds, which is usually the name of the portfolio management company such as Fidelity Investments (Fidelity). Families play an important role in the attributes and performance of individual OEFs. This section discusses a few of these family matters and offers some perspectives on their impact in the competitive investment product structure environment.

Having a family of funds under one advisor allows taking an industrial organizational view of the OEF. Ciccotello, Miles, and Walsh (2006) show that more focused families can achieve higher gross returns than families that offer funds across a wide range of investment objectives. The advantages of focus continue into net returns, reflecting economies in portfolio management, fund administration, and fund distribution. The intuition is that if a family offers a narrow range of funds, it can build efficient scale in that niche. That scale resides in security analysis and selection, reflected by higher gross returns and returns after advisory fees. The advantage is also reflected in fund administration, which is due to efficiencies in indirect costs such as producing fund reports and audit fees. Last, economies in distribution reflect the ability to have focused advertising and sales forces.

Focused families, however, do not have the opportunity to provide investors with a complete set of fund offerings. So broadening the array of offerings to include stock and bond funds, for example, serves investors with higher search costs by offering them a one-stop shop. The reduction in investor search costs is offset by the loss of the benefits of focus. Ciccotello et al. (2006) conclude that low search cost investors can build portfolios from different focused families and claim the benefits of fund family focus.

Ciccotello, Greene, and Walsh (2007) continue the analysis in a follow-on paper that examines supermarket distribution of OEFs. They find that OEFs from focused families experience significant increases in fund flows after they are added to no-transfer-fee supermarkets such as Schwab or Fidelity. The authors contend that the supermarket expands the investor base for the fund and levers the benefits of family focus. This is a distribution innovation with the potential of changing the structure of the OEF industry. Ciccotello et al. also observe a shift in fund entry into supermarkets over time. In the early days of the mutual fund supermarket, the supermarket added the well-known family name funds to its "shelves." More recently, the supermarket is adding the names of smaller, less well-known, focused family funds. These funds use the brand recognition and search cost reductions of the supermarket to lever their security selection skills. Thus, over time, the brand recognition of OEFs is migrating from families to supermarkets.

None of the other investment vehicles relies on a family structure to the same extent as OEFs do. Although a few CEF complexes such as Eaton Vance offer a wide variety of CEFs, most focus in a niche. Since CEFs have no daily flows, the spillovers seen in OEF families would not pertain. Separately managed accounts can "piggy back" on the reputation and security selection skill of a successful OEF advisor. But a separately managed account is typically not a pooled vehicle to the same extent as an OEF. Some ETF advisors such as ProFunds offer a wide variety of ETFs, but since most of those are passive vehicles, no security selection synergies exist across funds. However, synergies in administration, marketing, and in dealing with vendors for fund services may occur. Finally, the same advisor may offer several hedge funds but hedge funds do not typically attempt to provide a range of funds across asset classes so as to allow an investor to have a "one-stop shop" for portfolio construction.

As the OEF is rather unique in the family context, the institutional issues regarding family structure provide worthwhile research opportunities. Family affects both security selection and fund administration issues such as marketing and distribution. With the changes and advances in distribution of funds such as supermarkets, could brand recognition shift from the fund family to the supermarket? Will supermarkets in funds offer their own products much like supermarkets for groceries (e.g., think Kroger peas or Schwab funds)? How will supermarkets allocate "shelf space" to funds? While some might argue that these are marketing concerns and not finance issues, Bergstresser, Chalmers, and Tufano (2009) show that distribution channels and advice affect investor performance. Thus, the industrial organization of the OEF can influence such factors as fund flows and active management.

The Future of Mutual Funds: Challenges and Opportunities

Building off the prior section on the distinctive characteristics of OEFs, this section now turns to examining the future of OEFs. It begins with a specific institutional environment where OEFs are dominant—defined contribution (DC) retirement plans. The section then turns to examining how the issues of income tax, governance, and the evolution of markets will affect the OEF going forward.

DEFINED CONTRIBUTION RETIREMENT PLANS

As part of the author's graduate wealth management coursework, students are required to construct a personal (or household) balance sheet. The patterns provide insights into the current marriage of investments, investment vehicles, and asset location in a tax-deferred or ordinary after-tax account. Looking at the balance sheet of a typical upper middle-income retiree (current age equal to or greater than a normal retirement age of 67), the observer might often see little to no investment assets as the retiree has a traditional defined benefit (DB) pension. If the observer does see investments, they tend to be in individual securities such as stocks and bonds. That retiree came from an age without many DC retirement plans with OEFs as the investment options and stock brokers as the dominant advisors. Brokers in that time period tended to recommend individual stocks and bonds rather than funds.

Change that example to a typical upper middle-income household with spouses of age range 40 to 50 and an evolution occurs. First, more households in this age cohort have DC plans as the number of traditional pensions has declined substantially over the past two decades. Second, inside those DC retirement plans, OEFs are the dominant investment offering. OEFs have been the mainstay of DC retirement plans, and have grown as the DC world has grown over the past several decades. According to the Investment Company Institute (2013), out of the $13.0 trillion invested in mutual funds at the end of 2012, $5.3 trillion was in DC retirement plans and individual retirement accounts (IRAs).

Several reasons help to explain why OEFs are the mainstay for retirement plans. In a DC plan, the sponsor (typically the employer) owes the beneficiaries of the plans fiduciary duty regarding the plan. OEFs offer a diversified portfolio of investments. In contrast, think of the lack of diversification inherent with offering company stock in a retirement plan. If the stock crashes, the value decline hits the employee's retirement plan, their job security, and the real estate value in the company town where they have their home. Plan sponsors have duties to offer diversified portfolios of offerings and a mutual fund family can accomplish this duty. Thus, OEFs are prudent choices because they are diversified into many securities and the family structure offers choices across a range of asset classes and investment objectives.

OEFs also have a strong position in retirement plans because of the ease of periodic trading. Many participants in DC retirement plans purchase shares on a regular basis (e.g., monthly) by having a salary reduction done from their pay. Sometimes the employer matches this employee contribution. Together, the employee and employer contribution purchase the fund's shares at that day's NAV. This process works smoothly because no commissions are involved as in buying exchange-traded securities or funds. Similarly, when employees rebalance retirement accounts, the sale and purchase of another fund occurs without commission.

Having CEFs or ETFs in a retirement plan would create the need for having a (brokerage) platform in the plan to allow plan beneficiaries to buy and sell during the day. In contrast, the OEF has an end-of-day purchase or redemption protocol that involves trading with the fund itself at the closing NAV. Concerns over beneficiary trading along with record-keeping associated with that trading have meant that most retirement plans continue to offer OEFs as their primary investment vehicle.

Regulation has reinforced the OEF's strong position in retirement plans. The Pension Protection Act of 2006 established qualified default investment alternatives as a foundation in DC plans. Many plans now have a default option, which is a target-date mutual fund. A *target-date fund* (TDF) is an investment strategy where the asset allocation evolves through time to meet the changing risk and returns preferences of a cohort of individuals saving for retirement. A beneficiary who does not choose an investment will be defaulted into a target-date OEF that has an asset allocation appropriate to that beneficiary's age. Younger participants' TDFs have greater equity exposure, and that exposure declines (via the "glide slope" or "glide path") as that beneficiary grows closer to normal retirement age. An advantage of the target-date OEF is that the participant need not rebalance the account over time. The glide slope accomplishes the transition from a growth to an income-oriented portfolio. The growth of TDFs is testimony to the strong current position that OEFs have in DC plans. TDFs also have challenges such as layering of costs and agency issues with selecting funds that go within the fund. Vallapuzha (2011) provides an analysis and discussion of the TDF structure and its pros and cons.

Could the OEF's strong position in DC retirement plan erode over time? Returning to the financial planning example, consider that many millennials might favor ETFs to OEFs. ETFs are more modern and have received much more attention in recent years with their spectacular growth. Younger investors with greater risk tolerance enjoy the lower fees in ETFs and the ability to trade, often at low commissions. While retirement plan offerings remain mostly OEFs, some plans have opened a brokerage window to allow beneficiaries a wide variety of options including ETFs.

With DC retirement plan wealth mainly in OEFs, displacing the OEF in retirement plans is unlikely to occur anytime soon. Although sponsors will generally be reluctant to issue options that promote trading like ETFs, the options are likely to grow over time. Younger retirement plan beneficiaries who like low fees and ease of trading will probably lean more toward ETFs in the future. While trading has potential tax impacts, retirement plans are an excellent place to trade from a tax perspective since all realized gains are trapped inside the retirement account until the employee removes the assets from the tax-deferred location. Retirement accounts are also an excellent location to hold actively managed funds. Active management generally means more portfolio manager trading than passive management, meaning less tax efficiency. From a tax perspective, the former strategy is better suited to retirement accounts and the latter strategy to ordinary accounts.

Turning to institutional issues in retirement plans, the Pension Protection Act of 2006 tightened the requirements on retirement plan sponsors regarding duties to protect plan participants. One impact has been on integrated record-keeping for participants. As many plans have moved toward an "open architecture" that allows participants to own funds across families inside the plan, a challenge has arisen concerning the plan sponsor's ability to know a participant's complete plan holdings. This information might be necessary with regards to the approval of a plan loan, for example. Some assets might be in Fidelity funds in the plan, for example, while others are in TIAA-CREF funds. The need for an integrated or third party record-keeper thus grows. The result could be that funds are offered in much more of a supermarket style than in a fund family. This "breakdown" of the fund family might then lead to issues in brand recognition as discussed earlier in the chapter.

INCOME TAX

OEFs are pass-through vehicles for income tax purposes and are similar to most of the other investment structures mentioned in the chapter. As mentioned previously, however, tax considerations arise when the OEF is held in an ordinary account as opposed to a retirement account. There are two tax impacts. The first is that active managers tend to trade more often than passive managers, and actively managed funds thus tend to have more realized capital gains than passive funds do. This brings about a second tax consideration. If passive funds are not realizing gains over time, they can have large amounts of unrealized capital gains in them. Sale of these appreciated assets would result in realized capital gains, which when distributed would be shared pro rata by all the current investors in the fund.

OEFs are a mutual vehicle in this tax respect, as gains are shared. But not all investors may have the same tax appetite. Some might own the OEF in an ordinary account and have realized gains flow through to their current year taxes. Other investors might own the fund in a retirement account and be indifferent to realized and unrealized gains. Also, market conditions might affect taxes. In the case of large redemptions from an OEF, say in the midst of falling asset prices, the portfolio manager may be forced to sell a large amount of fund holdings. This triggers a large tax bill in a year where the fund has done very poorly. This outcome was indeed a nasty surprise for investors in large down market years such as 2008.

The threat of mutuality involving the tax treatment in the OEF stands in contrast to other investment structures. The separately managed account might not be pooled across investors regarding tax treatment and offers the advantage of tax-oriented tailoring (e.g., matching gains and losses) at the investor level. In an ETF, trading is between investors and so these trades do not force sales of the underlying securities in the fund. The situation is similar in a CEF. Thus, taxes are a bigger challenge for the OEF in ordinary accounts relative to most of its investment structure competitors.

MUTUAL FUND GOVERNANCE

Effective governance is important in OEFs as in operating companies. Similar to an operating company such as Apple or Exxon, an OEF is governed by a board of directors and shareholders elect the directors. Yet, boards of OEFs and operating companies differ in several ways. Consider a board's most important task, which in an operating company is the hiring and firing of the Chief Executive Officer (CEO). In an OEF, the most important job of the independent directors of a fund board is arguably to negotiate the annual advisory agreement. This is called the "15(c)" process, named after the applicable section of the 1940 Investment Company Act. This is an annual agreement that renews the contract of the fund's advisor. The advisor employs the portfolio managers and typically coordinates all of the other in-house and outside service providers that support the fund's administration.

Although replacing the CEO of an operating company is a major event, removing the CEO often leaves some or even all of the other members of management in place at least for the short run. The firm can continue to operate as management and workers carry on without the CEO. Nonrenewal of the fund advisor, however, is a much bigger deal. It means changing the entire portfolio and administrative support team for the fund at the same time. This rarely happens in OEFs.

What happens in the negotiations to renew the advisor? In short, a discussion occurs about price and performance. *Price* is the advisory fee the manager charges, considered in both absolute terms and relative to appropriate benchmarks. *Performance* is the fund's absolute and relative return measured against appropriate benchmarks. Fund advisors are highly concerned about beating benchmarks. Brown, Harlow, and Starks (1996) demonstrate that portfolio managers tend to behave as if they are in an annual tournament with their fund peers. Some of these tournament behaviors, such as risk shifting in mid-year depending upon whether relative performance is good or bad, may not be in investors' best interests.

If a fund has relatively low fees and good performance relative to its benchmarks, renewal seems to be indicated and fees look to be well earned and fair to shareholders. But what if a fund has high fees and poor performance? Should fees be cut? Or what if a fund has grown its AUM by a factor of 10, say from $100 million to $1 billion? One might argue that some of the fund's costs, in either portfolio management and/or in administration should decline in percentage-of-asset terms. These types of changes are a realization of an economy of scale.

OEF fund fees have become a hot issue in the last decade for several reasons. One is the negative fallout from the market timing and late trading scandal that broke in 2003 with Attorney General Spitzer's allegations regarding Canary Hedge Fund.

What came to light in the following several years was that some funds allowed certain investors to trade in excess of prospectus limitations. This was done in exchange for investing "sticky" assets in other funds. These agreements were not disclosed. Some allegations surfaced that the funds allowed certain investors to trade later than 4:00 p.m., thus giving them the stale price advantage discussed in a previous section. Settlement negotiations for violations of securities laws by OEF investment advisors sometimes brought added demands for advisory fee reductions. This opened the door to civil class actions claiming excessive fees, under Section 36(b) of the Investment Company Act.

Beyond the scandal, however, was a general concern for fees, especially in actively managed OEFs, that did not decline in percentage terms as AUM grew enormously. Also, the low interest rate environment that has existed over the last decade has raised concerns. Consider bond funds. An average fund fee of approximately 1 percent a year consumes much more of the fund's return when nominal interest rates are low. The extreme case is money market funds. Many currently pay basically zero percent interest net of fees.

In this environment, the pressure has been growing on boards to negotiate with advisors more aggressively regarding fees. The challenge for OEF governance is that inside a family of funds, the same individuals often comprise the board of every fund. So the same individuals could be the board for 100 different funds. This is technically 100 different discussions about fees. Moreover, it raises concerns that board members might be reluctant to "rock the boat" in one fund given they have a seat on the boards of other funds in the family. Total board member compensation received from the sum of all of the individual funds can be attractive, reaching several hundred thousand dollars in some cases.

Going forward, fees will be a major issue for all funds sold to the public. However, OEFs have the potential to grow their asset base and hence management fees dramatically from new inflows. Thus, OEF fees are a relatively more sensitive issue compared to other structures without new inflows, such as CEFs. Fees in separately managed accounts are either accepted by or negotiated with larger account individual investors. Thus, no board intermediary is necessary. To the extent that large account investors can take care of themselves, the fee concern is less. The situation is similar with hedge funds as they are normally owned only by sophisticated and/or qualified investors who can judge for themselves whether paying 2 percent of AUM per year plus 20 percent of returns over some benchmark is too high.

On the passive (index) investing side, the OEF is under fee pressure from the ETF. Some large ETFs that follow highly liquid indexes such as the S&P 500 index have continued to reduce fees, with some fees falling to under 10 basis points per year. OEF index funds tracking similar liquid benchmarks have tended not to decline as much, at least not across the board. In the low interest rate/low return environment, a difference of 20 to 30 basis points matters.

MUTUAL FUNDS AND MARKET EVOLUTION

This final subsection offers some high-level discussion on the evolution of markets and the resulting impact on OEFs. The goal is to highlight how markets may affect OEFs going forward. First, the number of stocks trading on public exchanges in the United

States is falling dramatically while the number of funds of all kinds (e.g., OEFs, CEFs, and ETFs) continues to grow. Ciccotello (2014) documents the decline in the number of publicly traded stocks over the past three decades. He examines 10 industries over the period 1966 to 2013 and observes that the decline in the number of publicly traded stocks from the respective industry peak to year-end 2013 is 60 percent for the sample as a whole. Meanwhile, the number of OEFs alone has roughly doubled since the early 1990s. Given these trends, generating alpha from active management might become more difficult. The trends suggest that many more funds are chasing far fewer stocks, which is a relevant topic for future research.

Second, stock exchanges are arguably becoming more fragmented and less transparent. Phenomena such as high-frequency trading (HFT) raise concerns about trade execution, especially during a time of market distress. For OEFs, HFT poses a challenge. OEFs typically trade in amounts that are much larger than retail investor trades. The differences might be orders of magnitude (e.g., 100 vs. 10,000 shares). If HFT does not harm small investors and is as profitable to the traders as some claim, then who is losing? If HFT is negatively affecting institutional traders such as OEFs, then this relationship leads to another challenge to active management.

Third, the growing number of passive vehicles (both OEFs and ETFs) is raising questions. With the growth of indexing approaching 25 percent of all trading, will passivity become a "self-fulfilling" phenomenon? In other words, will securities that have performed well continue to perform well because they have performed well? A similar issue arises with the growth of ETFs. Will the "basket trading" that accompanies these products raise the correlations among securities and ultimately among funds to the point where active management effects are overwhelmed or obscured?

Summary and Conclusions

This chapter provides an overview of distinctive attributes of OEFs and how they compare to the major investment structure alternatives: CEFs, separately managed accounts, ETFs, and hedge funds. OEFs are unique in that they can combine three features: (1) daily liquidity at the NAV with the fund as the counterparty, (2) active management in the search for mispriced securities by portfolio managers, and (3) membership in a family structure. The chapter discusses the trends and current issues arising from these three attributes. Daily pricing at the NAV presents challenges, especially with regard to staleness issues inherent when U.S.-domiciled funds hold stocks traded on other exchanges around the globe. Active management is also facing challenges from both passive alternatives and issues related to measuring performance. Regarding the latter, this chapter discusses issues related to DWRs versus TWRs. Family structure offers OEFs advantages in terms of low search cost opportunities for investors to build complete portfolios across asset classes, investment objectives, and styles.

The chapter then turns to an examination of the future of OEFs in the competitive alternative investment structure landscape. OEFs are strongly positioned as an investment vehicle in DC retirement plans, but face growing competition from ETFs in that venue. Taxes hamper the OEF in ordinary after-tax accounts due to the pooling treatment of gains. In contrast, separately managed accounts can offer investors tailored tax strategies. Governance is also an issue for OEFs going forward, as fund boards face increased calls to negotiate lower fees. Investment structures that have larger, more sophisticated clienteles, such as hedge funds or separately managed accounts, rely more on investors to negotiate terms. Finally, the evolving public stock market affects the future of stock OEFs. The number of publicly traded stocks is falling dramatically, HFT is increasing, and the correlation among the returns of individual stocks is increasing as index and basket trading becomes more prominent. All of these trends will challenge active management of the OEF in the future.

Discussion Questions

1. Identify three distinctive characteristics of OEFs and discuss how they position the structure within the range of alternatives.
2. Explain how the timing of inflows and outflows can affect OEF performance.
3. Discuss the advantages and disadvantages of using OEFs as the investment options in a DC retirement plan.
4. Evaluate how changes in the nature of stock exchanges and the number of firms that have listed securities on them could impact OEFs in the future.

References

Bergstresser, Daniel, John Chalmers, and Peter Tufano. 2009. "Assessing the Costs and Benefits of Brokers in the Mutual Fund Industry." *Review of Financial Studies* 22:10, 4129–4156.

Berk, Jonathan, and Richard Green. 2004. "Mutual Fund Flows and Performance in Rational Markets." *Journal of Political Economy* 112:6, 1269–1295.

Brown, Keith, Van Harlow, and Laura Starks. 1996. "Of Tournaments and Temptations: An Analysis of Managerial Incentives in the Mutual Fund Industry." *Journal of Finance* 51:1, 85–110.

Chalmers, John, Roger Edelen, and Gregory Kadlec. 2001. "On the Perils of Financial Intermediaries Setting Security Prices: The Mutual Fund Wild Card Option." *Journal of Finance* 56:6, 2209–2236.

Ciccotello, Conrad. 2014. "The State of the U.S. Public Corporation: More of an Evolution than an Eclipse." *Journal of Applied Corporate Finance* 26:4, 8–21.

Ciccotello, Conrad, Roger Edelen, Jason Greene, and Charles Hodges. 2002. "Trading at Stale Prices with Modern Technology: Policy Options for Mutual Funds in the Internet Age." *Virginia Journal of Law and Technology* 7:3, 6–37.

Ciccotello, Conrad, Jason Greene, Leng Greene, and David Rakowski. 2011. "Capacity and Factor Timing Effects in Active Portfolio Management." *Journal of Financial Markets* 14:3, 277–300.

Ciccotello, Conrad, Jason Greene, and Lori Walsh. 2007. "Supermarket Distribution and Brand Recognition of Open-End Mutual Funds." *Financial Services Review* 16:4, 309–326.

Ciccotello, Conrad, James Miles, and Lori Walsh. 2006. "Should Investors Choose Funds from Focused Families?" *Financial Services Review* 15:3, 247–264.

Dubofsky, David. 2010. "Mutual Fund Portfolio Trading and Investor Flow." *Journal of Banking and Finance* 34:4, 802–812.

Edelen, Roger. 1999. "Investor Flows and the Assessed Performance of Open-End Mutual Funds." *Journal of Financial Economics* 53:3, 439–466.

French, Kenneth. 2008. "Presidential Address: The Cost of Active Investing." *Journal of Finance* 63:4, 1537–1573.

Friesen, Geoffrey, and Travis Sapp. 2007. "Mutual Fund Flows and Investor Returns: An Empirical Examination of Fund Investor Timing Ability." *Journal of Banking and Finance* 31:7, 2796–2816.

Greene, Jason, and Charles Hodges, 2002. "The Dilution Impact of Daily Mutual Fund Flows on Open-End Mutual Funds." *Journal of Financial Economics* 65:1, 131–158.

Haslem, John A., H. Kent Baker, and David Smith. 2006. "Are Retail S&P 500 Index Funds a Financial Commodity? Insights for Investors." *Financial Services Review* 15:2, 99–116.

Investment Company Institute. 2013. *2012 Facts at a Glance*. Washington, DC: Investment Company Institute.

Kempf, Alexander, and Stefan Ruenzi. 2008. "Tournaments in Mutual Fund Families." *Review of Financial Studies* 21:2, 1013–1036.

Massa, Massimo. 2003. "How Do Family Strategies Affect Fund Performance? When Performance-Maximization Is Not the Only Game in Town." *Journal of Financial Economics* 67:2, 249–305.

Nanda, Vikram, Z. Jay Wang, and Lu Zheng. 2004. "Family Values and the Star Phenomenon." *Review of Financial Studies* 17:3, 667–698.

Rakowski, David. 2010. "Fund Flow Volatility and Performance." *Journal of Financial and Quantitative Analysis* 45:1, 223–237.

Reuter, Jonathan. 2006. "Are IPO Allocations for Sale? Evidence from Mutual Funds." *Journal of Finance* 61:5, 2289–2324.

Ritter, Jay. 1991. "The Long-Run Performance of Initial Public Offerings." *Journal of Finance* 46:1, 3–27.

Sirri, Erik, and Peter Tufano. 1998. "Costly Search and Mutual Fund Flows." *Journal of Finance* 53:5, 1589–1622.

Vallapuzha, Sandhya. 2011. " Agency Problems in Target-Date Funds." PhD dissertation, Georgia State University.

Wermers, Russell. 2000. "Mutual Fund Performance: An Empirical Decomposition into Stock-Picking Talent, Style, Transaction Costs, and Expenses." *Journal of Finance* 55:4, 1655–1695.

6

Target-Date Funds and Other Funds-of-Funds

ALISTAIR BYRNE
Vice President and Senior Defined Contribution Strategist, State Street Global Advisors, London

TREVOR OLIVER
Vice President, BlackRock, Seattle

Introduction

Target-date funds (TDFs) are a growing category of investment strategy used in defined contribution (DC) pension plans. DC plans play an increasing role in retirement income provision around the world. A DC plan comprises individual personal accounts in which participants can accumulate assets to fund their retirement. Participants make regular contributions into the plan and may receive matching contributions from their employer. In many countries, these contributions receive tax benefits (e.g., being made from pre-tax pay). The participant chooses where to invest the contributions from a range of fund options selected by the plan provider. However, many participants and often the vast majority of them do not exercise this choice and the funds are instead allocated to a default option chosen by the provider.

A conventional approach, with some theoretical support, is for DC participants to follow a lifecycle approach to asset allocation, holding risky assets while young and far from retirement and reducing the weight in risky assets as they age and approach retirement. This pattern is discussed in more detail in the section that follows on Lifecycle Investment Theory. TDFs exist to manage this asset allocation transition, with the participant investing in a single TDF, with the target date aligned to the intended retirement date, and the fund manager responsible for creating an asset allocation appropriate for the age of the investors. Most TDFs exist as funds-of-funds.

TDFs have seen substantial growth in DC plans, especially in the United States. Their "one-stop shop" nature is suitable where DC participants are not interested in managing their own asset allocation. The growth has also been driven by the 2006 Pension Protection Act "safe harbor" provisions, which categorize TDFs as appropriate defaults and provide plan fiduciaries with protections from lawsuits in the event that a TDF chosen by an appropriate process fails to deliver the returns required by participants.

Morningstar (2014) shows that mutual fund TDFs in the United States amounted to $650 billion of assets at the end of 2013, up from $100 billion in 2006. According to Bary (2014), TDF assets amounted to more than $1 trillion at year-end 2013, including Common Investment Trusts and mutual funds. This figure compares to $11 trillion of overall DC assets according to Towers Watson (2014). The growth of TDFs has been less pronounced in other markets but increasing attention has occurred, for example, in the United Kingdom.

The purpose of the chapter is to discuss TDFs and funds-of-funds. It begins by outlining the DC market and the role that TDFs play within it. Next, it discusses the evolution of TDFs and their main characteristics and variants. The chapter also covers other funds-of-funds, where the asset allocation does not follow a glidepath. The chapter ends with a summary and conclusions.

An Overview of Defined Contribution Pensions

Historically, a substantial part of employees' retirement income provision has come from *defined benefit (DB) pension plans* in which the employer promises a set percentage of the employee's final or average salary as a retirement income pension. While the employee may be required to make monetary contributions to be eligible for this benefit, the remaining costs and hence risks of meeting the pension promise lie with the sponsoring employer. For example, if participants live longer than expected or investment returns are lower than expected, the sponsoring employer is required to make up the funding shortfall. In the face of the rising cost and risk of this DB pension promise, many employers have switched to DC plans where the employer and employee both make contributions to the individual employee's account. These contributions are invested and the accumulated balance at retirement is available to fund the employee's retirement. The employee has no recourse to the employer if the accumulated balance falls short of the employee's needs or expectations.

According to Towers Watson (2014), the DC market represents 47.0 percent of the total global retirement assets of $32 trillion and has been growing at 8.8 percent a year over the past 10 years compared to 5.0 percent growth in DB assets. These figures show the most substantial DC assets in the United States, United Kingdom, and Australia.

While DC participants have a choice of investment funds, evidence from around the world suggests most DC participants are reluctant investors and are unengaged in investment decisions. Hence, plan sponsors have to nominate default investments for employees who do not make their own choice and ready-made packaged options are typically more popular with participants than creating their own portfolios from asset class fund building blocks.

Lifecycle Investment Theory

A considerable body of research is available on how individuals should invest to fund their retirement (Bodie 2003). Much of this work involves lifecycle investment and is based on the idea that the appropriate asset allocation varies by age. The appropriate portfolio for a young employee far from retirement is predominantly invested in riskier growth assets such as equities, but for employees closer to retirement, the majority of the portfolio should be in safer assets such as bonds and cash. For example, some financial advisors recommend a simple rule in which the allocation to equities equals 100 minus the participant's age. For those who do not want to manage this evolution themselves, TDFs exist as an "autopilot" means of achieving lifecycle investing for DC participants.

The justification for this lifecycle approach is that the participant's tolerance for risk decreases when approaching retirement. A participant close to retirement has less scope to make adjustments to respond to an unexpected investment loss. For example, less scope exists to change the planned retirement date, or to save more over the remaining period, to make up a shortfall in desired retirement income.

Each individual's personal balance sheet comprises a mix of *human capital*—future earnings based on the individual's skills and talents—and *financial capital* such as savings and investments. Younger individuals have a larger proportion of human capital (a long career ahead of them) but have little accumulated savings. Older individuals have accumulated savings, but less earning potential ahead of them. If human capital is assumed to be bond-like in nature because most people's labor income comprises regular payments that vary little over time, then this disparity can be balanced by younger investors allocating their limited financial capital to equities and reducing this allocation as the financial capital becomes large in relation to the human capital.

Balancing between human capital and financial capital can differ by age. As a first illustration, take an example where Joe is age 30, earns $60,000, has financial assets of $50,000, contributes 10 percent of his salary to the DC plan, and expects to retire at age 65. Using a 5 percent discount rate, the present value of future contributions is $108,000, so his financial capital equals 32 percent of overall wealth. In contrast, consider Mary, who is age 60, earns $80,000, has financial assets of $500,000, contributes 10 percent of her salary to the DC plan, and expects to retire at age 65. Again using a 5 percent discount rate, the present value her future contributions is $27,000, so her financial capital equals 95 percent of overall wealth.

A lifecycle asset allocation approach could also be justified if returns on risky assets are *mean reverting*, such that over longer time horizons losses can be expected to recover as markets mean revert. As the time horizon shortens, less scope for this recovery mechanism to work exists. While the logic of this justification is clear, more mixed views are available on the extent to which equity returns are mean reverting (Bodie 1995).

Safe Harbor Regulations

In the United States, DC plans grew up as supplementary to DB plans that historically were the main form of pension provision. This history has implications for the investment strategies used. Concern that participants would sue sponsors over investment losses led to using conservative defaults such as money market and stable value funds. While these funds do not generate high long-term returns, they minimized the risk of short-term losses and the resulting fiduciary issues for plan sponsors.

Additionally and somewhat contradictorily, some sponsors made DC contributions as their own company stock. Sponsors made this decision in part to align employees' incentives with the company's success and to create a friendly and stable pool of equity holders. While the resulting investments offer the potential for high long-term returns, they lack diversification and expose plan participants to substantial stock-specific risk. This approach also creates a strong correlation between participants' human capital and their investments. Employees' financial well-being is already tied to the financial performance of their employer and the performance of the industry in which they work. By investing their DC plan assets in company stock, they are exposed to taking a meaningful loss of their financial wealth at the same moment they experience loss in their human capital. For example, many DC plan members at Enron experienced this scenario when the company collapsed in 2001.

While these arguably inappropriate investment strategies were perhaps tolerable in a supplementary savings system in which other sources provide the bulk of retirement income, they become of greater concern where the DC plan accounts for the majority of expected retirement income.

The U.S. government's concern about this situation led to introducing safe harbor provisions to encourage plan sponsors and fiduciaries to provide more appropriate default strategies. The *safe harbor provisions* provide relief from legal liability for the outcomes of investment strategies that fall within the safe harbor provisions provided a reasonable process has been followed in selecting them. The safe harbor provisions exist as a key part of the Pension Protection Act 2006. A default falls within the safe harbor (i.e., it becomes a Qualified Default Investment Alternative or QDIA) if it is:

- A product with a mix of investments that takes into account the individual's age or retirement date (e.g., a TDF);
- An investment service that allocates to provide an asset mix that takes account of the individual's age or retirement date (e.g., a managed account);
- A product with a mix of investments that takes into account the characteristics of a group of individuals (e.g., a balanced fund), or
- A capital preservation product (e.g., cash fund) only in the first 120 days of membership.

For safe harbor provisions to apply, participants must have been given the option to make a fund choice, be notified of their investment in the QDIA, and be able to switch out of the QDIA into another investment should they choose to do so (Department of Labor 2007).

TDFs experienced substantial growth following the adoption of the safe harbor provisions. Despite a widely held belief among plan sponsors that TDFs were an appropriate investment strategy for DC participants, a fear of liability arising from an investment loss in the DC default investment caused sponsors to favor defaults with minimal risk of loss such as cash or stable value funds. Lifting this risk of litigation allowed plans to default their members into the investments they thought made the most sense from a retirement investing standpoint, rather than the one that minimized risk to the sponsor. Although other countries do not have formal safe harbor provisions, pension trustees in the United Kingdom, for example, have obligations to ensure the suitability of their chosen defaults for their participants.

Defining a Target-Date Fund

A TDF can be considered a series of services rolled into one product for the convenience of plan participants saving for retirement and the convenience of the pension plan sponsors and providers. First, TDFs are an investment strategy that provides risk-efficient exposure to a diversified range of asset classes. This packaged approach to asset allocation helps to mitigate some of the behavioral biases toward concentrated and inefficient portfolios that individual savers may construct on their own. However, TDFs are more than just a balanced fund in that they also become more conservatively invested over time to match the evolving investment needs and preferences of investors as they age. This framework makes TDFs a combination of investment management, portfolio oversight, and basic advice, all packaged together into a single product to deliver institutional style asset management to individual investors saving for retirement.

TDFs have various common, if not universal, features. They begin with a substantial weight in growth assets intended to generate returns. Historically, in the United States, this category has consisted primarily of domestic equity, but over time it has increasingly included amounts of foreign equities, as well as commodities, real estate investment trusts (REITS), and other alternative asset classes. From this initial aggressive allocation, the portfolios move to a more conservative asset allocation focusing on capital preservation and consisting primarily of fixed-income funds. The evolution from this initial portfolio to the final portfolio is called the *glidepath*. A range of solutions are available in the market in terms of when this "derisking" begins, when it ends, and how it evolves. These three elements—initial allocation, final allocation, and glidepath—effectively define a particular target-date solution.

Part of the reason this approach of providing the same asset allocation to many investors works is that people of the same age face similar needs regarding saving for retirement. While not completely identical, these investors are similar enough to be grouped together in age cohorts.

The Glidepath

Building portfolios and evolving them over time can be a complex process requiring knowledge, interest, and time. Within any large group of DC participants, some individuals possess all of these qualities and thus build their own portfolios, but most participants lack one or more of these qualities and the result is low levels of engagement in the allocation process. Even more concerning is that these decisions occur at the time of enrolment into the pension plan, which is a time when a relatively high level of engagement is expected. The level of engagement typically decreases from this point until near retirement when individuals begin to think concretely about their retirement plan. Thus, even if participants construct well-balanced efficient portfolios when they join the plan, they are unlikely to reallocate assets as market risk and correlation change or to systematically reduce risk through time, even if that is the appropriate investment strategy.

Not only do the preferences of retirement savers change over time but also investment markets themselves continue to evolve. This dynamic can lead to an expanding universe of investment opportunities that most retirement savers would be unlikely to be aware of unless they were dedicating a substantial amount of time to monitoring their retirement investments. A decade ago, most TDFs had relatively simple asset allocations consisting almost entirely of domestic equity and fixed income. More recently, TDFs have increasingly diversified their assets globally to decrease home bias and made greater use of alternative investment strategies. *Home bias* is the overweighting, relative to global market capitalization, of domestic assets. While the growth in use of alternative assets is partly due to the evolution of thinking about retirement investing, increasing levels of transparency and liquidity exist in these new asset classes, which make them more appropriate for individual investors. In addition, fees on alternative assets classes have reduced, making them a more attractive strategic holding. As the world gets smaller from an economic perspective, true diversification may become increasingly difficult to find, making professional management and continual oversight more important.

EXAMPLE GLIDEPATHS

At their core, TDFs are an evolving asset allocation designed to meet the changing needs of individuals saving for retirement as they progress through their career. This framework has resulted in some basic structural commonalities across global markets. TDFs typically begin with a heavy weight toward return-seeking assets such as equities and then move to a portfolio more focused on fixed income for capital preservation. This evolution from equity to fixed income is so central that many providers define the derisking of their portfolios not in terms of the expected standard deviation of returns, but rather, in terms of the equity/bond split.

The manner of this evolution is not completely consistent across markets or even within markets. The range of solutions in the United States is narrower than elsewhere, with glidepaths among the major institutional managers ranging from 85 to 95 percent equity for their initial allocation and landing point at the target date between 35 and 55 percent equity. Figure 6.1 shows some example glidepaths.

For the United States, looking at the institutional TDFs on offer provides a somewhat misleading view of the range of approaches on offer. Retail forms of TDFs, such as those found in Individual Retirement Accounts (IRAs), exhibit an even wider range of approaches.

Within the U.S. institutional market, a range of approaches is also available in terms of when the glidepaths reach their *land point*, which is the point where the asset allocation ceases to evolve. For reasons addressed in more detail later in the chapter, some providers freeze the asset allocation immediately at the point of expected retirement while others wait 10 or even 20 years post-retirement before they hold the allocation constant. Figure 6.2 provides some examples.

Another distinguishing feature of glidepaths among providers, across markets, and through time has been the building blocks used throughout the life of a TDF. The alternative assets included in TDFs vary by market. In the United States, such assets are often limited to commodities, inflation-protected bonds, and REITs, while in the United Kingdom they can also include asset allocation strategies similar to hedge funds.

Besides including alternative investments, another major trend in TDFs is a move away from home bias. While this trend has been especially strong in the equity portion of TDFs, another trend is the increasing number of providers including global fixed

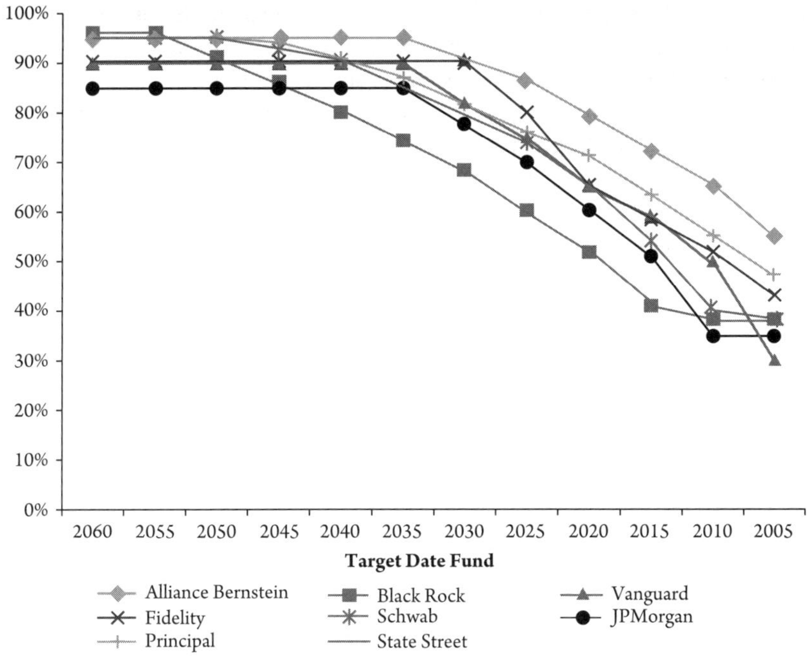

Figure 6.1 Equity Allocations of Major U.S. Target-Date Providers. This figure shows the asset allocation glidepaths of a selection of TDFs in the United States. They all switch from equities to lower risk assets as the target retirement date approaches, but some differences exist in the precise paths taken. Source: Morningstar 2012.

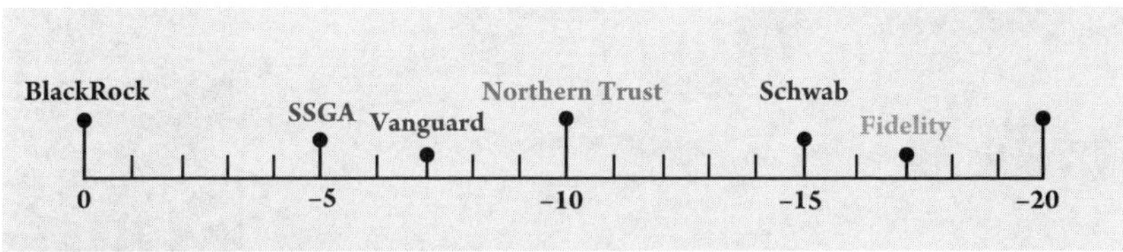

Figure 6.2 Landing Point Date of U.S. Target-Date Funds. A wide range of perspectives exists about when TDFs should reach their final landing point where asset allocation becomes static. Some land at the retirement date, while others continue to evolve for 15 or more years after retirement. The chart shows how many years after retirement the glidepaths of major U.S. TDF providers reach the landing point. Source: Morningstar 2012.

income. Early versions of TDFs were heavily, if not entirely, comprised of domestic securities. This composition was to provide technical ease and liquidity and to reflect the idea that the spending liability eventually faced by individuals would be denominated in their local currency, so taking on foreign assets presented an unnecessary risk factor. This view has changed over time and now reflects the belief that diversification benefits typically outweigh the currency risk.

In the United Kingdom, the government-created National Employment Savings Trust (NEST) pension plan has a unique feature in its TDF glidepath. Most TDFs start out with a high level of investment risk and reduce risk through time as the expected retirement date approaches. The NEST TDF begins with a relatively low-risk portfolio in the early years of membership, before moving to higher risk in the middle years of the participant's career and then derisking as retirement approaches. This initial lower risk phase is known as the "foundation stage" and exists to address a behavioral issue. The concern of the designers of the NEST glidepath was that participants who experience losses in their account due to market volatility in the earliest stages of retirement saving may opt out of the savings program altogether. By placing their initial investments in a relatively low risk portfolio, the chances of their account reducing in value due to financial market movements is greatly reduced and thus participants are more likely to continue their participation in the plan. Figure 6.3 shows the NEST glidepath.

Across different markets and providers, the ultimate question is whether the particular characteristics of TDF glidepath produce superior or inferior outcomes. Although some strategies or particular assets classes will perform well over any period, determining whether any one approach is objectively superior to the others is difficult. Most TDFs derive the majority of their returns from a diversified exposure to the equity market as a whole. Thus, if the market does well, TDFs do well; if the market does poorly, TDFs follow suit. Focusing on the details of a glidepath can distract from the key drivers of suitability: portfolio efficiency, total lifetime risk, and the end user's risk aversion. These primary factors determine outcomes and drive fit in selecting a TDF provider.

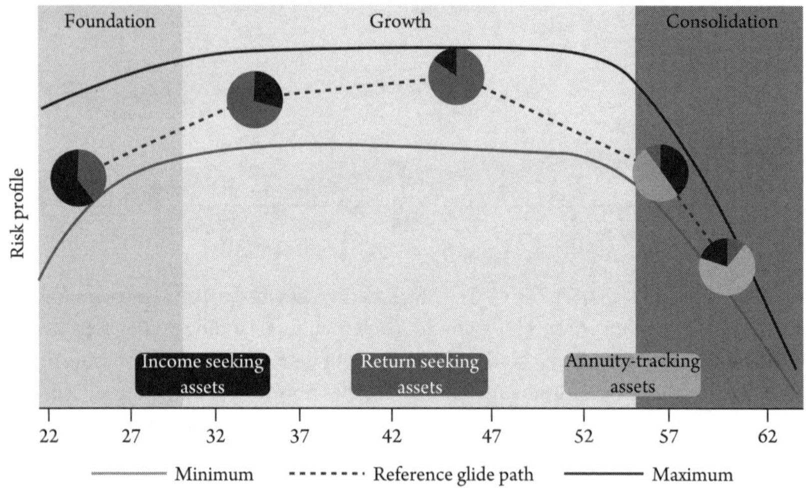

Figure 6.3 GLIDEPATH FOR NEST 2058 TARGET-DATE FUND. A key difference between the NEST strategy and other target-date approaches is the foundation stage, in which the initial asset allocation is relatively low risk. This assumption should reduce the probability of the participant seeing a reduction in their account balance early in their membership of the plan. Source: NEST 2012. © NEST Corporation 2012. Used with permission. The chart reflects the strategy in place in 2012.

To and Through Approaches

The decision to manage the glidepath asset allocation "to" versus "through" retirement remains one of the key differentiator between TDFs. A manager may hold the asset allocation constant after the expected retirement (i.e., the "to" approach) or continue the evolution post-retirement (i.e., the "through" approach) for various reasons. While the distinction between these two approaches is frequently drawn right at the point of retirement, this comparison misses much in the range of approaches among the strategies available in the marketplace. Although the consensus is that asset allocation should continue to evolve at least until the point of retirement, TDF providers within the "through" camp have a wide range of perspectives on how long this evolution should continue after retirement. Some of these "through" providers have an asset allocation that evolves for just 5 years post-retirement while others continue to evolve for 20 years. This means that some of the "through" managers are closer to the "to" managers in terms of actual investment strategy than they are to the more extreme versions of "through."

The lack of consensus of "to" versus "through" approach reflects the fact that a set of factors exists suggesting that evolution should end at retirement, while other considerations support continued evolution. The choice to be "to" or "through" comes down to one's own weighting on the relative importance of these various factors.

TO GLIDEPATHS

Although various arguments support a "to" glidepath, they typically consider human capital as previously discussed. *Human capital* is the present value of future earnings, or in retirement planning, future savings. This contrasts to *financial capital,* or existing savings, which can be used to purchase goods or invested. Because human capital is converted into financial capital steadily over one's working career, a little with each pay check, some view human capital as being rather bond-like, and therefore relatively low risk. Younger individuals hold large stocks of human capital but little financial capital. This means that their overall portfolio, regardless of how they invest their savings, is fairly low risk. As they convert their human capital into financial capital, risk is reduced in the portfolio to reflect this transition. The thinking behind a "to" glidepath is that once people reach retirement, they have completely depleted their human capital. If the changing mix of human versus financial capital is the driving force behind evolving asset allocation, then a need no longer exists to continue to evolve the asset allocation.

THROUGH RETIREMENT GLIDEPATHS

The thinking behind the "through" glidepath does not have the same unifying theme, which in part explains why a range of "through" approaches exists. Proponents of the "through" approach may also reference human capital arguments, but from the perspective that in early retirement, individuals retain the option of returning to the workforce and therefore have not totally drawn down their potential human capital.

Some empirical considerations are important. In the United States, a well-documented phenomenon is that many savers do not draw on their DC assets until several years into retirement, suggesting that demands on that pool of savings do not stabilize until several years post-retirement. Regulatory considerations in different markets sometimes compel DC investors to draw down their DC assets beginning at a specific age, often several years after standard retirement age. Aligning the timing for asset allocation stabilization with these types of regulation can be seen as trying to maintain consistency between the products and the regulatory environment in which they exist.

Finally, returning to theoretical considerations, TDF providers favoring a liability-driven approach to investing typically prefer a "through" approach. DC plan participants have an implicit liability equal to the cash flows required to support their spending in retirement. Because the value of those cash flows and the distance those cash flows extend into the future both decrease as an individual moves through retirement, the price sensitivity of the liability to changes in interest rates continues to evolve into retirement. The scenario means that a manager striving to control the asset-liability risk would continue to evolve the asset allocation into retirement to account for the continued evolution of the investment time horizon.

Custom Target-Date Funds

While much of the growth in the DC market to date has focused on "off-the-shelf" TDFs, custom TDFs have also received increasing attention. A *custom TDF* is a TDF built to suit a specific employer-sponsored pension plan. The industry recognizes that workers in the United Kingdom differ from those in Australia and the United States and no single approach is suitable for all those markets. Regulatory and cultural considerations must be considered when designing a TDF for a particular market. Customization thus extends this thinking to explore whether within these broad national systems enough differentiation exists in the needs and desires of the participants in a particular company's pension plan to warrant a customized TDF solution. Although various considerations can drive the decision to move to a custom solution, they generally can be placed into the following categories: (1) investment preferences, (2) demographics, (3) benefits programs, and (4) risk preferences.

INVESTMENT PREFERENCES

In many countries, a transition is occurring between providing DB and DC pension plans, with many companies having both types of plans. This transition means the pension plan has an existing investment staff that has managed and will continue to manage large amounts of assets on behalf of the organization's DB plan. In the process of managing these assets, the investment staff has formed views on asset classes and found fund managers they trust. Some organizations want to apply the same investment universe and managers to both the DC and DB plans. This creates consistency across the plans and allows them to leverage the work that is being done for the DB plan to benefit the DC plan. Also, marginal asset management fees typically decrease as assets increase. Thus, combining these two pools of capital for placement among managers can cause better pricing for both DB and DC plans. Hence, these organizations want to customize the TDF to be able to include their favored managers in the glidepath.

DEMOGRAPHICS

Demographics also play an important role in setting the asset allocation and evolution of risk in TDFs. Specific information on when the company's employees typically enter the workforce and when they retire can be used to determine how quickly investment risk should be reduced in the TDF over time and what duration of payment of retirement income it will need to support. This concern can be particularly relevant in industries requiring substantial education, causing people to begin work later, or in physically demanding jobs, such as mining, where workers may leave their jobs at younger ages. An important consideration is to make sure that the demographic characteristic in question applies to a large proportion of the workforce rather than just to a small group.

BENEFIT PROGRAMS

Another factor that can lead to the need for customization of a TDF is the nature of the employee benefits that the participants in the plan have exposure to. Management of investment risk in retirement savings should incorporate consideration of as much of an individual's retirement assets as possible and this includes DB pensions, which from an asset perspective look very much like a bond. Using a custom TDF allows information about employer-specific DB pensions to be included in the risk calculation and may suggest a more aggressive target-date asset allocation is appropriate. Because benefits programs change over time, different age groups might have different levels of DB. This difference can make an off-the-shelf product a poor fit, but a custom approach allows those different age cohorts to be placed on different glidepaths. For example, older workers who have some DB rights could be placed in a higher risk TDF than younger workers who will rely on a DC plan for a greater proportion of their retirement income. Besides DB pension plans, historical programs for purchasing company stock or cash/stable value investments can affect the risk to which participants are exposed and thus justify modifying the amount of risk taken in the TDF. For example, in plans where employees typically have large allocations to company stock, it may be prudent to use a lower risk TDF.

RISK PREFERENCES

Finally, risk preference is an important consideration. While TDF providers have built glidepaths that they believe represent the best trade-off of risk and return over time, the ability and willingness to withstand market volatility is an issue of preference. Like individuals, the institutions that sponsor DC plans and their participants have different levels of risk aversion. Some may prefer more aggressive asset allocations while others want more conservative approaches than they would find in an off-the-shelf product.

While many factors can lead to interest in custom TDFs, the relative importance of each factor varies from sponsor to sponsor. Whenever considering a custom strategy, remembering the benefits of an off-the-shelf strategy, which have substantially more scale, is important to ensure that the effort of customization truly benefits both the sponsoring entity and the underlying investors. Table 6.1 shows examples of potential customizations.

Table 6.1 **Examples of Target-Date Fund Customizations**

Rationale	*Issue*	*Customization*
Investment preferences	The investment office has a favored equity manager	Use open architecture for fund building blocks to incorporate the desired manager
Demographics	Employees typically retire earlier than the general population	Accelerated derisking to reach the desired retirement allocation at the expected retirement age
Benefits program	A high proportion of employees have substantial DB pension rights	Increase the equity allocation to reflect the bond-like allocation to DB
Risk preferences	The fiduciary committee has a conservative approach	Increase the fixed-income allocation across the glidepath to reduce risk

Note: A pension plan provider may want to use a custom TDF rather than an off-the-shelf version for various reasons. This table provides some reasons for customization and the resulting type of customization.

Dynamic Asset Allocation in Target-Date Funds

As previously discussed, the glidepath in TDFs involves a shift through time from risky assets such as equities to less volatile assets such as bonds. This transition is typically done mechanistically, in which the shift from equities to bonds follows a predetermined path. While this has the advantage of providing clarity as to the derisking path, it can be criticized for paying no attention to the circumstances of the cohort of participants, other than age and time to retirement, or to market conditions. For example, a cohort of DC participants reaching age 55 in the severe equity bear market of 2008, and facing record low long-term bond yields, might question the merit of a strategy that had them selling (arguably cheap) equities and buying (arguably expensive) bonds at that point in time. Some commentators suggest using more dynamic approaches to lifecycle switching that might produce better returns and more appropriate allocations.

One option would be to switch asset allocation based on achieved returns. Where the TDF has achieved a desired rate of return or accumulated level of wealth, the asset allocation could be switched from risky assets into safer assets. Where the target had not been achieved, the portfolio would remain in risky assets. An alternative approach would be for the switching to reflect the portfolio manager's subjective view on future returns. For example, switching out of equities and into bonds could be done earlier than the specified glidepath implies because equities had done well and were overvalued, with low expected returns. Equally, a switch into bonds could be postponed if the fund manager deems fixed-income assets to be unattractive. Scope also exists for

Table 6.2 **Outcomes of Dynamic Lifecycle Strategies**

Strategy	*Mean ($)*	*Median ($)*	*25th Percentile ($)*	*75th Percentile ($)*
Dynamic	2,243,825	1,762,712	988,573	2,695,902
Lifecycle	1,919,124	1,408,545	876,404	2,340,550
Constant 100 percent stocks	2,547,867	1,716,608	965,411	3,102,896
Constant balanced fund	1,276,875	1,118,547	799,502	1,573,030

Note: The table shows the distribution of wealth at retirement in U.S. dollars based on 10,000 simulations of the specified lifecycle investment strategy. The dynamic approach switches from equities to bonds in the last 10 years of plan membership only if the fund achieves the hurdle rate of return. The lifecycle strategy switches over the last 10 years irrespective of the achieved returns. The 100 percent stocks and balanced approaches each involve a static asset allocation through membership, rebalanced monthly.

Source: Adapted from Basu et al. 2011.

dynamic lifecycle investing to incorporate both approaches, taking account of achieved returns versus targets and also expectations of future returns.

Dynamic approaches to lifecycle switching raise some important risk management questions. For example, when an investor has gotten ahead of target in terms of accumulated wealth, DC participants or fiduciaries overseeing DC plans might be comfortable "banking" some of those unexpected gains in safe assets. However, they might be less comfortable with the idea that an investor who is behind target stays in risky assets closer to the intended retirement date, or in the extreme re-risks to catch up. In both cases, the risk of more losses that take the participant further off target may be unacceptable.

Basu, Byrne, and Drew (2011) analyze the results of a dynamic lifecycle strategy that switches from equities to bonds in the last 10 years of a 40-year plan membership only if a hurdle rate of return is achieved, compared to a mechanistic strategy that switches over the last 10 years of membership without reference to achieved performance. Table 6.2 shows the results including reference static strategies. The dynamic strategy produces better average outcomes than the standard lifecycle approach, while also limiting downside risk, as measured by the 25th percentile outcome.

Other Funds-of-Funds

While TDFs are a key category of funds-of-funds (FoFs), distinguished by their asset allocation glidepath, other types of FoFs exist and play an important role in the investment markets. FoFs enable effective diversification by allowing an FoF to invest in several underlying funds that are in themselves highly diversified. For example, an FoF could invest in the global bond fund with hundreds of holdings and a global equity fund with holdings in thousands of stocks. Even if an FoF is relatively small, it can benefit from the scale of the underlying funds.

Investment Management Association (IMA) (2014) statistics show assets under management (AUM) in FoFs in the United Kingdom amounted to £88 billion at the end of 2013. This is approximately 11 percent of the U.K. funds market, up from 5.5 percent in 2004. Many FoFs are mixed or balanced funds investing across a range of market sectors. According to the IMA, FoFs have benefited in particular from the growth of balanced and asset allocation funds since the financial crisis of 2007–2008. Investors appear to increasingly value the ability of their fund manager to switch from one asset class or market sector to another if conditions warrant.

Some FoFs are fettered in that the only underlying funds in which the FoF invests are funds managed by the same firm or fund complex that manages the FoF. Alternatively, an FoF can be run on an unfettered or open architecture basis where the FoF manager is free to invest in funds from external firms and fund complexes. In this case, diversification occurs both by manager and asset class. Thus, FoF managers can search for best in class managers across the asset classes and investment styles they want to include in the FoF. IMA statistics for the United Kingdom show that growth in unfettered funds in recent years has been substantially stronger than the growth in fettered funds.

While FoFs benefit from economies of scale and can create portfolios of best in class managers, the main potential disadvantage is that the investor incurs multiple levels of fees. Besides fees charged by the FoF manager, fees typically exist in the underlying funds. Whether the performance achieved offsets what has been referred to as "fees on fees" is an empirical question.

Brown, Goetzmann, and Liang (2003) study fees on fees in hedge funds to investigate if the role of the FoF manager adds value for investors. They note that the FoF manager provides professional oversight and expert selection of the underlying funds, in addition to providing diversification. While a cost in terms of additional fees occurs, the expectation is that the information advantage of the FoF manager in selecting the underlying funds would more than compensate for the additional fees. In fact, the authors find that the average performance of the underlying funds dominates the performance of FoFs, suggesting that any informational advantage does not offset the extra fees. Whether FoFs of mutual funds add enough value in selection to offset the drag from their additional fees requires further study.

Summary and Conclusions

With many retirement systems moving from a DB pension provision to DC individual savings plans, TDFs are playing a growing role in retirement income provision globally. Although variations in characteristics occur across different TDFs, some common features are central to what defines a TDF. All TDFs contain an evolving asset allocation designed to take individual retirement savers from an aggressive return-seeking portfolio when they are young to a more conservative capital preservation strategy as they approach retirement. This evolving asset allocation is called the glidepath of the strategy and the specific structure of this derisking is a key differentiator among TDFs. The TDF market continues to evolve and advance with customization, personalization, and dynamic asset allocation all being areas of current interest and research.

Several forces have led to the increase in importance of TDFs. Both empirical and theoretical evidence suggests that retirement savings accounts should reduce their volatility as retirement approaches. TDFs automate this process through the derisking embedded in their glidepaths and do so with efficiency and low cost. This evolution in the asset allocation to stay in line with the needs of investors through time makes TDFs a convenient one-stop shop for individual investors preparing for retirement. Because TDFs address the core investment problems and needs facing individuals saving for retirement while still allowing for the institutional pricing and governance oversight associated with DB investment strategies, regulators have increasingly favored them. This has resulted in supportive legislation, particularly for using TDFs as a default option. Finally, plan sponsors favor TDFs for the simplicity that they bring to their plan and their ability to deliver best practices to participants even as knowledge and understanding around how individuals should invest for retirement continues to evolve. With the three major agents of the retirement savings industry—individual participants, regulators, and sponsors—all favoring TDFs, they are experiencing much traction in the marketplace and their growth looks set to continue.

Discussion Questions

1. Define a TDF.
2. Explain the difference between a "to" and a "through" target-date glidepath.
3. Discuss the meaning of the Qualified Default Investment Alternative (QDIA) in the U.S. DC market.
4. Explain how the TDF implemented by NEST is unusual.
5. Identify four major factors contributing to the desire for customized TDFs.

References

Bary, Andrew. 2014. "Target Date Funds Take Over." *Barons,* July 5. Available at http://online.barrons.com/articles/SB50001424053111904544004579651134019266274.

Basu, Anup, Alistair Byrne, and Michael Drew. 2011. "Dynamic Lifecycle Strategies for Target Date Retirement Funds." *Journal of Portfolio Management* 37:2, 83–96.

Bodie, Zvi. 1995. "On the Risk of Stocks in the Long Run." *Financial Analysts Journal* 51:3, 18–22.

Bodie, Zvi. 2003. "Thoughts on the Future: Lifecycle Investing in Theory and Practice." *Financial Analysts Journal* 59:1, 13–26.

Brown, Stephen, William Goetzmann, and Bing Liang. 2003. "Fees on Fees in Funds of Funds." NBER Working Paper 9464, National Bureau of Economic Research.

Department of Labor. 2007. "Factsheet on Regulation Relating to Qualified Default Investment Alternatives in Participant Directed Individual Account Plans." Washington, DC: Department of Labor.

Investment Management Association. 2014. *Asset Management in the UK 2013–2014: The IMA Annual Survey.* London: Investment Management Association. Available at http://www.investmentfunds.org.uk/research/ima-annual-industry-survey/.

Morningstar. 2012. "2012 Target-Date Series Research Paper." Morningstar. Available at http://corporate.morningstar.com/us/documents/MethodologyDocuments/MethodologyPapers/TargetDateFundSurvey_2012.pdf.

Morningstar. 2014. "2014 Target-Date Series Research Paper." Morningstar. Available at http://corporate.morningstar.com/us/documents/MethodologyDocuments/MethodologyPapers/2014-Target-Date-Series-Research-Paper.pdf

NEST. 2012. "Developing and Delivering NEST's Investment Approach." NEST Corporation. Available at https://www.nestpensions.org.uk/schemeweb/NestWeb/includes/public/docs/Developing-and-delivering-NESTs-Investment-Approach,PDF.pdf

Towers Watson. 2014. "Global Pension Assets Study 2014." Towers Watson. Available at http://www.towerswatson.com/en-GB/Insights/IC-Types/Survey-Research-Results/2014/02/Global-Pensions-Asset-Study-2014.

7

Closed-End Funds

Z. JAY WANG

Associate Professor of Finance, Lundquist College of Business, University of Oregon

Introduction

A *closed-end fund* (CEF) is a publicly traded investment company. It raises capital through an initial public offering (IPO). The common shares are listed on an exchange for secondary market trading. A CEF's shareholders elect a board of directors with the fiduciary duty to hire an investment advisor to manage the fund's assets, to determine its compensation contract, and to monitor its performance on behalf of shareholders. Subject to the approval of the board, a CEF can issue new equity, which is typically through rights offerings. Most CEFs also have dividend reinvestment programs (DRIPs) in place to automatically issue new shares at a predetermined price for the reinvested dividend. CEFs may borrow up to a maximum of a 2 to 1 equity-to-debt ratio. Therefore, the organization structure of a CEF is similar to a publicly traded firm.

This chapter provides an overview of CEFs and reviews the literature on the relationship between agency problems, the effectiveness of internal and external governance mechanisms, and the CEF discount. The chapter is organized as follows. The next section discusses the organization structure of CEFs and focuses on how they differ from other investment vehicles. This is followed by a brief review of the history and current status of the CEF industry. Next, the chapter reviews the potential sources for the well-known closed-end fund discount puzzle and the related empirical evidence. Finally, the chapter discusses agency conflicts between CEF managers and investors and focuses on the effectiveness of both internal and external mechanisms to improve corporate governance in the CEF industry. The final section offers a summary and conclusions.

Organization Structure of Closed-End Funds

As an investment company, a CEF's assets are professionally managed under its investment objective and subject to the regulation of the 1940 Investment Company Act. CEFs offer investment services in various asset classes including domestic and international equity, taxable bond, municipal bond, and other securities. This framework makes CEFs a close "cousin" to open-end funds (OEFs), commonly called mutual funds. One important distinction though lies in the liquidity provision.

OEFs must meet the investors' liquidity needs on a daily basis at the closing net asset value (NAV). Should investors withdraw their investments, the fund has to honor their redemption requests by using its cash reserves or liquidating its investments. Conversely, if investors invest more capital into the fund, the fund does not have the discretion to turn down the request even if no obvious investment opportunities are available to absorb the additional capital. By contrast, CEFs are "closed" to investors' liquidity demands by organizational design. CEF investors can liquidate or expand their existing investments in a CEF only by trading the CEF shares with other investors in the secondary market.

In absence of the possibility of a massive withdrawal, CEFs can invest in less liquid securities. According to the Investment Company Institute (ICI) (2014), CEFs allocated 29 percent of their total assets to domestic equity at the end of 2013, but they allocated the remaining assets to less liquid asset classes including municipal bonds, domestic and international taxable bonds, and international equity.

Another closely related investment vehicle to CEFs is an exchange-traded fund (ETF). A typical ETF is created by a sponsor to track the performance of a specific index. For example, the first ever and still most popular and most liquid ETF is the SPDR S&P 500 ETF, created by State Street Global Advisor to track the performance of the S&P 500 index. In the process of ETF creation and redemption, the authorized participant (AP) plays the intermediation role between the EFT sponsor and the stock exchange. The AP is typically a large broker/dealer with a strong financial reputation. During the ETF creation, the AP assembles the basket of securities tracking a particular index for the sponsor for a specified number of ETF shares. The AP can then sell all or part of the ETF shares to investors on the stock exchange. The ETF redemption follows the reverse process. The AP purchases the ETF shares from the sellers on the stock exchange, returns the ETF shares to the sponsor for the underlying securities, and then puts the securities back into the secondary market. The creation and redemption process ensures that the price of ETF shares on the secondary market tracks closely to the NAV of the underlying securities. Otherwise, the AP can arbitrage away the mispricing by effectively changing the supply of ETF shares on the secondary market.

Although both CEFs and ETFs issue shares publicly traded on the secondary market, their underlying mechanisms differ. CEFs issue shares through IPOs and the number of outstanding shares is unaffected by the buying and selling activities on the secondary market. The trading by ETF investors, however, directly changes the number of outstanding shares in the creation and redemption process intermediated by the AP. When the share price deviates from the NAV due to a trade imbalance, the AP restores the balance by either creating or redeeming sufficient ETF shares. In the CEF world, no AP enforces the law of one price and the share price of a CEF could therefore deviate substantially from the NAV for extensive time periods. The *law of one price* states that two identical assets must sell for the same price. A later section contains a review of the possible sources of such deviation.

History and Current Status of the Closed-End Fund Industry

As Gabelli (2002) documents, the CEF industry has a long and volatile history. The first U.S. CEF was created in 1893, which was more than 30 years before forming the first OEF. Earlier CEFs were formed for raising capital to finance U.S. railroad construction. These CEFs were usually leveraged with bank loans or bond issuances. During the stock market boom in the 1920s, CEFs became a widely popular investment vehicle for small investors. By 1929 and before the stock market crash, about 700 CEFs existed with assets totaling $4.5 billion, compared to only 19 OEFs. The enthusiasm of investors to ride the soaring market for quick riches also invited some shady fund managers to explore pyramid schemes and manipulate CEF share prices. The stock market crash of 1929 wiped out many highly leveraged CEFs.

The ensuing financial regulation, especially the Investment Company Act of 1940, dramatically improved the transparency through better disclosure. The 1940 Act also curtailed the excess risk-taking by limiting the use of leverage by registered investment companies. The industry landscape also entered a new era with OEFs replacing CEFs as the dominate investment vehicle for the investor public.

As a casualty of the 1929 great crash, the investment community largely ignored the CEF structure and existing CEFs shriveled into almost oblivion over the next half century. However, in the mid- and late-1980s, some well-known portfolio managers including Charles Allmon, Martin Zweig, Chuck Royce, and Mario Gabelli brought new CEFs into the market. The spectacular performance of stock markets in emerging countries and the growing popularity of *sector funds* (i.e., funds investing in sectors such as energy, real estate, and infrastructure) drove the rebirth of CEFs during this period. Following the burst of the dot-com bubble, more *fixed-income CEFs* (i.e., funds investing in Treasury securities, corporate bonds, and municipal bonds) entered the market, mainly driven by investors' desire to look for higher returns in the historically low interest rate environment. The close-end structure has the unique advantage of investing in emerging markets, specific sectors, and fixed-income securities given the illiquid and less well diversified nature of the investments.

As Table 7.1 shows, the expansion of the CEF industry reached its peak in 2007 with 663 funds managing $312 billion in total assets. The financial crisis of 2007–2008 delivered a blow to the CEF industry and reduced its total assets to $184 billion. The ensuing years saw a steady recovery. By the end of 2013, the CEF industry had 599 funds managing $279 billion assets, still below its peak in 2007.

Several factors caused the limited recovery. First, before the financial crisis of 2007–2008, the auction-rated preferred stocks issued by CEFs accounted for more than 85 percent of total CEF debt. The collapse of the auction-rated preferred market in 2008 hindered the ability of CEFs to lever up their investments. According to Nohel, Todd, and Wang (2012), the average leverage ratio for equity CEFs dropped from more than 30 percent in 2008 to 23 percent in 2010. The ratio further declined to 19.8 percent in 2013 (Investment Company Institute 2014). The reduced usage of leverage directly contributed to the slow growth of total assets.

Table 7.1 **Year-End Total Assets and Total Number of Closed-End Funds, 2003 to 2013**

Year	*Total Assets ($ billions)*	*Number of Funds*
2003	214	583
2004	253	619
2005	276	635
2006	297	646
2007	312	663
2008	184	642
2009	223	627
2010	238	624
2011	243	632
2012	264	602
2013	279	599

Source: Investment Company Institute 2014.

Second, the shares of many CEFs traded at a substantial discount relative to the NAV, thus discouraging new issuance. The discount-laden funds attracted activists intending to force them to convert to the open-end structure or to be liquidated or merged. Activist investors also pressured many equity funds to adopt so-called managed distribution policies or regular share repurchase programs to narrow the discounts. While being effective in reducing the discounts, both policies resulted in considerably shrinking the total assets under management (AUM).

In terms of asset allocation, the majority of the CEF assets have been invested in fixed-income securities and international equities. This observation is consistent with the earlier discussion that the CEF structure provides more flexibility to invest in less liquid securities. Table 7.2 presents the percentage of CEF total assets allocated to each major asset category for 2003 and 2013. In 2003, the allocation to domestic equities was only 20 percent, compared to 70 percent to domestic fixed-income securities

Table 7.2 **Asset Allocation of Closed-End Funds, 2003 and 2013**

Asset Classes	*2003 (%)*	*2013 (%)*
Domestic equity	20	29
International equity	5	12
Domestic taxable bond	26	21
International bond	5	8
Domestic municipal bond	44	30

Source: Investment Company Institute 2014.

and 10 percent to international securities. In 2013, the allocation to domestic equities increased to 29 percent, but still far below the 71 percent allocated to fixed-income securities and international equities.

Sources of the Closed-End Fund Discount

CEFs are a cause célèbre in financial literature as they have generated a long list of perceived deviations from the efficient markets paradigm, also known as *puzzles*. All such puzzles stem from the fact that the market value of all the shares of a CEF (i.e., its capitalization) often differs from the NAV of its portfolio. A positive (negative) difference between the NAV and the capitalization, which is known as the discount (premium) and reported as the percentage difference normalized by the NAV, is an apparent arbitrage opportunity. Its presence raises issues of market efficiency and investor rationality. As for the size of the discount, various studies quote different averages for different time periods ranging anywhere from 4 to 15 percent (Lee, Shleifer, and Thaler 1990; Chay and Trzcinka 1999; Malkiel and Xu 2005; Cherkes, Sagi, and Stanton 2009). Based on Bloomberg data, the average discount for July 2014 was 6.93 percent.

Lee et al. (1990) document several puzzling facts in discount time-series data. First, new CEFs are initially sold in IPOs at a premium, whereas within 100 days the new CEFs trade at a discount. Second, discounts exhibit considerable variation both across funds and over time. Third, discounts exhibit mean reversion and are positively correlated with other funds. Fourth, discounts disappear immediately upon fund termination through open-ending, liquidation, or merger. Lee, Shleifer, and Thaler (1991) also observe that discounts narrow when small cap stocks are performing well, even though the CEFs may not invest in small cap stocks.

A large body of theoretical and empirical literature has emerged to explain the CEF discount puzzle. Dimson and Minio-Kozerski (1999) extensively review the early explanations and Cherkes (2012) surveys the most recent developments. The following discussion provides a comparison of two broad frameworks taking fundamentally different approaches to explain the discount puzzle. The first one is "investor sentiment" theory, which invokes the irrational behavior of small investors. The second approach uses the trade-off between managerial contribution and managerial rent extraction to offer a rational explanation.

INVESTOR IRRATIONALITY

The investor sentiment theory developed by Lee et al. (1991) is based on one empirical fact and two assumptions. The empirical fact is that small investors, who are sometimes referred to as noise traders, are the predominant investors in CEF shares. The two assumptions are that irrational bouts of optimism and pessimism drive small investors and this irrationality causes greater share price volatility that cannot be diversified. Investor sentiment risk has to be compensated for by an additional risk premium known as the *noise trader risk premium*.

Investor sentiment theory can explain several pieces of the discount puzzle. CEF shares have to trade at a discount to compensate for noise traders. Fluctuations in investor sentiment explain the co-movement and conversion to the mean. Investor optimism raises the prices of existing CEFs and creates demand for new CEFs.

One critic on the sentiment story is whether CEF discounts reflect investor sentiment. A direct verification of the theory requires an independent and not a CEF data-based measure of the sentiment. Qiu and Welch (2006) use various proxies for sentiment based on consumer confidence surveys. The results are surprising. The proxies for sentiment correlate with small stocks' returns but not with a CEF discount index. The authors conclude that sentiment may play a role in asset pricing, but the CEF discounts appear to be the wrong measure of sentiment.

MANAGERIAL CONTRIBUTION VERSUS MANAGEMENT FEES

Several recent papers offer a rational explanation based on the dynamic trade-off between managerial contribution and managerial rent extraction. The intuition is that the discount/premium is determined by whether the valuable services provided by fund managers outweigh the rent they extract as management fees. The capitalized value of management fees is therefore the source of discount. When the value of managerial contribution is zero, a discount must ensue. A source of value is required in order for a CEF to trade at a premium. Ross (2002) and Berk and Stanton (2007) suggest managerial ability as a source of value added, whereas Cherkes et al. (2009) build on value added by liquidity transformation.

Managerial Ability as the Source of Value

Ross (2002) and Berk and Stanton (2007) develop a rational model that links fund discounts to both management fees and investors' perception of managerial ability. Because both factors can be time varying, the fluctuation in the discount or premium depends on whether the perceived managerial ability outweighs the management fees. In this model, the abilities of a new manager are unknown to either the investors or the manager, and both parties learn about managerial ability over time based on job performance. The interplay among abilities, managerial compensation, and managerial renegotiation of contracts explains why the IPO premium is always followed by a discount and why the discount/premium fluctuates over time and across funds.

Liquidity Transformation as the Source of Value

Cherkes et al. (2009) provide a liquidity-based theory to explain CEF discounts. The theory builds on the empirical fact that the majority of CEFs primarily invest in illiquid assets (e.g., international equities, corporate bonds, and municipal bonds). The authors argue that the higher liquidity of CEF shares when compared with their holdings is a design feature. Specifically, CEFs transform illiquid asset holdings into liquid securities (i.e., CEF shares) to facilitate small investors, who otherwise do not have an economic way to invest in illiquid assets due to high transaction costs. Benveniste, Capozza, and Seguin (2001) supply an empirical estimate of the value added by this transformation: An exchange-traded real estate investment trust (REIT) increases the valuation of its illiquid assets by packaging them into an exchange-traded security. The authors determine that a REIT increases the value for the real estate assets by 12 to 22 percent.

According to the liquidity-based theory, a discount is simply the algebraic difference between the capitalized benefits of liquidity transformation and the capitalized value of management fees. The result can be positive (premium) or negative (discount) and varies across funds and over time. Benveniste et al. (2001) also build on works of Chordia (1996) and Nanda, Narayanan, and Warther (2000) to explain why funds that specialize in highly illiquid assets have to be closed.

Managerial ability and liquidity transformation are not the only sources of value added by CEFs. Another channel is through the *provision of leverage*. CEFs are distinct from OEFs in the flexibility of using leverage. Elton, Gruber, Blake, and Shachar (2013) use a large sample of bond CEFs to show that higher levered funds deliver better performance. They also compare OEFs and CEFs managed by the same portfolio manager and find that leverage, rather than liquidity, is the only distinct dimension.

A Laboratory for Corporate Governance Studies

A CEF is not only an investment company but also a publicly traded corporation. This blending makes the CEF industry a unique setting to study corporate governance. One big challenge for corporate finance research is how to estimate the costs of corporate management versus the value added by the management. The CEF industry offers several unique advantages. A CEF's NAV provides a simple measure of its "intrinsic value," whereas its market capitalization gives market evaluation of its value under current management. The difference between the share price and the NAV can be interpreted as the net present value (NPV) of the capitalized value added by fund managers (e.g., through superior investment skills, liquidity transformation, and provision of leverage) minus the capitalized value of rent they extract (e.g., through fees and private benefits). Therefore, the CEF discount/premium serves as a natural market-based measure of agency problems.

The fund managers' objective is to maximize the fee income and private benefits while enhancing their job security. This personal agenda may collide with shareholders' objective to maximize the return of their investments. The "closed" structure of a CEF could provide managers more freedom to extract rents compared to the open-end setting. The conflict intensifies when the rents extracted by entrenched fund managers exceed the value of their service. The following discussion reviews the extent of agency problems in the CEF industry and both the internal and external mechanisms used to ease the conflicts of interest between shareholders and fund managers.

AGENCY PROBLEMS IN THE CLOSED-END FUND INDUSTRY

Barclay, Holderness, and Pontiff (1993) use a set of 138 equity CEFs to analyze the agency problems when managers and their allies control large blocks of fund shares. They show that large management-affiliated block ownership is associated with a much wider discount. The authors then provide evidence that fund managers and their allied block holders enjoy various pecuniary benefits, which include (1) receiving salary as an employee of the fund; (2) relatives or close associates receiving salary as employees of the fund; (3) receiving fees for management or administration of the fund, payment for financial research, or commissions on executing trades for the fund; (4) purchasing activity by the fund of the IPO shares underwritten by the block holder; and (5) extending of voting rights associated with block holder's company shares held by the fund. Sometimes managers and block holders receive non-pecuniary benefits such as the fund carrying the family name of the block holder.

Given the managers' incentive to extract rents as fee income and private benefits, they naturally are opposed to any open-ending or liquidation proposal that will lead to relinquishing their control. When confronted with such attempts, managers are resistant. The battle for control can be costly and occur at the expense of CEF shareholders. For example, Barclay et al. (1993) report that David Schafer, president of Schafer Value Trust, spent $728,000 of the fund's resources on legal fees to stop an attempt to liquidate the fund in 1989. These fees represented about 1 percent of the total value of the fund and were almost as large as the $928,000 in management fees paid to Schafer Capital Management in 1989. If fund managers lack the incentives to improve shareholder value, changes can only come from other sources.

THE ROLE OF THE BOARD OF DIRECTORS

The next several sections review both internal and external mechanisms to address the agency conflicts. The board of directors of any public corporation has the fiduciary duty to effectively monitor fund managers and should be the major internal mechanism to reduce agency conflicts. Most studies on board efficacy focus on industrial corporations. However, as Del Guercio, Dann, and Partch (2003) note, the CEF industry can be a unique setting to study the effectiveness of monitoring by the board. First, the main responsibility of a CEF board is monitoring, as opposed to the board of an industrial corporation that often provides strategic expertise and advice to management. Second, the CEFs have highly visible measures of board effectiveness such as the approval of the advisory contract, share repurchase, dividend payout, and fund restructure. Third, unlike investors in OEFs, CEF investors cannot directly withdraw their investment from the fund with severe agency problems. Hence, an effective board of directors can substantially improve the welfare of CEF investors.

The Investment Company Act of 1940 has several regulations on the structure of a CEF board. Section 10(a) requires a minimum 40 percent of directors to be independent. Effective in February 2001, this minimum requirement increased to 50 percent. Also effective in February 2001, only the independent directors can select and nominate other independent directors. Any legal counsel for independent directors must be independent (i.e., not affiliated with the fund advisor). Another relevant regulation is Section 30(f) that requires all directors to disclose their beneficial ownership and compensation at both the fund and fund family level.

Some charter provisions also have direct impact on the effectiveness of board monitoring. Some CEFs have provisions specifically designed to deter takeovers. For example, a *staggered board* structure ensures that nobody can replace the majority of the board in one election. A *supermajority voting provision* requires a supermajority of shareholders to approve fund restructure proposals. Such anti-takeover provisions protect the entrenched fund managers and thus exacerbate agency problems. Conversely, some CEFs have specific charter provisions designed to reduce the discount. For example, a *lifeboat provision* specifies conditions contingent on the level of discounts that will trigger adopting certain dividend payout or share repurchase policy, or trigger a vote to the open-ending or liquidation proposal.

Del Guercio et al. (2003) collect board characteristics and charter provisions for 476 U.S. CEFs in existence at the end of 1996. Their main empirical finding suggests that board structure and independence are strongly related to the monitoring effectiveness of CEF boards. Funds with smaller board size, higher proportion of independent directors, lower director compensation, and a lifeboat provision tend to have lower expense ratios. Moreover, funds with smaller board size and annual election of all directors versus staggered boards tend to have smaller discounts. However, the proportion of independent director is unrelated to the discounts.

Gemmill and Thomas (2006) investigate how the governance structure affects management fees and fund discounts in U.K. CEFs. They find that management fees are higher when the board is larger and has fewer directors from outside of the fund family. The authors also find that discounts are wider if the management company or any block holder has a substantial long-term ownership stake, suggesting that investors are wary of entrenched management.

In summary, studies on the role of CEF boards on governance quality suggest considerable variation in monitoring effectiveness. Many CEF boards frequently compromise their fiduciary duties to rein in agency conflicts and fail to discipline fund managers, mainly due to their lack of independence from management companies. As Van Steenwyk (2012) notes, individuals who do not have the proper incentive to act in the best interests of shareholders sometimes occupy seats on the boards.

THE ROLE OF SHAREHOLDER ACTIVISM

The market for corporate control serves as an alternative discipline mechanism to the board that puts pressure on the management team to perform or risk removal. The research on corporate control market dates back to Manne (1965, p. 113), who states that "the lower the stock price, relative to what it could be with more efficient management, the more attractive the takeover becomes to those who believe that they can manage the company more efficiently." For CEFs, a persistently deep discount provides a convenient market-based measure of the extent of mismanagement.

In the past two decades, professional activist shareholders frequently target CEFs with large discounts. Examples include Opportunity Partners, which is a hedge fund run by Phillip Goldstein, City of London Investment Management, Lazard Freres & Co., Ron Olin's Deep Discount Advisors, and Harvard College. In a typical hostile control contest, activist shareholders first select a target fund to launch or threaten to launch a proxy fight. Their ultimate goal is to pressure the incumbent management into pursuing policies that reduce the discount. The strategic interaction between the activist shareholders and fund management decides the outcome of the control contest. The control contest in the CEF industry provides a rich setting to investigate the strategic behavior of both the activists and the targets and the effectiveness of corporate control contests on improving corporate governance.

Characteristics of Target Closed-End Funds

According to Van Steenwyk (2012), trading at a persistent and deep discount makes the CEF susceptible for possible activist attacks. One common request from activist shareholders is restructuring the board of directors. These activists often nominate themselves or close associates for the board seats. The activists are mainly concerned about the board's tie with the management company, the size of the board (too many directors), and the so-called "unitary" board (e.g., the same director serving on all funds offered by the management company).

Activist shareholders also consider advisory fees as another important factor. Gemmill and Thomas (2006) show that in the United Kingdom the relationship between advisory fees and investor return is not linear: a 1.00 percentage point increase in the advisory fee leads to a 1.50 percentage decrease in investor return. Even without an outright increase in the advisory fee, the management company can still receive higher payments by increasing the capital base. For example, some CEFs issue additional shares via rights offerings at a discount. This dilutes the wealth of existing shareholders while giving the management company a larger dollar amount of advisory fees. A higher advisory fee combined with low managerial ownership could further exacerbate the agency conflicts. In this case, the management company can enjoy the high pay without bearing much direct consequence of worse investment performance.

Two recent studies examine the determinants of activist attacks. Bradley, Brav, Goldstein, and Jiang (2010) and Cherkes, Sagi, and Wang (2014) show that CEFs trading at a sizable discount do not automatically become the targets of activist shareholders. Other strategic considerations are involved in selecting a prey. First, both the share liquidity and the underlying portfolio liquidity are important factors for consideration. The activist shareholders need to accumulate large enough blocks of shares to make their voices heard by the management company. Their ultimate goal is to profit from selling these shares after the discount narrows. Everything else equal, the activists would prefer funds with reasonable liquidity that allows them to buy and sell shares without having much of negative price impact. The asset liquidity of the underlying portfolio determines the cost of liquidating the fund. If the fund mainly invests in highly illiquid assets, then the high liquidation costs could decrease the gains that activist shareholders can derive from liquidating the fund assets. Hence, everything else equal, activists prefer to target CEFs with fairly liquid underlying asset portfolios.

Second, the composition of the shareholder base also matters. In most control contests, an activist shareholder accumulates a minority block of shares and then engages in communicating and persuading other shareholders to join the fight against the management company. Compared to the daunting and expensive task of convincing thousands of individual investors, forming a coalition force would be much easier and cheaper if other block institutions are present. The objectives of other block institutions play a crucial role here. If the block institutions enjoy various private benefits documented in Barclay et al. (1993), they are unlikely to vote against the management company. Hence, the activist shareholder would prefer to target CEFs owned by like-minded institutions with a track record of activism and/or no business relationship with the management company.

Finally, fund size, age, and the accumulated unrealized capital gains can also affect activist shareholders' decision. The threat from activist shareholders may decrease with fund size because it would be harder for individual investors to accumulate enough of a toehold to mount a shareholders' action. Older funds as measured by age may be more likely to be attacked because, consistent with Berk and Stanton (2007), investors require time to conclude that the management's added value is less than their advisory fees. Accumulating a large amount of unrealized capital gains may contribute to the discount due to potential tax liabilities (Malkiel 1977). The capital gains overhang increases the liquidation costs relative to the NAV, therefore discouraging the attack from activists.

Bradley et al. (2010) study activist attacks intending to open-ending for 142 U.S. domestic equity and international equity funds from 1988 to 2003. A total of 127 events occurred in this period. They find that the level of discount has a significant impact on the probability of open-ending attempts. The unconditional probability for a fund to be attacked in a given year is 13.3 percent. A 1.00 percentage point increase in the discount is associated with a 1.07 percentage point increase in the probability of being targeted for open-ending. Bradley et al. also show that the discount level is related to dividend yield, insider ownership, and lifeboat provision, suggesting that discount reflects the extent of agency problems. Even after controlling for the effect of discount, the governance quality index, which is based on the existence of a staggered board, the supermajority rule, and the ability of the board to call a special meeting, remains a significant factor explaining the probability of open-ending attacks. Specifically, the worse the governance quality, the higher is the probability for the fund to become a target of activist shareholders. Overall, the results suggest that shareholder activism mainly targets poorly governed CEFs that trade at deep discounts.

Cherkes et al. (2014) investigate 122 cases of activist attacks involving 62 equity CEFs from 1990 to 2006. They find that the probability of being attacked is significantly related to several fundamental characteristics. Funds with higher trading liquidity and more liquid underlying assets are more likely to be attacked, supporting the theory that both trading costs and liquidation costs play an important role in activist attacks. Management fees have a positive impact on the probability of being attacked, but are not always statistically significant across specifications. The effects of fund leverage and past risk-adjusted performance are both negative and statistically significant for the subsample of domestic equity funds. If using leverage and higher alpha add value to shareholders and proxy for managerial ability, such funds are less likely to be attacked by activists.

Actions Taken by Activist Shareholders

After accumulating an ownership stake in the target CEF, the activist shareholder typically submits a shareholder proposal demanding actions by the fund management company to narrow the discounts. Bradley et al. (2010) describe the actions taken by activist shareholders in a case study. In March 1997, Phillip Goldstein submitted a shareholder proposal to the annual shareholders meeting of the Emerging Germany Fund. In the proposal, he pointed out that (1) the fund shares had been trading at more than a 20 percent discount relative to the NAV and (2) the portfolio performance had been mediocre when compared to the relative indexes. He urged the board of directors to enhance shareholder value by expediting the process of open-ending the fund.

The board of directors issued an opposing statement and recommended shareholders to vote against Phillip Goldstein's proposal. The statement included several counterarguments. First, the board had just approved a new investment mandate and hired a new investment advisor. This advisor deserved to be given some time to implement its investment strategy and improve fund performance. Second, the board had considered some possible actions to narrow the discount, such as share repurchase, but did not believe they would be very effective. Third, open-ending, liquidation, or merging with another OEF would impose large costs on shareholders and reduce fund assets. The main message to shareholders was that the board would do nothing meaningful to reduce the discount.

Goldstein's proposal was defeated in the subsequent annual shareholders meeting. However, the voting record showed that the proposal gained substantial support from the shareholders. Out of the 6.3 million votes casted, more than 40 percent voted yes. Goldstein continued his quest. By the end of 1997, he formed an alliance with Ron Olin, another prominent activist investor, who runs Deep Discount Advisor, Inc. The two combined controlled 14 percent of the fund's outstanding shares. Additionally, three other block holders—Bankgesellschaft Berlin, FMR Corp., and Lazard Freres & Co.—were beneficial owners of 14, 10, and 10 percent, respectively, of the fund's outstanding shares. At least two of them had a previous record of being activist investors and thus would likely vote with Goldstein and Olin.

One year later, on March 27, 1998, Goldstein came back and struck again, this time with even stronger forces. He notified the board his intention to nominate himself and three others for elections as directors in the upcoming shareholders meeting. He also revealed his intention to submit shareholder proposals intended to fire the current investment advisor and open-end the fund. Goldstein was on a collision course with the board and fund management company. To build up his case and win support from more shareholders, he took his case to the Internet and discussed his shareholder proposals in various messages posted in the Internet discussion board. This strategy provided some ammunition for the fund management to fight back. Accusing Goldstein of violating the proxy solicitation rules and beneficial ownership disclosure provisions, the fund managers called off the upcoming annual shareholder meeting and filed a lawsuit against both Goldstein and Olin.

This response only briefly halted the proxy campaign. Throughout 1998, Olin continued to increase his holdings through two investment companies. By November 6, 1998, his beneficial ownership in the fund reached 14.5 percent. On the same day, Olin sent a letter to the fund and nominated three of his associates and himself for board seats in the next annual shareholder meeting. He also clarified that, if elected, the new board would open-end the fund.

Given the large beneficial holdings by the coalition of activist investors, they would clearly gain enough affirmative votes to fire the board and pass the open-ending proposal. The fund management gave up the fight and put together a package of proposals designed to open-end the fund. Shareholders approved the proposals in the annual meeting held on January 26, 1999, with the announcement that the fund would convert to an OEF at the close of business on May 3, 1999. Following the announcement, the discount relative to the NAV disappeared.

This case study highlights the important role of effective communication in a successful proxy battle. During hostile proxy contests, the incumbent boards and management companies rarely go away quietly without a fight to preserve their jobs, fee income, and other private benefits. Therefore, an important tactic is for activist investors to communicate their intentions and plans with other shareholders and to convince them to join the fight for their own interests. In the United States, the Security and Exchange Commission (SEC) lays out the rules governing the communication between shareholders during the proxy contests under the authority granted by Section 14(a) of the Securities Exchange Act of 1934. These rules determine the ease and costs of communication and coordination between shareholders born by the activist investor, and thus affect the probability of launching a successful proxy fight.

Bradley et al. (2010) provide a detailed review on the rule changes governing the shareholder communication during proxy contests. First enacted by the SEC in 1935 and later amended in 1956, the early rules required any party soliciting proxies to register and file all proxy materials for review before communicating with shareholders. These rules also imposed severe restrictions on any public communication between activists and shareholders. In 1992, the SEC enacted major revisions in proxy rules. The new rules relaxed the communication restrictions and essentially allowed independent shareholders to freely engage in communication without being monitored by the SEC.

Bradley et al. (2010) show that the frequency of activist attacks increased dramatically following the 1992 proxy reform. In the early 1990s, only 3 to 4 percent of the CEFs were subject to activist attacks. In the peak years of 1999 and 2002, the percentage rose to around 30 percent. They construct three proxies for the ease of communication among shareholders: turnover of CEF shares, average trade size of CEF shares, and the percentage of institutional holdings. The empirical results are consistent with the hypothesis that smaller costs of communication enhance activist attacks. Interestingly, the above effects are present only after the 1992 proxy reform. This provides convincing evidence that activist shareholders have taken advantage of the 1992 reform and dramatically increased the intensity of activism activities.

Strategic Responses from Closed-End Funds to Activist Attacks

The rising shareholder activism has put increasing pressure on CEF managers to narrow the discounts or risk losing their jobs. One obvious action is to repurchase shares in the open market. However, as acknowledged by the CEF managers and documented in several academic studies (Porter, Roenfeldt, and Sicherman 1999; An, Gemmill, and Thomas 2012), share repurchases only have a temporary boosting effect on the stock price and the discount reverts to the normal level soon after. Since the size and timing of share repurchases are at the discretion of the board and management company, the modest announcement effect reflects the stock market's uncertainty about the future actions taken by the fund. Hence, to have a long-term effect on the discount, fund managers needs to adopt something more committal. This leads to the emergence of the managed distribution policy (MDP).

The *MDP* is a commitment by the fund management company to pay a minimum annual dividend, regardless of the underlying portfolio performance. If the fund's earnings fall short of the MDP commitment, then partial asset liquidation may fund the shortfall. The average annual payout target is around 10 percent of the NAVs, ranging from a low of 5 percent to as high as 20 percent. As Johnson, Lin, and Song (2006) and Wang and Nanda (2011) show, the MDPs, especially the ones with high payout targets, have had remarkable success in reducing the long-run discounts. For the sample of 236 CEFs in Wang and Nanda, the average monthly median discount is only

0.86 percent for MDP funds between 1990 and 2006, compared to 10.19 percent for non-MDP funds.

Two hypotheses—signaling and agency costs—can both explain the effectiveness of MDPs. The signaling hypothesis of Johnson et al. (2006) argues that an MDP can serve as a costly signal of the fund's future NAV performance. Since MDP funds that perform poorly have to return capital to investors, only funds sufficiently confident of future performance would commit to such a dividend policy. The implication is that funds committing to a higher payout target should deliver better performance in the future. However, Wang and Nanda (2011) show that, for CEFs adopting aggressive payout targets (i.e., 10 percent and above), discounts tend to disappear, though no discernible improvement in NAV performance occurs relative to moderate payout or no payout commitment CEFs. This suggests that signaling is at best only part of the explanation for the effectiveness of MDPs.

The agency cost hypothesis provides an alternative explanation. The premise is that fund discounts reflect the rent extracted by fund managers over value added (Berk and Stanton 2007; Cherkes et al. 2009). As Wang and Nanda (2011) and Cherkes et al. (2014) explain, adopting MDPs can induce a direct wealth transfer from fund managers to shareholders. The reason is that MDPs can effectively reduce the managerial claim on fund assets since managers can no longer charge advisory fees on assets paid out to shareholders. This leads to an increase in shareholder value and thus a decrease in discounts. Cherkes et al. (2014) investigate the change in management fees during the three-year periods before and after the MDP adoption. They find that the impact of MDP adoption on managers in dollar terms is a loss of $0.46 million annually relative to managers of non-MDP funds and that the average discount for MDP funds drops by 5.29 percent relative to the matched non-MDP funds.

Since managerial compensation increases with fund size, CEF managers have little incentive to adopt policies that reduce fund assets. Adopting MDPs is thus expected to be involuntary and associated with actual or anticipated intervention by shareholders. Wang and Nanda (2011) conduct an event study to investigate the change in institutional holdings around the adoption of MDPs. They find that institutional investors accumulate a significant stake of fund shares from the fifth quarter before the MDP adoption to the third quarter after the MDP adoption. Starting from the fourth quarter after the MDP adoption, institutional investors significantly reduce their holdings. The timing of holding reduction coincides with the quarter when funds experience a large drop in discounts. The above findings are consistent with the notion that some institutional investors accumulate fund shares, influence the adoption of MDPs, and then unwind their positions once the discount is eliminated or turns into a premium.

The following case study in Wang and Nanda (2011) illustrates the impact of shareholder activism on the MDP adoption. The activist shareholder involved in the case is Bankgesellschaft Berlin AG (BBAG), a German bank. The CEF targeted by BBAG is Aberdeen Australia Equity Fund (AAE), a country fund primarily investing in Australian equities. On October 22, 2002, BBAG purchased 5,348,149 common shares of AAE from Mira, L.P. in a private transaction at a price of $5.14 per share. After the transaction, BBAG controlled more than 30 percent of the outstanding AAE common shares. In the "Purpose of Transaction" part of the 13-D filing, BBAG expressed concerns about the persistently high discount level and vowed to take necessary actions to pressure AAE's board. At that time, AAE shares were trading at a discount of more than 16 percent. On November 20, BBAG further increased its holdings to 31.40 percent and proposed to nominate its own candidates for board directors.

To fend off BBAG's challenge, AAE made an in-kind tender offer on February 19, 2003, for 40 percent of outstanding shares at a price equal to 90 percent of the NAV. BBAG applauded the greenmail and withdrew its board nominations. Due to the restriction of Investment Company Act of 1940, BBAG needed to get an exemptive order from the SEC to participate in the tender offer. However, on August 28, 2003, the SEC denied BBAG's request.

Unable to take part in the tender offer, BBAG became hostile again and notified AAE on January 16, 2004, that it intended to nominate three nominees of the bank to the board at the 2004 annual meeting. In response, AAE declared, on February 1, 2004, that it would implement an MDP with a 10 percent payout target. Soon after, with the discount narrowing and then turning into a premium, BBAG dropped its hostile actions against AAE, withdrew its own board nominations, and gradually unloaded its shares to realize trading profits. By December 2005, BBAG's beneficial ownership of AAE dropped to about 27 percent. By April 2007, BBAG controlled only 13.60 percent of AAE's common stock. On May 8, 2007, BBAG registered with the SEC to offer and sell all remaining 2,592,641 shares held by the bank at a maximum price of $15.91 per share.

Over the five-year period from 2002 to 2007, BBAG's engagement with AAE generated a handsome trading profit. BBAG established its position in AAE shares at an average cost between $5 and $6 a share. After successfully pressing AAE to adopt the MDP, the bank offloaded its shares at an average price of $11 to $16 a share. The total trading profit over the five-year period came to about $46.60 million or a 168.61 percent return on investment.

The MDP has undoubtedly become a frequently used policy among CEFs to deter activist attacks. Wang and Nanda (2011) show that more than 40 percent of closed-end equity funds in the United States adopted the MDPs by the end of 2006. Managers may adopt an MDP preemptively (before an activist emerges) or reactively (in response to the emergence of an activist). In recently years, most of new funds brought to the market had the MDPs in place at inception. As Cherkes et al. (2014) show, funds with preemptive MDPs are much less likely to be attacked by activists and subsequently be terminated through open-ending, liquidation, or merger. Conditional on being attacked by activists, funds reacting with MDPs also have a much lower likelihood of being terminated.

Not all CEFs adopt the MDPs. The decision of MDP adoption reflects the fund managers' trade-off between rent extraction and job security. Instead of risking the loss of control over the entire capital base, managers may rationally give up part of their rents to deter the emergence of activist attacks and/or influence the probability of the proxy fight success. The economic incentives for an activist to emerge are determined by fundamentals such as the cost of accumulating a substantial stake called a *toehold*, the cost of liquidation, the extent of agency problems, and the payout policy.

Cherkes et al. (2014) investigate determinants for the strategic interaction between activist attacks and the adoption of MDPs. They show that the same set of economic fundamentals simultaneously determines the likelihood of activist attacks and MDP adoptions. Specifically, funds with more liquid shares and underlying assets, higher management fees, lower leverage ratio, lower risk-adjusted past performance, and lower managerial ownership are more likely to adopt the MDPs. The results suggest that funds with bigger agency issues and lower costs of mounting proxy contests are more likely to adopt MDPs to fend off activist attacks.

Summary and Conclusions

CEFs are publicly traded investment companies. Compared to OEFs, CEFs are "closed" to investors' liquidity demand by organizational design. This feature provides CEFs a unique advantage of investing in less liquid securities such as international equities and municipal bonds. Another benefit from investing in CEFs is their use of leverage, which is typically not a feasible option for small investors. An appropriately levered CEF portfolio can enhance the return/risk trade-off for retail investors.

The CEF discount puzzle has touched off a lively and still ongoing debate in the efficient market literature. Investor sentiment theory argues that a discount reflects the additional compensation required for bearing noise trader risk arisen from investor irrationality. In contrast, several recent papers propose rational theories based on the trade-off between managerial value added and managerial rent extraction.

As publicly traded companies, CEFs provide researchers a rich setting to study corporate governance topics. Early studies focus on the agency conflicts between fund managers and shareholders and the monitoring effectiveness of boards of directors. Recent studies use the shareholder activism events involving CEFs to investigate the strategic behavior of both the activists and the targets and the effectiveness of corporate control contests on improving corporate governance.

Discussion Questions

1. Compare the organizational structure of CEFs with OEFs and discuss the main advantages of a closed-end structure.
2. Describe the empirical patterns for the CEF discount and discuss the behavioral and rational explanations.
3. Discuss the impact of 1992 proxy reform by the SEC on the shareholder activism in the CEF industry.
4. Discuss the effectiveness of the MDP on reducing the fund discount and fending off activist attack.

References

An, Jingfeng, Gordon Gemmill, and Dylan C. Thomas. 2012. "The Agency Effect of Repurchases on Closed-End Funds." *European Financial Management* 18:2, 240–270.

Barclay, Michael J., Clifford G. Holderness, and Jeffrey Pontiff. 1993. "Private Benefits from Block Ownership and Discounts on Closed-End Funds." *Journal of Financial Economics* 33:3, 263–291.

Benveniste, Lawrence, Dennis R. Capozza, and Paul J. Seguin. 2001. "The Value of Liquidity." *Real Estate Economics* 29:4, 633–660.
Berk, Jonathan B., and Richard Stanton. 2007. "Managerial Ability, Compensation, and the Closed-End Fund Discount." *Journal of Finance* 62:2, 529–556.
Bradley, Michael, Alon Brav, Itay Goldstein, and Wei Jiang. 2010. "Activist Arbitrage: A Study of Open-Ending Attempts of Closed-End Funds." *Journal of Financial Economics* 95:1, 1–19.
Chay, J. B., and Charles A. Trzcinka. 1999. "Managerial Performance and the Cross-Sectional Pricing of Closed-End Funds." *Journal of Financial Economics* 52:3, 379–408.
Cherkes, Martin. 2012. "Closed-End Funds: A Survey." *Annual Review of Financial Economics* 4, 431–445.
Cherkes, Martin, Jacob Sagi, and Richard Stanton. 2009. "A Liquidity-Based Theory of Closed-End Funds." *Review of Financial Studies* 22:1, 257–297.
Cherkes, Martin, Jacob Sagi, and Z. J. Wang. 2014. "Managed Distribution Policies in Closed-End Funds and Shareholder Activism." *Journal of Financial and Quantitative Analysis* 49:5–6, 1311–1337.
Chordia, Tarun. 1996. "The Structure of Mutual Fund Charges." *Journal of Financial Economics* 41:1, 3–39.
Del Guercio, Diane, Larry Y. Dann, and M. Megan Partch. 2003. "Governance and Boards of Directors in Closed-End Investment Companies." *Journal of Financial Economics* 69:1, 111–152.
Dimson, Elroy, and Carolina Minio-Kozerski. 1999. "Closed-End Funds: A Survey." *Financial Markets, Institutions & Instruments* 8:2, 1–41.
Elton, Edwin J., Martin J. Gruber, Christopher R. Blake, and Or Shachar. 2013. "Why Do Closed-End Bond Funds Exist? An Additional Explanation for the Growth in Domestic Closed-End Bond Funds." *Journal of Financial and Quantitative Analysis* 48:2, 405–425.
Gabelli, Mario J. 2002. "Closed-End Funds." Gabelli & Company, Inc. Available at http://www.gabelli.com/gab_pdf/articles/mario_clef040802.pdf.
Gemmill, Gordon, and Dylan C. Thomas. 2006. "The Impact of Corporate Governance on Closed-End Funds." *European Financial Management* 12:5, 725–746.
Investment Company Institute. 2014. *2014 Investment Company Fact Book: A Review of Trends and Activities in the U.S. Investment Company Industry*, 54th Edition, Washington, DC: Investment Company Institute. Available at http://www.ici.org/pdf/2014_factbook.pdf.
Johnson, Shane A., Ji-Chai Lin, and Kyojik Roy Song. 2006. "Dividend Policy, Signaling, and Discounts on Closed-End Funds." *Journal of Financial Economics* 81:3, 539–562.
Lee, Charles M. C., Andrei Shleifer, and Richard H. Thaler. 1990. "Anomalies: Closed-End Mutual Funds." *Journal of Economic Perspectives* 4:4, 153–164.
Lee, Charles M. C., Andrei Shleifer, and Richard H. Thaler. 1991. "Investor Sentiment and the Closed-End Fund Puzzle." *Journal of Finance* 46:1, 76–110
Malkiel, Burton G. 1977. "The Valuation of Closed-End Investment-Company Shares." *Journal of Finance* 32:3, 847–858.
Malkiel, Burton G., and Yexiao Xu. 2005. "The Persistence and Predictability of Closed-End Fund Discounts." Working Paper, Princeton University.
Manne, Henry G. 1965. "Mergers and the Market for Corporate Control." *Journal of Political Economy* 73:2, 110–120.
Nanda, Vikram, M. P Narayanan, and Vincent A. Warther. 2000. "Liquidity, Investment Ability, and Mutual Fund Structure." *Journal of Financial Economics* 57:3, 417–443.
Nohel, Tom, Steven Todd, and Z. J. Wang. 2012. "Leverage Decisions in Portfolio Management." Working Paper, University of Oregon.
Porter, Gary E., Rodney L. Roenfeldt, and Neil W. Sicherman. 1999. "The Value of Open Market Repurchases of Closed-End Fund Shares." *Journal of Business* 72:2, 257–276.
Qiu, Lily, and Ivo Welch. 2006. "Investor Sentiment Measures." Working Paper, Brown University.
Ross, Steven A. 2002. "Neoclassical Finance, Alternative Finance and the Closed-End Fund Puzzle." *European Financial Management* 8:2, 129–137.

Van Steenwyk, Jason. 2012. "A Survey of Shareholder Activism and Closed-End Mutual Funds." Available at http://www.pristineadvisers.com/ClosedEnd%20Funds%20and%20Shareholder%20Activism%20%20-%20September%2030,%202012.pdf.

Wang, Z. J., and Vikram Nanda. 2011. "Payout Policies and Closed-End Fund Discounts: Signaling, Agency Costs, and the Role of Institutional Investors." *Journal of Financial Intermediation* 20:4, 589–619.

8

Non-U.S. Closed-End Funds

DIMITRIS ANDRIOSOPOULOS

Senior Lecturer in Accounting and Finance, University of Strathclyde

MARY FLETCHER

Lecturer in Accounting and Finance, University of the West of Scotland

ANDREW MARSHALL

Professor of Finance, University of Strathclyde

Introduction

Closed-end funds (CEFs), also called investment trusts in the United Kingdom, were one of the first specialist financial intermediaries set up in the United Kingdom. Their aim was to provide small investors access to a managed diversified portfolio and to increase share ownership. From their origins in 1868 with the Foreign and Colonial Investment Trust, U.K. CEFs grew in popularity, spreading to the United States (Newlands 1997). Burton and Corner (1968) and Masey (1988) give insightful accounts of the turbulent history of CEFs.

This chapter focuses on the regulations and existing evidence on non-U.S. CEFs. Because of the impact of U.K. CEFs on this sector, this chapter concentrates mainly on research into U.K. CEFs. This chapter updates the earlier review of CEFs by Dimson and Minio-Kozerski (1999) and complements the reviews by Cherkes (2012) and Fletcher (2013) of U.S. CEFs and single-country CEFs.

The chapter is organized as follows. The next section discusses the current structure and regulation of U.K. CEFs, highlighting differences with the U.S. CEFs and recent regulatory changes. The following section considers non-U.S. CEFs, focusing on research relating to puzzling aspects of CEFs. The remaining two sections deal with studies of non-U.S. CEF performance and trading strategies and the final section concludes.

Current Structure and Regulation

NATURE OF CLOSED-END FUNDS

CEFs are similar to mutual funds, also called open-end funds (OEFs), which include unit trusts and open-ended investment companies (OEICs) in the United Kingdom, where they pool investor cash and usually invest it in domestic and/or foreign stock markets. Unlike OEFs, CEFs are public limited companies and are listed on stock exchanges. Therefore, CEFs provide investors with shares and the right to take part in the CEF's governance. A feature that distinguishes CEFs from OEFs is in their pricing structure. OEFs have a simple pricing structure, as the price reflects the value of the OEF's portfolio of assets. CEFs, however, have both a publicly available share price—the price at which the share trades on the stock market—and also a publicly available net asset value (NAV). The NAV is calculated by adding the value of the fund's investments (i.e., the portfolio of securities invested in by the fund, cash, and other net current assets) and deducting all of its liabilities. The total value of the assets is then divided by the number of shares to give the NAV. Table 8.1 shows the fund trades at a discount or premium when the share price differs from the NAV.

The causes and behavior of discounts and premiums are subject to much debate because they appear to violate the *law of one price* whereby assets of the same value should trade for the same price. While a discount makes CEFs cheaper to buy compared to buying the underlying assets, it can make them difficult to sell and, if the discount deepens, can put CEFs under the threat of a takeover or liquidation. However, an advantage of CEFs over OEFs, at least for the fund manager, is that CEFs do not have to redeem or buy back shares when the investor wants to sell them. This gives CEF managers greater freedom in their choice of investments and therefore they can tie up capital in less liquid asset classes.

COMPARISON OF U.K. AND U.S. CLOSED-END FUNDS

Both U.K. and U.S. CEFs have many similarities in structure and regulation. For example, in both the United Kingdom and the United States, shareholders of the CEF must pay income taxes on the dividends and capital gains distributed to them. However, differences also exist. In the United Kingdom, CEFs may retain up to 15 percent of their income from securities. U.S. CEFs must distribute almost all of their income and capital gains to shareholders. Another difference is the dominance of bond CEFs in the United States as opposed to the United Kingdom.

Table 8.1 **Closed-End Fund Discounts and Premiums**

	NAV per Share ($)	*Share Price ($)*	*(Discount)/Premium (%)*
CEF_X	10	8	(20)
CEF_Y	10	12	20

Note: This table shows how the difference between the NAV and share price results in a discount or premium.

Table 8.2 **Comparison of U.K. and U.S. Closed-End Fund Markets**

Fund Type	*Fund Category*	*Number of Companies*		*Total Assets*	*Total Net Assets*[a]
		U.K.	*U.S.*	*U.K. (£m)*	*U.S. ($m)*
Equity funds	Domestic	50	135	17,228	76,201
	International	89	74	40,477	19,318
	Single country	29	21	6,579	
	Private equity	17		11,603	
	Sector specialist	61	44	4,320	21,516
	Hedge funds	12		6,917	
	Equity and bond income	5		763	
	All equity funds	**263**	**253**	**98,748**	**117,034**
Property funds		24	17	8,073	3,439
Venture capital trusts		95		3,189	
Split capital trusts		19		6,420	
Bond funds	Fixed-income funds: Taxable		169		73,166
	Fixed-income funds: Tax-free		194		63,524
	All bond funds		**363**		**140,129**
	Total funds	**664**	**633**	**116,430**	**257,163**

Note: This table compares the number and value of equity and bond CEFs in the United Kingdom between January 1 and July 31, 2014, and in the United States between January 1 and August 31, 2014.

[a]The amount of assets in a fund after deducting all operating costs.

Source: Adapted from AIC 2014 and CEFA 2014b.

Table 8.2 shows 664 investment companies listed in the London Stock Exchange with total assets of £116,430 million. An *investment company* refers to both U.K.-domiciled CEFs and offshore CEFs. Table 8.2 includes data on U.S. CEFs to show that both sectors are of comparable size and that there are many bond funds in the United States, which feature marginally in the United Kingdom.

CAPITAL STRUCTURE

U.K. CEF managers have developed various share classes to appeal to different investors. Conventional CEFs issue only one class of ordinary shares. Most studies of CEFs are based on the analysis of a sample of ordinary shares of conventional CEFs because share classes can differ in terms of volatility and liquidity. Shareholders of conventional CEFs usually receive dividends and capital gains when they sell their shares.

Split capital CEFs issue more than one class of shares and are launched with a *wind-up date,* which is the date when the company will liquidate. Split trusts became popular in the United Kingdom in the 1990s but developed increasingly complex debt-laden structures. A large amount of cross-holding where CEFs held shares in other CEFs instead of investing in stock markets also increased the risk to investors. Split trusts offered high returns but investors were often ill-informed about the risks they were taking. When the market took a downturn in 2000 and 2001, a crisis of confidence forced many split capital CEFs to liquidate. An investigation by the Financial Services Authority (FSA), which was replaced by the Financial Conduct Authority (FCA) in April 2013, and the Treasury Select Committee resulted in changes to corporate governance, disclosure, and regulation. Following these formal investigations, the CEFs involved agreed to provide compensation to shareholders of just under £1 billion (Adams 2004).

U.K. CEFs often use leverage or gearing if markets are expected to rise. In August 2014, the Association Investment Companies (AIC) reported that the overall average gearing or leverage for conventional U.K. CEFs was 7 percent (AIC 2014). Leverage is a more pronounced feature in U.S. funds where 433 of the 633 funds listed have some level of leverage (CEFA 2014a). This finding contrasts with previous ones involving U.S. funds by Dimson and Minio-Kozerski (1999), who find an aggregate debt ratio of less than 1 percent. Only 11 of the 167 of equity funds studied report leveraged assets.

Besides increasing leverage, other ways in which CEFs can expand include issuing new shares or warrants or taking over other CEFs. If a company wants to contract, it can offer to buy back its shares. It may cancel the repurchased shares immediately or keep them "in treasury" for potential future new issues, an option available since December 2003. Buying back shares is another way a CEF can reduce a discount as it increases the value of the shares by reducing the number of shares while not affecting the NAV. Share buybacks have been allowed since 1980, but U.K. CEFs started using them more widely after a change in tax legislation in 1998. Some contend that share buybacks also reduce management fees and serve as means by which the directors can exert discipline over poorly performing managers (An, Gemmill, and Thomas 2012).

TAXATION

If a CEF is domiciled outside the United Kingdom, it is usually located in a taxation system where the company is treated as tax-exempt. U.K.-domiciled CEFs do not pay tax on the dividends they receive from U.K. companies and are not taxed on capital gains provided they comply with the regulations set out in the Corporation Tax Act 2010, Section 1158 (National Archives 2010). These exemptions allow management to change the portfolio without incurring capital gains tax on the transactions. U.K. CEFs can be liable to pay a 30 percent corporation tax on other forms of income. This tax can be reduced by offsetting expenses against taxes and by claiming double tax relief where income is taxed twice: once in the country where it arises and again in the United Kingdom. This tax status is why many CEFs have chosen an offshore base for their operations in recent years.

OWNERSHIP

Whereas individual investors mainly hold U.S. CEFs, institutions primarily hold U.K. CEFs. Substantial changes in the ownership of U.K. CEFs have occurred since the 1960s. An early survey by Burton and Corner (1968) of the ownership of CEFs with a capital of £25 million or more shows that individuals owned an average of 75.2 percent of the shares with institutions owning 24.8 percent. By 1986, the situation had reversed with institutions owning an average of 77.7 percent of the share capital of the same trusts, with individuals owning only 22.3 percent (Draper 1989). Draper contends that the reason for this change to OEFs is that OEFs are better able to market themselves efficiently to individual investors.

Although OEFs have overtaken CEFs as the preferred investment choice in the United Kingdom, the 2012 Retail Distribution Review (RDR) meant that Investment Advisers in the United Kingdom stopped receiving commissions for promoting certain investment products, particularly OEFs. CEFs are now operating in a more level playing field because the law removed the incentive for investment advisers to promote OEFs rather than CEFs. The recent growth in the U.K. CEF fund sector and the fall in the discount to 3.3 percent in August 2014 have partly been attributed to this regulatory change (Baron 2013; FT Adviser 2014). Another factor having a major impact on the sector is that many consumers are now buying shares in CEFs using direct-to-consumer (D2C) online platforms rather than via a broker (Stewart 2014).

The Closed-End Fund Puzzle

Various puzzling features are associated with CEFs that have caused much debate over the years. Lee, Shleifer, and Thaler (1991) identify the key anomalies of CEFs as the: (1) initial premium, (2) subsequent fall into a discount, and (3) fluctuations in the discount and its disappearance when the fund converts to an OEF. As much of the literature groups itself around these topics, the third topic of discount fluctuations, the following section discusses each of these areas. It also includes a separate section on performance studies and trading strategies.

PUZZLES 1 AND 2: THE INITIAL PREMIUM AND THE CHANGE INTO A DISCOUNT

Although studies such as Loughran, Ritter, and Rydqvist (1994) examine the puzzle of IPO underpricing for newly floated companies, only scant research exists on IPO underpricing in relation to CEFs. Following the work of Weiss (1989) for the United States, Levis and Thomas (1995) assess whether U.K. CEFs are underpriced relative to their subsequent performance and to other companies. They examine almost twice the number of funds and study their pricing over a longer period, specifically from 1989 to 1992. The particular interest in examining U.K. funds is the ownership difference. The authors point out that whereas institutional owners hold around 6 percent of U.S. CEFs, institutional owners hold around 70 percent of U.K. CEFs. Levis and Thomas find that underpricing exists for U.K. CEF IPOs with average first day returns of around 2 percent, which is much less than for industrial IPOs (13 percent).

Their findings show that the smaller degree of underpricing in CEFs is consistent with the lower uncertainty concerning the value of the assets. They also show that U.K. CEF IPOs have "hot" issue periods during which certain geographical areas are popular for investment, and that the IPOs take place when the premiums of existing funds with the same investment objectives are less negative. The initial premium drops into a discount by day 150 after the IPO and cumulative abnormal return (CAR) becomes negative by day 50. Levis and Thomas suggest that a better long-run after-performance of U.K. IPOs as opposed to U.S. IPOs is due to the greater institutional involvement in the U.K. CEF market.

Gemmill and Thomas (2013) return to the issue of CEF IPOs. They ask: Why do investors buy U.K. CEF IPOs despite the initial premium turning into a discount for most funds within a year? They investigate two major rational explanations for U.K. CEF IPO purchases based on an analysis of U.S. CEFs: (1) investors buy for managerial ability (Berk and Stanton 2007) and (2) investors buy for liquid access to less liquid assets (Cherkes, Sagi, and Stanton 2009). They also examine the alternative explanation of investor irrationality (Lee et al. 1991).

Gemmill and Thomas (2013) test the two elements required for Berk and Stanton's (2007) theory to hold against U.K. data: (1) the NAV has to outperform for the first years after the launch of the fund and (2) fees are raised or lowered according to the level of managerial performance. They do not find evidence of initial outperformance relative to either fund-specific benchmarks or to the market. Gemmill and Thomas also do not find that increasing fees (total expense ratios) are related to the NAV returns. They next test the liquidity and management fee trade-off theory of Cherkes et al. (2009) against U.K. data. Gemmill and Thomas do not find that U.K. funds are more liquid than the shares in which the fund invested so initial liquidity gain occurs. They also do not find that the liquidity of the assets in which the fund invested increase significantly over time, which is the reason suggested for the fall into discount. Instead, Gemmill and Thomas find evidence to support the sentiment hypothesis of Lee et al. (1991). They find that new issues are significantly related to both market-wide and sector-specific sentiment measures and that market-wide sentiment is a more significant factor in relation to the premium than managerial ability or liquidity.

PUZZLE 3: THE NATURE OF THE DISCOUNT AND ITS FLUCTUATIONS

Much of the non-CEF research into non-U.S. CEFs relates to the discount and focuses on why the discount occurs and why it fluctuates. Although some argue that investor sentiment plays a large role, others contend that the discount arises for rational reasons or that both play a role. For example, using a sample of 158 U.K. CEFs with OEF equivalents between 1991 and 1997, Gemmill and Thomas (2002) argue that a discount can arise because it reflects the present value of long-term managerial expenses, and that the discount persists because it rarely reaches the level at which arbitrage would be profitable. A premium can also occur, but if it becomes too high, new issues of funds in the same investment sector will produce competition and this will reduce the premium. However, they suggest that the subsequent fluctuations in the discount are due to changes in small investor sentiment. Examining the relationship between the discount and OEF flows, which is a measure of investor sentiment, into matched sectors, Gemmill and Thomas find a significant negative relationship between the discount and retail fund flows in most of the investment sectors, suggesting that investor sentiment affects discount fluctuations.

Findings elsewhere cast doubt on the role of the discount as an index of investor sentiment. Doukas and Milonas (2004) apply the same tests as Lee et al. (1991) on a sample of 16 Greek CEFs between 1997 and 2002. They find that sentiment, as proxied by the Greek CEF discount, does not enter into the return-generating process for small stocks. Halkos and Krintas (2006) also analyze 16 Greek CEFs from 1994 to 2004 using extracted factors that they then combine into behavioral and fundamental factors. They find evidence from regression analyses to support the influence of both on the discount of Greek CEFs.

Following up on the research of Gemmill and Thomas (2002), Copeland (2007) looks at arbitrage bounds in relation to the U.K. CEF discount. Like Gemmill and Thomas, he distinguishes between the long-term discount equilibrium and short-term fluctuations in his analysis of the discount. He analyzes 133 U.K. CEFs using weekly data from 1990 to 2004. Copeland (2007, pp. 328–329) finds that the U.K. CEF discount is non-stationary but also mean-reverting, suggesting a "long memory discount process." Supporting Gemmill and Thomas (2002), Copeland finds that a nonlinear price process may be present, which he models using smooth threshold auto regression (STAR) models. However, the author does not distinguish between CEFs with differing investment objectives, such as emerging market investment or U.K. investment, which could affect the discount.

Gemmill and Thomas (2011) revisit the arbitrage issue with a more recent example of U.K. and U.S. funds between 1988 and 2007. They argue that the discount in both markets persists because of arbitrage constraints, which are more severe in the United Kingdom, resulting from the possibility of new issues of CEFs in sectors where premiums occur. Besides arbitrage constraints, they find that premiums and discounts are more influenced by rational factors (liquidity and management fees) in the United Kingdom and by investor sentiment factors (dividend payout and idiosyncratic risk) in the United States. Gemmill and Thomas (2002, 2013) also find evidence of investor sentiment in the pricing of U.K. CEFs. Relative to the United States, however, the implication is that its impact is less severe.

If investors act upon sentiment instead of rational considerations, this implies that they make buying and selling decisions that are not based on changes in the fundamental value of the stock, but upon rumors and guesses. Looking more deeply into the role of investor sentiment in the pricing of U.K. CEFs, Agyei-Ampomah and Davies (2005) investigate whether excess price volatility exists in relation to the NAV in U.K. CEFs showing that investors are not responding rationally to changes in the fundamentals (changes in NAV) but instead are engaging in irrational noise trading. Examining 210 funds between 1970 and 1988, they also find excess price volatility in relation to the NAV in the United Kingdom although institutional investors mainly hold the funds. What is surprising about this finding is that it appears to contradict the argument that the excess volatility in U.S. CEFs (Pontiff 1997; Sias, Starks, and Tinic 2001) is due to the dominance of retail investors who act less rationally than informed institutional investors. The finding that U.K. CEFs show similar features of investor sentiment to U.S. funds, despite being held mostly by institutions, is a puzzle that has continued to engage researchers.

Due to the inherent transparency of CEFs, as their NAVs are made publicly available, the trading of the funds' share by their directors should therefore cause little or no price reaction. Based on Barber and Odean's (2008) notion of attention-grabbing news, Andriosopoulos, Steliaros, and Thomas (2015) assess the short impact of directors' trading on the stock price of U.K. CEFs from 1998 to 2008. The authors find that, contrary to directors' sell trades, directors' buy trades cause a significant and positive market reaction. They find that larger directors' purchases are associated with a higher market reaction especially in CEFs with higher information asymmetries due to their smaller capitalization and more ambiguous investment mandate such as investing in private equity and hedge funds. Also, the authors show that when the CEF chief executive officers (CEOs) or executive directors buy the funds' shares, a greater market reaction and a respective trading-volume increase occurs around the day of the purchase announcement. They argue that investors assume that CEOs and executive directors have greater "inside" knowledge about the CEF; hence, the purchases made by fund directors and CEOs serve as stronger signals to the market.

Given that many of the studies of U.K. CEFs find a role for investor sentiment, can investors use sentiment measures in the United Kingdom and elsewhere to predict CEF returns? Davies, Fletcher, and Marshall (2014a) analyze the predictive ability of consumer sentiment indices in relation to the U.K. closed-end country fund share price return and NAV return for 44 U.K. single-country CEFs between 1993 and 2009. They find that foreign country consumer sentiment index levels are a significant negative predictor of the share price and NAV return of CEFs over horizons up to one year. Their findings confirm research by Bodurtha, Kim, and Lee (1995) who find that the share price return of U.S. country CEFs is influenced by home (U.S.) market sentiment but more so by foreign market sentiment. Davies et al. (2014a) show that U.K. single-country CEFs are a good vehicle for diversification as their share prices reflect foreign market sentiment more than U.K. market sentiment. This result is consistent with that of Bekaert and Urias (1996), discussed in the next section, who find U.K. closed-end country funds are a better means of diversification than U.S. country funds.

Market-wide shocks can be a major source of price volatility and investor uncertainty. Fuertes and Thomas (2006) examine the reaction of CEF pricing to eight market-wide shocks between 1988 and 2003. In their examination of the share prices of 63 continuously traded CEFs, they find that U.K. CEF share prices overreact to changes in the NAV, supporting the evidence of Agyei-Ampomah and Davies (2005). They distinguish between negative and positive market-wide shocks and find that discounts widen after large negative market-wide shock and narrow after large positive market-wide shocks. In the aftermath of the shocks, Fuertes and Thomas report that the more widespread the shock, the longer prices take to recover. Their evidence also shows that small funds and funds that are more difficult to arbitrage take longer to recover from market shocks.

Market-wide shocks can also affect the openness of markets to foreign investment. Such increases in investment barriers can affect the prices of CEFs, as many CEFs invest internationally. Davies, Fletcher, and Marshall (2014b) examine the impact of changes in the levels of capital controls in emerging markets on a complete sample of 16 U.K.

CEFs investing in emerging markets between 1993 and 2009. They use the Edison and Warnock (2003) time-varying measure of availability of investment as a measure of a direct investment barrier. The authors also examine the role of indirect investment barriers such as illiquidity, inflation variability, and economic freedom. Their main finding is that when investment availability decreases, a significant decrease in the NAV returns and share price returns of U.K. closed-end country funds occurs. Further, their study shows some evidence for the impact of indirect measures of market segmentation upon closed-end country fund pricing.

In a more detailed study of liquidity related to U.K. CEFs, Davies, Fletcher, and Marshall (2013) examine the effect of changes in liquidity in both the U.K. CEF and the foreign country on the CEF premium. They divide the sample of 55 CEFs investing in single countries into those of established and emerging markets. Their main finding is that both country and fund illiquidity play highly significant roles in the premiums and discounts of U.K. country funds. In the sample of emerging market funds, they discover that country illiquidity is positively related to the premium, even with controlling variables. Fund illiquidity is not a significant factor. Developed market country funds provide a completely different picture. In developed market funds, they find that country illiquidity is not a significant factor, but fund illiquidity has a significant and negative impact. Davies et al. (2013) examine the closed-end country fund premiums and discounts during the financial crisis of 2007–2008. They find that the emerging market fund discount shows more stability whereas the discount of developed market funds widens markedly.

One way of reducing a widening discount is to repurchase shares. Buying back shares, a practice used by CEFs in the United Kingdom since 1998 although legal since 1980, is also a way in which a CEF can increase a premium as it increases the value of the shares by reducing the number of shares while the NAV is unaffected. Based on a study of 140 U.K. CEFs between 1996 and 2004, An et al. (2012) identify both an immediate effect on the share price in which the fund share price jumps slightly, and a longer term effect over the next four years when the fund share price and NAV show evidence of outperformance. They argue that as the repurchase reduces management fees, it serves as a means by which the directors exert discipline over poorly performing managers.

Gemmill and Thomas (2006) investigate further the impact of corporate governance in U.K. CEFs. In a study of 246 funds of which 39 are split capital funds between 1995 and 1998, they ask whether governance affects fund performance as proxied by management fees and the discount. Finding that lower returns follow higher fees, the authors then examine what influences the level of fees charged by the fund directors. They find that fees are higher when the number of directors is large, more "insider" directors are from within the same fund family, and the management company has less ownership. Gemmill and Thomas argue that this corresponds to a misalignment of the interests of managers and investors. They do not find evidence that managers can influence the level of the discount, as is often claimed. Instead, the authors find that the size of block holdings, both internal and external, affects the discount suggesting that investors are wary of large ownership groups.

Justifying management fees is one of the main challenges for CEF managers who promote their funds to investors on the basis that they provide both diversification and superior performance, which more than offsets the fees charged. As discussed in the next section, several studies on U.K. CEFs examine fund performance both compared to market benchmarks and OEFs.

Performance Studies

Leger (1997) presents an early analysis of the timing and selectivity of 72 continuously traded U.K. CEFs between 1974 and 1993 in four five-year non-overlapping samples. He uses various models to examine timing and selectivity. Using a generalized least squares (GLS) estimation method corrected for autocorrelation, he finds that not only is abnormal performance weak for both timing and selectivity but also that the timing performance is negative for a considerable proportion of CEFs. This evidence is consistent with findings for U.S. funds and substantiated by Bangassa (1999). One issue raised by this study, however, relates to the choice of a benchmark against which performance is measured. Although most U.K. CEFs invest internationally, they measure their performance against the U.K.-based Financial Times Stock Exchange (FTSE) All Share index.

In a more extensive performance study, Bangassa (1999) identifies a related CEF puzzle, applying to the United Kingdom: Why do U.K. institutions buy CEFs and pay annual fees when the large size of institutions allows them to obtain diversification and leverage at a lower cost than investing in CEFs? Using a sample of 79 U.K. CEFs from 1980 to 1994, he investigates whether U.K. CEFs provide evidence of managerial skill in stock picking and market timing that would justify their purchase by institutions. Bangassa uses five different measures of performance. The benchmarks the author uses for comparing the performance of U.K. CEFs are the FTSE All Share Index, an Investment Trust Index, and the Morgan Stanley Capital International (MSCI) World Index. Bangassa conducts the analysis by examining NAV performance as this should reflect stock picking and market timing and finds not only that market timing hardly exists but also evidence of poor market timing. One issue is that Bangassa uses U.K. and international benchmarks to evaluate performance which may not always be the most appropriate measure (e.g., for funds investing in the Far East as opposed to North America).

Bangassa, Su, and Joseph (2012) return to the subject of the performance of U.K CEFs in their selectivity and timing, this time using a sample of daily data from 218 CEFs between 1981 and 2009 including non-surviving funds. The authors compare the performance of the U.K. funds' share price returns to the FTSE All Share Index excess returns, as opposed to NAV returns. They use ordinary least squares (OLS) and a GARCH (1, 1) in-mean estimation to which they add factors for size, value, and momentum and find a clear difference depending on which model is used. One question that could be raised concerns using daily data to analyze U.K. CEFs. Whether the funds analyzed in Bangassa et al. (2012) change their portfolios daily is unclear. Indeed this level of turnover would be most unlikely with less liquid markets such as emerging markets.

A certain proportion of funds could have performed well because of luck rather than superior stock-picking ability or market timing. This is the subject of investigation in a paper on CEF performance by Bredin, Cuthbertson, Nitszche, and Thomas (2014). The authors apply the false discovery rate (FDR) to around 300 U.K. CEFs using monthly data between 1990 and 2013. Their aim is to estimate the percentage of "lucky funds" with statistically significant alphas, which are due to Type I error, and then to test the performance and performance persistence of portfolios. They measure performance against benchmark indices identified by the funds themselves, where available, which vary according to each fund's investment mandate. The authors use three different factor models: (1) an excess benchmark return model, (2) a one-factor benchmark model, and (3) a four-factor benchmark model.

Using NAV returns, Bredin et al. (2014) find that as much as 16 percent show truly positive alphas and about 3 percent show truly negative alphas. Evaluating performance, they discover that most funds (75 percent) are neither significantly above nor below their benchmarks. When they examine the subsequent performance of portfolios formed using alpha funds, their evidence shows the greatest level of persistence in performance when using the four-factor model and suggest that the use of leverage available to CEFs and hedge funds but not to OEFs may be one reason for the performance persistence.

Investors in CEFs, as in other sectors, may have diverse investment aims. Different clientele groups are likely to have dissimilar requirements for marginal utility growth. This factor is not usually considered when examining fund performance because funds are typically tested against a general benchmark, such as the FTSE All Share Index. Fletcher and Marshall (2014) assess the role of investor heterogeneity in relation to the performance of 221 U.K. CEFs investing in the U.K. between January 1990 and December 2010. They model performance using five linear factor models. Their evidence shows that the benchmark models do not capture a large proportion of the volatility of the excess fund returns, suggesting a significant influence of investor heterogeneity in evaluating fund performance. Unlike the previous study by Bredin et al. (2014), who find evidence of positive alphas when looking across all U.K. CEFs with a range of investment objectives, Fletcher and Marshall find that U.K. CEFs that invest in the U.K. stock market provide neither superior nor inferior performance.

Further evidence showing the impact of different investment clienteles on CEF fund pricing comes from research into Chinese CEFs. CEFs in China are held less widely and mostly by institutional investors. Since 2000, insurance firms and pension funds can invest in CEFs. Chan, Kot, and Li (2008) investigate how varying clienteles affect the discount behavior of 54 CEFs in mainland China during 2000 and 2003. The authors find strong evidence of investor concentration having a negative relationship with the CEF discount, suggesting that more widely held funds are less attractive to institutional investors. Finally, their evidence shows that investors prefer smaller CEFs paying more dividends.

One issue for those investing abroad is that the fund in which they invest should provide some benefit that is unavailable when investing directly in an index that covers the whole market. Bekaert and Urias (1996) consider the benefits of diversification using emerging market CEFs as compared with International Finance Corporation (IFC) investable indices. They measure diversification benefits relative to a set of mature market benchmark returns. Their sample consists of 43 U.S. closed-end country funds, of which 23 are emerging market funds, and 37 U.K. CEFs, including both single country funds and funds investing in more than one country, of which 19 are emerging market funds from 1986 to 1993. One original feature of the work is that they use mean-variance spanning tests. Another feature is the comparison between U.S. and U.K. funds. Their main finding is that U.K. emerging market funds provide diversification benefits that are statistically significant, but that comparable U.S. funds do not provide such benefits. Although Bekaert and Urias suggest that this difference may be due to differences in portfolio selection, they do not investigate this possibility in the study.

Trading Strategies

Can the presence of discounts be used to create a profitable trading strategy? Draper and Paudyal (1991) explore the possibilities of profiting from persistent discounts in the United Kingdom. Their study follows the study of U.S. funds by Thompson (1978), who finds significant outperformance by following a strategy of investing yearly in funds in proportion to the size of the discount. Draper and Paudyal find no evidence that such a strategy can be successful in the United Kingdom during the period 1983 to 1986. They also find some evidence to support a relationship between the discount and managerial variables but only mixed support for the number of directors (as a proxy for managerial resistance and agency costs) and not for expenses.

Gemmill and Thomas (2006) also find a relationship between the discount and management variables, finding that discounts are wider when the management is more concentrated. In their sample for 1996, they also find that expenses are negatively related to the U.K. CEF returns. Their results suggest that governance affects U.K. CEF pricing.

Cheng, Copeland, and O'Hanlon (1994) revisit the possibility of exploiting the U.K. CEF discount in a trading strategy that involves buying high discount shares and selling low discount shares. Analyzing a sample of 63 funds that survive between 1984 and 1990, they find that positive (negative) abnormal returns can be obtained by following this strategy. However, they note that short-selling constraints and transaction costs are likely to prevent this strategy from being profitable when put into practice.

Copeland and Wang (2000) consider whether forecasting models can work with U.K. CEFs to give accurate information that can be used for trading strategies. Using daily data from 1990 to 1993, they examine a sample of 55 continuously traded funds across various sectors. They use three models for forecasting changes in price and NAV. The authors find that the forecasts made using the vector auto regression (VAR) model as opposed to a random walk forecast are more accurate than those made using the error correction model (ECM). They also find that an asymmetric bi-GARCH model is even better. However, Copeland and Wang acknowledge some of the issues with acting on forecasts of CEF prices. The main one being that the sector suffers from thin trading and so rapid trades may not be feasible or profitable.

Bleaney (2004) also looks at forecasting and examines the extent to which past NAV returns can forecast current CEF discounts and therefore provide a basis for a profitable investment strategy. Using a sample of 55 U.K. CEFs between 1990 and 1999 across six investment sectors, Bleaney finds that discounts are negatively related to past NAV returns and the past discount. A puzzling finding of this research is that past NAV returns have the greatest impact on the discount one year later. The author suggests that this relationship may be because investors generally look at performance over the past year when making investment decisions. He considers that the costs of trading strategies based on past NAV returns and past discount make these trading strategies only marginally profitable. He investigates the possibilities of profitable arbitrage strategies by taking into account past NAV returns and the past discount. Consistent with previous studies such as Gemmill and Thomas (2002), Bleaney estimates the risks and cost of arbitrage and concludes that they constitute a sufficient barrier to deter such a strategy.

A factor that is often neglected in the above investment strategies is transaction costs. A study by Cakici, Tessitore, and Usmen (2002) is an exception. Using weekly discount and return data for U.S. and U.K. CEFs from 1991 to 2000, they examine the probability of the strategy of buying CEFs at discounts controlling for turnover and trading costs, so the model has a greater bearing on the reality of the investment process. They find that when transactions costs are low, portfolios that are frequently rebalanced and have less constrained turnover perform better than the benchmark and other portfolios. However, when transactions costs are high, portfolios with higher constraints on rebalancing and turnover perform better than the benchmark and other portfolios. The implication of their findings is that in a high-cost environment, CEF managers can profit by limiting turnover and rebalancing.

By using a strategy of investing in CEFs before the CEFs become OEFs, investors can often profit from the rise in share price at open-ending. Chen, Johnson, Lin, and Liu (2009) investigate the trading activity and performance of domestic and foreign investors trading before the open-ending of Taiwanese CEFs. In Taiwan, a CEF can call for a shareholder meeting for voting to change the fund's status to an OEF within three months of the effective date. The authors show that by buying all triggered funds after the effective date and selling them the day before the meeting a potential investor can gain significant abnormal returns. Chen et al. also find that foreign investors can exploit this useful public information earning significant excess returns by buying the CEF when the discount is large and selling the shares in the fund when the discount is reduced due to the gradual price conversion to the NAV. However, domestic investors in Taiwan, both retail and institutional, are net sellers or neutral, hence foregoing any significant excess returns.

Summary and Conclusions

This chapter reviewed non-U.S. CEFs focusing primarily on the United Kingdom. It discussed the following key differences between the current structure and regulation of U.K. CEFs compared to U.S. CEFs. First, U.S. CEFs are required to distribute substantially all of their dividend and capital gains income but U.K. CEFs may retain up to 15 percent of their income from selling securities and cannot distribute the surplus from selling assets as a dividend. Second, bond funds dominate the U.S. CEF sector, whereas the U.K. CEF sector does not currently have any purely bond funds. Third, retail investors primarily own U.S. CEFs, whereas institutional investors, such as pension and insurance funds, mainly own U.K. CEFs. Fourth, the key recent regulatory change affecting U.K. CEFs was the introduction of the RDR, which came into effect in December 2012. One result of the RDR was that U.K. financial advisers no longer had a financial incentive to promote OEFs as opposed to CEFs. Since then, U.K. CEFs have enjoyed a time of growth and the discount has decreased to an average of 3.3 percent across the sector (FT Adviser 2014).

This chapter also considered academic research on non-U.S. CEFs. The evidence shows an initial premium, referring to the CEF underpricing following their IPO, and the subsequent fall into a discount, where the U.K. findings support the role of investor sentiment although most investors in U.K. CEFs are institutions. Research findings also reveal fluctuations in the discount and its disappearance when the fund converts to an OEF. The majority of the research on non-U.S.-based CEFs supports the role of investor sentiment as a key factor influencing discount fluctuations, despite most U.K. CEFs being owned by institutions. Most U.K. studies focusing on performance show that U.K. CEFs do not outperform the U.K. stock market. Although evidence of underperformance exists, comparing the existing evidence is challenging due to differing samples, performance measures, and benchmarks employed. Finally, various studies examine trading strategies. Although profiting from a persistent discount should be possible in theory, most studies find that the costs of an arbitrage deter such a strategy.

Discussion Questions

1. Identify similarities and differences between U.S. and non-U.S. CEFs.
2. Discuss the U.S. and U.K. research evidence involving the rationale for the CEF discount.
3. Discuss whether investors obtain superior performance when investing in CEFs and, if not, the rationale for investing in CEFs.
4. Examine potentially effective trading strategies for CEFs.

References

AIC. 2014. "AIC Stats." July 31. Available at http://www.theaic.co.uk./sites/default/files/statistics/attachment/AICStats31Jul14.pdf.

Adams, Andrew. 2004. "The Crisis Unfolds." In Andrew Adams, ed., *The Split Capital Investment Trust Crisis*, 38–58. Chichester, U.K.: John Wiley & Sons, Inc.

Agyei-Ampomah, Samuel, and J. Richard Davies. 2005. "Excess Volatility and U.K. Investment Trusts. " *Journal of Business Finance and Accounting* 32:5, 1033–1061.

An, Jingfen, Gordon Gemmill, and Dylan C. Thomas. 2012. "The Agency Effect of Repurchases on Closed-End Funds." *European Financial Management* 18:2, 240–270.

Andriosopoulos, Dimitris, Michael Steliaros, and Dylan C. Thomas. 2015. "The Short Term Impact of Director Trading in U.K. Closed-End Funds." *European Journal of Finance*, 21:8, 672–690.

National Archives. 2010. "Corporation Tax Act 2010, Section 1158." Available at http://www.legislation.gov.uk/ukpga/2010/4/section/1158.

Bangassa, Kenbata. 1999. "Performance of U.K. Investment Trusts: 1980–1994." *Journal of Business Finance and Accounting* 26:9–10, 1141–1168.

Bangassa, Kenbata, Chen Su, and Nathan L. Joseph. 2012. "Selectivity and Timing Performance of U.K. Investment Trusts." *Journal of International Financial Markets Institutions and Money* 22:5, 1149–1175.

Barber, Brad M., and Terrance Odean. 2008. "All That Glitters: The Effect of Attention and News on the Buying Behavior of Individual and Institutional Investors." *Review of Financial Studies* 21:2, 785–818.

Baron, John. 2013. *Investment Trusts: Unlocking the City's Best Kept Secret*. Harlow, U.K.: Pearson.

Bekaert, Geert, and Michael S Urias. 1996. "Diversification, Integration and Emerging Market Closed-End Funds." *Journal of Finance* 51:3, 835–869.

Berk, Jonathan, and Richard Stanton. 2007. "Managerial Ability, Compensation and the Closed-End Fund Discount." *Journal of Finance* 62:2, 529–556.

Bleaney, Michael. 2004. "Past Returns and Investment Trust Discounts." *Journal of Business Finance and Accounting* 31:9–10, 1505–1523.

Bodurtha, James N., Dong-Soon Kim, and Charles M. C. Lee. 1995. "Closed-End Country Funds and US Market Sentiment." *Review of Financial Studies* 8:3, 879–918.

Bredin, Don, Keith Cuthbertson, Dirk Nitzsche, and Dylan C. Thomas. 2014. "Performance and Performance Persistence of U.K. Closed-End Equity Funds." *International Review of Financial Analysis* 34:1, 189–199.

Burton, Harry, and Desmond Carteret Corner. 1968. *Investment and Unit Trusts in Britain and America*. London: Elek Books.

CEFA. 2014a. "Leveraged Funds." August 27. Available at http://www.cefa.com/FundSelector/LeveragedFunds.fs.

CEFA. 2014b. "Lipper Classification Averages." August 26. Available at http://www.cefa.com/FundSelector/Classifications.fs.

Cakici, Nusret, Anthony Tessitore, and Nilufer Usmen. 2002. "Closed-End Funds and Turnover Restrictions." *Financial Analysts Journal* 58:3, 74–81.

Chan, Kalok, Hung Wan Kot, and Desmond Li. 2008. "Portfolio Concentration and Closed-End Fund Discounts: Evidence from the China Market." *Emerging Markets Review* 9:2, 129–143.

Chen, Li-Wen, Shane A. Johnson, Ji-Chai Lin, and Yu-Jane Liu. 2009. "Information, Sophistication and Foreign Versus Domestic Investors' Performances." *Journal of Banking and Finance* 33:9, 1636–1651.

Cheng, A., Laurence Copeland, and John O'Hanlon. 1994. "Investment Trust Discounts and Abnormal Returns: U.K. Evidence." *Journal of Business Finance and Accounting* 21:6, 813–831.

Cherkes, Martin. 2012. "Closed-End Funds: A Survey." *Annual Review of Financial Economics* 4:1, 431–445.

Cherkes, Martin, Jacob Sagi, and Richard Stanton. 2009. "A Liquidity-Based Theory of Closed-End Funds." *Review of Financial Studies* 22:1, 257–297.

Copeland, Laurence. 2007. "Arbitrage Bounds and the Time Series Properties of the Discount on U.K. Closed-End Funds." *Journal of Business Finance and Accounting* 34:1–2, 313–330.

Copeland, Laurence, and Ping Wang. 2000. "Forecasting the Returns on U.K. Investment Trusts: A Comparison." *European Journal of Finance* 6:3, 298–310.

Davies, J. Richard, Mary Fletcher, and Andrew Marshall. 2013. "Investigating the Role of Illiquidity in Explaining the U.K. Closed-End Country Fund Discount." *International Review of Financial Analysis* 30, 121–130.

Davies, J. Richard, Mary Fletcher, and Andrew Marshall. 2014a. "Does Sentiment Predict U.K. Closed-End Country Fund Pricing?" Working Paper. Available at http://dx.doi.org/10.2139/ssrn.2467180.

Davies, J. Richard, Mary Fletcher, and Andrew Marshall. 2014b. "Time Varying Investment Barriers and Closed-End Country Fund Pricing." Working Paper. Available at http://dx.doi.org/10.2139/ssrn.2467195.

Dimson, Elroy, and Carolina Minio-Kozerski. 1999. "Closed-End Funds: A Survey." *Financial Markets, Institutions and Instruments* 8:2, 1–41.

Doukas, John A., and Nikolaos T. Milonas. 2004. "Investor Sentiment and the Closed-End Fund Discount: Out Of Sample Evidence." *European Financial Management* 10:2, 235–266.

Draper, Paul. 1989. *The Investment Trust Industry in the U.K.: An Empirical Analysis*. Aldershot: Gower Press.

Draper, Paul, and Krishna Paudyal. 1991. "The Investment Trust Discount Revisited." *Journal of Business Finance and Accounting* 18:6, 791–805.

Edison, Hali J., and Francis E. Warnock. 2003. "A Simple Measure of the Intensity of Capital Controls." *Journal of Empirical Finance* 10:1–2, 81–103.

FT Adviser. 2014. "Special Report: Investment Trusts—August 2014." *FT Adviser*. Available at http://www.ftadviser.com/2014/08/04/our-publications/special-reports/investment-trusts-august-8WYK2gHItaLMT6Zv3fDU.K.M/article.html.

Fletcher, Mary. 2013. "Liquidity, Sentiment and Segmentation: A Survey of Closed-End Fund Literature." *Journal of Accounting and Management Information Systems* 12:4, 510–536.

Fletcher, Jonathan, and Andrew Marshall. 2014. "Investor Heterogeneity and the Cross-Section of U.K. Investment Trust Performance." *Journal of Financial Services Research* 45:1, 67–89.

Fuertes, Ana-Maria, and Dylan C. Thomas. 2006. "Large Market Shocks and Abnormal Closed-End Fund Price Behavior." *Journal of Banking and Finance* 30:9, 2517–2535.

Gemmill, Gordon, and Dylan C. Thomas. 2002. "Noise Trading, Costly Arbitrage and Asset Prices: Evidence from Closed-End Funds." *Journal of Finance* 57:6, 2571–2593.

Gemmill, Gordon, and Dylan C. Thomas. 2006. "The Impact of Corporate Governance on Closed-End Funds." *European Financial Management* 12:5, 725–746.

Gemmill, Gordon, and Dylan C. Thomas. 2011. " Arbitrage, Idiosyncratic Risk and the Rationality of Discounts on Closed-end Funds." Working Paper, University of Warwick.

Gemmill, Gordon, and Dylan C. Thomas. 2013. " What Explains IPOs of Closed-End Funds: Managerial Ability, Illiquidity, or Sentiment?" Working Paper, University of Warwick.

Halkos, George E., and Theodore N. Krintas. 2006. "Behavioural and Fundamental Explanations of Discounts on Closed End Funds: An Empirical Analysis." *Applied Financial Economics* 16:5, 395–404.

Lee, Charles M. C., Andrei Shleifer, and Richard H. Thaler. 1991. "Investor Sentiment and the Closed-End Fund Puzzle." *Journal of Finance* 46:1, 75–109.

Leger, Lawrence A. 1997. "U.K. Investment Trusts: Performance, Timing and Selectivity." *Applied Economics Letters* 4:4, 207–210.

Levis, Mario, and Dylan C. Thomas. 1995. "Investment Trust IPOs: Issuing Behaviour and Price Performance: Evidence from the London Stock Exchange." *Journal of Banking and Finance* 19:8, 1437–1458.

Loughran, Tim., Jay R. Ritter, and Kristian Rydqvist. 1994. "Initial Public Offerings: International Insights." *Pacific-Basin Finance Journal* 2:2–3, 165–200.

Masey, Angela. 1988. *Investment Trusts*. London: Financial Times Business Information.

Newlands, John. 1997. *Put Not Your Trust In Money*. London: Association of Investment Trust Companies.

Pontiff, Jeffrey. 1997. "Excess Volatility and Closed-End Funds." *American Economic Review* 87:1, 155–169.

Sias, Richard W., Laura T Starks, and Seha M. Tinic. 2001. "Is Noise Trader Risk Priced?" *Journal of Financial Research* 24:3, 311–329.

Stewart, Nyree. 2014. "Trusts Enjoy Boost in Platform Sales." *FT Advisor*. Available at http://www.ftadviser.com/2014/08/04/investments/wraps-and-platforms/trusts-enjoy-boost-in-platform-sales-yzPXlfha0JdxJlc6t6TN6J/article.html.

Thompson, Rex. 1978. "The Information Content of Discounts and Premiums on Closed-End Fund Shares." *Journal of Financial Economics* 6:2–3,151–186.

Weiss, Kathleen. 1989. "The Post-Offering Price Performance of Closed-End Funds." *Financial Management* 18:3, 57–67.

9

Exchange-Traded Funds

EHSAN NIKBAKHT

Professor of Finance, Frank G. Zarb School of Business, Hofstra University

KEITH PARETI

Regional Director, WisdomTree Asset Management

ANDREW C. SPIELER

Professor of Finance, Frank G. Zarb School of Business, Hofstra University

Introduction

The distinction of offering the first exchange-traded fund (ETF) belongs to Canada with the Toronto Index Participation Fund (TIP 35) introduced in 1989. In 1993, the first U.S. ETF began trading publicly tracking the S&P 500 index (ticker symbol SPY). Over the following two decades, the industry has experienced explosive growth with more than 1,600 ETFs trading worldwide and over 1,200 in the United States as of 2013 (Investment Company Institute 2014). With the large number of securities in a typical index, most investors cannot replicate an index. An ETF is a vehicle or "wrapper" that allows investors to gain exposure to the index indirectly with one security. Attempting to replicate an index and all its underlying holdings can be cumbersome and cost-prohibitive for investors. The ETF fund structure allows this broad stock representation to be established in one simple vehicle. Why should investors buy 500 stocks separately with 500 individual trades and commissions when they can buy a single ETF in one trade that owns all 500 stocks?

Figure 9.1 shows the dramatic increase in net assets under management (AUM) as well as the concomitant increase in ETFs. For example, AUM increased over 15 times between 2002 and 2013 from $102 billion to almost $1.7 trillion. Similarly, the number of ETFs has grown tenfold from 113 to 1,294 over the same period.

The purpose of this chapter is to provide a comprehensive understanding of ETFs. One of the primary objectives is to highlight the major differences between mutual funds and ETFs. The remainder of the chapter is organized as follows. The next section discusses the basics of ETFs followed by major sections on the creation and redemption process, legal framework, types of ETFs, issuing involving ETFs, growth of the ETF industry, and trends and initiatives in ETFs. The final section provides a summary and conclusions.

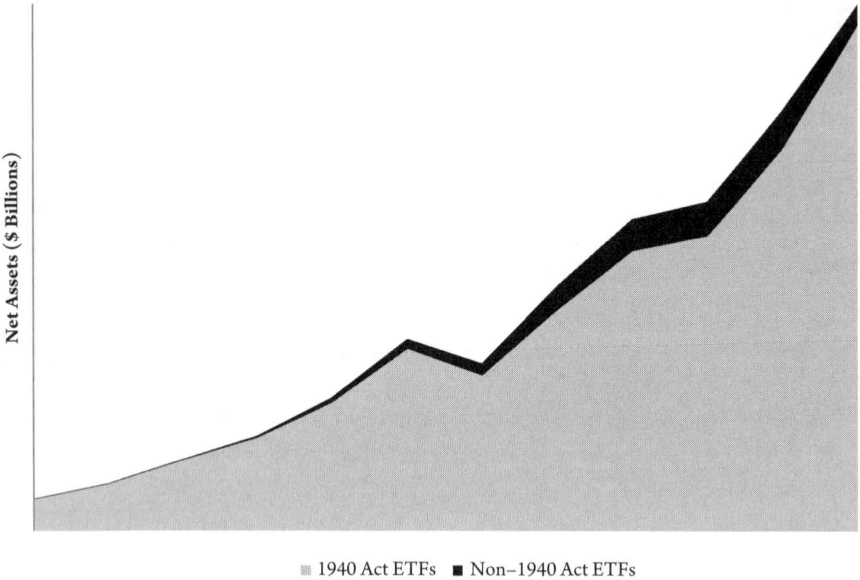

Year	2002	2003	2004	2005	2006	2007	2008	2009	2010	2011	2012	2013
# ETFs	113	119	152	204	359	629	728	797	923	1,134	1,194	1,294

Source: Investment Company Institute 2014.

Figure 9.1 Total Net Assets and Number of Exchange-Traded Funds, 2002 to 2013. The figure shows the total net assets for all outstanding ETFs and the number of outstanding ETFs.

Exchange-Traded Fund Basics

The typical ETF is a fund that tracks an index such as the S&P 500, NASDAQ, or Dow Jones Industrial Average (DJIA). An ETF trades similarly to an exchange-traded stock and has no investment minimum as opposed to mutual funds that have minimum investments typically in the $1,000 to $2,500 range. An *index* is a portfolio of securities with predefined weights (e.g., price-weighted, value-weighted, and float-adjusted) representing a particular market, sector, or asset class. An *ETF sponsor* is a financial institution that issues and manages the ETF and its assets. ETF sponsors introduce new ETFs when market demand is high and close ETFs when market demand is low. At the time of this writing, the five largest U.S. ETF sponsors in descending order of assets are iShares, State Street, Vanguard, Power Shares, and WisdomTree. Although dozens of other ETF sponsors exist, the aforementioned list represents some of the most recognizable and influential ETF sponsors. Table 9.1 provides a complete list of U.S.-based ETF sponsors as of 2014 (ETF.com 2014).

Table 9.1 **U.S.-Based Exchange-Traded Funds Issuers**

ETF Issuers		
AdvisorShares	FFCM	Northern Trust
ALPS	Fidelity	PIMCO
ARK	First Trust	Precidian
Arrow Investment Advisors	Franklin ETF Trust	ProShares
Barclays Capital	Global X	RBS Securities
BlackRock	Goldman Sachs	Recon Capital
Calamos Investments	GreenHaven	Renaissance Capital
Cambria	Guggenheim	RevenueShares
Charles Schwab	Highland Capital Management	Royal Bank of Canada
CitiGroup	Horizons	Russell
Columbia	Huntington Strategy Shares	SSgA
Compass EMP	IndexIQ	Teucrium
Credit Suisse	Invesco PowerShares	UBS
Deutsche Bank	JP Morgan	US Commodity Funds
Direxion	KraneShares	Van Eck
Emerging Global Shares	LocalShares	Vanguard
ETF Issuer Solutions	Merk	VelocityShares
ETF Securities	Merrill Lynch	WisdomTree
Exchange Traded Concepts	Millington Securities Inc.	
Factor Advisor	Morgan Stanley	

Source: ETF.com. 2014.

ETF sponsors generally follow two accepted strategies to create ETFs and track indexes: (1) physical replication and (2) synthetic replication. ETFs constructed based on *physical replication* are designed to own the actual underlying assets. Within the physical replication model, the two strategies used are full replication and optimization. *Full replication* is where the ETF holds every security in the index with its exact weighting. This is common with the most liquid indexes such as the S&P 500 index. *Optimization* is a replication model that requires the sponsor to purchase a subset of the index to reduce the number of holdings, decrease turnover, and lower trading costs. This strategy uses a sample of securities and has gained popularity from the ETF sponsor's point of view, especially for the less liquid areas of the market. For an index with 2,000 securities, the 500 smallest securities may comprise a very small percentage of the index. The ETF sponsor makes an operational decision in the best interest of the company on how to replicate the index by balancing the number of securities, and hence reduced trading costs, against increased tracking error. *Tracking error* is the volatility of the difference in returns between the ETF and its benchmark. Hence, a full replication ETF would have no tracking error aside from trading commissions. In this example, the hypothetical ETF could track an index with 2,000 constituents but hold only 1,500 securities in the ETF to optimize the efficiency of the fund. This type of optimized physical replication typically takes place within an asset class such as small cap emerging market equities because the ability to buy securities on some exchanges can be limited.

Synthetic replication is the second method used by ETF sponsors to track indexes. *Synthetic replication* is a form of replication that does not require the purchase of each underlying security in the index but rather enters into a swap. A *swap* is a bilateral agreement between two counterparties to exchange future cash flows. The purpose of this swap agreement is to exchange the performance of an agreed upon index or more generally any predefined basket between two parties without actually owning the underlying securities. This method is not as popular as physical replication, but represents an alternative way to gain access and exposure to a specific index through the ETF structure. For example, fixed-income ETFs, which are discussed later in this chapter, tend to use physical replication and optimization. This protocol is important for fixed-income indexes containing illiquid bonds.

Each method has advantages and disadvantages. A main risk of using synthetic replication is counterparty risk. *Counterparty risk* or *default risk* is the probability that the other party (i.e., the counterparty) will not perform as promised. For example, if one of the parties in the contract becomes insolvent, its ability to honor the contract could be jeopardized. A common way to mitigate counterparty risk is by posting collateral. *Collateral* is defined as the assets pledged to an ETF by a counterparty in which a separate custodian bank holds these assets. Collateral is typically used to provide a safety net in case a counterparty cannot meet its obligations. In normal functioning markets, no issues are involved with this process. In times of high volatility or financial crisis, these swap agreements could become an issue.

Creation and Redemption Process

An important difference between mutual funds and ETFs is the creation and redemption process associated with ETFs. Mutual fund investors interact directly with the mutual fund company such as Vanguard or Fidelity. ETF investors trade directly through an exchange. When shares need to be created in the mutual fund structure, the mutual fund company receives cash from investors and purchases the underlying securities. Conversely, authorized participants (APs) are financial institutions that have exclusive agreements with many ETF sponsors. Their primary role is to facilitate the creation/redemption process for ETFs. As the supply and demand of ETFs ebb and flow, APs act as middlemen between the investor and ETF sponsor that issues new units when demand is high and assets are increasing and retire existing units when demand is low and assets are decreasing. APs can streamline the process with new ETF units created and redeemed. Unlike mutual funds, ETFs use an "in-kind" creation/redemption process. The creation process occurs when an AP delivers the basket of stocks that makes up a creation unit in the exact quantity to the ETF sponsor in exchange for an ETF unit. The redemption process works in the same manner but in reverse. When a creation takes place, the ETF unit issued to the AP has then increased the shares outstanding in the ETF, which also inherently increases the ETF's AUM. Creation units typically occur with large size lots of approximately 50,000 shares that could equal one creation unit of an ETF. The *creation unit* is the basket that the fund takes in when APs add assets to the fund (Abner 2013).

Several issues arise when assets increase or decrease within the mutual fund structure. First, many transactions trigger taxable events when the mutual fund manager sells assets. The tax burden is proportionally distributed to all the mutual fund investors based on their ownership stake. In contrast, within the ETF structure, existing shareholders who do not sell their shares are typically unaffected. Under the ETF structure, investors maintain their cost basis and bear the tax consequences of their individual decision to sell their ETF shares independent of the managerial decision to create or redeem ETF units. The creation and redemption decision should be considered an operational function of the APs (Abner 2013). In contrast to the mutual fund, this benefit is unique to the ETF structure.

Legal Framework

Six types of structures comprise the exchange-traded product universe: (1) open-end funds (OEFs), (2) C-corporations, (3) unit investment trusts (UITs), (4) grantor trusts, (5) exchange-traded notes (ETNs), and (6) commodity pools. The legal framework is an extremely important issue for ETF construction because the difference between the six structures can potentially lead to holding restrictions, tax implications from K-1 issuance, use of debt instruments, and trading issues.

According to the U.S. Securities and Exchange Commission (SEC) (2013), ETFs are registered under the Investment Company Act of 1940 as OEFs or UITs in a similar manner as mutual funds. Over time, OEFs have gained in popularity with investors because of their flexible structure. They differ from CEFs that have a finite number of shares issued. CEFs also have traditional initial public offerings (IPOs), intraday trading, and prices that often differ from the net asset value (NAV). OEFs can create new shares if demand is high and redeem shares if demand is low. OEFs are typically registered under Section 18 of the Investment Company Act of 1940 (the 1940 Act).

C-Corporations are typically used for master limited partnerships and are treated similarly to traditional corporations. C-Corp mutual funds have no holding restrictions and are fully taxed at the entity level.

UITs differ from the other structures because they have an explicit expiration date and prohibit reinvesting dividends. UITs must also replicate an index but are registered under the 1940 Act similar to OEFs. Grantor trusts are registered under the Securities Act of 1933 and distribute dividends directly to the shareholders.

ETNs are fundamentally different from the other structures in two important ways: (1) ETNs are debt instruments and (2) ETNs are linked to a security or basket of securities. Similar to grantor trusts, ETNs are registered under the Securities Act of 1933, but the tax treatment is considered to be the same as a prepaid contract.

Commodity pools are sometimes classified as partnerships, are publicly traded, and have both general and limited partners. From an investment standpoint, the drawback to the limited partnership structure involves the tax consequences of potential K-1 issuance as opposed to the 1099 distribution.

Types of Exchange-Traded Funds

ETFs provide exposure to a wide variety of asset classes and sectors. A list of the broad categories covered includes broad-based domestic equity, domestic sector equity, global/international equity, bond, hybrid, and commodities. Figure 9.2 shows the amount invested (in $billions) within each category between 2011 and 2013. Only one net outflow is observed in the last set of bar graphs. In 2013, the commodity ETF asset class experienced the only outflow from any of the asset classes over this three-year

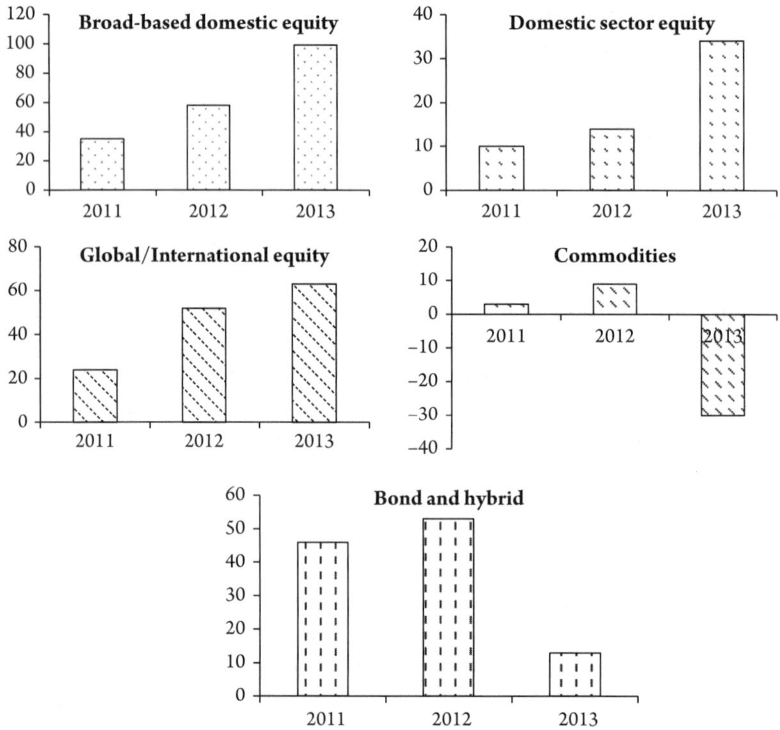

Figure 9.2 Net Issuance of Exchange-Traded Fund Shares by Investment Classification in Billions of Dollars, 2011 to 2013. These figures show the net issuance of ETF shares for each classification in each year.

Panel 1 Net Issuance of broad-based domestic equity ETF shares: Total $192 billion

Panel 2 Net Issuance of domestic sector equity ETF shares: Total $58 billion

Panel 3 Net Issuance of global/international ETF shares: Total $139 billion

Panel 4 Net Issuance of bond and hybrid ETF shares: Total $112 billion

Panel 5 Net Issuance of commodities ETF shares: Total $18 billion

Source: Investment Company Institute 2014.

Table 9.2 **Largest 10 Exchange-Traded Funds by Assets as of September 2014**

Symbol	*Name*	*Price ($)*	*Assets ($)*	*Average Volume*	*Sponsor*
SPY	SPDR S&P 500	197.90	185,010	89,695,164	SPDR
IVV	Core S&P 500 ETF	199.29	60,894	3,492,206	iShares
EFA	iShares MSCI EAFE ETF	64.77	54,129	13,502,867	iShares
VWO	Emerging Markets ETF	42.53	47,556	10,352,460	Vanguard
QQQ	QQQ	98.78	46,997	31,594,512	PowerShares
VTI	Total Stock Market ETF	101.90	45,737	1,876,097	Vanguard
EEM	iShares MSCI Emerging Markets ETF	42.42	40,114	50,109,316	iShares
GLD	SPDR Gold Trust	117.06	30,123	6,355,860	SPDR
IWF	iShares Russell 1000 Growth ETF	92.04	24,782	1,469,302	iShares
IWM	iShares Russell 2000 ETF	111.12	24,064	36,439,516	iShares

Note: The table shows the average daily volume of ETFs in $ millions.

Source: ETF Database 2014.

period. Investors can be fickle. Demand for a particular exposure can become very high or very low in a short period, which is evident from the $30 billion outflows from commodities in 2013.

Table 9.2 provides a list of the largest 10 ETFs including the sponsor based on AUM as of October 2014 (ETF Database 2014). Of the 10 ETFs listed, only one does not track an equity index, GLD. The GLD ETF is designed to track the spot price of gold bullion less expenses. This ETF was also the major contributor to the $30 billion ETF outflow illustrated in Figure 9.2. The other notable theme here is the market capitalization indexing trend. Many of these large ETFs based on AUM track a market capitalization index (e.g., the S&P 500 index). This methodology weights each component by its *market capitalization,* which is the stock price multiplied by the number of shares outstanding, to dictate the security's weight in the index. The higher the stock price runs up, the higher is the weight of that security in the index.

Many market participants refer to the S&P 500 index as the "beta" of the U.S. stock market. It is by far the most common benchmark for equity managers who want to compare their performance to the broader U.S. stock market. Theoretically, *beta,* which computationally is the asset covariance with the market scaled by market variance, measures the degree to which a stock tracks the overall market (e.g., the S&P 500 index). A beta of 1 indicates that the security's price tends to move in lock step with the market. A beta of less than 1 shows that the security's price tends to be less volatile than the market while a beta greater than 1 indicates that the security's price tends to be more volatile than the market.

TRADING EXCHANGE-TRADED FUNDS

One of the four primary benefits of ETFs is its intraday liquidity. Many retail and novice investors are not well versed on this topic and do not understand the trading mechanics of ETFs. Investors with a short holding period (i.e., less than a day) may favor an ETF over a mutual fund. A mutual fund cannot be purchased or sold intraday. As previously discussed, the authorized participant creates and redeems units of the ETF. APs, along with the liquidity-providing community (e.g., broker dealers, banks, and trading desks), are typically the screen markets (bid and ask quotes) on the exchange.

Comparing this process to a typical stock trade is useful. When investors start a buy transaction in a typical stock transaction on an exchange, they place a bid to buy, which is matched with an offer to sell. Therefore, a trade occurs when prices match on the same exchanges. With this stock trade, the screen market shows buyers and their bids with sellers and their offers. Conversely, an ETF transaction trades with an extra layer of complexity. This extra layer uses the assistance of the APs or liquidity providers including the institutional trading community. The bids and offers observed on the ETF trading screen are not always buyers and sellers, but rather, represent markets where liquidity providers and APs buy and sell the ETF with the size shown on the screens. This extra layer is important because liquidity providers are typically taking the other side of the trade. As additional market participants join, competition increases and allows the investor the potential for a tighter spread and a more efficient transaction. The increased level of competition limits the possibility of arbitrage, which is discussed in more detail later in the chapter.

In a similar vein, a brief discussion is needed to distinguish between screen liquidity and the underlying liquidity. *Screen liquidity* is the available price and depth observed on the collective screens. As expected, highly liquid ETFs see high trading volume and deeper markets. Only a small percentage of the ETFs are trading vehicles while the majority of ETFs are investment vehicles. What is the difference? *Trading vehicles* are the actively traded ETFs (e.g., SPY, GLD, and IWM) that trade at very high average daily volume levels, which are typically in the millions of shares. *Investment vehicles* are ETFs that do not have very high average daily volume and represent the balance of available ETFs. These ETFs might have high underlying liquidity, which can be accessed, but low screen liquidity because of a lack of daily screen trading volume.

In short, volume does not equal liquidity. *Daily volume* is the number of shares that traded in a particular day. ETFs are only as liquid as their underlying constituents. Hence, ETF liquidity equals trade capacity. When the screen market shows a wide bid-ask spread and low trading volume, it does not mean the ETF is illiquid but shows low volume. ETF liquidity can be found by placing liquidity providers and APs in competition with each other. This process is typically performed at the institutional level when a large institution takes a client's order and shops it around the street to large dealers. A wide bid-ask spread and small size on the screen can easily become a narrow spread with large size as market participants are competing for order flow. Such a trade typically occurs over the phone, and when a price and quantity are agreed upon, a trade is placed on the tape similar to a normal stock trade. Institutions refer to this process as using the *upstairs trading desk*, which is a secondary source of liquidity beyond the screens.

The cost of trading an ETF can vary. First, one important factor is the expense ratio, which the ETF sponsor takes from the fund on a daily basis. The *expense ratio* is an annual percentage calculation of fees paid to the ETF sponsor to compensate for fund operations. Another cost of trading an ETF is the premium or discount at which the ETF could trade during the trading day. A premium or discount occurs when the ETF deviates from its intraday NAV. ETFs have an inherent arbitrage mechanism built in because market makers and APs can capitalize on this deviation from an ETF's true underlying value. When an ETF trades above its NAV, it trades at a premium. Correspondingly, when an ETF trades below its NAV, it trades at a discount. Although this might be a large spread, arbitrageurs seek to capitalize on this opportunity effectively keeping the spread small. With this inherent arbitrage mechanism, traders who attempt to exploit this potential arbitrage opportunity minimize this spread. A mutual fund differs from an ETF in this case because an investor in a mutual fund transacts at the NAV after the close of the market.

A third cost is the *spread*, which is the difference between the bid and ask prices. For example, suppose an ETF has a spread of 6 cents ($50.00 – $50.06), implicitly assuming the fair value or NAV is $50.03. In this situation, the investor bears an additional cost to transact at non-NAV prices. If the investor pays the offer of $50.06, this has the investor purchasing the ETF at 3 cents above its fair value or NAV. After buying the ETF, if the investor chooses to immediately sell it at $50.00 (the screen bid), then the investor would suffer a round-trip loss of 6 cents (i.e., the investor paid $50.06 and sold at $50.00). This example illustrates that timing, trading, and prices can impact investment returns. Having the ability to dictate and control the holding period is an added benefit for ETFs. Investors use ETFs for many purposes from long-term investment vehicles to short-term daily trades.

ACTIVE VS. PASSIVE EXCHANGE-TRADED FUNDS

Until now, the primary discussion on ETFs focused on passive equity ETFs (i.e., ETFs that simply track or mimic an equity index). As ETFs evolved, so has their ability to engage in active investing. Actively managed ETFs started operating in 2008 (Hohorst 2014). An actively managed ETF does not track an index, which is likely to result in either outperformance or underperformance relative to its benchmark. The portfolio managers of actively managed ETFs have the freedom to buy and sell securities at their discretion. These ETFs are therefore more similar in spirit to mutual funds because most mutual funds do not track indexes. However, when compared to a mutual fund, actively managed ETFs continue to have the benefits of transparency, reduced costs, intraday liquidity, and increased tax efficiency (Katz 2004).

As ETFs continue to evolve, actively managed ETFs could be a compelling growth trend. For example, PIMCO has taken a successful mutual fund idea and created an ETF to deliver similar exposure. The ETF with ticker symbol BOND is the PIMCO Total Return Fund, which is the largest actively managed ETF with assets exceeding $2 billion as of October 2014. Fixed-income indexes are not nearly as large of a segment of the ETF universe as equity indexes. In fact, some fixed-income indexes have exposure to illiquid esoteric regions. Within these illiquid regions, some fixed-income ETFs do not track indexes and are thus considered actively managed.

A further development in the active vs. passive management debate involves Smart Beta ETFs. These ETFs are effectively bridging the gap between active and passive management and have some unique features to differentiate them from the typical market cap italization-weighted index. Smart Beta ETFs are likely to employ alternative weighting schemes such as fundamentally weighted, equally weighted, factor-based weighted, or low volatility weighted. WisdomTree manages a fundamentally weighted ETF with ticker DLN. Here, WisdomTree is dividend-weighting each constituent to reflect the proportionate shares based on the aggregate cash dividends each component company is projected to pay in the coming year based on the most recently declared dividend per share (WisdomTree.com 2014). This weighting scheme is updated annually. Guggenheim currently manages an equally-weighted ETF with ticker RSP, which equally weights each component in the S&P 500. iShares manages a low volatility ETF with ticker EEMV, which tracks a Minimum Volatility Index from MSCI (2014). MSCI combined its index and risk analytics expertise to construct the index's total risk-minimizing optimization using a MSCI parent index and the Barra Global Equity Model (GEM2) as the risk estimate input (MSCI Index website).

Debate exists over the preferred investment style (i.e., active or passive management) based on their performance. Standard & Poor's maintains records of historical indexes and mutual fund managers showing that passively managed ETFs typically provide better returns than those that are actively managed. For example, the five-year period before June 2014 was difficult for U.S. domestic equity managers. Less than 30 percent of managers across all capitalization and style categories delivered returns higher than their respective benchmarks (Soe 2014). These results showing only a minority of active managers outperforming their benchmarks only adds support to passive ETFs that track indexes.

Issues Involving Exchange-Traded Funds

This section examines several issues involving ETFs: tracking error, securities lending, and the arbitrage mechanism.

TRACKING ERROR

Within the ETF universe, *tracking error* is the annualized standard deviation of daily return differences between the return performance of the fund and its benchmark index. Tracking difference is another term similar to tracking error. *Tracking difference* is more simplistic and describes the difference between the index performance and the ETF performance.

Several factors can lead to tracking error. First, if the ETF tracked the index in lockstep (identically), the difference or tracking error between the ETF and the index should be the cost of the ETF. SPY is one of the most recognized and highly traded ETFs in the world. With an expense ratio of just 0.0945 percent, the ETF's tracking error is close to the fund's expense ratio, making the tracking error for SPY almost irrelevant.

A second source of tracking error arises from optimization. Some ETFs that track indexes do not own each security in the index but instead own a subset of securities to track the index as efficiently as possible. With a portion of the securities missing in the ETF, a difference exists between the index and the ETF returns.

A third source of tracking error is related to currency factors. Some ETFs own securities outside of their respective country and have a currency hedge overlay including currency swaps or non-deliverable forward contracts. Interest rates, volatility, and the continual rolling of the contracts can lead to tracking error.

A fourth factor is the *futures roll*, which is typical in commodity ETFs. As a futures contract approaches expiration, the ETF provider rolls the contract by selling the current position and opening a new position in a future month. Although this practice allows the ETF to have constant exposure to the commodity, it comes at the expense of potential tracking error in backwardation or contango markets. *Backwardation* is when the forward price trades below the spot price; *contango* occurs when the forward price is higher than the spot price. The roll of the contracts can lead to a positive or negative return, separate from the change (i.e., the return from the spot price of the commodity itself).

A potential fifth source of tracking error is timing. Throughout the day as securities fluctuate in price, the proportion of stocks in the index and ETF will ebb and flow. As securities are bought and sold, a potential drag occurs on ETF returns compared to index returns.

SECURITIES LENDING

To combat tracking error, many ETF sponsors take part in securities lending. *Securities lending* is when ETF sponsors lend out shares of the ETF's underlying holdings to allow other market participants to engage in a short position. A cost is associated with establishing a short stock position and the ETF sponsor can generate additional revenue with the fees charged for this service. This revenue could be placed entirely into the NAV of the ETF to help increase investor return. The ETF sponsor makes this operational decision, which can have a potential positive effect for the investor.

ARBITRAGE MECHANISM

Arbitrage is the simultaneous purchase and sale of an asset to create a riskless profit. Why is this important in the ETF landscape? ETFs that track an index have an embedded arbitrage mechanism in place that allows all market participants to potentially capitalize on this situation. Since the holdings are all publicly listed on the index website or the ETF sponsor website, traders can see if the value of the underlying basket (i.e., the *indicative value*) deviates from the screen market. To make a riskless profit, a trader could hold all the stocks in the basket and wait to see if the ETF price increases to a level higher than the indicative value. In this case, the trader would sell the ETF and buy the stocks in the basket with the same notional value on the purchase and sale. This process inherently keeps many ETFs trading very close to their fair value. More competition and participants lower the possibility of arbitrage because arbitrageurs expend greater attention and effort to capitalize on these rare opportunities.

By contrast, actively managed ETFs do not have the same arbitrage mechanism as passively managed ETFs. Since the portfolio manager is not tracking an index, arbitrageurs cannot definitively earn a riskless profit because they cannot be certain of the underlying basket holdings. Each day the portfolio manager can alter the actively managed ETF holdings.

Growth of the Exchange-Traded Funds Industry

The years following the introduction of the first ETF in 1993 resulted in very modest investor interest with low volume, low AUM, and few investment choices. However, the industry fundamentally changed after introducing the QQQ, which is the tracking stock of the NASDAQ 100 index. It quickly became one of the world's most traded securities with pre-market and after-hours trading across all major financial centers. Since then, the number of U.S. ETFs topped 1,200 with AUM over $1.6 trillion (Investment Company institute 2014). This phenomenal growth in both the AUM and number of products issued is important to consider.

INCLUDING EXCHANGE-TRADED FUNDS IN A PORTFOLIO

Hedge funds, institutional trading desks, and pension funds are not the only investors attracted to the ETF structure. Retail financial advisors and individual investors, who desire a low-cost, tax-efficient, transparent, and liquid investment vehicle, have shown tremendous interest. Additionally, the ease at which investors can access different regions of the world has substantially increased the popularity of ETFs. The ability to invest in very narrow sectors (e.g., the U.S. financial sector with ticker XLF), as well as the ability to leverage the U.S. financial sector investment three times (ticker FAS) is now available. Leveraged and inverse ETFs are discussed in more detail in the following chapter. Individuals who have brokerage accounts now have the same access for trading ETFs as institutional investors. Industry experts refer to this as "an equal playing field." Hence, the playing field is level for retail and institutional investors in this arena because the same quotes appear on their screens.

From an investment standpoint, a portfolio based on ETFs can be constructed easily and with ultimate flexibility. For example, financial advisors now can create a broadly diversified global asset allocation based using the following model. Consider the allocation below:

- 10 different ETFs each representing a sector of the Global Industry Classification Standard (GICS) sectors.
- Dividend paying only ETFs with holdings in high dividend yielding stocks.
- ETFs fitting size and style boxes such as large cap value, large cap growth, and mid cap value.
- International stock exposure with a specific country mix.
- Fixed-income ETFs with a certain coupon or maturity.
- Commodity ETFs with a specific metal exposure.

The ability to create a personalized portfolio including many asset classes has never been more accessible.

Trends and Initiatives in Exchange-Traded Funds

From the inception of the Investment Act of 1940, the legal and operational structures of investment companies have evolved in different directions to respond to the needs of the market and investors. However, to comply with the Act of 1940, the SEC must approve all modifications and initiatives. Many initiatives have occurred to construct an ETF portfolio to include various types of investments such as high-yield bonds, real estate investment trusts (REITs), limited partnerships, preferred stocks, and specific micro sectors such as solar energy and biotech. More recently, the SEC has reviewed a unique ETF, called the *exchange-traded managed funds (ETMF)*, which combines the favorable features of ETFs with those of mutual funds. This new product structure is also expected to address both the limitations of ETFs and mutual funds, creating a security with more flexibility in terms of pricing, trading, and taxation. Investors continuously look for new ways in which to differentiate their portfolios to maximize return and minimize taxes and fees.

ETFs are known for their transparency, low cost, tax benefits, intraday trading, and daily disclosure requirements. In contrast, mutual funds, due to more active management, may have higher costs and do not trade throughout the day on exchanges. ETFs are exempt from daily disclosure requirement, which provides an operational advantage to some investments managers who prefer less disclosure. Prominent market participants have proposed a new ETMF instrument, which is essentially a hybrid between these two instruments, that is exchange traded but not transparent.

EXCHANGE-TRADED MANAGED FUNDS

The SEC received the first version of the proposal for the ETMF in March 2013 and an amended proposal followed during summer 2014. The proposal focuses on an actively managed ETF based on a patent-pending algorithm. The new model proposes to use NAV-based trading to determine the trading value of the security each day. The NAV-based trading would allow investors to buy into the ETMF at a premium or discount to the NAV on any given day (Nadig 2013). An ETMF would also have a fund manager who carefully selects the appropriate securities and monitors the process as trading continues throughout the day. In this way, an ETF's structure incorporates both the diversification and active professional management features of a mutual fund. Furthermore, the lower costs and tax benefits of ETFs remain intact (Hansen 2006).

Although introduced in 2008, actively managed ETFs make up a small fraction of all ETFs. In early 2014, about 80 actively managed ETFs traded in the global market representing $15 billion AUM, which is a small amount compared to the ETF universe of $2 trillion (Fuhr 2013). The ETMF represents the next phase, which is the extension of a regular active ETF. Yet, concerns exist about confusion arising from the new hybrid status, disclosure requirements, the creation of a pricing model, and low liquidity of future ETMFs in the market, if approved by the SEC (Lydon 2014a).

The opponents of the proposal for ETMFs argue that the existing, small group of active ETFs has not been popular due to strict daily requirements, operating costs, and shortcomings in timely pricing. The advocates for this creative instrument propose a quarterly disclosure, which is similar to mutual funds, but different than the daily disclosure of the ETF. As discussed in previous sections, the majority of ETFs are passively managed and the holdings simply replicate an index, such as the DJIA and the S&P 500, or include a well-defined portfolio of stocks, bonds, REITs, and commodities. As a result, due to the high trading volume and liquidity, the pricing and daily disclosure requirements of classic ETFs are relatively simple with minimum operational costs. This may not prove to be the case for the ETMF. Therefore, the SEC application calls only for a quarterly disclosure with a lag no greater than two months (Eaton Vance Management 2013).

The provision for transparency and its implementation seems to be the most controversial section in the original 2013 SEC application proposal. For example, limiting the disclosure requirements to only four times a year could be a limitation from the perspective of an asset manager or an individual investor constructing a portfolio through the ETMF. Many opponents of the proposals express concern over the accuracy of the pricing model. A modified version of a NAV approach has been proposed for pricing because the NAV has traditionally been used when the disclosure is reported on a daily basis. Whether the NAV approach can accurately be modified for less frequent reporting (e.g., quarterly for an ETMF) is an issue. According to the ETMF proposal, the price of the ETMF would be determined by the NAV of the securities in the fund at the market close each day with a listed premium or discount (O'Neill 2014).

Opponents argue that applying NAV will be an impediment for investors who need current and updated information in managing a dynamic portfolio. Conversely, the proponents contend that the same limitation has always existed for other instruments such as mutual funds. However, mutual funds do not have a pricing problem because shares are not traded intraday. As requested in the latest 2014 filing with the SEC, the proposed ETMFs would trade intraday like a typical ETF with NASDAQ carefully monitoring the NAV. The beginning NAV is adjusted by adding a premium or subtracting a discount to determine the ending NAV. According to the proposal, the NAV would be determined at the end of the trading day when the intraday trades would be officially executed at the NAV of the ETMF. Such distinctions and similarities among regular ETFs, ETMFs, and mutual funds are the main source of disagreement and debate among industry proponents, opponents who are mainly competitors, and the regulatory agency.

Besides the delayed disclosure structure that replicates the requirements of a mutual fund, prospective sponsors of ETMFs claim that ETMFs retain the most important benefits of ETFs, namely lower transaction costs and tax relief. In the filing with the SEC, the sponsors cite a major advantage of the new instrument: ETMFs would minimize the transfer agency costs. According to industry reports (Schroeder 2013), a mutual fund's agency cost is on average, around 19 basis points of net assets annually, whereas an exchange-traded actively managed fund's cost would be less than one basis point of net assets annually. This expected substantial reduction in cost is extremely attractive to investors, boosting the total yield, despite the limitation and uncertainty of the NAV-based pricing model. Regarding taxation, unlike trading shares of common stock in the open market that requires paying taxes on capital gains, an ETMF would use in-kind distributions on securities to meet tax redemptions. Shares of an ETMF can be exchanged for a basket of securities of equal value rather than cash. The proposal under review by the SEC acknowledges that ETMFs could be purchased with a mix of securities of equal value to the ETMF, not necessarily cash.

Other market participants had previously considered creating a hybrid of ETFs and mutual funds similar to the pending 2013–2014 proposal. For example, Blackrock was unsuccessful in its September 2011 application to the SEC seeking to eliminate the daily disclosure requirement for ETFs. Some industry analysts believe that due to the SEC's rejection of the Blackrock proposal, the current proposal will remain as an innovative idea and a work in progress at least for several years going forward. However, this assessment may not be true. Blackrock's proposal, unrelated to the current proposal, did not include any modification to the NAV pricing. A new pricing model for the ETMF is a value added feature of the new proposal. A few other mutual funds have publically expressed interest in the ETMF similar to the structure that is currently under SEC review (Lydon 2014b).

A likely conclusion is that the market is taking the ETMF more seriously as a viable trading instrument than it did previously. However, the ETMF proposal will not be completed until the sponsors fully address the outstanding issues and concerns raised by both the SEC and NASDAQ, the self-regulatory organization (SRO) supporting the ETMFs. Usually, before listing and promoting a new product, the involved SRO performs an extensive survey of both buy and sell side organizations. The issues not fully resolved are discussed below.

Assuming the ETMF shares are approved and issued, only large institutional investors are expected to be able to purchase ETMF shares from an authorized issuer of ETMFs. The institutional investor would then act as a money manager for those shares as it trades on a stock exchange. In early 2014, the SRO supporting the ETMFs filed with the SEC outlining the proposed trading structure for the instrument. Then, Navigate Fund Solutions, a wholly owned subsidiary of Eaton Vance, which is the creator and the applicant of the proposal for the SEC, was formed to commercialize a patent and address the ETF transparency problems. At the time of this writing, the NASDAQ is prepared to list ETMF shares and some institutional investors expressed interest in taking advantage of the expected low cost of such managed funds (Jaffe 2014). On that note, the arrival could occur possibly by the time this book appears in print.

Summary and Conclusions

Over the last two decades, ETFs have become an important investment vehicle for both institutional and retail investors. The goal of this chapter was twofold. First, it provided some historical context to the explosive growth and variety of ETF offerings. Second, it discussed the legal structure as well as the advantages and disadvantages of stand-alone investments and those as part of a diversified portfolio. ETFs use a structure that benefits investors by their intraday trading liquidity, transparency, tax efficiency, and low expenses. Not all ETFs are created equal, and many of the firms that create ETFs continue to launch new strategies and products to attract additional investors via exposure to new asset classes and sectors.

Discussion Questions

1. Identify four main differences between mutual funds and ETFs.
2. Discuss why ETFs are considered tax-efficient vehicles and how their tax treatment differs from mutual funds.

3. Explain how passive, active, and Smart Beta ETFs differ.
4. Explain how individual investors, institutional investors, and financial advisors use ETFs.
5. Discuss whether a need exists for a hybrid ETF such as an ETMF.

References

Abner, David. 2013. "Understanding How ETF Portfolios Work." In *Visual Guide to ETFs*, 32–50. Hoboken, NJ: John Wiley & Sons, Inc.

Eaton Vance Management. 2013. SEC Form 40-APP. Available at http://www.sec.gov/Archives/edgar/data/1076598/000089843213000595/a40-app.htm.

ETF.com. 2014. "ETF Screener & Database and ETF Ratings." Available at http://www.etf.com/etfanalytics/etf-finder.

ETF Database. 2014. Available at http://www.etfdb.com.

Fuhr, Deborah. 2013. "2013: The Year of the Active ETF?" CNBC.com. Available at http://www.cnbc.com/id/100695142#.

Hansen, S. Wade. 2006. "Mutual Funds 101." *Forbes Magazine*. Available at http://www.forbes.com/2006/08/23/mutual-funds-in_wh_0822investools_inl.html.

Hohorst, James. 2014. "Keeping a Secret." Markit.com. Available at http://www.markit.com.

Investment Company Institute. 2014. *Investment Company Fact Book*, 56th Edition. Washington, DC: Investment Company Institute.

Jaffe, Chuck. 2014. "You May Want to Ignore the 'Next Big Thing' in Mutual Funds." MarketWatch. Available at http://www.marketwatch.com/story/the-next-big-thing-in-mutual-funds-2014–2006–30.

Katz, Jonathan. 2004. "SEC Concept Release: Actively Managed Exchange-Traded Funds." Washington, DC: Securities and Exchange Commission. Available at http://www.sec.gov/rules/concept/ic-25258.htm#seciii.

Lydon, Tom. 2014a. "Eaton Vance Files Amended Application for ETMFs Product." *ETF Trends*. Available at http://www.etftrends.com/2014/01/eaton-vance-files-amended-application-for-etmfs-product.

Lydon, Tom. 2014b. "ETMFs Could Change the Fund Industry." *ETF Trends*. Available at http://www.etftrends.com/2013/04/etmfs-could-change-the-fund-industry.

MSCI. 2014. "Global Minimum Volatility Indexes." Available at http://www.msci.com/products/indexes/strategy/factor/minimum_volatility/.

Nadig, Dave. 2013. "Exchange-Traded Managed Funds Fantasy." *ETF.com*. Available at http://www.etf.com/sections/blog/19909-exchange-traded-managed-funds-fantasy.html?nopaging=1.

O'Neill, Kevin. 2014. *Securities and Exchange Commission Release No. 34–72350*. Washington, DC: Securities and Exchange Commission. Available at http://www.sec.gov/rules/sro/nasdaq/2014/34–72350.pdf.

Schroeder, Mary. 2013. "An ETF with Non-Daily Disclosure?" *Money Management Executive*. Available at http://www.mmexecutive.com/issues/2010_69/An-ETF-With-Non-Daily-Disclosure-239462–239461.html.

Soe, Aye. 2014. "S&P Dow Jones Indices." *SPIVA US Scorecard*. Available at http://www.spindices.com/documents/spiva/spiva-us-mid-year-2014.pdf.

U.S. Securities and Exchange Commission. 2013. "Investor Bulletin: Exchange-Traded Funds (ETFs)." Office of Investor Education and Advocacy, Securities and Exchange Commission. Available at http://www.sec.gov/investor/alerts/etfs.pdf.

WisdomTree. 2014. "WisdomTree Large Cap Dividend Index." Available at http://www.wisdomtree.com/etfs/index-details.aspx?IndexID=5.

10

Leveraged and Inverse Exchange-Traded Funds

BENJAMIN AGUILAR
Senior Associate, Mergers & Acquisitions, Cathedral Consulting Group, LLC

MICHAEL BIANCO
Specialist, NASDAQ

CHRISTOPHER MILLIKEN
Vice President, Portfolio Management, Hennion & Walsh Asset Management

ANDREW C. SPIELER
Professor of Finance, Frank G. Zarb School of Business, Hofstra University

Introduction

Leveraged and inverse exchange-traded funds (LIETFs) are a growing segment of the exchange-trade fund (ETF) universe. Introduced in 2005, these funds combine the properties of a traditional ETF with a non-traditional return structure. Similar to traditional ETFs, leveraged ETFs (LETFs), often called 2X and 3X funds, track the performance of a specific index but magnify returns (ranging between two and three times) based on the amount of leverage used by the fund. For example, for every 1 percent daily increase in the underlying index, a 2X and 3X LETF returns 2 percent or 3 percent, respectively. Inverse ETFs (IETFs) allow for investors to maintain the equivalent of a short position by earning the inverse return of the underlying index. For example, for every –1 percent daily return in an index, an IETF returns a positive 1 percent. Leveraged and inverse return objectives can also coexist creating the potential for an investor to earn 2 percent or 3 percent for every –1 percent daily return in the underlying index.

Fund managers of LIETFs primarily use derivative contracts to meet their return objectives. These funds contain a mix of options, swaps, and futures contracts, which can provide managers with their desired leveraged and/or short exposure to virtually every asset class in the investment universe, including but not limited to equity, fixed-income, commodity, real estate, currency, and volatility. These indexes range from household names such as the S&P 500 index to the more obscure such as the Alerian MLP Infrastructure Index. Derivatives also provide the benefit of flexibility for the manager to enter or exit the position when it is deemed necessary.

As of September 2014, the number of LIETFs had grown to more than 260 and accounted for approximately 16 percent of all existing ETFs, which now total over 1,600 (ETFdb2014b). Equity ETFs currently offer the greatest variety of index coverage with 80 LETFs and 75 IETFs offered in the market today. The smallest group is real estate

Table 10.1 **Summary of U.S. Listed Leveraged and Inverse Exchange-Traded Funds by Asset Class**

		LIETFs by Asset Class		
ETF Asset Class	*Number of ETFs*	*Average Daily Trading Volume*	*AUM ($ millions)*	*Average Expense Ratio (%)*
Blend	2	15,567.50	41.68	1.00
Leveraged	1	26,998.00	31.05	0.85
Inverse	1	4,137.00	10.63	1.15
Bond	41	179,559.15	205,641.75	0.87
Leveraged	12	88,808.73	364.94	0.94
Inverse	29	215,211.11	205,276.81	0.79
Commodity	39	431,713.59	2,389.64	0.97
Leveraged	16	418,485.69	1,580.24	1.10
Inverse	23	440,915.61	809.40	0.84
Currency	11	29,171.82	564.77	0.89
Leveraged	6	4,773.17	40.74	0.89
Inverse	5	58,450.20	524.04	0.88
Real Estate	7	313,361.33	707.44	0.87
Leveraged	4	195,988.33	627.97	0.79
Inverse	3	117,373.00	79.47	0.95
Stock	155	743,456.25	24,978.51	0.97
Leveraged	80	506,315.09	14,294.12	0.92
Inverse	75	993,415.85	10,684.39	1.02
Volatility	8	5,986,601.25	2,098.74	1.08
Leveraged	3	10,497,712.67	648.62	1.06
Inverse	5	3,279,934.40	1,450.12	1.09
Grand Total	263	719,589.41	236,422.54	0.95

Note: This table summarizes the asset class coverage of LIETFs including some important characteristics of these products including AUM and the expense ratio.

Source: ETFdb 2014b.

offering only four LETFs and four IETFs. In terms of assets under management (AUM), equity LIETFs have the most AUM with $25 billion; conversely, real estate LIETFs have the least AUM with just shy of $700 million.

The annual cost associated with owning these products is known as the *expense ratio*, which is an annual management fee charged by fund issuers and based on the portfolio's net asset value (NAV). While ETFs are often associated with their low cost structure, investors find LIETFs cost slightly more to cover the expenses associated with developing and implementing their often complex strategies. Of the six primary asset classes, volatility-based LIETFs are the most expensive with an average expense ratio for the group of 1.08 percent, whereas bond and real estate LIETFs are the least expensive with an average expense ratio of 0.87 percent. Table 10.1 summarizes these costs along with other LIETFs characteristics.

LIETFs are a product of asset managers pushing innovation to provide their clients with strategies that meet their changing needs in an evolving investment universe. In their relatively short history, these funds have proven controversial due to their complex mechanics and path-dependent returns. This chapter explores the current regulatory landscape surrounding LIETFs and their characteristics, including risk and return, and also discusses their potential effects on the capital markets.

Growth

Products that offer investors the leveraged and/or inverse return of an underlying index as an ETF are relatively new. However, mutual funds have been offering this return structure to investors for more than 20 years. Rydex introduced the first leveraged mutual fund in 1993 with the Rydex Nova fund and the first inverse mutual fund in 1994 with the Rydex Ursa fund. The design of these open-end mutual funds was to produce 150 percent and –150 percent of the daily return of the S&P 500 index, respectively. In 2005, ETFs offering this return structure became available to investors when Swedish firm Xact issued the Xact Bull and Bear funds. Xact listed these funds on the NASDAQ OMX Stockholm exchange and offered investors 150 percent and –150 percent exposure of the daily return of the OMX Stockholm 30 (OMXS30) Index, which is a market-cap-weighted index of the 30 most actively traded issues on the Stockholm Stock Exchange (OMX Stockholm 30 Index 2014).

ProShares was the first provider to bring LIETFs to U.S. exchanges in June 2006(Spence 2006). Since then the products have grown rapidly both in terms of the number available and AUM. A dozen firms have now introduced their own versions with the largest providers being ProShares, Direxion, and Powershares (ETFdb 2014b). Table 10.2 lists the firms, number of products, and cumulative AUM.

Three years after ProShares introduced the first LIETFs traded in the United States, the firm announced it would bring to market the first ETFs aimed at delivering three times the exposure. The benchmark was the S&P 500 index. The firm launched the ProShares UltraPro S&P500 fund and the ProShares UltraPro Short S&P500 fund on the NYSE Arca on July 1, 2009. ProShares Group Chairman and CEO Michael Sapir's motivation for bringing the first triple-levered ETF to the market was that "as the

Table 10.2 **Overview of Leveraged and Inverse Exchange-Traded Fund Providers**

Firm Name	*Number of Fund Offerings*	*AUM ($ millions)*
Deutsche Asset Management	1	6.50
US Commodity Funds	1	11.30
JP Morgan	2	15.70
Van Eck	2	41.30
Advisor Shares	2	190.00
Barclays iPath	16	434.00
Credit Suisse	2	471.00
Powershares	24	637.00
UBS	12	1,494.00
Velocity Shares	14	2,170.00
Direxion	56	7,789.00
Proshares	131	24,827.00

Note: This table lists the largest U.S. LIETF sponsors by AUM and the number of LIETFs each firm offered on September 30, 2014.

Source: ETFdb 2014b.

leader in short and LETFs, [ProShares is] committed to giving investors more choices to manage risk and pursue returns"(ProShares 2009, p.1).

The products have since grown rapidly both in terms of the number available and AUM. As Figure 10.1 shows, seven LETFs and/or IETFs were available globally at the end of 2005, with a combined $141 million in AUM. By the end of May 2014, 893 such

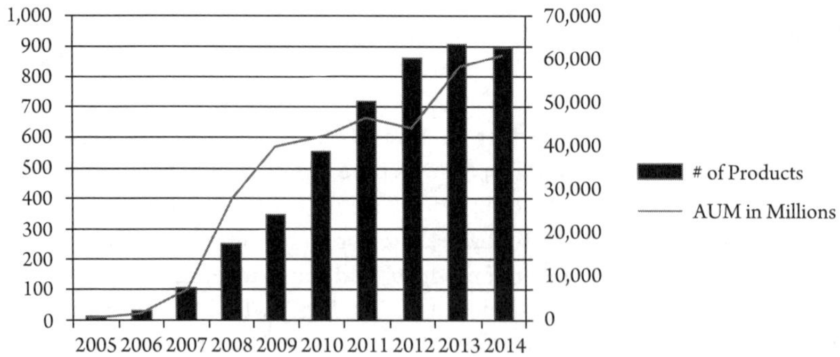

Figure 10.1 Global Growth of Leveraged and Inverse Exchange-Traded Funds. This figure illustrates the growth of LIETFs globally both in the number of products available and the cumulative amount of AUM. Source: Data obtained from Lydon 2014.

products existed, totaling $61 billion in assets. According to Lydon (2014),this figure represents an average annual increase of more than 71 percent in the number of funds and 96 percent in AUM. The number of funds and their AUM has exhibited an upward trend since these products entered the market in 2005. Of particular note is that this period spans the financial crisis of 2007–2008, when a large-scale unwinding of leverage in financial markets occurred globally. Through May 2014, while the number of funds modestly decreased after the start of the year, investor dollars have continued to flow into these products and AUM has risen.

Legal Issues

This section discusses the issues and misunderstandings commonly associated with LIETFs and regulators' attempts to educate the investing public. LIETFs are most commonly structured as open-end funds (OEFs). OEFs are registered with the Securities and Exchange Commission (SEC) under the Investment Company Act of 1940, and ETF providers must file for an exemption from certain provisions of the 1940 Act in order to operate. To a lesser extent, LIETFs are structured as debt instruments, in which case they are referred to as exchange-traded notes (ETNs). ETNs can avoid registration with the SEC under the Investment Company Act of 1940 allowing them to operate in a more opaque manner and use derivative strategies to a greater extent than their open-end counterparts. Regardless of the structural format the fund sponsor uses, LIETFs must register their securities with the SEC under the Securities Act of 1933.

Like other investment companies, LIETFs are required to draft a prospectus and make it available to investors. The fund must also file a registration statement with the SEC, which includes a prospectus that describes the investment to potential investors as well as a summary prospectus and statement of additional information (SAI). Shortly after these forms are filed with the SEC, they are made publically available. After an LIETF is successfully listed on an exchange and trading begins, the fund must file periodic financial data that are available to shareholders and potential investors (United States Senate 2014).

The Financial Industry Regulatory Authority (FINRA) has taken notice of investor use of and confusion over LIETFs and has especially called into question the suitability of the products for retail investors (ETFdb 2014a). Considering LIETFs' complex use of derivatives and path-dependent pricing mechanism, the likelihood that an individual investor has a strong understanding of these products is quite low. Individual investors are drawn to these products because of the ease with which they can implement hedging strategies and degree to which they can use leverage (Shum 2011).

The SEC Act of 1934 established margin requirements in the United States following the Great Depression. The Federal Reserve Board now sets these requirements. Investors are limited to borrowing no more than 50 percent of the value of their suitable assets (Humphries 2010). This restriction means that if investors hold strong bullish views about U.S. stocks, the most they could purchase would be 100 percent of their account, plus the additional 50 percent borrowed, making the exposure 150 percent.

Using a LETF, investors can, with a single purchase, achieve exposure of up to 300 percent using a fund such as the Direxion Daily S&P 500 Bull 3X, which promises to return three times the daily movement of the S&P500 index.

Besides being able to exceed current margin requirements, investors can implement short strategies, whereas before the introduction of IETFs, they may have lacked the expertise or faced restrictions (Anderson, Curcio, and Guirguis 2014). For example, funds such as ProShares Short S&P500 promise to deliver the opposite return of the daily movement of the S&P 500 index allowing investors to short the entire S&P 500 index while technically going long an equity investment.

Both the SEC and FINRA have taken steps to warn financial advisors and educate investors about LIETFs. In June 2009, for example, FINRA (2009, p. 1) released Regulatory Notice 09–31, which reminded those selling the products that:

> Recommendations to customers must be suitable and based on a full understanding of the terms and features of the product recommended; sales materials related to leveraged and inverse ETFs must be fair and accurate; and firms must have adequate supervisory procedures in place to ensure that these obligations are met.

In August 2009, the SEC and FINRA issued an investor alert titled "Leveraged and Inverse ETFs: Specialized Products with Extra Risks for Buy-and-Hold Investors." This release not only discusses the daily pricing objectives and background information but also provides examples of the inconsistency of the funds' stated daily return objective and the long-term performance (Securities Exchange Commission 2009).

LIETF providers were the targets of several lawsuits after the financial crisis of 2007–2008. Perhaps the most publicized example was in August 2009, when Labaton Sucharow LLP filed a class action lawsuit against ProShares UltraShort Real Estate Fund (SRS) (ProShares Investment Fraud Lawsuit 2009). The suit alleged that the registration statement of ProShares, the largest provider of LIETFs, contained misleading information and violated the Securities Act of 1933 (Labaton Sucharow LLP 2009). As described in the prospectus, the fund's objective is to deliver twice the daily inverse return of the Dow Jones U.S. Real Estate Index (DJREI). Investors, not understanding the path dependency of returns and the fact that as variability of returns increases, compound return decreases (Sullivan 2009), were expecting this objective to be achievable over a longer holding period. When the DJREI fell more than 39 percent between January 2 and December 17, 2008 and the fund SRS decreased more than 48 percent instead of increasing the 78 percent some expected, this market reaction shocked misinformed or uneducated shareholders. This lawsuit, however, was eventually dismissed in 2012 after Judge Koeltl ruled that the disclosures properly stated the objectives "in plain English" (Proshares 2012).

As financial innovation continues to change the way individuals and institutions invest, the regulatory bodies that govern and oversee financial markets will have to continually adapt. Additionally, closely monitoring the effect these products have on the capital markets is essential to ensure the integrity of the U.S. financial system.

Holding Period and Returns

When used properly, LIETFs can be effective tools for both achieving growth objectives and pursuing hedging strategies. While most funds clearly state the return objective in their marketing materials, investors would be wise to consult a fund's prospectus to confirm the holding period for its return objective. The majority of funds attempt to earn the multiple or inverse return of the underlying index over a single day. As a result, investors cannot expect to receive the stated return multiple for holdings periods that exceed the fund's reset period or frequency of *marking-to-market*, which is the process of adding gains to or subtracting losses from the margin account daily, based on the change in settlement prices from one day to the next.

Consider the following example summarized in Table 10.3. An investor purchases $10,000 worth of a 3X LETF that tracks Alpha Index having an initial value of 1,000. At the end of the first day, Alpha Index increases 1 percent to a value of 1,010. The ETF magnifies this increase by three times, increasing the investment value to $10,300, which is growth rate of 3 percent. If the investor exits the position at the end-of-day, he would achieve the ETF's stated target return before transaction fees and taxes. However, if this investor keeps his dollars in the ETF for an entire week, the ETF's overall weekly return would suffer from the oscillation of the index.

Continuing with this example for a second day, if Alpha Index experiences another 1 percent gain, the ending index value would be 1020.1 and the LETF investment would now be worth $10,609. Now, if Alpha Index falls by 1 percent for the next two consecutive days, its value at the end of the fourth day would be 999.8, and the value of the LETF investment would have fallen to $9,982.01. Finally, if on the fifth day the index ends the week on a positive note and increases 1 percent, the value would be 1009.798, and the value of the investment would be $10,281.47.

Table 10.3 **Index Return versus Performance of 3x Leveraged Exchange-Traded Funds**

	Alpha Index	*Article I.*	*3X ETF ($)*
Alpha Index	1000.00		10,000.00
Day 1 (1% gain)	1010.00		10,300.00
Day 2 (1% gain)	1020.10		10,609.00
Day 3 (1% loss)	1009.90		10,290.73
Day 4 (1% loss)	999.80		9,982.01
Day 5 (1% gain)	1009.80		10,281.47
Cumulative Five-Day % Return	0.98		2.81
3 times Cumulative Five-Day % Return	2.94		

Note: This table compares the difference in returns between a hypothetical index return and the return an investor would experience holding a 3x LETF over the same five-day period.

Source: Authors' calculations.

Recapping the week's return, the fund experienced three up days and two down days, and each day the Alpha Index moved in a corresponding direction by 1 percent. The ending value of the index on the fifth day was 1009.798, which represents a weekly return of 0.98 percent. The ending value of the 3X LETF investment was $10,281.47 or a weekly return of 2.815 percent. This return falls short of the 2.939 percent return some might expect by multiplying the index's weekly return by 3. The reason for the difference is that both the leverage in the fund and the effects of daily compounding magnified the fund's losses on the third and fourth days.

Consider the situation in which the Alpha Index experienced two weeks of alternating returns with each 1 percent daily gain followed by a 1 percent daily loss the return on the index after 10 days, with five up days and five down days would be –0.05 percent. If an investor owned a 3X LETF on the Alpha Index over that period, his return would not be –0.15 percent but rather –0.449 percent. Pushing out the effects of daily compounding and leverage a month would result in a loss on the index of –0.1 percent and a loss on the LETF investment of –0.9 percent. Extrapolating this process for a year assuming 250 trading days, the Alpha Index would have declined –1.24 percent and the ETF investment would have declined –10.64 percent.

This example shows returns for the LETF moving in the same direction as the underlying index. However, an index can increase in value over the course of the year while the LETF tracking that index can actually lose value. Assume the Alpha Index experienced a year-end rally and increased on the last day of trading by 2 percent. Holding all else constant and alternating the index with 1 percent daily gains followed by 1 percent daily losses except on the last day of trading, the yearly gain on the index would be 1.75 percent. Would investors owning a 3X LETF receive a 5.25 percent return? In fact, the return would be –2.35 percent and an investor who bought a LETF tracking an index that increased in value throughout the year would have lost money. This result is due to the effect leverage has on daily compounding and the path dependency of the ETF's returns. Tables 10.4 and 10.5 show the hypothetical difference between an index return and the return an investor would experience holding a 3x LETF for each of the four scenarios discussed in this section.

Historical Returns

The long-term return of LIETFs has the potential to deviate from the stated daily return objective. A quick review of the historical performance of these funds and their underlying benchmarks helps to illustrate the deviation in performance. For example, the SPDR ETF that tracks the S&P 500 index (*SPY*) has had a cumulative return of 61.8 percent between 2012 and 2014. Over that same period, the Powershares UltraPro S&P 500 (*UPRO*), which is designed to return three times the daily index return, had a cumulative return of 243.8 percent, or 3.9 times the index return. Conversely, the Direxion S&P 500 Bear 3x Fund (SPXS) had a cumulative return of –83.7 percent, the return multiple was 1.35 times the annual return (in absolute value) but was substantially less than three times the daily return objective (in absolute value). Table 10.6 provides a review of the actual performance and the returns of other popular indexes and associated LIETFs.

Table 10.4 **Two-Week and One-Month Return Patterns of a 3x Leveraged Exchange-Traded Fund**

Panel A. Two-Week Hypothetical Return			*Panel B. One-Month Hypothetical Return*		
Day	*Alpha Index*	*3x ETF Return ($)*	*Day*	*Alpha Index*	*3x ETF Return ($)*
0	1000.00	10,000.00	0	1000.00	10,000.00
1	1010.00	10,300.00	1	1010.00	10,300.00
2	999.90	9,991.00	2	999.90	9,991.00
3	1009.90	10,290.73	3	1009.90	10,290.73
4	999.80	9,982.01	4	999.80	9,982.01
5	1009.80	10,281.47	5	1009.80	10,281.47
6	999.70	9,973.02	6	999.70	9,973.02
7	1009.70	10,272.22	7	1009.70	10,272.22
8	999.60	9,964.05	8	999.60	9,964.05
9	1009.60	10,262.97	9	1009.60	10,262.97
10	999.50	9,955.08	10	999.50	9,955.08
Two-Week. Return (%)	−0.05	−0.45	11	1009.50	10,253.73
3x Two-Week Return (%)	−0.15		12	999.40	9,946.12
			13	1009.39	10,244.50
			14	999.30	9,937.17
			15	1009.29	10,235.28
			16	999.20	9,928.23
			17	1009.19	10,226.07
			18	999.10	9,919.29
			19	1009.09	10,216.87
			20	999.00	9,910.36
			One-Month Return (%)	−0.10	−0.90
			3x One-Month Return (%)	−0.30	

Note: Panels A and B shows the hypothetical difference between an index return and the return an investor would experience holding a 3x LETF. The holding periods represent investing in the LETF for both a two-week and a one-month period.

Source: Authors' calculations.

Table 10.5 **One-Year Return Patterns of a 3x Leveraged Exchange-Traded Funds**

	Panel A. One-Year Hypothetical Return				*Panel B. One-Year Hypothetical Return with Rally*		
	Day	*Alpha Index*	*3x ETF Return ($)*		*Day*	*Alpha Index*	*3x ETF Return ($)*
First 10 Days of Returns	0	1000.00	10,000.00	**First 10 Days of Returns**	0	1000.00	10,000.00
	1	1010.00	10,300.00		1	1010.00	10,300.00
	2	999.90	9,991.00		2	999.90	9,991.00
	3	1009.90	10,290.73		3	1009.90	10,290.73
	4	999.80	9,982.01		4	999.80	9,982.01
	5	1009.80	10,281.47		5	1009.80	10,281.47
	6	999.70	9,973.02		6	999.70	9,973.02
	7	1009.70	10,272.22		7	1009.70	10,272.22
	8	999.60	9,964.05		8	999.60	9,964.05
	9	1009.60	10,262.97		9	1009.60	10,262.97
	10	999.50	9,955.08		10	999.50	9,955.08

continued

Table 10.5 **(continued)**

	Panel A. One-Year Hypothetical Return				*Panel B. One-Year Hypothetical Return with Rally*		
	Day	*Alpha Index*	*3x ETF Return ($)*		*Day*	*Alpha Index*	*3x ETF Return ($)*
Last 10 Days of Returns	241	997.95	9,245.11	***Last 10 Days of Returns***	241	997.95	9,245.11
	242	987.97	8,967.76		242	987.97	8,967.76
	243	997.85	9,236.79		243	997.85	9,236.79
	244	987.87	8,959.69		244	987.87	8,959.69
	245	997.75	9,228.48		245	997.75	9,228.48
	246	987.77	8,951.63		246	987.77	8,951.63
	247	997.65	9,220.18		247	997.65	9,220.18
	248	987.68	8,943.57		248	987.68	8,943.57
	249	997.55	9,211.88		249	997.55	9,211.88
	250	987.58	8,935.52		250	1017.50	9,764.59
	One-Year Return (%)	−1.24	−10.64		One-Year Return (%)	1.75	−2.35
	3x One-Year Return (%)	−3.73			3x One-Year Return (%)	5.25	

Note: Panels A through B shows the hypothetical difference between an index return and the return an investor would experience holding a 3x LETF. The holding periods represent investing in the LETF for two separate one-year periods. Panel A assumes alternating daily returns of +1.0 and −1.0 percent. The Alpha Index in Panel B assumes the same alternating return pattern increases in value on the final two days of the year.

Table 10.6 **Historical Return versus a Multiple**

		Three-Year Actual					Three-Year Theoretical				
Index	*Plain Vanilla ETF (%)*	*–3x (%)*	*–2x (%)*	*–1x (%)*	*2x (%)*	*3x (%)*	*–3 (%)*	*–2 (%)*	*–1 (%)*	*2 (%)*	*3 (%)*
Nasdaq 100	65.13	–85.83	–71.17	–45.18	147.17	252.72	–195.39	–130.26	–65.13	130.26	195.39
S&P 500	61.84	–83.74	–68.02	–42.69	139.63	243.75	–185.52	–123.68	–61.84	123.68	185.52
Russell 2000	57.24	–87.25	–72.14	–45.10	117.87	181.32	–171.72	–114.48	–57.24	114.48	171.72
DJIA	48.84	–77.58	–61.84	–37.48	104.97	174.84	–146.52	–97.68	–48.84	97.68	146.52

Note: This table illustrates the difference between the actual performances of LETFs versus what might be expected by multiplying the return of the underlying index by the fund's leveraged or inverse multiplier.

Source: Bloomberg Terminal Data (September 30, 2014).

Rebalancing Frequency and Returns

Investors seeking to achieve the daily return objective of an LIETF for an extended period must adopt an active management approach. In order for investors to ensure their ETF position maintains the desired level of magnified exposure, they must sell shares after an increase and buy shares after a decrease. These actions reset the asset base in proportion with the target level of leverage.

Because active management strategies result in additional costs over buy-and-hold strategies, investors seeking to maximize ETF returns might explore the following approaches. The first approach is to implement a rebalancing strategy where investors might choose to rebalance their exposure on specific calendar frequency (e.g., monthly or quarterly) or when the ETF returns vary from the index returns by a pre-determined percentage (e.g.,±10 percent). Establishing a rebalancing corridor allows for the flexibility of moderate deviations of exposure that are sometimes only temporary, without requiring a daily adjustment of the number of shares that are held. This approach reduces the investor's transaction costs and the frequency of their taxable events (ProShares 2013).

The second approach is to consider using a monthly rebalanced LIETF. Fund providers such as Direxion now offer LIETFs with the objective of producing a specific leveraged return over a one-month period rather than a one-day period (Direxion Investments 2014). A key characteristic is that the fund's stated leverage is only achievable if investors purchase the ETF on the monthly rebalancing date. Because the fund is not rebalanced daily, investors who buy this type of fund mid-month cannot be certain their leverage will match the stated return objective in the prospectus. This difference is again due to the ETFs variability of returns throughout the month.

Consider the following example: A monthly 3X LETF returns 69 percent for the 30-day period against the Alpha Index return of 21 percent, for a leverage ratio of 3.29. An investor entering this investment on the first day of the 30-day period would experience the full magnification of returns, whereas an investor entering this investment on the fifteenth day would experience a different leverage ratio. Another investor's leveraged return is dependent upon the performance of the index and the nature of the fund (e.g., bull, bear, two times, and three times). Table 10.7 provides a summary table to illustrate this concept (Johnston 2012).

Enhancing Returns

LETFs provide investors with magnified exposure to a long position while only requiring a fraction of the capital. This framework leaves capital available for investment in other opportunities and might increase their overall return. Consider two investors who each own a portfolio valued at $10,000 currently consisting of cash. Both investors are bullish on the S&P 500 index and desire a return equal to 150 percent of the index's movement. On the first day, the first investor purchases $5,000 worth of the ProShares UltraPro S&P 500 3x Fund(UPRO), giving him the target 150 percent($15,000) worth of exposure to the index. The second investor must borrow $5,000 on margin at 4 percent interest and purchases $15,000 of the unleveraged SPDR S&P 500 ETF (SPY).

Table 10.7 **Leverage Ratio of 3x Monthly Rebalanced Exchange-Traded Fund**

The Differing Returns of Monthly 3X Leveraged ETFs Based on the Investor's Purchase Date									
	Alpha Index Value	*Alpha Index Return (%)*	*ETF Value ($)*	*ETF Return (%)*	*Alpha Index's 30-Day Return (%)*	*Investor 30-Day Return (%)*	*Investor 1 30-Day Leverage Ratio*	*Investor2 15-Day Return (%)*	*Investor 2 15-Day Leverage Ratio*
Day 1	1,000	—	1,000	—	—	—	—	—	—
Day 15	1,100	10	1,300	30	—	—	—	—	—
Day 30	1,210	10	1,690	30	21	69	3.29	30	1.43

Note: This table illustrates how the purchase date affects an investor's return when investing in a monthly rebalanced LETF.

Source: Johnston 2012.

Both investors have the same effective exposure to the index, but the first investor has only risked $5,000 while the second investor has risked $15,000 and introduced an additional cost of $200 margin interest. Also, the first investor has retained a $10,000 pool of capital that should earn the risk-free rate. As an alternative, this investor could use the funds to buy investments with less than perfect correlation to the S&P 500 index thereby reducing the overall amount of risk taken and increasing the portfolio's Sharpe ratio (Isaacman 2008). The *Sharpe ratio* is a measure of risk-adjusted performance that compares excess returns to the total risk of the account (i.e., portfolio), where total risk is measured by the account's standard deviation of returns.

Investors can also enhance their returns by using an IETF to profit from a negative outlook on an index. Traditionally, this process would require investors to short sell a basket of stocks that replicates the index. This action allows them to profit by selling the borrowed shares, waiting for the price to fall, and then buying the shares back at the lower price, profiting from the difference between the sale price and the purchase price. IETFs allow less technical investors to implement this strategy while also making the strategy available to more market participants.

IETFs also offer additional advantages to traditional short selling. First, IETFs track the performance of an entire index rather than a single stock. This strategy allows investors to profit from a negative outlook on a sector's overall performance rather than the performance of an individual equity security. Second, IETFs do not require borrowing shares and avoid subsequent interest charges that reduce a short seller's return. Third, IETFs require no posting of margin and limit an investor's loss to the amount of capital invested. By contrast, traditional short selling introduces the potential for margin calls and an "infinite" loss, when the investor is forced to repurchase shares at the market price, which theoretically have no upper bound. Fourth, a short seller must pay back any dividends earned on the borrowed shares, whereas IETF investors avoid this requirement. Finally, investors can own IETFs, which are technically a long equity position in a security traded on an exchange, in their Individual Retirement Accounts (IRAs). Doing so provides them with the ability to make a directional bet on an index that they expect to fall in value (Isaacman 2008).

Sophisticated investors may seek to combine long and short positions to achieve *alpha* or excess risk-adjusted return while minimizing beta (systematic risk). This goal is accomplished by matching a long position in a specific stock with a short position in the stock's sector. For example, an investor bearish on the overall financial sector yet bullish on Wells Fargo (WFC) could buy shares of WFC and simultaneously buy shares of ProShares Short Financials ETF (SEF), an IETF designed to return the inverse of the Dow Jones U.S. Financials Index. Together these investments reduce exposure to the financial sector's market risk, while allowing the investor to benefit from the returns of WFC. Thus, while strategies involving LIETFs carry the potential for higher return volatility, these products add a large degree of versatility for portfolio managers.

Expenses and Returns

Several different cost components are associated with the purchase and ownership of LIETFs. Perhaps the most well-known cost is the *expense ratio*. This fee is, on average,

0.95 percent but can range anywhere between 0.30 to 3.29 percent (ETFdb 2014b). Brokers also usually charge commissions for buying and selling ETF shares just as they would for the purchase of shares of a common stock and hence investors should consider these costs. They also should factor in the bid-ask spread when calculating return (Schwab 2014). A less actively traded ETF with lower volume and lower liquidity has a higher spread than a more actively traded ETF. Also, the spread reduces an investor's return when exiting the position.

Fund managers using derivatives such as options and futures often borrow and hold a cash position to mark-to-market and settle daily with ease and flexibility. The interest charged on the borrowed funds is an expense that is passed on to shareholders by a daily adjustment to the ETF's NAV and is typically around 1 to 2 basis points. A *basis point* is one-hundredth of one percent. Holding this investment for a single day does not materially affect the investment's return, but the longer an investor maintains the position, the greater is the drag on the investment's performance (Isaacman 2008).

Taxes are an expense that cannot be avoided unless the investor holds the investment in a tax-deferred or tax-exempt account. Effective strategies involving LIETFs often involve short-term holding periods, sometimes no more than one or two days. This strategy could cause a U.S. investor to be subject to a higher short-term capital gains rate than had the investment been held for 12 months or longer, which is the current threshold for a capital gain to be considered long-term.

The return structure of LIETFs involves a combination of the factors previously discussed. Experienced investors who understand the products' mechanics and components may find them useful in certain strategies but must be mindful of each of the variables associated with the fund's return including the effects of compounding, leverage, and expenses. These variables in isolation can lead to unexpected returns and when combined under the umbrella of LIETFs, the effects can magnify one another.

Risks to Shareholders

Investors in LIETFs should consider their risk exposure, including some risks that are not entirely obvious. The leveraged structure and use of derivatives inherent in the majority of LIETFs converge to create a unique risk profile for these products. Besides discussing the deviations of long-term returns from the stated daily return objectives reviewed previously, this section tries to build on the understanding of the sources of *tracking error*, which is the difference between the return of the fund and the underlying benchmark, and the different risk factors associated with these products (Lu, Wang, and Zhang 2009).

Investors in LIETFs are exposed to four elements of financial risk: (1) market risk, (2) credit risk, (3) liquidity risk, and (4) sovereign risk. The majority of LIETFs track equity indexes and all trade on stock exchanges. Therefore, the primary form of financial risk that LIETF investors face when the investment is considered in isolation is market risk. *Market risk*, also called *systematic risk*, is defined as change in an investment value because of an overall change in broad equity market prices. Market risk includes various sources including interest rates, recessions, and unpredictable events that cause major sell-offs in equity markets, the so-called "black swan." Eliminating market risk is impossible without using a hedging strategy to counter the equity market exposure.

Besides market risk, LIETF investors also face currency risk, which can create the potential for increased tracking error. *Currency risk* is the risk associated with the uncertainty about the exchange rate at which proceeds in the foreign currency can be converted into the investor's home currency. Many LIETFs enter into swap agreements with other ETF providers in which they receive a multiple of the return or inverse return a traditional ETF tracking the same underlying index. If the "counter" fund tracks the index of a foreign market, it may use American Depository Receipts (ADRs) and/or invest directly in a foreign exchange to achieve the desired exposure. Both of these investments carry currency risk. These underlying investments subject shareholders to fluctuations in the local currency if the fund manager does not hedge against changes in exchange rates. If the fund aims to fully hedge currency risk, implementing the hedge comes at the cost of investing in and rebalancing the derivative positions. These costs are in turn passed on to shareholders and lower the fund's return. If left unhedged, as exchange rates change, the total return of the fund will deviate from the foreign indexes return and could produce an unexpected result.

LIETF investors also face *credit risk*, which is the risk of loss caused by a counterparty's failure to make a timely payment or the change in value of a financial instrument based on changes in default risk. LIETFs use various derivatives to achieve their stated return objectives. Besides options and futures contracts, which trade on an exchange, a diverse lineup of over-the-counter (OTC) derivatives such as forwards and swaps exists. When an option and/or futures contract is bought or sold over a regulated exchange, such as the Chicago Board Options, delivery by the counterparty is guaranteed by the clearinghouse. The clearinghouse acts as the buyer to every seller and the seller to every buyer. As a result, the clearinghouse allows either side of the trade to reverse positions at a future date without having to contact the other side of the initial trade. This process allows investors or traders to enter the market knowing that they can reverse their position.

When investors enter into an OTC contract, however, they assume the risk that the other party fails to deliver and defaults on the promise made. This risk is called *default risk* or *counterparty risk*, which is the risk of loss if an issuer or counterparty does not fulfill its contractual obligations. Little immediate recourse is often available in the event of a default until court proceedings are completed. Although little empirical evidence shows that counterparty risk has a negative impact on LIETF returns, the use of derivatives by funds substantially increases this theoretical risk.

In a more traditional sense, investors in LIETFs that hold fixed-income securities also assume credit risk. Investing in funds that provide cash flows through periodic interest payments exposes the shareholder to the risk of not receiving the full payment of interest and/or principal on the specified payment date. This risk is measured by ratings companies such as Moody's and Standard & Poor's and is as a letter grade with AAA being the highest (best) rating and C being the lowest non-default rating.

Liquidity risk is yet another factor that exists for LIETF investors. *Liquidity risk* is the risk that a financial instrument cannot be bought or sold without a substantial concession in price because of the market's potential inability to efficiently accommodate the desired trading size. While the funds are traded on exchanges, which typically increase liquidity and make buying or selling easier for investors, funds that are traded less frequently and/or are more difficult to price can incur wider bid-ask spreads. Since LIETFs often gain exposure to leverage by using derivatives that are not traded in a secondary market, the price transparency of the fund's holdings may not be readily available. This type of derivatives exposure increases the difficulty for investors of accurately determining the fund's NAV. This outcome can cause a suboptimal environment for execution that may increase the bid-ask spread and further reduces returns driving up volatility (Phillip Capital 2014).

Funds that offer exposure to government-issued securities subject shareholders to *sovereign risk*, which is the risk that a government lacks the ability or willingness to pay its contractual debt obligations. In the past, some emerging markets have had problems covering interest and principal payments on their debt including the infamous 1998 Russian default and more recent sovereign debt problem in Argentina (Thomson Reuters 2014). As the foreign economies become more integrated, additional examples are likely to emerge and translate into a loss of value for debt holders.

Examining the mechanics of these funds shows how different forms of risk combine to create a unique risk profile. Besides these risks, other sources of tracking error exist. As previously discussed, for example, lengthening the holding period, due largely to an effect known as volatility drag, can adversely affect a fund. *Volatility drag* refers to the loss in value when a portfolio falls by say 10 percent and subsequently earns the same 10 percent, but ultimately returns less than the initial investment. While daily returns may or may not be achieved over the duration of a longer holding period, the disconnect between the levels of the tracked index and the ETF share price, combined with the effect of daily compounding, create divergences in the performance of an ETF and the index to which it is benchmarked. This divergence increases with the length of the holding period, due not only to volatility drag as demonstrated earlier but also from the mechanics of the fund itself.

Because investors frequently use derivatives to provide the desired exposure and derivative contracts have finite lives, the fund will likely have to roll the position forward and take a new position in a similar contract with a later expiration date to maintain its desired exposure. The difference in pricing between the previously held contract and the newly purchased contract can be positive or negative, depending on the underlying asset and the costs or benefits from physically holding it. The component of return that is affected by rolling over futures contracts is known as roll yield. *Roll yield* is the yield due to a difference between the spot price and futures price, or a difference between two futures prices with different expiration dates. If the asset is in *contango*, then the forward prices are higher than spot prices and the manager will have to pay a higher cost at expiration to invest in the longer term contract. This process will result in negative roll yield and can have a negative effect on the shareholders.

A longer holding period and high degree of leverage enhance the risks associated with LIETFs. As the holding period increases, each of the components of risk also has the potential to increase. A longer holding period results in a greater opportunity for negative and more substantial roll yield and higher rebalancing costs. Greater potential also exists for damage due to the four financial risks previously discussed and counterparty risk. Each of these factors blends together to create an uncommon risk profile.

Leverage has the effect of magnifying each individual source of risk and amplifying the total risk to shareholders.

The different sources of risk contribute to the volatility of a fund's returns, which can lead to tracking error. So far, this chapter identifies which risks these funds contain and how their composition and management produce a unique set of risk profiles. It also shows how increasing the length of the holding period increases these risks and that leverage increases overall risk levels. All of these factors put the value of a fund's share price at risk, which ultimately can lead to large and costly tracking error.

Effect on Market Volatility and Pricing

LIETFs have come into focus recently by regulators, industry experts, and the media as volatility increased during and after the financial crisis of 2007–2008. This time period includes the "flash crash" of May 2010 and August 2011 as the European sovereign debt problems took center stage. The *flash crash* was a U.S. stock market crash on May 6, 2010, in which the Dow Jones Industrial Average (DJIA) plunged about 1,000 points or about 9 percent but recovered those losses within minutes. In August 2011, stock markets experienced a sharp drop in stock prices across the United States, Middle East, Europe, and Asia. This fall resulted from several factors including fears of contagion of the European sovereign debt crisis to Spain and Italy, as well as concerns over France's current AAA rating, and also concerns about slow U.S. economic growth and its credit rating being downgraded.

The reason LIETFs have been called into question arises from their use of derivative contracts to replicate their stated return objective, which is often one, two, or three times the daily return or inverse of the daily return of a particular index. While LIETFs often replicate commodity and fixed-income markets, this chapter examines their effect on the U.S. stock market. This section reviews whether the construction and trading practices of LIETFs lead to a distortion in the pricing and volatility of the underlying securities and U.S. equity market as a whole.

Because marking-to-market for both future and swap contracts occurs at the end of the trading day, the counterparties to the derivative contracts adjust their hedges at the end of the day. To maintain the proper exposure, the counterparty must buy or sell the underlying security. This process is one of the contributing factors that leads to the increase in volume witnessed during the last hour of trading (Haryanto, Hejazi, Rodier, and Shum 2014).

Besides the increase in order flow resulting from the counterparties hedging, trading in the futures markets has a direct effect on the price and volatility of the associated equities. According to Anderson et al. (2014), futures trading increases the volatility of the underlying spot market. The Commodity Futures Trading Commission (CFTC) and SEC brought the relationship between price volatility of individual stocks and futures to the attention of the U.S. Joint Advisory Committee on Emerging Regulatory Issues in the wake of the infamous May 6, 2010, "flash crash." Although various factors contributed, perpetuated, and corrected the sharp sell-off and recovery in the U.S. stock market during the flash crash, some believe that the algorithmic trading that endeavored to profit from arbitrage and in turn keep futures contracts and security prices moving in lockstep played a role. A report confirmed that cross-market arbitrage between the S&P 500 E-mini contracts and the ETF SPY exists, and "price changes in the E-mini generally lead price changes in SPY and in the basket of underlying stocks"(CFTF and SEC 2010, p. 17).

Importance of Volatility

Much academic and governmental interest exists on the topic of volatility and what contributes to changes in the volatility of the overall stock market. According to Anderson et al. (2014, p. 1), "volatility is synonymous with risk and thus is central to the theory and practice of asset pricing, asset allocation, and risk management." Providers and proponents of LIETFs present the relatively small size of AUM as the central theorem of their argument that LIETFs do not adversely affect market volatility (United States Senate 2012). At the end of 2014, LIETFs held about $40 billion in AUM, accounting for a very low proportion of the total market capitalization on U.S. exchanges, which totaled more than $23 trillion in January 2014 (Bloomberg Terminal 2014).

Regardless of the relative size of LIETFs compared to the overall market, market volatility increased after these products were introduced in 2006 (Shum 2011). Although various contributing factors led to the increase in volatility since the financial crisis of 2007–2008, LIETFs have come under examination. For example, the Committee on Banking, Housing and Urban Affairs held a hearing in October 2011 on "Market Microstructure: Examination of Exchange Traded Funds"(United States Senate 2012). Understanding the effect that the introduction and growth of LIETFs have had on market volatility is a natural course of action considering their complex strategies and the increase focus on investor protection.

INCREASING VOLUME AND VOLATILITY

Fund managers trading in the futures market and counterparty hedging of derivative contracts both have the potential to increase volatility in the stock market and underlying equity securities (Tuzun 2014). LIETFs rebalance toward the end of the trading session anticipating derivative contracts being marked-to-market. While the amount of assets that are held in LIETFs is currently only 0.2 percent of the overall market, studies including Anderson et al. (2014) and Haryanto et al. (2014) show that they account for a substantial amount of end-of-day trading volume. Understanding how the counterparties in derivative contracts hedge their exposure is fundamental to understanding how the limited amount of assets in LIETFs contributes to the end-of-day volume. As swap counterparties hedge their positions, whether they are on the opposite side of long or short ETFs, they do so by trading in the same direction as the market. As the market increases in value, the counterparty to a long ETF must increase its exposure by purchasing stocks, whereas the counterparty to a short ETF must buy stocks in order to close out its short positions (Haryanto et al. 2014).

Haryanto et al. (2014, p. 3) estimate, "If the market moves by one percent during the day, leverage ETF rebalancing could account for up to 16.8 percent of the market-on-close volume." Although some difference of opinion exists about the size of the volume because of LIETFs, several studies provide similar results. For example, Tuzun (2014) reports that, in the last hour of trading, flows are 2 to 3 percent of volume for average large cap stocks and can be as large as 18 percent of volume for small cap stocks.

Besides the increase in trading volume, Anderson et al. (2014) conclude that the daily rebalancing of LIETFs leads to an increase in end-of-day price volatility. The authors also find both traditional ETFs and LIETFs significantly increase the volatility of the underlying U.S. real estate stock prices. Hatyanto et al. (2014) find a statistically significant increase in volatility at the end of the trading session, but this effect is only economically significant during days when the highest expected rebalancing volume occurs. Trainor (2010) counters this claim by noting that the increase in volatility can be explained spuriously.

Price Efficiencies

If investors feel strongly that a particular sector is overvalued and they are unable or lack the expertise to execute a short sale, they can avoid investing in that sector (Anderson et al. 2014). However, with the advent of IETFs, these same investors can go "long" from the standpoint that they are purchasing an investment that expresses their view, which is a return that is opposite the sector's daily movement. The underlying stock in this case will experience the negative price pressure associated with the futures activity initiated by the fund provider. With LETFs, besides achieving the desired direction of returns, the result can be enhanced to the upside or downside by a multiple of up to three times the daily movement of the index. Individual investors can now circumvent margin limits or even use those margin limits to increase their effective leverage over the three times exposure that some LETFs provide (Humphries 2010). In this way, LIETFs permit using sophisticated strategies that some investors otherwise would not be allowed or capable of implementing.

Price Distortions

As LIETFs grow in popularity so will the amount of trading volume by the providers and their counterparties. Besides the effect the timing and type of trading activity that is associated with fund rebalancing can have on volume and volatility, fund rebalancing also has the potential to distort prices.

Price momentum is the tendency for a security's price to continue to rise or fall as trading volume increases in the direction of the trend. This relationship can drive the stock price up or down as investors identify and follow trends. When traders recognize that a price has moved in one direction toward the end of a trading day without fundamental support, they usually conclude that momentum led to the movement. If, for example, at the end of a trading session a stock increases (decreases) in price by 25 basis points due to excessive buying (selling) caused by LIETF rebalancing, it will open the next day down (up) 25 basis points. Tuzun (2014) finds that prices revert the next day after LETF rebalancing.

Similarly, Trainor (2010) tests whether the magnitude of the previous day's final 30-minute decline is related to a positive reversal when the markets open for trading the next day. His evidence shows that for each 1 percent additional decline during the previous day's final 30 minutes, the opening is expected to be 0.023 percent higher the next day. Trainor concludes that this change is neither economically nor statistically significant.

In summary, anticipating the amount, timing, and direction of LETF rebalancing seems possible. This creates the opportunity for predatory traders to take advantage of fund rebalancing and distort prices by trading ahead of the counterparties to derivative contracts. Tuzun (2014) acknowledges this and states that all categories of the stock market show price reactions to LETF portfolio rebalancing, suggesting that LETFs and anticipatory traders in the same direction are stronger than the traders on the opposite side. He warns that this dynamic could be destabilizing. Haryanto et al. (2014) concludes that predatory traders could profit during days with large market swings by front running potential rebalancing trades. No trade is without risk. Thus, these predatory traders could find this strategy to be a losing proposition as the standard deviation of the potential profits from this strategy may also be large.

Summary and Conclusions

This chapter reviews the characteristics of LIETFs and how their unique attributes are changing the way investors access short and leveraged strategies. The additional flexibility offered to investors has both allowed the funds to grow in popularity and forced regulators to inform the investing public of the common misunderstanding associated with their return objectives. Given the complexity involved in the long-term performance of LIETFs, investors should educate themselves on the effects of compounding, leverage, and return path dependency before executing a specific trade. Investors should also implement a disciplined rebalancing strategy to achieve the desired exposure over time periods greater than a single day.

The potential yet inconclusive effects these products have on the pricing, volume, and volatility of the markets in which they trade is rightfully a cause for concern for those responsible for upholding the integrity of the financial system. Specific features of the underlying derivative holdings inherent in the majority of LIETFs have created the need for further research to better understand and monitor end-of-day trading patterns. As high frequency trading attracts more attention, so should the potential predatory trading techniques used to profit during fund rebalancing. Since a direct correlation exists between the AUM in a LIETF and the trading volume required during marking-to-market, these morally questionable algorithmic mechanisms may further disadvantage investors as products increase in size and popularity.

Although LIETFs are controversial, they enhance the ability of professional and individual investors to manage a portfolio or achieve a specific investment result. As with any financial instrument, investors should understand the costs and benefits of LIETFs. Time will determine if investors, traders, and regulators can find enough common ground to create an environment where LIETFs continue to flourish. However, history suggests that once a product is introduced and accepted by market participants, some version is likely to remain.

Discussion Questions

1. Identify several potential benefits of using LIETFs.
2. Discuss the most important risks that individual investors should know about LIETFs before investing.
3. Discuss why the market for LIETFs has grown so rapidly despite the risks associated with them.
4. Explain why the performance of a LIETF could differ substantially from its stated return objective.

References

Anderson, Randy, Richard Curcio, and Hany Guirguis. 2014. "Traditional ETFs." *Journal of Index Investing* 5:1, 12–31.

Bloomberg Terminal.2014. "Selected Data." New York: Bloomberg L.P.

CFTC and SEC. 2010. "Findings Regarding the Market Events of May 6, 2010." Report of the Staffs of the CFTC and SEC to the Joint Advisory Committee on Emerging Regulatory Issues.

Direxion Investments. 2014. "DXSLX DXSSX Monthly S&P 500 Bull & Bear 2x Funds." Available at http://www.direxioninvestments.com/products/direxion-monthly-sp-500-bull-2x-fund?exposure;funds=dxssx.

ETFdb. 2014a. "SEF-Short Financials." Available at http://etfdb.com/etf/SEF/.

ETFdb. 2014b. "Selected Data." Available at http://etfdb.com/screener/.

FINRA. 2009."Regulatory Notice 09–31." Available at https://www.finra.org/web/groups/industry/@ip/@reg/@notice/documents/notices/p118952.pdf.

Haryanto, Edgar, Walid Hejazi, Arthur Rodier, and Pauline Shum. 2014. "Intraday Share Price Volatility and Leveraged ETF Rebalancing." Available at http://papers.ssrn.com/sol3/papers.cfm?abstract_id=2161057.

Humphries, William M.2010. "Leveraged ETFs: The Trojan Horse Has Passed the Margin-Rule Gates." *Seattle University Law Review* 34:1, 299.

Isaacman, Max.2008. *Investing with Intelligent ETFs: Strategies for Profiting from the New Breed of Securities*. New York: McGraw-Hill.

Johnston, Michael. 2012. "Reviewing Three Different Types of Leveraged ETFs." Available at http://etfdb.com/2010/reviewing-three-different-types-of-leveraged-etfs.

Labaton Sucharow LLP. 2009. "Files Class Action Lawsuit against ProShares' UltraShort Real Estate ProShares Fund—SRS." Available at http://www.globenewswire.com/news-release/2009/08/06/402414/170818/en/Labaton-Sucharow-LLP-Files-Class-Action-Lawsuit-Against-ProShares-UltraShort-Real-Estate-ProShares-Fund-SRS.html.

Lu, Lei, Jun Wang, and Ge Zhang. 2009. "Long Term Performance of Leveraged ETFs." Available at http://ssrn.com/abstract=1344133.

Lydon, Tom. 2014. "Inverse, Leveraged ETFs See Slight Decline in Assets." Available at http://www.etftrends.com/2014/06/inverse-leveraged-etfs-see-slight-decline-in-assets/.

OMX Stockholm 30 Index. 2014. Available at https://indexes.nasdaqomx.com/Index/Overview/OMXS30.

Phillip Capital. 2014. "Selected Data." Available at http://www.phillipetf.com/ReadPage.aspx?id=65.

Proshares Investment Fraud Lawsuit. 2009. Available at http://www.forthepeople.com/class-action-lawyers/proshares-investment-fraud-lawsuit.

Proshares. 2009. "ProShares Launches First ETFs to Provide Triple Exposure to S&P 500." Available at http://www.proshares.com/news/49036466.html.

Proshares. 2012. "U.S. District Court Dismisses Class Action Lawsuit against ProShares." Available at hhtp://www.proshares.com/news/u_s_district_court_dismisses_class_action_lawsuit_against_proshares.html.

Proshares. 2013. "Rebalance Geared Fund Positions." Available at http://media.proshares.com/media/documents/rebalancing_leveraged_and_inverse_fund_positions.pdf.

Thomson Reuters. 2014. "Argentina Fails to Reach Debt Agreement, Default Looms." Available at http://www.reuters.com/article/2014/07/30/us-argentina-debt-idUSKBN0FZ0AM20140730.

Schwab. 2014. "Beyond the Expense Ratio: The Total Cost of Owning ETPs." Available at http://ims.schwab.wallst.com/repository/?doc=BeyondExpRatioTotalCostOwningETPsW.

Securities and Exchange Commission. 2009. "Leveraged and Inverse ETFs: Specialized Products with Extra Risks for Buy-and-Hold Investors." Available at http://www.sec.gov/investor/pubs/leveragedetfs-alert.htm.

Shum, Pauline.2011. "The Long and Short of Leveraged ETFs: The Financial Crisis and Performance Attribution." Available at http://www.cfainstitute.org/learning/products/publications/contributed/performance/Documents/leveraged_etfs_rf_op.pdf.

Spence, John, 2006. "ProFunds Prepares First Leveraged ETFs." Available at http://www.marketwatch.com/story/profunds-readies-first-leveraged-etfs.

Sullivan, Randy. 2009. " The Pitfalls of Leveraged and Inverse ETFs." *CFA Magazine*, May–July, 1.

Trainor, William Jr. 2010. "Do Leveraged ETFs Increase Volatility?" *Technology and Investment* 1:33, 215–220.

Tuzun, Tugkan. 2014. "Are Leveraged and Inverse ETFs the New Portfolio Insurers?" Washington, DC: Board of Governors of the Federal Reserve System. Available at http://www.federalreserve.gov/pubs/feds/2013/201348/201348abs.html/.

United States Senate. 2012. "Market Microstructure: Examination of Exchange-Traded Funds (ETFs)." Available at http://www.gpo.gov/fdsys/pkg/CHRG-112shrg74309/html/CHRG-112shrg74309.htm.

United States Senate. 2014. "Subcommittee on Securities, Insurance, and Investment of the Committee on Banking, Housing, and Urban Affairs." Available at http://www.banking.senate.gov/public/index.cfm?Fuseaction=Hearings.Hearing&Hearing_ID=ad4fdfb9-d589–584ac9–8829 0edf1ad8dc8d.

Part Three

CLASSIFICATION OF FUNDS BY PRINCIPAL INVESTMENTS

11

Money Market Mutual Funds

ANNA AGAPOVA
Associate Professor of Finance, Florida Atlantic University

Introduction

A *money market mutual fund* (MMMF) is an open-end mutual fund that invests in short-term debt securities such as U.S. Treasury bills and commercial paper. Investors widely consider MMMFs as safe as bank deposits yet providing a higher yield. They offer market rates less administrative expenses, redemption of full value upon demand, and limited check-writing privileges. This combination of return, safety, and liquidity was unavailable elsewhere at the time of their introduction in 1971.

However, investors' treatment of MMMF shares as cash equivalents is based only on their beliefs, since money market shares are equity stakes by law. These beliefs are due to three key distinct features of MMMF shares involving their: (1) stable net asset value (NAV), (2) liquidity, and (3) perceived safety. However, with no true subordinated capital at their disposal, MMMFs lack any true loss-absorbing capacity and, therefore, are susceptible to runs. In their 35-year history until 2008, MMMFs did not experience runs on their assets and performed as expected. In 2008, however, MMMFs experienced the first run. Since MMMFs are important providers of liquidity to financial intermediaries, such runs threaten the stability of the financial system.

This chapter reviews MMMFs' structure, performance, and role in the financial system. The remainder of the chapter is organized as follows. The first section reviews the history of MMMFs, while the second and third sections discuss the structure and types of MMMFs. Section four reviews analyses of funds' performance followed in section five by analyses of MMMFs' role in the stability of financial systems. The final section summarizes and draws conclusions.

The History of Money Market Mutual Funds

Although the first MMMF was introduced in the United States in 1971, it took a few years before the growth of this asset class increased. Before 1974, few MMMFs existed but their number grew to 35 by the end of 1975. MMMF assets remained stable at close to $4 billion during 1976 and 1977. The growth of the MMMF industry accelerated in

1978 with assets growing by over $2 billion in just the first five months of the year. By the middle of 1979, the total assets of MMMFs reached $25 billion. The rapid industry growth persisted into the 1980s (Stigum 1990).

Several factors explain the explosive growth of MMMFs in the late 1970s to early 1980s: (1) a market interest rate increase above the Regulation Q limits on bank deposit interest rates (Cook and Duffield 1979a, b; Silber 1983; Lam, Deb, and Fomby 1989), and (2) a need for an intermediary specializing exclusively in short-term assets and liabilities (Cook and Duffield 1979a, b; Whiting 1994).

A common belief is that MMMFs developed in response to interest rate ceilings imposed on banks and savings and loans institutions by Regulation Q, which was implemented in 1966. The regulation and the large minimum purchase requirements in the money market, which was $10,000 between 1969 and 1979, made MMMFs a primary means for providing easy access to money market yields to a diverse pool of institutional and individual investors. The view that MMMFs' creation was due to Regulation Q limitations implies that changes in certain government regulations would remove the incentive to invest in MMMFs.

In December 1982, Congress introduced an important deregulatory measure permitting banks to offer money market deposit accounts (MMDAs) free from an interest rate ceiling. Lam et al. (1989) find that introducing MMDAs led to a decline in the long-term demand for MMMFs. Yet, as Whiting (1994) shows, introducing MMDAs did not lead to restoring deposits to banking institutions because investors continued to hold funds with MMMFs. Thus, the growth in MMMFs resulted from a permanent change in the way institutional and individual investors manage their liquid assets. Specifically, the change in how investors participate in the money market resulted from advantages that MMMFs offer to investors through pooling large amounts of short-term funds: economies of scale, liquidity and divisibility, and diversification. Arguably, both the Regulation Q limitations and a need for an intermediary specializing exclusively in short-term assets and liabilities contributed to the initial growth of the MMMF industry. Continuation of MMMF growth after deregulation and their current popularity can be explained by the need for an intermediary specializing only on short-term assets and liabilities.

During the first decade of MMMF existence (1974–1984), total net assets (TNA) increased from $4 billion to $233 billion, representing the fastest percentage growth in the history of MMMFs. In the second decade (1985–1994), the industry nearly tripled in asset size to $611 billion while in the third decade (1995–2004) the assets ballooned to $1.9 trillion. The assets peaked at $3.8 trillion in 2008 and then declined to $2.7 trillion in 2013. Figure 11.1 illustrates the growth of MMMF assets in the United States (Investment Company Institute 2014).

MMMFs are a vital element of the U.S. financial markets. Until 2011, they were the second largest type of mutual fund, second only to equity mutual funds. In 2008, they briefly overtook the leading share of the mutual fund market, representing almost 40 percent. As of December 2013, MMMFs are the third largest mutual fund industry category by TNA with $2.7 trillion in assets and 18.1 percent in market share. Figures 11.2 and 11.3 illustrate mutual fund market composition and share of the money market, equity, bond, and hybrid mutual funds.

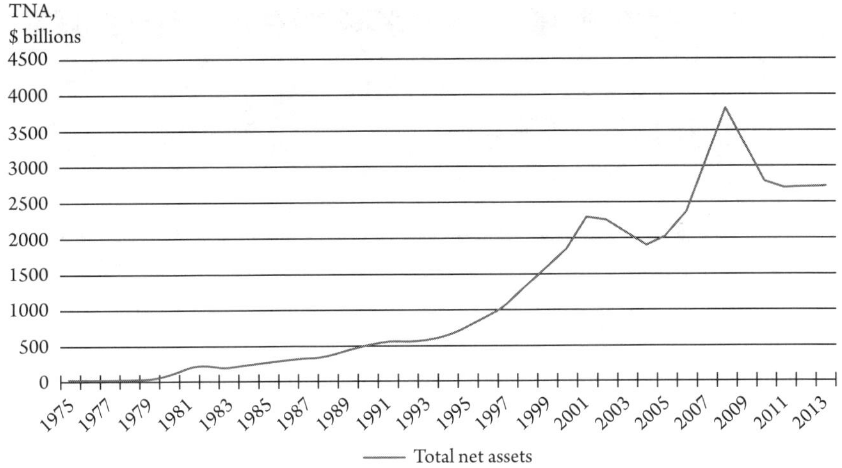

Figure 11.1 The Growth of Total Net Assets for Money Market Mutual Funds, 1975 to 2013.

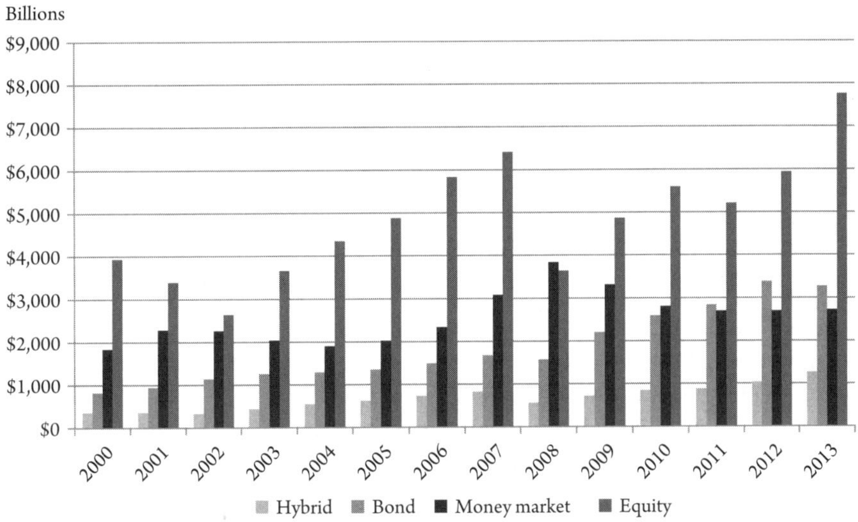

Figure 11.2 Mutual Funds Market Composition, 2000 to 2013. This figure illustrates the composition of mutual fund industry by TNA with the following investment objectives: hybrid, bond, money market, and equity funds.

The development of the European MMMF market lagged the U.S. market by about a decade. Similarly to that of the United States, the inception of the MMMF industry in Europe is attributed to the presence of interest rate limits on depositary accounts (Le Coz 2009). Despite disappearance of caps in 2004, European MMMFs still offer more attractive interest rates than bank deposits. As of 2010, the European MMMF market has grown into a EUR 1.3 trillion industry with 37 percent of the assets managed in France, 25 percent in Luxemburg, and about 23 percent in Ireland (Bengtsson 2013).

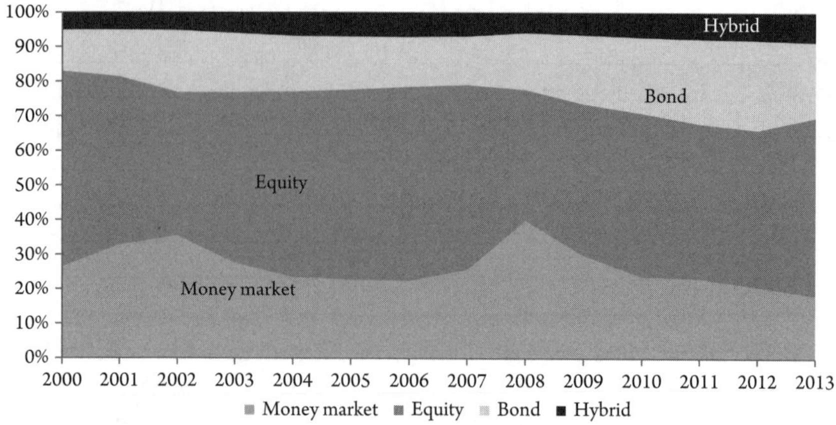

Figure 11.3 Mutual Fund Market Share, 2000 to 2013. This figure illustrates mutual fund market share in percentage by investment objective: hybrid, bond, money market, and equity funds.

Money Market Mutual Fund Structure

MMMFs are collective investment structures that invest in short-term, high credit quality debt instruments. They provide a considerable share of funding in the overnight and term money markets. In the United States, MMMFs are known as mutual funds, whereas in other countries they are called investment funds.

GOVERNING BODIES AND INVESTMENT RESTRICTIONS

Rule 2a-7 (17 CFR 270.2a-7) of the Investment Company Act of 1940 governs operations of U.S. MMMFs. Until May 5, 2010, the regulation limited MMMF holdings to short-term instruments with a remaining maturity of less than 397 days or with an average portfolio maturity of less than 90 days. Since May 2010, new regulation requires average portfolio maturity to be less than 60 days. The regulation also specifies the quality of instruments that MMMFs can hold in a portfolio, requiring funds to invest only in first tier (highest credit quality), and second tier securities with a maturity not exceeding 45 days. The rule also specifies the level of portfolio diversification: MMMFs must not hold more than 5 percent of total assets in any instrument of a single issuer with the highest quality, and only 0.5 percent of total assets in the second tier securities of any single issuer.

Until recently, the European Union has not had common regulation on what constitutes an MMMF. Typically, a European MMMF is organized as an Undertaking for Collective Investment in Transferable Securities (UCITS), which is a fund product regulated in terms of supervision, asset allocation, separation of management, and safekeeping of assets and later additions and amendments. European MMMFs are regulated by common UCITS legislation and supplemental regulations of the fund's domiciles. This dual regulation has led to substantial cross-European variations. For example, Irish-based MMMFs are similar to those in the United States. French MMMFs need approval by the securities regulation (i.e., the Autorité des marchés financiers) to classify a fund as an MMMF. German MMMFs are regulated under the European Central Bank's (ECB) definition of an MMMF. These MMMFs are defined as Collective Investment Undertakings (CIUs) and are considered to be close substitutes for bank deposits in terms of liquidity with primary investments in money market instruments and/or in other transferable debt instruments with a maturity of no more than one year.

Dollar-dominated funds domiciled in Europe generally voluntarily adopt the code of practice set by the Institutional Money Market Funds Association (IMMFA) for their investment guidelines. These guidelines are very similar to the restrictions set forth by Rule 2a-7, including a weighted average maturity of a portfolio limitation of no more than 60 days. Credit rating agencies rate many European MMMFs and may impose additional investment restrictions.

Given regulatory variation across Europe, restrictions on eligible assets vary substantially across MMMFs of different European countries. Portfolio assets are generally restricted to short-term, high-quality papers: short-term government bonds, certificates of deposit, time deposits, and repurchase agreements. However, European MMMFs can also invest in unsecured commercial paper and floating rate notes with large degrees of variation, leading to risk variations across different funds.

VALUATION METHODS

In the United States, Rule 2a-7 specifies the MMMF share price valuation method. According to the rule, the current price per share, for purposes of distribution, redemption, and repurchase may be computed using the amortized cost method or the penny-rounding method provided that the fund satisfies specific conditions.

The earlier rules governing MMMFs allowed two methods for valuing portfolio assets and calculating yields: the mark-to-market, which is no longer used in the United States but is used in Europe; and the amortized cost or straight-line accrual methods. Mark-to-market requires appraising portfolio assets as their estimated market value. When using the mark-to-market valuation method, three options are available to determine the share price:

- Maintain a constant share price, usually \$1, allowing variation in the number of shares owned by each shareholder. Interest income and capital appreciation net of expenses accrue to the shareholder as additional shares. In case of capital depreciation, the process can lead to a reduction in the number of shares.
- Maintain a constant share price and reflect changes in portfolio value by changing dividends. If losses and expenses exceed interest income, then the reduction of dividends occurs; if the reduction of dividends is insufficient, then the share price is reduced accordingly.
- Allow the NAV and the share price to fluctuate with market interest rates. Under this method, the effective yield depends on both dividends and share price.

The amortized method records the cost of a security on the date of purchase at its fair value and amortizes it on a straight-line basis as an increase in the value of the asset. In contrast to the mark-to-market method, amortized cost valuation does not allow changes in market interest rates to affect the value of the MMMF's portfolio. The amortized cost valuation leads to a constant share price. Both methods—mark-to-market and amortized cost—derive a fund's NAV as the difference between the calculated portfolio's asset value and net income (i.e., income minus expense). The MMMF's share price is the NAV divided by number of shares outstanding.

During the early days of the industry, most U.S. institutional investors preferred the amortized cost valuation method. Some even considered the mark-to-market valuation method unacceptable. Despite this preference, the Securities and Exchange Commission (SEC) has limited using the amortized cost valuation method to securities of 60 days or less to maturity and required the mark-to-market valuation method for securities with a longer maturity (Securities and Exchange Commission 1977). The reason for such directive was an argument that using the amortized cost on securities of longer than 60 days to maturity does not take into account changes in market value that may lead to a dilution of existing shareholders interests due to substantial net redemptions (purchases) if interest rates rise (fall). Lyon (1984) finds that significant dilution among institutional MMMF investors has taken place as a result of using the amortized cost valuation technique from August 1980 to September 1982.

As a compromise to institutional investors' push to use the amortized value method, the SEC allowed MMMFs to price their shares to the nearest one penny on a $1 share price ("penny-rounding") instead of the one-tenth of a penny accuracy previously required (Securities and Exchange Commission 1978). Penny-rounding, which is technically a third method used by many MMMFs available to the general public, is essentially the amortized cost method. Penny-rounding, like mark-to-market, values all securities with a remaining maturity greater than 60 days at market price, and less than 60 days on an amortized basis. MMMFs using this method are required to maintain a dollar-weighted average maturity of 120 days or less, of which no security has a maturity longer than one year, with a goal to minimize fluctuation in asset value. Penny-rounding allows an MMMF to report a share price of $1 as long as the fund's NAV is between of $0.9950 and $1.0050. The event of getting a share value outside of this interval, which is called "breaking the buck," is unlikely due to restrictions on the portfolio's maturity.

Unlike in the United States where all MMMFs are currently valued at a constant NAV, European MMMFs can be valued at either a constant net asset value (CNAV) or variable net asset value (VNAV). Given much variation in European MMMF regulation, the extent of using the constant versus variable valuation method among these MMMFs differs. Most Irish MMMFs are the highest rating CNAV funds that also abide by the IMMFA rules (Investment Company Institute 2009), which require additional mechanisms in place to manage exceptional events to protect their CNAVs. Such mechanisms include temporary suspension of redemptions, when the NAV cannot be calculated or when liquidity shortages occur, or redemption gates such as no more than 10 percent. Irish funds also limit deviation from $1 to 30 basis points, which is a stricter requirement than 50 basis points by Rule 2a-7. In case shadow pricing falls below the limit, the fund managers are required to take corrective actions, such as providing support to maintain a $1 NAV. All French and German MMMFs are variable NAV funds.

Money Market Mutual Fund Types

In the United States, MMMFs are generally categorized by investment strategy type. The three types of MMMFs are: (1) prime funds, which are taxable and invest mainly in short-term debt instruments issued by financial and non-financial companies, such as commercial paper, bank certificates of deposits (CDs), and floating rate notes; (2) government and Treasury funds, which are taxable and invest in U.S. Treasury and agency securities; and (3) tax-exempt funds, which invest in tax-exempt securities issued by state and local governments.

As of December 2013, prime funds managed $1.486 trillion in assets, government funds managed $0.962 trillion, and tax-exempt funds managed $0.271 trillion (Investment Company Institute, 2014). Figure 11.4 illustrates the trend and composition of MMMFs by their investment category.

Prime funds have always represented the largest share of all MMMF investment categories and have experienced tremendous growth starting from 1998. Table 11.1 presents the composition of the U.S. prime funds by their holdings. Prime funds invest in the following: U.S. Treasury bills, other Treasury securities, U.S. government agency issues, repurchase agreements (repos), certificates of deposits (CDs), Eurodollar CDs, commercial paper, bank notes, corporate notes, and other assets that include banker's acceptances, municipal securities, and cash reserves. The two largest holdings of prime funds are in commercial paper and CDs, with a proportion of commercial

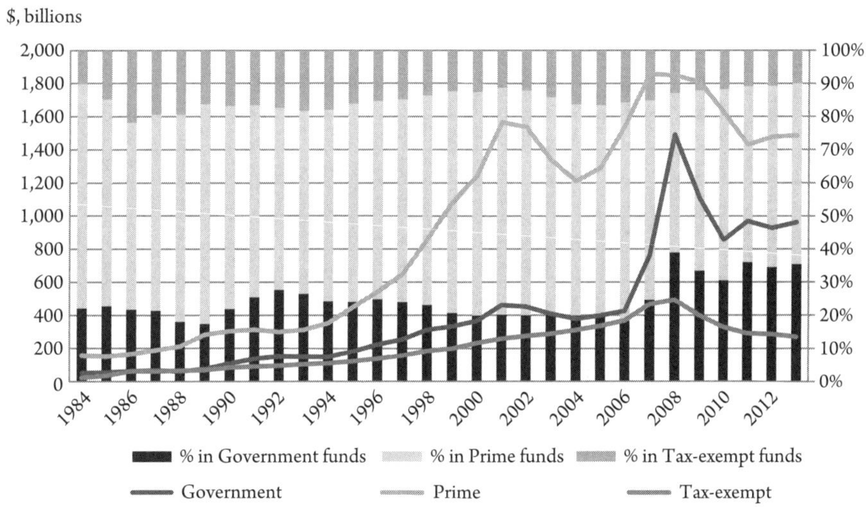

Figure 11.4 The Total Net Assets of Money Market Mutual Funds by Investment Category, 1984 to 2013. This figure illustrates the TNA and market share of MMMFs by investment category: government, prime, and tax-exempt.

Table 11.1 **Asset Composition of Taxable Prime Money Market Mutual Funds as a Percentage of Total Net Assets (Year-End), 1984 to 2013**

Year	Total Net Assets ($ millions)	U.S. Treasury Bills (%)	Other Treasury Securities (%)	U.S. Government Agency Issues (%)	Repurchase Agreements (%)	Certificates of Deposit (%)	Eurodollar CDs (%)	Commercial Paper (%)	Bank Notes[a] (%)	Corporate Notes[b] (%)	Other Assets[c] (%)	Average maturity Days
1984	$157,951	5.9	0.8	4.1	3.3	13.6	12.0	47.2	—	—	13.1	42
1985	151,849	4.6	1.0	6.1	3.1	10.0	10.2	55.4	—	—	9.5	42
1986	164,610	3.6	1.6	3.6	4.4	10.0	11.6	56.0	—	—	9.3	42
1987	187,087	1.0	0.9	6.5	4.8	16.2	8.9	52.3	—	—	9.4	34
1988	210,897	1.0	0.2	2.8	2.8	15.2	14.1	54.6	—	—	9.4	32
1989	283,939	1.3	0.8	2.0	2.8	14.4	9.3	62.3	—	—	7.1	43
1990	305,189	4.4	2.2	4.7	2.9	6.9	8.9	65.5	—	—	4.7	48
1991	314,346	5.7	2.9	4.2	3.7	10.6	6.9	60.1	—	—	5.8	56
1992	300,310	2.7	2.5	7.5	4.9	10.4	6.9	57.7	—	—	7.4	59
1993	312,701	2.6	2.4	11.9	5.9	8.0	3.2	52.6	—	—	13.3	58
1994	352,972	2.4	1.3	11.4	5.6	6.4	4.5	53.4	2.4	—	12.7	38
1995	449,829	1.4	0.9	9.2	6.2	8.9	4.5	52.5	3.7	—	12.7	60
1996	540,146	0.5	1.6	9.0	5.1	12.8	4.3	51.0	2.3	—	13.5	56
1997	647,005	0.4	0.5	5.4	5.3	14.7	3.7	52.0	3.2	—	14.8	57
1998	854,061	0.4	0.8	9.6	4.6	13.0	3.6	48.7	3.9	5.8	9.6	58
1999	1,079,523	0.3	0.3	6.8	4.8	12.8	3.9	49.2	3.1	8.4	10.4	49

continued

Table 11.1 **(continued)**

Year	*Total Net Assets ($ millions)*	*U.S. Treasury Bills (%)*	*Other Treasury Securities (%)*	*U.S. Government Agency Issues (%)*	*Repurchase Agreements (%)*	*Certificates of Deposit (%)*	*Eurodollar CDs (%)*	*Commercial Paper (%)*	*Bank Notes[a] (%)*	*Corporate Notes[b] (%)*	*Other Assets[c] (%)*	*Average maturity Days*
2000	1,243,598	0.3	0.1	5.9	3.9	11.7	6.6	50.9	3.6	10.5	6.5	53
2001	1,564,598	0.4	0.3	12.3	6.0	14.9	7.3	41.7	1.5	11.1	4.5	58
2002	1,535,621	1.3	0.3	11.8	8.1	13.8	7.0	40.1	1.4	12.0	4.2	54
2003	1,339,689	1.4	0.3	14.9	8.1	11.6	5.1	35.6	2.0	16.2	4.6	59
2004	1,209,995	0.3	0.1	12.0	8.5	14.1	5.7	33.9	2.6	17.9	4.9	41
2005	1,291,119	0.6	0.1	4.1	11.8	14.5	6.0	38.5	2.3	17.9	4.0	38
2006	1,542,584	0.1	0.2	2.9	9.9	13.9	4.4	39.6	2.2	21.6	5.2	49
2007	1,857,280	0.8	0.2	3.1	11.3	15.2	5.5	36.9	4.0	16.7	6.3	44
2008	1,848,349	1.9	0.5	12.7	8.4	21.5	4.7	34.1	3.1	9.3	3.8	47
2009	1,809,923	2.3	1.3	8.9	8.3	31.6	5.5	28.1	2.9	6.4	4.8	50
2010	1,618,896	2.7	1.9	7.8	12.8	28.6	6.7	24.3	3.2	6.2	5.8	44
2011	1,429,650	3.1	3.8	9.2	13.6	28.4	3.1	24.6	2.6	4.5	7.1	40
2012	1,477,347	3.4	4.2	6.9	16.8	29.5	3.0	23.1	3.5	3.5	6.1	45
2013	1,485,711	2.2	4.3	5.7	15.7	33.3	2.3	23.9	2.7	4.2	5.7	46

Note: This table provides asset composition of taxable prime MMMFs as a percentage of TNA between 1984 and 2013. The series excludes data for funds that invest primarily in other mutual funds. Components may not add to 100 percent because of rounding.

[a]Before 1994, other assets include bank notes.

[b]Before 1998, other assets include corporate notes.

[c]Other assets include banker's acceptances, municipal securities, and cash reserves.

Source: Investment Company Institute 2014.

paper holdings gradually declining between 1984 and 2013 and CD holdings increasing over the same period. Prime funds have also substantially increased holdings in repos after 2007. As of December 2013, commercial paper represented 23.9 percent, CDs 33.3 percent, and repos 15.7 percent of all holdings.

A substantial outflow from the prime funds and a substantial inflow into the government funds occurred in 2008, which was during the financial crisis. A separate section of this chapter provides an analysis of the 2008 events.

Table 11.2 illustrates the composition of U.S. government MMMFs by their holdings. Government MMMFs are similar to prime funds in that they invest in Treasury bills, other Treasury securities, U.S. government agency issues, and repurchase agreements (repos). The key difference between the two is in the proportions of the holdings: If prime funds hold only about 12 percent in the first three categories, government funds hold about 71 percent of their assets in these securities as of December 2013. Holdings of repos are material in both types of funds: 15.7 percent in prime funds and 27.9 percent in government funds.

Tax-exempt MMMFs represent the smallest share of the MMMF market in the United States, accounting for about 10 percent as of December 2013. This ranking has been historically consistent with an exception in 1986 (when tax-exempt MMMFs had the same share as government MMMFs at 22 percent). Tax-exempt MMMFs invest in short-term municipal securities or equivalent instruments and pay exempt-interest dividends. *Exempt-interest dividends* are the dividends that are exempt from federal income tax and, in some cases, state and local taxes.

The funds are also categorized by the type of distribution channel/investor: institutional and individual (retail). Institutional funds are designed for institutional investors such as bank trust departments, pensions, and corporations. Retail funds can be separated into three categories: (1) general purpose; (2) stockbroker-affiliated general purpose funds that are open to any investor; and (3) special purpose funds that are open to individuals who have a specific affiliation (e.g., customers of a certain bank). Before 2001, retail funds represented the larger portion of all MMMFs. In 2001, retail and institutional MMMFs each accounted for half of the market. After 2001, the proportion reversed with institutional MMMFs accounting for 66 percent of the market at the end of 2013 as Figure 11.5 shows. As of December 2013, retail and institutions funds held \$0.936 and \$1.782 trillion, respectively, in TNA.

U.S. non-financial businesses are important users of institutional MMMFs. In 2013, U.S. non-financial businesses' portion of cash balances held in MMMFs was 20 percent as Figure 11.6 shows. This portion peaked at 37 percent in 2008 and has declined thereafter.

A substantial difference exists in the proportion of prime and government MMMFs held by retail and institutional investors. Between 1996 and 2006, both retail and institutional government MMMF holdings were relatively flat and ranged between \$200 and \$300 billion TNA for retail and institutional investors, respectively. During 2008, retail government funds experienced a small temporary increase in the assets to \$300 billion, but returned to the previous \$200 billion level between 2009 and 2013.

Inflows of institutional government MMMFs reached \$599 billion during 2008 with TNA skyrocketing to \$1.2 trillion. This figure compares to average annual inflows of \$12 billion and the average TNA of \$233 billion between 1996 and 2006. The abnormal inflows of 2008 mark the only time when institutional government MMMFs'

Table 11.2 **Asset Composition of Taxable Government Money Market Mutual Funds as a Percentage of Total Net Assets (Year-End), 1984 to 2013**

Year	*TNA ($ in millions)*	*U.S. Treasury Bills (%)*	*Other Treasury Securities (%)*	*U.S. Government Agency Issues (%)*	*Repurchase Agreements (%)*	*Certificates of Deposit (%)*	*Eurodollar CDs (%)*	*Commercial Paper (%)*	*Bank Notes[a] (%)*	*Corporate Notes[b] (%)*	*Other Assets[c] (%)*	*Average maturity Days*
1984	51,800	21.0	7.5	20.4	33.9	4.3	4.3	7.3	—	—	1.3	46
1985	55,705	23.9	4.9	15.9	38.2	2.9	6.3	6.2			1.6	44
1986	63,736	22.8	7.9	14.4	39.1	4.1	4.9	4.3	—	—	2.5	51
1987	67,589	4.6	11.2	22.0	44.9	4.8	7.4	4.0	—	—	1.1	35
1988	61,298	5.0	9.7	20.5	58.4	1.2	0.1	3.2	—	—	2.0	28
1989	74,685	5.0	6.9	20.6	62.7	0.2	0.1	3.0	—	—	1.4	31
1990	109,376	11.1	12.2	20.6	45.7	0.0	0.0	0.3	—	—	9.9	46
1991	138,111	21.5	16.5	20.3	40.9	0.0	0.0	0.4	—	—	0.3	58
1992	151,043	26.0	16.5	21.6	34.7	0.0	0.0	0.5	—	—	0.6	55
1993	149,180	30.3	14.1	20.7	32.8	0.0	0.0	0.3	—	—	1.8	61
1994	148,139	24.4	12.6	26.3	34.0	0.0	0.0	0.4	0.0	—	2.1	37
1995	181,494	19.8	13.9	28.5	34.1	0.0	0.0	0.5	0.0	—	3.1	48
1996	223,790	17.7	18.5	25.4	35.2	0.0	0.1	0.7	0.0	—	2.4	49
1997	254,223	15.2	17.6	25.1	37.8	0.1	0.0	1.2	0.1	—	2.8	50
1998	312,907	14.3	17.7	30.4	33.4	0.3	0.0	1.7	0.1	0.2	2.0	52

continued

Table 11.2 **(continued)**

Year	TNA ($ in millions)	U.S. Treasury Bills (%)	Other Treasury Securities (%)	U.S. Government Agency Issues (%)	Repurchase Agreements (%)	Certificates of Deposit (%)	Eurodollar CDs (%)	Commercial Paper (%)	Bank Notes[a] (%)	Corporate Notes[b] (%)	Other Assets[c] (%)	Average maturity Days
1999	333,726	17.1	13.0	37.1	28.2	0.1	0.0	1.4	0.1	1.1	1.9	48
2000	367,780	14.2	10.1	32.0	37.9	0.0	0.0	1.6	0.1	1.2	2.9	45
2001	461,631	19.2	9.2	34.5	31.7	0.2	0.0	0.5	0.0	1.5	3.3	55
2002	453,157	20.5	6.4	33.2	35.5	0.1	0.0	0.5	0.0	1.7	2.1	52
2003	410,041	20.0	7.2	33.8	36.3	0.3	0.0	0.9	0.0	1.8	–0.3	52
2004	379,706	21.4	4.9	34.5	35.9	0.2	0.0	0.9	0.1	0.8	1.2	36
2005	399,330	15.8	4.4	28.1	50.0	0.0	0.0	0.2	0.1	0.8	0.5	27
2006	426,838	14.9	4.1	21.5	58.6	0.1	0.0	0.5	0.0	0.1	0.3	32
2007	760,389	16.3	5.1	24.1	53.7	0.3	0.0	0.2	0.0	0.0	0.2	31
2008	1,490,208	30.5	6.2	36.2	26.8	0.0	0.0	0.1	0.1	0.2	–0.1	48
2009	1,107,035	25.6	6.0	35.4	30.6	0.0	0.0	1.0	0.2	0.3	0.7	47
2010	855,021	22.9	8.5	33.3	33.0	0.0	0.0	0.9	0.1	0.4	0.9	47
2011	970,075	23.2	13.2	28.9	31.6	0.0	0.0	1.0	0.1	0.4	1.5	45
2012	928,749	25.6	12.6	26.7	33.0	0.0	0.0	0.7	0.0	0.1	1.4	46
2013	962,009	27.1	14.3	29.4	27.9	0.0	0.0	0.3	0.0	0.1	0.8	48

Note: This table provides asset composition of taxable government MMMFs as a percentage of TNA between 1984 and 2013. The series excludes data for funds that invest primarily in other mutual funds. Components may not add to 100 percent because of rounding.

[a]Before 1994, other assets include bank notes.

[b]Before 1998, other assets include corporate notes.

[c]Other assets include banker's acceptances, municipal securities, and cash reserves.

Source: Investment Company Institute 2014.

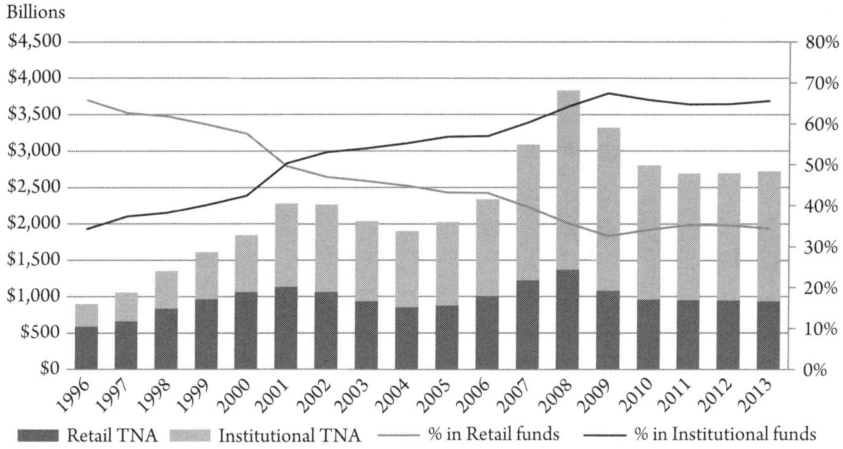

Figure 11.5 Retail versus Institutional Money Market Mutual Funds, 1996 to 2013. This figure illustrates the TNA and market share of MMMFs by investor type: retail and institutional.

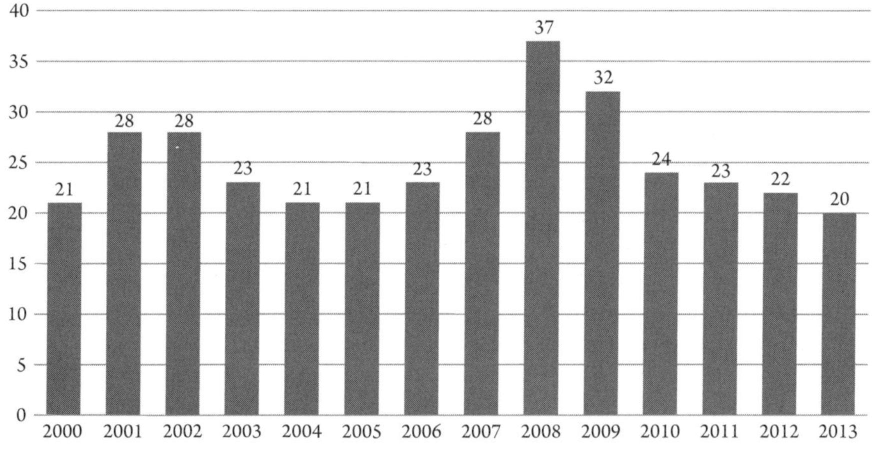

Figure 11.6 Percent of Businesses' Short-Term Assets in Money Market Mutual Funds, 2000 to 2013. This figure illustrates proportion of U.S. non-financial businesses' short-term assets in MMMFs. Note: U.S. non-financial businesses' short-term assets comprise foreign deposits, checkable deposits, time and savings deposits, MMMFs, repurchase agreements, and commercial paper. Source: Investment Company Institute 2014.

TNA surpassed prime MMMFs' TNA as shown in Figure 11.7. In that year, institutional prime MMMFs experienced outflows of $75.6 billion leading to a large drop in TNA to $1.07 trillion. Following the Reserve Prime Fund "breaking the buck" in October 2008, prime institutional MMMFs experienced their first "run" on the funds. Institutional prime MMMF investors transferred their funds to institutional government MMMFs. This flight to safety only occurred for institutional and not

Figure 11.7 TOTAL NET ASSETS OF RETAIL AND INSTITUTIONAL MONEY MARKET MUTUAL FUNDS BY INVESTMENT CATEGORY, 1996 TO 2013. This figure illustrates TNA of retail and institutional MMMFs by investment category: government and prime.

retail investors. Following 2009, the TNA declined in both institutional and retail prime MMMFs, with a sharper decline in institutional funds. The decline in TNA can be related to increased risk-taking in these funds as later discussed. Since 2008, an inverse relation exists between the level of TNA in prime and government institutional funds. This change suggests that after that period institutional MMMF investors started moving their money between these two investment categories of MMMFs as the risk level in prime MMMFs changes—primarily increases (Kacperczyk and Schnabl 2013).

Institutional investors comprise the vast majority of European MMMFs. For example, in France, 90 percent are institutional investors and most of the remaining investors are high net worth individuals. By contrast, German MMMFs are predominantly retail oriented (Le Coz 2009).

Given differences in regulations of European MMMFs, substantial variation exists across these MMMFs in types of funds offered based on their investment objectives. For example, in France, besides the two main categories of ordinary MMMFs—Eurozone MMMFs and International MMMFs, a large enhanced MMMF segment exists (Fitch Ratings 2008). Enhanced MMMFs, which are also called *dynamic, absolute performance,* or *absolute return* MMMFs, invest in riskier instruments such as uninsured commercial paper and floating rate notes. These funds try to fill a gap between traditional MMMFs and bond funds by pursuing higher returns by taking greater risks. They achieve that by investing in longer maturity and/or higher credit risk securities, such as short-term bonds, currencies, and, for less conservatively managed funds, collateralized debt obligations (CDOs) and commercial paper offered by structured investment vehicles (Fitch Ratings 2006).

Money Market Mutual Fund Performance

The net rate of return of MMMFs typically exceeds the rate on comparable bank deposits insured by the Federal Deposit Insurance Corporation (FDIC) (i.e., MMDAs). Koppenhaver (1999) shows that MMMFs usually earn less in net return than Treasury bills due to the MMMFs' annual management, distribution, and other fees required for fund operation. To achieve higher net returns, MMMF managers either adjust (waive) effective expenses that they charge their investors or assume either additional interest rate risk by extending the average maturity of the portfolio or additional credit risk by investing in commercial paper and variable rate notes.

Early studies on MMMFs focus on the ability of portfolio managers to predict interest rate fluctuations (i.e., exploit inefficiencies in the market through actively managing the maturity of portfolio holdings to achieve higher rates of return). They do so by examining the association between portfolios' average maturities and interest rate changes (Ferri and Oberhelman 1981; Domian 1992). Ferri and Oberhelman conclude that money fund managers consistently lengthened (shortened) the average duration of their portfolios ahead of a decrease (increase) in interest rates between November 1975 and July 1980. Domian finds the opposite result that fund managers changed average maturity as a response to interest rate changes between January 1982 and November 1986.

DeGennaro and Domian (1996) examine time-series differences in MMMFs' average maturities between January 1983 and December 1991. They conclude that managers select their target levels for interest rate risk and do not actively manage a portfolio's maturity to capture additional return. Based on their evidence, the authors contend that MMMF managers, in aggregate, do not have superior skill in forecasting interest rates. They conclude that investors should choose to invest in such funds based on management fees, expense ratios, and convenience features such as check-writing privileges. DeGennaro and Domian also suggest that MMMFs typically cannot outperform similar investments, such as bank deposits, without taking correspondingly larger risks.

Domian and Reichenstein (1998) examine the factors that affect the cross section of net returns and the persistence of relative returns through time. They view taxable MMMFs as a commodity. The authors find that the expense ratio is the most important factor in explaining the difference between funds' net returns, and that the relative returns of MMMFs show strong persistence.

Over a given period, MMMFs realize very similar gross returns, especially government MMMFs, yet deliver very different net returns to investors due to a wide variation in their fees (Bogle 1994; Domian and Reichenstein 1998; Fredman and Wiles 1998). Historical data show that a common practice among MMMF managers is to waive fees. Managers have waived fees since the late 1970s. Investors incur both upfront costs and ongoing costs. Upfront costs include any kind of load fees (front or back). MMMFs automatically deduct ongoing fees such as contractual management fees from gross returns. MMMF managers most commonly adjust ongoing expenses to change the net returns. To avoid a fixed structure of nominally flat fees, managers charge higher contractual fees and then selectively waive these fees throughout the year. Christoffersen (2001) finds that variation in fee waivers is significant and relates to differences in relative performance. She also argues that the effectiveness of waivers to improve performance differs between retail and institutional funds. Christoffersen finds that from 1990 to 1995, almost 80 percent of institutional funds waived fees while only 55 percent of retail funds did so.

During periods of ultra-low yields in the money market, fee waiving is widespread, setting a record in 2009. That year, which was characterized by a flight to safety, resulted in Treasury rates and federal fund target rates dipping to historic lows. A *flight to safety* occurs during periods when risk aversion increases and thus investors seek less risky securities. MMMF managers relied on partial fee waiving to increase net returns to shareholders. According to an iMoneyNet (2009) report that surveyed 1,677 funds, 82.7 percent absorbed at least some expenses in the second quarter of 2009. Among taxable MMMFs, 82.9 percent waived the fees. Government retail and government institutional funds had the largest increase in the number of funds that waived fees during this quarter: 93.4 percent of government retail funds waived their fees (an increase from 65.9 percent from the previous year), and 85.1 percent of government institutional funds waived their fees (an increase from 68.4 percent from the previous year). Prime funds increasingly used this practice during that time: 83.2 percent of prime retail MMMFs waived their fees (an increase from 54.2 percent from the previous year), and 73.7 percent of prime institutional MMMFs waived their fees. More prime institutional funds have been able to maintain their fees because the yields were not as low as in government MMMFs and in prime retail funds. Higher risk-taking behavior helps to explain the better performance of prime institutional funds during that period (Kacperczyk and Schnabl 2013).

Whiting (1994) suggests that MMMFs are not just a commodity and MMMF expenses are not the only determinant of cross-sectional returns. Capon, Fitzsimons, and Prince (1996) argue that investors may have a range of selection criteria beyond the fund's risk and return. Thus, for MMMFs, additional factors can include the possibility of emergency expenditure, unexpected investment opportunities (Agapova 2011), planned transactions, management of overall portfolio risk, and the attractiveness of a money market return. The implication of different roles that MMMFs play for investors is that the cost of switching to another money fund can lead to money fund operators charging expenses without losing existing customers to better performing funds. Thus, MMMFs are not just a financial commodity from the investor's point of view.

Christoffersen and Musto (2002) examine investor self-selection and the implied demand curve differences for money fund services to explain the cross-sectional differences of MMMF fees between 1988 and 1997. The authors contend that taxable money fund performance reflects the persistence in fees and that an investor clientele exists that is relatively insensitive to the level of fund fees. Christoffersen and Musto also find that direct distribution channels are cheaper for MMMF investors than for MMMFs whose investors are sought by brokers or other intermediaries. Further, their evidence shows that money funds charge more after merging with funds having an investor base that is relatively less fee sensitive.

Before the financial crisis of 2007–2008, investors generally considered MMMFs to be a safe investment with the main goal of capital preservation. Before August 2007, the yields of money market instruments were almost the same as the yields of U.S. Treasuries. Since regulation restricts MMMFs to investing in money market instruments, those restrictions led to limits in risk-taking by MMMFs as they were investing in similar instruments with similar yields. As a result, early studies focus on explaining variation in MMMF net returns with differences in fees across MMMFs. However, starting in August 2007, several events in the market led to changes in risk and yields of some money market instruments (Kacperczyk and Schnabl 2013). Change in risks and yields among money market instruments after August 2007 gave money fund managers an opportunity to increase fund returns by assuming more credit and/or interest rate risk.

Christoffersen (2001), Christoffersen and Musto (2002), Kacperczyk and Schnabl (2013), and Chernenko and Sunderam (2014) document a strong performance-flow relationship among MMMFs that created incentives for MMMFs to take more risk. Kacperczyk and Schnabl document a substantial increase in risk-taking by institutional prime MMMFs between 2007 and 2010, with funds sponsored by financial intermediaries with more money fund business taking even more risk. However, the authors do not find these results on risk-taking for retail prime funds. Instead, they find that retail investors are much less sensitive to yield differentials than institutional investors. Kacperczyk and Schnabl also find that risk-taking gradually disappears after government unlimited insurance on MMMF investments after Lehman's default.

McCabe (2010), Schmidt, Timmermann, and Wermers (2014), and Strahan and Tanyeri (2015) show that during the financial crisis of 2007–2008, investors concentrated MMMF redemptions among risky funds, suggesting that investors had knowledge about MMMF portfolio quality.

The Role of Money Market Mutual Funds in the Financial System

Before October 2008, investors considered MMMFs as low-risk, short-term highly liquid investments comparable to bank deposits. An important feature of MMMFs is that they are not guaranteed or insured by any government agency or fund sponsor. Investors can lose money in MMMFs but they rarely do. In the 40-year history of the MMMF industry, only two MMMFs have not returned the full $1 a share. In 1994, the Denver-based Community Banker's U.S. Government Money Market Fund reported a NAV below $1 and ultimately investors recovered about 96 cents on the dollar. The fund was tailored only to institutional investors. The event did not lead to widespread outflows from MMMFs largely because no vast U.S. financial crisis took place in 1994. In September 2008, the Reserve Primary Fund, a $60 billion MMMF, held large quantities of Lehman Brothers' debt. The following day after Lehman failed on September 15, the Reserve Fund "broke the buck" and returned only 99 cents on the dollar as investors redeemed billions of dollars almost immediately. The important difference from the first case is that the Reserve Fund's failure happened during a widespread financial crisis when the liquidity in the money market dried up, causing money market investors, including MMMFs, to have problems selling assets. On the next day, run-like behavior spread to many other institutional prime MMMFs.

As history shows, without deposit insurance, MMMFs are vulnerable to runs if they are expected to "break the buck" while market liquidity substantially diminishes. As market events of September 2008 show, breaking the buck can lead to market runs on MMMFs and to the destabilization of financial systems. Prime MMMFs are an important source of short-term financing for both financial and non-financial firms. In 2008, U.S. non-financial businesses' held 37 percent of their cash balances in MMMFs. Instabilities related to MMMFs, such as runs on the funds, played a central role in the financial crisis of 2007–2008 and in a smaller scale run during the 2011 European banking crisis.

The consequences of the MMMF run in September 2008 appeared so catastrophic that the Treasury Department and the Federal Reserve intervened on September 19. They announced two programs aimed at stabilizing MMMFs and providing liquidity to short-term funding markets. The Treasury's Temporary Guarantee Program for Money Market Funds (TGP) provided, for the first time, unlimited insurance to existing balances on registered 2a-7 MMMFs using the Exchange Stabilization Fund, similar to deposit insurance with banks. The program opened on September 29, 2008, and closed on September 18, 2009.

The Federal Reserve also announced the Asset-Backed Commercial Paper Money Market Mutual Fund Liquidity Facility (AMLF). The purpose of the AMLF was to (1) increase the liquidity of the asset-backed commercial paper market, and (2) provide a means for MMMFs to sell assets without having to suffer fire sale costs to meet the wave of redemptions. AMLF began operations on September 22, 2008, and concluded on February 1, 2010. The intervention was successful in stopping the run, but transferred the entire risk of the $3 trillion MMMF industry to the Federal government. Duygan-Bump, Parkinson, Rosengren, Suarez, and Willen (2013) examine the effect of AMLF in separation from other policies that took place at that time. They find that this facility helped stabilize asset outflows from MMMFs and reduced asset-backed commercial paper yields significantly.

As Chernenko and Suderam (2014) show, the quiet run on MMMFs of 2011 resulting from the European sovereign debt crisis had a negative spillover effect on the broader economy. The authors show important frictions in MMMFs lending that can transmit distress across firms. Their evidence shows that risk-taking by MMMFs through lending to eurozone banks created large investor redemptions in the summer of 2011 that reduced the ability of non-European firms to raise short-term financing.

In 2010, the SEC adopted amendments to Rule 2a-7 that strengthened MMMF standards for liquidity, credit quality, maturity, and transparency. The SEC is still working to develop new policies and regulations intended to correct structural flaws in MMMFs to prevent future runs. Policies discussed include introducing a VNAV structure as well as fees and gates.

Summary and Conclusions

This chapter summarizes the history, structure, and recent developments in the MMMF industry. MMMFs are an important element of the financial system. They emerged as a financial intermediary that pools deposits to buy large-denomination money market securities. MMMFs initially offered market rates less administrative expenses, redemption of full value upon demand, and limited check-writing privileges. This provides a combination of return, safety, and liquidity then unavailable elsewhere. From the early

1970s until the financial crisis of 2007–2008, MMMFs performed as intended and provided easy access to money markets for individual investors and liquidity and short-term financing to financial and non-financial firms. However, MMMFs experienced runs in 2008 and 2011, creating instability in the financial system. New regulations helped to strengthened MMMF standards for liquidity, credit quality, maturity, and transparency and the Treasury Department and the Federal Reserve took temporary measures to insure the stability of the money markets.

Discussion Questions

1. Discuss why MMMFs developed.
2. Explain how MMMFs maintain a constant $1 a share NAV.
3. Discuss why money fund managers sometimes waive fees.
4. Discuss how the current MMMF structure can create runs on funds.

References

Agapova, Anna. 2011. "The Role of Money Market Mutual Funds in Mutual Fund Families." *Journal of Applied Finance* 21:1, 87–102.

Bengtsson, Elias. 2013. "Shadow Banking and Financial Stability: European Money Market Funds in the Global Financial Crisis." *Journal of International Money and Finance* 32, 579–594.

Bogle, John C. 1994. *Bogle on Mutual Funds: New Prospective for the Intelligent Investor*. Burr Ridge, IL: Irwin.

Capon, Noel, Gavan J. Fitzsimons, and Russ Alan Prince. 1996. "An Individual Level Analysis of the Mutual Fund Investment Decision." *Journal of Financial Services Research* 10:1, 59–82.

Chernenko, Sergey, and Adi Sunderam, 2014. "Frictions in Shadow Banking: Evidence from the Lending Behavior of Money Market Funds." *Review of Financial Studies* 27:6, 1717–1750.

Christoffersen, Susan. 2001. "Why Do Money Fund Managers Voluntarily Waive Their Fees?" *Journal of Finance* 56:3, 1117–1140.

Christoffersen, Susan, and David K. Musto. 2002. "Demand Curves and the Pricing of Money Management." *Review of Financial Studies* 15:5, 1499–1524.

Cook, Timothy Q., and Jeremy G. Duffield 1979a. "Average Cost of Money Market Funds." *Economic Review*, Federal Reserve Bank of Richmond 65:July/August, 32–39.

Cook, Timothy Q., and Jeremy G. Duffield. 1979b. "Money Market Mutual Funds: A Reaction to Government Regulation or a Lasting Financial Innovation?" *Economic Review*, Federal Reserve Bank of Richmond 65:July/August, 15–31.

DeGennaro, Ramon P., and Dale L. Domian. 1996. "Market Efficiency and Money Market Fund Portfolio Managers: Beliefs versus Reality." *Financial Review* 31:2, 453–474.

Domian, Dale L. 1992. "Money Market Mutual Fund Maturity and Interest Rates." *Journal of Money, Credit, and Banking* 24:4, 519–527

Domian, Dale L., and William Reichenstein 1998. "Performance and Persistence in Money Market Fund Returns." *Financial Services Review* 6:3, 169–183.

Duygan-Bump, Burcu, Patrick Parkinson, Eric Rosengren, Gustavo A. Suarez, and Paul Willen. 2013. "How Effective Were the Federal Reserve Emergency Liquidity Facilities? Evidence from the Asset-Backed Commercial Paper Money Market Mutual Fund Liquidity Facility." *Journal of Finance* 68:2, 715–737.

Ferri, Michael, and H. Dennis Oberhelman. 1981. "A Study of the Management of Money Market Mutual Funds: 1975–1980." *Financial Management* 10:4, 24–29.

Fitch Ratings. 2006. "French Money Market Funds." May 23. Available at http://www.alacrastore.com/fitch-credit-research/French-Money-Market-Funds-275636_report_frame.

Fitch Ratings. 2008. "French Asset Management Industry—Dynamics and Challenges." Fund and Asset Manager Rating Group. December 2003. Available at http://www.alacrastore.com/fitch-credit-research/French-Asset-Management-Industry-Dynamics-and-Challenges-416872_report_frame.

Fredman, Albert J., and Russ Wiles. 1998. *How Mutual Funds Work.* Paramus, NJ: Prentice-Hall.

IMoneyNet. 2009. "Money Fund Expense Report." IMoneyNet 23:2, 1–247. Available at http://www.imoneynet.com/files/Publication_News/mfer.pdf.

Investment Company Act of 1940, rule 2a-7 (17 CFR 270.2a-7). Available at http://www.ecfr.gov/cgi-bin/text-idx?SID=4806ecc5a3033db8889d493aa7ebae87&node=se17.4.270_12a_67&rgn=div8.

Investment Company Institute. 2009. *2009 Investment Company Fact Book,* 49th Edition. Washington, DC: Investment Company Institute. Available at http://www.ici.org/pdf/2009_factbook.pdf.

Investment Company Institute. 2014. *2014 Investment Company Fact Book,* 54th Edition. Washington, DC: Investment Company Institute. Available at http://www.ici.org/pdf/2014_factbook.pdf.

Kacperczyk, Marcin, and Philipp Schnabl. 2013. "How Safe Are Money Market Funds." *Quarterly Journal of Economics* 128:3, 1073–1122.

Koppenhaver, Gary D. 1999. "Circle Unbroken: Bank-Affiliated Money Market Mutual Funds. Global Financial Crises: Implications for Banking and Regulation." Proceedings of the 35th Annual Conference on Bank Structure and Competition, Federal Reserve Bank of Chicago, May, 430–447.

Lam, Chun H., Rajat Deb, and Tom Fomby. 1989. "Deregulation and the Demand for Money Market Mutual Funds." *Journal of Macroeconomics* 11:2, 297–308.

Le Coz, Gail, 2009. "Importance of Definition." *Finance Director Europe.* August. 17. Available at http://www.the-financedirector.com/features/feature63565/.

Lyon, Andrew B. 1984. "Money Market Funds and Shareholder Dilution." *Journal of Finance* 39:4, 1011–1020.

McCabe, Patrick E. 2010. "The Section of Money Market Fund Risks and Financial Crises." Finance and Economics Discussion Series Working Paper 2010–51, Federal Reserve Board. Available at http://www.federalreserve.gov/pubs/feds/2010/201051/201051pap.pdf.

Schmidt, Lawrence, Allan Timmermann, and Russ Wermers. 2014. "Runs on Money Market Funds." Working Paper. University of California San Diego and, University of Maryland.

Securities and Exchange Commission. 1977. SEC Release, No. IC-9786, May 31. Washington, DC. Securities and Exchange Commission.

Securities and Exchange Commission. 1978. SEC Release, No. ICA 10451, October 26. Washington, DC: Securities and Exchange Commission.

Silber, William L. 1983. "The Process of Financial Innovation." *American Economic Review* 73:2, 89–95.

Stigum, Marcia. 1990. *The Money Market,* 3rd Edition. Homewood, IL: Dow Jones-Irwin.

Strahan, Philip E., and Basak Tanyeri. 2015. "Once Burned, Twice Shy: Money Market Fund Responses to a Systemic Liquidity Shock." *Journal of Financial and Quantitative Analysis,* forthcoming.

Whiting, Cathleen. 1994. "Persistence in Regulatory Innovation: MMFs and Financial Intermediaries." *Journal of Economic Behavior and Organization* 23:3, 321–342.

12

Bond Mutual Funds

SANDEEP SINGH
Professor of Finance, College at Brockport, State University of New York (SUNY)

Introduction

According to the Investment Company Institute (2014), investors worldwide held mutual fund assets worth \$30 trillion at the end of 2013. Investors in the United States held \$17 trillion including about \$5 trillion in bond funds. This total did not include additional amounts invested through hybrid (balanced) funds. Investors also had about \$165 billion in bond market investments through closed-end funds (CEFs) and \$246 billion through bond exchange-traded funds (ETFs).

Investors can gain exposure to the fixed-income asset class in four major ways:

- *Create a portfolio of fixed-income securities.* This method has the benefit of being tailored to an investor's goals. It is also the preferred method if an investor has a defined liability or a set of liabilities that has to be met (e.g., for a defined benefit (DB) plan seeking to meet retirement obligations). For individual investors, a self-managed portfolio of individual bonds makes sense only beyond a specific asset size and only if they plan to make a certain number of transactions while managing the portfolio (Reipe 2000). It seems intuitive that over time the optimal asset size and the volume/frequency of trading will be affected by changing conditions like liquidity and transactions costs in the bond market.
- *Buy shares in an open-end bond mutual fund.* Here, investors delegate the portfolio management to a professional and pay a management fee for the service. When pursuing this choice, investors must make decisions such as determining an appropriate fund with investment objectives that match those of the investor. In addition, the investor has to choose an appropriate benchmark to measure a fund manager's performance if the fund is actively managed.
- *Buy shares of a closed-end fund.* After an initial offering, these funds are traded in the secondary market among investors. With CEFs, the discount or premium from the fund's net asset value (NAV) acts as an additional source of return and risk for investors.
- *Acquire an ETF or unit investment trust (UIT).* ETFs do not suffer from the shortcoming of trading only at the end of the day or at a wide premium or discount from the NAV, and can be sold short or purchased on margin. Most bond ETFs provide

investors with indexing opportunities and actively managed bond ETFs are rare and in their infancy. *UITs* are a hybrid security with characteristics of both CEFs and open-end funds (OEFs), have a fixed number of shares that trade on the secondary market, and typically have finite lives. Eventually the unit trust company liquidates the shares and returns the money to the shareholders. UITs are particularly popular with fixed-income investors. More recently, finite life ETFs are slowly encroaching on the market previously dominated by UITs.

Managers of equity portfolios face somewhat different circumstances than those faced by managers of fixed-income portfolios. Most fixed-income securities have a finite life, while most open-end fixed-income funds and most ETFs are perpetual securities. Whether a portfolio is actively or passively managed, the bond fund manager faces the reality of reinvesting funds from maturing bonds. The challenge is to create a perpetual portfolio from a set of securities with finite lives. Comparatively, most equity securities are perpetual and not subject to time decay. Liquidity in the bond market is also a relevant issue in fixed-income portfolio management, especially for those portfolios that are benchmarked to broader indexes. For example, the Barclays Capital U.S. Aggregate Bond Index has about 8,200 constituent bonds and thus replicating the return of such an index is challenging.

With the possible exception of high yield bonds and a few exotic securities, a bond portfolio's change in value is a function of its *duration*, which is a measure of a portfolio's price sensitivity to changes in interest rates (yields). While incorporating views on other aspects such as sectors and individual issues, the challenge for an active manager is to manage the portfolio duration such that the total return of the portfolio exceeds that of the benchmark. Although a fixed-income mutual fund's performance is evaluated on a total return basis and often compared to a benchmark return, most bond portfolios are managed on an interest rate sensitivity (duration) basis and other subsidiary active bets such as issue selection and sector weightings. Ultimately, interest rate sensitivity remains the major driver of performance for most bond portfolios. For actively managed equity portfolios, there rarely is a single factor that affects portfolio performance so significantly and consistently over time as does duration for fixed-income portfolios.

Bond mutual funds form an integral part of most individual investor portfolios. Besides being a reliable source of income, bond mutual funds play a vital role in managing portfolio volatility and risk. The bond market comprises securities differing in risk and maturities. At one end of the risk spectrum are securities with low default probabilities issued by stable governments, while volatile high yield bonds and exotic securities such as inverse floaters, interest only (IO), and principal only (PO) securities are at the other end. An *inverse floater* is a security that usually provides the holder a return that moves in a direction opposite to that of a floating rate instrument. For example, a floater may pay 10 percent minus the yield on a 10-year Treasury note. Therefore, when interest rates go up, the yield on the inverse floater goes down and vice versa, which is opposite that of a traditional floating rate bond. Theoretically, the return and price of an inverse floater goes up in a declining interest rate environment. A coupon-bearing bond is sometimes stripped of its coupon and the principal portions and then the coupon portion (IO) and the principal portion (PO) is traded separately in the bond market. Bond mutual funds cater to investors seeking exposure to each of the wide array of segments in the bond market. Given that each sector has unique characteristics, each may require different skill sets from the bond mutual fund manager.

The goal in this chapter is to examine bond mutual funds. The first section discusses performance evaluation of bond mutual funds. This discussion is followed by an overview of the unique characteristics of various segments of the bond mutual fund market. The same section also discusses the empirical findings in each segment of the bond mutual fund market, and guidelines for institutional decision-makers and individual investors considering investing in each segment. The final section offers some concluding remarks including suggestions for future research.

Bond Mutual Fund Performance Evaluation

Measuring and benchmarking investment performance of bond mutual funds pose unique challenges. In the United States, all mutual funds open to the public are subject to the Investment Companies Act of 1940, which requires funds to report their performance compared to a selected benchmark or provide an explanation for not maintaining a benchmark comparison. Most actively managed bond funds are benchmarked to a widely reported index.

Although bond indexes are useful barometers of market performance and convey valuable information to the investing public, they usually are not good benchmarks for performance evaluation of actively managed bond funds for several reasons. First, many segments of the bond market often lack liquidity. Some bonds do not trade on a given day, so the pricing entity has to "matrix price" the bond, which does not reflect an actual trade price. *Matrix pricing* involves arriving at a hypothetical (presumably close to the actual) price based on the traded price of similar securities. Second, some bonds that are traded may also face the problem of "stale pricing" meaning the trade might have occurred a few hours before and hence may not reflect current market conditions. Third, the index against which an active bond mutual fund's performance is benchmarked is unstable due to the very nature of its constituent bonds. Unlike stocks in stock indexes that are perpetual securities and are mostly liquid, bonds mature and are therefore subject to time decay.

Finally, additional issues involve bonds being called or refunded. A *call feature* gives the issuer the right to redeem the bond before maturity at a predetermined price. A call is usually an undesirable event for the holder because it denies the holder future coupons and possible capital gains. Issuers usually call bonds when interest rates drop, which subjects the bond holder to reinvestment risk. *Reinvestment risk* is the risk of reinvesting coupon income or principal at a rate less than the original coupon or purchase rate. In a *refunding,* the issuer replaces an existing issue with new bonds often carrying lower yields. Given the multiple issues noted above, risk-adjusted performance comparison of an actively managed bond fund to an index is tentative at best because of relative instability and imprecise pricing of the benchmark and the fund portfolio.

The challenge required for a passive bond mutual fund manager to match the performance of an index is no less daunting. One issue involves liquidity. If bonds in the index are infrequently traded, the indexed fund manager cannot implement a full replication and has to resort to cell matching or optimization techniques. In a *full replication method*, the manager holds all the index securities exactly in the same weight in the portfolio. In *cell matching*, the index is divided into cells (e.g., cells based on sectors and maturity) and the manager largely tries to populate each cell with a similar, though not exactly the same, bond. In an *optimization technique*, the manager matches the statistical properties of the index, albeit with far fewer securities. For example, the manager usually matches duration, convexity, average rating, and expected volatility. Even full replication is bound to be subject to some tracking error, especially when the index is not investable and not subject to transaction costs and management fees. *Tracking error* measures the deviation of portfolio returns from benchmark returns.

A key dimension of bond portfolio management is duration management. A portfolio manager's success often depends on the ability to manage a portfolio's duration vis-à-vis the duration of a known set of liabilities or of an index. For an actively managed bond fund, the mismatch of duration is often deliberate depending on the manager's outlook on interest rates and their term structure. The manager of an actively managed bond fund has more latitude because bond mutual funds are usually not constrained to meeting one or a set of liabilities. The only restraint originates from the restrictions placed on the fund through its objectives or the benchmark against which the portfolio's performance is to be compared.

Given these challenges, measuring bond mutual fund performance has attracted the attention of empiricists. In an early study on the topic, Blake, Elton, and Gruber (1993) use two sets of bond return data for both linear and nonlinear evaluation models. Similar to the findings of many equity mutual fund performance studies, bond fund returns lagged those of the index after adjusting for risk. The authors also find a one-for-one relationship between expenses and returns. Nonlinear models confirm no presence of forecasting ability for bond mutual fund managers.

Investment grade bonds are perhaps more homogeneous than a group of large cap stocks. Active managers of investment grade bond portfolios have difficulty distinguishing themselves in terms of performance. According to various studies such as Blake et al. (1993) and Philpot (2000), past performance has no predictive ability regarding future mutual fund performance. Philpot, Hearth, Rimbey, and Schulman (1998) find some economies of scale in bond mutual funds. Chen, Ferson, and Peters (2010) show that bond mutual funds, in aggregate, can time the market, but this benefit vanishes once adjusting the returns for expenses. In a study of 3,549 bond mutual funds, Huij and Denwall (2008) find economically and statistically significant persistence of superior/inferior risk-adjusted performance (alpha) in the top and bottom deciles of the sample.

From 1997 to 2003, fund portfolio duration and operating expenses drove taxable bond mutual fund performance positively and negatively, respectively. Redman and Gullet (2007) show that average duration and fund expenses are also primary drivers of municipal bond fund performance. The authors conclude that fund managers enhance returns for shareholders.

Window dressing is a phenomenon in which the manager of an actively managed bond mutual fund buys securities that have recently performed well and sells securities that have recently performed poorly from the portfolio close to the end of a performance reporting period. Because managers have to report their portfolios at the end of the reporting period (usually each quarter), window dressing occurs when a publicly reported portfolio shows that the manager is holding securities that have recently performed well, signaling superior selection skills. In a study of Spanish mutual funds investing in fixed-income securities, Ortiz, Sarto, and Vicente (2012) find no pervasive practice of window dressing. However, limited window dressing is shown to be more prevalent in larger sized mutual funds.

Despite the lack of evidence on performance persistence in bond funds, investors continue to chase the so-called "hot hands" managers. *Hot hands* refer to managers who have a streak of good performance that cannot be explained by a string of mere luck. The hot hand phenomenon is analogous to home run hitting streak in baseball or a very high free throw shooting percentage in basketball for periods of time. Fulkerson, Jordan, and Riley (2013) show that investors chase performance, and funds with superior performance experience additional inflows showing some ability by investors to distinguish and reward expected performance. The most chased-after funds were those with superior performance as inflows instead of outflows for poorly performing funds.

Overall, the evidence shows a lack of support for the notion that performance is sufficient to justify the additional expenses of actively managed bond mutual funds. Indexing for bond portfolios, even with its many challenges, seems to be a better and cheaper way to acquire exposure to fixed-income markets, as long as investors have realistic expectations from their investments.

Segments of the Bond Mutual Fund Market

Classifying the bond mutual fund segments is complicated because of the fluid dimensions of issuers, time to maturity, and risk. Some bond mutual funds can easily be classified into two or more categories. Morningstar Inc., a mutual fund advisory service, provides the most widely used classifications. Individual investors use the Morningstar Style Boxes® to understand the fund manager's investment style. A manager's style is predominantly a broad metric for indicating the nature of securities held by the manager in the portfolio reflective of manager's investment philosophy and/or mandate. For bond mutual funds, the style box is created on risk and interest rate sensitivity dimensions. Another popular metric is the Morningstar Star ratings in which Morningstar assigns a mutual fund a star rating that ranges from one to five stars based on past risk-adjusted performance among its peer group. For this peer group comparison, each mutual fund is assigned to a category (Morningstar 2014). For bond mutual funds, the two broad categories are taxable and municipal. Taxable bond fund categories comprise 17 subcategories ranging from long government bonds to nontraditional bonds. By contrast, municipal bond funds comprise 16 subcategories encompassing a range of national municipal bond funds to state specific bond funds. These two sets of categorizations form the basis for the overall discussion in this chapter.

At the end of the first quarter in 2014, the Securities Industries and Financial Markets Association (SIFMA) (2014) estimated the size of outstanding bonds in the U.S. bond market at about $40 trillion, with the Treasury segment as the largest with $12 trillion in outstanding securities. Table 12.1 shows the growth of the bond market in the United States between 1980 and 2014. The size of the bond market over this

Table 12.1 **U.S. Debt Market**

End of Year	*Municipal*	*Treasury*	*Mortgage Related*	*Corporate Debt*	*Federal Agency Securities*	*Money Markets*	*Asset Backed*	*Total*
1980	399.4	623.2	111.4	458.6	164.3	780.0		2,536.9
1985	859.5	1,437.7	399.9	776.6	261.0	847.0	1.2	4,582.9
1990	1,178.6	2,195.8	1,340.1	1,350.3	421.5	1,156.8	66.2	7,709.4
1995	1,268.2	3,307.2	2,432.1	2,100.9	924.0	1,177.3	214.9	11,424.6
2000	1,480.7	2,951.9	4,119.3	3,504.5	1,853.7	2,813.9	699.6	17,423.6
2005	3,019.3	4,165.9	7,206.4	5,120.9	2,616.0	3,535.9	2,047.4	27,711.7
2010	3,772.1	8,853.0	8,976.5	7,971.9	2,538.8	2,980.8	1,465.7	36,559.0
2011	3,719.4	9,928.4	9,043.9	8,295.4	2,326.9	2,719.3	1,331.9	37,365.2
2012	3,714.4	11,046.1	8,816.6	8,985.2	2,095.8	2,612.3	1,255.8	38,526.2
2013	3,671.2	11,854.4	8,718.8	9,617.3	2,058.3	2,713.7	1,279.8	39,913.6
2014 (Q1)	3,660.8	12,120.5	8,714.7	9,798.7	1,946.9	2,802.8	1,355.0	40,399.3

Note: This table provides various outstanding bonds in the United States for selected years (in billion $).

Source: Securities Industry and Financial Markets Association 2014.

period has substantially increased from about $2.5 trillion to $40.4 trillion. This increase represents a compounded growth rate of about 8.7 percent a year. Yet, the growth in Treasury and corporate debt has been even greater. Reflecting sustained budget deficits and increased borrowing by the U.S. government, outstanding Treasuries have grown from $399 billion at the end of 1980 to $11.85 trillion at the end of 2013, representing an annual growth rate of 10.8 percent. The comparable numbers for corporate debt are $457 billion and $9.62 trillion, respectively, implying an annual growth rate of 9.67 percent.

This chapter discusses the characteristics and research on the following bond fund categories: (1) government bond mutual funds, (2) investment grade corporate bond funds, (3) high yield bond funds, (4) municipal bond funds, (5) asset-backed and convertible bond mutual funds, (6) international and global bond funds, (7) indexed bond mutual funds, and (8) closed-end bond funds.

GOVERNMENT BOND MUTUAL FUNDS

Using issuers as the basis for classifying government bond mutual funds often results in having four broad and often overlapping categories. The first category comprises funds that hold a broad category of government bonds, which include Treasuries and securities issued by government agencies and government-sponsored enterprises (GSEs) such as the Government National Mortgage Association (GNMA or Ginnie Mae) or the Tennessee Valley Authority (TVA). The second category contains government bond funds holding only Treasuries, and the third focuses only on securities issued by agencies of the U.S. government. The fourth category of bond funds is more recent. These funds specialize in holding what is popularly referred to as Treasury Inflation Protection Securities (TIPS), which the U.S. Department of the Treasury began issuing in January 1997. With TIPS, the principal (par) value of the underlying bond is adjusted for the U.S. inflation rate, as measured by the non-seasonally adjusted U.S. City Average All Items Consumer Price Index for All Urban Consumers (i.e., CPI-U), but the coupon rate remains fixed. The coupon rate is called the "real rate" because it is the rate that investors ultimately earn above the inflation rate, assuming that the bond was purchased for par.

Some funds specialize in holding government debt of other countries or "sovereigns." These funds can also be included in the government bond mutual fund category, but they usually appear in the global and international bond fund categories owing to additional currency and political risks. Mortgage-backed securities (MBSs) issued by agencies or companies sponsored by the U.S. government are usually discussed as a part of mutual fund investing in asset-backed securities (ABSs) though such securities can also be held by funds with a government bond mandate.

Treasury securities represent the borrowing of the U.S. government, which is the largest issuer of debt securities. Treasuries are backed by the full faith and credit of the U.S. government and coupon payments from these securities are exempt from state and local income taxes in the United States. These securities are also *non-callable*, which means that the issuer does not have the right to retire the issue before the stated maturity date. On the risk spectrum, investors consider these securities as having the lowest default risk and therefore they usually carry the lowest yields. Market participants often consider yields on these securities as the benchmark rate owing to the perceived absence of default risk. Yields on securities with credit risk are derived from the yield of these securities, as the yield on Treasuries is widely used as the base rate for other instruments.

The U.S. government issues four types of traded securities: Treasury bills, notes, bonds, and TIPS. *Treasury bills* are discount instruments (analogous to short-term zero-coupon bonds) representing short-term borrowing of the U.S. government with a maturity at issuance of one year or less. *Treasury notes* and *Treasury bonds* are intermediate-term (i.e., a maturity at issuance greater than one year but not greater than 10 years) and long-term (i.e., a maturity at issuance greater than 10 years) instruments, respectively, and are fixed coupon-bearing instruments. As mentioned previously, TIPS are coupon securities whose principal's reference rate is the CPI-U. Thus, most investors consider TIPS as the best proxy for an intermediate and longer term risk-free asset as other securities carry the risk of loss of purchasing power, once getting into intermediate and longer term holding periods.

The factors driving equity returns and bond returns may differ. This difference is especially true for mutual funds that primarily hold Treasury securities and high-quality straight agency debt. According to Ferson, Henry, and Kisgen (2006), the level of short-term interest rates, slope, and convexity of the term structure might best explain performance of government bond funds. *Convexity* refers to the nonlinear nature of the term structure of interest rates and is measured through the fixed yield on seven-, three-, and one-year Treasury securities. They use a stochastic discount factor (SDF) framework to study actively managed government bond funds from 1986 to 2006. Their evidence shows that the higher level of short-term interest rates is positively related to fund performance. Lower convexity of term structure of interest rates positively affects fund performance, but it is the least relevant of the three (level, slope, and convexity). The SDFs are better able to predict conditional performance of bond mutual funds than segregations based on size, age, expenses, or other traditional characteristics.

Huang and Wang (2014) identify potential benefits of superior timing ability from specialization in the Treasury bond mutual fund market. While the authors find short-term timing ability by Treasury bond fund managers, this ability was not evident once adjusting managerial action for public information. For example, once performance is adjusted for a manager's action resulting from release of public information (e.g., CPI releases), timing ability was not evident. Huang and Wang report some evidence of superior timing ability in managers specializing in Treasury only bond funds as opposed to those investing in Treasury, straight agency, and agency MBSs.

Treasury and straight agency debt by themselves are largely homogeneous securities. The markets for both have substantial liquidity, which makes exploiting market inefficiencies virtually impossible. These securities do not have any significant credit risk and thus lack the possibility of market participants mispricing bonds based on inaccurate assessment of credit risk. Excess risk-adjusted returns can only be derived from accurately forecasting unexpected changes in the yield curve or taking duration risks. Forecasting unexpected interest rate changes is a challenging task for which few managers have a good long-term record of success. Thus, the likelihood that additional active management returns can justify the additional fee is slim. The advice in this regard is to create a portfolio of individual bonds instead of buying mutual funds, portfolio size permitting, especially when a liability structure has to be met. The temptation to outperform the Treasury and straight agency market should be resisted because consistent outperformance is a difficult endeavor in this segment.

INVESTMENT GRADE CORPORATE BOND FUNDS

Bonds issued by corporate entities carrying the top four ratings (Aaa to Baa for Moody's and AAA to BBB for Standard & Poor's) constitute the investment universe of such mutual funds. The corporate bond market is classified based on the broad industry in which the issuer operates. On this dimension, issuers are usually classified into three categories: industrials, financials, and utilities.

Comer and Rodriguez (2013) provide a comparative analysis of investment grade corporate bond funds and government bond funds between 1994 and 2009. Their evidence shows that corporate bond funds outperform Treasury bond funds between 8 to 53 basis points a year on a risk-adjusted basis. Expenses alone cannot explain the difference in performance. Comer and Rodriguez also show that differences in risk-adjusted performance drive fund flows.

Cici and Gibson (2012) use a holdings-based analysis of bond mutual funds. In a holdings-based analysis, researchers look at the securities held by the mutual fund manager. This helps analyze the ability of managers to identify mispriced bonds, absent factors that are beyond a manager's control. By contrast, returns-based analysis includes factors beyond the fund manager's control, such as fund flows that cannot be controlled by the manager but affects performance. Although Cici and Gibson show that the benefits of active management cannot justify the costs, they offer some evidence of timing ability by managers of bond mutual funds. This weak timing ability contradicts strong evidence of perverse timing ability by managers of high-quality corporate bond mutual funds. Boney, Comer, and Kelly (2009) offer evidence of the inability to reallocate between cash and bonds within sectors to generate superior risk-adjusted returns in investment grade corporate bond mutual funds.

Droms and Walker (2006) provide evidence of the persistence of corporate and government bond mutual fund returns between 1990 and 1999. Both short-term positive and negative performance seems to persist though the direction of interest rates seems to drive the direction of the persistence.

The evidence on European corporate bond funds is similar regarding risk-adjusted benchmark comparative performance. Using both conditional and unconditional models, Silva, Cortez, and Armada (2003) offer evidence that these funds cannot outperform passive strategies. Using single or multi-index models does not alter the conclusion, but as expected, multi-index models provide better explanatory power.

Even after considering credit risk, the investment grade corporate bond market appears to be efficient, which substantially reduces the opportunities to exploit mispriced credit or anticipate changes in ratings. Once again, low-cost indexing seems to be the preferred route when seeking investments in high grade corporate bonds.

HIGH YIELD BOND FUNDS

High yield bond funds characterize the bond market segment most associated with volatility, perhaps at par with funds that primarily hold bonds with embedded options such as mortgage backed securities and other ABSs. A substantial body of empirical evidence on high yield bond mutual performance is available.

Most performance evaluation of mutual funds is based on a benchmark. Owing to the equity-like nature of high yield bonds, expecting an uncomplicated comparison to the benchmark is tempting but unrealistic. In practice, choosing an appropriate benchmark for such funds is difficult. For the high yield bond segment, especially actively managed high yield bond funds, any widely quoted benchmark might be inappropriate, because it may not accurately represent the manager's style. The liquidity issues in the high yield bond market are important. A later section of this chapter provides further discussion of some of these issues. Given the challenges of liquidity and style fit, Fridson (1992) concludes that the best benchmark might be a custom benchmark because it can be tailored to the manager's true style.

According to Bailey, Richards, and Tierney (2007), a valid benchmark should be: (1) unambiguous, (2) measurable, (3) appropriate, (4) reflective of current investment opinions, (5) prescribed in advance, (6) investable, and (7) accountable. One of many distinctions in the high yield bond market is the lack of liquidity in many segments and over-the-counter (OTC) dealer market making. When liquidity is absent, some bonds in the benchmark have to be matrix priced. Very few investors are likely to sell at a low, distressed price. This dilemma makes measuring returns erroneous because this inaccurate price becomes part of the manager's return calculation. The fact that a security is hypothetically priced, even when the actual trade might never take place at this price, skews actual performance measurement, as a trade may never happen at the price that is used to calculate the return. Besides the liquidity and style fit issues, additional shortcomings are associated with using widely quoted benchmarks for high yield bond funds. In fact, Levine, Drucker, and Rosenthal (2010) remark that no benchmark can accurately evaluate a high yield bond mutual fund's performance. Many of the seven characteristics of a valid benchmark previously listed are rarely met. Investors need to consider these challenges when evaluating empirical evidence on actively managed high yield bond funds.

Cornell and Green (1991) conduct one of the first studies of low-grade bond funds. They find that over the long run, the performance of such bond funds is comparable to those funds that primarily invest in high-grade bonds after adjusting both samples for risk. While low-grade bond funds are less sensitive to interest rate changes due to their shorter duration, they are more sensitive to equity prices because of their higher credit risk. Using data between 1977 and 1989, however, Blume, Keim, and Patel (1991) find that returns on low-grade bond portfolios exceed those of higher grade bond portfolios but lag equity returns. No relationship exists between the age of the bonds in the portfolio and realized returns. Finally, the authors find no evidence of systematic under- or overpricing in the low-grade bond market.

Trainor (2010) analyzes actively managed high yield bond funds that have a performance record of at least 10 years. Ignoring survivorship bias, he finds that compared to the CSFB High Yield Bond Index, the performance of actively managed funds lagged by about 160 basis points. However, the analysis has limited significance because traditional factors that are relevant in explaining mutual fund performance (e.g., expense ratios) have limited explanatory power with these high yield bond funds.

Using a style-based analysis based on Sharpe's method, Domian and Reichenstein (2008) find that high yield bond fund performance can be attributed to a mix of bond, stock, and cash returns. Performance of these funds persists for short periods when measured using the Sharpe ratio in which the monthly returns have been adjusted for serial correlation. However, Lipton and Kish (2010) find that managers of actively managed high yield bond mutual funds do not add value on a risk-adjusted basis.

This sector of the bond market is perhaps most sensitive to economic growth. During expansionary economic cycles, credit spreads on these bonds narrow and these funds perform well. An opportunity for good credit analysis may also add value to investors' returns. The possible benefits of active management are substantial in this segment, but identifying a superior active manager ex ante remains as challenging as in any mutual fund segment. Controlling fund expenses and using an appropriate benchmark to evaluate performance are two guidelines appropriate for investors seeking active high yield bond fund management.

MUNICIPAL BOND MUTUAL FUNDS

Municipal bond mutual funds are distinctive in three aspects. First, the market is highly U.S. centric, meaning non-U.S. investors find other U.S. bond segments more desirable than the municipal (muni) bond market. Unlike Treasuries and agency debt that is in great demand by foreign governments and non-U.S. domiciled investors, high net worth individual investors, who are primarily U.S. domiciled individuals, dominate the municipal bond segment. The primary reason involves the tax status of the coupon payments, which is the second distinctive feature of this segment of the bond market. Pozen (2002) shows how coupon payments from a municipal bond may be tax-exempt on multiple governmental levels. A municipal bond coupon free from only federal tax is denoted as *single tax-free,* while one whose coupon is without both federal and state income tax liability is called *double tax-free.* A *triple tax-free municipal bond* is one with coupon payments free from federal, state, and local (county, town or city) income taxes. Finally, yields traditionally are among the lowest in this segment because of the tax-exempt status of cash flows.

Municipal bonds can be general obligations (GOs) or revenue. GOs are usually backed by the full faith and credit of the municipality, while revenue bonds are backed by the cash flows of a particular project such as a toll highway or receipts from airport operations. Like corporate and sovereign bonds, most municipal bonds carry a credit rating and cover the full spectrum of risk.

Some municipal bond issues carry additional credit enhancement in the form of *monoline insurance,* which is insurance that promises to compensate investors in the event the issuer cannot make coupon payments or defaults on repaying the principal. Investors should treat such insurance with trepidation because in the event of large sustained defaults the insurance may not be able to cover all losses. For example, during the financial crisis of 2007–2008, these insurance companies became highly vulnerable to economic distress. Lai and Zhang (2013) find that the benefits of insurance initially accrued to issuers as insured bonds carried yields lower than uninsured bonds between 2001 and 2010. However, this benefit vanished during the years of the financial crisis.

Empirical research on municipal bond funds is sparse. Elyasiani and Jia (2011) study closed-end municipal bond fund performance between 1994 and 2004. Their findings show greater persistence in the performance of municipal bond funds than equity and other bond funds although this persistence varies over time. They also find that the dividend yield of the funds is significant in explaining persistently superior performance. For bond funds, the dividend yield essentially is the coupon income from the underlying bonds being paid as dividends by the fund.

Municipal bond funds are usually part of a tax strategy and in most cases single state municipal bonds are more attractive to individual investors than national bond funds because a larger proportion of the yield is likely to be exempt from state income taxes. This is especially valuable for residents of states with punitive income taxes such as California and New York. However, national municipal bond funds offer the benefits of diversification and therefore provide some investment efficiency benefits. Sacrificing yields in favor of bond insurance may not be a prudent strategy in many circumstances because collection on such coverage might be difficult in the occurrence of tail events, such as the ones experienced during the financial crisis. UITs are also a popular method for gaining diversified municipal bond exposure by individual investors.

ASSET-BACKED SECURITIES AND CONVERTIBLE BOND MUTUAL FUNDS

Mutual funds investing in ABSs contain securities whose cash flows are derived from a pool of securities or claims such as mortgages or credit card receivables. *Convertible bond mutual funds* are funds that invest in bonds giving the holder the option of converting all or part of the bond into common equity of the issuer. The value of such bonds is derived from the value of the assets underlying the securities (e.g., the stock price of the issuer with the convertible bond and the value of the asset such as mortgages and credit card receivables for ABSs). Valuing the bonds usually involves determining the value of both the straight security and the embedded option. For the holder of a convertible bond, this embedded option is a long position in a call option written by the issuer.

Given the challenges of valuing such complex securities held by these mutual funds, the temptation exists to assume that a manager with superior analytical skills can consistently outperform a passive benchmark and therefore justify the higher fees. Domian and Reichenstein (2009) study 16 convertible bond mutual funds between 1998 and 2007. They find that the returns from such funds parallel the returns of a portfolio comprising 60 percent stocks, 30 percent bonds, and 10 percent cash. The equivalent underlying stock exposure of these funds has a small cap and growth tilt in terms of style.

Ferson, Kisgen, and Henry (2006) study various segments of the bond market including mutual funds and funds that invest in ABSs. They use an SDF framework conditioned on ex ante economic states to derive an SDF alpha that measures a manager's investment skill and ability to add value. The choice of passive benchmarks and a two-factor model shows that actively managed fixed-income mutual funds lagged behind their benchmark in the majority of states between 1985 and 1999. When credit spreads are high, such bond funds perform better while performance lags in states where short-term interest rates are high or industrial capacity utilization is high.

Mortgage funds lag the GNMA index in all states. Fund performance shows greater heterogeneity based on style as compared to classifications based on traditional measures such as expense ratios.

Although some persistence exists in the short-term performance for high yield bond funds, it is absent for convertible bonds funds. Moreover, managers cannot stand out in terms of performance in the long run. Philpot (2000) presents evidence supporting the lack of such persistence for convertible and global bond funds.

Most convertible bond and ABS funds form part of a multi-fund core strategy or are the plus part of a core plus strategy. In most cases, given the unique and specialized nature of such securities, having such funds as the primary core of a core plus strategy is questionable. However, MBSs form a substantial portion of the Barclay's Aggregate Bond Index. Given the complex nature of the securities underlying these funds, some might logically recommend actively managed funds although the limited empirical evidence still cannot support such a recommendation.

INTERNATIONAL AND GLOBAL BOND FUNDS

For a U.S. based investor, *international or global funds* are mutual funds based in the United States that mandate investing in securities issued by entities outside of the United States. In the United States, a global fund can hold both U.S. and non-U.S. securities while an international fund usually holds only non-U.S. securities. This distinction may be unique to the United States because in other markets all funds that hold non-domestic securities are classified as international. Usually no "global" nomenclature occurs in these markets.

As with equity funds holding non-U.S. stocks, exchange rate movement provides another source of risk and return for these funds. For unhedged portfolios, during the holding period, a stronger domestic currency hurts returns while a weaker domestic currency enhances them. The cost of actively managing global or international portfolios is higher because both transaction and research costs are likely to be higher in non-U.S. markets. Moreover, the U.S. bond market dwarfs other fixed-income markets. However, in the recent past, the European bond market grew substantially in size and often provided a competitive venue for issuers of debt. Investors find the lure of holding non-U.S. bonds enticing for various reasons. Besides the traditional benefit of diversification resulting from a low correlation among returns in different markets, relatively higher returns form the primary attraction for investing in global or international bond funds. The notion is that because of differing economic cycles and low correlations, the impact of the higher risk of these markets is lessened without an associated sacrifice in expected returns. The low interest rate environment of developed economies and accommodative policies of central banks of these countries further spur investors to seek non-U.S. bond markets. The primary source of this attraction is the relatively higher yields in these markets, even though a major portion of these higher returns may come from taking on greater risks.

As with other mutual funds, Gallo and Lockwood (1997) find that actively managed international bond funds do not perform better than a single or multi-index passive benchmark between 1988 and 1994. However, within the sub-period from 1988 to 1991, the managers outperform their benchmarks. The authors report that a multi-index benchmark model is more appropriate for performance evaluation than a single index benchmark. Performance rankings of funds over the sample period differ under the two (single and multi-) index evaluations and show inter-temporally unstable rankings.

In a study of 188 global bond funds from 1993 to 2004, Polwitoon and Tawatnuntachai (2006) find that performance is below that of the benchmark but by less than the expense ratio. Returns increased by 0.5 to 1.0 percent annually without increasing risk as compared to similar domestic funds. This finding implies increased portfolio efficiency through these funds. Some evidence exists of short-term performance persistence and as indicated by enhanced returns, such funds provide diversification benefits to U.S. investors.

Polwitoon and Tawatnuntachai (2008) also study emerging market bond funds over the period 1996 to 2005. Their evidence shows that as a group, emerging market bond fund returns exceed those of domestic funds on a risk-adjusted basis. Investing in such funds offers diversification benefits. Their results are robust across non-conditional models over the entire evaluation period, and in conditional models when restricting the holding period to 36 months. Fund size and high initial minimum investment requirements increase performance but not on a risk-adjusted basis.

Given the growing economic importance of non-U.S. markets, such mutual funds may form an essential part of long-term core portfolios for some investors. For longer investment horizons, holding unhedged portfolios may be advisable because currency returns in the long run likely net out to zero. Also, managers have limited ability to consistently and accurately forecast exchange rates. Although active management may offer some benefits, investors in international and global bond funds need to be wary of expenses, which decrease returns. Risk-seeking investors could look to this segment for adjusting risk exposures during periods when expected returns from equity markets are unattractive.

INDEXED BOND MUTUAL FUNDS

As previously mentioned, empirical evidence on open-end bond mutual funds generally shows that active managers cannot consistently outperform their benchmarks on a risk-adjusted basis. In part, this result may be because of the largely homogeneous nature of the bond market. Such evidence makes a strong argument in favor of indexing bond portfolios. With indexing, the manager tries to match the total return of an index. One objective of an indexed bond mutual fund manager is to minimize the *tracking error*, which in this context is the deviation of the mutual fund return from the benchmark return. Accomplishing this objective is easier in theory than in practice. A bond index is not investable and not subject to management fees. Not all issues in an index are traded every trading day and some issues mature or are called, creating the need for replacements. This replacement process and other mentioned obstacles, create challenges for the manager in replicating the index returns.

Despite the difficulties noted, managers of passive bond mutual funds have additional tools to match benchmark returns that are unavailable to managers of a passive equity mutual fund. If managers of passively managed bond mutual funds can successfully match the various durations (e.g., modified, key rate, and effective) and convexity of the index over time, then possible tracking error largely results from fees and unanticipated changes in a portfolio constituent's returns and spreads.

Some challenges exist in using broad bond indexes for benchmarking and for matching portfolio performance though. Equity indexes as proxy investment portfolios are attractive for two reasons. First, active managers generally cannot beat passive indexes. Second, such indexes broadly constitute the market, which according to portfolio theory are likely to be a proxy for efficient portfolios. According to Granito (1987), however, conventional bond index portfolios do not represent the market portfolio and therefore are not risk-return efficient or optimal.

The index committee closely guards changes in constituents of some widely used equity index portfolios and index exclusion and inclusion of stocks are often regarded as subjective. An example of this practice is the S&P 500 index. Such exclusion and inclusion result in an unexpected price decline in the stock being removed from the index and an increase in the price of the equity being added. Dbouk and Kryzanowski (2009) find similar evidence for bond indexes. Adding or removing a corporate bond from the index results in a positive or negative effect on the return of the bond in question. However, such actions do not affect the equity prices of the issuer and show a lack of importance of this information of such action for stock holders.

Given the challenges with bond indexes, liquidity, and stale pricing issues in the bond market, some logical advice would be to use mutual funds that are not benchmarked to broad bond indexes. Bond index mutual funds that are benchmarked to custom indexes might be preferable because they can better meet the criterion for a valid benchmark. If the goal is to broadly mimic the returns of the bond market, then creating a composite benchmark comprising narrowly focused sub-indexes may be worthwhile. This alternative may be better than indexing to a benchmark with more than 8,000 constituents given the problems highlighted with mimicking such indexes.

CLOSED-END BOND FUNDS

Closed-end bond funds remain a popular investment vehicle. At the end of 2013, bond funds constituted about 59 percent of the $279 billion in closed-end fund assets (Investment Company Institute 2014). These funds have a fixed number of shares and subsequent to the initial public offering (IPO) trading of shares takes place in the secondary market. CEFs may trade at a discount or premium from their NAVs.

Malhotra, Martin, and McLeod (2003) show that CEFs are a more expensive investment option vis-à-vis open-end bond mutual funds. Economic theory suggests that a product delivering the same benefit with a higher cost will eventually be priced out of existence. However, CEFs not only exist, they thrive and grow as indicated earlier. According to Elton, Gruber, Blake, and Shachar (2013), CEFs provide investors with an opportunity to leverage at low cost through margin loans, which might explain why many CEFs sell at a discount from their NAVs. Unrealized capital appreciation and investor sentiment hypotheses primarily drive the discounts on closed-end bond funds. CEF price discounts are also directly related to expenses and foreign holdings. According to Noronha and Rubin (1995), proxies for the asset allocation decision, such as the difference between stock and bond returns, also affect the direction of the discount.

CEFs are inefficient vehicles for a broad investment. They meet particular and limited needs and should be treated as specialty assets. Investors should avoid the enticement of capturing fund discounts or premiums because the additional cost rarely justifies the benefit. Moreover, the ability to leverage is now available with ETFs, which are more efficient both on a transactional and pricing basis.

Summary and Conclusions

Active mutual fund managers typically cannot justify their fees and provide risk-adjusted performance superior to their benchmarks. However, performance evaluation of bond portfolios is much less reliable compared to equity portfolios due to liquidity, maturity, and transactional factors in the bond market. Although some evidence of short-term performance persistence for actively managed bond portfolios exists, similar evidence does not exist for longer term performance persistence.

Empirical evidence on bond mutual funds provides several guidelines for investing. Given the homogeneity and the inability of active managers to distinguish themselves, investors should temper their expectations of trying to outperform the market over extended periods of time. While indexing may be a prescribed strategy for investors seeking exposure to high-quality credit issues, indexing of lower grade bond exposure and portfolios with substantial optionality is challenging due to liquidity and pricing concerns. A portfolio of individual bonds might be the preferred alternative in this case if the size of the portfolio negates the lack of economies of scale. Failing this, the goal should be to find actively managed funds that are appropriately benchmarked (i.e., the benchmark appropriately captures the style of the fund manager).

Compared to equity mutual funds, research on various aspects of bond mutual funds is relatively small. With about $5 trillion in bond exposure through OEFs, many questions still remain to be answered. For example, given the size of transaction costs related to individual bond trading (e.g., brokerage fees and bid-ask spreads) and mutual fund costs (e.g., expense ratios) what might be the optimal size of a self-managed bond portfolio? Because problems exist with comparing performance to bond indexes, can researchers develop a widely accepted method of evaluating bond portfolio performance that the investing public can understand? With the increasing use of electronic trading and improved price disclosures, accessing better quality and substantially more data on fixed-income markets is now possible. Many segments of the bond mutual fund market remain virtually untouched from empirical testing. The municipal bond fund market is one such example.

Discussion Questions

1. Identify four vehicles for investors to acquire exposure to the fixed-income market and describe advantages and disadvantages of each.
2. Discuss the challenges faced by bond index mutual fund managers compared with equity indexing.

3. Define window dressing and discuss its occurrence in bond mutual funds.
4. Describe the dimensions available for analyzing the bond mutual fund market.
5. Describe the universe of securities available to municipal bond mutual fund managers.

References

Bailey, Jeffery V., Thomas M. Richards, and David E. Tierney. 2007. "Evaluating Portfolio Performance." In John L. Maginn, Donald L. Tuttle, Jerry E. Pinto, and Dennis W. McLeavey, eds., *Managing Investment Portfolios: A Dynamic Process*, 717–782. Hoboken, NJ: John Wiley & Sons, Inc.

Blake, Christopher R., Edwin J. Elton, and Martin J. Gruber. 1993. "The Performance of Bond Mutual Funds." *Journal of Business* 66:3, 371–403.

Blume, Marshall E., Donald B. Keim, and Sandeep A. Patel. 1991. "Returns and Volatility of Low-Grade Bonds 1977–1989." *Journal of Finance* 46:1, 49–74.

Boney, Vaneesha, George Comer, and Lynne Kelly. 2009. "Timing the Investment Grade Securities Market: Evidence from High Quality Bond Funds." *Journal of Empirical Finance* 16:1, 55–69.

Chen Yong, Wayne E. Ferson, and Helen Peters. 2010. "Measuring the Timing Ability and Performance of Bond Mutual Funds." *Journal of Financial Economics* 98:1, 72–89.

Cici, Gjergji, and Scott Gibson. 2012. "The Performance of Corporate Bond Mutual Funds: Evidence Based on Security-Level Holdings." *Journal of Financial and Quantitative Analysis* 47:1, 159–178.

Comer, George, and Javier Rodriguez. 2013. "A Comparison of Corporate versus Government Bond Funds." *Journal of Economics and Finance* 37:4, 495–510.

Cornell, Bradford J., and Kevin Green. 1991. "The Investment Performance of Low-Grade Bond Funds." *Journal of Finance* 46:1, 29–48.

Dbouk, Wassim, and Lawrence Kryzanowski. 2009. "Impact of Bond Index Revisions." *Applied Financial Economics* 19:9, 693–702.

Domian, Dale L., and William Reichenstein. 2008. "Returns-Based Style Analysis of High Yield Bond Funds." *Journal of Fixed Income* 17:4, 72–87.

Domian, Dale L., and William Reichenstein. 2009. "Returns-based Style Analysis of Convertible Bond Funds." *Journal of Fixed Income* 18:3, 52–64.

Droms, William G., and David A. Walker. 2006. "Performance Persistence of Fixed Income Mutual Funds." *Journal of Economics and Finance* 30:3, 347–355.

Elton, Edwin J., Martin J. Gruber, Christopher R. Blake, and Or Shachar. 2013. "Why Do Closed-End Bond Funds Exist? An Additional Explanation for the Growth in Domestic Closed-End Bond Funds." *Journal of Financial and Quantitative Analysis* 48:2, 405–425.

Elyasiani, Elyas, and Jingy Jia. 2011. "Performance Persistence of Closed-End Funds." *Review of Quantitative Finance and Accounting* 37:3, 381–408.

Ferson, Wayne E., Tyler R. Henry, and Darren J. Kisgen. 2006. "Evaluating Government Bond Fund Performance with Stochastic Discount Factors." *Review of Financial Studies* 19:2, 423–456.

Ferson, Wayne E., Darren J. Kisgen, and Tyler R. Henry. 2006. "Fixed Income Fund Performance across States." *Research in Finance* 23, 1–62.

Fridson, Martin S. 1992. "High-Yield Indexes and Benchmark Portfolios." *Journal of Portfolio Management* 18:2, 77–83.

Fulkerson, Jon A., Bradford D. Jordan, and Timothy B. Riley. 2013. "Return Chasing in Bond Funds." *Journal of Fixed Income* 22:4, 90–103.

Gallo, John G., and Larry J. Lockwood. 1997. "The Performance of International Bond Funds." *International Review of Economics & Finance* 6:1, 17–36.

Granito, Michael R. 1987. "The Problem with Bond Index Funds." *Journal of Portfolio Management* 13:4, 42–48.

Huang, Jing-Zhi, and Ying Wang. 2014. "Timing Ability of Government Bond Fund Managers: Evidence from Portfolio Holdings." *Management Science* 60:4, 2091–2109.

Huij, Joop, and Jeroen Denwall. 2008. "'Hot Hands' in Bond Funds." *Journal of Banking & Finance* 32:4, 559–572.

Investment Company Institute. 2014. *Investment Company Fact Book*, 54th Edition. Washington, DC: Investment Company Institute.

Lai, Van Son, and Xueying Zhang. 2013. "On the Value of Municipal Bond Insurance: An Empirical Analysis." *Financial Markets, Institutions & Instruments* 22:4, 209–228.

Levine, Robert, Eve Drucker, and Steven Rosenthal. 2010. "The Problems and Challenges of High-Yield Bond Benchmarking." *Journal of Portfolio Management* 36:4, 93–98.

Lipton, Amy F., and Richard J. Kisch. 2010. "Robust Performance Measures for High Yield Bond Funds." *Quarterly Review of Economics and Finance* 50:3, 332–340.

Malhotra, D. K., Rand Martin, and Robert W. McLeod. 2003. "Investment Selection and Open- and Closed-End Bond Fund Expenses." *Journal of Business and Economic Studies* 9:1, 42–65.

Morningstar Inc. 2014. *The Morningstar Category Classifications*. Chicago: Morningstar Inc.

Noronha, Gregory M., and Bruce L. Rubin. 1995. "Closed-End Bond Fund Discounts: Agency Costs, Investor Sentiment and Portfolio Content." *Journal of Economics and Finance* 19:2, 29–45.

Ortiz, Cristina, José Luis Sarto, and Luis Vicente. 2012. "Portfolios in Disguise? Window Dressing in Bond Fund Holdings." *Journal of Banking & Finance* 36:2, 418–427.

Philpot, James. 2000. "Performance Persistence and Management Skill in Non-conventional Bond Mutual Funds." *Financial Services Review* 9:3, 247–259.

Philpot, James, Douglas Hearth, James N. Rimbey, and Craig T. Schulman. 1998. "Active Management, Fund Size, and Bond Mutual Fund Returns." *Financial Review* 33:2, 115–126.

Polwitoon, Sirapat, and Oranee Tawatnuntachai. 2006. "Diversification Benefits and Persistence of US-Based Global Bond Funds." *Journal of Banking & Finance* 30:10, 2767–2786.

Polwitoon, Sirapat, and Oranee Tawatnuntachai. 2008. "Emerging Market Bond Funds: A Comprehensive Analysis." *Financial Review* 43:1, 51–84.

Pozen, Robert C. 2002. *The Mutual Fund Business*, 2nd Edition. Boston, MA: Houghton Mifflin Company.

Redman Arnold L., and Nell S. Gullet. 2007 "Impact of Fund, Management and Market Characteristics on Bond Mutual Fund Performance." *Journal of Asset Management* 7:6, 429–442.

Reipe, Mark W. 2000. "Portfolio Size and the Bond Funds vs. Bonds Decision." *Journal of Financial Planning* 13:2, 36–38.

Securities Industry and Financial Markets Association. 2014. "Outstanding U.S. Bond Market Debt." Available at http://www.sifma.org/research/statistics.aspx.

Silva, Florinda, Maria do Céu Cortez, and Manuel R. Armada. 2003. "Conditioning Information and European Bond Fund Performance." *European Financial Management* 9:2, 201–230.

Trainor, William J. 2010. "Performance Measurement of High Yield Bond Mutual Funds." *Management Research Review* 33:6, 609–616.

13

Stock Mutual Funds

GRADY PERDUE
Professor of Finance, University of Houston–Clear Lake

Introduction

Equity mutual funds are one of the primary investment vehicles used by individual investors in both brokerage accounts and self-managed retirement accounts. According to the Investment Company Institute (2014), $15 trillion was invested in U.S.-based mutual funds including money market funds as of year-end 2013, with 38 percent of that wealth in domestic equity funds and another 14 percent in world equity funds. U.S.-based equity funds received about $160 billion in net cash inflows in 2013.

The major attraction of equity funds is the potential for strong long-run returns for investors. Many investors are familiar with Morningstar, Inc. (2014) data that reports the performance of multiple asset classes in the U.S. financial markets across approximately the past nine decades. The 10.1 percent historical geometric mean return for large company stocks from 1926 through 2013 and an even greater mean return for small company stocks suggests that equity investing could be an attractive asset class for long-term investors who believe that they can wait out the down markets such as 2008 and 2009.

Research shows that asset allocation is the major determinant of a portfolio's risk-return characteristics (Brinson, Hood, and Beebower 1986; Brinson, Singer, and Beebower 1991; Ibbotson and Kaplan 2000). For example, the asset allocation in an equity fund's portfolio is almost entirely equities with some differences in cash allocations from one fund to the next. Since asset allocation is essentially the same from one equity fund to the next, portfolio managers and money management companies that create the funds control variables that help explain the differences in risk, return, and other characteristics between any two funds. Examples of such variables include fees, security selection, portfolio turnover, and tilting the portfolio toward a particular sector or sub-market.

One factor that distinguishes equity mutual funds from closed-end equity funds or other equity-type investment companies is that shares of equity funds do not trade on a secondary market. As these shares are not traded through an organized market, investors are effectively prevented from using certain portfolio management strategies that are connected with the ownership of individual common stocks such as stop-loss orders. Since certain portfolio management strategies that investors in individual stocks might use are unavailable to mutual fund investors, investors must rely more on their asset allocation strategies and the selection of superior performing funds to reach their investment goals.

Before determining how to select appropriate mutual funds, an investor should take several steps. First, the investor should establish financial goals and have both target monetary values for funding these goals and the appropriate time horizons for accumulating the required wealth. Next, the investor should specify the accepted level of risk and expected level of return on the portfolio. Third, the investor should apply the information gathered in the first two steps to develop an asset allocation strategy. Finally, the investor should determine which mutual funds to include in the portfolio.

The purpose of investing is to meet future needs and to accomplish future goals. Unfortunately, knowing exactly what will happen to an investment in the future is impossible. That lack of foreknowledge is the uncertainty or risk associated with any investment. So investors strive to mitigate risks, while seeking to earn a required rate of return to reach investment goals. For mutual fund investors, this process requires selecting funds that will meet specific risk and return requirements.

Investors should look beyond their intuitive feelings to select funds that will perform well. Fortunately, research suggests an alternative to simple intuition is possible. For example, studies by Hendricks, Patel, and Zeckhauser (1993) as well as Fortin and Michelson (2010) address the connection between a mutual fund's past and future performance. The central finding in this literature is that past performance can be somewhat predictive of future performance.

This chapter examines current research as it relates to selecting equity mutual funds. The rest of the chapter is organized into four sections. The first section discusses the search for positive alphas, which investors seek for their funds and portfolios. *Alpha* is a risk-adjusted return above that of the benchmark. If the investor can construct a portfolio that produces a positive alpha, then the portfolio has superior performance relative to other portfolios with similar risk. The next section explores alternate methods to examine mutual funds using evaluation approaches other than alpha. Many of these alternate approaches are better known to the general investing community and more frequently used by individual investors. This section also explores measurement issues with alpha. The third section discusses the stock selection ability of mutual fund managers. Given that most equity funds target a particular segment of the equity market (e.g., domestic small capitalization), asset allocation decisions are virtually taken away from the manager. In this case, the only control that a manager exerts over the portfolio is security selection. If the manager cannot offer superior buy and sell decisions, then active management provides no value to investors. The final section provides a summary and conclusions.

The Search for Alpha

If past performance can be predictive of future performance, then an accurate measurement of past performance is essential for predicting future performance. So investors should consider the best method to evaluate past performance of an equity mutual fund. A widely accepted means of assessing the performance of a portfolio is using alpha, developed by Jensen (1968). This investment evaluation tool allows the investor to make a risk-adjusted comparison of the performance of an investment to what the capital asset pricing model (CAPM) shows should happen. Equation 13.1 shows the model used to calculate alpha:

$$\alpha = R_p - \left[R_f + \beta_p\left(R_m - R_f\right)\right], \tag{13.1}$$

where alpha, α, is the difference between a portfolio's actual return and the return that the CAPM shows should be earned; R_p is the portfolio return; R_f is the risk-free rate; β_p is the portfolio beta; and R_m is the market return. A positive alpha represents superior performance and a negative alpha represents inferior performance. A zero alpha means that the portfolio earned the return that the CAPM indicated it should earn.

Several recent studies examine the continued use of alpha to select mutual funds. For example, Budiono and Martens (2010) use fund characteristics to predict future mutual fund return performance. Using the results of previous studies, the authors examine the following: (1) the alpha of the fund's portfolio across the three preceding years, (2) the *t*-statistic of that alpha, (3) the fund's expense ratio, (4) the portfolio's size, (5) the age (time) since the fund's inception, (6) the portfolio's turnover rate, and (7) volatility as measured by the standard deviation of returns. Using monthly data between 1962 and 2006, they divide the data into two subsets using the first subset to ascertain the key predictive variables and the second set to confirm their results. Budiono and Martens find three significant variables in predicting future performance: alpha (representing past performance), the *t*-statistic of the alpha, and the turnover ratio. Each variable is positively correlated with favorable future performance.

Fama and French (1993) developed a model used to derive each fund's alpha. Equation 13.2 shows the Fama–French three-factor model for individual securities:

$$R_{it} - R_{ft} = a_i + b_{i1}\left(R_{mt} - R_{ft}\right) + b_{i2}SMB_t + b_{i3}HML_t + e_{it}. \tag{13.2}$$

The first factor is the same market risk factor in the CAPM. The second factor is Small Minus Big (SMB), which is the return on a portfolio of small minus large capitalization (cap) stocks in which the two portfolios have approximately the same average book-to-market (BM) ratio. The third factor is High Minus Low (HML). This factor is the return on a portfolio of high minus low BM value companies of about the same size. The remaining alpha is the portion of the return that could not be explained by the three factors. According to Fama and French, the results of their research show that their multifactor model does a better job of explaining non-diversifiable risk than a single factor model.

The Carhart (1997) model extends the Fama and French (1993) three-factor model by adding a fourth factor called *momentum*, which measures the tendency of a company's stock to continue doing well or poorly in the market. Carhart uses a momentum factor previously described by Grinblatt and Titman (1992) as the tendency for a well performing fund to continue to do so during the next year. More recent studies such as Fortin and Michelson (2010) continue to confirm that finding. Equation 13.3 shows Carhart's revised model:

$$R_{it} - R_{ft} = a_i + b_{i1}\left(R_{mt} - R_{ft}\right) + b_{i2}SMB_t + b_{i3}HML_t + b_{i4}MOM_t + e_{it}. \qquad (13.3)$$

The momentum factor (MOM) added to the preceding three-factor model is the one-year momentum in stock returns. Carhart reports that this additional variable enhances the model's explanatory power. His version of the model is sometimes referenced as the Fama and French four-factor model.

Budiono and Martens (2010) test their results against the momentum model developed by Carhart (1997) and against a passive buy-and-hold market index strategy using the S&P 500 index. Their results show that their model using alpha, turnover, and the *t*-statistic of alpha, outperforms both the four-factor momentum model and the passive market index strategy. Their analysis does not include tax considerations. Since the higher return funds that their model recommends also tend to be higher turnover funds, an investor using mutual funds might need to distinguish between those funds with the best performance and those with the best after-tax performance.

Increasingly more research on using alpha in portfolio evaluation has allowed scholars to gain greater understanding of its usefulness as a performance measurement. According to Barras, Scaillet, and Wermers (2010), many alphas contain false information. Their argument is that investors should view a fund that produces a positive alpha through pure luck differently from one that produces a positive alpha as the result of skilled management. While some investors might perceive a positive return is a positive return regardless of the alpha source, alpha's predictive power would differ if based on luck instead of the fund manager's skill. Skill has a much greater chance of continued success than luck.

The Barras et al. (2010) data set comprises a group of 2,076 domestic equity mutual funds each having at least 60 months of operation between 1975 and 2006. The data set includes 1,304 growth funds, 388 aggressive growth funds, and 384 growth and income funds. They analyze the funds after allowing for expenses. Barras et al. divide these funds into three groups. The first group includes those funds with a negative alpha, consisting of unskilled managers who are unable to produce returns to cover trading costs and expenses. The second group comprises funds with an alpha of zero, consisting of funds with managers who are just able to cover trading costs and expenses. The last group contains funds with skilled managers who could cover their trading costs and expenses and still produce a positive alpha for investors.

Barras et al. (2010) use the *t*-statistic of each fund's alpha as the performance measure, which is the same variable used by Budiono and Martens (2010). Barras et al. examine the *p*-value associated with each fund's *t*-statistic, knowing that the *p*-values of skilled and unskilled managers are very small. They use the data to find "false discoveries." After reclassifying funds properly with no false alphas, they determine that 75.4 percent of the funds are zero alpha funds, and 24 percent of the funds exhibit negative alphas. That leaves only 0.6 percent of the funds as possessing truly positive alphas. Their evidence shows that no growth funds have skilled managers, only 3.9 percent of the aggressive growth funds have skilled managers, and none of the growth and income funds have skilled managers as represented by positive alphas.

Reworking their analysis into rolling five-year periods, Barras et al. (2010) find other notable results. For example, they initially report as many as 14.4 percent of managers can be classified as skilled because of positive alphas, but as their analysis proceeds that rate declines to only 0.6 percent. Why? They note two problems. First, no funds created in the 1990s show skilled management as evidenced by positive alpha. These managers did not show superior stock-picking skills. Second, many of the funds that were created before 1990 start with positive alphas but all have zero or negative alphas by the end of the study period. Perhaps this finding results from the tendency of investors to flood successful managers with new funds that they cannot successfully invest. Nonetheless, the percentage of funds with skilled managers who produce positive alpha erodes sharply during the 1990s. This conclusion may be consistent with a similar finding of Amman and Verhofen (2009) about the market becoming increasingly efficient.

To complete their analysis, Barras et al. (2010) repeat their study using pre-expense data. Using these data would show if a fund manager has superior stock selection skills, but still could not earn enough return to cover expenses. Although the authors previously report that only 0.6 percent of the funds have positive alphas, the portion of the data set with positive alphas increases to 9.6 percent in this study. Nevertheless, 9.6 percent remains a distressingly low percent because it indicates that 93.4 percent of active managers have zero or negative alphas even when calculating alphas gross of fees.

In summary, an important component of the analysis is that the portion of active managers who consistently select successful stocks is very small. After fees and on a risk-adjusted basis, Barras et al. (2010) find that almost no managers produce a positive alpha for their investors.

Previous studies assume that a positive alpha represents outperformance and a negative alpha means underperformance. This approach is based on the assumption that the relevant index benchmark has an implicit alpha of zero. But Costa and Jakob (2006) and Cremers, Petajisto, and Zitzewitz (2008) establish that the four-factor model could report positive or negative alphas for indexes because of the weighting of the indexes toward one or more of the four factors in the model. Indexes have alphas different from zero because a fund could underperform relative to its passive benchmark index even with a negative alpha and could still offer superior performance relative to its index.

Using a data set of 211 growth and income funds from the CRSP Survivor-Bias-Free U.S. Mutual Fund database, Costa and Jakob (2010) examine monthly data for the 48 months between 2004 and 2007. During this period, 28 of the 211 funds outperform the index after fees with no adjustment for risk. They apply the four-factor model to each fund as done in previous studies. Costa and Jakob report that the mean alpha for the funds is –0.15 percent or –1.8 percent if annualized, implying that most of the funds underperform the index on a risk-adjusted basis. With the application of the four-factor model, the researchers find only four positive alphas, which are not statistically different from zero. The remaining 207 funds have negative alphas, with 172 of those being significantly different than zero.

Costa and Jakob's (2010) contribution derives from their next step of analyzing each fund to that of the S&P 500 index benchmark. Using the four-factor model, they find the index has a statistically significant negative alpha based on the t-test. Then they apply a pair-wise F-test to compare the four-factor coefficients from the funds against those of the index. The results show that two funds significantly outperform the index while 138 funds significantly underperform. The results on the remaining funds are not statistically significantly different from zero. These results are different from the testing fund performance based on the initial application of the four-factor model. As in their expanded analysis, both the number of funds with either significantly positive or significantly negative alphas increases. Adding the benchmark to their overall evaluation process allows for an improved performance measurement of the fund's active manager.

Costa and Jakob (2011) use the same method to determine if funds are using the correct benchmark. Working with 70 equity mutual funds using the S&P 500 index as their benchmark, the authors use a four-factor model to compare characteristics to those of the S&P 500 index and 17 other equity market indexes. Their findings show that some funds either growth or value orientations that differ from the S&P 500 index. Return data show that 65 of the 70 funds outperform the S&P 500 index, but this analysis also reports that the S&P 500 index is not the best benchmarks for almost all of the funds. In the 60-month study period ending in December 2009, they report that when applying their method and using the correct indexes, less than 9 percent of the 70 funds have both positive and significant performance.

Continuing with research related to the three- and four-factor models, Elton, Gruber, and Blake (2011) observe that the standard way to estimate a portfolio beta is to separately measure the beta of each asset and then find the beta of the portfolio as the weighted beta of the assets in the portfolio. The alternative is to use time series regression to regress the returns of the portfolio against the returns of the market index to find the beta. The results of the two approaches should only be the same if the assets comprising the portfolio remain unchanged, meaning the manager does not engage in trading with the portfolio. If an active manager changes the composition of the portfolio, the two approaches would measure different portfolio betas. Elton et al. seek to determine whether using betas and alphas found based on the portfolio's holdings can do a better job of selecting funds than if the betas and alphas are derived directly from portfolio returns.

Using a Morningstar data set of non-index equity funds with monthly data between 1994 and 2005, Elton et al. (2011) estimate betas using the monthly compositions of the funds in their data set. They also explore the predictability of the data using quarterly, semiannual, and annual portfolio compositions, but eventually report that monthly data predict more accurately ex post alphas. They then calculate alphas of funds using the three-factor and four-factor models. For the models, they use both the betas they calculate based on portfolio holdings and by regression analysis as did Fama and French (1993) and Carhart (1997). Their evidence shows that they could more accurately predict superior fund performance in subsequent periods using the betas and alphas derived from portfolio holdings data. They also note that using more frequent holdings data (e.g., monthly rather than quarterly) results in superior predictive ability.

Beyond Alpha

Beyond using alpha to evaluate equity mutual fund portfolio performance, Brooks and Porter (2012) note the importance of using *performance attribution*, also called *attribution analysis*, to determine how a manager's sector and security selection contribute to the performance of the fund's portfolio against the fund's self-selected and perhaps customized benchmark. *Performance* or *attribution analysis* is the separation of the fund's performance into the portions of that performance that come from the overall performance of the market. The two portions of the attribution analysis consist of the manager's sector allocation and the individual security selection in the portfolio. The outcomes of that attribution analysis are key components in determining managerial compensation, as the sector allocations and security selections are what the manager actually contributes to the portfolio's management. Performance attribution analysis is important because it segregates sector allocation decisions from security selection decisions, whereas the studies previously described combine the two into what is treated as security selection. This analysis helps to explain the source of alpha beyond simply measuring it.

Studying attribution analysis requires having a custom benchmark that a fund uses as the "bogey" against which the manager's sector and security selection decisions can be compared. Although Brooks and Porter (2012) lack that information, they arrive at a reasonable proxy for each fund's benchmark. The authors compare each fund against its bogey benchmark and the CRSP index, which is similar to the Wilshire 5000 index. They find that the funds have a slightly higher return and "materially less" risk relative to a passive portfolio, primarily due to their ability to outperform passive management during the 2001–2002 bear market. They also find that some managers exhibit superior sector selection skills but the gains are eroded by poor security selection decisions. Mid-cap, small cap blend, and value funds outperform the CRSP index with superior stock and sector selection decisions throughout the study period. Large cap and growth funds exhibit poor security selection skills when measured against the CRSP index. Overall, managers do not exhibit strong security selection skills.

Although the academic community tends to focus on the three- and four-factor models in recent years, the Sharpe ratio remains the best known and most widely used portfolio evaluation tool. Investors also use other evaluation techniques such as the Treynor ratio and the information ratio.

Ornelas, Silva, and Fernandes (2012) compare mutual fund rankings by comparing the Sharpe ratio with 13 other performance measures. The study shows that different ratios report different information about the same portfolio, showing that the chosen performance measurement tool can determine the relative ranking of the analyzed funds. The major premise of this study is that using the standard deviation of returns in the Sharpe measure presupposes a normal distribution of returns. However, the authors contend that return distributions are often non-normal, which makes using the standard deviation and Sharpe ratio inappropriate. The first major reason they cite for this problem is that certain non-equity assets held in some portfolios have non-symmetric distributions that skew a portfolio's distribution. Second, they observe that the use of leverage or the manager's changing the portfolio's composition could also skew a portfolio's returns. With the excessive presence of non-normal assets, the portfolio's returns might be quite skewed. Given the absence of those factors, their argument for alternative performance evaluation methods is much weaker.

This perspective is not mere speculation. Investors seek returns, but are also concerned about risk. Do equity portfolio managers tend to vary the risk level in their portfolios? If the risk measure does not properly describe a portfolio's risk, then this could affect any risk-adjusted portfolio evaluation.

Researchers have addressed this matter in the mutual fund "tournament" literature. The theory in that literature posits that fund managers are in a performance competition. Performance is important to managers and their companies because good performance attracts more investable funds from investors, which increases compensation for the manager and profits for the management company. Using monthly data between 1980 and 1991, Brown, Harlow, and Starks (1996) report that underperforming fund managers in the first half of the year tend to have a larger standard deviation of returns in the second half of the year than do superior performing managers. This behavior could be interpreted as taking on more risk hoping to increase performance. Examining monthly data between 1983 and 1993, Chevalier and Ellison (1997) find that underperforming funds increase volatility relative to their benchmarks in the last quarter of the year.

Two more recent studies address whether managers change risk levels due to performance. Amman and Verhofen (2009) use multiple risk measures to explore changes in risk-taking. Using data between 2001 and 2005, they quantify fund performance using a four-factor model. Their results show that better performing funds start with a higher level of volatility than underperforming funds and also are more likely to increase risk as the year progresses. They also find that as the year progresses, the more successful funds decrease their market risk or beta. Additionally, Amman and Verhofen report that successful funds increase their allocation to small cap firms and to momentum stocks during the year. Unsuccessful funds shift their portfolios toward large cap companies and low momentum investments. Successful growth funds increase their growth allocation, and successful value funds increase their value allocation. Funds unsuccessfully pursuing a growth or value strategy increase their allocation to the alternate strategy. Amman and Verhofen also examine whether managers change tracking error with their benchmark, showing increasing active or passive portfolio management. Successful funds make little change in what they are doing, but underperforming funds decrease tracking error showing a more passive, benchmark-like strategy.

During their study period, Amman and Verhofen (2009) note that the dispersion of returns and alphas decrease among the 8,000 funds researched. They hypothesize that the decrease in alphas might show that markets became more efficient over the period. If they are correct, their observation on returns and alphas is consistent with the work of Bhojraj, Cho, and Yehuda (2012), who discuss major regulatory changes during that timeframe that would reduce a manager's ability to generate abnormal positive returns.

First, the Securities and Exchange Commission (SEC) implemented Regulation FD (Fair Disclosure) in 2000, which reduced the ability of mutual fund managers to get non-public information. Second, the SEC, New York Attorney General, and other organizations jointly announced in December 2002 an initial settlement greatly restricting the sale of investment information by investment banking firms to mutual funds. This announcement included enforcement actions and fines against 10 large financial firms.

Finally, in September 2003, the "market timing" and "late trading" scandals rocked the mutual fund industry, resulting in increased industry examination. The market timing scandal involved funds that permitted favored clients to engage in frequent trading to take advantage of short-term market fluctuations, even though the fund documents prohibited such trading. The late trading scandal involved Bank of America's Nations Funds, which allowed a hedge fund to purchase mutual fund shares after the market closed. Bhojraj et al. find a decline in the stock selection abilities of mutual fund managers in the large fund families affected by these three factors.

Chen and Pennacchi (2009) also examine the potential tendency of portfolio managers to shift risk in the middle of the year. Using monthly data, they study the changes in the portfolios of more than 6,000 funds classified as having growth portfolios or growth and income portfolios between 1962 and early 2006. The authors report no evidence that underperforming funds increase the standard deviation of their returns, but instead find that such funds actually decrease the standard deviation. However, Chen and Pennacchi find the same increase in tracking error among underperforming funds as Amman and Verhofen (2009) report.

Ornelas et al. (2012) examine a group of fixed-income, equity, and asset allocation mutual funds between January 1998 and August 2008. Although they include various measures, their study focuses on the manipulation proof performance measure (Ingersoll, Spiegel, Goetzmann, and Welch 2007), because it provides significantly different results from the Sharpe ratio. Many other evaluation tools produce results that are highly correlated with the results from the Sharpe ratio, resulting in similar fund ranking regardless of the analytical tools used.

According to Ornelas et al. (2012), different evaluation tools can produce different results particularly if using the manipulation proof performance measure (MPPM). They argue that trading strategies and varying portfolio compositions can cause portfolios to have return distributions that are not normally distributed, so analysis techniques that are based on assumed normal distributions are not appropriate. The MPPM is designed to allow for these factors, and so it potentially ranks funds in different order than other techniques. This conclusion suggests that investors should ensure their evaluation tools are consistent with the behavior of the assets in the evaluated portfolios. A tool that works well evaluating one fund may not work well when evaluating another fund with different assets in its portfolio.

Betker and Sheehan (2013) address the issue of how the results of single and multiple factor models differ when ascertaining the alphas of mutual funds. They note that practitioners use the Jensen (1968) single factor model rather than the multiple factor models that have gained prominence in the academic community. In their study, Betker and Sheehan use Jensen's model with several different individual indexes, the Fama and French (1993) three-factor model, and the Carhart (1997) four-factor model. For the single factor model, they use the S&P 500 index as the first single factor index, a "best fit" index taken from the Russell indexes, and a custom index that is a weighted average of the Russell Large Growth, Large Value, Small Growth, and Small Value indexes plus the Citigroup three-month Treasury-bill index. The authors use these single and multiple factor models to analyze mutual funds in the Zephyr database, which reports monthly mutual fund returns between 1991 and 2010. After eliminating index funds and other types of funds, their final data set comprises 2,703 mutual funds.

Betker and Sheehan (2013) find that single factor models each produce significantly higher mean and median alphas than those found using multiple factor models.

Their evidence also shows that, when using the S&P 500 index as a proxy for the market portfolio, the single factor model consistently produces higher alphas than when using the Russell indexes. Since the single factor models produce positive median alphas and the multiple factor models produce negative alphas, this implies entirely different conclusions about the performance of the average fund manager. Using best fit indexes for the single factor models, the alphas are very similar to the multiple factor models for large cap growth and large cap value. However, when turning to small cap indexes, the single factor models produce average alphas that exceed the multiple factor alphas by more than 200 basis points.

Investors should consider relative rankings. For example, is a mutual fund that a single factor model finds to be a top quartile fund also a top quartile fund when evaluated using multiple factor models? Betker and Sheehan (2013) find that with 5-year and 10-year alphas when a fund is ranked as a top or bottom quartile fund by the single factor models, about 25 percent of the time the four-factor model ranks the fund in a different quartile. When they rank funds as top quartile by the single factor model using any of the proposed indexes, 26 percent of the funds are also ranked in one of the other three quartiles by the four-factor model.

Betker and Sheenan (2013) also explore whether positive alphas persist from one period to the next. Although alphas are computed using historical data, investors hope that these alphas also show strong future performance. The authors find that single factor alphas are more likely to show persistently positive alpha from one period to the next, with about 58 percent of funds with positive alphas in one period showing positive alphas in the next period. However, the multiple factor models do not show evidence of the persistence of positive alphas in consecutive periods. Interestingly, the multiple factor models show persistence in negative alphas from one period to the next, with over 62 percent of funds with negative alphas in one period showing negative alphas in the next.

Betker and Sheenan (2013) conclude that single factor alpha models tend to give different results than multiple factor models about the performance of mutual funds. Using single factor models, individual investors and their financial advisors are potentially misled about mutual fund performance on both historical and future performance. Betker and Sheenan contend that the investing public is better served using multiple factor models.

Stock Selection

Substantial research attempts to determine if mutual fund managers can effectively pick stocks. Studies often find that an overwhelming percentage of funds have zero or negative alphas. This evidence suggests that portfolio managers are not good enough at stock selection to produce the positive alphas that investors typically desire. Since most stock funds target a segment of the equity market such as large cap growth companies, the fund manager can only contribute stock and sector selection without abandoning the fund's stated objectives and asset allocation. Even if the manager is successful at sector selection but adds no value through stock selection, is that enough to overcome the costs of active management relative to a market index?

Baker, Litov, Wachter, and Wurgler (2010) address a manager's ability to select stocks by examining mutual fund stock trades made before earning announcements. They describe the ability to successfully trade stocks as being able to buy stocks that have high returns at their quarterly earnings announcement and sell stocks that yield low returns when earnings are announced. Working with a data set from Thompson Financial spanning 1980 to 2005, Baker et al. find that managers increase the weights of stocks with higher returns in portfolios but decrease the weights of stocks with lower returns. In fact, a disproportionate share of overall returns is generated around the time of earnings announcements, with 18 to 51 percent of abnormal returns for the whole year coming from these transactions. The study includes the implementation of the SEC's Regulation FD in late 2000. Baker et al. find some evidence suggesting that Regulation FD may affect the ability of managers to select stocks. However, they insist that further research is needed to verify any correlation between their data and the new regulation.

Studies offer mixed results regarding the performance record of managers of mutual funds engaged in socially responsible investing (SRI). For example, Ferruz, Muñoz, and Vargas (2012) investigate if managers of religiously based funds perform as well as conventional managers. They do not examine whether such managers can produce positive alphas, but whether their performance is similar to conventional managers. The authors acknowledge that SRI mutual funds differ because they may exclude different stocks due to their focus on a separate set of social issues. For example, for one fund the list of acceptable investments might be related to environmental issues, while another fund is concerned with avoiding the "sin" industries including tobacco, alcohol, and gambling, while another fund may only invest in firms that show good corporate governance practices. Ferruz et al. focus on religiously based funds so they may reach different conclusions than if they examine other SRI funds.

Ferruz et al. (2012) examine a group of 50 religiously based mutual funds between January and September 2010. The authors pair these religious funds against a set of 119 conventional equity funds controlling for age and size. Using the Carhart (1997) four-factor model, their analysis shows that religious managers underperform conventional mangers. Although managers of religious funds do not show evidence of being able to time the market, conventional managers do show some timing ability based on investment style related to company size and BM valuations. Both conventional and religious fund managers cannot pick stocks, but this is only statistically significant for religious fund managers. Ferruz et al. attribute this primarily to the fact that most religious funds use a negative screen that excludes many well performing investments that conventional funds may include in their portfolios. Given this reduced data set, religious fund managers are not skilled enough at stock selection to compensate for this constraint.

Fulkerson (2013) examines how successful managers time their trades. He analyzes data between 1980 and 2007 taken from the Thomson Reuters Financial Network database, CRSP Survivor-Bias-Free Mutual Fund database, and a few other data sources. The results differ between the first and second parts of his data set. From 1980 to1994, Fulkerson provides some evidence that managers have limited ability to pick industries but better ability to pick winners and losers within an industry. However, he finds no ability of industry selection or individual investment selection between 1995 and 2007 or the overall study period.

Petajisto (2013) offers an alternative view of active stock selection by equity fund managers. He explores what he calls *active share*, which is the percent of the portfolio that differs from the benchmark. Active share differs from tracking error in that active share involves stock selection while tracking error measures the systematic factor risk.

Petajisto (2013) analyzes more than 2,700 funds between 1980 and 2009 using multiple databases. The results show that index funds held about 20 percent of mutual fund assets by the end of 2009 and closet indexers managed about another third of the assets. A *closet indexer* is a manager who supposedly actively manages a portfolio but is in fact investing a substantial portion of the portfolio in the passive benchmark index. As a result, the manager can earn higher fees charged for active management on the full portfolio while producing benchmark-like returns by investing a large percentage of the portfolio in the passive benchmark.

Petajisto (2013) offers an example of a fund with a 33 percent active share (implying a 67 percent passive share) and a 1.5 percent management fee on all invested funds effectively amounting to a 4.5 percent active management fee on the active portion of the portfolio. He explains that this is one of the primary reasons that these closet indexers consistently underperform the index. A manager cannot essentially hold the index, charge an active management fee, and consistently outperform the index.

Petajisto (2013) divides active managers into five groups depending on what percentage of their respective portfolios represents true active management. The first (bottom) quintile represents the group of managers with zero to 20 percent of their managed funds in active investments. This indicates that 80 percent or more of the portfolio is invested in the benchmark index, despite it being an actively managed fund. The fifth (top) quintile contains the funds in which 80 to 100 percent of the portfolio holds active positions, so that only between zero and 20 percent of the portfolio of any of these funds is invested in the benchmark index. Using gross returns, he finds that the average fund outperforms its benchmark by 0.96 percent and has a four-factor model alpha of 0.31 percent. Using net returns, the average fund underperforms its benchmark by –0.41 percent and has a four-factor alpha of –0.71. Only the top quintile of funds based on active management has a net of fees positive return and positive alpha. Petajisto also examines persistence of performance and finds that it is fairly consistent across the four more active quintiles but not among the extreme closet indexers.

In summary, Petajisto (2013) recommends that investors only consider investing in two types of funds: pure index funds or pure active management funds. The inability of closet indexers to overcome active management fees with only partial active management increases the difficulty for other funds to produce the positive returns and positive alphas that most investors seek.

Summary and Conclusions

When engaging in investment activities, investors should seek to earn their required rate of return and do so with the least amount of risk possible to meet their long-term financial goals. To accomplish this goal, investors must make critical investment management decisions when selecting individual investments or investment vehicles.

To reach their financial goals, many investors seek to add investments to their portfolios that will produce positive alpha. Alpha represents superior risk-adjusted performance. Investors who add alpha to their portfolios and earn their required rate of return are minimizing their risks. Yet, adding alpha involves two difficulties. First, many studies find that accomplishing this goal is quite difficult. Research shows that very few mutual funds actually produce positive alphas for their investors. This inability to produce positive alphas stems from either a lack of managerial skill or highly efficient markets.

Alternately, investors use other approaches beyond trying to find investments that will produce positive alpha. The ability of mutual fund managers to engage successfully in stock selection is crucial to the concept of active management. Most equity fund managers have little or no control over asset allocations and many are restricted to investing in certain areas of the equity market. Thus, the one tool that they have to produce a positive alpha is successful stock selection. Yet, many studies show that most managers do not possess that ability. This represents a serious and direct challenge to active portfolio management. Managers with no control over asset allocation and little or no ability to successfully pick stocks should not earn an active management fee, although some do.

In short, many investors have invested with managers who are not giving them the risk-adjusted performance that they pay to receive. Some sources estimate that nearly 20 percent of money invested in equity funds are in index funds (Investment Company Institute, 2014). Given the research evidence previously discussed, this percentage should probably be higher. While some managers can produce long-run alphas, such managers are in the vast minority. Unless an investor can locate and invest with such a rare manager, indexing seems to be a better option for investors.

Discussion Questions

1. Define alpha.
2. Discuss issues with measuring alpha.
3. Define performance attribution.
4. Explain how trading distorts risk analysis.
5. Explain closet indexing.

References

Amman, Manuel, and Michael Verhofen. 2009. "The Impact of Prior Performance on the Risk-Taking of Mutual Fund Managers." *Annals of Finance* 5:1, 69–90.

Baker, Malcolm, Lubornir Litov, Jessica A. Wachter, and Jeffrey Wurgler. 2010. "Can Mutual Fund Managers Pick Stocks? Evidence from Their Trades Prior to Earnings Announcements." *Journal of Financial and Quantitative Analysis* 45:5, 1111–1131.

Barras, Laurent, Olivier Scaillet, and Russ Wermers. 2010. "False Discoveries in Mutual Fund Performance: Measuring Luck in Estimated Alphas." *Journal of Finance* 65:1, 179–216.

Betker, Brian, and Joseph Sheehan. 2013. "A Comparison of Single Factor and Multiple Factor Alphas Used in Measuring Mutual Fund Performance." *Financial Services Review* 22:4, 349–365.

Bhojraj, Sanjeev, Young Jun Cho, and Nir Yehuda. 2012. "Mutual Fund Family Size and Mutual Fund Performance: The Role of Regulatory Changes." *Journal of Accounting Research* 50:3, 647–684.

Brinson, Gary P., L. Randolph Hood, and Gilbert Beebower. 1986. "Determinants of Portfolio Performance." *Financial Analysts Journal* 42:4, 39–48.

Brinson, Gary P., Brian D. Singer, and Gilbert Beebower. 1991. "Determinants of Portfolio Performance II: An Update." *Financial Analysts Journal* 47:3, 40–48.

Brooks, LeRoy D., and Gary E. Porter. 2012. "Mutual Fund Performance Attribution: 1994–2005." *Financial Services Review* 21:3, 259–273.

Brown, Keith, W. V. Harlow, and Laura Starks. 1996. "Of Tournaments and Temptations: An Analysis of Managerial Incentives in the Mutual Fund Industry." *Journal of Finance* 51:1, 85–110.

Budiono, Diana, and Martin Martens. 2010. "Mutual Fund Selection Based on Funds Characteristics." *Journal of Financial Research* 33:3, 249–265.

Carhart, Mark. 1997. "On Persistence in Mutual Fund Performance." *Journal of Finance* 52:1, 57–82.

Chen, Hsiu-lang, and George C. Pennacchi. 2009. "Does Prior Performance Affect a Mutual Fund's Choice of Risk? Theory and Further Empirical Evidence." *Journal of Financial and Quantitative Analysis* 44:4, 745–775.

Chevalier, Judith, and Glenn Ellison. 1997. "Risk Taking by Mutual Funds as a Response to Incentives." *Journal of Political Economy* 105:6, 1167–1200.

Costa, Bruce, and Keith Jakob. 2006. "Do Stock Indexes Have Abnormal Performance?" *Journal of Performance Measurement* 11:1, 8–18.

Costa, Bruce, and Keith Jakob. 2010. "Enhanced Performance Measurement of Mutual Funds: Running the Benchmark Index through the Hurdles." *Journal of Applied Finance* 20:1, 95–102.

Costa, Bruce, and Keith Jakob. 2011. "Are Mutual Fund Managers Selecting the Right Benchmark Index?" *Financial Services Review* 20:2, 129–143.

Cremers, Martijn, Antti Petajisto, and Eric Zitzewitz. 2008. "Should Benchmark Indices Have Alpha? Revisiting Performance Evaluation." Social Science Research Network Working Paper 1108856. Available at http://papers.ssrn.com/sol3/papers.cfm?abstract_id=1108856.

Elton, Edwin J., Martin J. Gruber, and Christopher R. Blake. 2011. "Holdings Data, Security Returns, and the Selection of Superior Mutual Funds." *Journal of Financial and Quantitative Analysis* 46:2, 341–367.

Fama, Eugene, and Kenneth French. 1993. "Common Risk Factors in the Returns on Stocks and Bonds." *Journal of Financial Economics* 33:1, 3–56.

Ferruz, Luis, Fernando Muñoz, and María Vargas. 2012. "Managerial Abilities: Evidence from Religious Mutual Fund Managers." *Journal of Business Ethics* 105:4, 503–517.

Fortin, Rich, and Stuart Michelson. 2010. "Mutual Fund Performance Persistence: Still True?" *Academy of Accounting and Financial Studies Journal* 14:4, 29–41.

Fulkerson, Jon A. 2013. "Is Timing Everything? The Value of Mutual Fund Manager Trades." *Financial Management* 42:2, 243–261.

Grinblatt, Mark, and Sheridan Titman. 1992. "The Persistence of Mutual Fund Performance." *Journal of Finance* 47:5, 1977–1984.

Hendricks, Darryll, Jayendu Patel, and Richard Zeckhauser. 1993. "Hot Hands in Mutual Funds: Short-Run Persistence in Relative Performance, 1974–1988." *Journal of Finance* 48:1, 93–130.

Ibbotson, Roger C., and Paul D. Kaplan. 2000. "Does Asset Allocation Policy Explain 40, 90, or 100 Percent of Performance?" *Financial Analysts Journal* 56:1, 26–33.

Ingersoll, Jonathan, Matthew Spiegel, William Goetzmann, and Ivo Welch. 2007. "Portfolio Performance Manipulation and Manipulation-Proof Performance Measures." *Review of Financial Studies* 20:5, 1503–1546.

Investment Company Institute. 2014. *2014 Investment Company Fact Book*. Washington, DC: Investment Company Institute.

Jensen, Michael C. 1968. "The Performance of Mutual Funds in the Period 1945–1964." *Journal of Finance* 23:2, 389–416.

Morningstar, Inc. 2014. *Ibbotson SBBI 2014 Classic Yearbook*. Chicago: Morningstar.

Ornelas, Jose Renato Haas, Antonio Francisco Silva, and Jose Luiz Barros Fernandes. 2012. "Yes, the Choice of Performance Measures Does Matter for Ranking of US Mutual Funds." *International Journal of Finance and Economics* 17:1, 61–72.

Petajisto, Antti. 2013. "Active Share and Mutual Fund Performance." *Financial Analysts Journal* 69:4, 73–93.

14

Socially Responsible Mutual Funds

EDDY JUNARSIN

Associate Professor of Finance, Universitas Gadjah Mada

ENRICO LIBERT

Research Assistant, Universitas Gadjah Mada

FRENDY

PhD candidate, Nagoya University

Introduction

In his seminal article, Friedman (1970) argues that the main goal of large public corporations is shareholder wealth maximization, which implies that managers in such organizations should give little consideration to social criteria when evaluating investment opportunities. However, management and stakeholders of modern corporations have to constantly design and implement business decisions with real ethical and social consequences. Although investment activities that emphasize social or ethical performance are still deemed a niche market in finance, socially responsible investing (SRI) has been growing rapidly in recent decades as public concerns about environment and ethical corporate behavior increase (Baker and Nofsinger 2012).

The investment paradigm of conventional mutual funds prioritizes the most optimum return given a certain risk level. Modern portfolio theory postulates that rational investors should only consider risk and return trade-offs when selecting the most optimum diversification of assets. Different from conventional investments, the underlying philosophy behind SRI is that investment decisions should take into account both financial and non-financial considerations, with the foci on non-financial matters given to ethical, social, environmental, and moral concerns. However, socially responsible mutual funds (SRMFs) only include investments whose desirable social attributes qualify for the inclusion into a portfolio after screening out socially undesirable securities (Reyes and Grieb 1998). Besides the risk and return diversification requirements, SRMFs investment managers are also required to perform several steps of ethical screenings for potential assets. Managers of firms with a substantial amount of SRI face an additional demand for information, which may differ markedly from typical financial-oriented metrics requested by traditional investors.

Consistent with the growing awareness on social responsibility and environmental protection issues, investors have extended their interests in implementing social responsibility criteria in their portfolios, including mutual funds. A mutual fund is considered socially responsible if its investment portfolio satisfies several "good" social and financial criteria. A *socially responsible investment* can be defined as an investment in companies whose actions support social objectives deemed desirable by investors such as reducing environmental pollution and enacting fair labor policies (Rosen, Sandler, and Shani 1991). Specifically, SRMFs are characterized by extensive use of various "social screens" in their investment selections to the mutual funds' portfolios. Other instances of companies that may be excluded from SRMFs are firms in the so-called "sin industries," such as tobacco products, gambling, firearms, and companies with poor human rights or environmental records (Edwards and Samant 2003).

Investors now have choices in creating portfolios with profit and positive social and environmental impacts by incorporating environmental, social, and governance (ESG) criteria as well as ethical considerations. Investors have taken actions so that corporate management considers their demands and carries out changes in its firm. SRI is not a new phenomenon but has evolved since the 1960s to gain its current popularity. Due to an increase in education and globalization, investors now have voiced some concerns about their investment choices and balanced financial returns with reducing environmental and social damage. Thus, whether SRI is an ethical decision or an act of prudence, investors should give it serious consideration in their decision processes. For investors concerned with financial performance, existing empirical evidence generally shows that no statistically significant difference exists between conventional investments and SRI (Kreander, Gray, Power, and Sinclair 2005; Bauer, Derwall, and Otten 2007; Cortez, Silva, and Areal 2009, 2012; Humphrey and Lee 2011).

This chapter provides an overview of SRI and SRMF. The rest of the chapter has the following organization. The first section of this chapter defines SRI and SRMFs. This is followed by sections that examine the types and structure of SRMFs, the sustainability paradigm and SRMF criteria, and strategies for constructing portfolios. Then, the chapter reviews the academic literature on international SRMFs performance and discusses trends and potential development of SRMFs. The next section examines challenges and opportunities faced by both mutual funds managers. The final section offers a summary and conclusions.

Defining Socially Responsible Investing and Socially Responsible Mutual Funds

According to Social Investment Forum (2003, p. 3), the meaning of SRI varies across place and time:

> Socially responsible investing (SRI) is an investment process that considers social and environmental consequences of investments, both positive and negative, within the context of rigorous financial analysis. It is a process of identifying and investing in companies that meet certain standards of corporate social responsibility (CSR) and is increasingly practiced internationally.

The Social Investment Forum is a U.S. organization that represents professionals, firms, institutions, and others engaged in SRI. However, because of the growing emphasis on sustainability, the forum changed its name to the Forum for Sustainable and Responsible Investment (US SIF) on June 9, 2011 (Hinchcliff 2011). US SIF now is part of Global Sustainable Investment Alliance (GSIA) along with the European Sustainable Investment Forum (Eurosif), Social Investment Organization (SIO), Responsible Investment Association of Australasia (RIAA), Association for Sustainable and Responsible Investment in Asia (ASRIA), among others. SRI evolved into sustainable and responsible investing or investment. According to Italian SIF in Eurosif (2014, p. 49):

> Sustainable and Responsible Investment is a medium- to long-term investment strategy which, in the evaluation of companies and institutions, combines financial analysis with a robust environmental, social and governance (ESG) analysis, with the aim to create value for the benefits of investors and the society as a whole.

Another view of SRI is that it involves investments that take into account the financial analysis and sustainability paradigm and/or ESG analysis as part of its decision-making process. Hence, a *socially responsible mutual fund* is a mutual fund that takes into account the financial analysis and sustainability paradigm and/or ESG analysis when developing a portfolio. The GSIA members work hard to bring the standards of SRI and SRMF definitions along with strategies, which are discussed later.

Types and Structure of Socially Responsible Mutual Funds

When modern SRMFs were established in the United States in the early 1970s, investment managers did not have standardized criteria to evaluate socially responsible investments. However, the fund managers used similar evaluation criteria, relying on data disclosed by the firms. Based on the survey of eight socially responsible U.S. mutual funds between 1983 and 1986, the social performance of an asset was measured using these six criteria (Rockness and Williams 1988): (1) environmental protection, (2) equal employment opportunity, (3) treatment of employees, (4) business relations with repressive regimes, (5) product innovation, and (6) defense/weaponry development.

According to Fung, Law, and Yau (2010), SRI portfolios can be divided into four general categories: (1) environmental, (2) religious or ethical, (3) social, and (4) corporate governance. The environmental portfolios, often called "green investments," raise the issues of global warming, climate change, carbon emission, and other environmental problems. The religious or ethical portfolios screen out "sin stocks" such as tobacco, weaponry, and alcohol products. Stocks categorized as "sin stocks" may vary across countries due to different local religions and ethical values that might affect the judgment. The social portfolios are based on labor and human rights issues. Corporate governance portfolios focus on firms that show good corporate citizenship and sound corporate governance practices.

The total amount of assets based on SRI at the end of 2011 had increased by 22 percent since the end of 2009 (US SIF Foundation 2012) and the same phenomenon also prevailed in Europe. In fact, institutional investors drove the substantial growth of the SRI investor base over time. The conjecture that institutional investors will be the primary future of SRI is likely to come to pass because assets of European institutional investors constituted 96.6 percent of total European investors' assets in 2013, expanding from 94.1 percent in 2011 (Eurosif 2014). Institutional investors can be segmented into two sub-markets: (1) value-driven organizations such as nongovernmental organizations (NGOs), foundations, charities, churches, endowments, and religious groups; and (2) traditional institutional investors such as insurance companies and pension funds.

Both value-driven organizations and traditional institutions can create SRMF portfolios since SRI has become more mainstream. From a behavioral perspective, the motivation of socially responsible investors is quite diverse such as aligning investment decisions with moral or philosophical stances and enacting political actions through shareholder activism. Two broad motivations characterize why investors choose SRMFs (Schueth 2003): (1) "feeling good" investors, who put their money to work in a manner more closely aligned with their personal values and priorities; and (2) "activist" investors, who believe that their investments can contribute to positive social and environmental changes. Using their capital power to influence corporate policy, socially responsible investors could stymie the growth of socially unacceptable industries such as defense or tobacco firms by constraining the amount of available capital.

Socially responsible investors have heterogeneous risk and return preferences (Berry and Yeung 2013). Some are unwilling to make a trade-off for high financial return in the place of poor ethical/social performance. Meanwhile, another subset of socially conscious investors is more willing to make a trade-off between financial performance and social performance (Pava and Krausz 1996). The investors of both SRMFs and conventional mutual funds are more loyal to their SRMFs than to their conventional funds (Peifer 2014). This characteristic suggests that a corporation's ethical behavior attracts more patient investment capital. Patient investors hold their assets longer although the performance of socially responsible firms tends to be inferior compared to that of non-socially responsible firms.

Active socially responsible investors could engage in shareholder advocacy and/or activism. Under this process, shareholders of a listed company, under the provision of securities legislations in various jurisdictions, can require its members to meet and vote on specified resolutions (Haigh and Hazelton 2004). Investment managers can increase the attractiveness of their funds to socially responsible investors by claiming that those investors who put capital in their investment products can directly contribute to the betterment of society. However, Haigh and Hazelton conclude that SRMFs are ineffective at initiating corporate changes while showing similar performance to conventional funds.

The composition of assets in SRMFs does not differ markedly from that of conventional funds regarding the characteristics of the assets held, portfolio diversification, and variable effects of diversification (Bello 2005). However, based on tests of differences between SRMFs and conventional funds, evidence shows that the estimated industry betas between the two groups differ significantly (Benson, Brailsford, and Humphrey

2006). Despite similar performance, the returns on SRMFs are generated through different industry exposures, which is consistent with holding different portfolio positions. This result contradicts public critics who view SRMFs as mere marketing ploy in the form of rebranding conventional funds.

Sustainability Paradigm and Socially Responsible Mutual Fund Criteria

The three pillars of sustainability comprising the environmental, social, and economic components became a powerful mantra for businesses (Fiksel, Eason, and Frederickson 2012). Such issues as Nike's labor practices, child labor and slavery in the chocolate industry, McDonald's health issues, and global warming and climate change raised several questions for corporate stakeholders. Should corporations only focus on maximizing stockholder wealth? Do firms face consequences for making investment decisions without considering negative social effects? As people became more aware of social and environmental issues and learned from their past experiences, investors became more accepting of the sustainability paradigm. Hence, these three pillars can provide general criteria for constructing SRMF portfolios.

ENVIRONMENTAL PILLAR

A business requires raw materials and natural resources to operate. The salient purpose of the environmental pillar is to ensure that adequate resources will be available in the future. This pillar can be translated into the following three criteria: (1) natural resource consumption where firms disclose use of water, mineral, energy, materials, and renewable energy; (2) corporate environment management, which covers waste management, pollution prevention, site and facility recovery; and (3) ecological protection policy disclosure for firms with environmentally sensitive operations, such as disclosure on affected threatened species, sustainable fisheries yield, and algae index.

SOCIAL PILLAR

The social environment provides market and human resources. This pillar purports to make sure that sufficient markets and good productivity will be available in the future. Accordingly, businesses should pay attention to social development. The social pillar can be categorized into the following three criteria: (1) fair labor policy, which support equal opportunity, worker rights, and reasonable worker wage; (2) corporate social responsibility activities on charity, education, and community development; and (3) consumer protection policy, which covers product safety and commitment to fair trade and fair competition.

ECONOMIC PILLAR

The economic motive is the heart of all profit-centered organizations. A company accomplishes its economic objective by managing costs efficiently, increasing revenues, and harnessing new technologies through research and development. SRMF managers use the ESG framework to supplement the value of economic goals with governance factors, such as independent audits, good management structure, transparency, and fair executive compensation. Since different firms operate in different sectors, the governance criteria used to evaluate their performance should be relevant to their industry. For instance, an agricultural company should place greater emphasis on waste management, pollution prevention, and water preservation whereas a shoe manufacturer should put more emphasis on worker rights and the standard of living. The sustainability framework known as the ESG framework is beneficial when constructing SRMF portfolios as it considers the relevant environmental, social, and governance factors.

Strategies for Constructing Socially Responsible Mutual Fund Portfolios

Constructing SRMF portfolios requires a different strategy from other conventional portfolios. Besides balancing financial aspects such as risk, return, and the time horizon, an SRMF must consider non-financial aspects of the firm. Because of SRMF growth in the previous decade, many strategies are available from different SRMF managers to establish portfolios. Five common approaches are available for creating SRMF portfolios: (1) screening, (2) best-in-class, (3) thematic, (4) ESG integration, and (5) engagement (Social Investment Forum 2003; Global Sustainable Investment Alliance 2012; US SIF Foundation 2012; Eurosif 2014).

SCREENING

Negative screens and positive screens are two major methods of screening assets used to create SRI portfolios (Renneboog, Horst, and Zhang 2008). A typical negative screen can be applied to an initial asset pool such as the S&P 500 index stocks to exclude alcohol, tobacco, gambling, and defense industries or companies with poor performance in labor relations or environmental protection. The positive screen process involves selecting shares that meet superior CSR standards. The most common positive screen focuses on corporate governance, labor relations, environment, sustainability, and cultural diversity. Many SRMF managers also combine the ESG framework with positive or negative screening. For example, negative environmental screening removes assets with poor environmental performance. By contrast, positive social screening includes assets with good social performance.

Another method of screening assets is to apply *norms-based screening.* This method involves screening investments against minimum standards of business practices based on international norms set by organizations or institutions such as the United Nations Global Compact (UNGC) and the OECD Guidelines for Multinational Corporations and International Treaties.

BEST-IN-CLASS

The best-in-class strategy compares a firm's social and environmental performance in the same predetermined group or sector and then ranks the firms. This strategy allows investors to select a company based on its relative rating to others. Many consider the best-in-class strategy stronger and more sophisticated than a simple screening strategy because it provides a rating and more transparent judgment that enable investors to select the best firm and avoid the rest. Many SRMF managers use the ESG framework to choose high-performing ESG compliant companies of which the top ranked are considered the best-in-class. A newer development in the best-in-class strategy is using a financially weighted best-in-class, which combines financial performance and the ESG components into its weighted rating system. With this strategy, investors can easily pick the best firm regarding overall performance.

THEMATIC INVESTMENT

Thematic investment is an investment approach that identifies themes and trends that are influencing or likely to influence the economy and financial markets. Such themes include social, political, technological, and environmental issues. However, the most popular theme is the sustainability theme. A *sustainability themed investment* is an investment specifically related to the three pillars of sustainability and may include such areas as climate change, energy efficiency, clean energy, green technology, or sustainable agriculture.

ESG INTEGRATION

ESG integration is an integrated approach that includes ESG factors into conventional financial analysis. The integrated approach uses mathematical models and quantitative analysis that may vary for each SRMF manager. Today, the ESG integration is the second most used strategy in the world (Global Sustainable Investment Alliance 2012). The rise in the popularity of ESG integration is mainly because SRMF institutions are trying harder to integrate extra-financial components into their traditional financial analysis.

ENGAGEMENT

The purpose of engagement is to encourage management to improve how their firms positively affect the environment and society. Current shareholders can also participate in a firm's decision-making via research, dialogues, direction, and guidance. This strategy requires a critical amount of capital invested before investors can be involved in the decision-making process. When engagement is not a viable option, more confrontational forms of interaction and shareholder advocacy can be conducted. For example, investors can submit shareholder resolutions, vote at annual meetings, and launch a public campaign against specific corporate practices. One benefit of being a shareholder is the right to vote. Since most shareholders cannot or do not want to attend annual and special meetings at which the voting occurs, SRMF managers often use proxy votes to manage the votes of SRMF investors. In the past, a proxy vote used mail or e-mail as its main channel, but today a proxy vote can easily be carried out via a web-based system.

Screening, best-in-class, and ESG integration strategies attract "feel good" investors, whereas the thematic and engagement strategies attract "activist" investors. Also, some social investment forums add impact/community investing into their strategies. *Impact/community investing* is a targeted investment typically made in private markets and aimed at solving social or environmental problems. Impact investing includes *community investing,* in which capital is specifically directed to traditionally underserved individuals or communities, or financing provided to businesses with clear social or environmental purposes. Hence, this strategy uses a private equity fund or venture capital structure.

Table 14.1 compares the strategies among SRI forums. In terms of popularity, the exclusion strategy constitutes 35.3 percent of total European professionally managed assets, followed by ESG integration (26.9 percent), norms-based screening (18.7 percent), engagement and voting (16.9 percent), best-in-class (1.8 percent), sustainability themed (0.3 percent), and impact investing (0.1 percent) (Global Sustainable Investment Alliance 2012).

Table 14.1 **Comparison among Socially Responsible Investment Strategies**

Eurosif	*GSIA-equivalent*	*PRI-equivalent*	*EFAMA-equivalent*
Exclusion	ESG negative screening	ESG Negative/ exclusionary screening	Negative screening or exclusion
Norms-based screening	Norms-based screening	Norms-based screening	Norms-based approach
Best-in-class selection	ESG positive screening and best-in-class	ESG positive screening and best-in-class	Best-in-class policy
Sustainability themed	Sustainability themed	ESG-themed Investments	Thematic investment
ESG integration	ESG integration	Integration of ESG issues	n/a
Engagement and voting	Corporate engagement and shareholder action	Engagement (three types)	Engagement (voting)
Impact investing	Impact/Community investing	n/a	n/a

Note: This table compares the socially responsible asset management strategies used by four SRI institutions: the European Social Investment Forum (Eurosif), Global Sustainable Investment Alliance (GSIA), The United Nations-supported Principles for Responsible Investment (PRI), and European Fund and Asset Management Association (EFAMA).

Source: Eurosif 2014.

Empirical Evidence on Socially Responsible Mutual Funds

This section presents empirical evidence across global investment markets related to SRMFs. A growing number of empirical studies have accompanied the growing popularity of SRMFs. These studies tend to focus on the financial performance of SRMFs.

EMPIRICAL EVIDENCE: THE UNITED STATES AND CANADA

The historical origin of ethical investing in the United States can be traced back to the religious philosophy of Methodist and Quaker immigrants (Schueth 2003). Traces of this history are still evident in the widespread practices of avoiding "sin stocks" by the majority of socially conscious U.S. investors. The development of modern SRI started in the 1960s and rapidly gained national attention in the 1980s due to several events. As the anti–Vietnam War, civil and labor rights, women's equality, and anti-nuclear movements intensified during the 1960s, more investors became aware of SRI (Cooper and Schlegelmilch 1993).

The 1980s saw a massive social movement to boycott investing in companies related to pro-apartheid South African government. Headlines on environmental disasters of the Bhopal gas tragedy, Chernobyl nuclear meltdown, and Exxon Valdez oil spill also raised the concerns among many investors over how their funds could positively contribute to a better environment. The source of rapid growth for SRI largely resulted from investor demand, as big financial institutions on Wall Street have not aggressively promoted SRMFs to their clients (Schueth 2003).

During the next few decades, research interest on the characteristics and performance of SRMFs grew alongside the rapid growth of U.S. SRMFs. An early survey by Rosen et al. (1991) on the characteristics of individual investors in U.S. SRMFs shows that they are younger and better educated than conventional investors. Although these investors are particularly concerned about the environmental and labor performance of the firms in which they invest, they still prioritize the financial performance of assets over more ethical corporate behavior. According to Cortez, Silva, and Areal (2009, 2012), U.S. and European SRMFs generally show neutral performance pertaining to both conventional and socially responsible benchmarks.

Limited evidence is available about SRMFs in Canada. For example, Bauer, Derwall, and Otten (2007) examine the performance and risk sensitivity of Canadian ethical mutual funds documents. They find that any performance differential between ethical mutual funds and their conventional peers is insignificant. In 2000, the number of institutional investors in Canada was still low compared to that of retail investors, but since 2010 institutional investors have increased steadily and recorded the strongest growth in the Canadian markets.

EMPIRICAL EVIDENCE: EUROPE

The growth of SRMFs in the United Kingdom began in 1990s with over 30 mutual funds having a combined market value of GBP400 million (Cooper and Schlegelmilch

1993). In 2005, SRI assets in Europe grew to $1.4 trillion, representing 10 to 15 percent of European funds under management (Renneboog et al. 2008). In 2012, Europe held the largest market for global sustainable investment with 64.5 percent, followed by the United States (27.6 percent) and Canada (4.3 percent) (Global Sustainable Investment Alliance 2012).

Similar to other regions, European studies on SRMFs often focus on financial performance. For example, Schröder (2004) investigates 16 German and Swiss funds and 30 U.S. SRMFs. The results show that socially screened assets have no clear disadvantage over conventional assets and their risk-adjusted performances are similar. Furthermore, Kreander, Gray, Power, and Sinclair (2005) examine the performance of 60 European funds from four countries: 34 U.K. funds, 14 Swedish funds, 8 German funds, and 4 Dutch funds. Their findings confirm no difference exists between the performances of ethical and non-ethical funds and neither type of fund displays any ability to time the market.

EMPIRICAL EVIDENCE: AUSTRALIA AND ASIA

Sustainable investments in Australia and Asia only contribute 1.9 percent to the global sustainable investment (Global Sustainable Investment Alliance 2012). Although this percentage is relatively small, the development in Australia has mirrored the rapid growth of SRMFs in both the United States and the United Kingdom. Research in Australia also investigates the financial performance of SRI funds compared to that of conventional funds. For example, Jones, van der Laan, Frost, and Loftus (2008), who study 89 ethical funds in Australia between 1986 and 2005, find that ethical funds significantly underperform the market in Australia. Humphrey and Lee (2011) also study Australian equity funds but find no significant difference between the returns of SRI and conventional funds. However, the authors did find weak evidence that funds with more screens overall attain better risk-adjusted performance. Although positive screening significantly reduces the funds' risk, negative screening lowers the funds' capability of forming diversified portfolios.

A few studies examine SRI funds in Japan, which represents only 0.1 percent to the global sustainable investment. Recently, sustainable investment in Japan has suffered from the impact of long-term stagnation of Japanese listed equities. Jin, Mitchell, and Piggott (2006) study Japanese SRI using the Morningstar SRI Japan and FTSE4Good Japan indices, and emphasize the potential roles for SRIs in pension portfolios. Their results show that SRI involves some financial sacrifices but provides a possible reduction in exposure to overall market risk. Therefore, this study does not support the conjecture that Japanese pension participants would benefit from investing in SRI-based portfolios.

Socially Responsible Mutual Fund Performance and Measurement

According to Hamilton, Jo, and Statman (1993), finance theory can explain empirical findings about the difference in expected return between SRMFs and conventional mutual funds. If empirical results show no difference in risk-adjusted return between those two types of funds, then the performance of SRMFs is not being considered when pricing the assets. According to Hamilton et al. and Reyes and Grieb (1998), investors do not experience either a positive or negative performance trade-off when they invest in SRMFs over conventional mutual funds. This evidence suggests that the market does not price the value of social and ethical performance inherent in SRMFs.

To date, research on SRMFs concentrates on the relative performance of return. The majority of studies compare the realized risk-adjusted return on SRMFs with that of conventional funds. Prior research shows evidence that on a risk-adjusted basis; no statistically significant difference exists in short-term performance between those two types of assets. This finding is a reasonably consistent result across the range of studies despite some differences in methodology and time period.

For example, Pava and Krausz (1996) and Shank, Manullang, and Hill (2005) find that although short-term performance of SRMFs shows no significant difference over conventional assets, the long-term financial performance of SRMFs is statistically higher than the market indexes. Bauer, Koedijk, and Otten (2005) examine the performance of 103 German, U.K., and U.S. ethical mutual funds between 1990 and 2001. They find that SRMFs underperform in the beginning of the observation period but experience a similar rate of return to conventional mutual funds in the latter period. Statman (2000) finds that when compared to the performance of S&P 500 index from 1990 to 1998, the return on SRMFs was actually worse.

Statman and Glushkov (2009) propose three hypotheses to address the relative returns on stocks of both socially responsible companies and conventional companies. First, the "doing good but not well" hypothesis posits that the expected return on SRMFs is lower than that on conventional stocks. Second, the "doing good while doing well" hypothesis states that the expected return on socially responsible stocks is higher than that on conventional stocks. Third, the "no effect" hypothesis states that the expected return of socially responsible stocks is equal to that on conventional stocks.

Typical socially responsible portfolios, such as the DS 400, are tilted toward stocks of companies with high scores on social responsibility characteristics. According to Statman and Glushkov (2009), KLD Research and Analytics (KLD) analyzed stock returns on socially responsible companies from 1992 to 2007. It reports that companies with socially responsible characteristics have a slight advantage, which is consistent with the "doing good while doing well" hypothesis. However, when excluding sin stocks from typical socially responsible portfolios, socially responsible portfolios are at a relative performance disadvantage compared to conventional portfolios. This finding is consistent with the "doing good but no well" hypothesis. The advantage from the tilt toward stocks of companies with high social responsibility scores is largely offset by the disadvantage from excluding sin stocks. Accordingly, the net effect is consistent with the "no effect" hypothesis.

Overall, existing empirical evidence conclusively show that the financial performance of SRIs is similar to that of conventional funds. Irrespective of the benchmark techniques used by researchers (e.g., the capital assets pricing model (Jensen's (1968) alpha), Fama and French's (1993) three-factor model, or Carhart's (1997) four-factor model), they provide overwhelming evidence that the financial performance of

SRMFs is not significantly different relative to their conventional peers or benchmarked index (Revelli and Viviani 2014).

Several hypotheses explain the similar financial returns between SRI and conventional portfolios. First, because the exclusion method of SRMFs removes a large number of stocks, portfolio construction is limited and consequently the optimum diversification of stocks cannot be achieved. However, an efficient portfolio can still be constructed, even if exclusion has been performed. In this case, the constructed SRMF portfolio may consist of stocks as in a conventional portfolio but with a lower risk preference. Thus, no difference exists on a risk-adjusted basis. Second, sin stocks tend to have higher betas and hence higher expected returns. Removing sin stocks leads to a lower portfolio beta and thus lower expected returns. Therefore, in a bull market, portfolios with higher betas should outperform those with lower betas. In a bear market, portfolios with lower betas should outperform those with higher betas. These relationships may explain why SRMFs and conventional funds perform similarly in a long time horizon and stable market.

Nevertheless, those research phenomena raise a new question about SRMF performance measurement. Why do researchers mainly focus on SRMF financial performance compared to their conventional peers? Freedman (2010, p. 39) tells the following story. A police officer finds an intoxicated man late at night crawling on his hands and knees on a sidewalk under a streetlight. When questioned, the man says that he is looking for his wallet. When the officer asks if he is sure that he dropped the wallet here, the man replies that he actually dropped it across the street. “Then why are you looking over here?” asks the befuddled officer. “Because the light’s better here,” explains the man.

Although the question on the financial performance of SRMFs is important, researchers have seemingly paid too much attention to this area perhaps because financial performance is easier to measure. The phenomenon known as the “streetlight effect” or “drunkard’s search” is an observational bias when researchers are looking for whatever they are searching in a place where it is most convenient (Capelle-Blancard and Monjon 2012). This behavior leads to producing the right answers to a wrong question. The SRMF performance and measurement should analyze both financial and extra-financial performance. The extra-financial performance is much harder to measure but is more relevant to the SRMF philosophy. The extra-financial factors might affect the company in the long run but not in the short run. Future research should examine whether SRMFs could affect brand loyalty, firm reputation, shareholder satisfaction, government policies, and research and development.

Trends and Future Developments

Compared to traditional investors whose investment criteria of earnings-oriented performance do not change in the short run, the criteria of SRI constantly adapt to the national or global changes in social, political, and environmental concerns. An example of this behavior occurred during late 1980s when the majority of SRIs expressed concern over whether their investments supported the pro-apartheid government in South Africa. As a result, SRMFs excluded firms with business or investment relationships in South Africa from their portfolios. Meeting several criteria may help to persuade more corporations to adopt the concept of stakeholder value maximization. For example, these criteria could include making corporate social performance measureable and maintaining a sustainable balance between financial and social goals.

A recent European survey by Eurosif (2014) covering institutional and retail assets from 13 distinct European markets shows that the demand from institutional investors remains the largest share of SRI demand in 2014, even though the proportion has fallen compared to 2012. On the contrary, materiality is the biggest growing driver between 2012 and 2014. Materiality determination is not limited to financial (quantitative) information. A matter is material if it is likely that the information will affect decisions of a reasonable person. In the future, instead of relying only financial information as the main consideration in decision-making, investors should also consider using extra-financial information.

This Eurosif (2014) survey also finds that impact investing is the most preferable asset management strategy in the European SRI market, surpassing both the exclusion and engagement strategy by a large margin. The increasing use of the exclusion strategy is understandable since the strategy can be easily applied and reasonably used to compare assets across regions. The rapid growth of engagement can be interpreted as an increase in investors' willingness to participate in a firm's decision-making process.

Upon realizing the trends in materiality, impact investing, exclusion, and engagement, SRMF managers can harness or manage the trends to include specific investments in their portfolios. SRMF managers and SRI institutions should conduct new research on the performance measurement of extra-financial factors that may reinforce the materiality. If empirical studies can show that SRMFs help make the world better, then conventional investors may shift to SRMFs. Consequently, SRIs and SRMFs could grow and become more typical. At that time, asset managers could begin incorporating both financial and extra-financial components into analysis. If this scenario develops, then a gradual shift could occur from SRI as an instrument of moral philosophy for "good" investors to an instrument for mainstream investors who recognize that immoral behavior of companies hurts their investments.

Opportunities for Socially Responsible Mutual Funds

SRMF managers can potentially exploit several elements associated with the changing trends in business practices. External factors such as market, social, and technology seem favorable to SRMF growth. Three main drivers from the external factors are: (1) growth of mutual funds, (2) an increase in environmental and social concerns, and (3) rapid technological development.

GROWTH OF MUTUAL FUNDS

U.S. mutual funds had total net assets of $11.831 trillion in 2010, which increased to $15.017 trillion in 2013 (Investment Company Institute 2014). The impressive growth of mutual funds shows that the market size is increasing. At the same time, investor tastes continue to change, prompting mutual fund managers to consider new products

		Market Share	
		High	**Low**
Growth	**High**	★ Star	? Question Mark
	Low	$ Cash Cow	X Pet

Figure 14.1 THE BOSTON CONSULTING GROUP (PORTFOLIO GROWTH-SHARE) MATRIX. This figure shows four types of assets of a diversified company where a quadrant represents different categories of assets as categorized by their growth and market share. The star quadrant represents assets with high market share and growth potential. The question mark quadrant includes assets with low market share and high growth, which can be changed to the star quadrant with additional investment. The cash cow quadrant contains assets with mature assets that provide positive cash flow to the company with low future growth. The pet quadrant represents failed investment projects.
Source: Henderson 1970.

to meet investor demand. As the market grows, SRMFs have an opportunity to reach out to niche markets to receive additional funds. With good promotion and marketing strategies, SRMFs can expand their market share in a growing mutual funds market. The impressive growth of mutual funds is occurring not only in the United States but also worldwide.

The Boston Consulting Group (BCG) matrix is based on the product life cycle theory that can be used to determine what priorities should be given in the product portfolio (Henderson 1970). It has two dimensions: market share and market growth. This tool is helpful when analyzing the position of SRMFs in terms of market share and market growth. Using the BCG matrix, SRMFs could be positioned in the question mark quadrant (see Figure 14.1). As the market expands, SRMF leaders should leverage their market share to gather funds and become a "star" in the BCG matrix. This vision is possible considering the increase in environmental and social concerns. In the future, SRMFs have the potential of becoming a market leader in the mutual funds market.

INCREASE IN ENVIRONMENTAL AND SOCIAL CONCERNS

The rapid growth of SRI can be construed as investors being more concerned about social and environmental issues. Moreover, growing assets under the engagement strategy show that some investors also want to participate actively in a firm's decision-making process. Today's business differs from decades ago when no international standards, such as ISO 9000 quality management, ISO 14,000 environmental management, ISO 26,000 social responsibility, ISO 50,001 energy management, and ISO 20,121 sustainable events existed. The pressure from government and stakeholders helped to shape conventional firms into sustainable businesses. A change in investors' mindset to conform to that of society and the government could lead investors to seek sustainable investments as SRIs.

RAPID TECHNOLOGICAL DEVELOPMENT

Benson et al. (2006) show that SRI investors often invest in the information and communications technology industry. Therefore, they should be attracted to technological development. Some SRMF managers have also created portfolios with technological themes such as energy and green technologies. With the rapid development of technology, the money they invest may eventually attract new investors interested in technology. Technological development also brings out new companies that can enrich the SRMF portfolios.

Issues and Challenges of Socially Responsible Mutual Funds

SRMFs face additional challenges that other mutual funds do not have. The issues vary from the approaches of portfolio construction to the benefits and effects on society. In the past, issues put forward by SRMF investors were value-driven but are now becoming more performance-driven. SRMF investors want to know the extent to which companies are prepared and organized to address new environmental and social challenges and related strategic and corporate governance issues.

FINANCIAL BENEFITS

As previously discussed, SRMFs do not show superior financial performance compared to conventional funds. However, some studies find that investing in SRMFs result in lower returns because of excluding potentially profitable options from the portfolio. Modern portfolio theory as proposed by Markowitz (1952) postulates that a portfolio is deemed efficient if it has a higher expected return for its risk level. Because of that disadvantage, SRMF managers must be able to pick the best stocks associated with risk, expected return, and the ESG rank to create efficient portfolios. From a time horizon perspective, SRMFs might be more suitable for long-term investors because SRMFs are more likely to include firms with higher sustainability. The sustainability concept relies on the idea that a business should be a going concern and this concept would affect a company's profitability. For short-term or mid-term investments, SRMFs may underperform conventional mutual funds because the limited number of assets qualified as socially responsible restricts investment managers' ability to optimize SRMF returns from short-term market fluctuation. Accordingly, convincing investors to select SRMFs if they can invest in conventional mutual funds and give to charity from their profits could be a challenge.

ASYMMETRIC INFORMATION

SRMF managers often access the firm's social and environmental information from its CSR or annual reports despite their questionable accuracy and objectivity. Such reports may be flawed for several reasons. First, firms tend to enhance their reports by exaggerating their CSR activities. This action creates a false positive, in which fund managers think that a firm is good enough and should pass the positive screening. Second, no generally accepted standards exist for creating CSR reports. Unlike accounting that can be standardized, audited, and analyzed, the accuracy and accountability of CSR reports are still vague. Third, unlike financial reports, CSR reports are not mandatory in some countries. Therefore, a firm's CSR actions might not be well documented. This creates a false negative, where fund managers think that the firm is not good enough and should fail negative screening. Since the information received by managers or investors may differ from reality, why apply the ESG screen at all? This issue arises because without accurate information, any approach of screening becomes questionable.

SHAREHOLDER ENGAGEMENT OR ACTIVISM

As previously discussed, engagement strategies require investing considerable capital before managers and investors can participate in a firm's decision-making process. However, no guarantee exists that these parties can smoothly execute such a dialogue. This strategy often raises different problems within the firm because the ESG criteria may not be aligned with the firm's current vision, mission, and strategy. Also, activism may threaten the firm's stability and reduce its performance. Managing proxy votes within the mutual fund can also be challenging as unhappy investors can simply divest their funds and invest elsewhere.

Encouraging shareholder activism can be beneficial to the development of capital markets. Corporate governance systems that advocate shareholder activism are more likely to attract both domestic and foreign capital because investors prefer to invest in corporate governance systems under which they can have an active influence over corporate management (Wen 2009). The ability of SRMF managers to connect socially responsible investors and management in an effective and efficient way is the key to solving this issue.

SOCIALLY RESPONSIBLE MUTUAL FUND IMPACTS ON THE ENVIRONMENT

Skeptics still are not convinced as to whether investing in SRMFs makes a substantial impact on the environment, mainly due to the lack of empirical research on extra-financial performance. For instance, no evidence shows that such firms behave more ethically. The skeptics argue that SRMFs are just a marketing ploy and merely conventional funds in disguise. Prior research indicating that no difference in performance occurs between SRMFs and conventional mutual funds reinforces this belief. A salient challenge for SRMF researchers is to determine whether investing in SRMFs affects extra-financial performance.

Many ways are available to address these issues. With the labor issue, for instance, researchers can create questionnaires on the standard of living, worker rights, and equal opportunity and compare the results between socially responsible firms and conventional firms. For the environmental case, researchers can measure such variables as the amount of resources, waste, and the quality of waste management when comparing their findings. This kind of research may counter skeptics' arguments and lead to SRMF investors being more confident that their investments help create a better world.

Key Success Factors for Socially Responsible Mutual Fund Managers

Differences exist between managing SRMFs and conventional mutual funds. The main focus of conventional funds is to create efficient portfolios in terms of expected return and risk and then match those portfolios to various investors' risk preferences. SRMFs involve additional considerations. Successful SRMF managers must possess additional screening ability, engagement management, and documentation ability.

SCREENING ABILITY

Screening ability is the heart of SRMFs. To effectively screen, managers must gather accurate and detailed data related to companies' social responsibility activities. Even with an exclusion strategy, managers still need to avoid the false negative error. The inability to get accurate data results in a failure to construct a good portfolio. Managers must be able to set unbiased standards for screening and choose the best strategy for constructing a particular portfolio. Because strategies have different consequences, managers must balance the trade-offs among the chosen strategies regarding risk, return, and the impact of social responsibility on society.

MANAGING ENGAGEMENT

Managing engagement and advocacy is often challenging. First, managers must determine both the style and level of engagement to use. Low engagement may bring more stability whereas high engagement may create less stability inside a company. Managers should realize that because the company's shareholders have different interests, they may not cooperate or engage with SRMF managers. The role of SRMF managers here is similar to an intermediary who connects SRMF investors with corporate management and other shareholders, implying that managers may have to attend the company's meetings and other decision-making discussions. Conducting proxy votes also requires some weighted vote values based on the amount of assets held. Achieving this goal can be solved by a web-based proxy vote.

DOCUMENTATION ABILITY

Conventional mutual fund managers publish financial performance reports of their funds including the fund's net asset value (NAV) and historical performance. However, only providing financial performance reports is insufficient for SRMF investors because they are not only motivated by a firm's financial performance, but also by its social responsibility performance. Investors need to be informed of a company's recent CSR activities and the extent to which the company incorporates CSR. Writing reports that discuss SRMF strategies in a clear and concise way is often challenging for SRMF managers.

Summary and Conclusions

SRMFs have been growing rapidly in recent decades as public concern about the environment and ethical corporate behavior increases. SRMFs take into account financial analysis and the sustainability paradigm and/or the ESG analysis into their decision-making process.

Constructing SRMF portfolios requires different strategies from conventional portfolios. Besides balancing the financial aspects such as risk, return, and time horizon, SRMFs must consider non-financial facets of the firm. Although numerous strategies are available to managers to construct SRMF portfolios, the most common strategies are: (1) screening, (2) best-in-class, (3) thematic, (4) ESG integration, and (5) engagement. The screening, best-in-class, and ESG integration strategies attract "feel good" investors while the thematic and engagement strategies appeal to "activist" investors.

Studies tend to focus on comparing the financial performance between SRMFs and conventional funds. Despite a few exceptions, research typically shows no statistically significant difference in performance between the two fund types on a risk-adjusted basis.

Cameron (1963, p. 13) notes that "not everything that counts can be counted, and not everything that can be counted counts." Although the financial performance of SRMFs matters, it represents only one dimension when comparing SRMFs to conventional funds. Thus, SRMF performance and measurement mechanisms should analyze both financial and extra-financial performance. Extra-financial performance is much more difficult to measure but is more relevant to the SRMF philosophy.

In the future, conventional asset managers may incorporate both financial and extra-financial components into their analyses. Whether a gradual shift will occur from SRI being an instrument of moral philosophy to SRI being an instrument for mainstream investors who recognize that immoral behavior of companies hurts their investments remains to be seen. Nonetheless, successful SRMF managers are likely to conduct additional screening, engagement management, and documentation activities.

Discussion Questions

1. Friedman contends that a necessary trade-off exists between corporate "social responsibilities" and corporate profits. Provide an argument against this view.
2. Explain whether a best strategy exists for constructing SRMF portfolios.
3. Discuss several hypotheses to explain why the performance between SRMFs and conventional funds may differ significantly on a risk-adjusted basis.
4. Discuss whether SRMFs are likely to remain a niche financial product in the future.

References

Baker, H. Kent, and John R. Nofsinger, eds. 2012. *Socially Responsible Finance and Investing.* Hoboken, NJ: John Wiley & Sons, Inc.

Bauer, Rob., Jeroen Derwall, and Rogér Otten. 2007. "The Ethical Mutual Fund Performance Debate: New Evidence from Canada." *Journal of Business Ethics* 70:2, 111–124.

Bauer, Rob, Kees Koedijk, and Rogér Otten. 2005. "International Evidence on Ethical Mutual Fund Performance and Investment Style." *Journal of Banking & Finance* 29:7, 1751–1767.

Bello, Zakri Y. 2005. "Socially Responsible Investing and Portfolio Diversification." *Journal of Financial Research* 28:1, 41–57.

Benson, Karen L., Timothy J. Brailsford, and Jacquelyn E. Humphrey. 2006. "Do Socially Responsible Fund Managers Really Invest Differently?" *Journal of Business Ethics* 65:4, 337–357.

Berry, Robert H., and Fannie Yeung. 2013. "Are Investors Willing to Sacrifice Cash for Morality?" *Journal of Business Ethics* 117:3, 477–492.

Cameron, William B. 1963. *Informal Sociology: A Casual Introduction to Sociological Thinking.* New York: Random House.

Capelle-Blancard, Gunther, and Stéphanie Monjon. 2012. "Trends in the Literature on Socially Responsible Investment: Looking for the Keys under the Lamppost." *Business Ethics: A European Review* 21:3, 239–250.

Carhart, Mark M. 1997. "On Persistence in Mutual Fund Performance." *Journal of Finance* 52:1, 57–82.

Cooper, Marc, and Bodo Schlegelmilch. 1993. "FOCUS: Key Issues in Ethical Investment." *Business Ethics: A European Review* 2:4, 213–227.

Cortez, Maria C., Florinda Silva, and Nelson Areal. 2009. "The Performance of European Socially Responsible Funds." *Journal of Business Ethics* 87:4, 573–588.

Cortez, Maria C., Florinda Silva, and Nelson Areal. 2012. "Socially Responsible Investing in the Global Market: The Performance of US and European Funds" *International Journal of Finance & Economics* 17:3, 254–271.

Edwards, Ed, and Ajay Samant. 2003. "Investing with a Conscience: An Evaluation of the Risk-Adjusted Performance of Socially Responsible Mutual Funds." *American Journal of Business* 18:1, 51–60.

Eurosif. 2014. "European SRI Study 2014." Available at http://www.eurosif.org/wp-content/uploads/2014/09/Eurosif-SRI-Study-20142.pdf.

Fama, Eugene F., and Kenneth R. French. 1993. "Common Risk Factors in Stock and Bond Returns." *Journal of Financial Economics* 33, 3–56.

Fiksel, Joseph, Tarsha Eason, and Herbert Frederickson. 2012. "A Framework for Sustainability Indicators at EPA." Available at http://www.epa.gov/sustainability/docs/framework-for-sustainability-indicators-at-epa.pdf.

Freedman, David H. 2010. *Wrong: Why Experts Keep Failing Us.* New York: Hachette Book Group, Inc.

Friedman, Milton. 1970. "A Friedman Doctrine—The Social Responsibility of Business Is to Increase Its Profits." *New York Times Magazine*, September 13, 32–33, 123–125.

Fung, Hung-Gay, Sheryl A. Law, and Jot Yau. 2010. *Socially Responsible Investment in a Global Environment*. Northampton, MA: Edward Elgar Publishing, Inc.

Global Sustainable Investment Alliance. 2012. "Global Sustainable Investment Review 2012." Available at http://gsiareview2012.gsi-alliance.org/pubData/source/Global%20Sustainable%20Investement%20Alliance.pdf.

Haigh, Matthew, and James Hazelton. 2004. "Financial Markets: A Tool for Social Responsibility?" *Journal of Business Ethics* 52:1, 59–71.

Hamilton, Sally, Hoje Jo, and Meir Statman. 1993. "Doing Well While Doing Good? The Investment Performance of Socially Responsible Mutual Funds." *Financial Analysts Journal* 49:6, 62–66.

Henderson, Bruce. 1970. "The Product Portfolio." Available at https://www.bcgperspectives.com/content/classics/strategy_the_product_portfolio/.

Hinchcliff, Dorothy. 2011. "Social Investment Forum Changes Its Name to US SIF." Available at http://www.fa-mag.com/news/social-investment-forum-changes-its-name-to-us-sif-7556.html.

Humphrey, Jacquelyn E., and Darren D. Lee. 2011. "Australian Socially Responsible Funds: Performance, Risk and Screening Intensity." *Journal of Business Ethics* 102:4, 519–535.

Investment Company Institute. 2014. *2014 Investment Company Fact Book*, 54th Edition. Washington, DC: Investment Company Institute. Available at http://www.ici.org/pdf/2014_factbook.pdf.

Jensen, Michael C. 1968. "The Performance of Mutual Funds in the Period 1945–1964." *Journal of Finance* 23:2, 389–415.

Jin, Henry H., Olivia S. Mitchell, and John Piggott. 2006. "Socially Responsible Investment in Japanese Pensions." *Pacific-Basin Finance Journal* 14:5, 427–438.

Jones, Stewart, Sandra van der Laan, Geoff Frost, and Janice Loftus. 2008. "The Investment Performance of Socially Responsible Investment Funds in Australia." *Journal of Business Ethics* 80:2, 181–203.

Kreander, Niklas, Rob H. Gray, David M. Power, and Donald C. Sinclair. 2005. "Evaluating the Performance of Ethical and Non-Ethical Funds: A Matched Pair Analysis." *Journal of Business Finance & Accounting* 32:7–8, 1465–1493.

Markowitz, Harry. 1952. "Portfolio Selection." *Journal of Finance* 7:1, 77–91.

Pava, Moses L., and Joshua Krausz. 1996. "The Association between Corporate Social-Responsibility and Financial Performance: The Paradox of Social Cost." *Journal of Business Ethics* 15:3, 321–357.

Peifer, Jared L. 2014. "Fund Loyalty among Socially Responsible Investors: The Importance of the Economic and Ethical Domains." *Journal of Business Ethics* 121:4, 635–649.

Renneboog, Luc, Jenke Ter Horst, and Chendi Zhang. 2008. "Socially Responsible Investments: Institutional Aspects, Performance, and Investor Behavior." *Journal of Banking & Finance* 32:9, 1723–1742.

Revelli, Christophe, and Jean-Laurent Viviani. 2014, "Financial Performance of Socially Responsible Investing (SRI): What Have We Learned? A Meta-analysis." *Business Ethics: A European Review* 24:2,158–185.

Reyes, Mario G., and Terrance Grieb. 1998. "The External Performance of Socially-Responsible Mutual Funds." *American Business Review* 16:1, 1–7.

Rockness, Joanne, and Paul F. Williams. 1988. "A Descriptive Study of Social Responsibility Mutual Funds." *Accounting, Organizations and Society* 13:4, 397–411.

Rosen, Barry N., Dennis M. Sandler, and David Shani. 1991. "Social Issues and Socially Responsible Investment Behavior: A Preliminary Empirical Investigation." *Journal of Consumer Affairs* 25:2, 221–234.

Schröder, Michael. 2004. "The Performance of Socially Responsible Investments: Investment Funds and Indices." *Financial Markets and Portfolio Management* 18:2, 122–142.

Schueth, Steve. 2003. "Socially Responsible Investing in the United States." *Journal of Business Ethics* 43:3, 189–194.

Shank, Todd, Daryl Manullang, and Ron Hill. 2005. "Doing Well While Doing Good Revisited: A Study of Socially Responsible Firms' Short-Term versus Long-term Performance." *Managerial Finance* 30:8, 33–46.

Social Investment Forum. 2003. "2003 Report on Socially Responsible Investing Trends in the United States." Available at http://www.ussif.org/files/Publications/03_Trends_Report.pdf.

Statman, Meir. 2000. "Socially Responsible Mutual Funds." *Financial Analysts Journal* 56:3, 30–39.

Statman, Meir, and Denys Glushkov. 2009. "The Wages of Social Responsibility." *Financial Analysts Journal* 65:4, 33–46.

US SIF Foundation. 2012. "Report on Sustainable and Responsible Investing Trends in the United States 2012." Available at http://www.ussif.org/files/Publications/12_Trends_Exec_Summary.pdf.

Wen, Shuangge. 2009. "Institutional Investor Activism on Socially Responsible Investment: Effects and Expectations." *Business Ethics: A European Review* 18:3, 308–333.

15

Mutual Funds: Management Styles, Social Responsibility, Performance, and Efficiency

TAMAS BARKO
Researcher, Tilburg University

LUC RENNEBOOG
Professor of Corporate Finance, Tilburg University and European Corporate Governance Institute

Introduction

The mutual fund industry is a sizable part of the overall financial markets, with $30 trillion of its $156 trillion in total net assets globally at the end of 2013 (Investment Company Institute 2014; Ro 2014). Mutual funds have been growing in popularity in the past decade worldwide. Both the number of active mutual funds and their total net assets have been increasing. Despite the financial crisis of 2007–2008, the mutual fund market rebounded, surpassing its pre-crisis level by 2013. New money invested in financial markets continues to go to mutual funds but the growth rate has slowed recently.

In principle, the sheer size of the mutual fund industry should ensure that investors can select a fund that meets their return objectives and risk-aversion level. However, research suggests that even two similar funds can generate substantially different returns, due to managerial actions, investor biases, or other imperfections. This chapter presents an overview of the structure and type of mutual funds, management techniques, fund performance and efficiency, and behavioral biases of fund managers and investors. As responsibly managed mutual funds represent a non-trivial segment of active fund management, the chapter has a special focus on socially responsible mutual funds.

The remainder of the chapter is organized as follows. The next section describes the mutual fund industry, distinguishes between active and passive fund management, and explains the characteristics of socially responsible investments funds. Subsequently, the performance of mutual funds is analyzed, discussing the measurement, drivers, and sources of mutual fund returns. The final section offers a summary and conclusions.

The Mutual Fund Industry

The term *mutual fund* is the common name for an open-end fund (OEF) or open-end investment company. Investors in OEFs can sell their shares back to the fund at the end of every trading day at the net asset value (NAV). Mutual funds are the most common investment vehicles today, with more than $30 trillion in assets under management (AUM) worldwide and over $15 trillion in the United States alone (Investment Company Institute 2014). Figure 15.1 shows that the amount of active mutual funds and their AUM have increased since the early 2000s. Despite a drop in 2008 caused by the financial crisis of 2007–2008, the levels of 2013 now surpass their pre-crisis standard.

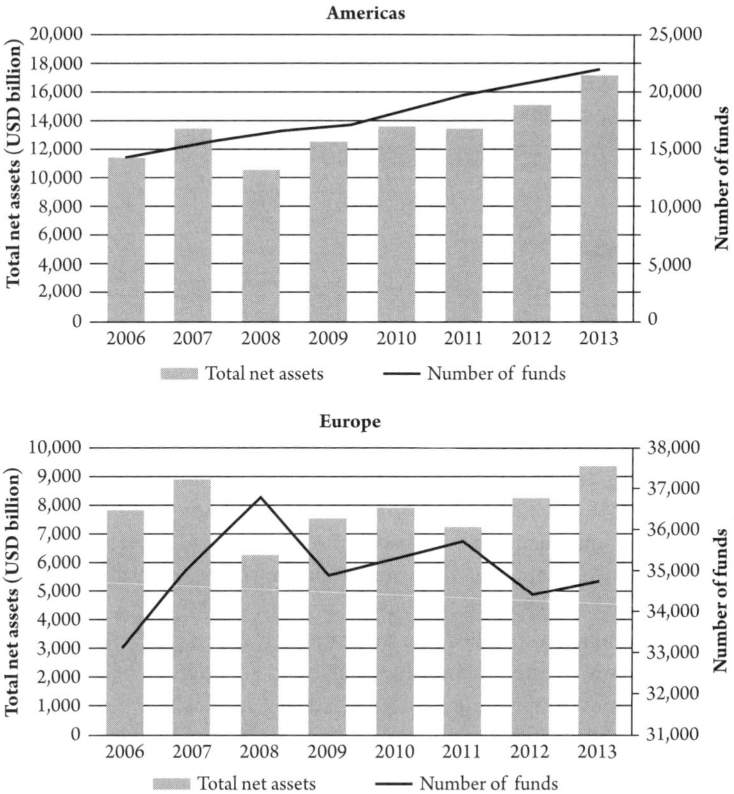

Figure 15.1 Number of Active Mutual Funds and Their Total Nets Assets by Region. These figures show the size of the mutual fund industry by major geographical areas between 2000 and 2013. In each figure, the left axis refers to total net assets held (in $ billions), while the right axis shows the number of active funds. Source: The graphs are based on data provided by the Investment Company Institute 2014.

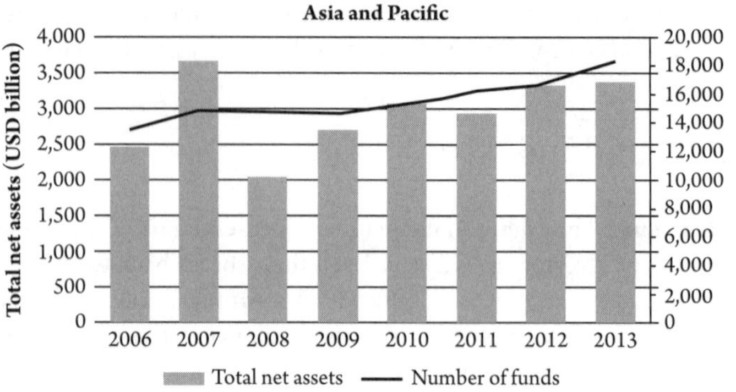

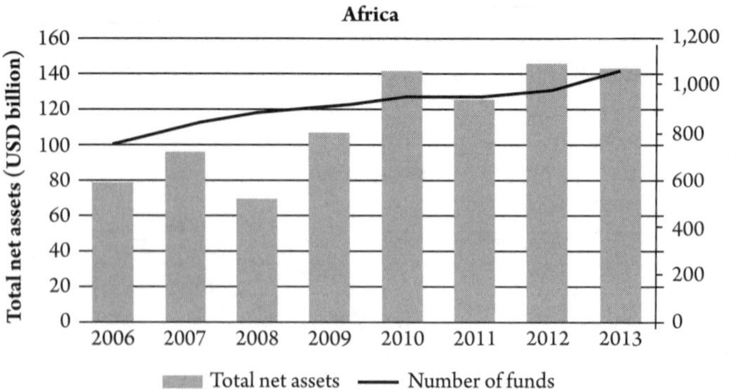

Figure 15.1 (continued)

The figure also reveals that North America has the largest concentration of funds and Europe has the highest number of funds.

Management companies typically manage a family of mutual funds and collect fees in exchange for offering funds to investors. These fees include *front- and back-end loads* (i.e., the commission paid for purchasing and redeeming fund shares, respectively), operating expenses, as well as marketing expenses, which are called 12b-1 fees in the United States. The fund manager or advisor carries out the daily operations of a mutual fund. The advisor can be appointed within the management company, but operations can also be outsourced to specialized advisory firms.

Each mutual fund has a specified investment policy, which is described in the fund's prospectus. For example, fixed-income funds invest in government or corporate bonds. However, some funds adopt more focused strategies such as being allowed to invest only in large capitalization stocks of a certain industry. Mutual funds are typically categorized into money market, equity, fixed-income, and hybrid funds, based on the assets they hold in their portfolios. Money market funds adopt a short-term focus, typically around one month, while other types of funds invest for the longer run. Figure 15.2 shows the net flows to short- and long-term funds: the financial crisis in 2007–2008 triggered a net outflow from equity, bond, and hybrid funds into money market funds, whereas investors made the reverse investment decisions in following years.

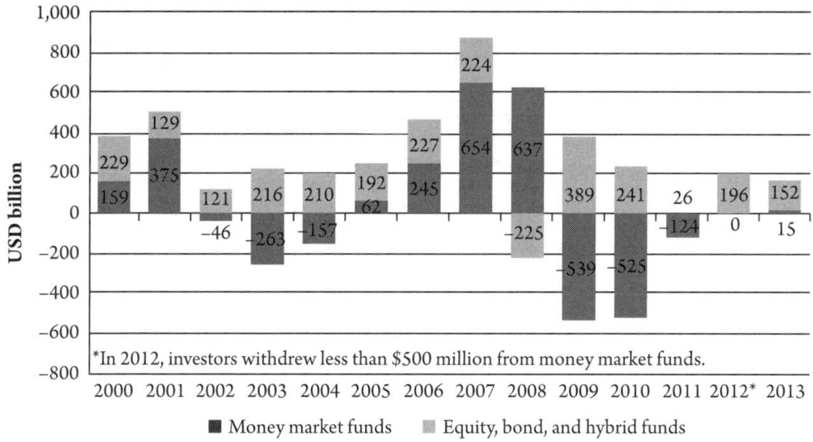

Figure 15.2 NET NEW CASH FLOWS TO U.S. MUTUAL FUNDS. The figure shows the annual breakdown of net new cash flows to U.S. mutual funds by the asset classes to which the funds invest. All numbers are in USD billions. Source: The graph is based on data provided by the Investment Company Institute 2014.

ACTIVE VERSUS PASSIVE MANAGEMENT

The quality of mutual fund management is a key component to a fund's success. Mutual funds are managed either actively or passively. Passive management or indexed investing is the simplest form of operation. In this case, a fund's holdings mirror the composition of a market index such as the Vanguard 500 fund, which invests in stocks of the S&P 500 index. This investment strategy ensures that management is simple: operational expenses, portfolio turnover, and trading costs are low, and holding a market index provides direct diversification benefits. Indexed mutual funds are becoming increasingly popular. For example, as Figure 15.3 shows, the market share of indexed funds in the United States was close to 20 percent at the end of 2013.

The objective of active management is to form portfolios that attain higher returns than the market. Managers of actively managed mutual funds typically try to pick stocks that they forecast to outperform the market. Active management strategies are diverse. Some funds focus on momentum, others on growth stocks, or on specific industries (Kacperczyk, Sialm, and Zheng 2005). However, a specific type of active investment that has gained traction in recent decades is sustainable investment. Socially responsible investments (SRIs) aim to produce financial returns that are sustainable in the long run while considering the interests of stakeholders in the economy and focusing on environmental, social, and governance (ESG) issues. According to a US SIF (2012) report, responsible investments amounted to $3.74 trillion in the United States alone. Another form of active fund management is investor activism in which managers directly engage the companies they include in their portfolios. The activist funds intend to improve those firms' operations to generate higher portfolio returns. For example, the Hermes UK Focus Fund successfully engaged companies by changing the board structure, requesting divestments from unprofitable businesses, and

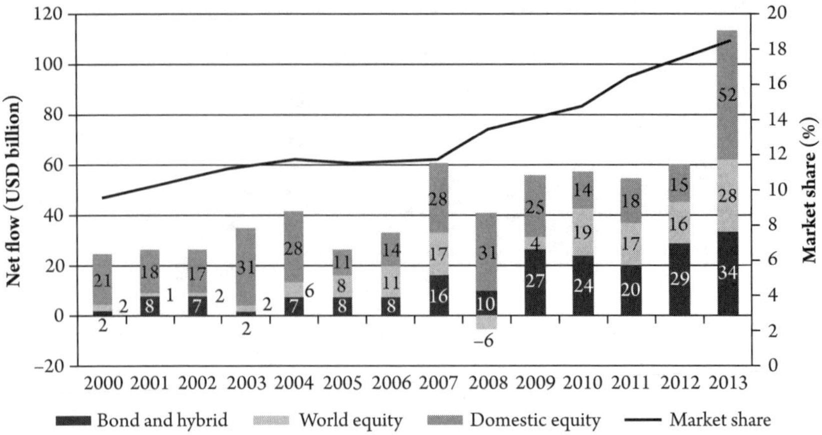

Figure 15.3 NET NEW FLOW TO AND MARKET SHARE OF U.S. INDEXED MUTUAL FUNDS. The figure shows the net new flows to U.S. indexed mutual funds by the assets invested by the funds and the market share of U.S. indexed funds relative to the U.S. mutual fund industry. The left axis shows the amount of flows (in USD billions) and the right axis shows the market share (in percentage). Source: The graph is based on data provided by the Investment Company Institute 2014.

splitting up companies to release the conglomerate discount (Becht, Franks, Mayer, and Rossi, 2010).

The popularity of passive or index mutual funds resulted in a new investment vehicle called exchange-traded funds (ETFs). The main difference between mutual funds and ETFs is that the latter enable investors to trade index portfolios just as they would trade any stock. Passive mutual funds are priced once a day after markets close, whereas ETFs are priced throughout the day and can be traded whenever the markets are open (based on supply and demand). Thus, an advantage of ETFs is that they combine the convenient simplicity of indexed mutual funds with the liquidity of stocks. Figure 15.4 shows the growing popularity of ETFs. From January 2007 to December 2013, investors withdrew capital from actively managed U.S. equity mutual funds and transferred it to indexed equity funds and ETFs. The figure shows that ETFs attracted about twice as much capital as indexed mutual funds.

SOCIALLY RESPONSIBLE MUTUAL FUNDS

Social responsibility roots lie in Jewish, Catholic, and Islamic religions. However, SRI gained momentum and public interest starting in the 1960s. The merits of Martin Luther King's anti-discriminatory arguments, growing opposition against the Vietnam War, and increase in the power of labor unions paved the way of today's SRI. The first modern SRI vehicle was Pax World Fund, a mutual fund founded in 1971 as a response to growing concerns of socially responsible investors. Since introducing the Pax World Fund, SRI has expanded from a niche to mainstream market strategy. According to recent SRI reports, total AUM reached \$3.74 trillion in the United States (US SIF 2012) and \$6.72 trillion in Europe (Eurosif 2014).

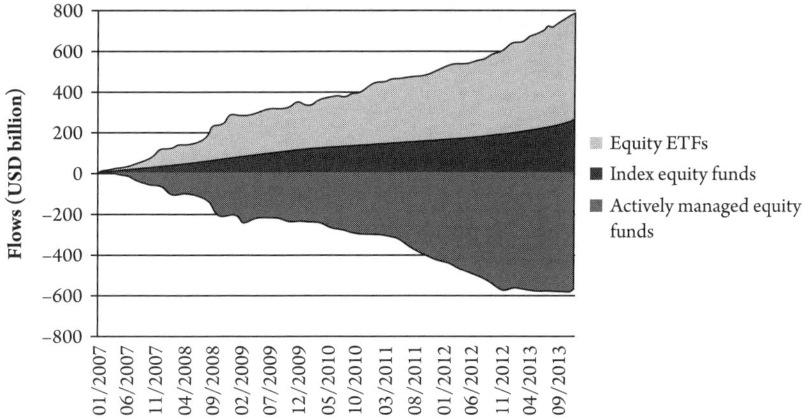

Figure 15.4 CUMULATIVE FLOWS TO U.S. DOMESTIC EQUITY MUTUAL FUNDS AND EXCHANGE-TRADED FUNDS. The figure shows the cumulative flows to U.S. domestic equity mutual funds and ETFs between 2007 and 2013. All numbers are in USD billions.
Source: The graph is based on data provided by the Investment Company Institute 2014.

Investors who intend to engage in SRI generally use a set of screens to identify their investment universe. The screening starts from a general pool such as an MSCI country index. After filtering out companies not meeting SRI standards on various aspects of ESG issues, fund managers form portfolios using the usual financial portfolio optimization methods. Renneboog, Horst, and Zhang (2008b) differentiate four distinct types or generations of screens:

- *Negative screens.* Negative screening is the most basic type with origins in religion. Negative screens eliminate stocks that are involved in "sin" industries such as alcohol, tobacco, military, weaponry, abortion, and pornography.
- *Positive screens.* Fund managers use positive screens to select companies that meet above average standards in such areas as protecting the environment, promoting human rights, and providing sustainable investments. A branch of positive screens is the *best-in-class approach*, in which all companies are ranked within an industry and a certain quantile, meeting the requirements, is selected.
- *Sustainable investing screens.* Fund managers often combines negative and positive screens to yield the so-called "transversal" (Capelle-Blancard and Monjon 2014), "sustainable" or "triple bottom line" (i.e., people, planet, and profit) screens.
- *Sustainable investing and social activism screens.* The fourth generation of ethical funds combines the sustainable investing approach (third generation) with shareholder activism. In this case, portfolio managers or the companies specialized in granting ethical labels attempt to influence the company's policies through direct dialogue with the management or with voting rights at annual general meetings.

Using a proprietary data set, Dimson, Karakas, and Li (2014) show that mutual funds can indeed create value to investors when they engage their portfolio companies to improve the firms' social responsibility. According to a Eurosif (2014) report, most European funds have active pro-social voting policies in place, representing about 40 percent of AUM.

Performance

Accurately measuring the performance and returns of investment vehicles is important because a large portion of global wealth is invested in mutual funds. Since the performance of mutual funds affects personal (retirement) wealth, public wealth, and corporate finance decisions, the topic attracts considerable academic research.

EFFICIENCY

The neoclassical view on efficient markets implies that an optimal portfolio generates the highest possible return for a given level of risk. *Mutual fund efficiency* means that funds produce returns for investors in line with the risk level of the fund. Investors primarily buy mutual funds because of the presumed superior risk-return trade-off and professional management. Because professional management is costly and mutual fund managers cannot predict the market accurately, the realized returns can be considerably lower than the return on the benchmark portfolio. The mutual fund industry has various strategies to combat this problem. For example, passive funds try to mimic their benchmark portfolio as closely as possible, charging low management fees. By contrast, managers of active funds aim to pick stocks with good upside potential, but they typically charge more.

Socially responsible funds use non-financial criteria to identify stocks that can outperform their peers. According to the efficient market hypothesis (EMH) and the classic risk-return relationship, SRI funds face great difficulty trying to continually outperform their conventional peers. Screening portfolios based on public information such as corporate social responsibility (CSR) issues cannot generate abnormal returns unless the SRI screening processes generate value-relevant information unavailable to investors and not yet priced.

SRI fund managers claim that their SRI stock-picking skills generate better risk-adjusted returns than conventional mutual funds. Two arguments support this "outperformance" hypothesis. First, sound social and environmental performance signals good managerial quality, which translates into favorable financial performance. Ferrell, Liang, and Renneboog (2014) confirm, while controlling for endogeneity problems, that well-managed firms (i.e., those with few agency problems) adopt a CSR policy that is value-enhancing. Still, while CSR can create value at the firm level, this does not necessarily mean that SRI funds apply the appropriate corporate weights in their portfolios to maximize fund returns and ignore the costs of active management that erode net returns. Second, social and environmental screening may identify firms that could be less subject to rare negative events such as corporate social crises or environmental disasters, and hence provide (unpriced) insurance against those events, which financial markets tend to undervalue. A key assumption underlying the "outperformance" hypothesis is that the stock markets misprice information on CSR in the short run.

Financial economists have long questioned whether active or passive management is more beneficial to investors and the economy. French (2008) argues that U.S. investors spend 67 basis points of their returns each year on active management and price discovery. In the United States, this foregone return between 1980 and 2006 translates into a cost of 10 percent of the total market capitalization in 2006. Similarly, Fama and French (2010) show that the aggregate portfolio of actively managed mutual funds is close to the market portfolio. By the law of one price, the aggregate return of actively managed funds should be the same as the market return if markets are efficient. However, due to the costs associated with active management, investors earn lower returns than the market return. Some funds are capable of generating superior returns, but on average, investors would benefit more from holding an indexed fund.

As Wurgler (2010) points out, index investing also accompanies its own economic costs and consequences. He contends that if passive management is the dominant investment style, then many of the well-documented market anomalies are exacerbated and carried over directly to corporate investment decisions and eventually to the entire economy. Specifically, the positive effects of index inclusion and the negative effects of exclusion and detachment are magnified. In both cases a firm's access to capital changes dramatically, although its fundamentals stay the same. When a firm is enlisted as a member of an index, such as the S&P 500, it has easier access to capital. In contrast, exclusion from an index generates a negative effect that might lead to underinvestment due to a reduced access to financial resources. Strictly indexed investing can exacerbate the effects of bubbles and crashes.

PERFORMANCE MEASUREMENT

To estimate the performance of active and passive mutual funds requires examining risk-adjusted returns. Risk-adjusted returns are calculated using a factor model such as the CAPM model shown in Equation 15.1:

$$r_{i,t} - r_{f,t} = \alpha_{i,CAPM} + \beta_i\left(r_{M,t} - r_{f,t}\right) + \varepsilon_{i,t}, \tag{15.1}$$

where $r_{i,t}$ is the return on the fund; $r_{f,t}$ is the risk-free rate; $r_{m,t}$ is the return on the relevant market index; and $\alpha_{i,CAPM} + \varepsilon_{i,t}$ is the fund's adjusted risk-adjusted return.

Another conventionally applied model is the three-factor model (Fama and French 1993) to which Carhart (1997) added a fourth factor, namely the momentum, as shown in Equation 15.2:

$$r_{i,t}-r_{f,t} = \alpha_{i,FFC}+\beta_{M,i}\left(r_{M,t} - r_{f,t}\right)+\beta_{SMB,i}r_{SMB,t}+\beta_{HML,i}r_{HML,t}+\beta_{MOM,i}r_{MOM,t}+\varepsilon_{i,t}, \tag{15.2}$$

where $\beta_{SMB,i}$ is the return on a portfolio that goes long in small market cap stocks and short in large capitalization stocks; $\beta_{HML,i}$ is the return on a portfolio long in low market-to-book ratio stocks and short in high market-to-book ratio stocks; and $\beta_{MOM,i}$ is the return on a portfolio that is long in stocks that outperformed the market in the past year and short in stocks that underperformed.

Adding further factors to Equations 15.1 and 15.2, such as fixed-income return factors or return factors on socially responsible portfolios (Renneboog, Horst, and

Zhang 2008a), is possible. However, whether the search for additional factors is productive is questionable given that most empirically discovered factors could be considered the result of data mining (Harvey, Liu, and Zhu, 2014).

Specifying the correct benchmark to evaluate the performance of mutual funds is important. For index funds, this choice is simply their self-reported benchmark. Yet, for actively managed funds, selecting the appropriate benchmark can be more complicated. Although actively managed funds also designate their benchmarks in their prospectuses, several studies report that these are not the best performance measures. For example, Leite and Ceu Cortez (2014) find in a sample of European SRI mutual funds that SRI funds track their self-appointed benchmarks poorly and their performance is better aligned with conventional market indices. Sensoy (2009) claims that one-third of U.S. mutual funds use their self-designated benchmarks as a marketing tool to attract investor flow, while in fact other indices are better aligned with their holdings. Furthermore, even if the benchmarks are truthfully disclosed, they can yield upward biased alpha estimates. As Cremers, Petajisto, and Zitzewitz (2013) acknowledge, factor models yield significant positive alphas even for indices such as the S&P 500 and Russell 2000 because factors are disproportionately weighted toward small cap stocks that performed well historically. Thus, evaluating performance based on correctly specified factors and tradable benchmarks is critical.

Despite the fact that risk-adjusted performance evaluation is the primary method in evaluating fund performance, Berk and Binsbergen (2014) propose that this method does not fully capture the value created by mutual funds. Since returns are calculated as capital gains, bigger funds have greater difficulty generating large risk-adjusted returns than smaller funds. As well-performing funds get substantially larger, managerial skill and performance are reflected in fund size rather than alphas.

MUTUAL FUND RETURNS

Research evidence often shows that mutual funds do not add value, on average, because their risk-adjusted returns net of fees are lower than the benchmark return. Ferreira, Keswani, Miguel and Ramos (2013) provide a comprehensive overview of mutual fund performance worldwide and study actively managed mutual funds from 27 countries. Their results show that mutual funds underperform the market but reveal important differences across countries. In the United States, for example, funds show diminishing returns to scale, but this effect is not present in some other countries. Furthermore, funds located in countries with a liquid stock market and strong legal institutions display better performance.

Other international studies also find that the average mutual fund underperforms.

Eling and Faust (2010) evaluate fund performance in many emerging markets and find that funds fail to deliver positive alphas. Bialkowski and Otten (2011) also conclude that Polish funds underperform, they also show that local management firms enjoy an informational advantage over their international counterparts.

As Table 15.1 shows, the average mutual fund has a four-factor risk-adjusted return that is about 0.1 percent lower than its benchmark. The table also reveals that mutual funds hold more assets (2653 vs. 706) in their portfolio and are riskier (33.3 vs. 31.5 percent) compared to their benchmarks.

Table 15.1 **Characteristics of Global Mutual Funds and Their Holdings**

Variable	*Mean*	*Median*	*Standard Deviation*	*Minimum*	*Maximum*	*Obs.*
Active share	0.705	0.743	0.219	0	1	67,195
Pure-ETF active share	0.704	0.743	0.224	0	1	52,984
Minimum active share	0.668	0.701	0.207	0	1	66,893
Explicit indexing (% by country)	0.128	0.087	0.111	0	0.957	67,195
Closet indexing (% by country)	0.331	0.323	0.148	0	1	67,195
Total net assets ($ millions)	634	115	3,128	0	193,453	67,195
Family total net assets ($ millions)	20,824	4,228	72,265	0	832,483	67,184
Fund age	10.7	8.5	9.4	−8.8	86.4	67,195
Flows	0.140	−0.035	0.729	−0.856	4.788	60,461
Benchmark-adjusted return	0.000	−0.006	0.084	−0.282	0.331	66,104
Benchmark-adjusted four-factor alphas	−0.001	−0.004	0.079	−0.260	0.282	56,991
Excess return four-factor alphas	−0.001	−0.016	0.122	−0.317	0.497	57,460
Number of stocks (benchmark)	706	498	857	10	8,322	67,195
Volatility (benchmark)	0.315	0.312	0.104	0.134	1.478	67,195
Number of stocks	2,653	1,538	2,989	40	7,720	66,663
Volatility	0.333	0.325	0.103	0.164	0.649	66,663

Note: This table presents descriptive statistics for global mutual funds and their holdings for the period 2002 to 2010. Active share represents the percentage of holdings different from the benchmark index. Fund age is in years. Flow is the change in total net assets, net of internal growth.

Source: Cremers et al. 2013.

How do socially responsible funds compare to their benchmarks and conventional mutual funds? Studies in this area reach different conclusions. The general consensus is that SRI funds have returns similar to their conventional peers. Yet, SRI funds that are managed by specialized management firms and are more active in portfolio selection significantly outperform conventional mutual funds (Statman 2000; Gil-Bazo, Ruiz-Verdu, and Santos 2010). Table 15.2 provides a comprehensive overview of studies conducted on socially responsible mutual funds.

If mutual funds consistently underperform, then rational investors should not use these investment vehicles. Yet, in some circumstances fund managers may be able to use their expertise to generate superior returns. In line with this argument, Kosowski (2011) shows that the underperformance of mutual funds relative to their benchmarks is due to their counter-cyclical nature. Between 1962 and 2005, U.S. equity mutual funds consistently outperformed their benchmarks in times of recession, but generated insignificant or negative alphas in expansion periods. Although Nofsinger and Varma (2014) document similar results, they find that this outperformance is even more pronounced for SRI mutual funds.

An important aspect of mutual fund performance and efficiency is the cost associated with management. Even if risk-adjusted returns are positive, investors can lose money if management fees are disproportionately high. Studying the fees charged by mutual funds around the world, Khorana, Servaes, and Tufano (2009) find substantial differences among countries. Fees tend to differ by investment objectives, while larger funds and fund families charge less. The authors also find that investor protection implies lower fund fees and funds in countries with more developed capital markets charge less.

SOURCES OF GOOD PERFORMANCE

The previous section shows that the average mutual fund does not outperform the market. As markets are not perfectly efficient, active managers may exploit inefficiencies to generate superior returns. For example, stocks that are more difficult to analyze and more expensive to trade should earn higher returns (Schultz, 2010), which may enable skilled managers to capitalize on these stocks.

Active management involves unobserved managerial actions that may create value for investors. These managerial actions such as security selection, trading and rebalancing, and market timing are difficult to identify and track because mutual funds are only required to disclose their holdings and returns at the end of every quarter. Researchers address this problem with different measures. Cremers and Petajisto (2009) use a measure called *active share,* which is the proportion of holdings that differs from the benchmark index holding. Others examine the *return gap,* which is the difference between the reported fund return and the return on a portfolio with previously disclosed holdings (Kacperczyk, Sialm, and Zheng 2008; Cici, Gibson, and Moussawi 2010).

An important aspect of active management that concerns SRI funds is screening intensity. SRI funds can screen using a few or many screens and can also focus on specific types of screens. The screening information can come from different sources such as in-house research or third-party information. Barnett and Salomon (2006) provide the first paper to examine the role of screens. They find a curvilinear relationship between the number of screens and fund performance: applying more than one screen

Table 15.2 **Empirical Findings of Studies on Socially Responsible Investment Mutual Funds**

Study	*Country*	*Findings*
Luther, Matatk, and Comer (1992)	U.K.	The alphas of ethical funds have a mean of 0.03 percent a month, which is not significantly different from zero. Ethical funds have relatively high portfolio weights on small cap companies.
Luther and Matatko (1994)	U.K.	The alphas of ethical funds are measured against the FTSE All share index or against a small cap index. The SRI portfolio is biased toward small caps. The average alphas measured in both ways are not significantly different from zero.
Hamilton, Jo, and Statman (1993)	U.S.	For 17 SRI funds established before 1985, the average alpha is –0.06 percent a month, which is higher than the average monthly alpha (–0.14 percent) of 170 non-SRI funds. The difference is not significant. For the 15 SRI funds with shorter history (i.e., established after 1985), the average alpha is –0.28 percent a month, which is worse than the average monthly alpha (–0.04 percent) of the corresponding 150 non-SRI funds.
Mallin, Saadouni, and Briston (1995)	U.K.	The monthly alphas of ethical funds range from –0.28 to 1.21 percent, while 22 out of the 29 alphas are positive. Alphas of non-ethical funds, 23 of which are positive, ranging from –0.41 to 1.56 percent a month. The difference is not statistically significant.
Gregory, Matatko, and Luther (1997)	U.K.	The alphas of ethical funds range from –0.71 to 0.24 percent a month and almost all are not significant. Most of the ethical funds have a significant exposure to the small cap factor.
Goldreyer and Diltz (1999)	U.S.	The average alpha of 29 SRI equity funds is –0.49 percent a year, whereas that of 20 non-SRI equity funds is 2.78 percent. The difference is not significant.
Statman (2000)	U.S.	The average monthly alpha is –0.42 percent for SRI funds and –0.62 percent for non-SRI funds; the difference is not significant.
Schröder (2004)	Germany, Switzerland, and U.S.	The monthly alphas range from –2.06 to 0.87 percent. Of the 46 alphas, 38 are negative; only four are significant at the 0.05 level. SRI funds do not significantly underperform the benchmark portfolio consisting of both large stocks and small stocks.

Table 15.2 **(continued)**

Study	*Country*	*Findings*
Kreander, Gray, Power, and Sinclair (2005)	Europe	The average alphas of SRI and non-SRI funds are 0.20 and 0.12 percent a month, respectively, and the difference is statistically insignificant. The market-timing coefficients are similar for the two types of funds (–0.29 vs. –0.28), and each is significant at the 0.05 level. The signs of the timing coefficients are negative, which implies that both SRI and non-SRI fund managers time the market in the wrong direction.
Bauer, Koedijk, and Otten (2005)	Germany, U.K., and U.S.	The average monthly alphas of SRI funds are 0.29, 0.09, and –0.05% percent for Germany, U.K. domestic, and U.S. domestic funds, respectively. The U.S. domestic ethical funds significantly underperform conventional domestic funds, while for U.S. international funds the difference in returns between ethical and conventional funds is insignificant. The U.K. ethical funds, both domestic and international funds, significantly outperform conventional funds. The difference in average alphas between German SRI and non-SRI funds is insignificant.
Geczy, Stambaugh, and Levin (2006)	U.S.	The monthly alpha of the SRI portfolio is higher than that of the non-SRI portfolio (0.21 vs. 0.08 percent), but the difference is insignificant. Meanwhile, the risk exposure of the SRI portfolio to the size factor (SMB factor) is higher than that of the non-SRI portfolio (0.20 vs. 0.16).
Bauer, Otten, and Rad (2006)	Australia	Domestic ethical funds underperform domestic conventional funds by –1.56 percent a year. International ethical funds outperform their conventional peers by 3.31 percent a year. None of these differences is significant.
Bauer, Derwall, and Otten (2007)	Canada	The difference in average alphas is insignificant between the SRI funds and non-SRI funds (–0.21 vs. –0.18 percent a month).
Barnett and Salomon (2006)	U.S.	When the number of social screens used by an SRI fund increases, the fund's annual return declines at first, but rebounds as the number of screens reaches a maximum.
Renneboog, Horst, and Zhang (2008a)	Worldwide	SRI funds in many European and Asia-Pacific countries strongly underperform domestic benchmark portfolios. SRI investors are unable to identify the funds that will outperform in the future, whereas they show some fund-selection ability in identifying ethical funds that will perform poorly in the future. Finally, the screening activities of SRI funds have a significant impact on funds' risk-adjusted returns and loadings on risk factors.

Derwall and Koedijk (2009)	U.S.	SRI bond fund performance is similar to conventional funds, but balanced SRI funds significantly outperform conventional funds by 1.3 percent a year.
M. Cortez et al. (2009)	7 EU countries	No difference compared to conventional funds.
Lee, Humphrey, Benson, and Ahn (2010)	U.S.	Screening reduces risk-adjusted returns by 70 basis points. More screening leads to incorporating less risky stocks in the portfolio.
Gil-Bazo, Ruiz-Verdu, and Santos (2010)	U.S.	SRI funds run by specialized management companies outperform matched conventional funds by 2.70 percent.
Climent and Soriano (2011)	U.S.	Environmental funds underperform conventional funds, the difference diminishes but in more recent subsamples.
Renneboog, Horst, and Zhang (2011)	Worldwide	SRI fund flow is less sensitive to past negative returns, implying that SRI investors also invest in SRI funds for nonfinancial reasons (e.g., to obtain a "moral" dividend). SRI investors cannot identify future winners, but they do chase past winners.
Peifer (2011)	U.S.	Religiously affiliated funds have less volatile fund flows than other SRI or conventional funds.
Cortez, Silva, and Areal (2012)	U.S., 7 EU countries	No difference compared to conventional funds; alphas are time-invariant.
In, Kim, Park, Kim, and Kim (2014)	U.S.	Competition between SRI mutual funds and the growth of the segment does not erode returns.
Nofsinger and Varma (2014)	U.S.	In expansion periods, conventional funds outperform SRI funds by 0.67 to 0.95 percent. In crises, this relationship is reversed, the difference being 1.61 to 1.70 percent. SRI funds that use positive screens outperform their both their SRI and conventional peers.
Capelle-Blancard and Monjon (2014)	France	SRI fund returns are not different from conventional funds. The number of screens decreases returns.

Source: Renneboog et al. 2008b, but further updated by the authors of this chapter.

erodes return up to a certain threshold, at which the relationship becomes positive. Although some researchers report similar findings such as Capelle-Blancard and Monjon (2014), others including Renneboog et al. (2008a) and Renneboog, Horst, and Zhang (2011) document a negative relationship. Gil-Bazo et al. (2010) consider screening intensity irrelevant. Others note that the best-in-class approach has a significantly positive effect, as well as other focused screens, such as religion or employee relations (Statman and Glushkov 2009; Edmans 2011). According to Gil-Bazo et al. (2010) and Renneboog et al. (2011), if the management company is specialized in SRI or applies an in-house research team, their funds yield positive excess returns.

Stock-Picking

Active management can only add value if fund managers can select stocks that consistently outperform the market. Most studies find that some active managers are successful at security selection (Cuthbertson, Nitzsche, and O'Sullivan 2008; Kacperczyk et al. 2008). According to Cuthbertson, Nitzsche, and O'Sullivan (2010), only 5 percent of active managers in the United States and United Kingdom can consistently create value and whose performance is not attributable to sheer luck. By contrast, about 20 percent of active managers destroy value and 75 percent do not outperform indexed funds.

Baker, Litov, Wachter, and Wurgler (2010) examine the performance of stocks held and traded by fund managers at subsequent corporate earnings announcements. They find that managers are capable of selecting superior stocks for their funds. The results show that stocks purchased and held by funds significantly outperform sells around the next earnings announcement. This implies that mutual fund managers can forecast earnings-related fundamentals.

Research shows that managers exhibit better stock-picking ability in industries with which they are familiar (Kacperczyk et al. 2005; Jiang, Yau, and Tong 2007), as funds that are concentrated in one industry generally outperform their peers with broader holdings. Yet, Pool, Stoffman, and Yonker (2012) document a familiarity effect in portfolio choice. They find that U.S. managers have a *home bias* in that they overweight stocks from their home states, which, on average, leads to underperformance.

Some consensus exists among fund managers about the stocks that are likely to perform well in the future (Gupta-Murkerjee 2013). Active funds that ex ante hold the ex post consensus portfolio earn higher returns than those funds that deviate the most from the consensus. The ex post consensus portfolio outperforms the average mutual fund by a significant margin (7 percent annually). Copycat funds that quickly mimic the consensus portfolio also earn positive returns but cannot consistently outperform the market. Nonetheless, copycat funds still perform better than the average actively managed fund (Verbeek and Wang 2013). Furthermore, once the consensus becomes widely available, returns generated by skilled managers also dissipate. Jiang, Verbeek, and Want (2014) argue that the mandatory disclosure of holdings is detrimental to skilled managers.

After examining the level of activity exerted by fund managers, Cremers and Petajisto (2009) find that funds with the highest active share significantly outperform their peers and that this performance is persistent. Non-index funds with the lowest active share or "closet indexing" underperform their benchmarks. Similarly, Cremers, Ferreira, Matos and Starks (2013) and Petajisto (2013) find international evidence that true active management can create value, but low active share funds cannot outperform explicitly indexed funds. Explicit indexing improves competition in the mutual fund industry and hence lowers management fees. Apparently, truly active funds increase market efficiency but funds that use the notion of active management only as a marketing tool destroy value. However, not all types of truly active management increase performance. For example, active management that induces large shifts in a fund's risk level leads to subpar returns (Huang, Sialm, and Zhang 2011).

Managerial Incentives

Although investors benefit from higher returns, fund managers also enjoy benefits from good performance by receiving higher salaries or a share of fund management fees. As with any venture, managers can potentially expropriate private benefits of control (e.g., excessive trading just for the sake of trading). Thus, managerial incentives should be well aligned in order to maximize the utility of both investors and managers. Aligning incentives is even more important, when management firms outsource daily operations to advisory firms. Chen, Hong, Jiang, and Kubik (2013) find that outsourcing leads to disproportionately high risk-taking in the United States because outside managers are not well incentivized to maximize investor returns. This excessive risk-taking and excessive trading have a negative effect on expected returns and performance in many cases.

Massa and Patgiri (2009) show that higher incentive contracts, on average, induce fund managers to increase their risk-taking, which reduces the typical fund's probability of survival. Yet, the managers who are skilled and receive high incentives can persistently beat the market and their lower incentivized peers through frequently rebalancing portfolios. Furthermore, managers who have higher personal stakes in their funds tend to perform better because their incentives are closely aligned with those of investors (Evans 2008). As Warner and Wu (2011) note, incentive contracts are not constant over time. Typically, compensation increases following good past performance and especially in fund families in which one or more star performers are present. Decreases in compensation, however, are not associated with extreme poor performance but with economies of scale.

The size of mutual funds and the size and structure of funds families matter not only for compensation but also for incentives. Larger fund families typically employ more managers and also manage more types of funds such as hedge funds. This is called *side-by-side management* which occurs when firms or managers simultaneously manage hedge funds and mutual funds. Such management can negatively affect performance. In particular, when managers try to align mutual fund holdings with the holdings of their successful hedge fund, the mutual fund tends to underperform otherwise comparable funds (Cici et al. 2010). Also, managers in large fund families tend to compete with one another and try to outperform their fellow managers. This results in excessive risk-taking especially among those managers whose competitive position, in terms of return performance, is low relative to their peers within the fund family (Kempf and Ruenzi 2008). Pikulina (2014) studies the impact of contractual incentives on the behavior of mutual fund managers in annual tournaments. As a response to poor performance in the relative mutual funds' performance ranks in the first half of the year, fund managers with high-incentive contracts make larger risk adjustments during the second half of the year.

Chasing Returns and Investor Flows

Skilled and successful managers can create value for investors, but the question remains whether investors can identify these managers. The efficiency of the mutual fund industry depends not only on fund managers but also on investors who can reward good (expected) performance by investing more money in the right fund. Fully rational investors would invest in funds based on observable characteristics, such as the risk-return trade-off, style, and expenses. Yet, research shows that investors tend to incorrectly infer managerial skill. Instead of taking tangible parameters into account, they chase past returns (Friesen and Sapp 2007; Ivkovic and Weisbenner 2009; Bailey, Kumar, and Ng 2011). Furthermore, investors tend not to react immediately to information on performance, but with a lag of several months, especially in case of highly marketed funds (Goriaev, Nijman, and Werker 2008). Funds that invest in "hot stocks" which are in great public demand (Frazzini and Lamont, 2008) and whose Morningstar rating increases (Del Guercio and Tkac 2008) also experience a wave of irrational flows, which ultimately does not yield better performance. Some funds try to capitalize on these irrational flows by investing disproportionately in active management and marketing directly to retail investors (Del Guercio and Reuter 2014).

Several studies measure the sensitivity of flows to past returns for socially responsible funds (Benson and Humphrey 2008; Renneboog et al. 2011). These studies all find that SRI fund flows are less sensitive to returns than conventional funds. Apparently, ethical investors are less likely to chase returns and are even willing to accept lower returns as long as the fund's portfolio is aligned with their non-financial investment objectives. In, Kim, Park, Kim, and Kim (2014) show that the flows to SRI funds are stable even when competition from similar funds increases. They find that SRI funds even increased their fees as new funds entered the market, but their performance did not deteriorate. This result implies the socially responsible fund industry does not have the key features of a competitive market.

Contrary to the market of socially responsible funds, the market of conventional funds is highly competitive. To get ahead of competition, funds are actively marketed. As Khorana and Servaes (2012) document, actively managed mutual funds can gain market share through innovation, marketing, and price competition. Innovation is especially rewarded if the new investment style is substantially differentiated from that of incumbent funds.

Summary and Conclusions

This chapter provides a review of the literature on active and passive mutual funds with a special emphasis on SRI funds. The mutual fund industry is a large and important slice of the financial market. While passively managed mutual funds track a market index, active management aims to form portfolios that can outperform the market. Which management technique is better and more efficient is a difficult question. The general consensus in the literature is that the average passive mutual fund performs better than the typical active fund. However, active managers with superior skills can potentially outperform the market, but these skilled managers represent only 5 percent of the industry. These well-performing managers are typically very skilled, have a good performance record, and focus on industries they know well and have experience with. Managers tend to perform better if they are well incentivized or if they have personal stakes in the fund that they manage. The efficiency of the mutual fund market depends both on the funds and investors. While some investors can rationally invest in low-cost funds with good risk-return trade-offs, others tend to incorrectly identify luck as managerial skill and consequently chase past returns.

Discussion Questions

1. Distinguish between active and passive mutual funds.
2. Discuss the types of active investing and screening for socially responsible funds.
3. Identify the potential benefits and concerns of indexed investing.
4. Discuss several measures of active management.

References

Bailey, Warren, Alok Kumar, and David Ng. 2011. "Behavioral Biases of Mutual Fund Investors." *Journal of Financial Economics* 102:1, 1–27.

Baker, Malcolm, Lubomir Litov, Jessica A. Wachter, and Jeffrey Wurgler. 2010. "Can Mutual Fund Managers Pick Stocks? Evidence from Their Trades Prior to Earnings Announcements." *Journal of Financial and Quantitative Analysis* 45:5, 1111–1131.

Barnett, Michael L., and Robert M. Salomon. 2006. "Beyond Dichotomy: The Curvilinear Relationship between Social Responsibility and Financial Performance." *Strategic Management Journal* 27:11, 1101–1122.

Bauer, Rob, Jeroen Derwall, and Rogér Otten. 2007. "The Ethical Mutual Fund Performance Debate: New Evidence from Canada." *Journal of Business Ethics* 70:2, 111–124.

Bauer, Rob, Kees Koedijk, and Rogér Otten. 2005. "International Evidence on Ethical Mutual Fund Performance and Investment Style." *Journal of Banking & Finance* 29:7, 1751–1767.

Bauer, Rob, Rogér Otten, and Alireza Tourani Rad. 2006. "Ethical Investing in Australia: Is There a Financial Penalty?" *Pacific-Basin Finance Journal* 14:1, 33–48.

Becht, Marco, Julian Franks, Colin Mayer, and Stefano Rossi. 2010. "Returns to Shareholder Activism: Evidence from a Clinical Study of the Hermes UK Focus Funds." *Review of Financial Studies* 23:3, 3093–3129.

Benson, Karen, and Jacquelyn E. Humphrey. 2008. "Socially Responsible Investment Funds: Investor Reaction to Current and Past Returns." *Journal of Banking & Finance* 32:9, 1850–1859.

Berk, Jonathan B., and Jules H. van Binsbergen. 2014. "Measuring Skill in the Mutual Fund Industry." Working Paper, National Bureau of Economic Research 18184.

Bialkowski, Jedrzej, and Rogér Otten. 2011. "Emerging Market Mutual Fund Performance: Evidence from Poland." *North American Journal of Economics and Finance* 22:2, 118–130.

Capelle-Blancard, Gunther, and Stéphanie Monjon. 2014. "The Performance of Socially Responsible Funds: Does the Screening Process Matter?" *European Financial Management* 20:3, 494–520.

Carhart, Mark M. 1997. "On Persistence in Mutual Fund Performance." *Journal of Finance* 52:1, 57–82.

Chen, Joseph, Harrison Hong, Wenxi Jiang, and Jeffrey D. Kubik. 2013. "Outsourcing Mutual Fund Management: Firm Boundaries, Incentives, and Performance." *Journal of Finance* 68:2, 523–558.

Cici, Gjergji, Scott Gibson, and Rabin Moussawi. 2010. "Mutual Fund Performance When Parent Firms Simultaneously Manage Hedge Funds." *Journal of Financial Intermediation* 19:2, 169–187.

Climent, Francisco, and Pilar Soriano. 2011. "Green and Good? The Investment Performance of US Environmental Mutual Funds." *Journal of Business Ethics* 103:2, 275–287.

Cortez, Maria Ceu, Florinda Silva, and Nelson Areal. 2009. "The Performance of European Socially Responsible Funds." *Journal of Business Ethics* 87:4, 573–588.

Cortez, Maria Céu, Florinda Silva, and Nelson Areal. 2012. "Socially Responsible Investing in the Global Market: The Performance of US and European Funds." *International Journal of Finance & Economics* 17:3, 254–271.

Cremers, Martijn, Miguel A. Ferreira, Pedro Matos, and Laura Starks. 2013. "The Mutual Fund Industry Worldwide: Explicit and Closet Indexing, Fees, and Performance." Working Paper, University of Notre Dame.

Cremers, Martijn, and Antti Petajisto. 2009. "How Active Is Your Fund Manager? A New Measure That Predicts Performance." *Review of Financial Studies* 22:9, 3329–3365.

Cremers, Martijn, Antti Petajisto, and Eric Zitzewitz. 2013. "Should Benchmark Indices Have Alpha? Revisiting Performance Evaluation." *Critical Finance Review* 2:1, 1–48.

Cuthbertson, Keith, Dirk Nitzsche, and Niall O'Sullivan. 2010. "Mutual Fund Performance: Measurement and Evidence." *Financial Markets, Institutions & Instruments* 19:2, 95–187.

Cuthbertson, Keith, Dirk Nitzsche, and Niall O'Sullivan. 2008. "UK Mutual Fund Performance: Skill or Luck?" *Journal of Empirical Finance* 15:4, 613–634.

Del Guercio, Diane, and Jonathan Reuter. 2014. "Mutual Fund Performance and the Incentive to Generate Alpha." *Journal of Finance* 69:4, 1673–1704.

Del Guercio, Diane, and Paula A. Tkac. 2008. "Star Power: The Effect of Morningstar Ratings on Mutual Fund Flow." *Journal of Financial and Quantitative Analysis* 43:4, 907–936.

Derwall, Jeroen, and Kees Koedijk. 2009. "Socially Responsible Fixed-Income Funds." *Journal of Business Finance & Accounting* 36:1–2, 210–229.

Dimson, Elroy, Oguzhan Karakas, and Xi Li. 2014. "Active Ownership." Working Paper, London Business School.

Edmans, Alex. 2011. "Does the Stock Market Fully Value Intangibles? Employee Satisfaction and Equity Prices." *Journal of Financial Economics* 101:3, 621–640.

Eling, Martin, and Roger Faust. 2010. "The Performance of Hedge Funds and Mutual Funds in Emerging Markets." *Journal of Banking & Finance* 34:8, 1993–2009.

Eurosif. 2014. " European SRI Study." Eurosif.

Evans, Allison L. 2008. "Portfolio Manager Ownership and Mutual Fund Performance." *Financial Management* 37:3, 513–534.

Fama, Eugene F., and Kenneth R. French. 1993. "Common Risk Factors in the Returns on Stocks and Bonds." *Journal of Financial Economics* 33:1, 3–56.

Fama, Eugene F., and Kenneth R. French. 2010. "Luck versus Skill in the Cross-Section of Mutual Fund Returns." *Journal of Finance* 65:5, 1915–1947.

Ferreira, Miguel A., Aneel Keswani, Antonio F. Miguel, and Sofia B. Ramos. 2013. "The Determinants of Mutual Fund Performance: A Cross-Country Study." *Review of Finance* 17: 2, 483–525.

Ferrell, Allen, Hao Liang, and Luc Renneboog. 2014. "Socially Responsible Firms." Working Paper, ECGI, 432/2014.

Frazzini, Andrea, and Owen A. Lamont. 2008. "Dumb Money: Mutual Fund Flows and the Cross-Section of Stock Returns." *Journal of Financial Economics* 88:2, 299–322.

French, Kenneth R. 2008. "Presidential Address: The Cost of Active Investing." *Journal of Finance* 63:4, 1537–1573.

Friesen, Geoffrey C., and Travis R. A. Sapp. 2007. "Mutual Fund Flows and Investor Returns: An Empirical Examination of Fund Investor Timing Ability." *Journal of Banking & Finance* 31: 9, 2796–2816.

Geczy, Christopher C., Robert F. Stambaugh, and David Levin. 2006. *Investing in Socially Responsible Mutual Funds*. Philadelphia, PA: Rodney L. White Center for Financial Research, The Wharton School, University of Pennsylvania.

Gil-Bazo, Javier, Pablo Ruiz-Verdu, and Andre A. P. Santos. 2010. "The Performance of Socially Responsible Mutual Funds: The Role of Fees and Management Companies." *Journal of Business Ethics* 94:2, 243–263.

Goldreyer, Elizabeth F., and J. David Diltz. 1999. "The Performance of Socially Responsible Mutual Funds: Incorporating Sociopolitical Information in Portfolio Selection." *Managerial Finance* 25:1, 23–36.

Goriaev, Alexei, Theo E. Nijman, and Bas J. M. Werker. 2008. "Performance Information Dissemination in the Mutual Fund Industry." *Journal of Financial Markets* 11: 2, 144–159.

Gregory, Alan, John Matatko, and Robert Luther. 1997. "Ethical Unit Trust Financial Performance: Small Company Effects and Fund Size Effects." *Journal of Business Finance & Accounting* 24:5, 705–725.

Gupta-Murkerjee, Swasti. 2013. "When Active Fund Managers Deviate from Their Peers: Implications for Fund Performance." *Journal of Banking & Finance* 37:4, 1286–1305.

Hamilton, Sally, Hoje Jo, and Meir Statman. 1993. "Doing Well While Doing Good? The Investment Performance of Socially Responsible Mutual Funds." *Financial Analysts Journal* 49:6, 62–66.

Harvey, Campbell R., Yan Liu, and Heqing Zhu. 2014. ". . . and the Cross-Section of Expected Returns." Working Paper, National Bureau of Economic Research 20592.

Huang, Jennifer, Clemens Sialm, and Hanjiang Zhang. 2011. "Risk Shifting and Mutual Fund Performance." *Review of Financial Studies* 24:8, 2575–2616.

In, Francis, Martin Kim, Raphael Jonghyeon Park, Sangbae Kim, and Tong Suk Kim. 2014. "Competition of Socially Responsible and Conventional Mutual Funds and Its Impact on Fund Performance." *Journal of Banking & Finance* 44: 3, 160–176.

Investment Company Institute. 2014. *2014 Investment Company Fact Book: A Review of Trends and Activity in the Investment Company Industry*. Washington, DC: Investment Company Institute. Available at http://www.icifactbook.org.

Ivkovic, Zoran, and Scott Weisbenner. 2009. "Individual Investor Mutual Fund Flows." *Journal of Financial Economics* 92:2, 223–237.

Jiang, Hao, Marno Verbeek, and Yu Wang. 2014. "Information Content When Mutual Funds Deviate from Benchmarks." *Management Science* 60:8, 2038–2053.

Jiang, George J., Tong Yao, and Yu Tong. 2007. "Do Mutual Funds Time the Market? Evidence from Portfolio Holdings." *Journal of Financial Economics* 86:3, 724–758.

Kacperczyk, Marcin, Clemens Sialm, and Lu Zheng. 2005. "On the Industry Concentration of Actively Managed Mutual Funds." *Journal of Finance* 60:4, 1983–2011.

Kacperczyk, Marcin, Clemens Sialm, and Lu Zheng. 2008. "Unobserved Actions of Mutual Funds." *Review of Financial Studies* 21:6, 2379–2416.

Kempf, Alexander, and Stefan Ruenzi. 2008. "Tournaments in Mutual Fund Families." *Review of Financial Studies* 21:2, 1013–1036.

Khorana, Ajay, and Henri Servaes. 2012. "What Drives Market Share in the Mutual Fund Industry?" *Review of Finance* 16:1, 81–113.

Khorana, Ajay, Henri Servaes, and Peter Tufano. 2009. "Mutual Fund Fees around the World." *Review of Financial Studies* 22:3, 1279–1310.

Kosowski, Robert. 2011. "Do Mutual Funds Perform When It Matters Most to Investors? US Mutual Fund Performance and Risk in Recessions and Expansions." *Quarterly Journal of Finance* 1:3, 607–664.

Kreander, Niklas, Robert H. Gray, David M. Power, and C. Donald Sinclair. 2005. "Evaluating the Performance of Ethical and Non-Ethical Funds: A Matched Pair Analysis." *Journal of Business Finance & Accounting* 32:7–8, 1465–1493.

Lee, Darren D., Jacquelyn E. Humphrey, Karen L. Benson, and Jason Y. K. Ahn. 2010. "Socially Responsible Investment Fund Performance: The Impact of Screening Intensity." *Accounting & Finance* 50: 2, 351–370.

Leite, Paulo, and Maria Ceu Cortez. 2014. "Style and Performance of International Socially Responsible Funds in Europe." *Research in International Business and Finance* 30: 1, 248–267.

Luther, Robert G., and John Matatko. 1994. "The Performance of Ethical Unit Trusts: Choosing an Appropriate Benchmark." *British Accounting Review* 26:1, 77–89.

Luther, Robert G., John Matatko, and Desmond C. Corner. 1992. "The Investment Performance of UK "Ethical" Unit Trusts." *Accounting, Auditing & Accountability Journal* 5: 4, 57–70.

Mallin, Chris A., Brahim Saadouni, and Robert J. Briston. 1995. "The Financial Performance of Ethical Investment Funds." *Journal of Business Finance & Accounting* 22: 4, 483–496.

Massa, Massimo, and Rajdeep Patgiri. 2009. "Incentives and Mutual Fund Performance: Higher Performance or Just Higher Risk Taking?" *Review of Financial Studies* 22:5, 1777–1815.

Nofsinger, Josh, and Abhishek Varma. 2014. "Socially Responsible Mutual Funds and Market Crises." *Journal of Banking & Finance* 48, 180–193.

Peifer, Jared L. 2011. "Morality in the Financial Market? A Look at Religiously Affiliated Mutual Funds in the USA." *Socio-Economic Review* 9:2, 235–259.

Petajisto, Antti. 2013. "Active Share and Mutual Fund Performance." *Financial Analysts Journal* 69:4, 73–93.

Pikulina, Elena. 2014. "Contractual and Tournament Incentives in the Mutual Fund Industry." Working Paper, Tilburg University.

Pool, Veronika, Noah Stoffman, and Scott E. Yonker. 2012. "No Place Like Home: Familiarity in Mutual Fund Manager Portfolio Choice." *Review of Financial Studies* 25: 8, 2563–2599.

Renneboog, Luc, Jenke Ter Horst, and Chendi Zhang. 2008a. "The Price of Ethics and Stakeholder Governance: The Performance of Socially Responsible Mutual Funds." *Journal of Corporate Finance* 14: 3, 302–322.

Renneboog, Luc, Jenke Ter Horst, and Chendi Zhang. 2008b. "Socially Responsible Investments: Institutional Aspects, Performance, and Investor Behavior." *Journal of Banking & Finance* 32:9, 1723–1742.

Renneboog, Luc, Jenke Ter Horst, and Chendi Zhang. 2011. "Is Ethical Money Financially Smart? Nonfinancial Attributes and Money Flows of Socially Responsible Investment Funds." *Journal of Financial Intermediation* 20: 4, 562–588.

Ro, Sam. 2014. "Chart of the Day: The Rise of The $156 Trillion Market for Global Financial Assets." Available at http://www.businessinsider.com/156-trillion-global-financial-assets-2014-2013.

Schröder, Michael. 2004. "The Performance of Socially Responsible Investments: Investment Funds and Indices." *Financial Markets and Portfolio Management* 18:2, 122–142.

Schultz, Paul. 2010. "Rational Cross-Sectional Differences in Market Efficiency: Evidence from Mutual Fund Returns." *Journal of Financial and Quantitative Analysis* 45:4, 847–881.

Sensoy, Berk A. 2009. "Performance Evaluation and Self-Designated Benchmark Indexes in the Mutual Fund Industry." *Journal of Financial Economics* 92:1, 25–39.

Statman, Meir. 2000. "Socially Responsible Mutual Funds." *Financial Analysts Journal* 56:3, 30–39.

Statman, Meir, and Denys Glushkov. 2009. "The Wages of Social Responsibility." *Financial Analysts Journal* 65:4, 33–46.

US SIF. 2012. " Sustainable and Responsible Investing Trends in the United States." US SIF.

Verbeek, Marno, and Yu Wang. 2013. "Better than the Original? The Relative Success of Copycat Funds." *Journal of Banking & Finance* 37:9, 3454–3471.

Warner, Jerold B., and Joanna Shuang Wu. 2011. "Why Do Mutual Fund Advisory Contracts Change? Performance, Growth, and Spillover Effects." *Journal of Finance* 66:1, 271–306.

Wurgler, Jeffrey. 2010. "On the Economic Consequences of Index-Linked Investing." Working Paper, National Bureau of Economic Research 16376.

Part Four

ASSET ALLOCATION AND PERFORMANCE OF MUTUAL FUNDS

16

Strategic Asset Allocation and Rebalancing

LAURA ANDREU
Associate Professor of Finance, University of Zaragoza

JOSÉ LUIS SARTO
Associate Professor of Finance, University of Zaragoza

Introduction

This chapter discusses the importance of strategic asset allocation (SAA) in the portfolio management process. It describes the principles of determining an appropriate SAA for investment portfolios and explains how asset classes should be defined to evaluate the consequences of including them in the SAA of individual or institutional investors. The chapter shows the major approaches to determine the SAA of collective investment portfolios such as mutual funds. It also shows that the return of collective portfolios can be split by the returns of the main asset classes in which mutual funds are invested. The chapter introduces an empirical application by using a sample of eurozone equity funds. According to the investment policy of eurozone's analyzed funds, more than 75 percent of their portfolios have to be invested in equity assets. Hence, the benchmark selected as representative of the equity investment is relevant. After an analysis of the correlation between different benchmarks, the proposed style model includes the Euro Stoxx 50 index, one fixed-income index, and a benchmark representative of cash and cash equivalents. The proposed model has strong explanatory power (i.e., the returns of the benchmarks explain more than 86 percent of the portfolio returns). The chapter then analyzes the style allocation in different time periods according to the market status (bull or bear market) to capture the tactical asset allocations and therefore, the rebalancing strategies of portfolio managers. Hence, the chapter discusses how to rebalance the SAA to control a portfolio's risk.

The remainder of the chapter is organized as follows. After a brief literature review of studies analyzing the importance of asset allocation policy, an SAA is defined. The next section discusses how standard finance determines the SAA of investors and introduces some concepts and biases detected in behavioral finance studies that advisors should consider when making SAA recommendations to investors. The following two sections review the different methods of determining an SAA and define a method to determine the SAA of mutual funds. Next, an empirical application of the SAA to Spanish eurozone equity mutual funds is presented followed by a discussion of the empirical findings obtained for the entire time period analyzed and for the different sub-periods. The final section concludes the chapter by discussing the study's results and implications.

Determining Investment Policy

Determining investment policy is one of the most important steps in portfolio and wealth management. Since the seminal studies of Brinson, Hood and Beebower (1986) and Brinson, Singer, and Beebower (1991), an extensive debate has occurred about the contribution of asset allocation policy to portfolio performance. Using quarterly returns of a sample of U.S. pension funds, the authors find that the variation of strategic policy determines more than 90 percent of the variability of the returns. Therefore, the active management abilities of market timing and security selection explain only a small proportion of the variability of pension fund returns.

However, both academics and professional investors have misinterpreted these findings, creating a controversy that stems from using the results to answer inappropriate questions. Jahnke (1997) argues that Brinson et al. (1986, 1991) analyze the wrong information, focusing on the return variability explained by asset allocation rather than on the level of return.

Hensel, Ezra, and Ilkiw (1991) show that Brinson et al.'s (1986, 1991) results are a consequence of the variation of capital markets, not of the strategic policy allocated by each pension fund. They also claim that the importance attributed to asset allocation depends on the benchmark used for the comparison. Ibbotson and Kaplan (2000) support this finding and clarify the misinterpretation by addressing three different questions to determine the importance of an SAA:

1. How much of the variability of returns over time does asset allocation explain?
2. How much of the variation in returns among funds do differences in strategic policy explain?
3. What proportion of the level of return does asset allocation explain?

To answer these questions and therefore determine the contribution of asset allocation to fund performance, Ibbotson and Kaplan (2000) analyze 10 years of monthly returns for 94 U.S. balanced mutual funds and 5 years of quarterly returns for 58 pension funds. Using three different analyses, they find that strategic policy explains, on average, about 90 percent of the variability of returns over time, about 40 percent of the variation in returns among funds, and nearly 100 percent of the total return obtained. None of these questions address an investor's real interest, which is to determine the consequences of asset allocation decisions on portfolio performance.

The analysis of the return that active management adds to merely passively tracking a strategic policy portfolio provides information about the performance consequences of asset allocation. Nevertheless, investors need to keep in mind their own specific risk and return objectives and establish an SAA that they expect to satisfy both.

Xiong, Ibbotson, Idzorek, and Chen (2010) examine the relative importance of asset allocation policy versus active portfolio management in explaining variability in performance. They conclude that after removing the market movements, both asset allocation and active management are equally important in determining portfolio return differences within a peer group.

Defining Asset Allocation

Portfolio investment policies focus on setting the main strategic allocations according to the portfolio investors' objectives in terms of return expectations, risk tolerance, and investment constraints (Sharpe, Chen, Pinto, and McLeavey 2007). Frequently, a portfolio's policy is specified as target percentages for the main asset classes and a range of permissible values. Hence, the investment policy is (1) a mechanism used by managers to align a portfolio's risk profile with an investor's financial objectives and (2) a process through which investors provide information about their desired long-term exposure to systematic risk.

According to Sharpe et al. (2007), many investment advisors rely on experience and rules of thumb in making SAA recommendations. Some common approaches to asset allocation are: (1) using a 60/40 stock/bond asset allocation as a starting point for an average investor's asset allocation, and (2) increasing the allocation to bonds as risk aversion increases. Hence, if investors are less risk-averse, this mix of assets is likely to include a considerable proportion of equity securities. If investors are more risk-averse, the portfolio is likely to place greater emphasis on fixed-income securities because a higher exposure to these securities reduces the portfolio's interim volatility over the investors' time horizons and conservative investors highly value low volatility. Investors with longer time horizons should increase their allocation to stocks. The logic behind this reallocation is that stocks are less risky to hold in the long run than the short run. The percentage allocation to equities is a decreasing function of an investor's age. This strategy is based on the premise that young investors should adopt more aggressive asset allocations than older investors.

Strategic asset allocation refers to determining how much of a portfolio's assets should be invested in each target asset type. For instance, when considering a balanced portfolio of traditional assets, the main decision of the portfolio's SAA is to determine the portfolio weight that should be invested in equity, fixed-income, and cash or equivalents. In this framework, the target weights may vary according to different factors such as the investor's risk tolerance and investment time horizon.

An *asset class* is a group of assets with similar characteristics. Selecting asset classes as inputs of an SAA is an important decision with long-term effects on a portfolio's return and risk. The specification of asset classes should follow three major criteria. First, assets within an asset class should be relatively homogeneous in terms of their characteristics. Second, asset classes should be mutually exclusive. Similar asset classes should reduce the effectiveness of an SAA in controlling risk and return expectations. Third, including different asset classes in a portfolio should result in diversification.

According to these criteria, traditional asset classes include both domestic and international common equity and fixed-income, real estate, and cash and cash equivalents. When investing in international markets, investors should consider both systematic risk and currency risk. Exchange rate fluctuations affect both the total return and volatility of return of any non-domestic currency asset. Thus, investors in international markets must form expectations about exchange rates. A simpler approach based on the main asset types—equity, fixed-income, and cash—is refined according to the specific objectives of the portfolio and its investors. Because these asset classes have different levels of risk and return, each behaves differently over time.

An adequate SAA should determine not only the amount invested in equity assets but also the target markets (e.g., domestic vs. international markets and developed vs. emerging markets) and the target sectors (e.g., telecommunications, banking, and manufacturing). Specifying the type of equity in which the portfolio is concentrated (e.g., large cap vs. small cap stocks and high vs. low book-to-market ratio companies) is also desirable. Determining the appropriate SAA is of primary importance followed by selecting business sectors and individual securities.

An SAA should consider both the weight invested in fixed-income assets and the types of fixed-income assets (e.g., government vs. corporate debt, long-term vs. short-term assets, and high vs. low grade debt). Using an SAA, a manager or investor can protect against losses. As Markowitz (1952) notes, one advantage of diversification is that the returns of the three major asset classes are not highly correlated. Market conditions that affect the returns of one asset class may have a lesser effect on the returns of other asset classes.

An SAA is important because it can affect whether a portfolio meets its established financial goals. For example, if the portfolio has insufficient risk exposure, the investment may not earn a sufficient return to meet its goal. Besides focusing a portfolio's SAA on these long-term weights of the target asset types, considering short-term variations in these portfolio weights is also desirable. These short-term adjustments to asset class weights based on short-term predictions of relative performance among asset classes make up *tactical asset allocation* (TAA).

Arnott, Burns, Plaxco, and Moore (2007) stress the importance of distinguishing between changes to the portfolio's policy itself due to changes in the investors' investment objectives and constraints and changes in their long-term capital market expectations. The authors also show the relevance of adjusting the actual portfolio to the SAA when asset prices move the portfolio weights away from the target weights beyond the tolerable limit. Thus, monitoring the portfolio's investment policy is a relevant and continuous task for managers. This process is important because an investor's objectives can change over time due to changing income, liquidity requirements, time horizons, tax circumstances, and laws and regulations.

These possible changes require managers to evaluate events and trends affecting prospects of individual holdings and asset classes and their suitability for attaining an investor's objectives leading to changes in the investment policy. Similarly, managers also evaluate changes in asset values that create unintended divergences from an investor's SAA, which requires rebalancing to maintain the required ratio of asset classes (e.g., 60 percent equity and 40 percent fixed-income).

TAA implies rebalancing the proportions of the portfolio's target asset types based on short-term predictions of performance among asset classes. For instance, managers should increase (reduce) the portfolio weight invested in equity assets in expected bullish (bearish) markets, changing the proportions invested in fixed-income assets and/or in cash. When rebalancing a portfolio, mutual fund managers should review the investments within each asset allocation category and the associated transaction costs and tax consequences.

A common reason for changing the SAA and rebalancing the portfolio results from both changing market conditions and time horizons. For example, history suggests that investors planning for retirement should invest a smaller percentage of their pension plan in stocks and a larger percentage in bonds and cash equivalents as they get closer to retirement.

Standard and Behavioral Finance

Standard finance theory views investors as rational decision-makers who strive to maximize their utility. Standard finance only considers risk and return in the utility function with return as a positive variable and risk as a negative variable. In contrast, behavioral finance, which is grounded in psychology, focuses on describing individual behaviors because information distribution and the characteristics of financial markets influence their investment decisions.

The majority of research on asset allocation is in the context of standard finance. Investment advisors often focus their recommendations about asset allocation on such factors as their clients' investment goals, needs, and reactions to losses. Many studies document historical phenomena in securities markets that contradict the efficient market hypothesis (EMH) and cannot be captured in models based on the perfectly rational behavior of investors (Jegadeesh and Titman 1993; Shiller 2003). Behavioral finance recognizes a psychological element in financial decision-making and challenges the traditional models that assume that investors weigh risk and return rationally and act without biases.

Behavioral finance studies provide evidence that individual investors suffer from different biases such as overconfidence, mental accounting, and the disposition effect. *Overconfidence* is the tendency of individuals to overestimate the accuracy of their forecasts or investment decisions. Thaler (1985) describes *mental accounting* as the process whereby people evaluate economic outcomes. This theory posits that people mentally frame assets as belonging to current income, current wealth, or future income, which has implications for their behavior as the accounts are non-fungible. This behavior has implications for SAAs because investors who suffer from mental accounting look at their different investments narrowly rather than as a portfolio.

When developing an SAA, investment advisors and management companies need to be aware that investors worry more about avoiding losses than acquiring gains, which is a concept explained by loss aversion theory. For example, the *disposition effect* (Odean 1998) shows that investors are less willing to recognize losses, which they would be forced to do if they sold assets that have fallen in value. Conversely, they are more willing to recognize gains. This behavior is irrational based on standard finance because the future performance of equity is unrelated to its purchase price. Logically, investors should be more likely to sell "losers" to exploit tax reductions on capital gains (Shefrin and Statman 1985).

Behavioral finance also asserts that investors are sensitive to *regret*, which is the pain that comes when a decision results in a negative outcome. The fear of regret may play a role in actual asset allocation decisions because regret avoidance may limit divergence from the average asset allocation of peers if the investor is sensitive to peer comparisons.

Similarly, behavioral finance introduces the concept of *herding* in financial markets in which market participants tend to imitate others who are supposedly better informed, acting sometimes like a herd. Although herding behavior is occasionally associated with irrational behavior, recent research in economics suggests that rationality and emotion are complementary in decision-making (Taffler and Tuckett 2010).

The rich theoretical literature suggests different reasons within the context of agency theory to explain herding behavior. The compensation-reputation scheme can justify imitation strategies because the payoff to a single manager depends on the decisions of others (Scharfstein and Stein 1990; Trueman 1994). Therefore, an unprofitable decision is not as bad for one's reputation when other agents make the same mistake. Other studies explain this behavior in terms of correlated private information signals and information acquisition (Froot, Scharfstein, and Stein 1992; Hirshleifer, Subrahmanyam, and Titman 1994). Researchers also explain herding behavior as an informational cascade in which the recommendation of an analyst or the investment of a trader influences the recommendations of subsequent financial agents and traders (Banerjee 1992; Bikhchandani, Hirshleifer, and Welch 1992). For example, Andreu, Ortiz, and Sarto (2009) analyze the herding behavior in the SAA of portfolio managers, finding this behavior among U.K. pension managers and its persistence over time.

Asset allocation involves determining an optimal asset allocation for the total portfolio of a given investor. However, if investors display mental accounting, they look at their portfolios narrowly in pieces rather than as one portfolio. For this reason, investment advisors should consider these behavioral issues when determining the optimal SAA of each investor.

Methods of Determining a Strategic Asset Allocation

Different quantitative and qualitative approaches are available to determine the appropriate portfolio asset allocation. These approaches can be categorized into SAA methods based on portfolio holdings information and historical portfolio return data.

Portfolio holding is important because it provides information about the different assets held by the portfolio and their respective weights during a certain period (e.g., monthly or quarterly) depending on the disclosure date requirements of each country and the fiscal year. However, return data are more available and can be collected with greater frequency (e.g., daily returns). This wealth of data permits calculating more accurate results of the SAAs of each portfolio along with the variation of these allocations over time to detect the short-term tactical adjustments in allocation levels.

Analyzing portfolio holdings may convey misleading results if managers engage in window dressing practices. *Window dressing* is a strategy that portfolio managers use near the end of a reporting period to improve the appearance of the portfolio performance before reporting it to investors or shareholders. Thus, the portfolio holdings reported on a quarterly basis may not be representative of the current holdings (Lakonishok, Shleifer, Thaler, and Vishny 1991).

Various models are available using return data including efficient frontiers based on the mean-variance approach (Markowitz 1952), multifactor models including different risk factors of equity assets such models by Fama and French (1993) and Carhart (1997), and strategic style models as proposed by Sharpe (1992). Both academics and practitioners widely use the Sharpe style analysis model (De Roon, Nijman, and Horst 2004; Harri and Brorsen 2004).

This chapter applies Sharpe's model because it incorporates not only different equity allocations but also strategic assets such as fixed-income or cash investments. Sharpe's return-based style analysis (RBSA) reflects the overall SAA while the multifactor models gather the different styles of equity assets such as big versus small cap and high versus low book-to-market ratios. Some authors propose more sophisticated factor models to capture the investment in fixed-income assets (Elton, Gruber, and Blake 1999). Additionally, an RBSA can offer a wider perspective given that it permits managers to include assets of different markets, countries, and economic sectors.

Determining the Strategic Asset Allocation of Mutual Funds

This section introduces the methodology proposed by Sharpe (1992) and modified by De Roon et al. (2004) to determine the SAA. RBSA has become a standard technique for inferring the SAA of collective portfolios. This method attempts to explain the return obtained by a portfolio such as a mutual fund or pension fund by analyzing the returns of a set of benchmarks or indexes that represent the different investment opportunities in which the portfolio managers usually invest. Therefore, Sharpe's SAA model is a multifactor model subject to two restrictions that are discussed later.

Equation 16.1 shows the general RBSA model:

$$\begin{aligned} R_t^p &= \beta_1^p R_{1t} + \beta_2^p R_{2t} + \cdots + \beta_n^p R_{nt} + \varepsilon_t^p \\ \textit{subject to } &\sum_{j=1}^{n} \beta_j^p = 1 \qquad , \\ &\beta_j^p > 0 \text{ j} = 1,2, \ldots, \text{n} \end{aligned} \tag{16.1}$$

Where R_t^p is the gross return of mutual fund p in month t; R_t^j is the gross return of the benchmark representative of style j in month t; β_j^p is the style weight of the basic asset class j of mutual fund p; and ε_t^p is the residual return not captured by the model. Therefore, the SAA of mutual fund p is given by the set of β_j^p that better explains the portfolio return.

The analysis comprises a quadratic optimization of a style model to get the average sensitivity of the portfolio returns to different benchmarks. As a result, the best explanation for a portfolio's return is given by the weights that minimize the residual variance of the model subject to two constraints. First, the weights are non-negative because short sales are not allowed in equity mutual funds (positivity constraint). Second, the weights sum to one because the whole portfolio must be invested (portfolio constraint). When analyzing hedge funds, the positivity constraint is relaxed because these portfolios can take important positions in derivatives (Fung and Hsieh 1997; Agarwal and Naik 2000).

De Roon et al. (2004) call this model, including the above-mentioned restrictions, "strong style analysis." They show that this model leads to better estimates of portfolio SAA when it complies with these restrictions. Additionally, De Roon et al. and Harri and Brorsen (2004) also introduce a constant (β_0^p) in Equation 16.1 that captures the management abilities of portfolio managers. If β_0^p is positive, this means that the portfolio return is higher than the return that could be obtained through the benchmarks proposed. Therefore, the fund manager has management skills and adds value. β_0^p captures the return that active management adds to the passive tracking of the portfolio style.

To carry out the empirical analysis to determine the SAA of mutual funds requires having return data on the mutual funds analyzed and the different asset classes in these portfolios. Thus, a relevant issue is to define the benchmarks representative of the different asset classes contained in the mutual funds. As Sharpe (1992), Lobosco and DiBartolomeo (1997), Ben Dor, Jagannathan, and Meier (2003), and Ferruz and Vicente (2005) note, the benchmarks selected to determine the SAAs must fulfill the following requirements. The benchmarks must be exclusive (i.e., exclude any securities that already form part of any other benchmark being considered), exhaustive (i.e., include as many strategic assets as possible), and independent (i.e., have a low correlation among the benchmarks).

If these requirements are not fulfilled, separating the individual explanatory effects of each strategic asset class from the overall return obtained by the portfolio analyzed is impossible. The study in this chapter uses the Sharpe (1992) model with the procedures previously described.

First, the correlations of the different benchmarks proposed are analyzed to capture the main asset classes in which eurozone equity mutual funds invest their portfolios. Then, the most appropriate asset classes are selected based on the previously mentioned characteristics of independence, exhaustiveness, and exclusiveness. Third, the RBSA is applied to the mutual funds to determine the SAA of each portfolio. Finally, to detect the TAA or rebalancing of the SAA carried out by the portfolios, the study splits the time period analyzed depending on the market condition (bear market or bull market). The TAA analysis examines how mutual fund managers adjust the percentage invested in different assets, which are mainly equity, fixed-income, and cash, according to the market status and their short-term expectations. Hence, the aim of the rebalancing analysis carried out is twofold: (1) to smooth or decrease the volatility of mutual fund returns in bear markets and (2) to take advantage of equity returns in bull markets by considering the strategic investment style imposed on the portfolios according to the risk tolerance of the investors.

Application to Spanish Equity Mutual Funds

This study uses the Spanish Securities Exchange Commission (Comisión Nacional del Mercado de Valores, CNMV) mutual fund data set to examine the SAA of collective portfolios and their rebalancing. This database provides information on monthly fund returns and other fund characteristics such as total net assets (TNA) and the number of investors for all Spanish mutual funds in existence in a given period regardless of the disappearance of some mutual funds over time. Therefore, this database is free of survivorship bias.

This analysis focuses on actively managed eurozone equity funds. The sample includes 188 funds that report at least two years of monthly returns over the sample period June 1999 to December 2011 to get robust estimations. Since the purpose of this examination is to analyze the SAA and rebalancing from a managerial perspective, computing the gross returns of the portfolios is important as opposed to using net returns that are relevant from an investor's perspective. Thus, the model compares the gross returns of the mutual funds examined with the returns of the benchmarks/indexes selected to verify that the proposed SAA model explains the portfolio's returns.

Once the mutual funds' gross returns are calculated, the next step is to identify the primary prospectus benchmark of the mutual funds. The Morningstar database is the source of this information. Next, the correlation among the benchmarks most representative of the different asset classes is analyzed to propose a model that fulfills the independence, exclusiveness, and exhaustiveness requirements imposed by Sharpe (1992). Different benchmarks related to equity, fixed-income, and cash or cash equivalents are examined.

Table 16.1 shows some annual descriptive statistics for Spanish mutual funds. It reports the TNA managed by eurozone equity funds, the number of investors, and the number of funds in existence from 1999 to 2011. The figures of TNA, number

Table 16.1 **Annual Descriptive Statistics for Spanish Mutual Funds**

Year	*TNA (000 €)*	*Number of Investors*	*Number of Equity Mutual Funds*	*Average Returns (%)*	*Euro Stoxx 50 Average Returns (%)*
1999	206,196	8,012,123	2,153	2.30	4.16
2000	182,842	7,655,441	2,425	−0.68	−0.41
2001	177,849	7,448,815	2,540	−1.15	−1.41
2002	170,814	7,142,193	2,487	−3.11	−2.81
2003	197,857	7,731,354	2,623	1.59	−1.66
2004	219,731	8,148,140	2,654	0.80	−0.92
2005	245,887	8,477,425	2,616	1.94	−1.90
2006	254,306	8,819,809	2,794	1.30	−1.54
2007	238,699	8,264,240	3,051	0.81	−0.56
2008	167,655	6,147,542	2,505	−3.73	−4.05
2009	162,567	5,608,725	1,926	2.23	−1.99
2010	138,080	5,320,522	2,345	0.33	−0.16
2011	127,772	4,922,063	2,670	−0.96	−1.03

Note: This table shows annual descriptive statistics for a sample of Spanish mutual funds. Specifically, the table lists the total net assets (TNA) managed by eurozone equity funds, number of investors that save their money in these portfolios, and number of funds between 1999 and 2011. The table also reports the average annual returns of the portfolios and the average returns of the Euro Stoxx 50 (an equity index).

of investors, and number of funds tended to grow until 2007 and then steadily decreased from 2008 until 2011 as a consequence of the global financial crisis. Table 16.1 also reports average annual returns for the portfolios examined and the Euro Stoxx 50 index, which is an index representative of eurozone equity assets. These figures reflect the status of the European equity market. Negative annual returns occur during 2000, 2001, and 2002, which was a bear market. The following years before the global financial crisis in 2008 were during a bull market, resulting in positive annual returns.

In relation to the benchmark returns, the study uses monthly returns on domestic and foreign benchmarks obtained from DataStream. Analistas Financieros Internacionales (AFI) provides the returns on Treasury bills, one-day Treasury-bill repos, and other fixed-income securities.

The study uses different benchmarks for the three main asset classes: equity, fixed-income, and cash. The Euro Stoxx 50 and Ibex 35 indexes represent equity. Spanish public debt with different maturities (five years, three years, and one year) serve as the benchmarks for fixed-income investments. The one-day Treasury-bill repo serves as a proxy for cash and cash equivalents return. Table 16.2 shows the correlation among the benchmarks used to select those that fulfill the requirements of independence, exclusiveness, and exhaustiveness.

Table 16.2 **Benchmark Correlations**

	Euro Stoxx 50	*Ibex 35*	*Five-year Spanish Public Debt*	*Three-year Spanish Public Debt*	*One-year Spanish Public Debt*	*Cash*
Euro Stoxx 50	1	0.870**	–0.195*	–0.198*	–0.188*	–0.167*
Ibex 35		1	–0.030	–0.038	–0.045	–0.134
Five-year Spanish Public Debt			1	0.976	0.826	0.071
Three-year Spanish Public Debt				1	0.860	0.099
One-year Spanish Public Debt					1	0.271**
Cash						1

Note: This table shows the correlation between the benchmarks initially chosen to determine the SAAs of eurozone equity funds.

*, ** Statistically significant at the 0.05 and 0.01 levels, respectively.

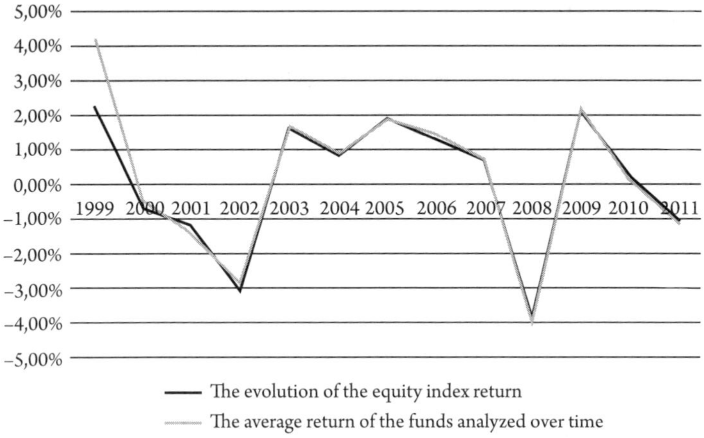

Figure 16.1 Annual Average Return of Eurozone Equity Funds and the Euro Stoxx 50. The figure shows the evolution of the equity index return (black line) and the average return of the funds analyzed over time (grey line). It also shows that the Euro Stoxx 50 is an appropriate benchmark to explain the return of the portfolios analyzed.

The findings show a high level of correlation between the two equity benchmarks (Euro Stoxx 50 and Ibex 35). Given that the portfolios analyzed are eurozone equity funds and that Euro Stoxx 50 is the prospectus benchmark of 40 percent of the funds analyzed, this study uses the Euro Stoxx 50 as the benchmark. Figure 16.1 shows the evolution of the equity index return and the average return of the funds analyzed over time. The figure shows that the Euro Stoxx 50 is an appropriate benchmark to explain the return of the portfolios analyzed.

Figure 16.1 also shows the different stages undergone by eurozone equity between 1999 and 2011. Specifically, the graph depicts a bearish trend until 2003. The "dot-com" bubble characterized this period during which the Euro Stoxx 50 went from a 4 percent to a –3 percent return. During the bull period, the market return was around 1 to 2 percent until 2008, when the global financial crisis began.

Fixed-income benchmarks (i.e., five-, three-, and one-year Spanish public debt) show high correlations. The study uses three-year public debt as the benchmark for fixed-income investments because one-year public debt shows a high correlation with cash and cash equivalents and five-year public debt can be a long time horizon for eurozone equity funds. Equation 16.2 shows the proposed SAA model:

$$R_t^p = \beta_1^p R_{EuroStoxx\text{-}50t} + \beta_2^p R_{3\text{-}ySpanishPublicDebtt} + \beta_3^p R_{\text{Cash}\ t} + \varepsilon_t^p$$
$$\textit{subject to} \sum_{j=1}^{3} \beta_j^p = 1 \qquad (16.2)$$
$$\beta_j^p > 0$$

The style model proposed is not limited to equity factors such as size and book-to-market indexes as in previous research examining style investing (Teo and Woo 2004).

Empirical Findings

Table 16.3 shows descriptive statistics of SAA estimates for the Spanish mutual funds investing in eurozone equities for the entire sample period (1999 to 2011) and the determination coefficient of the style model proposed. Table 16.3 also shows that the style model proposed to capture the SAA of Spanish mutual funds is appropriate given that the average R^2 is above 86 percent. Furthermore, the average value of the equity beta is 85.33 percent, which is above the 75 percent of equity investment required by the CNMV to equity mutual funds. The betas reported in the RBSA are not portfolio holdings. The RBSA betas represent the style allocated by the fund. For example, a mutual fund with 90 percent of the portfolio in domestic stocks can show a beta in the domestic equity benchmark used in the RBSA higher or lower than 90 percent. The value of the equity beta of the RBSA depends on the type of stocks in which the fund invests and is higher than the 90 percent if the stocks are aggressive and lower if the stocks are defensive. The results also show that 65.96 percent of the mutual funds have a positive value of β_0. This figure is only positive and statistically significant in five mutual funds, suggesting that very few fund managers add value even before charging their fees to institutional and individual investors.

To determine the rebalancing strategies of Spanish mutual fund portfolios, the analysis carries out the RBSA for different periods to capture the asset allocation in different market conditions (i.e., bear and bull periods). Specifically, the study considers three periods: (1) a bear period from April 2000 to March 2003, (2) a bull period from April 2003 to December 2007, and (3) a period from January 2008 to December 2011 capturing the impact of the global financial crisis.

Table 16.4 shows descriptive statistics about the SAA followed by Spanish equity mutual funds investing in eurozone equity for the different sub-periods examined. To carry out the analysis in the different subsamples, mutual funds were required to have at least 30 observations to get robust estimations of the SAAs. The equity investment is analyzed in more detail than fixed-income and cash because it is the most relevant decision in eurozone equity funds and explains the majority of the return obtained by the portfolios analyzed.

Table 16.3 **Summary Statistics of the Strategic Asset Allocation of Spanish Mutual Funds Investing in Eurozone Equity**

	β_0	β_1	β_2	β_3	R^2
Average	0.16	85.33	3.77	9.47	86.10
Median	0.20	89.00	0.00	6.10	91.90
Maximum	1.31	100.00	42.30	50.70	99.80
Minimum	-1.30	49.30	0.00	0.00	44.20
Standard Deviation	0.38	12.02	8.19	11.19	12.23

Note: This table shows some descriptive statistics of the SAA to equities (β_1), fixed-income (β_2), and cash (β_3) and the adjusted coefficient of determination (R^2) of the Spanish mutual funds investing in eurozone equities. The figures are expressed in percentages.

Table 16.4 **Comparison of the Equity Investment during Different Periods**

Bear Period: 2000 to 2003	β_0	β_1	β_2	β_3	R^2
Average	–0.06	86.29	3.10	10.61	89.20
Median	–0.10	90.00	0.00	4.70	93.90
Maximum	1.10	100.00	34.20	46.00	99.90
Minimum	–0.80	54.00	0.00	0.00	55.30
Bull Period: 2003 to 2007	β_0	β_1	β_2	β_3	R^2
Average	0.33	87.63	5.76	6.61	85.93
Median	0.20	91.85	0.00	1.80	93.55
Maximum	1.80	100.00	46.00	36.20	99.30
Minimum	–0.30	49.20	0.00	0.00	26.10
Global Financial Crisis: 2008 to 2011	β_0	β_1	β_2	β_3	R^2
Average	0.26	88.48	2.89	8.63	89.70
Median	0.20	92.20	0.00	4.35	93.65
Maximum	1.20	100.00	40.30	59.80	99.10
Minimum	–0.50	40.20	0.00	0.00	54.10

Note: This table shows the investment exposures of eurozone equity funds for the entire time period examined (1999 to 2011) and the three different sub-periods: a bear period (2000 to 2003), a bull period (2003 to 2007), and the global financial crisis (2008 to 2011). The figures are expressed in percentages.

Table 16.4 reports that the average investment in equity is 86.29, 87.63, and 88.48 percent for the bear period (2000 to 2003), the bull period (2003 to 2008), and the global financial crisis (2008 to 2011), respectively. Although the magnitude of these figures is not very different, it suggests that in the first market trend transition (i.e., from the bear market to the bull market), some Spanish mutual fund managers increased exposure to the equity market expecting that the equity market would perform well in the future. Therefore, those portfolio managers who increased their market exposure made correct decisions. Some managers increased their market exposure more than 15 percent. Others increased their average exposure to fixed-income securities and reduced the percentage invested in cash or cash equivalents.

However, this is not the case in the second change (i.e., from the bull market to the global financial crisis). Mutual funds and portfolio managers did not foresee the beginning of the global financial crisis because they continued to increase, on average, their market exposure instead of decreasing equity exposure given how the equity market performed during the following years. Only a few funds reduced their market exposure. The minimum investment in equities takes the smaller value during this period. Therefore, some portfolio managers either anticipated the bad behavior of equity markets or were simply lucky.

Regarding the value added by portfolio managers, more than 38 percent of the managers beat the market during the bear period on a gross basis, while this figure was more than 93 percent during the bull period. However, gross returns ignore the impact of management fees and other expenses that mutual funds charge to investors. Using net returns, the major conclusion is that portfolio managers do not add value to their investors, which is generally consistent with the financial literature (Jensen 1968; Carhart 1997).

Summary and Conclusions

Creating an SAA is an important task for managers. This chapter explains the importance of an SAA as an investment strategy that aims to balance risk and reward by including different assets in portfolios under the risk tolerance and investment horizon of investors. The three main asset classes—equities, fixed-income, and cash and equivalents—have different levels of risk and return and therefore each asset type behaves differently over time. No simple formula can provide the optimal asset allocation for each mutual fund or for every individual.

The chapter explains a methodology that mutual fund investors can follow to identify the exposure of different financial products to the main asset classes. Thus, investors can make their investment decisions over time according to an appropriate SAA because their financial needs change over time. This methodology is illustrated using Spanish mutual funds.

The empirical findings show that eurozone equity funds invest more than 85 percent of portfolios in the Euro Stoxx 50 index, which is consistent with their investment policy of eurozone equity since the CNMV requires that the portfolios must invest at least 75 percent of their assets in equities. Specifically, the average SAA is 85 percent in equity, 5 percent in fixed-income, and 10 percent in cash. The results also show that managers of more than 65 percent of the funds add value on a gross basis but this value is not statistically significant. However, an analysis based on gross returns overstates performance because it excludes management fees and other charges that considerably reduce actual returns. In fact, Spanish mutual fund managers cannot add value based on net returns. This finding is consistent with previous financial literature reporting that active management rarely adds value when accounting for fees and expenses.

Finally, the chapter analyzes different time periods to capture the TAA and rebalancing strategies followed by mutual fund investors. Equity allocation is the most relevant aspect of portfolio management. Therefore, analyzing its evolution over time helps to detect whether portfolio managers have market timing abilities. One interpretation of the evidence suggests that some managers of Spanish mutual funds could successfully time the market before the bull period analyzed (2003 to 2008) because they increased their market exposure before the good performance of the equity market. Another possibility is that they were simply lucky. However, these managers were unsuccessful in timing the market before the beginning of the global financial crisis. The past returns obtained by the portfolios can provide a general idea about portfolio allocation because the portfolio returns are a combination of the returns of the different assets in which the portfolio managers invest. Because an SAA varies over time, determining the impact and consequences of rebalancing is important.

Discussion Questions

1. Define SAA and TAA.
2. Explain the steps needed to determine a portfolio's SAA.
3. Identify the three characteristics of an effective benchmark for an SAA analysis.
4. Discuss the importance of rebalancing a portfolio.

References

Agarwal, Vikas, and Narayan Y. Naik. 2000. "Generalised Style Analysis of Hedge Funds." *Journal of Asset Management* 1:1, 93–109.

Andreu, Laura, Cristina Ortiz, and José L. Sarto. 2009. "Herding Behavior in Strategic Asset Allocations: New Approaches on Quantitative and Intertemporal Imitation." *Applied Financial Economics* 20:19, 1649–1659.

Arnott, Robert D., Terence E. Burns, Lisa Plaxco, and Philip Moore. 2007. "Monitoring and Rebalancing." In John L. Maginn, Donald L. Tuttle, Jerald E. Pinto, and Dennis W. McLeavey, eds., *Managing Investment Portfolios: A Dynamic Process*, 682–716. Hoboken, NJ: John Wiley & Sons, Inc.

Banerjee, Abhijit V. 1992. "A Simple Model of Herd Behavior." *Quarterly Journal of Economics* 107:3, 797–817.

Ben Dor, Arik, Ravi Jagannathan, and Iwan Meier. 2003. "Understanding Mutual Fund and Hedge Fund Styles Using Return-Based Style Analysis." *Journal of Investment Management* 1:1, 94–134.

Bikhchandani, Sushil, David Hirshleifer, and Ivo Welch. 1992. "A Theory of Fads, Fashion, Custom, and Cultural Change as Informational Cascades." *Journal of Political Economy* 100:5, 992–1026.

Brinson, Gary P., L. Randolph Hood, and Gilbert L. Beebower. 1986. "Determinants of Portfolio Performance." *Financial Analysts Journal* 42:4, 39–48.

Brinson, Gary P., Brian D. Singer, and Gilbert L. Beebower. 1991. "Determinants of Portfolio Performance II: An Update." *Financial Analysts Journal* 47:3, 40–48.

Carhart, Mark M. 1997. "On Persistence in Mutual Fund Performance." *Journal of Finance* 52:1, 57–82.

De Roon, Frans A., Theo E. Nijman, and Jenke R. ter Horst. 2004. "Evaluating Style Analysis." *Journal of Empirical Finance* 11:1, 29–53.

Elton, Edwin J., Martin J. Gruber, and Christopher R. Blake. 1999. "Common Factors in Active and Passive Portfolios." *European Finance Review* 3:1, 53–78.

Fama, Eugene F., and Kenneth R. French. 1993. "Common Risk Factors in the Returns on Stocks and Bonds." *Journal of Financial Economics* 33:1, 3–56.

Ferruz, Luis, and Luis A. Vicente. 2005. "Effects of Multicollinearity on the Definition of Mutual Funds' Strategic Style: The Spanish Case." *Applied Economics Letters* 12:9, 553–556.

Froot, Kenneth A., David S. Scharfstein, and Jeremy C. Stein. 1992. "Herd on the Street: Informational Inefficiencies in a Market with Short-Term Speculation." *Journal of Finance* 47:4, 1461–1484.

Fung, William, and David A. Hsieh. 1997. "Empirical Characteristics of Dynamic Trading Strategies: The Case of Hedge Funds." *Review of Financial Studies* 10:2, 275–302.

Harri, Ardian, and Wade Brorsen. 2004. "Performance Persistence and the Source of Returns for Hedge Funds." *Applied Financial Economics* 14:2, 131–141.

Hensel, Chris R., D. Don Ezra, and John H. Ilkiw. 1991. "The Importance of the Asset Allocation Decision." *Financial Analysts Journal* 47:4, 65–72.

Hirshleifer, David, Avanidhar Subrahmanyam, and Sheridan Titman. 1994. "Security Analysis and Trading Patterns When Some Investors Receive Information before Others." *Journal of Finance* 49:5, 1665–1698.

Ibbotson, Roger G., and Paul D. Kaplan. 2000. "Does Asset Allocation Policy Explain 40, 90 or 100 Percent of Performance?" *Financial Analyst Journal* 56:1, 26–33.

Jahnke, William. 1997. "The Asset Allocation Hoax." *Journal of Financial Planning* 10:1, 109–113.

Jegadeesh, Narasimhan, and Sherdan Titman. 1993. "Returns to Buying Winners and Selling Losers: Implications for Stock Market Efficiency." *Journal of Finance* 48:1, 65–92.

Jensen, Michael C. 1968. "The Performance of Mutual Funds in the Period 1945–1964." *Journal of Finance* 23:2, 389–416.

Lakonishok, Josef, Andrei Shleifer, Richard H. Thaler, and Robert W. Vishny. 1991. "Window Dressing by Pension Fund Managers." *American Economic Review* 81:2, 227–231.

Lobosco, Angelo, and Dan DiBartolomeo. 1997. "Approximating the Confidence Intervals for Sharpe Style Weights." *Financial Analysts Journal* 53:4, 80–85.

Markowitz, Harry M. 1952. "Portfolio Selection." *Journal of Finance* 7:1, 77–91.

Odean Terrance. 1998. "Are Investors Reluctant to Realize Their Losses?" *Journal of Finance* 53:5, 1775–1798.

Scharfstein, David S., and Jeremy C. Stein. 1990. "Herd Behavior and Investment." *American Economic Review* 80:3, 465–479.

Sharpe, William F. 1992. "Asset Allocation: Management Style and Performance Measurement." *Journal of Portfolio Management* 18:2, 7–19.

Sharpe, William F., Peng Chen, Jerald E. Pinto, and, Dennis W. McLeavey. 2007. "Asset Allocation." In John L. Maginn, Donald L. Tuttle, Jerald E. Pinto, and Dennis W. McLeavey, eds., *Managing Investment Portfolios: A Dynamic Process*, 230–327. Hoboken, NJ: John Wiley & Sons, Inc.

Shefrin, Hersh, and Meir Statman. 1985. "The Disposition to Sell Winners Too Early and Ride Losers Too Long: Theory and Evidence." *Journal of Finance* 40:3, 777–790.

Shiller, Robert J. 2003. "From Efficient Markets Theory to Behavioral Finance." *Journal of Economic Perspectives* 17:1, 83–104.

Taffler, Richard J., and David A. Tuckett. 2010. "Emotional Finance: The Role of the Unconscious in Financial Decisions." In H. Kent Baker and John R. Nofsinger, eds., *Behavioral Finance: Investors, Corporations, and Markets*, 95–112. Hoboken, NJ: John Wiley & Sons, Inc.

Teo, Melvyn, and Sung-Jun Woo. 2004. "Style Effects in the Cross-Section of Stock Returns." *Journal of Financial Economics* 74:2, 367–398.

Thaler, Richard H. 1985. "Mental Accounting and Consumer Choice." *Marketing Science* 4:3, 199–214.

Trueman, Brett. 1994. "Analyst Forecasts and Herding Behavior." *Review of Financial Studies* 7:1, 97–124.

Xiong, James X., Roger G. Ibbotson, Thomas M. Idzorek, and Peng Chen. 2010. "The Equal Importance of Asset Allocation and Active Management." *Financial Analysts Journal* 66:2, 21–30.

17

Building and Monitoring Mutual Fund Portfolios

LARRY J. PRATHER
John Massey Endowed Chair and Professor of Finance, Southeastern Oklahoma State University

HAN-SHENG CHEN
Assistant Professor of Finance, Southeastern Oklahoma State University

YING-CHOU LIN
Assistant Professor of Finance, Southeastern Oklahoma State University

Introduction

Building and monitoring mutual fund portfolios is a daunting task because individual investors face many choices. According to the Investment Company Institute (2014), worldwide investments in mutual funds totaled $30 trillion at the end of 2013. Investments included $15 trillion in 8,974 open-end funds (OEFs), $1.675 trillion in 1,332 exchange-traded funds (ETFs), $279 billion in 599 closed-end funds (CEFs), and $87 billion 5,552 unit investment trusts (UITs).

Many investor decisions require in-depth knowledge, which adds to the complexity of selecting mutual funds. Previous chapters discuss the nuances of various types of pooled investments such as OEFs, CEFs, ETFs, and UITs. Although each of these investment vehicles shares some commonalities, they also possess key differences that may influence an investor's preference for one type of vehicle over another for their specific purpose and holding period. Such choices have important implications for trading and managing individual investments within the portfolio.

Other important choices include determining which asset classes to include in the portfolio and deciding whether to actively or passively manage funds. Previous chapters examine the characteristics of many asset classes such as money market mutual funds, bond funds, and stock or equity funds. This information is vital because investors must choose both the asset classes and their weightings.

Once investors make these choices, they can use a screener to search for specific criteria to identify potential investments for the portfolio. After completing the screening process, investors should research competing funds in each asset category. Ideally, this process should produce a short list of funds in each desired asset class. Investors can use this list of funds to create a portfolio with optimal risk.

This chapter shows how investors can use a money market mutual fund in conjunction with the optimal risky mutual fund portfolio to create a risk-return relationship that maximizes investor utility. It also presents useful information for making mutual fund portfolio management decisions. The remainder of the chapter is organized as follows. The next section discusses choices that investors may confront such as choosing between actively or passively managed funds, load and no-load funds, and management structures. The following section discusses portfolio construction including reviewing portfolio risk and return, using Excel to form optimal risky portfolios, assessing risk aversion, and creating a utility-maximizing portfolio for an investor. The final section concludes by discussing the need to monitor and periodically rebalance a portfolio.

Investor Choices, Sources of Information, and Screening

Smart, Gitman, and Joehnk (2014) point out that portfolio management primarily involves two issues: asset allocation and security selection. Although the fund manager makes security selection decisions for the fund, an investor must decide which funds to hold for each asset class. Therefore, the investor should first concentrate on which asset classes to hold and then focus on how best to hold those asset classes.

Before building a portfolio, an investor must decide on the portfolio's composition. This decision can be complex because each investor can have different needs about key portfolio attributes. For example, does the investor want to trade funds frequently or rebalance the portfolio once or twice per year? Does the investor prefer using OEFs to ensure trading at the net asset value (NAV) at the close of any trading day, or to use CEFs to speculate on a change in the premium or discount from NAV? Or does the investor prefer ETFs that allow trading at or very near the NAV any time the market is open?

THE CHOICE BETWEEN ACTIVE AND PASSIVE MANAGEMENT

Investors' preferences for actively or passively managed funds depend on their view of the efficient market hypothesis (EMH). According to the EMH, all securities are fairly priced because current stock prices include all information. Because information is already incorporated in current prices, attempts to identify incorrectly priced securities are futile. Therefore, under the EMH, consistently outperforming the market on a risk-adjusted basis is impossible.

Empirical research suggests that actively managed mutual funds fail to consistently outperform the market (Treynor and Mazuy 1966; Veit and Cheney 1982; Kon 1983; Chang and Lewellen 1984; Henriksson 1984; Lehmann and Modest 1987; Grinblatt and Titman 1989, 1994; Cumby and Glen 1990; Gruber 1996; Daniel, Grinblatt, Titman, and Wermers 1997; Becker, Ferson, Myers, and Schill 1999). All fail to find evidence of market-timing ability. However, that does not rule out a particular fund from having superior performance in any year or even a sustained number of years. Whether superior performance persists is a question of interest to investors. Malkiel (1995) reports some persistent performance of mutual funds during the 1970s that basically disappeared by the 1980s. Carhart (1997) agrees that mutual funds exhibit little persistence but finds that most persistent performance is poor performance. Thus, investors might be better off choosing index funds and diversifying among asset classes.

THE CHOICE BETWEEN LOAD FUNDS, NO-LOAD FUNDS, AND EXCHANGE-TRADED FUNDS

A *load fund* is a fund that charges a fee to purchase (front-end load) or sell (back-end load) the fund, whereas a *no-load fund* is a fund that does not charge fees to purchase or sell shares. Choosing between such funds is becoming increasingly difficult because many underlying portfolios are being sold with multiple share classes (e.g., front-end load, back-end load, or no load). The share classes with loads have lower annual expenses than no-load funds because funds use the load charges to pay distributions costs. No-load funds must also pay distribution costs so they charge higher annual fees to generate this revenue. Thus, investors may need to evaluate whether they should pay a load to receive lower annual fees.

Bodie, Kane, and Marcus (2014) show how to make that choice when the underlying portfolio is identical and how the intended investment horizon affects the choice. Prather, Chu, Mazumder, and Topuz (2009) extend Bodie et al.'s process to choose between mutual funds and ETFs with identical underlying portfolios. The process of making the choice between competing assets is detailed below and centers on how loads or spreads and commissions change the amount of money that is invested in return-generating securities, how annual fee differentials affect net returns, and how back-end load fees or costs affect net terminal wealth. Investors should use this process to make these choices.

Prather et al. (2009) show that the choice between S&P 500 index funds and S&P 500 ETFs can be framed as the choice among front-end load (class "A"), back-end load (class "B"), and no-load (class "C") shares of a selected mutual fund. This outcome is because the only difference between the investments is the magnitude and type of costs and fees that investors must pay to buy, hold, or redeem the shares. This process is explained in the following section and investors should use this process to evaluate funds to include in their portfolio.

Unlike mutual funds, ETFs can be traded like shares of stock in that they can be sold short and bought on margin. ETFs function similarly to an index fund but ETFs have lower expense ratios because of lower management and distribution costs. However, a disadvantage of ETFs is that they require investors to incur trading costs, which include commissions and bid-ask spreads. Because ETFs trade like shares of stock, investors can use price contingent orders such as limit, stop, and trailing stop orders to manage transactions and can buy or sell securities without waiting for the market closing price.

Given these complexities, choosing between classes of funds or within a fund class and an ETF can be confusing. If one index fund has lower front-end load fees, back-end load fees, operating expenses, and 12b-1 fees, the choice would be easy because the optimal choice would dominate all other index investment choices. *The 12b-1 fees* are annual recurring fees deducted from the assets of the fund to cover distribution costs. Without dominance in fees, decision-makers must examine which index alternative provides the highest net terminal wealth (NTW) by computing its value in Equation 17.1:

$$NTW = NI\,(1 + NPR)^n, \tag{17.1}$$

where *NI* is the net investment; *NPR* is the net periodic return; and *n* is the number of investment periods. If the mutual fund has a contingent deferred sales charge (i.e., a back-end load or class "B" shares), the terminal wealth must be multiplied by $(1 - BL)$, where *BL* is the percentage back-end load to compute NTW. For ETFs, the commission for selling the shares must be subtracted from the terminal wealth to compute NTW.

Given any gross investment amount, the net investment and net periodic returns will differ between the investments if load and fee differentials exist. The net investment in class "C" shares is the investor's total investment because the investor does not pay a load. However, for class "A" shares, only part of the initial investment amount is invested and the remainder is the load fee. Thus, Equation 17.2 shows that the net investment in a load fund is:

$$NI = GI\,(1 - L), \tag{17.2}$$

where *GI* is the gross amount available for investment and *L* is the load percentage.

Modifying this approach to evaluate an ETF is straightforward. Because investors buy an ETF at the dealer's ask price and sell it at the dealer's bid price, this spread is similar to a front-end load. Purchasing an ETF involves a flat commission fee. Thus, Equation 17.3 shows that *NI* for evaluating ETFs is:

$$NI = (GI - C)(1 - S), \tag{17.3}$$

where *GI* is the gross amount to be invested; *C* is the commission; and *S* is the bid-ask spread percentage.

To illustrate, assume that a fund offers Class A and B shares on the same underlying portfolio. The portfolio's historical annual return of 10 percent is expected to continue into the future. The Class A shares have a front-end load of 6 percent while the Class B shares have a back-end load of 5 percent that decreases by 1 percentage point per year until it reaches zero at the end of five years and an annual 12b-1 fee of 0.5 percent. If an investor's investment horizon is four years, which share class is a better choice?

To determine the best share class, the investor can compute which alternative results in the highest NTW. Assume that the investor has \$1,000 to invest. The initial investment in Class A shares is \$940 net of the 6 percent front-end load. After four years, the portfolio will be worth $\$940(1.10)^4 = \$1{,}376.25$.

With Class B shares the full \$1,000 is invested, but the annual 0.5 percent 12b-1 fee must be subtracted from the expected average portfolio return. Thus, the return net of 12b-1 fees will be 9.5 percent. The investor will pay a 1 percent back-end load fee if the fund is sold after four years. After four years the portfolio value will be $\$1{,}000(1.095)^4 = \$1{,}437.66$. However, after paying the back-end load fee, the investor will receive $\$1{,}437.66(0.99) = \$1{,}423.28$. Class B shares are the better choice if the investor's investment horizon is four years.

The choice can be more complicated. Many competing funds exist that hold different underlying portfolios in the same asset class. Thus, this approach is unsuitable without adjusting for potential risk differences. Just because two portfolios share the same investment objective class does not ensure that the risk of these portfolios is the same. Najand and Prather (1999) study mutual funds during a 10-year period and report that risk is heterogeneous within the investment objective class for several commonly used investment classification sources. Therefore, a more general question is whether investors recoup load fees or whether they would be better off selecting no-load funds for their portfolio. Agarwal and Prather (1997) evaluate a broad sample of mutual funds to determine whether load funds exhibit significantly higher returns so that the investor can recoup load fees over time. The authors find no evidence that investors recoup load fees.

THE CHOICE OF MANAGEMENT STRUCTURE

Prather and Middleton (2006) examine the security selection and market timing differentials of funds managed by individuals and teams. Classical decision-making theory suggests that decisions made by an individual or a team of decision-makers should lead to the same performance outcome. Conversely, behavioral decision-making theory argues that teams would form different expectations, resulting in superior performance outcomes. Prather and Middleton's analysis suggests that managerial structure is not an important selection criterion.

TAX EFFICIENCY AND TURNOVER

If the portfolio is tax-sheltered, tax efficiency may not be a concern. However, if the portfolio is not tax-sheltered, the investor may want to consider the tax efficiency of the funds. Funds with high turnover have high realized capital gains making them tax inefficient. Thus, turnover may be a factor to consider when setting up a screen to find a list of competing funds. Turnover is reported in the annual report, prospectus, semi-annual report, and from other mutual fund investment sources. Bodie et al. (2014) compute turnover by dividing the assets sold and then replaced by the average total assets.

IMPORTANT SOURCES OF INFORMATION ABOUT MUTUAL FUNDS

Investors can find important information on mutual funds from four major sources.

- *Mutual fund prospectus and annual shareholder report*. The Security and Exchange Commission (SEC) requires that a prospectus disclose a mutual fund's organization, investment objectives and policies, major risks, fees and expenses, and past performance. If investors desire greater detail, they can request the fund's Statement of Additional Information (SAI). Investors should also read a fund's semi-annual and annual reports because they contain information such as current performance, audited financial statement, and management compensation to determine if the fund has met its goals. These documents are available on a mutual fund's website or Electronic Data Gathering, Analysis, and Retrieval (EDGAR) mutual fund filing (http://www.sec.gov/edgar/searchedgar/mutualsearch.html).

- *Morningstar*. Morningstar is an independent investment search and management company that provides investment data and advice to the public. Its mutual fund data include a unique "style box" and "star rating" feature. Both investors and financial experts have embraced Morningstar for many years. Morningstar's tools not only help investors assess each fund's performance and risk but also simplify making comparisons among funds. This information is available on Morningstar's website (http://www.morningstar.com/Cover/Funds.aspx).
- *Lipper Leaders*. Lipper Leaders is a Thomson Reuters company that provides global mutual fund data and online screening tools (http://www.lipperleaders.com). It has a rating function that allows investors to measure a fund's success against five metrics: (1) total return, (2) consistent returns, (3) preservation, (4) tax efficiency, and (5) expense relative to other funds.
- *Kiplinger mutual fund finder*. Kiplinger publishes business forecasts and finance advice. Through its online mutual fund finder investors can search for a mutual fund that meets specific criteria (http://www.kiplinger.com/tool/).

With thousands of mutual funds available, selecting suitable funds to build a portfolio can be challenging for investors. Pozen and Hamacher (2011) suggest that investors should consider their liquidity needs, time horizon, return expectations, and risk tolerance. Next, investors should start with asset allocation and investment style by using screening tools such as Morningstar's Fund Screener to create a short list of possible funds that meets their criteria. Then, investors should assess each fund's background, investment objective, investment portfolio, turnover, performance, risk, and tax efficiency. Other issues that merit attention are a fund's corporate governance and manager's credentials. Although whether fund managers have superior stock-picking skills is still being debated (Jensen 1968; Lucas 1978; Chen, Jegadeesh, and Wermers 2000; Fama and French 2010), studies find that funds with better corporate governance are more likely to have better future performance (Wellman and Zhou 2008; Chen and Huang 2011).

When constructing a portfolio, investors should avoid various pitfalls:

- Investors often select a fund based on past performance. Coombes (2013) reports that 47 percent of mutual fund investors primarily rely on past performance to make their investment decision. However, Malkiel (1995) and Carhart (1997) argue that superior past performance does not persist.
- Investors frequently construct overly diversified portfolios. A study conducted by Morningstar (2014) finds that an extremely diversified portfolio including eight different asset classes does not outperform a mutual fund portfolio comprising a broadly diversified mix of U.S. stocks and bonds. Retail investors often do not have the time and knowledge to monitor many funds.
- Investors repeatedly chase funds with large asset size. Large actively managed funds have problems with liquidity (Chen, Hong, Huang, and Kubik 2004; Yan 2008) and organizational diseconomies such as hierarchy costs (Chen et al. 2004), which erode their performance. This effect is more pronounced among small cap funds.

- Investors often ignore the effects of expenses. Even small expenses or charges decrease fund returns. Malkiel (1995), Carhart (1997), and Dellva and Olson (1998) find that the fees investors pay to mutual funds for stock-picking ability do not result in higher risk-adjusted returns. Thus, investors should focus on funds with low 12b-1 fees and low or no-load fees.

Basics of Building the Most Satisfying Portfolio

This section discusses the process of building mutual fund portfolios. It begins by reviewing how portfolio risk and return are computed and illustrating the benefits of diversification. Next, the section explains the process of using Excel to form optimal risky portfolios. Once an optimal risky portfolio is formed, the investor's risk aversion is used as an input to create a utility-maximizing portfolio.

RISK AND RETURN OF MUTUAL FUND PORTFOLIOS

Finance textbooks often stress that investors should only care about two variables: risk and return. This section discusses principles of portfolio risk and return that are generally covered in financial management and investments textbooks such as Bodie et al. (2014), Brigham and Ehrhardt (2014), or Smart et al. (2014).

As Equation 17.4 shows, the return of a mutual fund portfolio is the market value weighted average of the returns of the mutual funds making up the portfolio:

$$R_p = W_a\,(R_a) + W_b\,(R_b), \tag{17.4}$$

where R_p is the return on the portfolio; W_a and W_b are the market value weights of the portfolio invested in funds "a" and "b"; and R_a and R_b are the expected returns of funds "a" and "b."

The risk of a portfolio is its variability of returns and can be computed as shown in Equation 17.5:

$$\sigma_p^2 = W_a^2\sigma_a^2 + W_b^2\sigma_b^2 + 2W_aW_b\sigma_a\sigma_b\rho_{a,b}, \tag{17.5}$$

where σ_p^2 is the variance of the portfolio; W_a^2 and $W_b^2$are the squared market value weights for funds "a" and "b"; σ_a^2 and σ_b^2 are the variance of the returns of funds "a" and "b"; σ_a and σ_b are the standard deviations of the returns of fund "a" and "b"; and ρ_{ab} is the correlation between funds "a" and "b." Standard deviation is an alternative measure of total risk and is computed by taking the square root of variance. Standard deviation is often preferred because it keeps measuring risk and return in the same units (percent). If variance is used, the risk measure is in squared units.

Risk, return, and diversification require further discussion. For example, assume that an investor can choose between two potential funds. Each fund has an expected return of 15 percent and the investor can invest in one or both funds. Now look at the return and risk for three potential scenarios (1) put all the money in fund "a"; (2) put all the money in fund "b"; or (3) split the money evenly between funds "a" and "b."

The returns for the three scenarios are:
Scenario (1) put all the money in fund "a" as illustrated in Equation 17.6:

$$R_{pa} = 1(0.15) + 0(0.15) = 0.15. \tag{17.6}$$

Scenario (2) put all the money in fund "b" as illustrated in Equation 17.7:

$$R_{pb} = 0(0.15) + 1(0.15) = 0.15. \tag{17.7}$$

Scenario (3) split the money evenly between funds "a" and "b" as shown in Equation 17.8:

$$R_{pa,b} = 0.5(0.15) + 0.5(0.15) = 0.15. \tag{17.8}$$

In this example, the average return is 15 percent regardless of how the money is invested. Therefore, diversification does nothing to influence expected return in this case. So, if diversification is beneficial, it must affect the risk of the portfolio.

Assume that the total risk, σ^2, is the same for each investment and is (0.25) and the standard deviation, σ, is 0.5.

Now, compute the risk from the three scenarios:

Scenario (1) put all the money in fund "a" resulting in total risk shown in Equation 17.9:

$$\sigma_p^2 = (1)^2(0.25) + (0)^2(0.25) + 2(1)(0)(0.5)(0.5)() = 0.25. \tag{17.9}$$

Note that the correlation between "a" and "b" is not needed because the last term drops out of the equation because of the zero weight for mutual fund "b."

Scenario (2) puts all the money in fund "b" resulting in total risk shown in Equation 17.10:

$$\sigma_p^2 = (0)^2(0.25) + (1)^2(0.25) + 2(0)(1)(0.5)(0.5)() = 0.25. \tag{17.10}$$

Again, the correlation between fund "a" and "b" is not needed because of the zero weight for fund "a."

Scenario (3) splits the investment evenly between funds "a" and "b" with total risk as shown in Equation 17.11:

$$\sigma_p^2 = (0.5)^2(0.25) + (0.5)^2(0.25) + 2(0.5)(0.5)(0.5)(0.5)() = ? \tag{17.11}$$

Unfortunately, an answer cannot be computed without knowing the correlation coefficient between funds "a" and "b." Although the correlation coefficient was not provided, the boundaries of correlation are + 1 (perfectly positively correlated) to −1 (perfectly negatively correlated). The first and third scenarios illustrate this point. The second scenario will be a correlation coefficient of zero. Therefore, if $\rho_{a,b} = +1$, the Equation 17.12 can be used to compute the total risk:

$$\sigma_p^2 = (0.5)^2(0.25) + (0.5)^2(0.25) + 2(0.5)(0.5)(0.5)(0.5)(1) = 0.25. \tag{17.12}$$

This is the same result that was achieved without diversification. Thus, no benefit exists to diversification between investment choices when the perfect positive correlation exists. If $\rho_{a,b} = 0$, then Equation 17.13 can be used to calculate the total risk:

$$\sigma_p^2 = (0.5)^2(0.25) + (0.5)^2(0.25) + 2(0.5)(0.5)(0.5)(0.5)(0) = 0.125. \tag{17.13}$$

With zero correlation, risk was cut in half from 0.25 to 0.125. If $\rho_{a,b} = -1$, then Equation 17.14 can be used to calculate total risk:

$$\sigma_p^2 = (0.5)^2(0.25) + (0.5)^2(0.25) + 2\,(0.5)(0.5)(0.5)(0.5)(-1) = 0. \tag{17.14}$$

With perfect negative correlation, all risk is eliminated. Thus, if an investor diversifies into an asset class that is not perfectly correlated with the returns of the current portfolio, the risk of the portfolio can be reduced.

When portfolio size increases, the portfolio return formula does not change. It remains the market value weighted average of the returns of the investments in the portfolio. However, the formula for portfolio variance changes when portfolio size increases. Besides adding a squared market value weight for the additional investment times the investments variance, another covariance term is needed for each possible combination of assets. For example, for a portfolio with four securities, Equation 17.15 shows the corresponding formula:

$$\begin{aligned}\sigma_p^2 = {} & W_a^2\sigma_a^2 + W_b^2\sigma_b^2 + W_c^2\sigma_c^2 + W_d^2\sigma_d^2 + 2W_aW_b\sigma_a\sigma_b\rho_{a,b} + 2W_aW_c\sigma_a\sigma_c\rho_{a,c} \\ & + 2W_aW_d\sigma_a\sigma_d\rho_{a,d} + 2W_bW_c\sigma_b\sigma_c\rho_{b,c} + 2W_bW_d\sigma_b\sigma_d\rho_{b,d} + 2W_cW_d\sigma_c\sigma_d\rho_{c,d}.\end{aligned} \tag{17.15}$$

Computing the expected risk of a portfolio is important in practice as will be discussed later. Finding a perfectly negatively correlated security to add to the portfolio is difficult, if not impossible. Various asset classes are less than perfectly correlated. As Solnik (1974) shows, both diversifying within a country and between countries is important because of the potential diversification effects.

Deciding what asset classes to include in the portfolio and in what proportion is the heart of the portfolio management decision. According to Brinson, Hood, and Beebower (1986) and Brinson, Singer, and Beebower (1991), more than 90 percent of a portfolio's return is due to asset allocation decisions. More recent studies, such as Ibbotson and Kaplan (2000) and Xiong, Ibbotson, Idzorek, and Chen (2010), point out that asset allocation may not be as important in explaining variation in returns across various funds as previously believed. Yet, Ibbotson (2010) concludes asset allocation is still a very important aspect.

RISK, RETURN, AND CORRELATIONS OF MAJOR ASSET CLASSES

When investors evaluate mutual fund performance, they need to realize that the return and risk is likely to be similar to that of the asset class in which the fund invests. Table 17.1 summarizes the historical annual return and risk for asset classes during

Table 17.1 **Summary Statistics of Realized Returns, 1926 to 2013**

Series	*Geometric Mean (%)*	*Arithmetic Mean (%)*	*Standard Deviation (%)*
Large cap stocks	10.1	12.1	20.2
Small cap stocks	12.3	16.9	32.3
Long-term corporate bonds	6.0	6.3	8.4
Long-term government bonds	5.5	5.9	9.8
Intermediate-term government bonds	5.3	5.4	5.7
U.S. Treasury bills	3.5	3.5	3.1
Inflation	3.0	3.0	4.1

Note: This table presents summary statistics of the average annual returns on each asset class and inflation rates between 1926 and 2013.

Source: Morningstar 2014.

the period 1926 to 2013. It reveals that stock investments earn higher average returns than bond investments. Specifically, small company stocks produce the highest average return 12.3 percent (16.9 percent) but also carry the highest risk (32.3 percent), as measured by standard deviation.

Table 17.2 illustrates the benefits of diversification. The returns of long-term corporate bonds are highly correlated with returns of long- to intermediate-term government bonds. This is not surprising because inflation strongly influences bond prices and yields. Table 17.2 also shows a negative correlation between the returns of large and small capitalization stocks and the returns of government bonds. Thus, investors can reduce portfolio risk by having portfolios that contain both stocks and bonds.

FORMING OPTIMAL RISKY PORTFOLIOS

Markowitz (1952) sets a tone in modern portfolio theory by asserting that investors should make investment decisions using the mean, variance, and covariance (or correlation) of securities, and this concept is widely accepted in investment textbooks such as Smart et al. (2014). The optimization of risky portfolios focuses on two aspects: maximizing returns while holding risk constant or minimizing risks while maintaining the same level of returns. The goal of portfolio optimization is to maximize portfolio return per unit of risk. With a risk-free asset, this can be simplified to maximizing the *Sharpe ratio* of a portfolio, which is its excess returns per unit of total portfolio risk, illustrated in Equation 17.16.

Maximizing the Sharpe ratio is tricky with a mutual fund investment because OEFs cannot engage in short sales. The following maximization problem shown in Equation 17.16 defines the optimization of a mutual fund portfolio:

$$\max \vartheta = \frac{E(r_w) - c}{\sigma_w}, \tag{17.16}$$

Table 17.2 **Correlations of Historical Annual Returns, 1926 to 2013**

Series	*Large Cap Stocks*	*Small Cap Stocks*	*Long-Term Corporate Bonds*	*Long-Term Government Bonds*	*Intermediate-Term Government Bonds*	*U.S. Treasury Bills*	*Inflation*
Large cap stocks	1.00						
Small cap stocks	0.80	1.00					
Long-term corporate bonds	0.14	0.05	1.00				
Long-term government bonds	–0.01	–0.10	0.89	1.00			
Intermediate-term government bonds	–0.03	–0.12	0.87	0.89	1.00		
U.S. Treasury bills	–0.02	–0.10	0.17	0.20	0.46	1.00	
Inflation	0.02	0.05	–0.15	–0.13	0.01	0.41	1.00

Note: This table presents the annual correlations of returns for asset return series and inflation rates between 1926 and 2013.

Source: Morningstar 2014.

given the relationships in Equations 17.17 through Equation 17.22:

$$\sum_{i=1}^{N} w_i = 1 w_i \geq 0, i = 1,2,\ldots,N, \tag{17.17}$$

where

$$E(r_w) = w^T \times R = \sum_{i=1}^{N} w_i E(r_i), \tag{17.18}$$

$$\sigma_w = \sqrt{w^T S W} = \sqrt{\sum_{i=1}^{N}\sum_{j=1}^{N} w_i w_j \sigma_{ij}}\,, \tag{17.19}$$

$$W = \begin{bmatrix} w_1 \\ w_2 \\ \vdots \\ w_N \end{bmatrix}, \tag{17.20}$$

$$R = \begin{bmatrix} E(r_1) \\ E(r_2) \\ \vdots \\ E(r_N) \end{bmatrix}, \tag{17.21}$$

and

$$S = \begin{bmatrix} \sigma_{11} & \cdots & \sigma_1 N \\ \cdots & \ddots & \vdots \\ \sigma_{N1} & \cdots & \sigma_{NN} \end{bmatrix}, \tag{17.22}$$

where w_i is the market value weight invested in fund i; $E(r_i)$ is the expected rate of return of fund i; σ_{ij} is the covariance between fund i and fund j; and c is a constant. Changing c permits finding infinite combinations of w_i and therefore creating the efficient frontier with the selected mutual fund investments. The *efficient frontier* is a plot of the risk and return of portfolio combinations that have the highest return for any given level of risk. Thus, these portfolios dominate all other choices in terms of return for a given level of risk. If the risk-free rate is used for c, a theoretical optimal risky portfolio may be found by solving the problem above. To better illustrate the application of portfolio optimization in practice, an example is provided next using Microsoft Excel.

First, assume that an investor has selected four funds based on his investment objectives. The funds are the Vanguard Market Neutral Fund (VMNFX), Vanguard Long-Term Bond Index Fund (VBLTX), Vanguard Selected Value Fund (VASVX), and Vanguard Health Fund (VGHAX). To construct an optimal portfolio, the investor gets historical returns over some period such as January 2003 to December 2013 in this example. Figure 17.1 shows the summary statistics.

The investor then solves the constrained optimal problem 17.16. This task can be accomplished in Excel using the Solver tool. In Figure 17.2, the process begins with an arbitrary portfolio. For example, a portfolio equally split among the four target funds. The portfolio mean and standard deviation (σ) may be computed using Equations 17.18 and 17.19, respectively. The goal of the optimization is to maximize the Sharpe ratio of the portfolio as shown in Equation 17.16. Therefore, the ratio is computed so that the optimal solution can be derived in the next step. The risk-free rate in this case is assumed to be 0.02 percent.

As stated in Equation 17.16, the optimization problem the investor faces is to maximize the Sharpe ratio ϑ (theta) in this example. The Solver function in Excel can find the maximum, minimum, or a specified number in a specific cell (in this case, ϑ in cell J21) by changing parameters. The parameters are cells J13 to J16, which are the investment weights in each of the selected funds. One or more constraints may be added to the Solver to further limit solutions. By adding two constraints as Figure 17.3 shows, the weights obtained are all positive (no short sales) and the sum of the weights is 100 percent. Note that this optimization does not consider higher moments of the return distribution (e.g., skewness and kurtosis), time-varying parameters, or investors' behavioral biases.

	A	B	C	D	E	F	G	H	I	J	K
1	**SUMMARY STATISTICS-SELECTED FUNDS**										
2											
3	**Monthly Statistics**	VMNFX	VBLTX	VASVX	VGHAX			**Annualized Variance-Covariance Matrix**			
4	Average	0.13%	0.54%	1.10%	1.03%			VMNFX	VBLTX	VASVX	VGHAX
5	Standard Deviation	1.51%	2.85%	4.50%	3.49%		VMNFX	0.0030	−0.0003	0.0006	0.0005
6	Variance	0.0002	0.0008	0.0020	0.0012		VBLTX	−0.0003	0.0107	0.0003	0.0015
7							VASVX	0.0006	0.0003	0.0268	0.0164
8	**Annualized**						VGHAX	0.0005	0.0015	0.0164	0.0161
9	Average	1.60%	6.49%	13.20%	12.41%						
10	Standard Deviation	5.24%	9.86%	15.59%	12.11%						
11	Variance	0.0027	0.0097	0.0243	0.0147						
12											
13											
14											

Figure 17.1 SUMMARY STATISTICS FOR SELECTED FUNDS. This figure shows summary statistics of the sample funds including Vanguard Market Neutral Fund (VMNFX), Vanguard Long-Term Bond Index Fund (VBLTX), Vanguard Selected Value Fund (VASVX), and Vanguard Health Fund (VGHAX).

	I	J	K	L	M	N	O	P	Q
1		MUTUAL FUND PORTFOLIO OPTIMIZATION							
2									
3		Annualized Variance-Covariance Matrix						Means	
4		17932	31242	31270	31185				
5	VMNFX	0.0030	–0.0003	0.0006	0.0005		VMNFX	1.60%	
6	VBLTX	–0.0003	0.0107	0.0003	0.0015		VBLTX	6.49%	
7	VASVX	0.0006	0.0003	0.0268	0.0164		VASVX	13.20%	
8	VGHAX	0.0005	0.0015	0.0164	0.0161		VGHAX	12.41%	
9									
10	**Constant**	0.02%							
11									
12	**Weight**								
13	VMNFX	25.00%							
14	VBLTX	25.00%							
15	VASVX	25.00%							
16	VGHAX	25.00%							
17	**Total**	100%							
18									
19	**Portfolio Mean**	8.43% <- {=MMULT(TRANSPOSE(J13:J16),P5:P8)}							
20	**Portfolio Standard Deviation**	7.69% <- {=SQRT(MMULT(TRANSPOSE(J13:J16),MMULT(J5:M8,J13:J16)))}							
21	**ϑ (Theta, Sharpe ratio)**	1.0938 <- =(J19–J10)/J20							
22									

Figure 17.2 An Arbitrary Portfolio. The figure shows the mean return and standard deviation of an arbitrary portfolio that invests equally in each of four sample funds. The formulas for calculating the portfolio mean return, standard deviation, and Sharpe ratio are also shown.

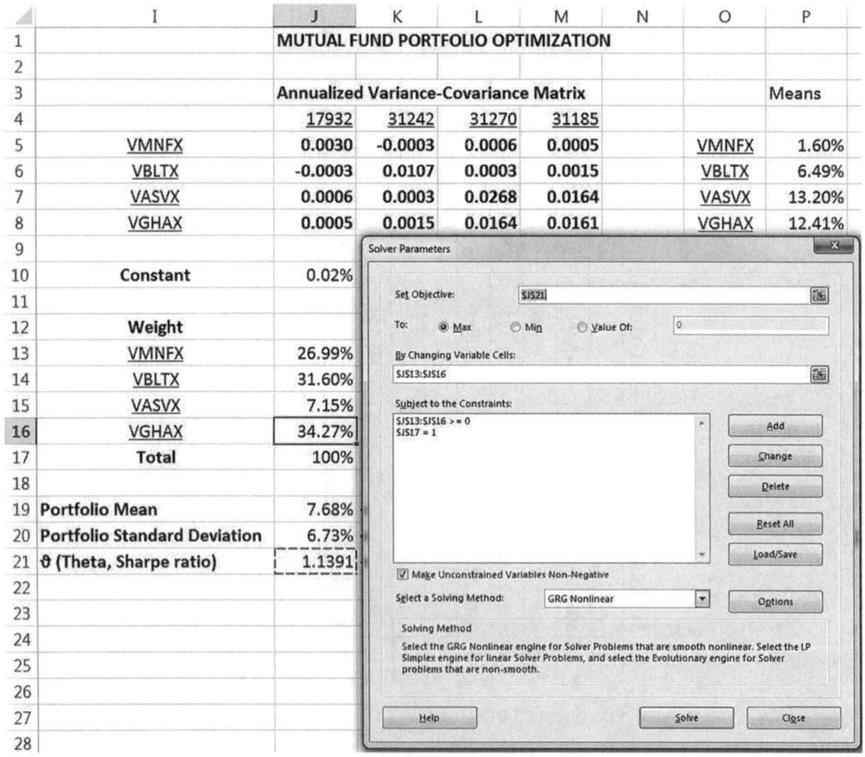

Figure 17.3 Using Solver to Create an Optimal Portfolio without Short Sales. This figure illustrates the use of the Solver function in Excel to find the optimal weights by maximizing the Sharpe ratio, where the weights are subject to non-negative constraint.

ASSESSING RISK AVERSION AND UTILITY

Investors need to choose among competing combinations and should do so considering their own risk tolerance (risk attitudes). While an investor's risk attitudes could be risk-averse, risk-neutral, or risk-loving, a common assumption is that most investors are *risk-averse.* A *risk-averse investor* is simply one who dislikes uncertainties or assuming risk (i.e., prefers less risk to more risk for a given level of return). The optimal portfolios have the highest expected returns given the degree of risk or lowest degree of risk given the level of return. Choosing among competing optimal portfolios is a risk and return trade-off. Thus, the choice depends on the investors' risk aversion.

Risk and risk aversion are used to decide how to allocate wealth among competing investment opportunities. One example is deciding how to allocate wealth between risky and risk-free assets. Therefore, after identifying the optimal risky portfolio, it can be combined with a money market mutual fund (a proxy for a risk-free asset) to form a portfolio that maximizes an investor's utility. Investors hold different portfolios due to their differing attitudes toward risk.

Examining how to choose among competing alternatives is important while maximizing the investor's satisfaction. Thus, the goal is to maximize the investor's utility. Equation 17.23 is a commonly used utility function based on an investor's investment outcome:

$$U = E(r) - \tfrac{1}{2}A\sigma^2, \qquad (17.23)$$

where U is the investor's utility; $E(r)$ is the expected return of the portfolio; $\tfrac{1}{2}$ is a constant scaling factor; A is the investor's risk tolerance or risk aversion score; and σ^2 is the portfolio variance. This formula reveals that utility changes are intuitive. An investor prefers to have a higher expected return, but feels penalized to bear a higher degree of risk, as measured by the portfolio variance. As the expected return of a portfolio increases, so does the investor's utility, ceteris paribus. An investor's utility decreases as risk increases. However, the decrease depends on the investor's risk aversion score A. Some investors place a large penalty on a portfolio for an increase in risk, as represented by a higher A, while other investors place much less of a penalty for a risk increase. More than one portfolio could be equally satisfying for an investor.

Several methods are available to estimate an investor's risk aversion. One method is to use a questionnaire such as the sample questionnaire provided by Bodie et al. (2014). Based on an investor's responses, the questionnaire provides a score to classify the investor into one of three categories: (1) conservative, (2) moderate, and (3) aggressive. More complex questionnaires could be used to get an accurate and specific risk aversion coefficient for an individual investor.

CREATING UTILITY-MAXIMIZING PORTFOLIOS

The optimal risky portfolio derived in the previous section does not account for the investor's risk preference. Although the portfolios are optimized based on Markowitz's mean-variance analysis, the ultimate choice still depends on the investor's risk attitude. The mutual fund separation theorem (Cass and Stiglitz 1970; Ross 1978; Chamberlain

1983) states that investors who are making optimal investment choices between a set of risky assets and a risk-free security should all hold the same portfolio of risky assets and their risk attitude does not influence the relative proportion of funds invested across different risky assets. Thus, the risk-preference-adjusted optimization does not need to re-create the optimal weights among risky assets. It simply needs to find the appropriate weights for the risk-free asset and the optimal risky portfolio. An optimal risky portfolio is created based on objective information including the expected risk and return, and a utility-maximizing portfolio mixes the optimal risky portfolio with the risk-free asset and is based on the investor's subjective risk preference.

The task is to quantify an investor's risk preference, which is typically done with a utility function. The previous section presented a common utility function. Therefore, Equation 17.24 shows an objective function:

$$\max U = E\left(r_p\right) - \tfrac{1}{2}A\sigma^2 p, \tag{17.24}$$

where r_p is the portfolio's expected rate of return and σ_p^2 is the portfolio's expected variance. An investor allocates capital between the optimal risky portfolio and risk-free asset. Assume that the weight invested in the optimal risky portfolio is x. Thus, Equations 17.25 and 17.26 describe the expected rate of return $E(r_p)$ and expected variance $\sigma^2{}_p$ for the portfolio, respectively:

$$E\left(r_p\right) = xE(r_w) + (1 - x)\, r_f = r_f + x\left(E(r_w) - r_f\right), \tag{17.25}$$

$$\sigma_p^2 = x^2\sigma_w^2 \tag{17.26}$$

The target function of the maximization problem becomes Equation 17.27:

$$\max U = r_f + x\left(E(r_w) - r_f\right) - \tfrac{1}{2}Ax^2\sigma_w^2. \tag{17.27}$$

To find the optimal weight (x) that is needed to maximize an investor's utility, the first order derivative of the expression regarding x should be set at zero as shown in Equation 17.28. By doing so, an optimal weight (x) may be computed in Equation 17.29:

$$\frac{dU}{dx} = \left(E(r_w) - r_f\right) - Ax\sigma_w^2 = 0, \tag{17.28}$$

$$x^* = \left(E(r_w) - r_f\right)/(A?_w^2). \tag{17.29}$$

Assume that an investor, with a coefficient of risk aversion of 4 wants to determine an optimal allocation between the optimal risky portfolio and the risk-free asset. The following inputs are obtained: $E\left(r_w\right) = 12\%$, $I\sigma_w^2 = 20\%$, and $r_f = 3\%$. Substitute the numbers into Equation 17.29: $x^- = \frac{12\% - 3\%}{4 \times 20\%2} = 56.25\%$. Thus, the optimal weight in the risky portfolio is 56.25 percent and that of risk-free asset is 43.75 percent.

MONITORING, EVALUATING, AND REBALANCING

After the portfolio is established, it needs to be monitored, evaluated, and rebalanced when situational changes occur. *Rebalancing* is the act of selling some assets and using the proceeds to purchase other assets to maintain target market value weights. Routinely monitoring mutual funds in a portfolio is important for two reasons. First, monitoring helps investors keep their mutual fund portfolio in line with their investment objectives. As previously discussed, investors create their portfolio with specific investment objectives. When the list of funds meeting the investment criteria changes, an investor must consider including new funds that become available and/or excluding existing funds that no longer meet the criteria. The need for such changes may arise due to management turnover in a mutual fund, failure to meet a fund's investment objectives, or excessive tracking error. Without disciplined monitoring, investors fail to identify in a timely manner the need for change or take proper actions. Second, monitoring and subsequent rebalancing actions serve as a form of governance of mutual funds. As Fama and Jensen (1983) note, the feature that mutual fund investors may redeem their shares at the NAV at the end of any business day is close to a "partial takeover or liquidation," and therefore reduces the need of other forms of governance.

Evans and Fahlenbrach (2012) document reducing agency problems with greater monitoring by examining *mutual fund twins,* which are retail mutual funds that offer a separate mutual fund or separate account to institutional investors, but share the same managers following the same strategies. The authors find that retail funds with an institutional twin outperform other retail funds by 1.5 percent annually, which suggests that investors in retail funds with an institutional twin benefit from more rigorous monitoring by institutional investors. Their findings provide empirical support for Fama and Jensen (1983).

However, previous research also documents that investors, especially retail investors, use only simple performance measures such as raw return to evaluate funds (Sirri and Tufano 1998; Del Guercio and Tkac 2002; Evans and Fahlenbrach 2012). As both Sirri and Tufano and Del Guercio and Tkac note, investors respond disproportionally to winners and are reluctant to withdraw funds from losers. These findings suggest that investors should use better measures in evaluating funds such as expenses and risk-adjusted performance and should respond to both good and poor performance.

A frequently asked question about rebalancing is "when." A typical motivation for rebalancing is that superior or inferior performance in a specific asset class results in the portfolio deviating from its original optimal asset allocation. This scenario requires investors to sell funds from asset classes with superior performance and buy funds from asset classes with poor performance. Doing so restores the portfolio to its original optimal weights. The frequency of rebalancing depends both on the level of the deviation and investor preference.

O'Brien (2006) suggests four simple rebalancing strategies: (1) periodic rebalancing, (2) threshold rebalancing, (3) range rebalancing, and (4) active rebalancing. *Periodic rebalancing* is evaluating and rebalancing the portfolio on a regular schedule such as once a year. With *threshold rebalancing,* portfolios are rebalanced to target allocations once an asset class has appreciated or depreciated by a predetermined amount. *Range rebalancing* is similar to threshold rebalancing but allows certain range in target allocation to offer more flexibility. With both threshold and range rebalancing strategies, a predetermined amount of value change would trigger rebalancing. *Active rebalancing* is a rebalancing strategy that focuses on optimal weights across broad asset classes such as equity versus fixed-income securities while allowing investors to actively shift among sub-asset classes. These strategies can be combined.

Arnott and Lovell (1993), Buetow, Sellers, Trotter, Hunt, and Shipple (2002), and Plaxco and Arnott (2002) report a benefit of more frequent periodic rebalancing. Plaxco and Arnott contend that threshold rebalancing is not as effective as periodic rebalancing because threshold rebalancing relies only on ad hoc information and thus fails to respond proactively to expectations to the future returns. As Buetow et al. show, a mixed strategy combining both periodic and threshold rebalancing increases value. Whichever strategy or combination of strategies is used, an investor needs a disciplined rebalancing policy to keep the mutual fund portfolio aligned with investment goals. However, the literature does not provide an unambiguous solution to the best rebalancing strategy.

Once the frequency of rebalancing is established, the investor might benefit by attempting to time trades. Some benefit may accrue by considering some potentially beneficial return patterns and using that information to time the rebalancing. The two factors that the investor might want to consider are day-of-the-week effects and cross-autocorrelations. *Day-of-the-week effects* refer to the documented daily return patterns that exist. For example, Mondays frequently have negative returns, whereas Friday returns are typically positive. *Cross-autocorrelations* are documented patterns in security returns between markets. Presumably, this occurs because the release of new information affects prices. However, information release can only influence markets that are open for trading. Therefore, such information will not affect prices in markets that are closed until they resume trading.

Miller, Prather, and Mazumder (2003) review the Monday effect and investigate a day-of-the-week effect among 10 investment objective classifications of mutual funds. The *Monday effect* is the observation that Monday returns are often negative. These day-of-the-week effects are market anomalies that violate the semi-strong form of the efficient market hypothesis (EMH). As Miller et al. (2003) report, a negative average return occurs on Monday for 6 of the 10 investment objective classifications of mutual funds. Mazumder, Chu, Miller, and Prather (2008) perform a similar analysis for international ETFs and report that 7 of the 18 countries examined have a negative average return on Monday. Thus, Monday may be a better day to buy than to sell.

Another empirical regularity is that returns from many countries exhibit cross-autocorrelation. Researchers have investigated the exploitability of this phenomenon for TIAA/CREF variable annuities (Miller and Prather 2000), international ETFs (Chu, Mazumder, Miller, and Prather 2007), and mutual funds (Miller, Prather, and Mazumder 2008). The combined findings suggest that as information is released in one market, the prices of its securities will change to reflect the new information. However, foreign markets closed at the time of the information release will not exhibit a price change until the next trading day. Thus, timing already planned trades to take advantage of these predictable return patterns might increase return and reduce risk.

Finally, regularly evaluating an investor's attitude toward risks is essential because an investor's risk preference may be time-varying. This relationship is especially true when special events occur such as retirement, marriage, or the birth of a child because important life events might alter an investor's risk preference. Consequently, an investor may need to rebalance because of these life changes.

Summary and Conclusions

This chapter reviews the factors that make building, monitoring, and rebalancing mutual fund portfolios such a complex task. It then addresses many applied topics that investors may want to consider by reviewing the literature about the choice between actively managed or passively managed funds, and fees, expenses, tax efficiency, turnover, and management structure.

The chapter also covers how to compute the risk and return of managed portfolios and illustrates the benefits of diversification. After presenting the theory, it is operationalized by using the Solver function in Excel. Using the Solver function in Excel provides investors with a step-by-step process to form their optimal risky portfolio. After discussing how to form an optimal risky portfolio, the chapter addresses risk aversion and utility as a prelude to forming utility-maximizing portfolios. The chapter concludes by examining the topics of monitoring portfolio performance and when and why to rebalance a portfolio.

Below are the 10 major "take-aways" from this chapter.

1. Investors should understand the nuances of pooled investments because they affect the management of investments within the portfolio.
2. Investors should determine the asset classes to hold in their portfolios.
3. Investors should use index funds rather than actively managed funds because evidence fails to show that actively managed funds can outperform the market.
4. Investors should compare funds with differing fee structures or OEFs and ETFs by following the process discussed in this chapter.
5. Investors should not give too much attention to a fund's management structure because it does not seem to be an important variable in explaining performance.
6. Investors should consider low-cost funds because loads and fees affect performance.
7. Investors should consider turnover for portfolios that are not tax-sheltered.
8. Investors can use Excel to form an optimal risky portfolio.
9. After forming an optimal risky portfolio, investors should create a utility-maximizing portfolio if they know their risk aversion.
10. Investors should monitor and rebalance their portfolio periodically to maintain optimal market value weights.

Discussion Questions

1. Discuss the fees and expenses of mutual funds and their impact on returns.
2. Identify mistakes that investors should avoid when selecting mutual funds.
3. Discuss the evidence on whether actively managed funds outperform the market.
4. Explain how to compute turnover and its importance when screening funds.

References

Agarwal, Vinod B., and Larry J. Prather. 1997. "Economic Rents and Mutual Fund Performance: An Empirical Investigation." *Journal of Economics and Finance* 21:2, 67–73.

Arnott, Robert D., and Robert D. Lovell. 1993. "Rebalancing: Why? When? How Often?" *Journal of Investing* 2:1, 5–10.

Becker, Connie, Wayne Ferson, David H. Myers, and Michael J. Schill. 1999. "Conditional Market Timing with Benchmark Investors." *Journal of Financial Economics* 52:1, 119–148.

Bodie, Zvi, Alex Kane, and Alan J. Marcus. 2014. *Investments,* 10th Edition. New York: McGraw-Hill Education.

Brigham, Eugene F., and Michael C. Ehrhardt. 2014. *Financial Management: Theory and Practice,* 14th Edition. Mason, OH: South-Western, Cengage Learning.

Brinson, Gary P., L. Randolph Hood, and Gilbert L. Beebower. 1986. "Determinants of Portfolio Performance." *Financial Analysts Journal* 42:4, 39–44.

Brinson, Gary P., Brian D. Singer, and Gilbert L. Beebower. 1991. "Determinants of Portfolio Performance II: An Update." *Financial Analysts Journal* 47:3, 40–48.

Buetow, Gerald W. Jr., Ronald Sellers, Donald Trotter, Elaine Hunt, and Willie A. Whipple, Jr. 2002. "The Benefits of Rebalancing." *Journal of Portfolio Management* 28:2, 23–32.

Carhart, Mark M. 1997. "On Persistence in Mutual Fund Performance." *Journal of Finance* 52:1, 57–82.

Cass, David, and Joseph E. Stiglitz. 1970. "The Structure of Investor Preferences and Asset Returns, and Separability in Portfolio Allocation: A Contribution to the Pure Theory of Mutual Funds." *Journal of Economic Theory* 2:2, 122–160.

Chamberlain, Gary. 1983. "A Characterization of the Distributions That Imply Mean-Variance Utility Functions." *Journal of Economic Theory* 29:1, 185–201.

Chang, Eric C., and Wilbur G. Lewellen. 1984. "Market Timing and Mutual Fund Investment Performance." *Journal of Business* 57:1, 57–72.

Chen, Carl R., and Ying Huang. 2011. "Mutual Fund Governance and Performance: A Quantile Regression Analysis of Morningstar's Stewardship Grade." *Corporate Governance: An International Review* 19:4, 311–333.

Chen, Hsiu-Lang, Narasimhan Jegadeesh, and Russ Wermers. 2000. "The Value of Active Mutual Fund Management: An Examination of the Stockholdings and Trades of Fund Managers." *Journal of Financial and Quantitative Analysis* 35:3, 343–368.

Chen, Joseph, Harrison Hong, Ming Huang, and Jeffrey D. Kubik. 2004. "Does Fund Size Erode Mutual Fund Performance? The Role of Liquidity and Organization." *American Economic Review* 94:5, 1276–1302.

Chu, Ting-Heng, M. Imtiaz Mazumder, Edward M. Miller, and Larry J. Prather. 2007. "Exploitable Cross Autocorrelations among iShares." *Financial Services Review* 16:4, 293–308.

Coombes, Andrea. 2013. "Bad Ways to Pick a Mutual Fund." *Wall Street Journal* Web, October 27. Available at http://www.wsj.com/articles/SB10001424052702304069604579155403080501672.

Cumby, Robert E., and Jack D. Glen. 1990. "Evaluating the Performance of International Mutual Funds." *Journal of Finance* 45:2, 497–521.

Daniel, Kent, Mark Grinblatt, Sheridan Titman, and Russ Wermers. 1997. "Measuring Mutual Fund Performance with Characteristic-Based Benchmarks." *Journal of Finance* 52:3, 1035–1058.

Del Guercio, Diane, and Paula A. Tkac. 2002. "The Determinants of the Flow of Funds of Managed Portfolios: Mutual Funds vs. Pension Funds." *Journal of Financial and Quantitative Analysis* 37:4, 523–557.

Dellva, Wilfred L., and Gerard T. Olson. 1998. "The Relationship between Mutual Fund Fees and Expenses and Their Effects on Performance." *Financial Review* 33:1, 85–104.

Evans, Richard B., and Rüdiger Fahlenbrach. 2012. "Institutional Investors and Mutual Fund Governance: Evidence from Retail-Institutional Fund Twins." *Review of Financial Studies* 25:12, 3530–3571.

Fama, Eugene F., and Kenneth R. French. 2010. "Luck Versus Skill in the Cross-Section of Mutual Fund Returns." *Journal of Finance* 65:5, 1915–1947.

Fama, Eugene F., and Michael C. Jensen. 1983. "Separation of Ownership and Control." *Journal of Law and Economics* 26:2, 301–325.

Grinblatt, Mark, and Sheridan Titman. 1989. "Portfolio Performance Evaluation: Old Issues and New Insights." *Review of Financial Studies* 2:3, 396–421.

Grinblatt, Mark, and Sheridan Titman. 1994. "A Study of Monthly Mutual Fund Returns and Performance Evaluation Techniques." *Journal of Financial and Quantitative Analysis* 29:3, 419–444.

Gruber, Martin J. 1996. "Another Puzzle: The Growth in Actively Managed Mutual Funds." *Journal of Finance* 51:3, 783–810.

Henriksson, Roy D. 1984. "Market Timing and Mutual Fund Performance: An Empirical Investigation." *Journal of Business* 57:1, 73–96.

Ibbotson, Roger G. 2010. "The Importance of Asset Allocation." *Financial Analysts Journal* 66:2, 18–20.

Ibbotson, Roger G., and Paul D. Kaplan. 2000. "Does Asset Allocation Policy Explain 40, 90, or 100 Percent of Performance?" *Financial Analysts Journal* 56:1, 26–33.

Investment Company Institute. 2014. *Investment Company Factbook: A Review of Trends and Activities in the U.S. Investment Company Industry*, 54th Edition. Washington, DC: Investment Company Institute.

Jensen, Michael C. 1968. "The Performance of Mutual Funds in the Period 1945–1964." *Journal of Finance* 23:2, 389–416.

Kon, Stanley J. 1983. "The Market-Timing Performance of Mutual Fund Managers." *Journal of Business* 56:3, 323–347.

Lehmann, Bruce N., and David M. Modest. 1987. "Mutual Fund Performance Evaluation: A Comparison of Benchmarks and Benchmark Comparisons." *Journal of Finance* 42:2, 233–265.

Lucas, Robert E., Jr. 1978. "On the Size Distribution of Business Firms." *Bell Journal of Economics* 9:2, 508–523.

Malkiel, Burton G. 1995. "Returns from Investing in Equity Mutual Funds 1971–1991." *Journal of Finance* 50:2, 549–572.

Markowitz, Harry. 1952. "Portfolio Selection." *Journal of Finance* 7:1, 77–91.

Mazumder, M. Imtiaz, Ting-Heng Chu, Edward M. Miller, and Larry J. Prather. 2008. "International Day-of-the-Week Effects: An Empirical Examination of iShares." *International Review of Financial Analysis* 17:4, 699–715.

Miller, Edward M., and Larry J. Prather. 2000. "Exploitable Patterns in Retirement Annuity Returns: Evidence from TIAA/CREF." *Financial Services Review* 9:3, 219–230.

Miller, Edward M., Larry J. Prather, and M. Imtiaz Mazumder. 2003. "Day-of-the-Week Effects among Mutual Funds." *Quarterly Journal of Business and Economics* 42:3, 113–128.

Miller, Edward M., Larry J. Prather, and M. Imtiaz Mazumder. 2008. "Cross-Autocorrelations among Asset Classes: Evidence from the Mutual Fund Industry." *Managerial Finance* 34:11, 756–771.

Morningstar. 2014. *Ibbotson SBBI 2014 Classic Yearbook*. Chicago: Morningstar, Inc.

Najand, Mohammad, and Larry J. Prather. 1999. "The Risk Level Discriminatory Power of Mutual Fund Investment Objectives: Additional Evidence." *Journal of Financial Markets* 2:3, 307–328.

O'Brien, John. 2006. "Rebalancing: A Tool for Managing Portfolio Risk." *Journal of Financial Service Professionals* 60:3, 62–68.

Plaxco, Lisa M., and Robert D. Arnott. 2002. "Rebalancing a Global Policy Benchmark." *Journal of Portfolio Management* 28:2, 9–22.

Pozen, Robert, and Theresa Hamacher. 2011. *The Fund Industry: How Your Money Is Managed*. Hoboken, NJ: John Wiley & Sons, Inc.

Prather, Larry J., and Karen L. Middleton. 2006. "Timing and Selectivity of Mutual Fund Managers: An Empirical Test of the Behavioral Decision-Making Theory." *Journal of Empirical Finance* 13:3, 249–273.

Prather, Larry J., Ting-Heng Chu, M. Imtiaz Mazumder, and John C. Topuz. 2009. "Index Funds or ETFs: The Case of the S&P 500 for Individual Investors." *Financial Services Review* 18:3, 213–230.

Ross, Stephen A. 1978. "Mutual Fund Separation in Financial Theory—The Separating Distributions." *Journal of Economic Theory* 17:2, 254–286.

Sirri, Erik R., and Peter Tufano. 1998. "Costly Search and Mutual Fund Flows." *Journal of Finance* 53:5, 1589–1622.

Smart, Scott B., Lawrence J. Gitman, and Michael D. Joehnk. 2014. *Fundamentals of Investing*, 12th Edition. Upper Saddle River, NJ: Pearson Education.

Solnik, Bruno H. 1974. "Why Not Diversify Internationally Rather Than Domestically?" *Financial Analysts Journal* 51:1, 48–54.

Treynor, Jack L., and Kay K. Mazuy. 1966. "Can Mutual Funds Outguess the Market?" *Harvard Business Review* 44:4, 131–136.

Veit, E. Theodore, and John M. Cheney. 1982. "Are Mutual Funds Market Timers?" *Journal of Portfolio Management* 8:2, 35–42.

Wellman, Jay W., and Jian Zhou. 2008. "Corporate Governance and Mutual Fund Performance: A First Look at the Morningstar Stewardship Grades." Working Paper, SUNY at Binghamton.

Xiong, James X., Roger G. Ibbotson, Thomas M. Idzorek, and Peng Chen. 2010. "The Equal Importance of Asset Allocation and Active Management." *Financial Analysts Journal* 66:2, 22–30.

Yan, Xuemin. 2008. "Liquidity, Investment Style, and the Relation between Fund Size and Fund Performance." *Journal of Financial and Quantitative Analysis* 43:3, 741–768.

18

Analyzing Mutual Funds

BRUCE A. COSTA
Professor of Finance, Chair of Accounting and Finance Department, University of Montana

KEITH JAKOB
Donald and Carol Jean Byrnes Professor of Finance, University of Montana

Introduction

As an investment vehicle, mutual funds or open-end funds (OEFs) offer an inexpensive and relatively easy process to build a well-diversified portfolio. Many investors struggle with deciding which mutual funds to choose for their portfolio. Sorting through and selecting funds from the thousands available can be difficult. To help investors with this process, various firms, organizations, and websites offer advice to simplify this task. An important aspect of the mutual fund selection process involves understanding mutual fund performance. At first glance, measuring or getting a fund's raw historical performance appears easy. Adjusting those returns for investment fees and other costs is also straightforward. Yet, both practitioners and academics often struggle with moving beyond simple return metrics to objectively measure the quality and risk-adjusted performance of mutual funds.

This chapter describes popular tools and methods available to investors to help analyze and select mutual funds. The chapter includes various ratio analyses and regression models as well as quantitative and qualitative risk metrics available from Morningstar, a well-known mutual fund evaluation firm.

The remainder of the chapter is organized as follows. The first section explores the main concepts of performance measurement. It discusses numerical approaches to assess mutual fund risk and return. The section then explains several tools including the coefficient of variation (CV), Sharpe ratio, and Treynor ratio, which measure relative fund performance as dimensionless ratios. Using a unique transformation by scaling the portfolio risk to a fixed level for all investments, the M^2 measure is no longer dimensionless and shows the percentage of risk-adjusted performance above or below the market portfolio. Jensen's single factor model alpha and the Carhart multifactor model are regression-based metrics used to quantify risk-adjusted performance in percentage terms. Next, the section presents extensions to the Carhart model, which is the most popular model of risk-adjusted mutual fund performance. The second section discusses the quantitative and qualitative risk metrics available from Morningstar. The final section presents a detailed example with three years of recent data for two mutual funds including the corresponding market data. Many of the analyses discussed are performed using Microsoft Excel on the first of the two mutual funds. The remaining fund data are left for the discussion questions at the end of chapter.

Quantitative Performance Metrics

Three key aspects relate to the practice of mutual fund management and analysis: (1) asset allocation, (2) security selection, and (3) fund performance. While measuring the raw performance of a mutual fund is straightforward, both practitioners and academics struggle with how to accurately measure risk-adjusted mutual fund performance. A nominal performance benchmark is the typical starting point to evaluate the risk-adjusted mutual fund performance of fund managers. For example, U.S. large capitalization domestic equity mutual funds typically use the Standard & Poor's 500 index (S&P 500) as their performance benchmark. Funds with overall investment characteristics that do not closely match the characteristics of the S&P 500 index should use different indexes that better fit their investment strategy as performance benchmarks. Although mutual fund prospectuses report both mutual fund returns and those for a specified benchmark index, comparing the two returns does not control for the differences in the inherent risks. To measure performance while controlling for portfolio risk, a large body of academic literature focuses on developing measures to better understand the risk-return trade-off by using ratio analysis and various regression models designed to measure risk-adjusted returns.

RATIOS AND RELATED MEASURES

An early metric for evaluating the relative dispersion in a distribution is the coefficient of variation. Developed by Karl Pearson in the 1800s (Pearson 1896), the CV can be used in a financial framework to assess the risk-return trade-off of a mutual fund investment. Equation 18.1 shows the CV formula:

$$CV_p = \frac{\sigma_p}{r_p}, \qquad (18.1)$$

where CV_p is the coefficient of variation for portfolio p; r_p is the portfolio return; and σ_p is the portfolio's standard deviation.

The CV provides a numerical but dimensionless value of the risk or volatility assumed by the investor per unit of return received. The CV is a total risk to total return ratio. In this model, the standard deviation of returns in the numerator captures the total risk of the mutual fund portfolio, including both systematic (market) risk and idiosyncratic (firm-specific) risk. The mutual fund portfolio holding period return in the denominator is the total return of the portfolio for the period being analyzed. Within this framework, a smaller CV can be interpreted as better relative fund performance during the sample period. For example, assume the same one-year holding period for two mutual funds. If fund A has a return of 10 percent and a standard deviation of the fund returns of 20 percent, its CV ratio would be 2.0. If fund B has a return of 20 percent and a standard deviation of the fund returns of 20 percent, its CV ratio would be 1.0. The lower ratio for fund B shows better relative performance. This example shows how to calculate and interpret the relative returns for comparison. Changing either the fund return or its standard deviation of returns (dispersion) influences the ratio.

In the 1960s, both academics and practitioners recognized several drawbacks of the CV as a risk-return measure. Over the next several decades, they developed alternative methods to account for the risk-return trade-off in mutual fund investing. William F. Sharpe, the recipient of the Nobel Memorial Prize in Economic Sciences in 1990, developed one of the earlier measures for evaluating risk-adjusted mutual fund manager performance. Sharpe (1966) introduced a metric now commonly called the *Sharpe ratio,* which is calculated by subtracting the periodic risk-free rate from the periodic rate of return of a portfolio and dividing the result by the standard deviation of the portfolio returns. Equation 18.2 shows the formula for the Sharpe ratio:

$$S_p = \frac{r_p - r_f}{\sigma_p}, \tag{18.2}$$

where S_p is the Sharpe ratio for a portfolio p; r_p is the portfolio return; r_f is the risk-free rate; and σ_p is the portfolio's standard deviation.

The Sharpe ratio is a straightforward reward-to-risk metric. The basic structure of this ratio differs slightly from the CV. Mutual fund returns are now in the numerator and fund risk is now in the denominator. The fund's returns are adjusted by the risk-free rate. The numerator for this metric represents the reward for investing in a risky portfolio. In this revised framework, the risk-free rate can be earned without taking on risk. Therefore, risk-taking investors are only interested in the return earned above the risk-free rate. This differs from the total return measure in CV. In the Sharpe ratio, the reward is only the return above the risk-free rate, which is also called the *market risk premium* of the portfolio. The denominator in the Sharpe ratio represents the portfolio risk an investor faces for earning the reward. The risk metric used for the Sharpe ratio is the volatility or dispersion of the portfolio measured as standard deviation of returns. This is unchanged from the risk metric in the CV. Again, standard deviation captures the total risk of the portfolio including both systematic and idiosyncratic risk.

Like the CV, using the Sharpe ratio leads to a dimensionless metric for evaluating relative fund manager performance. In this case, a larger Sharpe ratio can be interpreted as relatively better risk-adjusted performance because the numerator and denominator are flipped. For example, given a risk-free rate of 3 percent, a mutual fund return of 13 percent, and a standard deviation of the fund return of 20 percent, the Sharpe ratio would be 0.5. For a second fund during the same holding period, with the same risk-free rate of 3 percent, a fund return of 23 percent, and a standard deviation of the fund return of 20 percent, the Sharpe ratio would be 1.0. The Sharpe ratio allows for a direct risk-adjusted comparison of funds regardless of their risk characteristics. A higher Sharpe ratio shows relatively better historic risk-adjusted performance (i.e., more reward per unit of portfolio risk). In this example, the second fund offers twice as large a reward per unit of risk over the holding period.

The Treynor ratio (Treynor 1965) is a similar reward-to-risk style metric. It has the identical reward or risk premium measure as the Sharpe ratio in the numerator, but uses a different portfolio volatility or risk measure in the denominator. This ratio uses beta, β_p, or systematic risk of the portfolio in the denominator. Beta is a measure of the sensitivity of an investment or portfolio to movements in the overall market and is a linear risk measure. The Treynor ratio assumes that firm-specific or idiosyncratic risk can be completely diversified away and is therefore irrelevant in the overall reward-to-risk analysis. Equation 18.3 presents the formula for the Treynor ratio:

$$T_p = \frac{r_p - r_f}{\beta_p}, \tag{18.3}$$

where T_p is the Treynor ratio for a portfolio p; r_p is the portfolio return; r_f is the risk-free rate; and β_p is the portfolio's systematic risk (beta).

Using the Treynor ratio also leads to a dimensionless metric for evaluating relative fund manager performance. Similar to the Sharpe ratio, a larger Treynor ratio can be interpreted as relatively better fund manager risk-adjusted performance. The Sharpe and Treynor ratios are popular and useful tools but they both have a similar limitation. That is, they do not specifically quantify the amount of value added to the portfolio by the mutual fund portfolio manager. Both ratios result in dimensionless quantities that are difficult to interpret, except in a relative sense. Because the outputs from the CV, Sharpe ratio, and Treynor ratio are all dimensionless, these metrics cannot be effectively used in a stand-alone context. A portfolio's risk-adjusted performance cannot be judged on its own using these measures. The ratios can only be used to rank the relative performance of multiple portfolios.

In response to the drawbacks of these measures of relative performance, Franco Modigliani, a 1985 Nobel Laureate, and his granddaughter Leah Modigliani developed a measure called M-squared (M^2). They began their analysis by looking at Sharpe ratios for mutual funds with identical levels of total risk measured by standard deviation. In these unique cases, the numerator of the Sharpe ratio becomes the only factor contributing to any performance difference between two funds. Modigliani and Modigliani (1997) propose creating an improved risk-adjustment method so the standard deviations of all portfolios analyzed match identically with that of the market portfolio. This distinctive transformation to each fund is made by creating a new adjusted portfolio, p^*, from combining the original portfolio, p, and the risk-free asset, r_f. The weight of p in the new portfolio, p^*, is $w_p = \sigma_m/\sigma_p$. The weight of the risk-free asset in portfolio p^* is $w_{rf} = 1 - w_p$. After this transformation, the adjusted portfolio p^* and the market portfolio have the identical standard deviation. This means the numerators of their Sharpe ratios can be used as the sole source of the risk-adjusted return comparison. For calculation, M^2 simplifies to the market portfolio standard deviation multiplied by the difference between the Sharpe ratios of the mutual fund and the market portfolio. Equation 18.4 shows the M^2 formula:

$$M^2 = \left(r_{p*} - r_f\right) - \left(r_m - r_f\right) = \sigma_m\left(S_p - S_m\right), \tag{18.4}$$

where r_{p^*} is the adjusted portfolio return; r_f is the risk-free rate; r_m is the market return; σ_m is the market standard deviation; S_p is the Sharpe ratio of portfolio p; and S_m is the Sharpe ratio of the market.

As an example, given r_f of 3 percent, r_p of 23 percent, σ_p of 20 percent, r_m of 15 percent, and σ_m of 10 percent, the Sharpe ratios for the mutual fund portfolio and the market portfolio would be 1.0 and 1.2, respectively. Therefore, $M^2 = \sigma_m(S_p - S_m) =$ 10 percent $(-0.2) = -2.0$ percent. Although the relative underperformance of the fund portfolio regarding the market portfolio is already clear from their Sharpe ratios, the precise amount of this relative underperformance is not easily interpreted because the Sharpe ratios are dimensionless.

M^2 is a straightforward metric where the ranking and performance level is observable in percentage terms. Percentages are more intuitive and easier to comprehend by fund managers and investors. Also, percentages can be simply interpreted as an absolute measure of risk-adjusted performance instead of a relative measure. By scaling the portfolio risk to a fixed level for all investments, M^2 is no longer dimensionless, but shows the percentage of risk-adjusted performance above or below the market portfolio. This transformation creates a stand-alone percentage-based measure of risk-adjusted performance for all funds analyzed. In this example, once the mutual fund data are adjusted to the market risk, portfolio p^* underperformed the market by 2 percentage points during the period analyzed.

THE CAPITAL ASSET PRICING MODEL

Another pioneering work in risk-adjusted mutual fund performance measurement appears in the seminal paper of Jensen (1968). Jensen used a method based on the Capital Asset Pricing Model (CAPM) to measure mutual fund manager risk-adjusted performance. Treynor (1961, 1962), Sharpe (1964), Lintner (1965a, b), and Mossin (1966) independently developed the CAPM. Their work on the CAPM built on earlier work of Markowitz (1952, 1959) related to diversification and modern portfolio theory. The CAPM attempts to describe the relationship between risk and return for financial securities. Equation 18.5 shows the CAPM equation:

$$E(R_j) = R_f + \beta_j[E(R_M) - R_f], \tag{18.5}$$

where $E(R_j)$ is the expected return on the financial asset j; R_f is the risk-free rate; β_j is the sensitivity of the return of the financial asset j with respect to overall market returns (beta); $E(R_M)$ is the expected return on the market; and $[E(R_M) - R_f]$ is the market risk premium.

In the CAPM, the expected return for any asset depends on three inputs: (1) the risk-free rate, (2) market risk premium, and (3) beta. The risk-free rate for the CAPM is often proxied by a U.S. Treasury security such as the 30-day Treasury-bill (T-bill) rate. Regardless of asset risk, investors expect to be compensated at some minimum level for placing money in an investment over a specified period of time. This minimum compensation level is represented by the risk-free rate. The market risk premium represents the additional return investors expect for investing in a risky set of assets. Many U.S. equity models use the S&P 500 index as a proxy for the market portfolio. For example, the market risk premium can be the difference between the return on the S&P 500 index and the 30-day T-bill rate.

Finally, the beta coefficient is a measure of volatility and systematic risk. It represents the sensitivity of the asset's returns to the market's returns. *Systematic risk* is the risk that cannot be diversified away within a portfolio framework. By definition, the market has a beta of 1. Riskier assets and portfolios have higher betas and less risky assets have lower betas. The CAPM assumes that these three factors explain all the returns associated with a particular investment, which is an overly simplistic assumption.

JENSEN'S ALPHA

Jensen (1968) modified the CAPM for testing the performance of actively managed mutual fund portfolios. An allowance for the fund manager's forecasting ability is added to the model by not constraining the estimating regression to pass through the origin. In this framework, an additional variable called alpha (α) captures the fund manager's contribution to expected return. Equation 18.6 shows the equation for Jensen's alpha:

$$E(R_j) - R_f = \alpha_j + \beta_j[E(R_M) - R_f], \tag{18.6}$$

where $E(R_j)$ is the expected return on the financial asset; R_f is the risk-free rate; α_j is the fund manager's contribution to expected return; β_j is the sensitivity of the return of the financial asset j with respect to overall market portfolio returns (beta); and $E(R_M)$ is the expected return on the market portfolio $[E(R_M) - R_f]$ = market risk premium.

Following this method, the regression intercept, alpha (α), is designed to capture a mutual funds' risk-adjusted net return. Unlike the dimensionless Sharpe and Treynor ratios, Jensen's alpha quantifies in percentage terms the level an active manager underperforms or outperforms the overall financial market on a risk-adjusted basis. At first glance this may appear nearly identical to the overall goals of M^2. However, using M^2, the fund's risk-adjusted performance is calculated by modifying the risk of the mutual fund portfolio to the risk level of the market portfolio. Essentially, the fund portfolio is adjusted to behave more like the market portfolio. With the Jensen's alpha regression method, no risk level transformation is performed on the fund portfolio itself. The risk-adjusted performance is calculated for the actual mutual fund portfolio at its specified level of risk. In the Jensen's alpha regression model, the expected return related to the market is raised or lowered by the level of the beta coefficient.

To determine an alpha for a mutual fund, analysts often begin with at least 36 monthly returns for the mutual fund, the market index portfolio, and the risk-free rate. Subtracting the corresponding monthly risk-free rate from the mutual fund's monthly returns creates the dependent variable (y). Subtracting the monthly risk-free rate from the monthly market index return creates the independent variable (x). The regression output provides an intercept, or α, and β. The alpha value represents the manager's monthly risk-adjusted contribution in percentage terms to the overall mutual fund performance. The beta coefficient represents the level of systematic or market risk held by the fund during the period under examination.

This framework is helpful relative to the ratio metric methodologies. In the regression framework, the beta coefficient helps to clarify the level of market risk that is being used by the fund management, while the alpha coefficient quantifies the abnormal performance at that level of risk. The regression method allows an investor to look at these two separate but crucial aspects of a mutual fund within one tractable model. The beta coefficient shows whether the portfolio manager has chosen an inherently riskier or less risky portfolio relative to the market benchmark, whereas alpha shows the risk-adjusted abnormal performance of the fund's portfolio. If a fund has riskier assets than the market in its portfolio, the beta coefficient will be greater than one. Using this model, Jensen finds that, on average, actively managed mutual funds have negative and significant alphas and therefore, on a risk-adjusted basis, the average mutual fund underperforms the market.

MULTIFACTOR REGRESSION MODELS

The CAPM uses several key assumptions. It is a single factor model and it requires that the market includes all assets and be observable. It also assumes that markets are efficient where prices reflect all available information. The critique of the CAPM by Roll (1977) questioned whether the CAPM is sufficient for determining asset risk and return. His critique led many academics to consider alternative multifactor models that would more accurately explain financial asset returns. In a seminal paper, Fama and French (1993) identify five common risk factors associated with the overall returns of stocks and bonds. Three of the five common risk factors used in their model are equity related: a market return measure, firm size measure, and book-to-market factor. The two other factors are bond-market factors and are tied to bond maturity and bond default risks.

Gruber (1996) develops a four-factor model, composed of a similar set of three stock-market related factors and a bond factor to examine mutual fund manager performance. Based on the observed alphas of his four-factor model, Gruber reports that the average actively managed fund has negative risk-adjusted manager performance.

Carhart (1997) presents another four-factor risk-adjusted performance model that uses three Fama–French stock-market related factors, as well as an additional factor intended to capture Jegadeesh and Titman's one-year momentum anomaly. Jegadeesh and Titman (1993) document several strategies in which buying stocks that have performed well in the past and selling stocks that have performed poorly in the past can create significantly positive returns over 3- to 12-month holding periods. Using the Carhart model, an alpha similar to the alpha in both Jensen (1968) and Gruber (1996) is designed to capture the risk-adjusted net return of a mutual fund. The Carhart four-factor model is the most widely used risk-adjusted performance metric for mutual fund returns. Equation 18.7 shows the Carhart four-factor model:

$$r_i = \alpha_i + \beta_{1i}RMRF_t + \beta_{2i}SMB_t + \beta_{3i}HML_t + \beta_{4i}WML_t, \qquad (18.7)$$

where r_i is the monthly mutual fund return minus the 30-day T-bill return; *RMRF* is the market risk factor and is the excess return on the market index; and *SMB, HML,* and *WML* are returns on value-weighted zero-investment, factor-mimicking portfolios for size, book-to-market equity, and one-year momentum in stock returns, respectively.

RMRF is essentially the market risk premium as discussed in explaining the CAPM. *SMB, HML,* and *WML* are additional factors used to capture other sources of risk. The *SMB* factor stands for "Small Minus Big." This factor captures the well-known *small firm effect,* which is a theory stating that firms with a low market capitalization tend to outperform larger firms. *HML* stands for "High Minus Low." This factor captures differences in return between value and growth stocks. High book-to-market ratio firms are considered value stocks, while low book-to-market firms are growth stocks. This difference in returns is sometimes called the *value premium.* The *WML* factor stands for "Winners Minus Losers." This factor captures the momentum premium exhibited by the return differences between past winners and losers. French's (2014) website provides empirical data sets and more complete descriptions of the construction methodologies of these factors.

Many studies using the Carhart four-factor model report statistically significant abnormal performance for fund managers. On a net of fees basis, the average abnormal performance is almost always significantly negative (Carhart 1997; Bollen and Busse 2005; Fama and French 2008, 2010). In the Carhart regression framework, the factor weighting for each risk coefficient explains how much of each type of risk (market, *SMB, HML,* or *WML*) the fund manager uses, and the alpha coefficient quantifies the abnormal performance remaining after adjusting for the four risk factors.

The search for the best fund performance measurement model continues. Some studies question whether the Carhart model might spuriously find significant alphas even with unmanaged portfolios or indexes. For example, Costa and Jakob (2006) and Cremers, Petajisto, and Zitzewitz (2012) both confirm that the Fama and French (1993) and Carhart (1997) models produce statistically significant nonzero alphas for unmanaged portfolios, including the S&P 500 index and the Russell 2000 index. Both sets of authors propose enhanced methods to help deal with these spurious results.

Costa and Jakob (2010) introduce a method to compare the alphas and coefficients from each fund with the alpha and coefficients from the relevant benchmark index using a pair-wise F-test. When comparing alphas, the F-test shows whether the manager statistically outperforms or underperforms the relevant benchmark index over the specified holding period. The Carhart method assumes the alpha from the four-factor model is zero for the benchmark index, but Costa and Jakob (2006) and Cremers et al. (2012) show that this is not the case.

In Costa and Jakob (2010), the relevant benchmark index coefficients are subtracted from the original four-factor coefficients for each fund and then a pair-wise F-test is performed to measure the statistical difference between the alphas of each fund and the index. This F-test gives a more accurate sign of manager's contribution to fund performance relative to the correct benchmark. Using their method, the number of fund managers that underperform or outperform the benchmark changes dramatically. In a similar vein, Cremers et al. (2012) recommend that researchers use their index-based seven-factor model or their four-factor model, both of which are adjusted for relevant benchmark indexes.

Morningstar: A Practitioner Approach

Besides those ratios and models, other online resources are available to further investigate mutual fund performance. Although many of the tools are publicly available without cost, some require a fee. The performance evaluation tools are proprietary and their exact analytical methodologies are not publicly disclosed. The Morningstar Corporation has some of the most extensive tools currently available. This section focuses on some of their most popular products.

Morningstar divides its analysis into two distinct areas: (1) the Morningstar Rating™ for mutual funds focuses on a mutual fund's past performance and (2) the newer Morningstar Medalist™ Funds Rating system has a forward-looking perspective. Morningstar introduced its star rating system in 1985, which was one of the first commercially available products for evaluating risk- and cost-adjusted return. The ratings use a scale of one to five stars, and originally evaluated a fund's past performance relative to other funds within the same asset class from a set of six broad asset classes. In 1996, Morningstar refined its categories and created Category Rating™ as a tool to be used with their star ratings. Morningstar further enhanced the star rating system in 2002 by refining the broad asset classes to smaller category groups and using a new measure of risk-adjusted return.

The current category-based rating groups allow investors to compare performance of funds that use similar investment strategies. About 90 proprietary Morningstar categories are currently available. Since the investment objective stated in a fund's prospectus may not reflect how the fund actually invests, the Morningstar category is determined based on the actual underlying securities in the fund. Categories are available for municipal, domestic, and international funds. They cover equities, bonds, commodities, and target-date funds.

To further evaluate fund type, Morningstar also has its proprietary Morningstar Style Box. The nine-square grid provides the investor with a graphical representation of the "investment style" of the mutual fund. The Style Box classifies funds on the vertical axis according to the market value of the securities within the fund (i.e., large-capitalization stocks, mid-capitalization stocks, or small-capitalization stocks). On the horizontal axis, the Style Box designates whether the underlying stocks are from the growth, blend, or value categories. The growth versus value measure for Morningstar is proprietary, but it is based on growth metrics such as the price/earnings (P/E) ratio and dividend yield of the assets within the portfolio. Typically, growth stocks have higher P/E ratios and lower dividend payouts.

Because most investors are risk-averse, the Morningstar rating system considers the variations in a fund's monthly performance. Morningstar believes that most investors are more concerned with losses than with equally large gains. This concept is consistent with the behavioral finance literature related to expected utility theory (Kahneman and Tversky 1979; Barberis and Thaler 2003). The rating system therefore places a larger negative emphasis on downward movements in the portfolio's net asset value (NAV) and rewards fund managers for consistent performance.

The Morningstar Rating™ system assigns funds a star rating based on their overall Morningstar risk-adjusted return measure. Since fees are important, Morningstar's measure also accounts for all sales charges, loads, and redemption fees. Funds can be given a star rating of between one and five stars. The lowest 10 percent of funds ranked receive a one-star rating. The next 22.5 percent of funds receive a two-star rating. The next 35 percent of the funds receive a three-star rating. The next 22.5 percent receive a four-star rating, and the top 10 percent of funds analyzed receive a five-star rating. Depending on the fund's age, it is rated for up to three periods: the trailing 3, 5, and 10 years. The overall fund rating is based on combining these sub-period ratings.

The Morningstar rating system is a historical look at the past performance of a mutual fund. For a forward-looking perspective, Morningstar added a new research segment called Morningstar Medalist. Medalist funds are those that Morningstar believes will have an edge over their peers in the long term. Morningstar medalists are funds that have a Morningstar Analyst Rating of Bronze, Silver, or Gold. Morningstar analysts assign ratings on a five-tier scale with three positive ratings of Gold, Silver, and Bronze, a Neutral rating, and a Negative rating. The top three rating levels suggest that the funds will outperform other funds in their category, as well as appropriate risk-adjusted benchmarks over the next five or more years.

The Morningstar Analyst Rating system is based on five different aspects of the fund. These areas include examining the (1) fund management team, (2) management process, (3) parent organization, (4) fund's price and expenses, and (5) past and future expected performance.

A Real-World Example

This section provides three years of recent data for two mutual funds. Many of the analyses from the previous sections are performed using Microsoft Excel on the first of the two mutual funds. The second fund's data are left for analysis within the discussion questions. The first fund, Fidelity Magellan Fund (FMAGX), is a large capitalization equity fund managed by Fidelity Investments (Fidelity). As of August 2014, FMAGX had $16.7 billion of portfolio net assets under management (AUM). The second fund, The Oakmark Class II Fund (OARMX), is also a large capitalization equity fund managed by Oakmark Funds. As of August 2014, the portfolio had $16.8 billion net AUM.

Table 18.1 shows an Excel worksheet that contains the monthly return data for FMAGX, OARMX, and the S&P 500 Total Return Index (^SP500TR). The S&P500 Total Return Index is an appropriate benchmark because the typical S&P 500 index does not adjust for dividend distributions. The 36 monthly returns from July 2011 through June 2014 are created using the historically adjusted closing prices available from Yahoo Finance. The monthly returns are calculated based on the adjusted closing prices from the last day of trading for each month. The table also includes the U.S. Research Database monthly Carhart factors and the risk-free rate data available directly from French's (2014) website.

For the CV analysis, the total period return and the standard deviation of the monthly returns are computed from the complete set of the monthly returns for the fund. One way to calculate total return is to use the array formula = *PRODUCT*(1 + *B*2:*B*37)–*1* in Excel. To use an array formula in Excel, press CTRL + SHIFT + ENTER to properly enter the formulas into the workbook. The standard deviation measure is for a sample of returns, so the recommended formula is = *STDEV.S*(*B*2:*B*37). To calculate

Table 18.1 **Monthly Return Data and Risk Factors**

Date	*FMAGX*	*OARMX*	*^SP500TR*	*RF*	*Mkt-RF*	*SMB*	*HML*	*Mom*
June-14	0.026187	0.025132	0.020656325	0	0.0259	0.0299	–0.0066	0.0061
May-14	0.030767	0.026731	0.023476236	0	0.0206	–0.0187	–0.0038	0.0099
April-14	–0.01142	–0.00323	0.007391476	0	–0.0019	–0.0419	0.0157	–0.039
March-14	–0.0114	0.01596	0.008403587	0	0.004	–0.0183	0.0467	–0.0324
February-14	0.051976	0.046847	0.045745794	0	0.0465	0.0032	–0.0048	0.0207
January-14	–0.01881	–0.03904	–0.034576048	0	–0.0328	0.0084	–0.0186	0.0173
December-13	0.025074	0.029994	0.025317591	0	0.0281	–0.0043	–0.0015	0.0011
November-13	0.034884	0.036987	0.030473951	0	0.0312	0.0134	–0.0033	0.0048
October-13	0.042624	0.043692	0.045967242	0	0.0417	–0.0156	0.0131	0.0019
September-13	0.04216	0.034489	0.031358286	0	0.0376	0.0285	–0.0159	0.0299
August-13	–0.01866	–0.02513	–0.028961318	0	–0.0269	0.0029	–0.0246	0.0007
July-13	0.06624	0.05567	0.050886461	0	0.0566	0.0187	0.0074	0.0172
June-13	–0.01683	–0.01254	–0.013428115	0	–0.0121	0.0123	–0.0044	0.0066
May-13	0.035856	0.046929	0.023390073	0	0.0281	0.0195	0.0132	–0.0188
April-13	0.01002	0.01889	0.0192668	0	0.0156	–0.024	0.0041	0.0035
March-13	0.031296	0.029162	0.037502996	0	0.0403	0.0083	–0.0006	0.0209
February-13	0.006987	0.007755	0.013575485	0	0.0128	–0.0039	0.0029	0.0147

continued

Table 18.1 **(continued)**

Date	*FMAGX*	*OARMX*	*^SP500TR*	*RF*	*Mkt-RF*	*SMB*	*HML*	*Mom*
January-13	0.050765	0.056034	0.05179601	0	0.0558	0.0047	0.0131	−0.0191
December-12	0.007713	0.023153	0.009114279	0.0001	0.0118	0.0162	0.0325	−0.0296
November-12	0.009695	0.004875	0.005799369	0.0001	0.0077	0.0067	−0.011	0.0033
October-12	−0.02586	0.000887	−0.018465112	0.0001	−0.0175	−0.0107	0.0414	0.001
September-12	0.032119	0.020367	0.025842651	0.0001	0.0274	0.0049	0.0157	−0.0102
August-12	0.033355	0.031031	0.022523387	0.0001	0.0256	0.0071	0.0055	−0.0246
July-12	0.011694	0.009896	0.013888713	0	0.0079	−0.026	0.0002	0.0306
June-12	0.033673	0.045835	0.041202511	0	0.0388	0.0082	0.0048	−0.0116
May-12	−0.07181	−0.07478	−0.060101349	0.0001	−0.062	−0.0012	0.0011	0.0664
April-12	−0.01188	−0.00318	−0.00627399	0	−0.0084	−0.0062	−0.0017	0.0381
March-12	0.035761	0.032864	0.032907961	0	0.0311	−0.0024	−0.0006	0.0145
February-12	0.059805	0.04952	0.043241758	0	0.0443	−0.0164	0.0004	−0.0039
January-12	0.060081	0.055108	0.044813659	0	0.0506	0.0253	−0.0216	−0.0794
December-11	−0.00276	0.006278	0.01022891	0	0.0074	−0.0057	0.0154	0.0188
November-11	−0.02263	−0.00933	−0.002208413	0	−0.0026	−0.0026	−0.0016	0.0397
October-11	0.108743	0.113387	0.109292051	0	0.1134	0.0359	−0.0092	−0.0141
September-11	−0.11664	−0.06677	−0.070296324	0	−0.076	−0.0372	−0.0099	−0.0255
August-11	−0.07712	−0.05472	−0.054324068	0.0001	−0.06	−0.033	−0.0157	−0.0035
July-11	−0.0144	−0.02772	−0.020333146	0	−0.0234	−0.0143	−0.0114	0.0004

Note: The table contains monthly return data for FMAGX, OARMX, and the S&P 500 Total Return Index (^SP500TR). The 36 monthly returns from July 2011 through June 2014 are created using the historically adjusted closing prices available from Yahoo Finance. The table includes monthly Carhart factors and the risk-free rate data available directly from French's (2014) website.

Table 18.2 **Return and Risk Metrics**

Return and Risk Metrics	*FMAGX*	*SP500TR*
Total return	47.99%	58.46%
Standard deviation	4.32%	3.54%
Coefficient of variation (CV)	0.09	0.06
Sharpe ratio	11.08	16.50
M^2	−19.18%	

Note: The table contains the results for the total return, standard deviation of return, CV, Sharpe ratio, and M^2 for FMAGX and ^SP500TR. For the period analyzed, FMAGX underperformed the benchmark index with respect to total returns. FMAGX's higher CV, lower Sharpe ratio, and negative M^2 all indicate negative risk-adjusted performance relative to SP500TR.

the fund's Sharpe ratio, the total period return for the T-bill risk-free rate proxy is also required. To calculate the dimensional M^2 measure for the fund requires computing the standard deviation and Sharpe ratio for the S&P 500. Table 18.2 contains the results for the standard deviation, total return, CV, Sharpe ratio, and M^2 for FMAGX and ^SP500TR. For the period analyzed, FMAGX underperformed the benchmark index regarding total returns. FMAGX's higher CV, lower Sharpe ratio, and negative M^2 all show negative risk-adjusted performance relative to SP500TR.

For the Treynor ratio, the regression based on the CAPM model must be used to calculate the beta coefficient in the denominator of the ratio. Table 18.3 contains the regression output for FMAGX minus the risk-free rate regressed on the market return minus the risk-free rate from French's (2014) website. The regression beta of 1.13 indicates that FMAGX is riskier than the overall market portfolio. Beta is the risk metric used in the Treynor ratio. FMAGX's lower Treynor ratio suggests a lower reward-to-risk measure relative to the SP500TR index. The alpha of the regression model is Jensen's alpha, which measures abnormal performance above and beyond the market proxy. In this case the alpha is negative and statistically significant suggesting that FMAGX underperformed the market on a risk-adjusted basis by 0.3475 percent per month over the 36-month holding period.

Table 18.4 contains the Carhart four-factor regression output for FMAGX. The alpha represents the risk-adjusted abnormal return and the factor loadings on each of the Carhart factors indicate the level of the different risk characteristics of the fund. Using the Carhart model, the alpha remains negative but is no longer statistically significant. This finding suggests that FMAGX management did not outperform or underperform the market on a risk-adjusted basis, and the four risk factors capture the FMAGX's overall returns. The coefficient on $Mkt - RF$ is greater than one and statistically significant. This coefficient suggests that FMAGX held a riskier portfolio than the overall market. The *SMB* coefficient is positive but insignificant. While insignificant, the slightly positive coefficient suggests that the portfolio may be weighted more toward smaller capitalization stocks. The negative but insignificant loading on *HML* is consistent with a more growth-oriented portfolio. Finally, the positive but insignificant coefficient on the momentum factor suggests the portfolio tends to hold momentum stocks. With the Carhart model for FMAGX, the only statistically significant risk factor is the market.

Table 18.3 **The CAPM and Treynor Ratio**

Regression Statistics								
Multiple R	0.97370704							
R Square	0.9481054							
Adjusted R Square	0.946579089							
Standard Error	0.009996235							
Observations	36							
ANOVA								
	df	***SS***	***MS***	***F***	***Significance F***			
Regression	1	0.06207065	0.06207065	621.1741467	1.99985E-23			
Residual	34	0.00339744	9.99247E-05					
Total	35	0.06546809						
	Coefficients	***Standard Error***	***t Stat***	***P-value***	***Lower 95%***	***Upper 95%***	***Lower 95.0%***	***Upper 95.0%***
Intercept	−0.00347532	0.001775873	−1.956964219	0.058603601	−0.007084328	0.000133688	−0.007084328	0.000133688
Mkt-RF	1.132322022	0.045432148	24.92336548	1.99985E-23	1.039992789	1.224651255	1.039992789	1.224651255
Treynor FMAGX	0.423215806							
Treynor ^SP500TR	0.583920116							

Note: The table contains the regression output for FMAGX minus the risk-free rate regressed on the market return minus the risk-free rate using data from French's (2014) website. The beta of 1.13 shows that FMAGX is riskier than the market. FMAGX's lower Treynor ratio suggests a lower reward-to-risk measure relative to the SP500TR index. Jensen's alpha, which is the measure of abnormal performance above the market proxy, is negative and statistically significant suggesting that FMAGX underperformed the market on a risk-adjusted basis by 0.3475 percent per month over the 36-month holding period.

Table 18.4 **The Carhart Model Regression**

Carhart Model					
SUMMARY OUTPUT					
Regression Statistics					
Multiple R	0.976731629				
R Square	0.954004675				
Adjusted R Square	0.948069795				
Standard Error	0.009855776				
Observations	36				
ANOVA					
	df	***SS***	***MS***	***F***	***Significance F***
Regression	4	0.062456864	0.015614216	160.7453862	2.95368E-20
Residual	31	0.003011226	9.71363E-05		
Total	35	0.06546809			

continued

Table 18.4 **(continued)**

	Coefficients	*Standard Error*	*t Stat*	*P-value*	*Lower 95%*	*Upper 95%*	*Lower 95.0%*	*Upper 95.0%*
Intercept	−0.002939987	0.001843076	−1.595151922	0.120824132	−0.006698965	0.000818992	−0.006698965	0.000818992
Mkt-RF	1.116564127	0.056687391	19.69686934	4.37249E-19	1.000949432	1.232178823	1.000949432	1.232178823
SMB	0.089113552	0.111295901	0.800690335	0.429405045	−0.137875935	0.316103039	−0.137875935	0.316103039
HML	−0.156716654	0.111720658	−1.402754483	0.170626345	−0.38457244	0.071139131	−0.38457244	0.071139131
Mom	0.023637278	0.066528862	0.355293594	0.72477578	−0.11204923	0.159323787	−0.11204923	0.159323787

Note: The table contains the Carhart four-factor regression output for FMAGX. The intercept or alpha represents the risk-adjusted abnormal return, and the factor loadings on each of the Carhart factors indicate the level of the different risk characteristics of the fund. The alpha is negative but not statistically significant. This suggests that FMAGX management did not outperform or underperform the market on a risk-adjusted basis. The significant coefficient on *Mkt – RF* suggests that FMAGX held a riskier portfolio than the overall market. In this sample period for FMAGX, the only statistically significant risk factor is the market.

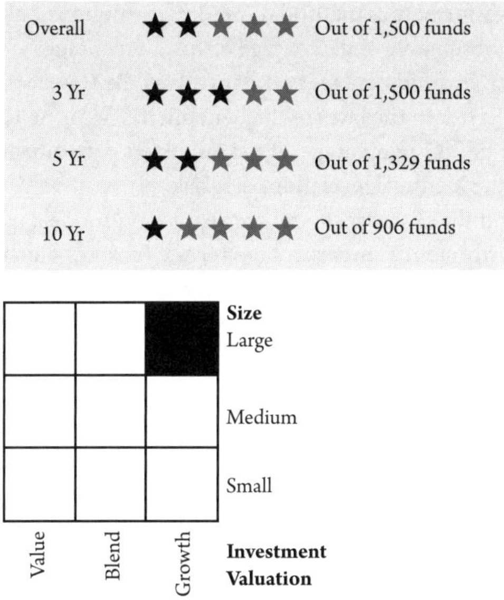

Figure 18.1 MORNINGSTAR STAR RATING AND STYLE BOX. The figure contains the Morningstar ratings and Style Box for the Fidelity Magellan Fund (FMAGX) as of August 2014. FMAGX has an overall star rating of two out of five stars. The Style Box indicates that the fund is weighted heavily in large capitalization growth stocks. Source: Fidelity Investments (October 2014).

Figure 18.1 contains Morningstar Star Rating information and the Morningstar Style Box for FMAGX. FMAGX has two stars for the Star Rating system. As discussed previously, the lowest 10 percent of funds ranked by Morningstar receive a one-star rating. The next 22.5 percent of funds receive a two-star rating. In the Style Box FMAGX is located in the top-right quadrant, which according to Morningstar suggests that the fund has a large capitalization growth-oriented portfolio.

Summary and Conclusions

This chapter examines widely used metrics to analyze mutual fund performance and to better understand the risk-return trade-off related to mutual fund investing. Measurements of mutual fund relative risk-adjusted performance are evaluated with common dimensionless ratios including the CV, Sharpe ratio, and Treynor ratio. The CV is a basic total risk to total return measure. The Sharpe and Treynor ratios incorporate the concept of reward into the analysis framework. The Sharpe ratio analyzes reward vs. total risk, while the Treynor ratio focuses on investment reward relative to only systematic risk. The CV, Sharpe, and Treynor ratios all have a common limitation due to their structure. All three metrics are dimensionless and can only be used in the framework of relative risk-adjusted performance evaluation by comparing one fund to another and using the same sample period.

M^2 uses a risk transformation method to modify the dimensionless Sharpe ratio of a fund into a measure observable in percentage terms. Percentages are more intuitive and easier to comprehend by fund managers and investors. By transforming and scaling the mutual fund portfolio risk to the level of the benchmark, M^2 is no longer dimensionless and shows the total period percentage of risk-adjusted performance compared to the market portfolio at the identical level of market risk.

Jensen's alpha and the Carhart model are regression models used to further quantify risk-adjusted performance in percentage terms. Jensen's alpha is calculated using regression analysis based on the CAPM. The regression intercept, alpha (α), captures the risk-adjusted net return of the mutual fund. Jensen's alpha precisely quantifies in percentages the level an active manager underperforms or outperforms the overall financial market on a risk-adjusted basis. M^2 and Jensen's alpha are related, but differ in their method of analysis. M^2 calculates risk-adjusted abnormal performance by modifying the risk of the subject mutual fund portfolio to the risk level of the market portfolio. In other words, M^2 is the level of risk-adjusted performance when the risk level of the mutual fund portfolio is scaled down or up to the level of the market. With the Jensen's alpha regression method, no risk level transformation is performed. The risk-adjusted performance is calculated for the actual mutual fund portfolio at its specified level of risk. The Jensen's alpha method gives the additional benefit of providing the beta for the mutual fund portfolio. The beta shows the amount of market risk being held in the mutual fund portfolio.

The Carhart model expands on the regression model concept and adds three additional independent variables to the regression process. Along with the market risk premium, the model adds the *SMB, HML,* and momentum factors. These factors are designed to capture well-documented investment risks associated with firm size or market capitalization, value vs. growth investing, and momentum investing. The alpha generated by the Carhart model is a metric of risk-adjusted excess return of the mutual fund based on the four risk factors in Carhart's model instead of the single risk factor in Jensen's model. The factor loadings on each of the four factors show the amount of the particular risk characteristic within the mutual fund portfolio. The chapter also discusses several extensions to the Carhart regression approach where model misspecifications related to index portfolios are handled in various ways.

The next portion of the chapter discussed the quantitative and qualitative risk metrics available from corporations such as Morningstar. The Morningstar Rating™ system assigns funds a star rating based on an overall Morningstar risk-adjusted return measure. Morningstar's proprietary rating process considers historical fund performance. Mutual funds are categorized and ranked based on historical fund performance and given an overall star rating based on the findings. Funds with more stars indicate better historically performing funds. Morningstar also has its proprietary Morningstar Style Box. The nine-square grid provides the investor with a graphical representation of the mutual fund's "investment style." The Style Box classifies funds on the vertical axis according to the market value of the securities within the fund. On the horizontal axis, the Style Box designates whether the underlying stocks are from growth, blend, or value categories.

For a forward-looking perspective, Morningstar added a new research segment called Morningstar Medalist. Medalist funds are those that Morningstar believes will have an edge over their peers in the long term. Morningstar medalists are funds that have a Morningstar Analyst Rating of Bronze, Silver, or Gold.

The final section of the chapter focuses on a real-world example with risk-adjusted performance analysis on the Fidelity Magellan mutual fund and the Standard and Poor's 500 Total Return Index. Data from the publicly available sources on Yahoo Finance and French's (2014) website are collected and analyzed with the various ratio and regression model techniques.

Discussion Questions

1. Calculate the total return, standard deviation of returns, CV, Sharpe ratio, and M^2 for OARMX. Compare the answers for OARMX to those found in the chapter for FMAGX and the market benchmark index ^SP500TR.
2. Use a single factor CAPM regression analysis to calculate Jensen's alpha and beta for OARMX.
3. Use the beta from the CAPM regression analysis to calculate the Treynor ratio for OARMX. Compare this Treynor ratio to those in the chapter found for FMAGX and the market index ^SP500TR.
4. Discuss the meaning and significance of Jensen's alpha for OARMX and whether OARMX's management team added value.
5. Use the four-factor regression approach for OARMX to calculate the Carhart alpha and factor loadings for *Mkt – RF, SMB, HML,* and momentum.
6. Discuss the direction and significance of the Carhart alpha and factor loadings and whether OARMX's management team added value.

References

Barberis, Nicholas, and Richard Thaler. 2003. "A Survey of Behavioral Finance." In George M. Constantinides, Milton Harris, and René M. Stulz, eds., *Handbook of the Economics of Finance* 1, 1053–1128. Amsterdam: Elsevier Science B.V.

Bollen, Nicolas P. B., and Jeffrey A. Busse. 2005. "Short-Term Persistence in Mutual Fund Performance." *Review of Financial Studies* 18:2, 569–597.

Carhart, Mark. 1997. "On Persistence in Mutual Fund Performance." *Journal of Finance* 52:1, 57–82.

Costa, Bruce A., and Keith Jakob, 2006. "Do Stock Indexes Have Abnormal Performance?" *Journal of Performance Measurement* 11:1, 8–22.

Costa, Bruce A., and Keith Jakob. 2010. "Enhanced Performance Measurement of Mutual Funds: Running the Benchmark Index through the Hurdles." *Journal of Applied Finance* 20:1, 95–102.

Cremers, Martijn, Antti Petajisto, and Eric Zitzewitz. 2012. "Should Benchmark Indices Have Alpha? Revisiting Performance Evaluation." *Critical Finance Review* 2:1, 1–48.

Fama, Eugene, and Kenneth French. 1993. "Common Risk Factors in the Returns on Stocks and Bonds." *Journal of Financial Economics* 33:1, 3–56.

Fama, Eugene, and Kenneth French. 2008. "Mutual Fund Performance." *Journal of Finance* 63:1, 389–416.

Fama, Eugene, and Kenneth French. 2010. "Luck versus Skill in the Cross-section of Mutual Fund Returns." *Journal of Finance* 65:5, 1915–1947.

French, Kenneth. 2014. Database. Available at http://mba.tuck.dartmouth.edu/pages/faculty/ken.french/data_library.html.

Gruber, Martin. 1996. "Another Puzzle: The Growth in Actively Managed Mutual Funds." *Journal of Finance* 51:3, 783–810.

Jegadeesh, Narasimhan, and Sheridan Titman. 1993 "Returns to Buying Winners and Selling Losers: Implications for Stock Market Efficiency." *Journal of Finance* 48:1, 65–91.

Jensen, Michael. 1968. "The Performance of Mutual Funds in the Period 1945–1964." *Journal of Finance* 23:2, 389–416.

Kahneman, Daniel, and Amos Tversky. 1979. "Prospect Theory: An Analysis of Decision under Risk." *Econometrica: Journal of the Econometric Society* 47:2, 263–291.

Lintner, John. 1965a. "The Valuation of Risk Assets and the Selection of Risky Investments in Stock Portfolios and Capital Budgets." *Review of Economics and Statistics* 57:1, 13–37.

Lintner, John. 1965b. "Security Prices, Risk, and Maximal Gains from Diversification." *Journal of Finance* 20:4, 587–615.

Markowitz, Harry. 1952. "Portfolio Selection." *Journal of Finance* 7:1, 77–91.

Markowitz, Harry. 1959. *Portfolio Selection: Efficient Diversification of Investments*. New York: John Wiley & Sons.

Modigliani, Franco, and Leah Modigliani. 1997. "Risk-Adjusted Performance." *Journal of Portfolio Management* 23:2, 45–54.

Mossin, Jan. 1966. "Equilibrium in a Capital Asset Market." *Econometrica: Journal of the Econometric Society* 34:4, 768–783.

Pearson, Karl. 1896. "Mathematical Contributions to the Theory of Evolution—On a Form of Spurious Correlation Which May Arise When Indices Are Used in the Measurement of Organs." *Proceedings of the Royal Society of London* 60:1, 489–498.

Roll, Richard. 1977. "A Critique of the Asset Pricing Theory's Tests." *Journal of Financial Economics* 4:2, 129–176.

Sharpe, William F. 1964. "Capital Asset Prices: A Theory of Market Equilibrium under Conditions of Risk." *Journal of Finance* 19:3, 425–442.

Sharpe, William F. 1966. "Mutual Fund Performance." *Journal of Business* 39:1, 119–138.

Treynor, Jack L. 1961. " Market Value, Time, and Risk." Unpublished Manuscript, 95–209.

Treynor, Jack L. 1962. " Toward a Theory of Market Value of Risky Assets." Unpublished Manuscript.

Treynor, Jack L. 1965. "How to Rate Management of Investment Funds." *Harvard Business Review* 43:1, 63–75.

19

Predicting Mutual Fund Performance

MATTHEW R. MOREY
Professor and New York Stock Exchange Research Scholar, Pace University

Introduction

Choosing the right mutual fund is an important decision for individual investors. If an individual chooses correctly, it could mean retiring early, sending children to better schools, and gaining financial independence. However, the wrong choice can mean working well beyond the normal retirement age, having fewer educational options for children, and experiencing the limitations and worries associated with not being financially independent. The difference in the 10-year annualized total return between the lowest performing and best performing surviving large growth funds as of the December 31, 2013, is 10.3 percent a year. The lowest growth fund had an annualized return of 1.57 percent and the highest had an 11.89 percent return (Morningstar 2014). Put another way, if an employee started with $100,000 in a retirement account 10 years ago, the $100,000 would have turned into $116,857 in the lowest performing fund versus $307,547 in the highest performing fund.

This example shows the importance of identifying mutual funds that will outperform. This chapter provides a survey of the literature to identify factors predicting mutual fund outperformance for U.S. equity funds. Here, *outperformance* refers to funds that consistently perform better than their benchmark indices. Although some factors appear to help investors predict better performance, much dissonance occurs in the literature. A study may report robust evidence of a certain factor predicting fund outperformance, while another offers contradictory or statistically insignificant evidence on the same factor.

Kosowski, Timmermann, White, and Wermers (2006) and Fama and French (2010) illustrate this frustration. They examine the question of the degree to which mutual fund outperformance is due to manager skill as opposed to luck. Kosowski et al. examine 25 years of mutual fund data and find outperformance is not due to luck. That is, sampling variability cannot solely explain outperformance. Instead, they find that the performance of some mutual fund managers exhibits superior skill. If investors can find these fund managers, then their portfolios are likely to outperform. It also means that some managers are worth paying higher fees for their skills. Conversely, Fama and French, using somewhat different techniques and time periods than Kosowski et al., find that the performance of few funds shows evidence of manager skill.

Instead, outperformance, if it exists at all, is based more on luck than skill. If fund performance rarely reflects managerial skill, then the search to find a winning fund is much harder, if not impossible.

The rest of this chapter is organized as follows. It begins by surveying basic factors reported in the literature to predict fund outperformance in U.S. equity funds. These include expenses, loads, turnover, past performance, and mutual fund ratings. Next, the chapter examines less obvious issues such as the degree to which the fund is actively managed, fund size, fund family size, and fund governance. Then, the chapter examines whether fund manager characteristics, such as manager education, tenure, and age, have any ability to predict outperformance. Finally, the chapter concludes by providing an opinion about using indicators of fund performance.

Factors That May Predict Equity Mutual Fund Outperformance

This section describes factors used to predict mutual fund performance in the literature. The first section examines how some basic factors such as fees, trading costs, and past performance predict future performance. The second section investigates how some less well-known factors such as mutual fund ratings and fund manager characteristics predict future performance.

EXPENSES, LOADS, AND OTHER FEES

Academics agree that the best known predictor of mutual fund outperformance is expenses. Expenses are measured by the fund's *expense ratio,* which is the percentage of fund assets that pay for operating expenses, management fees, administrative fees, and all other asset-based costs incurred by the fund, except brokerage costs. Carhart (1997), Dellva and Olson (1998), O'Neal (2004), Haslem, Baker, and Smith (2008), and Gil-Bazo and Ruiz-Verdu (2009) all document that funds with low expense ratios outperform other funds. Arguably, Carhart's research on fees and performance is the most influential. In a study that examines almost 2,000 U.S. equity mutual funds between 1962 and 1993, he finds that for every 1 percent increase in expense ratios there is a 1.54 percent decrease in fund performance. More recent research by Gil-Bazo and Ruiz-Verdu examine U.S. equity funds between 1962 and 2005 and find results similar to Carhart. They report the startlingly result that funds with the worse before-fee performance charge higher expense ratios.

The prevailing view in the mutual fund field is that if investors want to use only one measure to predict outperformance, they are best served by using the expense ratio as low expense funds appear to outperform other funds. As evidence of this claim, the Financial Research Corporation (2002) examines 10 different factors to determine which are effective at predicting mutual fund outperformance including past performance, Morningstar ratings, expense ratios, turnover, and manager tenure. Of the 10 factors, only the fund's expense ratio can consistently predict future fund outperformance. In a study using data between 2005 and 2009, Kinnel (2010) finds comparable results.

Similar to expense ratios, research shows that *load fees,* which are fees levied on the purchase or sale of mutual fund shares, also help to predict fund outperformance.

Carhart (1997), Dellva and Olson (1998), Morey (2003), O'Neal (2004), and Haslem et al. (2008) find a negative relationship between loads and future performance. Funds with no or low loads exhibit consistently better performance than high load funds. Carhart finds load funds underperform no-load funds by 80 basis points a year. Haslem et al. document that other types of fees predict performance, such as *12b-1 fees,* which are annual marketing or distribution fees on a mutual fund, and range from 0.25 and 1.00 percent (the maximum allowed) of a fund's net assets.

Yet, other studies show that expenses and loads do not always predict outperformance. According to Cremers and Petajisto (2009) and Petajisto (2013), what matters most in terms of performance is the degree to which fund holdings differ from the stated benchmark, not expenses and loads. These authors find that some actively managed funds with higher expenses and loads actually outperform. These results are based on long time periods so such findings do not seem to be an artifact of the time period. This research suggests that expenses and loads alone do not always show outperformance. Similarly, Wermers (2000) and Kosowski et al. (2006) find that some managers are more skillful and thus charge higher expenses. They find that some higher expense funds are worth the costs as the managers' skill enables the fund to outperform.

Further evidence suggests that increases in certain types of fees actually predict better performance. One such feature is the *redemption fee,* which is a fee applied to shares held for short periods. The purpose of such a fee is to limit investors' ability to time the market, forcing them to hold the fund for longer periods. Dellva and Olson (1998), Finke, Nanigian, and Waller (2009), Ismailescu and Morey (2012) all find a positive relationship between the size and duration of the redemption fee and fund performance. The main reason for a positive relationship is that the redemption fee allows funds to hold lower amounts of cash to deal with redemptions. Rather than holding cash, the fund puts more money into investments that outperform cash over the long run.

Another type of fee that seems to predict better fund performance is an *incentive fee,* which is a fee that investors pay to reward management for strong performance. Elton, Gruber, and Blake (2003) find that funds offering managerial incentive fees have higher risk-adjusted returns. The authors contend that incentive fees are beneficial because they attract better managers who might earn more. These results are similar to those of Cremers, Driessen, Maenhout, and Weinbaum (2009), who find that funds that have directors with a high ownership stake in the fund, or "skin in the game," significantly outperform funds that have directors with low or no ownership stake.

In sum, researchers find a negative relationship between both expenses and loads and fund outperformance, but recent research shows that this is not always the case as some active fund managers may consistently outperform and hence are worth their fees. Also, certain types of fees such as redemption fees and manager incentive fees are beneficial to performance.

TURNOVER AND TRADING COST

Turnover cost is another type of cost that has been examined in terms of its ability to predict fund performance. The *turnover ratio* measures the percentage of the portfolio's holdings that has changed over the past year. As with the other factors that appear to predict outperformance, the turnover ratio has a mixed history to predict fund performance. Ippolito (1989), Elton, Gruber, Das, and Hlavka (1993), and Chen, Hong, Huang, and Kubik (2004) find no significant relationship between the turnover ratio and fund outperformance. Grinblatt and Titman (1994), Wermers (2000), Chen, Jegadeesh, and Wermers (2000), and Kacperczyk, Sialm, and Zheng (2008) find a positive relationship between the turnover ratio and fund outperformance. Others such as Carhart (1997) and Ang, Chen, and Lin (1998) report a significant negative relationship between the turnover ratio and outperformance. Thus, the turnover ratio does not seem to be a consistent predictor of fund outperformance.

Edelen, Evans, and Kadlec (2013) suggest that the turnover ratio does not incorporate all of the true trading costs. When other costs are considered, these trading costs are predictive of outperformance (i.e., higher trading costs mean worse performance). Specifically, the authors find that the turnover ratio does not account for the so-called *differential cost of fund trades*, which are the costs of trading related to fund size and the type of stock that is being traded (i.e., small cap versus large cap). For example, a larger small cap fund with 50 percent turnover will have much higher costs than a much smaller large cap fund with 100 percent turnover, despite having lower turnover. This result occurs because small cap stocks are less liquid and thus more expensive to trade. To deal with this issue, Edelen et al. devise an adjustment to the turnover rate called *position-adjusted turnover*, which multiplies each fund's turnover by its relative position size. The relative position size is equal to its mean position size (i.e., the total net assets divided by number of holdings) divided by the mean position size of all funds in its market cap category.

Investors can calculate the position-adjusted turnover using data from Morningstar or other data providers. Edelen et al. (2013) document a strong negative relationship between fund performance and turnover. More precisely, they find that funds in the highest quintile of trading costs underperform those funds in the lowest quintile of trading costs by 178 basis points a year. Trading costs may differ depending upon the style of the fund. While the average fund charges investors about 1.44 percent a year in trading costs, the typical small and large cap funds charge 3.17 percent and 0.84 percent, respectively.

Trading cost, as measured by position-adjusted turnover, appears predictive of fund outperformance. However, the study by Edelen et al. (2013) has yet to be replicated or rebutted. As explained, other earlier studies show mixed evidence on whether turnover predicts outperformance.

PAST PERFORMANCE

Past risk-adjusted performance is one of the popular methods used to predict mutual fund performance because investors can simply project past outperformance into the future. Similar to other factors, the research evidence on the effectiveness of this method varies considerably.

Research by Grinblatt and Titman (1992), Hendricks, Patel, and Zeckhauser (1993), and Elton, Gruber, and Blake (1996) find some performance persistence. Their research shows that fund outperformance persists in the next year (Hendricks et al.), over the next three years (Elton et al.), and the next five years (Grinblatt and Titman). These studies also find that poor performance also persists: a poorly performing fund today is likely to underperform in the near future.

Research by Grinblatt, Titman, and Wermers (1995) and Carhart (1997) find that outperformance persistence is due to *momentum stocks*, which are stocks that are previous winners. Carhart determines that the extra transaction costs of buying these momentum stocks offset the gains from following this strategy. He concludes that the best past performance funds earn back their expenses and transaction costs. While performance persists, it does not mean much for investors after expenses and fees. The only performance that is predictive of future results is that of poor performance as losing funds continue to underperform in the future.

More recent studies such as Bollen and Busse (2005) and Fama and French (2010) find similar results to those reported by Carhart (1997). The general consensus is that good performance persists, but for only one to two quarters after controlling for momentum, while poor performance may persist for many years due to high expenses and fees. While using past strong risk-adjusted performance to guide investment decisions can work in very short horizons of one or two quarters, little consistency in predictive ability exists beyond this horizon. Yet, the evidence is clear that investors should avoid poorly performing funds because this performance may persist for many years.

MUTUAL FUND RATINGS

Reviewing mutual fund advertisements suggests that investors do not appear to choose a fund based on expenses, turnover, or even past performance, but on mutual fund ratings. Private providers calculate these ratings using some combination of risk-adjusted past performance. The most famous of the rating systems is Morningstar, which started rating funds in 1986. Other well-known rating providers include Lipper, Value Line, and Standard & Poor's Corporation. Mutual fund rating systems use simple metrics to rate funds, which inherently appeal to investors. For example, Morningstar ratings use star ratings to rate funds, which range from one star (the lowest) to five stars (the highest). These star ratings are alluring to investors because they can use one simple measure to make a complex decision. These ratings are so popular that they are often the only evidence of past winning performance in many well-known mutual fund advertisements. Fund companies such as American Century, Dreyfus, Fidelity, Franklin Resources, Northern Funds, and Strong Funds have all run advertisements emphasizing star ratings rather than their own return history.

Evidence from academic research also shows that investors recognize the importance of mutual fund ratings. Del Guercio and Tkac (2008) find that the Morningstar's star rating has a significant effect on fund flows. They find that a fund's initial 5-star rating produces inflows of 53 percent above the normal flow. In contrast, funds with rating downgrades experience significant outflows beyond what would normally be expected.

Given the importance of these ratings to investors, ample research examines whether the ratings from Morningstar and other rating systems have predictive ability (Blake and Morey 2000; Morey 2002a, b, 2005; Morey and Gottesman 2006). Similar to other previously discussed factors, ratings do not consistently show outperformance. For example, Blake and Morey find that highly rated funds do not subsequently outperform average rated mutual funds. The 5-star funds (the top-rated funds) perform about the same as 3-star rated funds (median-rated funds) after being rated. These findings are robust over one-, three-, and five-year horizons. Phillips and Kinniry (2010) also find similar results in a study sponsored by Vanguard.

By contrast, Morey and Gottesman (2006) examine the predictive ability of an updated Morningstar rating system created in 2002. Over a short, three-year horizon, they find evidence supporting the notion that the new Morningstar rating system can predict future performance. Their evidence shows that higher rated funds significantly outperform lower rated funds. The effect is relatively monotonic as even the next-to-lowest rated funds (2-star funds) significantly outperform the lowest rated funds (1-star funds).

In sum, more recent evidence shows that ratings can predict fund performance, albeit only for a three-year period and based on a new rating system. Earlier studies, however, find that mutual fund ratings have a mixed ability to predict outperformance.

ACTIVENESS OF MUTUAL FUNDS

Measuring the activeness of a mutual fund portfolio to predict future performance has recently received considerable attention. *Activeness* refers to how portfolio's holdings differ from the benchmark index. Kacperczyk, Sialm, and Zheng (2005), Cremers and Petajisto (2009), Cremers, Ferreira, Matos, and Starks (2011), and Petajisto (2013) all document in various ways that the activeness of a portfolio is a good predictor of risk-adjusted mutual fund performance. The more the fund composition consistently deviates from the composition of the benchmark index, the better is the risk-adjusted performance. The explanation for outperformance is that active fund managers can pick better stocks (stock selection), engage in factor or market timing, or both.

Measuring a fund's activeness can be complex. The traditional measure of activeness is to use *tracking error*, which measures the volatility of the difference between a portfolio return and its benchmark index return. However, Cremers and Petajisto (2009) maintain that tracking error is inappropriate as a measure of activeness. They explain their rationale by providing an example with two funds. First, consider a stock picker fund that tries to generate alpha (i.e., a measure of percentage returns in excess of those from a portfolio that has the same beta) by selecting various stocks across many different industries. Second, consider a sector rotation fund that tries to time the industry and sectors to outperform the market but at the same time holds diverse and thus passive positions in those sectors. The stock picker fund will have substantially lower tracking error than the sector rotation fund not because it is less active, but because it is more diversified across different industries. Hence, tracking error as a measure of activeness is inappropriate as stock picker funds are labeled as less active than they are.

To remedy this situation, Cremers and Petajisto (2009) create a new measure of activeness called *active share*, which measures the degree to which the fund's portfolio deviates from the underlying benchmark portfolio. Active share is depicted using Equation 19.1:

$$= \frac{1}{2} \sum_{i=1}^{n} \left| w_{fund,i} - w_{index,i} \right|, \tag{19.1}$$

where $w_{fund,i}$ is the weight of stock i in the fund's portfolio; $w_{index,i}$ is the weight of the same stock in the fund's benchmark index; and the sum is computed over the universe of all assets. Unlike tracking error, this measure does not minimize the activeness of stock-picker funds as it clearly shows the difference in holdings of a fund versus its benchmark index.

Using this active share measure, Cremers and Petajisto (2009) find very strong evidence that active share predicts performance. Over the period 1990 to 2003, they find that U.S. equity funds with consistently high active share measures outperform all other funds over many different horizon periods. They also identify the funds with high active share that outperform their benchmark indexes by 1.13 percent a year after fees and expenses while funds with the lowest active shares underperform their benchmarks by 1.42 percent a year after fees and expenses.

Cremers and Petajisto (2009) find a negative relationship between size and fund performance. Hence, smaller funds predict better performance than larger funds. Similar to Carhart (1997), Cremers and Petajisto also find that the prior one-year risk-adjusted fund performance predicts future one-year performance. Using these size and prior one-year performance results along with active share, they find the most impressive findings of all: funds with the highest active share, smallest assets, and best one-year performance outperform their benchmarks by 6.5 percent a year net of fees and expenses. Hence, Cremers and Petajisto conclude that investors trying to predict winning funds should pick funds with high active share, small fund size, and strong prior one-year returns. Other factors such as expenses are not as important as these factors.

In a follow-up paper, Petajisto (2013) examines the data from January 1990 to December 2009 and finds very similar results to those reported by Cremers and Petajisto (2009). He also examines the performance of these high active share funds during the financial crisis. He finds that over the period January 2008 to December 2009, the high active share funds perform extremely well; funds with the highest active share outperform their benchmarks by 6.09 percent net of fees and expenses.

While the above would seem to show strong support for active share as a predictor of fund performance, a study on Vanguard by Schlanger, Philips, and LaBarge (2012) contradicts the idea. Using later data from 2001 to 2011, they replicate the analysis of Cremer and Petajisto (2009) and Petajisto (2013). Rather than finding a positive relationship between fund performance and active share, they find no significant relationship between fund activeness and performance. Schlanger et al. (2012, p. 13) state: "Active share by itself does not indicate whether a fund will outperform an unmanaged benchmark." This study seems to suggest that active share is not always a predictor of fund performance. The results of Cremers and Petajisto may be time-specific and not robust to later time periods. Hence, some evidence suggests that activeness matters to mutual fund outperformance, while a more recent finding suggests that activeness does not indicate outperformance.

FUND SIZE

Another possible predictor of mutual fund outperformance is fund size. As with other factors, the evidence of size as an effective measure is mixed. Considerable research shows a negative relationship between fund size and fund performance. For example, Chen et al. (2004) examine U.S. diversified mutual funds between 1962 and 1999. They find that a two standard deviation increase in the log of a fund's total assets under management (AUM) in one month decreases monthly risk-adjusted performance by 5.4 to 7.7 basis points in the following month's fund return. This finding means that the largest 2.5 percent of funds in the sample are underperforming the smallest 2.5 percent of funds by 65 to 96 basis points a year because of size alone. Using more recent data, Bhojraj, Cho, and Yehuda (2012) also find a strong negative relationship between size and fund performance.

Chen et al. (2004) investigate the impact of fund style on the relationship between fund size and fund performance. They find that the effect of size on performance is most notable in funds that hold small company stocks but is insignificant for other styles of funds. This finding leads them to conclude that the main reason for the negative impact of size on fund performance is due to liquidity factors. A small-sized fund can invest all of its money in its best ideas because the small size of the fund's positions will not influence the price of those stocks. Moreover, the fund's small size allows the fund to take the optimal amount of the stock. Conversely, a large-sized fund cannot invest in small company stocks without taking very large positions that will affect the stock's price and thus hurt fund performance. Large funds also may have to take bigger positions in the stock than is optimal. Petajisto (2013) finds that large funds are more likely to be *closet index funds* (i.e., to hold a portfolio close to an index despite being actively managed), than other funds because their size forces them to invest in more stocks, thus making them closer to an index fund.

While the result in the previous paragraph seems to make a compelling case for a negative relationship between size and performance, considerable evidence contradicts this idea. Studies by Haslem et al. (2008) and Elton, Gruber, and Blake (2012) find that size and performance are positively related. For example, Elton et al. examine data from 1999 to 2009 and find that risk-adjusted performance increases, albeit weakly, as fund size increases. To explain these findings, the authors note that since expense ratios and management fees decline with size, larger funds should exhibit better post-expense performance.

As previously discussed, fund size is a confounding factor for investors to use when trying to predict fund performance. Two lessons are available for investors trying to predict fund performance based on fund size. First, if an investor is considering a small cap fund, selecting a small-sized fund makes sense. A smaller size allows the fund to more easily invest in small companies without affecting the company's stock price and thus enhances fund performance. Second, if an investor believes that more active funds achieve better performance, then an argument exists for investing in smaller funds because smaller size is typically associated with more active funds. The smaller size allows fund managers to pick the stocks they prefer and in the amounts optimal for the fund. Larger funds, by their size alone, have greater difficulty being substantially different from their underlying benchmark index. Third, for funds other than small cap funds, size does not seem to be a significant factor in predicting outperformance. Yet, some evidence indicates that smaller funds underperform and large funds may be more appropriate for styles other than small cap.

FUND FAMILY SIZE

Fund family size is another issue relating to size. Chen et al. (2004) find a strong positive relationship between the size of the fund family and fund performance. However, the association between fund family size and fund performance is inconsistent. Bhojraj et al. (2012) find that the positive relationship between fund family size and fund performance disappears after 2000. Their explanation is that large institutional investors such as those in large mutual fund families used to receive information from companies before being disclosed to the general public. This allowed the funds in the fund family to have better performance than other funds. In 2000, the Securities and Exchange Commission (SEC) instituted a policy called Regulation Federal Disclosure, which eliminated selective disclosures of information to analysts and institutional investors. After 2000, large fund families did not have an informational advantage over other funds, which led to a decline in their performance. The improved performance of funds in large fund families reported by Chen et al. seems to result from better access to information received before 2000. After the SEC implemented its disclosure requirement, such performance benefits receded.

FUND GOVERNANCE

Fund governance is another characteristic used by researchers to predict performance. Better governed funds should produce better returns for their investors. The assumption is that better governed funds will have better boards of directors that will force the fund to be investor-driven rather than sales-driven. Thus, such funds should pursue policies that consistently have the best interests of the investors in mind. For example, they can close funds that are too large, keep fees fair, and implement redemption fees to stop market timing. These funds could also avoid using *soft dollars* (i.e., benefits provided to an asset manager by a broker-dealer as a result of commissions generated from financial transaction executed by the broker-dealer for client accounts or funds managed by the asset manager). Adopting such policies should improve fund performance. Additionally, better governed funds are likely to better mentor their employees, reward performance and hard work, and listen to employees' views. Thus, these funds should attract and retain top employees and get their employees to work harder than those who work for funds with weaker governance. This differential effort should also enhance fund performance.

Despite these explanations, empirical results on the relationship between governance and fund performance are mixed. Various studies investigate the quality of the board of directors and fund performance (Tufano and Sevick 1997; Del Guercio, Dann, and Partch 2003; Ferris and Yan 2007; Khorana, Tufano, and Wedge 2007; Ding and Wermers 2012). Evidence shows that funds with better boards have lower fees and are more likely to replace poorly performing managers. Yet, such studies also find that the improvement in fund performance from better governance is marginal. For example, Ferris and Yan find that better governance via more independent directors is not significantly related to fund performance.

Another area of research related to fund governance and performance examines the Morningstar Stewardship rating. In 2004, in response to the market-timing and late-trading scandals, Morningstar developed stewardship ratings that rates fund governance. These governance ratings examine five factors of fund governance: (1) board quality, (2) fees, (3) managerial incentives, (4) regulatory issues, and (5) corporate culture. Wellman and Zhou (2008) and Gottesman and Morey (2012) examine the relationship between these stewardship ratings and fund performance and find mixed results. Using two years of data, Wellman and Zhou find some evidence of better governance ratings predicting better fund performance. Yet, using six years of data, Gottesman and Morey find little consistency in the relationship between any of the Morningstar governance factors and fund performance. These results are robust to different performance metrics, time horizons, samples, and adjustments for survivorship bias.

Studies suggest good fund governance does not clearly show better future fund performance. Perhaps good governance allows a fund to avoid a scandal such as the market-timing and late-trading scandals, but it does not guarantee better fund performance.

MANAGER CHARACTERISTICS

This section surveys the literature on the relationship between characteristics of fund managers and performance. These managerial characteristics include education, age, and tenure,

Manager Education

Research examines whether a fund manager's educational background is useful in predicting fund performance. Some evidence shows that manager education matters to fund performance. For example, Golec (1996) and Chevalier and Ellison (1999) use the mean Scholastic Aptitude Test (SAT) score of the school the fund manager attended. They find that funds with managers who attend schools requiring higher mean SAT scores have significantly better risk-adjusted performance than other funds.

Similarly, Gottesman and Morey (2006) find the same effect when examining prestige of the business school that the fund manager attended. They examine the mean Graduate Management Aptitude Test (GMAT) of the business school and whether the school ranks among the *Business Week* Top 30 MBA programs. Gottesman and Morey find a positive and significant relationship between the mean GMAT score of the MBA program from which the fund manager graduated and fund performance between 2000 and 2003.

These results suggest that, after controlling for various effects, a positive relationship exists between the prestige of the fund manager's education and fund performance. One explanation for these results is that managers from more prestigious undergraduate or graduate programs are more intelligent than other managers. Acceptance into a top program requires performing well on standardized tests, possibly implying higher intelligence. This higher intelligence allows the fund manager to outperform. Alternatively, the social connections attained at more prestigious schools could allow for better performance. One can easily imagine a scenario where a mutual fund manager from a top program gets allocations of initial public offerings (IPOs) from a school friend working at an investment bank, while the low-prestige education manager lacks such social connections.

Cohen, Fazzini and Malloy (2008) examine connections between mutual fund managers and corporate board members via shared education networks. They find that portfolio managers place larger bets on firms to which they connect in terms of education (so-called *connected stocks*) and that these connected investments perform significantly better relative to their non-connected investments. Cohen et al. find that a portfolio of connected stocks outperforms non-connected stocks by up to 7.8 percent a year.

If the benefits from education came from access to information rather than intelligence, then the Regulation Fair Disclosure Act that took effect in 2000 should have caused a reduction in information asymmetry that resulted from better social connections. As evidence of this point, Cohen et al. (2008) find that the benefits of having a connected portfolio drop substantially after October 2000, which occur after implementing the Regulation Fair Disclosure Act.

Gottesman and Morey (2006) also discover that some other education variables are unrelated to fund performance. Specifically, they find that whether the manager attained a Chartered Financial Analyst (CFA) designation or holds either a non-MBA masters-level graduate degree or a PhD are generally unrelated to mutual fund performance. These results lend support to the idea that social connections and not experience or education allow managers from prestigious schools to perform better.

Using manager education to predict fund performance can be problematic. Some evidence shows that manager education matters when examining data from the 1990s and early 2000s. Yet, given the new regulations on disclosure, any benefits that might accrue from having a manager with a prestigious education may have disappeared as these benefits seem to be largely due to social connections rather than intelligence.

Manager Age and Tenure

Research evidence is also available on relationships among manager age, tenure, and fund performance. In terms of fund manager age, Golec (1996) and Chevalier and Ellison (1999) find a negative relationship between fund manager age and fund performance. For example, Chevalier and Ellison find that an 8.6 basis point reduction in performance occurs with every additional increase of a fund manager's age. They attribute this to two factors: (1) younger managers work harder because they are more likely to be fired than older managers and (2) younger managers may be better educated than older managers. Chevelier and Ellison also contend that older managers with high performance may have exited the mutual fund industry for hedge funds or other institutional money funds and as a result the remaining older fund managers are inferior. Using more updated data, Gottesman and Morey (2006) find very similar results to those of Chevalier and Ellison regarding manager age and fund performance.

Although some research indicates that funds with younger fund managers may outperform, other evidence suggests that this outperformance may simply be because younger mutual fund managers are more likely to chase momentum stocks. Greenwood and Nagel (2009) find that younger mutual fund managers disproportionately invested in high tech stocks during the peak of the late 1990s stock market bubble and exhibited trend-chasing behavior by increasing their technology stock holdings after quarters with high technology stock returns. Thus, the earlier results showing younger managers perform better than older managers are likely the result of momentum investing rather than managerial skill.

In terms of manager tenure, interpreting the results requires caution. Although Golec (1996) finds a positive relationship between manager tenure and performance, Chevalier and Ellison (1999), Costa, Jakob, and Porter (2006), and Gottesman and Morey (2006) all report that manager tenure is not consistently related to fund performance. Apparently, experience itself is not a consistent predictor of fund outperformance.

Summary and Conclusions

This literature survey reveals much dissonance on what predicts equity mutual fund outperformance. Industry experts often consider expenses and trading costs as the main factors when trying to predict fund performance. Although considerable research shows that lower expenses and trading costs improve performance, other studies suggest that expenses are justified as some high expense managers earn their fees with better performance. Some expenses such as redemption and incentive fees enhance performance. For most factors examined, several sides exist of whether a specific factor predicts outperformance. For example, one study shows that a factor predicts fund outperformance while another reports an opposing finding. This occurs with expenses, turnover, past performance, mutual fund ratings, activeness, fund and family size, fund governance, and various managerial characteristics.

The dissonance is open for interpretation. Even if markets are inefficient, timing the market is very difficult and consequently finding consistent factors that predict outperformance is nearly impossible. Combining this bias with short sample periods creates a recipe for conflicting results.

Some factors appear to help predict outperformance. First, small investors are often better off owning a small fund. These small cap/small-sized funds typically have better performance than small cap/large-sized fund. The small size means that the fund can invest all of its money in its best ideas and take the optimal amount of that stock. Conversely, a large fund may have to invest in other companies that the fund does not favor as much due to its large size.

Second, redemption fees and manager incentive fees help performance. The redemption fees enhance performance because they reduce redemptions and allow the manager to hold less cash. Manager incentive fees seem to work as they incentivize managers to perform well.

Third, some short-term persistence appears in performance but only for several quarters. If investors buy funds based on strong performance for the past one or two quarters, they may gain some outperformance for only a short period in the future. Beyond these factors, few consistently predict outperformance.

Discussion Questions

1. Identify the factors that are most likely to predict fund outperformance.
2. Explain the term *active share* and why it might predict future performance.

3. Discuss how the Regulation Fair Disclosure Act of 2000 affected fund family size and mutual fund performance.
4. Discuss whether some mutual fund managers exhibit skill or luck when they outperform.

References

Ang, James S., Carl R. Chen, and James Wuh Lin. 1998. "Mutual Fund Manager's Efforts and Performance." *Journal of Investing* 7:4, 68–75.

Bhojraj, Sanjeev, Young Jun Cho, and Nir Yehuda. 2012. "Mutual Fund Family Size and Mutual Fund Performance: The Role of Regulatory Changes." *Journal of Accounting Research* 50:3, 647–684,

Blake, Christopher, and Matthew Morey. 2000. "Morningstar Ratings and Mutual Fund Performance." *Journal of Financial and Quantitative Analysis* 35:3, 451–483.

Bollen, Nicolas P. B., and Jeffrey A. Busse. 2005. "Short-Term Persistence in Mutual Fund Performance." *Review of Financial Studies* 18:2, 569–597.

Carhart, Mark. 1997. "On Persistence in Mutual Fund Performance." *Journal of Finance* 52:1, 57–82.

Chen, Joseph, Harrison Hong, Ming Huang, and Jeffrey D. Kubik. 2004. "Does Fund Size Erode Mutual Fund Performance? The Role of Liquidity and Organization." *American Economic Review* 94:5, 1276–1302.

Chen, Hsiu-Lang, Narasimhan Jegadeesh, and Russ Wermers. 2000. "The Value of Active Mutual Fund Management: An Examination of the Stockholdings and Trades of Fund Managers." *Journal of Financial and Quantitative Analysis* 35:3, 343–368.

Chevalier, Judith A., and Glenn D. Ellison. 1999. "Are Some Mutual Fund Managers Better Than Others? Cross-Sectional Patterns in Behavior and Performance." *Journal of Finance* 54:2, 875–899.

Cohen, Lauren, Andrea Fazzini, and Christopher Malloy. 2008. "The Small World of Investing: Board Connections and Mutual Fund Returns." *Journal of Political Economy* 116:5, 951–979.

Costa, Bruce A., Keith Jakob, and Gary E. Porter. 2006. "Mutual Fund Performance and Changing Market Trends 1990–2001: Does Manager Experience Matter?" *Journal of Investing* 15:2, 79–86.

Cremers, Martijn, Joost Driessen, Pascal Maenhout, and David Weinbaum. 2009. "Does Skin in the Game Matter? Director Incentives and Governance in the Mutual Fund Industry." *Journal of Financial and Quantitative Analysis* 44:6, 1345–1373.

Cremers, Martijn, Miguel Ferreira, Pedro Matos, and Laura Starks, 2011. "The Mutual Fund Industry Worldwide: Explicit and Closet Indexing, Fees and Performance." Working Paper, University of Notre Dame.

Cremers, Martijn, and Antti Petajisto. 2009. "How Active Is Your Fund Manager? A New Measure That Predicts Performance." *Review of Financial Studies* 22:9, 3329–3365.

Del Guercio, Diane, Larry Y. Dann, and M. Megan Partch. 2003. "Governance and Boards of Directors in Closed-End Investment Companies." *Journal of Financial Economics* 69:1, 111–152.

Del Guercio, Diane, and Paula A. Tkac. 2008. "Star Power: The Effect of Morningstar Ratings on Mutual Fund Flow." *Journal of Financial and Quantitative Analysis* 43:4, 907–936.

Dellva, Wilfred L., and Gerard T. Olson. 1998. "The Relationship between Mutual Fund Fees and Expenses and Their Effects on Performance." *Financial Review* 33:1, 85–104.

Ding, Bill, and Russ Wermers. 2012. "Mutual Fund Performance and Governance Structure: The Role of Portfolio Managers and Boards of Directors." Working Paper, University of Maryland.

Edelen, Roger, Richard Evans, and Greg Kadlec. 2013. "Shedding Light on 'Invisible' Costs: Trading Costs and Mutual Fund Performance." *Financial Analysts Journal* 69:1, 33–44.

Elton, Edwin J., Martin J. Gruber, and Christopher R. Blake. 1996. "The Persistence of Risk-Adjusted Mutual Fund Performance." *Journal of Business* 69:1, 133–157.

Elton, Edwin J., Martin J. Gruber, and Christopher R. Blake. 2003. "Incentive Fees and Mutual Funds." *Journal of Finance* 58:2, 779–804.

Elton, Edwin J., Martin J. Gruber, and Christopher R. Blake. 2012. "Does Mutual Fund Size Matter? The Relationship between Size and Performance." *Review of Asset Pricing Studies* 2:1, 31–55.

Elton, Edwin J., Martin J. Gruber, Sanjiv Das, and Matthew Hlavka. 1993. "Efficiency with Costly Information: A Reinterpretation of Evidence from Managed Portfolios." *Review of Financial Studies* 6:1, 1–22.

Fama, Eugene, and Kenneth French. 2010. "Luck versus Skill in the Cross-Section of Mutual Fund Returns." *Journal of Finance* 65:5, 1915–1947.

Ferris, Stephen, and Xuemin Yan. 2007. "Do Independent Directors and Chairmen Matter? The Role of Boards of Directors in Mutual Fund Governance." *Journal of Corporate Finance* 13:2–3, 392–420.

Financial Research Corporation. 2002. *Predicting Mutual Fund Performance II: After the Bear*. Boston: Financial Research Corporation Publications.

Finke, Michael, David Nanigian, and William Waller. 2009. "Redemption Fees: Reward for Punishment." Working Paper, Texas Tech University.

Gil-Bazo, Javier, and Pablo Ruiz-Verdu. 2009. "The Relation between Price and Performance in the Mutual Fund Industry." *Journal of Finance* 64:5, 2153–2183.

Golec, Joseph. 1996. "The Effects of Mutual Fund Managers' Characteristics on Portfolio Performance, Risk and Fees." *Financial Services Review* 5:2, 134–149.

Gottesman, Aron, and Matthew Morey. 2006. "Manager Education and Mutual Fund Performance." *Journal of Empirical Finance* 13:2, 145–182.

Gottesman, Aron, and Matthew Morey. 2012. "Does a Mutual Fund's Corporate Culture Predict Fund Performance." *Review of Financial Economics* 21:2, 69–81.

Greenwood, Robin, and Stefan Nagel. 2009. "Inexperienced Investors and Bubbles." *Journal of Financial Economics* 93:2, 239–258.

Grinblatt, Mark, and Sheridan Titman. 1992. "The Persistence of Mutual Fund Performance." *Journal of Finance* 47:5, 1977–1984.

Grinblatt, Mark, and Sheridan Titman. 1994. "A Study of Monthly Mutual Fund Returns and Performance Evaluation Techniques." *Journal of Financial and Quantitative Analysis* 29:3, 419–444.

Grinblatt, Mark, Sheridan Titman, and Russ Wermers. 1995. "Momentum Investment Strategies, Portfolio Performance, and Herding: A Study of Mutual Fund Behavior." *American Economic Review* 85:5, 1088–1105.

Haslem, John A., H. Kent Baker, and David M. Smith. 2008. "Performance and Characteristics of Actively Managed Retail Equity Mutual Funds with Diverse Expense Ratios." *Financial Services Review* 17:1, 49–68.

Hendricks, Darryll, Jayendu Patel, and Richard Zeckhauser. 1993. "Hot Hands in Mutual Funds: Short Run Persistence of Performance, 1974–1988." *Journal of Finance* 48:1, 93–130.

Ippolito, Richard. 1989. "Efficiency with Costly Information: A Study of Mutual Fund Performance, 1965–1984." *Quarterly Journal of Economics* 104:1, 1–23.

Ismailescu, Iuliana, and Matthew Morey. 2012. "Redemption Fees and the Risk-Adjusted Performance of International Equity Mutual Funds." *Journal of Investment Management* 10:3, 21–33.

Kacperczyk, Marcin, Clemens Sialm, and Lu Zheng. 2005. "On the Industry Concentration of Actively Managed Equity Mutual Funds." *Journal of Finance* 60:4, 1983–2011.

Kacperczyk, Marcin, Clemens Sialm, and Lu Zheng. 2008. "Unobserved Actions of Mutual Funds." *Review of Financial Studies* 21:6, 2379–2416.

Khorana, Ajay, Peter Tufano, and Lei Wedge. 2007. "Board Structure, Mergers and Shareholder Wealth: A Study of the Mutual Fund Industry." *Journal of Financial Economics* 85:2, 571–598.

Kinnel, Russell. 2010. "How Expense Ratios and Star Ratings Predict Success." *Morningstar Fund Investor* 18:12, 1–2.

Kosowski, Robert, Allan Timmermann, Hal White, and Russ Wermers. 2006. "Can Mutual Fund 'Stars' Really Pick Stocks? New Evidence from a Bootstrap Analysis." *Journal of Finance* 61:6, 2551–2595.

Morey, Matthew. 2002a. "Mutual Fund Age and Morningstar Ratings." *Financial Analyst Journal* 58:2, 56–63.

Morey, Matthew. 2002b. "Rating the Raters: An Investigation into Mutual Fund Rating Services." *Journal of Investment Consulting* 5:2, 30–50.

Morey, Matthew. 2003. "Should You Carry the Load? A Comprehensive Analysis of the Out-of-Sample Performance of Load and No-Load Mutual Funds." *Journal of Banking and Finance* 27:7, 1245–1271.

Morey, Matthew, 2005. "The Kiss of Death: A 5-Star Morningstar Rating?" *Journal of Investment Management* 3:2, 41–52.

Morey, Matthew, and Aron Gottesman. 2006. "Morningstar Mutual Fund Ratings Redux." *Journal of Investment Consulting* 8:1, 25–42.

Morningstar Principia Data. 2014. January. Chicago: Morningstar.

O'Neal, Edward S. 2004. "Purchase and Redemption Patterns of U.S. Equity Mutual Funds." *Financial Management* 33:1, 63–90.

Petajisto, Antti. 2013. "Active Share and Mutual Fund Performance." *Financial Analysts Journal* 69:4, 73–93.

Phillips, Christopher, and Francis M. Kinniry. 2010. "Mutual Fund Ratings and Future Performance." Working Paper, Vanguard Investments.

Schlanger, Todd, Christopher B. Philips, and Karin Peterson LaBarge. 2012. "The Search for Outperformance: Evaluating Active Share." Working Paper, Vanguard Investments.

Tufano, Peter, and Matthew Sevick. 1997. "Board Structure and Fee-Setting in the U.S. Mutual Fund Industry." *Journal of Financial Economic* 46:3, 321–356.

Wellman, Jay W., and Jian Zhou. 2008. "Corporate Governance and Mutual Fund Performance: A First Look at the Morningstar Stewardship Grades." Working Paper, SUNY at Binghamton.

Wermers, Russ. 2000. "Mutual Fund Performance: An Empirical Decomposition into Stock-Picking Talent, Style, Transaction Costs, and Expenses." *Journal of Finance* 55:4, 1655–1703.

20

Evaluating Mutual Fund Performance within the Stochastic Discount Framework

JONATHAN FLETCHER
Professor, University of Strathclyde

Introduction

Chen and Knez (1996) develop the general framework to evaluate fund performance within the stochastic discount factor approach. Ferson (2003) and Cochrane (2005) provide reviews of the stochastic discount factor approach to asset pricing. A *stochastic discount factor* is a random variable that can be used to discount random payoffs across different states of the world to estimate the expected value or cost of the payoff given the information available to investors. The attraction of the stochastic discount factor approach is that most asset pricing models can be written as alternative candidate models of the candidate stochastic discount factor. Most existing performance measures can be derived as special cases of the stochastic discount factor approach (Chen and Knez 1996; Ferson 2010, 2013a, b).

This chapter presents an overview of the stochastic discount factor approach to evaluate mutual fund performance. The chapter begins with evaluating fund performance within the stochastic discount factor approach. It next considers the two main approaches used to construct candidate stochastic discount factor models to evaluate fund performance. The chapter then examines the weight-based performance measures of Ferson and Mo (2013) in which the portfolio weights held by mutual funds are available. The chapter concludes with a review of empirical evidence of mutual fund performance using the stochastic discount factor approach.

Evaluating Fund Performance

Ross (1978), Harrison and Kreps (1979), and Hansen and Richard (1987), among others, show that if the law of one price (LOP) holds in financial markets, then a stochastic discount factor m_{t+1}, shown in Equation 20.1, exists such that:

$$p_{it} = E\left(m_{t+1}x_{it+1} \mid Z_t\right) \textit{ for } i = 1, \ldots, N, \tag{20.1}$$

where p_{it} is the cost of asset i at time t; x_{it+1} is the payoff of asset i at time $t + 1$; Z_t is the information set available to investors at time t; and N is the number of *primitive assets*, which is the set of assets in which investors can trade. Equation 20.1 states that the cost of any asset i at time t is equal to the conditional expected value of the risk-adjusted payoff at time $t + 1$. The LOP states that any two assets with identical payoffs must sell for the same price. If financial markets satisfy the no arbitrage (NA) restriction, where any asset with the probability of a positive payoff in at least one state and zero otherwise must sell for a positive price, then m_{t+1} will be positive in every state of nature (Cochrane 2005).

When the payoff of asset i equals the gross return (1 + return) of asset i (R_{it}), the cost will equal one. When the payoff of asset i equals the excess return of asset i (r_{it}), the cost will equal zero. Using the definition of covariance with gross returns, Equation 20.1 can be rewritten as:

$$E\left(R_{it+1}|Z_t\right) = 1/E\left(m_{t+1}|Z_t\right) - \left[cov\left(m_{t+1}, R_{it+1}|Z_t\right)/E\left(m_{t+1}|Z_t\right)\right]. \quad (20.2)$$

Equation 20.2 states that the conditional expected gross return on asset i depends upon two terms: $1/E\left(m_{t+1}|Z_t\right)$ and $cov\left(m_{t+1}, R_{it+1}|Z_t\right)/E\left(m_{t+1}|Z_t\right)$. The $cov\left(m_{t+1}, R_{it+1}|Z_t\right)$ term captures the risk adjustment implied by the stochastic discount factor. Assets with a negative conditional covariance between m_{t+1} and gross returns have higher conditional expected gross returns.

Chen and Knez (1996) develop the stochastic discount factor approach to evaluate fund performance. Consider a fund manager who trades in the N primitive assets using information set Ω_t, which includes Z_t. The gross return by the fund is given by $R_{pt+1} = x(\Omega_t)'R_{t+1}$, where $x(\Omega_t)$ is the $(N,1)$ vector of optimal weights in the primitive assets, which are assumed to sum to 1 and R_{t+1} is the $(N,1)$ vector of gross returns of the N primitive assets. The uninformed investor (client) also trades in the N primitive assets. Whereas the uninformed investor does not use any public information and, Z_t is a constant. Chen and Knez show that Equation 20.3 gives the fund's unconditional performance:

$$\alpha_p = E\left(m_{t+1}R_{pt+1}\right) - 1, \quad (20.3)$$

where α_p is zero, the fund has neutral performance. When α_p is positive (negative), the fund is interpreted as having superior (inferior) performance. When uninformed investors use public information, Equation 20.4 gives the fund's conditional performance:

$$\alpha_{pt} = E\left(m_{t+1}R_{pt+1}|Z_t\right) - 1. \quad (20.4)$$

Ferson (2013b) points out that $\alpha_p = E\left(\alpha_{pt}\right)$.

Two main approaches are available to estimate the conditional performance of the fund α_{pt}. De Souza and Lynch (2012) model α_{pt} as a linear function of Z_t. Ferson, Henry, and Kisgen (2006a) model α_{pt} using dummy variables of Z_t. To show both approaches, assume Z_t only comprises one lagged information variable, such as the *term spread* which is the difference in the yields between long-term and short-term government bonds. De Souza and Lynch assume that α_{pt} is a linear function of Z_t

given by $\alpha_{pt} = a_0 + a_1 Z_t$, and Ferson et al. assume that $\alpha_{pt} = a_0 + a_L D_L + a_H D_H$, where D_L and D_H are dummy variables for Z_t, which equals 1 when Z_t is lower than normal (D_L) and equals 1 when Z_t is higher (D_H). Ferson et al. allow the fund's conditional performance to vary across only three states, but point out that more dummy variables could be used.

The fund performance measures in Equations 20.3 and 20.4 use the gross returns of the fund. If the fund's excess returns are used $r_{pt+1} = R_{pt+1} - R_{Bt+1}$, where R_{Bt+1} is the gross return at time $t + 1$ of a given benchmark return such as the risk-free return, then the performance measures become $\alpha_p = E(m_{t+1} r_{pt+1})$ and $\alpha_{pt} = E(m_{t+1} r_{pt+1} | Z_t)$. Ferson et al. (2006a) point out that if $m_t + 1$ correctly prices R_{Bt+1}, then using either the gross returns or excess returns of the fund will result in the same α_p.

Ferson (2013b) highlights the link between the stochastic discount factor alpha and the alpha from traditional performance measures such as Jensen (1968). Suppose the traditional alpha is defined as $E(R_{pt+1} - R_{Bt+1} | Z_t)$. The R_{Bt+1} for the Jensen measure using the capital asset pricing model (CAPM) is given by $(1 - b_p) R_{ft+1} + b_p R_{mt+1}$, where R_{ft+1} is the gross risk-free return at time, $t + 1$; $R_{mt} + 1$ is the gross return of the market portfolio at time $t + 1$; and b_p is the fund's market beta from the time-series regression of the excess fund returns (over the risk-free return) on a constant and the excess returns on the market index. The benchmark return passively combines the risk-free asset and the market portfolio that has the same b_p as the fund. This can be generalized to multifactor models.

Ferson (2013b) shows that α_{pt} can be written as Equation 20.5:

$$\alpha_{pt} = E(m_{t+1} | Z_t)\, E(R_{pt+1} - R_{Bt+1} | Z_t) + Cov(m_{t+1}, R_{pt+1} - R_{Bt+1} | Z_t) \qquad (20.5)$$

or if Z_t is a constant $\alpha_p = E(m_{t+1}) E(R_{pt+1} - R_{Bt+1}) + Cov(m_{t+1}, R_{pt+1} - R_{Bt+1})$. *If* $Cov(m_{t+1}, R_{pt+1} - R_{Bt+1}) = 0$, then α_p will equal the traditional alpha ignoring $E(m_t + 1)$, which is a number just below 1 (Cochrane 2005). The $cov(m_{t+1}, R_{pt+1} - R_{Bt+1})$ term will only equal 0 when $cov(m_{t+1}, R_{pt+1}) = cov(m_{t+1}, R_{Bt+1})$. When this condition holds or when $cov(m_{t+1}, R_{pt+1} | Z_t) = cov(m_{t+1}, R_{Bt+1} | Z_t))$, Ferson defines R_{Bt+1} as an appropriate benchmark.

Interpreting fund performance depends upon how fund returns are measured. Aragon and Ferson (2008) define investment ability as the situation in which the fund has a positive α_p when returns are measured gross of all trading costs and expenses. When the fund returns are measured net of all trading costs and expenses and the fund delivers a positive α_p, Aragon and Ferson define this process as capturing the value added to investors. A fund manager might have investment ability but not add value to investors either by excessive trading or by charging high expenses.

Chen and Knez (1996) explore the conditions that define an admissible performance measure. The key condition is that any trading strategy that can be achieved by an uninformed investor should be given zero performance. This condition is satisfied whenever m_{t+1} correctly prices the N primitive assets. Chen and Knez and Farnsworth, Ferson, Jackson, and Todd (2002) show that when Equation 20.1 holds for m_{t+1}, then $\alpha_{pt} = 0$ for funds that trade without cost in the N primitive assets using only the information in Z_t. The existence of an admissible performance measure is equivalent to the existence of an admissible stochastic discount factor.

Chen and Knez (1996) show that for admissible performance measures to exist, the LOP must hold in financial markets. When the admissible stochastic discount factors are positive in every state of nature, NA admissible stochastic discount factors provide NA admissible performance measures. When markets are incomplete (i.e., when an investor cannot buy any contingent claim), the fund's performance value is not unique unless the fund is given zero performance by every admissible stochastic discount factor. This situation only arises when the payoff of the fund's portfolio can be perfectly replicated by a portfolio of the primitive assets. Chen and Knez show that fund performance is essentially arbitrary when using LOP admissible stochastic discount factors. The same fund can be given positive performance by one LOP admissible stochastic discount factor and a negative performance by another.

When using NA admissible stochastic discount factors to evaluate fund performance, Chen and Knez (1996) show that fund performance is still sensitive to the NA admissible stochastic discount factor used. However, if the fund is given positive performance by an NA admissible stochastic discount factor, then Chen and Knez show that the fund adds value at the margin for at least one investor. This result follows, as an NA admissible stochastic discount factor can be viewed as the marginal utility growth for a client since positive stochastic discount factors are an implication of optimal investment/consumption decisions. Ahn, Cao, and Chretien (2009) extend the analysis of Chen and Knez and derive the lower and upper performance bounds for a fund implied by the set of NA admissible stochastic discount factors that correctly price the primitive assets.

The analysis of Chen and Knez (1996) and the empirical results in Ahn et al. (2009) imply that fund performance is likely to be sensitive to the NA admissible stochastic discount factor used. This relationship mirrors the sensitivity of fund performance to the benchmark model from traditional performance measures such as Lehmann and Modest (1987). Yet, in the latter case, the benchmark models used to evaluate fund performance are often inadmissible as they do not correctly price the N primitive assets (Hodrick and Zhang 2001) and can often take on negative stochastic discount factor values, which contradicts the NA restriction (Wang and Zhang 2012).

Ferson and Lin (2014) extend the analysis by Chen and Knez (1996) by addressing whether a client should buy a positive alpha fund. Ferson and Lin assume that the client makes optimal investment and consumption decisions at each time t to maximize a time-separable, concave, and increasing utility function, which is captured by an indirect value function. The client will trade in the N primitive assets until Equation 20.1 holds using $m_{t+1} = \beta J'(W_{t+1}) / u'(C_t)$, where β is the subjective discount factor of the client; $J(W_{t+1})$ is the indirect utility function of wealth at time $t + 1$; and $u(C_t)$ is the utility of consumption at time t. The stochastic discount factor captures the client's marginal utility growth.

Ferson and Lin (2014) assume that the client has the opportunity of investing in a fund that trades in the N primitive assets and provides a gross return $R_{pt+1} = x(\Omega_t)'R_{t+1}$. Where $\alpha_{pt} \neq 0$, the client will adjust their optimal consumption/investment decisions to the new opportunity until $\alpha_{pt} = 0$. Proposition 1 of their paper derives the optimal amount that the client invests in the fund and shows that the client will buy the fund if $\alpha_{pt} > 0$. This result holds regardless of the reason the fund's alpha is positive, which is an encouraging result given the problems of interpreting traditional alphas

(Ferson 2013a, b). Ferson (2013b) shows that if the indirect value function is a quadratic function of wealth, then an informed investor will generate a positive alpha.

According to the analysis of Ferson and Lin (2014), the relevant benchmark is the marginal utility of the client. However, when markets are incomplete, marginal utility growth will vary across clients, so fund performance is clientele-specific. Investor heterogeneity in terms of different marginal utility growth implies that different investors could evaluate the same fund in different ways. Ferson (2013a, 2013b) argues that developing clientele-specific performance measures is an important issue in future fund performance research.

Approaches to Evaluating Fund Performance

Two main approaches are available when proposing candidate stochastic discount factor models to evaluate fund performance. The first approach is to use a stochastic discount factor from a specific asset pricing model such as the CAPM or consumption CAPM. The second approach is to use a stochastic discount factor based on weaker economic restrictions than a full parametric asset pricing model such as the LOP and NA restrictions as used by Chen and Knez (1996). This section considers both approaches.

The most popular stochastic discount factor models to evaluate fund performance are linear factor models. Linear factor models such as the CAPM or multifactor models such as the arbitrage pricing theory (APT) (Ross 1976) and the inter-temporal CAPM (Merton 1973) imply that the stochastic discount factor is a linear function of the K factors in the model given by Equation 20.6:

$$m_{t+1} = a_t + \Sigma_{k=1}{}^{K} b_{kt} f_{kt+1}, \tag{20.6}$$

where a_t is the constant term; b_{kt} is the slope coefficient on the kth factor, $k = 1, \ldots K$; f_{kt+1} is the value of the kth factor at time $t + 1$; and K is the number of factors in the model. The stochastic discount factor coefficients a_t and b_{kt} are time-varying and are functions of the investors' information set at time t. In Equation 20.6, the stochastic discount factor is defined as a conditional factor model. If a_t and b_{kt} are constant over time, the model is known as an *unconditional factor model.*

To implement the conditional factor models in Equation 20.6, the standard approach used by Cochrane (1996) and Jagannathan and Wang (1996) among others is to model a_t and b_t as a linear function of a few lagged information variables in Z_t. To illustrate using the conditional CAPM, define z_t as the value of a single lagged information variable in Z_t and assume that $a_t = a_0 + a_1 z_t$ and $b_t = b_0 + b_1 z_t$. These assumptions imply that the corresponding conditional CAPM stochastic discount factor is given by Equation 20.7:

$$m_{t+1} = a_0 + a_1 z_t + b_0 r_{mt+1} + b_1 z_t r_{mt+1}, \tag{20.7}$$

where r_{mt+1} is the excess return on the market portfolio at time $t + 1$. Cochrane (1996, 2005) define the $z_t r_{mt+1}$ term as a scaled factor. A concern about this approach when $K > 1$ is that the number of coefficients in the stochastic discount factor can increase sharply by including more lagged information variables, increasing the danger of over fitting the data (Hodrick and Zhang 2001; Dittmar 2002).

The econometric method used to estimate the stochastic discount factor coefficients in the linear factor models and fund performance is to use the generalized method of moments (GMM) estimation of Hansen (1982). GMM is an extremely flexible estimation tool that relies on weak distributional assumptions, which do not require normality, and the statistical tests can be corrected for heteroskedasticity and/or serial correlation. A two-step approach can be used to evaluate fund performance. First, the parameters in the stochastic discount factor are estimated to minimize a weighted sum of squared pricing errors of the N primitive assets. Second, using the fitted values of the stochastic discount factor from step one, the fund's performance can then be evaluated using the sample versions of Equations 20.3 and 20.4. An alternative approach is to estimate the parameters in the stochastic discount factor and fund performance jointly as Farnsworth et al. (2002) do. They point out that the joint approach is much more efficient since estimation error of stochastic discount factor parameters is considered in the standard errors of the fund performance measures.

Farnsworth et al. (2002) offer several implementation issues when using the stochastic discount factor approach to evaluate fund performance. The gross returns on a short-term Treasury bill should be included as one of the primitive assets to tie down the expected value of the candidate stochastic discount factor to be slightly less than one (Dahlquist and Soderlind 1999). When using linear factor models with traded factors, the stochastic discount factor model should be estimated to correctly price not only the gross returns of the Treasury bill but also the excess returns of the factors in the model. This pricing can be accomplished by including the gross returns on the short-term Treasury bill and the excess returns on the K factors in the set of primitive assets as in De Souza and Lynch (2012) and Ferson and Mo (2013). However, this approach does not guarantee that the factor model will correctly price a broader range of primitive assets.

Farnsworth et al. (2002) show that when estimating fund performance as in Equation 20.3 using the GMM, both the estimated fund performance and the standard error are invariant to the number of funds in the GMM estimation. As a result, the GMM estimation can be conducted for one fund at a time. Ferson et al. (2006a) generalize this result when estimating the conditional time-varying fund performance.

The main downside of using linear factor models to evaluate fund performance is that the model might be an inadmissible model, thus assigning non-zero performance to passive trading strategies that involve no skill. Chan, Dimmock, and Lakonishok (2009) and Cremers, Petajisto, and Zitzewitz (2013) highlight problems in using both the Fama and French (1993) and Carhart (1997) models in fund performance. Cremers et al. find that different passive benchmark indexes have significant performance relative to both models.

The second main approach to evaluate fund performance is to estimate stochastic discount factors based on weaker economic restrictions than a full asset pricing model. Chen and Knez (1996) use the minimum second moment LOP and NA admissible stochastic discount factors of Hansen and Jagannathan (1991) to evaluate U.S. mutual fund performance (Dahlquist and Soderlind 1999). Hansen and Jagannathan develop volatility bounds of admissible stochastic discount factors in a given set of N primitive assets. The unconditional LOP volatility bounds using gross asset returns are solved as finding m_{t+1} in Equation 20.8 such that:

$$Min\ Var(m_{t+1})\ subject\ to\ E(m_{t+1}R_{it+1}) = 1\ for\ i = 1, \ldots, N\ and\ E(m_{t+1}) = Target\ E(m). \tag{20.8}$$

The NA volatility bounds are estimated by adding the restriction $m_{t+1} \geq 0$. Ahn et al. (2009) propose the maximum variance NA admissible stochastic discount factor to evaluate fund performance, which is given by the admissible stochastic discount factor with the highest volatility for a given target $E(m)$. Almeida and Garcia (2013a, 2013b) develop an alternative approach to using the Hansen and Jagannathan (1991) volatility bounds using minimum discrepancy (M_D) admissible stochastic discount factors to evaluate hedge fund performance, which takes into account higher moments of NA admissible stochastic discount factors.

Chretien and Kammoun (2013) use the good-deal bounds of Cochrane and Saa-Requejo (2000) to assess mutual fund performance. The good-deal bounds of Cochrane and Saa-Requejo place a restriction on the second moment of admissible stochastic discount factors $E(m^2)$ by restricting the maximum Sharpe (1966) ratio available in the economy. Equation 20.9 gives the performance measure used by Chretien and Kammoun:

$$\alpha_p = sup(m_{t+1})\, E\left(m_{t+1}R_{pt+1}\right) - 1, \tag{20.9}$$

subject to $E\left(m_{t+1}R_{it+1}\right) = 1$ for $I = 1, \ldots, N$ and $E\left(m_{t+1}{}^2\right) \leq (1+h^2)/R^2{}_f$, where h is the maximum Sharpe ratio allowed and R_f is the gross risk-free return. Chretien and Kammoun interpret their performance measure as the performance of the mutual fund's best clientele, linking to the analysis of Ferson and Lin (2014). However, without the NA restriction, the admissible stochastic discount factor can take on negative fitted values.

The advantage of using admissible stochastic discount factors to evaluate fund performance is that they avoid the "bad model" problem of Fama (1998) that affects linear factor models. The admissible stochastic discount factor might have poor pricing performance in a different set of primitive assets. The choice of the primitive assets used is critical. The set of primitive assets should reflect the investment opportunities available to the fund manager (Chen and Knez 1996).

Whether using linear factor models or admissible stochastic discount factors, the set of payoffs provided by primitive assets can be extended to incorporate the effect of conditioning information. Cochrane (1996, 2005) shows that the unconditional implications of conditioning information can be included by augmenting the investment universe of the N payoffs to include additional scaled payoffs. Scaled payoffs are created by multiplying each of the N payoffs by each of the lagged information variables in Z_t. The investment universe now contains N^*L payoffs, where L is the number of lagged information variables. Cochrane points out that the scaled payoffs for any z_t in Z_t is the payoff of a dynamic trading strategy. Given the large number of potential payoffs available, studies typically only use a few lagged information variables.

Weight-Based Performance Measures

When researchers or investors have access to the fund's portfolio weights, they can use weight-based performance measures to evaluate performance. Ferson (2013a) shows that by substituting $R_{pt+1} = x(\Omega_t)'R_{t+1}$ into Equation 20.4 and using the covariance decomposition, then Equation 20.10 emerges:

$$\alpha_{pt} = cov\left(m_{t+1}R_{t+1}'x(\Omega_t)|Z_t\right). \quad (20.10)$$

If Z_t is a constant, then $\alpha_p = cov(m_{t+1}R_{t+1}'x(\Omega_t))$. The stochastic discount factor alpha is equal to the covariance between $m_{t+1}R_{t+1}$ and $x(\Omega_t)$. Ferson points out that this measure differs from the traditional weight-based measures of Grinblatt and Titman (1993) and Daniel, Grinblatt, Titman, and Wermers (1997), which ignore the risk adjustment implied by the stochastic discount factor m_{t+1}. Ferson (2013b) shows that the traditional weight-based measures are only appropriate under restrictive conditions.

Ferson and Mo (2013) develop the first weight-based performance measures using the stochastic discount factor approach and provide a decomposition of overall fund performance into different components. They assume a linear factor model for the stochastic discount factor, although nonlinear stochastic discount factor models can be used. Ferson and Mo estimate the coefficients to price the excess K factor returns and the gross risk-free return correctly.

Ferson and Mo (2013) provide a decomposition of fund performance by regressing the excess returns of the N individual assets in which the fund invests, on the K factor excess returns as Equation 20.11:

$$r_{t+1} = a_0 + br_{Bt+1} + u_{t+1}, \quad (20.11)$$

where r_{t+1} is a $(N,1)$ matrix of excess returns at time $t+1$; r_{Bt+1} is a $(K,1)$ vector of excess returns of the K factors are time $t+1$; β is a (N,K) matrix of factor betas; and u_{t+1} is a $(N,1)$ matrix of residuals at time $t+1$. Suppressing the time subscript, Ferson and Mo define the idiosyncratic returns as $v = a_0 + u$. A fund manager forms a portfolio of the N assets (x) $r_p = (x'b)r_B + x'v$, where $w' = x'b$ are the fund's asset allocation weights relative to the K factors. They estimate the asset allocation weights using a bottom-up approach with daily excess returns on the N assets and K factors.

Ferson and Mo (2013) show that substituting the formulae for r_p into the definition of the stochastic discount factor α_p (unconditional) gives the decomposition for α_p in Equation 20.12:

$$\alpha_p = aCov(w'r_B) - b'E\left[(r_Br_B' - E(r_Br_B))\,w\right] + E[(a - b'r_B)x'v]. \quad (20.12)$$

The first term in Equation 20.12 captures the fund's level timing ability for the K factors (α_m). The second term captures the fund's volatility timing ability fund for the K factors (α_σ). The last term captures the fund's stock selection ability (α_s). Ferson and Mo compare their weight-based measures with the traditional weight-based measures. The Grinblatt and Titman (1993) weight-based measure misses the volatility timing component and part of the stock selection component of fund performance.

The characteristics selectivity (CS) measure of Daniel et al. (1997) also misses part of the stock selection component.

Ferson and Mo (2013) use the GMM to estimate their weight-based measures of fund performance. The attraction of their approach is that beyond estimating the stochastic discount factor coefficients in the linear factor model, only three parameters need to be estimated for a given fund. Overall fund performance is given by $\alpha_p = \alpha_m + \alpha_\sigma + \alpha_s$ and standard errors can be computed using the delta method. Ferson and Mo also use conditional factor models to evaluate fund performance. Their implicit assumption is that the linear factor models correctly price the N primitive assets; otherwise problems of interpretation may occur based on inadmissible stochastic discount factor models. The attraction of using weight-based performance measures is that they can capture the fund manager's investment ability, since the fund returns are gross of all trading costs and expenses (Aragon and Ferson 2008). Using weight-based performance measures will likely continue to grow in mutual fund performance research.

Empirical Evidence

This section provides a short survey of mutual fund performance, primarily focusing on U.S. mutual funds, using the stochastic discount factor approach. Chen and Knez (1996) evaluate the performance of 68 U.S. equity mutual funds between January 1968 and December 1989 using their unconditional LOP and NA measures and their conditional LOP measure. The set of primitive assets includes the gross returns on 12 industry portfolios. They add scaled gross returns for the conditional LOP measure using the lagged one-month Treasury-bill yield, the dividend yield on the NYSE market index, and the term spread. Chen and Knez find no evidence of significant superior performance ability by the average fund or for different investment sectors of funds. Annually, the average fund LOP α_p is −1.026 percent and the average NA α_p is −1.03 percent.

Two issues arise with the findings of Chen and Knez (1996). The first issue is that they do not include the gross return of a Treasury bill in their set of primitive assets. Dahlquist and Soderlind (1999) show that a failure to do so can result in evaluating fund performance using a mean-variance inefficient benchmark with the LOP measure. The second issue is that Farnsworth et al. (2002) show that the LOP-based measures of Chen and Knez delivers negative performance to artificial stock selection strategies without skill.

Farnsworth et al. (2002) conduct an extensive study of the sensitivity of fund performance relative to alternative stochastic discount factor models. They consider four groups of stochastic discount factor models. The first group consists of linear factor models based on the CAPM, Fama and French (1993), a three-factor portfolio model in which the factors include the index excess returns on the S&P 500, long-term government bonds, and low-grade corporate bonds, a three-factor APT model using statistical factors, and a four-factor economic model. Farnsworth et al. use both unconditional and conditional factor models. The second and third groups of models are the unconditional and conditional Chen and Knez (1996) LOP measure and the numeraire portfolio of Long (1990). The final model is the nonlinear stochastic discount factor model of Bakshi and Chen (1998).

Farnsworth et al. (2002) estimate the stochastic discount factor models using the gross returns and scaled gross returns of the Treasury bill, two long-term bond portfolios, large cap, small cap, value, growth, momentum, and contrarian stock portfolios. They construct the scaled gross returns using short-term interest rates and the market dividend yield as the lagged information variables. Farnsworth et al. construct artificial stock selection and market-timing strategies to assess how well the stochastic discount factor models can assign zero performance to trading strategies with no skill and identify significant superior performance for strategies with varying degrees of skill. Their evidence shows a downward bias in the models when evaluating the performance of stock selection strategies with no skill, with an average underperformance of –0.19 percent for unconditional models and –0.12 percent for conditional models. Most of the models, except the numeraire portfolio and economic factor model, can detect significant superior performance in the stock selection and market-timing strategies with skill.

Farnsworth et al. (2002) use different stochastic discount factor models to evaluate the performance of 188 equity mutual funds between 1977 and 1993.The average fund performance across models is –0.06 percent for unconditional models and –0.09 percent for conditional models. The results show little evidence of significant superior performance by individual funds. Farnsworth et al. point out that after adding back annual expenses and a proxy for trading costs, the average fund performs better than the artificial trading strategies with no skill. The performance of the funds is insensitive to the choice of the stochastic discount factor model as the performance measures across funds are highly positively correlated with one another. This finding is interesting given the sensitivity of regression-based performance measures to the chosen benchmark model as in Lehmann and Modest (1987). Fletcher and Forbes (2004) find similar results in U.K. equity open-end mutual funds.

Ferson et al. (2006a) evaluate the conditional performance of U.S. government bond mutual funds using stochastic discount factors based on continuous time term structure models between 1986 and 2000. The term structure models used include the one-factor, two-factor, and three-factor affine models, as well as the Brennan and Schwartz (1979) two-factor model. Ferson et al. use reduced form versions of the models where m_{t+1} is an exponential function of the underlying factors in the model. Applying the continuous time models to monthly data leads to additional time-averaged factors in the stochastic discount factor. Ferson et al. contend that the time-averaged factors help to control for interim trading bias in which the fund manager trades more often than the return observation interval (Goetzmann, Ingersoll, and Ivkovic 2000; Ferson and Khang 2002).

Ferson et al. (2006a) examine the ability of the alternative term structure models to correctly price passive bond portfolios and dynamic trading strategies, which allow for interim trading. They find that that the three-factor affine model is the most reliable model among those considered. Ferson et al. also find that the equal-weighted portfolio of all government bond funds relative to the three-factor affine model has negative conditional performance, which is statistically significant in some states due to low standard errors but is not large in economic terms.

Ferson, Kisgen, and Henry (2006b) examine the conditional performance of U.S. fixed income mutual funds between 1985 and 1999 using a similar approach to Ferson et al. (2006a). They extend the default-free term structure stochastic discount factor models in Ferson et al. (2006a) to include an additional factor to account because fixed-income funds hold securities subject to default risk and mortgage prepayment risk. Ferson et al. (2006b) consider additional factors, such as the credit spread, industrial production, and corporate illiquidity, for which they only use one additional factor at a time in the stochastic discount factor model. They use the stochastic discount factor models to evaluate the conditional performance of equal-weighted portfolios of bond funds sorted by investment sector and fund characteristics such as size and expenses, among others. Their evidence shows little cross-sectional variation in conditional performance across the characteristic sorted bond portfolios. Conditional performance varies more across the investment sector portfolios. Mortgage funds have significant negative conditional performance in several states relative to the different stochastic discount factor models.

Ahn et al. (2009) assess the performance of 320 U.S. funds between January 1984 and December 1997 using their NA performance bounds. The NA performance bounds are estimated using NA admissible stochastic discount factors from a set of primitive assets including the gross returns of 20 industry portfolios, short-term and long-term bond portfolios, and scaled gross returns of the 22 portfolios using the lagged credit spread and dividend yield on the CRSP value-weighted market index. The expected value of the NA admissible stochastic discount factors is equal to the inverse of the average gross return of the one-month Treasury bill during the sample period. Ahn et al. find that the NA performance bounds for individual funds are wide. Out of the 320 funds, 80.3 percent have NA performance bounds near zero, suggesting that fund performance is sensitive to the NA admissible stochastic discount factor used. Most of the remaining funds are assigned negative performance. Considering sampling error of the bounds at the 5 percent significance level, Ahn et al. find 49 funds have significant, negative performance at the lower NA bound and neutral performance at the upper NA bound. However, 33 funds have a significant, positive upper NA bound and a neutral, lower NA bound. Fletcher and Ntozi-Obwale (2008) find similar results to Ahn et al. in U.K. equity open-end funds.

The results in Ahn et al. (2009) show that mutual fund performance becomes more favorable when evaluating the fund performance using the upper NA bound. The difference between the lower and upper NA performance bounds is wide suggesting a wide range in estimated performance exists by a given fund. Different investors can evaluate the same fund very differently.

Ferson and Lin (2014) examine the impact of investor heterogeneity on traditional regression-based performance measures and find an economically significant impact. The disagreement among investors is as important as the chosen factor model used to evaluate fund performance and the sampling error in the traditional alphas. Fletcher and Marshall (2014) find similar results in U.K. equity closed-end funds.

Bessler, Drobetz, and Zimmermann (2009) examine the performance of German equity mutual funds between January 1994 and December 2003 and Gusset and Zimmermann (2012) evaluate Swiss equity mutual funds between January 2000 and August 2011. Both studies use similar stochastic discount factor models as

Farnsworth et al. (2002) and also compare the stochastic discount factor performance measures to the regression-based performance measures. Both studies find negative average performance by funds, which is much more negative when using the stochastic discount factor approach. Bessler et al. maintain that the difference in performance between the stochastic discount factor and regression approaches for a given linear factor model stems from using a large set of primitive assets to estimate stochastic discount factor models. For the CAPM, when the stochastic discount factor model is estimated to only correctly price the gross Treasury-bill return and the excess market return, the performance between the two approaches is similar.

De Souza and Lynch (2012) examine whether the conditional performance of U.S. equity mutual funds is counter-cyclical by using equal weighted portfolios of funds sorted by investment sector and size. Several studies such as those conducted by Moskowitz (2000), Kosowski (2011), and Kacperczyk, van Nieuwerburgh, and Veldkamp (2014 find that mutual funds perform better in recessions using the NBER recession indicators, despite negative overall fund performance. De Souza and Lynch criticize these conditional performance studies, since they use information, such as the NBER recession indicator, which is unavailable to investors in real time. They advocate using lagged information variables to evaluate conditional fund performance since they are known to investors in real time.

De Souza and Lynch (2012) evaluate conditional fund performance relative to the Fama and French (1993) and Carhart (1997) factor models using the lagged dividend yield on the New York Stock Exchange (NYSE) market index and the term spread, in which only one lagged information variable is used at a time. Their approach uses the GMM approach of Lynch and Wachter (2013, which allows for different lengths of time-series between the data. De Souza and Lynch estimate the stochastic discount factor models using data available from January 1927. The sector/size portfolios of funds have different start dates. De Souza and Lynch find that conditional performance of fund portfolios is often time-varying. However, in contrast to Moskowitz (2000), Kosowski (2011), and Kacperczyk et al. (2014), no robust pattern occurs in the time variation of fund performance. In some cases, the fund portfolios have counter-cyclical performance but in others the performance is pro-cyclical.

Ferson and Mo (2013) evaluate the performance of mutual fund portfolios using their weight-based performance measures using the Carhart (1997) model as the stochastic discount factor in their main tests. When sorting fund portfolios by fund characteristics such as expenses, turnover, return gap of Kacperczyk, Sialm, and Zheng (2008), and the active share of Cremers and Petajisto (2009), neutral performance occurs using the weight-based measures. However, fund portfolios sorted by the factor model R^2 of Amihud and Goyenko (2013) lead to significant differences in performance across fund portfolios. The decile portfolio of funds with the lowest R^2 provides significantly higher total performance than the decile portfolio of funds with the highest R^2, but no significant differences exist in the individual components of performance between the two portfolios. The low R^2 portfolio provides a significant positive total performance at the 0.10 level but none of the individual components are statistically significant. When sorting funds by their reaction to market volatility by changing their market beta, the decile portfolio with the most active response to volatility provides significant positive stock selection ability and total performance.

Chretien and Kammoun (2013) evaluate the performance of 2,786 U.S. mutual funds between January 1984 and December 2012 using their fund's best clientele performance measure. They also estimate the performance of the funds using the Chen and Knez (1996) LOP measure. Chretien and Kammoun use three alternative sets of primitive assets: the gross returns on the Treasury bill and either 10 industry portfolios, six size/book-to-market portfolios, and the market index. When estimating the conditional performance of the funds, they add scaled gross returns on the market using the lagged dividend yield on the S&P 500 index, three-month Treasury-bill yield, term spread, and default spread. To implement the good-deal bounds performance measure, Chretien and Kammoun specify an upper bound of the maximum Sharpe performance to be equal to $h^* + 0.5h_{Mkt}$ or $h^* + h_{Mkt}$, where h^* is the maximum Sharpe performance from the set of primitive assets and h_{Mkt} is the Sharpe performance of the market index.

Chretien and Kammoun (2013) find that when using the LOP performance measure, the average fund has significant negative performance. When using the false discovery rate (FDR) of Barras, Scaillet and Wermers (2010), no funds have superior performance. The FDR approach allows the researcher to adjust the findings of individual fund performance to control for the case where funds have significant performance but the true performance of the funds is zero (false discoveries). In contrast, when evaluating funds using their best clientele measure, the average fund has significantly superior performance and many individual funds have superior performance even after adjusting for the FDR. The results are robust to the different sets of primitive assets and the choice of the maximum Sharpe performance. The difference between the two measures highlights the large disagreement between investors that can result when evaluating the same fund and supports Ahn et al. (2009) and Ferson and Lin (2014).

Summary and Conclusions

This chapter summarizes the stochastic discount factor approach to fund performance. Using this approach has many benefits. First, any asset pricing model implies a candidate model of the stochastic discount factor. Second, the stochastic discount factor approach can be adapted to evaluate the performance of any managed fund, not only for mutual funds but also for hedge funds and private equity funds. Third, as Ferson (2013b) shows, the stochastic discount factor approach can be used as a unifying approach in assessing the different performance measures that have been proposed in the literature.

The empirical findings of studies using linear factor models of the stochastic discount factor suggest that the average fund does not provide significant value added to investors and the number of funds with significant superior performance is small. These results are similar to regression-based studies but with some differences. First, fund performance appears less sensitive to the stochastic discount factor model used, compared to regression-based studies. Second, even for linear factor models, important differences can occur in performance between the two approaches as reflected in Bessler et al. (2009) and Gusset and Zimmermann (2012). The differences stem from the set of payoffs used to estimate the stochastic discount factor models. A fuller comparison of the two approaches is worthy of further research.

Using the stochastic discount factor approach to evaluate fund performance shows a striking result that fund performance is more favorable when accounting for investor heterogeneity (Ahn et al. 2009; Ferson and Lin 2014) or using performance measures based on weaker economic restrictions (Chretien and Kammoun 2013). These studies raise the distinct possibility that funds add value for at least one clientele of investors. Research is likely to continue along these lines and extending this analysis to weight-based performance measures could be worthwhile.

Discussion Questions

1. Describe the stochastic discount factor approach to evaluating mutual fund performance.
2. Evaluate the alternative approaches used to estimate stochastic discount factors to evaluate fund performance.
3. Discuss the weight-based performance measures of Ferson and Mo (2013).
4. Discuss empirical results from mutual fund performance studies using the stochastic discount factor approach.

References

Ahn, Dong H., Henry H. Cao, and Stephane Chretien. 2009. "Portfolio Performance Measurement: A No Arbitrage Bounds Approach." *European Financial Management* 15:2, 298–339.

Almeida, Caio, and Rene Garcia. 2013a. "Robust Assessment of Hedge Fund Performance through Nonparametric Discounting." Working Paper, Graduate School of Economics, Getulio Vargas Foundation.

Almeida, Caio, and Rene Garcia. 2013b. "Robust Economic Implications of Nonlinear Pricing Kernels." Working Paper, Graduate School of Economics, Getulio Vargas Foundation.

Amihud, Yakov, and Ruslan Goyenko. 2013. "Mutual Fund's R^2 as Predictor of Performance." *Review of Financial Studies* 26:3, 667–695.

Aragon, George, and Wayne E. Ferson. 2008. "Portfolio Performance Evaluation." *Foundations and Trends in Finance* 2:1, 83–190.

Bakshi, Gurdip S., and Zhiwu Chen.1998. "Asset Pricing without Consumption or Market Portfolio Data." Working Paper, University of Maryland.

Barras, Laurent, Oliver Scaillet, and Russ Wermers. 2010. "False Discoveries in Mutual Fund Performance." *Journal of Finance* 65:1, 179–216.

Bessler, Wolfgang, Wolfgang Drobetz, and Heinz Zimmermann. 2009. "Conditional Performance Evaluation for German Equity Mutual Funds." *European Journal of Finance* 15:3, 287–316.

Brennan, Michael J., and Eduardo Schwartz. 1979. "A Continuous Time Approach to the Pricing of Bonds." *Journal of Banking and Finance* 3:2, 133–155.

Carhart, Mark M. 1997. "On Persistence in Mutual Fund Performance." *Journal of Finance* 52:1, 57–82.

Chan, Louis K. C., Stephen G. Dimmock, and Josef Lakonishok. 2009. "Benchmarking Money Manager Performance: Issues and Evidence." *Review of Financial Studies* 22:11, 4553–4599.

Chen, Zhiwu, and Peter J. Knez. 1996. "Portfolio Performance Measurement: Theory and Applications." *Review of Financial Studies* 9:2, 511–555.

Chretien, Stephane, and Manel Kammoun. 2013. "Mutual Fund Performance Evaluation and Best Clienteles." Working Paper, Laval University.

Cochrane, John H. 1996. "A Cross-Sectional Test of an Investment Based Asset Pricing Model." *Journal of Political Economy* 104:3, 572–621.

Cochrane, John H. 2005. *Asset Pricing*, Revised Edition. Princeton, NJ: Princeton University Press.

Cochrane, John H., and Jesus Saa-Requejo. 2000. "Beyond Arbitrage: Good-Deal Asset Price Bounds in Incomplete Markets." *Journal of Political Economy* 108:1, 79–119.

Cremers, Martijn, and Antti Petajisto. 2009. "How Active Is Your Fund Manager? A New Measure That Predicts Performance." *Review of Financial Studies* 22:9, 3329–3365.

Cremers, Martijn, Antti Petajisto, and Eric Zitzewitz. 2013. "Should Benchmark Indices Have Alpha: Revisiting Performance Evaluation." *Critical Finance Review* 2:1, 1–48.

Dahlquist, Magnus, and Paul Soderlind. 1999. "Evaluating Portfolio Performance with Stochastic Discount Factors." *Journal of Business* 72:3, 347–383.

Daniel, Kent, Mark Grinblatt, Sheridan Titman, and Russ Wermers. 1997. "Measuring Mutual Fund Performance with Characteristic Based Benchmarks." *Journal of Finance* 52:3, 1035–1058.

De Souza, Andre, and Anthony W. Lynch. 2012. "Does Mutual Fund Performance Vary over the Business Cycle?" Working Paper, New York University.

Dittmar, Robert F. 2002. "Nonlinear Pricing Kernels, Kurtosis Preference and Cross-Section of Equity Returns." *Journal of Finance* 57:1, 369–403.

Fama, Eugene F. 1998. "Market Efficiency, Long-Term Returns, and Behavioral Finance." *Journal of Financial Economics* 49:3, 283–306.

Fama, Eugene F., and Kenneth R. French. 1993. "Common Risk Factors in the Returns on Bonds and Stocks." *Journal of Financial Economics* 33:1, 3–56.

Farnsworth, Heber, Wayne E. Ferson, David Jackson, and Steven Todd. 2002. "Performance Evaluation with Stochastic Discount Factors." *Journal of Business* 75:3, 473–505.

Ferson, Wayne E. 2003. "Tests of Multifactor Pricing Models, Volatility Bounds and Portfolio Performance." In George M. Constantinides, Milton Harris, and René Stulz, eds., *Handbook of the Economics of Finance*, 743–800. Amsterdam: Elsevier Science.

Ferson, Wayne E. 2010. "Investment Performance Evaluation." *Annual Reviews of Financial Economics* 2:1, 207–234.

Ferson, Wayne E. 2013a. "Ruminations on Investment Performance Measurement." *European Financial Management* 19:1, 4–13.

Ferson, Wayne E. 2013b. "Investment Performance: A Review and Synthesis." In George M. Constantinides, Milton Harris, and René Stulz, eds., *Handbook of the Economics of Finance*, 959–1000. Amsterdam: Elsevier Science.

Ferson, Wayne E., Tyler R. Henry, and Darren J. Kisgen. 2006a. "Evaluating Government Bond Fund Performance with Stochastic Discount Factors." *Review of Financial Studies* 19:2, 423–456.

Ferson, Wayne E., and Kenneth Khang. 2002. "Conditional Performance Measurement Using Portfolio Weights: Evidence for Pension Funds." *Journal of Financial Economics* 65:2, 249–282.

Ferson, Wayne E., Darren J. Kisgen, and Tyler R. Henry. 2006b. "Fixed Income Fund Performance across Economic States." *Research in Finance* 23:1, 1–62.

Ferson, Wayne E., and Jerchern Lin. 2014. "Alpha and Performance Measurement: The Effects of Investor Disagreement and Heterogeneity." *Journal of Finance*, 69:4, 1565–1596.

Ferson, Wayne E., and Haitao Mo. 2013. "Measuring Performance with Market and Volatility Timing and Selectivity." Working Paper, University of Southern California.

Fletcher, Jonathan, and David Forbes. 2004. "Performance Evaluation of U.K. Unit Trusts within the Stochastic Discount Factor Approach." *Journal of Financial Research* 27:2, 289–306.

Fletcher, Jonathan, and Andrew P. Marshall. 2014. "Investor Heterogeneity and the Cross-Section of U.K. Investment Trust Performance." *Journal of Financial Services Research* 45:1, 67–89.

Fletcher, Jonathan, and Patricia Ntozi-Obwale. 2008. "Arbitrage Bounds and U.K. Unit Trust Performance." *Journal of Business Finance and Accounting* 35:3–4, 580–600.

Goetzmann, William N., Jonathan Ingersoll, and Zoran Ivkovic. 2000. "Monthly Measurement of Daily Timers." *Journal of Financial and Quantitative Analysis* 35:3, 257–290.

Grinblatt, Mark, and Sheridan Titman. 1993. "Performance Measurement without Benchmarks: An Examination of Mutual Fund Returns." *Journal of Business* 60:1, 97–112.

Gusset Jonas, and Heinz Zimmermann. 2012. "Why Not Use SDF Rather Than Beta Models in Performance Measurement." Working Paper, University of Basel.

Hansen, Lars P. 1982. "Large Sample Properties of Generalized Method of Moments Estimators." *Econometrica* 50:4, 1029–1054.

Hansen, Lars P., and Ravi Jagannathan. 1991. "Implications of Security Market Data for Models of Dynamic Economies." *Journal of Political Economy* 99:2, 225–262.

Hansen, Lars P., and Scott F. R. Richard. 1987. "The Role of Conditioning Information in Deducing Testable Restrictions Implied by Dynamic Asset Pricing Models." *Econometrica* 55:3, 587–613.

Harrison, Michael J., and David M. Kreps. 1979. "Martingales and Arbitrage in Multi-Period Securities Markets." *Journal of Economic Theory* 20:3, 381–408.

Hodrick, Robert J., and Xiaoyan Zhang. 2001. "Evaluating the Specification Errors of Asset Pricing Models." *Journal of Financial Economics* 62:2, 327–376.

Jagannathan, Ravi, and Zhenyu Wang. 1996. "The Conditional CAPM and the Cross-Section of Expected Returns." *Journal of Finance* 51:1, 3–53.

Jensen, Michael C. 1968. "The Performance of Mutual Funds in the Period 1945–1964." *Journal of Finance* 23:2, 389–416.

Kacperczyk, Marcin, Clemens Sialm, and Lu Zheng. 2008. "Unobserved Actions of Mutual Funds." *Review of Financial Studies* 21:6, 2379–2416.

Kacperczyk, Marcin, Stijn van Nieuwerburgh, and Laura Veldkamp. 2014. "Time-Varying Fund Manager Skill." *Journal of Finance* 69:4, 1455–1484.

Kosowski, Robert. 2011. "Do Mutual Funds Perform When It Matters Most to Investors? US Mutual Fund Performance and Risk in Recessions and Expansions." *Quarterly Journal of Finance* 1:3, 607–664.

Lehmann, Bruce N., and David M. Modest. 1987. "Mutual Fund Performance Evaluation: A Comparison of Benchmarks and Benchmark Comparisons." *Journal of Finance* 42:2, 233–265.

Long, John B. 1990. "The Numeraire Portfolio." *Journal of Financial Economics* 26:1, 29–70.

Lynch, Anthony W., and Jessica Wachter. 2013. "Using Samples of Unequal Length in Generalized Method of Moments Estimation." *Journal of Financial and Quantitative Analysis* 48:1, 277–307.

Merton, Robert C. 1973. "An Intertemporal Capital Asset Pricing Model." *Econometrica* 41:5, 867–887.

Moskowitz, Tobias J. 2000. "Discussion: Mutual Fund Performance: An Empirical Decomposition into Stock Picking Talent, Style, Transaction Costs, and Expenses." *Journal of Finance* 55:4, 1695–1703.

Ross, Stephen A. 1976. "The Arbitrage Theory of Capital Asset Pricing." *Journal of Economic Theory* 13:3, 341–360.

Ross, Stephen A. 1978. "A Simple Approach to the Valuation of Risky Streams." *Journal of Business* 51:3, 453–475.

Sharpe, William F. 1966. "Mutual Fund Performance." *Journal of Business* 39:1, 119–138.

Wang, Zhenyu, and Xioayan Zhang. 2012. "Empirical Evaluation of Asset Pricing Models: Arbitrage and Pricing Errors in Contingent Claims." *Journal of Empirical Finance* 19:1, 65–78.

21

Mutual Fund Risk

ROBERTO SAVONA
Associate Professor of Financial Markets and Institutions, University of Brescia

ORESTE AULETA
Head of Wrapping and Product Management, Eurizon Capital SGR

FILIPPO STEFANINI
Head of Hedge Funds and Manager Selection, Eurizon Capital SGR

Introduction

Mutual funds are portfolios designed to meet the specific needs of investors. Therefore, analyzing the investment strategies implemented by these financial vehicles requires inspecting what investors need in terms of risk-return targets. Investment styles evolve over time toward more sophisticated strategies because money managers adapt their strategies to the investor demand. This view is consistent with Barberis and Shleifer (2003, p. 164) who state, "If money managers are responsive to their clients, they will create products that correspond to the categories those clients like to use."

Operationally, mutual funds can be conceived as financial vehicles following specific investment strategies wrapped in a legal entity within a legal domicile. Investors delegate specific investment strategies conditional on their own risk appetite and return expectations to fund managers to implement. Managers establish positions in markets operating in changing conditions, forming portfolios in which the risk-return profile should match the utility function of investors. However, information asymmetry affects the investor–manager relationship because investors do not know in real time the evolving portfolio composition based on market dynamics.

As Chevalier and Ellison (1997) discuss, investors want to maximize risk-adjusted expected returns, while mutual fund companies want to maximize their fund value and have incentives to increase fund inflows. This fosters a classic agency problem. Since the information that fund managers possess and how they use it are not directly observable, investors have only a partial view about portfolio risks, including how they change over time, and how they are managed. Mutual fund risks derive from portfolio market exposures with the governance and organizational structures assumed by the legal entity. A formal risk evaluation process is needed to understand and measure all risks of mutual funds. This process includes conducting quantitative assessments and qualitative evaluations, offering a clear view of the risk spectrum, investigating past performance and operational activity, forming expectation on the future risk-return profile, and considering how managers are expected to operate within the entity.

This chapter examines the risk measurement and evaluation processes of mutual funds, including the analysis of market and operational risks. The chapter offers an analytical approach to quantitatively and qualitatively assess various risks faced by mutual funds. In a sense, the chapter presents a pragmatic approach to realize a "mutual fund risk anatomy." Specifically, it presents (1) how to proceed with the quantitative analysis of mutual fund risks and then describes the main results within the financial due diligence section; and (2) how to carry out an effective qualitative analysis of the main risks faced by mutual funds, which is summarized within the operational due diligence section. The mutual fund risk anatomy is conceived with the goal to help managers make the right investment decisions considering all risks connected to these choices.

The remainder of the chapter has the following organization. The next section introduces the theoretical framework to describe the mutual fund dynamics over time. This is followed by a discussion of the mutual fund risk evaluation process. The next two sections discuss financial and operational due diligence. The final section provides a summary and conclusions.

A Theoretical Framework for Mutual Fund Dynamics

Formalizing a theoretical framework for mutual funds is important because an effective approach to inspect quantitative and qualitative mutual fund risks should be justified by a solid theory. Before discussing how mutual fund risks are scrutinized in the industry, the theoretical assumptions underlying the theoretical framework is described in the following section.

Amisano and Savona (2008) discuss how the theoretical framework in the mutual fund literature, which is commonly used to describe how fund managers invest over time, relates to Admati, Bhattacharya, Pfleiderer, and Ross (1986). Specifically, money managers are assumed to be single-period investors who maximize the conditional expectation of an increasing, concave objective function that depends on excess returns of the risk-free rate, $r_p = R_p - R_f$, where R_p denotes the return of the managed portfolio and R_f is the return of the risk-free asset. The expectation of portfolio return is conditional on a set of instrumental variables, Z_t, and a private signal about the future performance of the market, S_t. The instrumental variables are those "instruments" used by money managers to forecast equity and bond returns, such as the credit spread (computed as the yield difference between Moody's BAA and AAA-rated corporate bonds), the dividend yield of the stock index (e.g., the S&P 500 index for the U.S. market), the term spread (usually measured as the difference between a five-year and a one-month Treasury-bill yield). The private signal is the "proprietary" informative set that managers use to take strategic decisions about changes in their portfolio allocation.

In such a framework, Becker, Ferson, Myers, and Schill (1999) show that the maximization problem can be simplified by assuming that portfolio managers choose between the risky market portfolio with return R_m and the risk-free asset. Hence, $R_p = R_f - wR_m$, where w is the weight of the market portfolio. In this setting, money managers adjust their market exposure w, trying to maximize their portfolio return in each period t, given the common information Z and the private information S.

As Chen, Ferson, and Peters (2006) note, since w evolves over time depending on both common instruments and the private signal, the return of the managed portfolio with market-timing ability should exhibit a convex pattern relative to the benchmark return. Classical market-timing approaches give convincing theoretical reasons for such functional form, which can be expressed by a quadratic function of the market returns (Treynor and Mazuy 1966) or an "isomorphic correspondence" to some non-linear option strategies payoff (Henriksson and Merton 1981). However, empirical evidence is contradictory and often shows anomalous negative market timing. Other problems also arise between selectivity and market timing. Glosten and Jagannathan (1994) point out that spurious market timing may be latent in the negative correlation between the two components if managers take long put option positions, which move down the beta portfolio when stock returns are low. Grinblatt and Titman (1989) highlight problems in performance measurement when a fund's beta varies without any active portfolio rebalancing.

Thus, the market portfolio R_m assumes a central role in the modeling process. Money managers modulate their risk over time depending on their targets expressed in relative terms, and the performance of mutual funds are measured and evaluated as risk-adjusted returns. The market portfolio is the benchmark for the mutual fund representing the investment style followed by the manager. Knowing the strategy followed by the manager is of fundamental importance as the asset allocation and the investment objectives assumed by the fund are used to select an unbiased benchmark to estimate the risk profile of manager. When the strategy is highly dynamic and no benchmark is clearly specified, such a complexity reflects on the non-linearity in returns, which increases the difficulty of uncovering how the returns are generated.

To reduce this problem, two strategies are available. The first strategy is to construct ad hoc benchmarks, replicating the payoff profile of the fund. Fung and Hsieh (2001), propose using primitive trading strategies to inspect the hedge fund performance. Primitive trading strategies are option-based benchmarks designed to describe non-linearity in returns and contextualized within a clear-cut economic framework tracing back to Merton's (1981) insight that the payoff of a perfect market timer should be identical to the payoff from owning a call option on the market. The isomorphic approximation of investment strategies to option-based trading strategies allows bypassing the unreliability problem connected to linear models when using passive benchmarks. Since the intrinsic non-linearity of hedge fund returns is moved onto the explanatory factors, which act as proxies of the complex and often unobservable trading strategies, a simple linear multivariate regression can be used effectively to describe the behavior of fund returns.

A second strategy focuses on risk loadings modeling them as time-varying to handle shifts in the coefficient estimate. A common approach is to estimate betas by state space models (Kalman filter), which allows risk loading to change over time possibly also depending on some macroeconomic factors (Amisano and Savona 2008; Mamaysky, Spiegel, and Zhang 2008).

This framework highlights the importance of an appropriate asset pricing model to inspect the risk-return profile of mutual fund managers. First, the one-period time horizon over which measuring the performance is used since managers are assumed to maximize portfolio returns each period. Second, an effective market benchmark should be specified to measure performance that accounts for managerial strategy. Third, the asset pricing model should include a framework recognizing that money managers alter their portfolio allocation based upon some market variables. Fourth, since inferring portfolio weights and their changes over time is extremely complex from a statistical viewpoint, knowing in advance the time-varying asset allocation helps the risk assessment of mutual funds. All these points are considered to formalize a step-by-step mutual fund risk evaluation process discussed in the following section.

The Mutual Fund Risk Evaluation Process

Fund managers implement different investment strategies with various risk profiles. These strategies range from passive to absolute return, based on different targets relative to their own benchmark (i.e., benchmark replication for passive strategies and benchmark outperformance for active strategies). Therefore, mutual fund dynamics incorporate *market risks*, related to market dynamics, and *operational risks*, deriving from the inner functioning of the legal entity and its governance structure. In order for mutual fund activities to be profitable and operationally effective, both risk categories need to be identified, measured, and managed in a unified, holistic way. As a result, the risk evaluation process of mutual funds is a complex process, which includes quantitative and qualitative assessment of many relevant issues related to the life of a mutual fund, leading to both financial and operational due diligence.

INVESTMENT STRATEGY

The evaluation process starts by focusing on the investment strategy and how it can be wrapped properly in a certain legal structure. For an investor focusing on an illiquidity premia-based strategy, it is difficult to be properly wrapped in a daily liquidity fund without creating a liquidity mismatch between assets and liabilities. Many financial analysts classify mutual funds by their investment styles derived from classic descriptors including small cap, mid-cap, large cap, aggressive growth, income, and capital appreciation indicators. As a result, investors believe that these styles attributes are informative and think of them as stable fund characteristics.

Most mutual fund investment companies offer different portfolios to match various risk-return profiles. Conversely, mutual fund clients are interested in being informed on how aggressively their money is managed as well as the main asset classes chosen by the fund. As a result, the disclosure of these characteristics has become so important that sometimes a fund is identified by its investment style (e.g., value or growth), which enters as a part of the fund name itself. Mutual fund investment styles and trading strategies play a fundamental role in mutual fund selection. Mutual fund performance evaluation depends strictly on the styles and strategies assumed by the manager.

Plan sponsors need to establish benchmarks, which serve as reasonable return targets to assess the achievement of their portfolio managers. To accomplish this task, the systematic style component must be subtracted from the ex post total return to determine *skill*, which is the proportion of return that is to be attributed solely to superior active management or above average talent (Fama 1972). Rational investors will pay higher fees only if this superior ability is in some sense unambiguously evident. However, this unambiguous evidence is far from being simple to determine. Mutual fund managers are rewarded relative their benchmarks, mimicking the behavior of broad, naive combinations of investable assets. These benchmarking practices could induce fund returns to remain closely related to their benchmarks, which reflect an investment mandate. Mutual funds returns are then expected to be highly correlated to the performances of the main asset classes in the market. Money managers are subject to institutional restrictions such as no short selling constraints and limited access to leverage. These restrictions explain why selecting the appropriate style benchmarks for mutual funds is so important.

BENCHMARK SELECTION

Risk-adjusted returns are evaluated relative to a benchmark that should reflect the fund's investment style philosophy and consider the long-run asset allocation assumed by the manager and his style dynamics, detecting possible style drifts. Detecting the relevant track records based on style and benchmark changes occurring over time is essential to this process. The need for market benchmarks in the performance measurement activity is extremely important in the mutual fund industry. Many studies discuss the importance of incentive systems (Starks 1987; Brown, Harlow, and Starks 1996; Schultz 1996; Admati and Pfleiderer 1997) and performance measurement models (Becker et al. 1999).

Performance-measurement-based benchmarks are prone to selection bias. Having a global view in terms of market location and broad asset classes, the mutual fund industry can be mapped within some major asset classes, with corresponding benchmark proxies thereby offering a possible list of market indices to be used in relative performance measurement and evaluation. This list includes the:

- *Euro bond market*. The JP Morgan Government Bond Index EMU is primarily used as a proxy for Euro bond market. The index selects its components from all government bonds, excluding floating rate notes, perpetuals, bonds targeted at the domestic market for tax purposes, and bonds with less than one year remaining to maturity. Index constituents are also subject to liquidity requirements so as to reflect the performance of actively traded issues with no price bias related to illiquid instruments.
- *Euro equity market*. The STOXX Europe 600 Index, which is a subset of the STOXX Global 1800 Index, is the main reference. This index represents large, mid, and small cap companies selected based on the free-float market capitalization criterion across 18 Euro countries (Austria, Belgium, Czech Republic, Denmark, Finland, France, Germany, Greece, Ireland, Italy, Luxembourg, the Netherlands, Norway, Portugal, Spain, Sweden, Switzerland, and the United Kingdom).
- *U.S. equity market*. The most widely used proxy is the S&P 500 index, which is consistent with other equity indices selected for the other equity-based asset classes in terms of free-float weighting scheme.

- *Equity emerging markets*. The MSCI Emerging Markets Index serves as the proxy including large and mid-cap companies across 21 emerging markets. The index includes 824 (the number varies over time) constituents and represents about 85 percent of the free-float-adjusted market capitalization in each country.
- *Commodities*. The common proxy is the Bloomberg Commodity Index Total Return based on the Bloomberg Commodity Index, which tracks the return on fully collateralized positions in the underlying commodity futures. The index reflects the return of underlying commodity futures price movements only. It is composed of commodities traded on U.S. exchanges, except for aluminum, nickel, and zinc, which trade on the London Metal Exchange (LME).
- *Bond emerging markets*. This usual proxy for this asset class is the JP Morgan Government Bond Index-Emerging Markets Global, which tracks emerging market debt issued by the governments of emerging markets in local currency. This "global" version is composed by those countries having open access to international investors.
- *High-yield bond market*. Market traders choose the Barclays Global High-Yield Index, which provides a broad-based measure of the global high-yield fixed-income markets. It represents the union of the following indices: U.S. High-Yield, Pan-European High-Yield, U.S. Emerging Markets High-Yield, and Pan-European Emerging. Securities included in the index are classified as high yield if the middle rating of Moody's, Fitch, and S&P is Ba1, BB+, and BB+, respectively, or below.
- *U.S. corporate bond market*. As a proxy, money managers use the Barclays U.S. Corporate Investment Grade Total Return Index (sub-index of the Barclays U.S. Credit Index), which includes USD-denominated securities publicly issued by U.S. and non-U.S. industrial, utility, and financial issuers that meet the specified maturity, liquidity, and quality requirements. This broad-based benchmark measures the investment grade, USD-denominated, fixed-rate, taxable corporate bond market.

FEES

Most early studies find that the after-fee alphas of mutual funds are zero or negative (Jensen 1968; Elton, Gruber, Das, and Hlavka 1993; Brown and Goetzmann 1995; Gruber 1996). *Alpha* refers to an excess risk-adjusted return. Even if an investor chooses an excellent investment strategy, an outstanding investment manager, and the proper legal structure, fees that are too expensive compared to the value added by the manager can nullify these efforts.

Although fees can be evaluated when buying or selling a fund, a swing price or an anti-dilution levy may be added to transaction costs. The *swing price* is an alternative NAV calculation method established to create fairness of treatment between continuing investors and redeeming investors. The valuation does not include a subscription commission or a refund commission, but with a new industry standard introduced to protect existing investors allowing the subscribing or refunding investors be the only ones bearing the portfolio unwinding costs. Swing pricing is a widely accepted anti-dilution standard used on Luxembourg-domiciled funds. The Association of the Luxembourg Fund Industry (ALFI 2006a, b, 2011) has published two best practice brochures on the subject.

An *anti-dilution levy* is a fee charged to investors buying or selling shares of a fund to offset the effects on the NAV of subscriptions or redemptions. Such a market practice is a way to protect continuing investors and to charge subscribing or redeeming investors for bid-ask spreads paid to invest or disinvest from the underlying securities, which may or may not be liquid at the time of the trade. In most cases the board of directors of the investment company decides the amount for the swing price. In others, the amount is fixed and can be viewed as a subscription or a redemption fee as it is not dependent on market conditions.

LIQUIDITY RISK

When fund managers cannot sell their holdings easily and quickly, they can incur portfolio large losses resulting in fund collapses in extreme cases. Indeed, portfolio losses can activate liquidity spirals, since losses lead to redemptions, which in turn spur more losses since the fund manager has to sell securities at fire-sale prices. This scenario defines the liquidity risk of mutual funds. The financial crisis of 2007–2008 highlighted the need for a better understanding of the liquidity risk of financial securities and institutions such as mutual funds. Liquidity is a risk factor whose premium varies over time. Therefore, assessing if the liquidity level of the assets is coherent with the liquidity level of the liabilities is important. This task is difficult in case of multi-asset funds: many prospectuses include a paragraph about *redemption gates,* which refer to multiple redemption payment dates since such provisions can be triggered in special cases.

Another important complexity of investing in mutual funds is the risk of not investing or divesting on the desired *dealing date,* which refers to the date when a subscription or redemption order is executed. Cut-off times exist regarding the ability for the order to be executed on a certain date. If the order is submitted before 11:00 a.m., then today's net asset value (NAV) is used, otherwise the following day's NAV is used. Notice periods also exist for both for subscriptions and redemptions.

CREDIT RISK

The search for yield has led many investment managers to invest in high-yield bonds rated as CCC (assigned by S&P or Fitch), subordinated bonds, non-agency mortgages, or even bank loans leading to settlement risks. On this last point, consider that bank loans can have complex settlement, mostly manual, which includes loan transfer restrictions in the bank load document allowing for stoppage of the transfer to a not linked counterparty (i.e., an activist hedge fund). As a result, financial vehicles that offer daily liquidity on those securities should include specific clauses within the prospectus stating that liquidity could be monthly while such events occur. This issue is relevant because such a possibility can happen even if loans are highly liquid. Bank loans are ineligible securities under the Undertakings for Collective Investment in Transferable Securities (UCITS) regulatory framework because they are not considered as transferable securities, but UCITS funds can invest up to 10 percent in bank loans.

Financial Due Diligence: Mutual Fund Performance Evaluation

Mutual fund risk quantification is first assessed based on past returns. Ex post analysis helps to understand the fund's main risk-return drivers (*risk factors*) and how the fund has behaved over time conditional on market dynamics (*risk dynamics*), which allow for analyzing the performance in both negative and positive market scenarios (*market-timing ability*).

The quantitative analysis of the fund's risk-return profile includes many activities necessary to correctly evaluate ex post portfolio returns and form ex ante expectation of risk-return dynamics. Some recent studies argue that the possibility exists of identifying funds with the skill to generate future risk-adjusted performance based on certain fund characteristics such as: (1) the styles that funds follow (Daniel, Grinblatt, Titman, and Wermers 1997); (2) the location of the stocks that funds hold (Coval and Moskowitz 2001); (3) the extent to which manager's decisions resemble the decisions of other managers with distinguished performance records (Cohen, Coval, and Pástor 2005); and (4) the industry concentration of fund holdings (Kacperczyk, Sialm, and Zheng 2005). Quantitatively assessing all risk drivers of a fund in the right way is important based on several factors discussed in the following sections.

DATA

Analyzing fund data can be challenging. Most funds have up to 20 or 30 different share classes with different performances. For example, a fund may accumulate share class or distribution share class, U.S. dollar-hedged, Euro-hedged, institutional share class or retail share class, and duration-hedged share class. Any combination of these increases the difficulty of picking the right one. Hence, the risks in picking the wrong share class of the fund should not be neglected. Not all the funds use the same prices for the same securities. Indeed, securities priced at their "market close" are difficult to compute because financial markets across the globe are open all day long. In theory, the possibility exists of pricing mutual funds by distinguishing, for example, between funds with NAVs calculated at 12:00 noon or 5:00 p.m. in London. With global funds that invest in securities listed in the United States, Europe, and Japan, this pricing is impossible, and therefore NAVs could be normalized to correctly compare different mutual funds. Computationally, the data set should collect the exact point in time when NAVs are calculated and then estimate how they changed based on the market price dynamics.

DECOMPOSING MUTUAL FUND RISKS (A): RETURN-BASED ANALYSIS

When mutual funds are evaluated relative to benchmarks, investment risk can be decomposed into *total risk,* which is connected to the uncertainty of the entire portfolio returns; and *active risk* or *tracking error,* which measures the uncertainty surrounding the portfolio's performance regarding its benchmark. *Active risk* is an estimate of the dispersion of excess returns of each fund relative to the benchmark and is used to measure the relative level of risk assumed by the fund. Common practice separates *ex post tracking error volatility* (TEV), which provides a risk measure of historical excess returns, from *ex ante TEV*, which represents superior active risk management as an estimate of the future dispersion around the benchmark based on current portfolio allocation. Mathematically, excess returns (relative to the risk-free rate) for a generic *i*th asset can be expressed as a linear function of *K* common risk factors in Equation 21.1:

$$r_i = \sum_{k=1}^{K} X_{ik} f_k + u_i, \tag{21.1}$$

where *X* denotes exposures of asset *i* toward factor *f*; *r* is the excess return relative to the risk-free rate; and *u* is the idiosyncratic or asset-specific risk. Portfolio risk can thus be computed based on covariance matrix in Equation 21.2:

$$V = XFX^T + \Delta, \tag{21.2}$$

where *V* is the portfolio variance; *F* is the covariance matrix of the *K* factors; and Δ is the covariance matrix of error terms *u*. Now, having a portfolio vector (q) and a benchmark vector (b) with $h = q - b$ denoting the vector representing the difference of the asset weights of portfolio relative to its benchmark, the TEV can be computed as shown in Equation 21.3.

$$TEV = \sqrt{h^T V h}, \tag{21.3}$$

where *V* is computed according to Equation 21.2. Thus, TEV can be decomposed into two main components: (1) *factor risk*, $\sqrt{h^T (XFX^T)\, h}$, and (2) *specific risk*, $\sqrt{h^T \Delta h}$. Finally, Equation 21.4 assesses the risk contribution (RC) played by each *K* factor relative to the total TEV.

$$RC_k = \frac{\partial TEV}{\partial h} = \frac{h_k^T V h}{\sqrt{h^T V h}}, \tag{21.4}$$

where h_k^T is the transposed *h* vector with all zeros except the *k*th factor of interest.

TEV analysis and the corresponding decomposition are impossible when mutual funds are absolute return based. In this case, the funds do not have specific benchmarks and the Sharpe ratio (Sharpe 1966) is usually computed assessing how many units of excess return have been generated per unit of volatility, as measured by the standard deviation of the portfolio. The Sharpe ratio is a mean-reverting characteristic of a fund because, on average, periods of strong excess returns are followed by periods of poorer performances. Furthermore, quantitatively disentangling alpha from betas is necessary, which is often complicated because alternative betas can be masked as alpha (e.g., by exposure to merger arbitrage spread, exposure to peripheral countries in Europe, exposure to momentum stocks, and exposure to minimum volatility stocks).

DECOMPOSING MUTUAL FUND RISKS (B): PORTFOLIO WEIGHT-BASED ANALYSIS

Decomposing risks for mutual funds when portfolio allocation is known is far more informative than TEV analysis. Having information on the actual portfolio allocation enables investors or analysts to execute a performance attribution analysis and attribute the mutual fund's excess return relative to its own benchmark or to some main drivers of performance. Brinson, Hood, and Beebower (1986) identify three main components shown in Equation 21.5 for each main asset class: (1) allocation, (2) selection, and (3) the interaction between allocation and selection. Equations 21.6, 21.7, and 21.8 define each subcomponent:

$$r_q^j - r_b^j \equiv r_h = ER_{allocation} + ER_{selection} + ER_{\text{interaction}} \tag{21.5}$$

with

$$ER_{allocation} = h_j^T \left(r_b^j \right), \tag{21.6}$$

$$ER_{selection} = q_j^T \left(r_h^j \right), \tag{21.7}$$

$$ER_{\text{interaction}} = b^T \left(r_h^j \right), \tag{21.8}$$

where q and b are vector weight for jth asset class; r_q and r_b are the corresponding vectors of single assets returns of jth asset class; h is the vector representing the difference in weights (portfolio minus benchmark); and r_h is the vector representing the difference in single asset returns (portfolio minus benchmark). An active risk measure can be computed and is more informative than that based on a multifactor asset pricing model (Equation 21.1), based on actual rather than estimates of portfolio loadings.

When assessing the fund volatility or the active risk, understanding risk diversification used in portfolio construction is important. In extreme market conditions, volatility contributions of the underlying securities are additive and the diversification that usually emerges from correlations among the different securities does not occur. In the following example, the diversification effect is particularly important because it often reduces the risk by 25 percent. Only in extreme market conditions will the diversification effect become negligible. In that case, all volatilities underlying the portfolio become additive. Figure 21.1 illustrates that in extreme cases, the variance-covariance matrix morphs and becomes a matrix where all correlations are one and in the diagonal are single security variances as.

When evaluating the risk of a fund, investors should keep in mind how much the portfolio manager relies on diversification to reduce the overall risk because the diversification effect can suddenly disappear in extreme market conditions implying that losses can be much greater than expected. For example, for a portfolio in which the securities are positively correlated to each other, the volatility is the sum of all volatility contributions. However, if the securities exhibit negative correlations, the overall volatility results from the subtraction of volatility contributions of securities with negative correlations. In extreme market conditions, these negative contributions

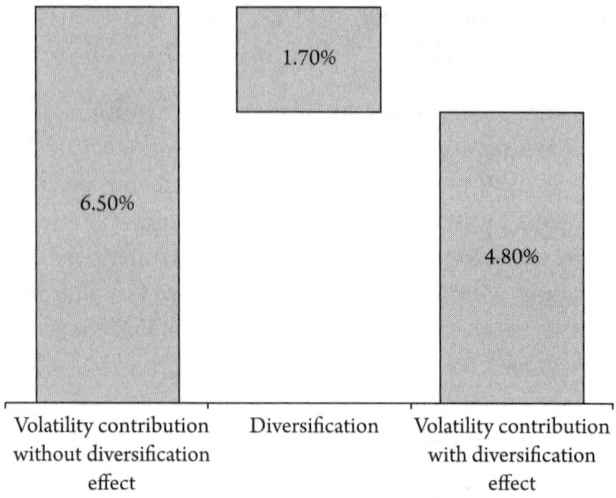

Figure 21.1 VOLATILITY AND DIVERSIFICATION. The figure presents an example of the volatility decomposition of a mutual fund and shows the contribution played by the diversification effect.

should be additive because correlations analysis may be ineffective in extreme circumstances. Thus, analyses differ if the volatility measure is determined by using sums or sums and subtractions. For the same reason, even funds with the same volatility but with different levels of gross exposures may exhibit different behavior in extreme market conditions.

The analysis of actual performances is the best way to see how fund managers react in different market conditions. With longer track records, *drawdown analysis,* which is the analysis of the peak-to-trough decline during a specific period, becomes more valuable, both on an absolute and relative basis compared to the benchmark. Drawdown analysis is particularly useful in discovering the fund manager's discipline in tough market conditions. It shows whether a *stop-loss policy,* which is a strategy designed to limit investor's loss that consists in selling positions when certain threshold of loss are triggered, is in place and whether this policy has been successful. Drawdown analysis also shows whether the fund manager has cut the losing positions or added to them during the drawdown. In this case, an a-priori successful formula does not exist. Fund management is about the dilemma of establishing a contrarian position by "topping-up" losing positions (i.e., adding to a losing position) and "top-slice" winning positions (i.e., reducing a winning position) or engaging in an opposite strategy (i.e., following the trend through momentum-based strategies). Both cases require anticipating the fund manager's actions during a drawdown.

MUTUAL FUND RISK MAPPING

A taxonomy of risk factors for both equity and fixed-income mutual funds should be executed in the same platform as an effective risk-mapping decomposition, along the mathematical rules previously discussed. The following risk factor classification, based on BarraOne, which is a multi-asset platform for total plan risk and performance commercialized by the MSCI index (MSCI Barra 2010), covers a list of possible risk sources pointing to some main risk dimensions.

- Fund-specific risk dimensions
  - Equity-based mutual funds
    - *Geographic market location.* The worldwide markets are segmented into Europe, North America, Japan, Pacific ex Japan, and emerging.
    - *Industry sectors.* A possible list includes energy, materials, industrials, consumer discretionary, consumer staples, healthcare, financials, information technology, telecommunications, utilities, and miscellaneous.
    - *Equity Style.* The Fama-French factors large versus small cap and growth versus value cap.
  - Fixed-income-based mutual funds
    - *Geographic market location.* The markets are segmented based on the issuer type.
    - *Government bonds including inflation linked-types.* The markets are segmented into the United States, EURO emerging markets, and developed markets.
    - *Corporate bonds also defined as spread bonds.* These bonds are segmented into Corporate Investment Grade (IG), Corporate High Yield (HY), agency/supranational, and emerging markets spread.
    - *Curve risks.* Term structures are usually estimated for sovereign issuers and swap curves in worldwide local markets. The factors reflect the moves of term structures including: (1) *shift moves,* when rates change in parallel; (2) *twist moves,* when short and long rates move in opposite directions, steepening or flattening; and (3) *butterfly moves,* when the curvature of the term structure changes or flexes.
    - *Swap spread risk.* This risk is commonly proxied by the monthly change in the average spread between the swap and Treasury-bill curve. Two types of risk sources pertain to this classification: (1) *market-wide spread risk,* which arises from changes in the general spread level of a market segment (e.g., the spreads of BB-rated or BBB-rated bonds might widen); and (2) *credit event risk,* which is related to individual issuers concerning their own probability of default.

- Overall risk dimensions
  - *Currency risk.* Currency exchange rate volatilities and correlations can affect well diversified equity and bond portfolios of international investors. Non-linear volatility movements and co-movements are substantial and need to be modeled based on GARCH methodology, also computing the sensitivity of portfolio to both currency risk sources (i.e., volatility and correlations).
  - *Investment style.* This risk quantifies the exposures of benchmark portfolio's sensitivities to factors. For equity-based mutual funds, exposure is expressed in standard deviations or percent of portfolio values for industries. For fixed-income-based mutual funds, exposures are measured as the portfolio's sensitivity to shocks in term structures or spread curves, which are usually assumed and studied as duration.

Table 21.1 presents an example of a mutual fund risk mapping and reports statistics about risk decomposition of a U.S. equity mutual fund based on ex ante expectation

Table 21.1 **An Example of the Risk Decomposition of a U.S. Equity Mutual Fund**

Main Risk Dimension	*Specific Risk Dimension*	*Portfolio Exposure (%)*	*Contribution to Active Risk (%)*
Geographical Market Location	World Developed	96.35	18.9
	Europe	4.55	3.5
	North America	91.80	15.4
	Japan	–	0.0
	Pacific ex Japan	–	0.0
	Emerging	0.04	0.0
Equity Industry Sectors	Energy	3.59	–3.0
	Materials	1.54	–2.5
	Industrials	13.24	5.9
	Consumer discretionary	10.67	–0.5
	Consumer staples	0.77	–4.5
	Health care	30.52	21.0
	Financials	5.80	–6.9
	Information technology	30.24	11.3
	Telecommunications	–	–1.7
	Utilities	–	–0.2
Equity Style	Large versus small cap	–1.04	11.7
	Growth versus value cap	–0.23	–0.2
Currency	EUR	1.40	0.3
	USD	94.73	0.0
	JPY	–	0.0
	GBP	–	0.0
	Developed currency	3.83	0.6
	Emerging currency	0.04	0.0
Investment Style	Momentum	0.15	0.2
	Volatility	0.88	38.1
	Local styles	–0.98	12.1

continued

Table 21.1 **(continued)**

Contribution to Active Risk by Main Risk Dimensions		
	%	*Contribution in %*
Industry	1.18	18.9
Style	3.86	62.0
Selection	1.14	18.3
Currency	0.05	0.8
Total	6.23	100.0

Note: The table presents the risk decomposition of a mutual fund focused on U.S. equities reporting portfolio exposures and contributions to active risk in percentage form.

of market dynamics using actual asset allocation. As Table 21.1 shows, the mutual fund portfolio exposures are mostly focused on North America (91.80 percent) with enough sector diversification, ranging from Information Technology to Healthcare both accounting for around 30.00 percent and includes Industrials (13.24 percent), Consumer Discretionary (10.67 percent), Financials (5.80 percent), Energy (3.59 percent), Materials (1.54 percent), and Consumer Staples (0.77 percent). Total exposures in Table 21.1 do not account for 100.00 percent but only 96.39 percent because cash is not included among exposures, which accounts for the remaining 3.61 percent of exposures.

Based on this allocation, U.S. dollar exposure (94.73 percent) drives currency risk. Momentum and volatility show positive sensitivities, while local style loading is negative. The active risk is 6.23 percent with the following contributions: (1) Industry at 18.90 percent; (2) Style (investment and equity) at 62.00 percent; (3) Currency at 0.80 percent; and (4) Selection at 18.30 percent. Much of the active risk derives from Equity and Investment Style, with volatility accounting for 38.1 percent, and Local Style together with Large versus Small Cap showing similar contributions, 12.10 percent and 11.70 percent, respectively.

Industry plays an important role as well, with Healthcare and Information Technology showing higher contributions (21.00 and 11.30 percent, respectively) moving in tandem with their corresponding portfolio loadings. Idiosyncratic risk contribution (Selection), which is the residual of the multifactor pricing model as shown in Equation 21.1, is high enough to suggest the manager is active and not passive as with an exchange-traded fund (ETF), which translates into deviations of returns against the benchmark, more often positive than negative.

Operational Due Diligence

While operational risk is mainly connected to hedge funds, some collateral issues are important for mutual funds that deserve monitoring. Mutual funds can contain physical securities so-called *cash-based* or they can be *swap-based*. In the first case, to enhance returns, the money manager may lend securities and receive a fee and collateral. In the second case, a portfolio containing physical securities will show one line item, the swap registration, and then many lines for the securities posted as collateral.

Operational due diligence on the swap is complex and time-consuming because all the legal contracts (i.e., International Swaps and Derivatives Association (ISDA) and Credit Support Annex (CSA) agreements), must be collected to understand if the swap is based on standard terms. The same requirements exist for lending, in which verification is required if an International Securities Lending Association (ISLA) agreement is in place with the split of revenues perceived by the fund and by the Lending Agent/Asset Management Company and the amount of assets lent previously.

In the mutual fund industry, innovation continues because many investment managers try to offer new strategies or to invest in new securities to gain market share and to exploit new investment opportunities. New investment solutions often challenge regulatory limits. Sometimes, a clear attempt to circumvent the spirit of the regulation exists. For example, consider the use of equities of closed-end funds that invest in asset classes not allowed by UCITS funds, such as offshore hedge funds or distressed securities or loans. Even in many prospectuses of UCITS funds, clauses exist related to the suspension of redemptions such as redemption gates. Redemption gates allow the investment manager to pay only a maximum percentage of the amount redeemed in line with the usual redemption terms (i.e., 10 percent of the amount redeemed) on the applicable redemption date and to postpone the payment of the remainder to the following dealing dates. That is, the first 10 percent is paid on the first redemption date and another 10 percent is paid on the following redemption date so that the total amount is paid on 10 consecutive redemption dates. The risk in these circumstances is to remain exposed to market risks more than expected, also having a delay in the redemption payment.

Two further issues need to be considered: (1) the settlement of a subscription and (2) a redemption order for funds with daily liquidity exits with 10 days' notice and that publish the NAV with five days' delay. Would an investor still consider a fund as a daily liquidity fund? Hence, investors need to consider the notice period for subscriptions and redemptions together with cut-off times.

Summary and Conclusions

Mutual fund risks are connected to the strategies followed by the money managers, spanning the spectrum from passive to absolute return strategies. Market risks, connected to market dynamics, and operational risks, related to the functioning of the legal entity, are intrinsically linked to the mutual fund and need to be mapped, measured, and evaluated. This chapter presents the complex mutual fund risk evaluation process including quantitative assessments and qualitative evaluations, which together offer a clear understanding of mutual fund risks. By quantitatively and qualitatively processing all risk factors faced by mutual funds, analysts monitor a list of relevant issues that leads them to realize financial and operational due diligences.

Mutual fund risk quantification is primarily assessed based on returns. Conducting ex post and ex ante analyses helps investors and analysts understand a fund's main risk-return drivers (risk factors), how it behaves over time conditional on market dynamics (risk dynamics), and how the performance should be viewed in both negative and positive market scenarios (market-timing ability). To do this requires the following: (1) identifying a reference benchmark to compare the risk-return profile in relative terms; (2) formalizing a mathematical model to disentangle all components of mutual fund risk; and (3) identifying a taxonomy of risk factors for both equity and fixed-income mutual funds to execute an effective risk-mapping decomposition.

Operational due diligence starts by reviewing official fund documents to verify whether a fund satisfies some issues such as fund administration, internal pricing rules, fund liquidity, and internal audit procedures. Recent financial innovations, including management account platforms and novel mutual fund strategies, lead to considering the operational risks that indirectly affect financial vehicles such as mutual funds. While the review of the risks of mutual funds offered in this chapter is not exhaustive, it shows how investing in mutual funds became a complex issue and requires reading offering documents and paying attention to details.

Discussion Questions

1. Describe the main points of financial due diligence for a mutual fund.
2. Discuss how to quantitatively decompose mutual fund risks.
3. Identify the elements of an effective risk-mapping strategy for mutual funds.
4. Discuss the rationale behind the methodology called "swing pricing."

References

Admati, Anat R., Sudipto Bhattacharya, Paul Pfleiderer, and Stephen A. Ross. 1986. "On Timing and Selectivity." *Journal of Finance* 41:3, 715–730.

Admati, Anat R., and Paul Pfleiderer. 1997. "Does It All Add Up? Benchmarks and the Compensation of Portfolio Managers." *Journal of Business* 70:3, 323–350.

Amisano, Gianni, and Roberto Savona. 2008. "Imperfect Predictability and Mutual Fund Dynamics: How Managers Use Predictors in Changing Systematic Risk." European Central Bank, Working Paper No. 881, March, 1–53.

Association of Luxembourg Fund Industry. 2006a. "Swing Pricing." Available at http://www.alfi.lu/sites/alfi.lu/files/ALFI_Swing_Pricing.pdf.

Association of Luxembourg Fund Industry. 2006b. "Swing Pricing." Available at http://www.alfi.lu/sites/alfi.lu/files/file/Alfi%20guidelines%20and%20recommendations/ALFI%20Swing%20Pricing_2006-2010-27.pdf.

Association of Luxembourg Fund Industry. 2011. "Annual Report 2010–2011". Available at http://www.alfi.lu//sites/alfi.lu/files/files/Annual%20report/alfi_rapport2011_web.pdf.

Barberis, Nicholas, and Andrei Shleifer. 2003. "Style Investing." *Journal of Financial Economics* 68:2, 161–199.

Becker, Connie, Wayne Ferson, David H. Myers, and Michael J. Schill. 1999. "Conditional Market Timing with Benchmark Investors." *Journal of Financial Economics* 52:1, 119–148.

Brinson, Gary P., Randolph L. Hood, and Gilbert L. Beebower. 1986. "Determinants of Portfolio Performance." *Financial Analysts Journal* 42:4, 39–44.

Brown, Stephen J., and William N. Goetzmann. 1995. "Performance Persistence." *Journal of Finance* 50:2, 679–698.

Brown, Keith C., W. V. Harlow, and Laura T. Starks. 1996. "Of Tournaments and Temptations: An Analysis of Managerial Incentives in the Mutual Fund Industry." *Journal of Finance* 51:1, 85–110.

Chen, Yong, Wayne Ferson, and Helen Peters. 2006. "Measuring the Timing Ability of Fixed Income Mutual Funds." Working Paper, Boston College.

Chevalier, Judith, and Glen Ellison. 1997. "Risk Taking by Mutual Funds as a Response to Incentives." *Journal of Political Economy* 105:6, 1167–1200.

Cohen, Randolph, Joshua D. Coval, and Luboš Pástor. 2005. "Judging Fund Managers by the Company They Keep." *Journal of Finance* 60:3, 1057–1096.

Coval, Joshua D., and Tobias J. Moskowitz. 2001. "The Geography of Investment: Informed Trading and Asset Prices." *Journal of Political Economy* 109:41, 811–841.

Daniel, Kent, Mark Grinblatt, Sheridan Titman, and Russ Wermers. 1997. "Measuring Mutual Fund Performance with Characteristic-Based Benchmarks." *Journal of Finance* 52:3, 1035–1058.

Elton Edwin J., Martin J. Gruber, Sanjiv Das, and Matthew Hlavka. 1993. "Efficiency with Costly Information: A Reinterpretation of Evidence from Manager Portfolios." *Review of Financial Studies* 6:1, 1–23.

Fama, Eugene F. 1972. "Components of Investment Performance." *Journal of Finance* 27:3, 551–567.

Fung, William, and David A. Hsieh. 2001. "The Risk in Hedge Fund Strategies: Theory and Evidence from Trend Followers." *Review of Financial Studies* 14:2, 313–341.

Glosten, Lawrence, and Ravi Jagannathan. 1994. "A Contingent Claims Approach to Performance Evaluation." *Journal of Empirical Finance* 1:2, 133–166.

Grinblatt, Mark, and Sheridan Titman. 1989. "Portfolio Performance Evaluation: Old Issues and New Insights." *Review of Financial Studies* 2:3, 396–422.

Gruber, Martin J. 1996. "Another Puzzle: The Growth in Actively Managed Mutual Funds." *Journal of Finance* 51:3, 783–810.

Henriksson, Roy D., and Robert C. Merton. 1981. "On Market Timing and Investment Performance II: Statistical Procedures for Evaluating Forecasting Skills." *Journal of Business* 54:4, 513–534.

Jensen, Michael C. 1968. "The Performance of Mutual Funds in the Period 1945–1964." *Journal of Finance* 23:2, 389–416.

Kacperczyk, Marcin, Clemens Sialm, and Lu Zheng. 2005. "On the Industry Concentration of Actively Managed Equity Mutual Funds." *Journal of Finance* 60:4, 1983–2011.

Mamaysky, Harry, Matthew J. Spiegel, and Hong Zhang. 2008. "Estimating the Dynamics of Mutual Fund Alphas and Betas." *Review of Financial Studies* 21:1, 223–264.

Merton, Robert C. 1981. "On Market Timing and Investment Performance. I. An Equilibrium Theory of Value for Market Forecasts." *Journal of Business* 54:3, 363–406.

MSCI Barra. 2010. "BarraOne Analytics Guide." Available at http://www.mscibarra.com.

Schultz, Ellen E. 1996. "Vanguard Bucks Trend by Cutting Fund Fees." *Wall Street Journal*, January 30, c1–c25.

Sharpe, William F. 1966. "Mutual Fund Performance." *Journal of Business* 39:1, 119–138.

Starks, Laura T. 1987. "Performance Incentive Fees: An Agency Theoretic Approach." *Journal of Financial and Quantitative Analysis* 22:1, 17–32.

Treynor, Jack L., and Kay K. Mazuy. 1966. "Can Mutual Funds Outguess the Market?" *Harvard Business Review* 44:4, 131–136.

Part Five

FUND STRUCTURE

22

Organization, Structure, and Services of Mutual Funds

MARK POTTER
Associate Professor of Finance and Finance Division Chair, Babson College

Introduction

Investing in portfolios of assets has been around for at least hundreds of years. Yet, only since the 1980s has the mutual fund industry changed its product and service structure to serve a broader array of clients—namely the middle and upper-middle class. This shift has mainly occurred either directly or through defined contribution (DC) plans, pension plans, or college savings vehicles. Because of the wider target demographic, the government has become more extensively involved in regulating these "public" savings vehicles. Surprisingly, the structure of mutual funds has stayed largely consistent over 100 years, but the service aspect has changed dramatically over the same period. Because of the wealth of data now available, researchers can examine the links among the structure of fund management firms, mutual funds, performance, and risk-taking activities. This chapter describes the organization and structure of mutual funds and fund firms, and explores the major research that has been done in this area.

The rest of the chapter has the following organization. The next section covers the organization of mutual funds, including how they are structured and the important related entities. The following section contains a discussion about the services provided by funds and fund firms, as well as a description of the current drivers of the fund management industry. Finally, the chapter contains a summary and conclusion section.

Organization of Fund Sponsors and Mutual Funds

The prevalence of investment in mutual funds is extensive. The origin of funds' setups have roots in the 1700s and were originally designed to democratize investments to provide smaller investors with a mechanism to own corporations previously reserved for large capitalists. According to the Investment Company Institute (2014), the

United States alone had 800 fund sponsors by the end of 2013. Yet, the top 25 fund complexes owned 72 percent of the total market share. These complexes consist mainly of familiar names including Vanguard, Fidelity, BlackRock, Janus, American, and Franklin Templeton. This group contains a mix of publicly and privately owned firms. Regardless of the volume of firms, families, funds, and ownership types, these registered investment companies have a common theme and a fair amount of consistency around how they operate.

Registered investment companies take the form of among four structures: open-end, closed-end, unit investment trusts, and exchange-traded. The other investment companies differ from Open-end funds along many dimensions.

- *Open-end funds (OEFs)*. The term mutual fund normally refers to an open-end fund, which is a key innovation that separates what the fund owns from who owns the fund. Specifically, the fund receives a pool of capital from investors and uses the pool to purchase ownership in various securities. The fund stands ready to allow investors the flexibility to redeem their fund shares with some potential constraints.
- *Closed-end funds (CEFs)*. A closed-end fund, also call a closed-end investment company, issues a fixed number of shares that require investors to buy and sell shares of the CEFs directly from other investors. Thus, the prices of shares of the CEFs can deviate from the underlying value of the shares themselves.
- *Unit investment trusts (UITs)*. Unit investment trusts also issue a fixed number of shares although these shares are redeemable, and the sponsor generally maintains a market in these shares to provide a buffer that does not force the portfolio to constantly liquidate small amounts of securities it owns.
- *Exchange-traded funds (ETFs)*. Exchange-traded funds can be set up structurally as an OEF or a UIT, offering investors the opportunity to buy and sell shares of the ETF during the day as opposed to waiting until after the market closes, when the shares of OEFs are ultimately priced.

Mutual funds are organized in a legal framework that is either a corporation or a trust. According to the Investment Company Institute (2014), 90 percent of mutual funds are organized as Massachusetts business trusts (38 percent), Delaware statutory trusts (37 percent), or Maryland corporations (15 percent). The remaining 10 percent of funds is set up mainly as trusts in other states, or as limited liability partnerships. One primary driver of how funds are organized is history and momentum. For example, Massachusetts was the first state to house a mutual fund, which provided a model for others to follow. More recently, changes to laws in Delaware and Maryland created more consistency with mutual fund regulations and that has driven most new funds to be set up in those domiciles.

How Mutual Funds Are Structured

A *mutual fund* is a legal entity whose objective is to receive capital from investors, pool it, and invest the capital into securities according to a pre-determined objective. Those who have a relationship to the mutual fund include: (1) fund shareholders, (2) board of directors or trustees, (3) fund sponsor or investment advisor, (4) fund administrator, (5) underwriter, (6) transfer agent, (7) custodian, and (8) independent accountant.

FUND SHAREHOLDERS

A fund's shareholders consist of individuals or companies who have bought shares of the mutual fund. The number of outstanding shares at any given point in time is a function of several factors: (1) the demand for the fund and any restrictions the fund has on ownership such as minimum investment size, (2) whether it is closed to all or new investors, and (3) whether investors can purchase the shares directly or through other possible distribution channels. The number of shares can range substantially among funds, from a few hundred shares outstanding for the Switzerland Cap Weighted Index Fund to more than 100 million shares for the Vanguard 500 Index Fund.

Multiple share classes also exist for most mutual funds. They typically differ by distribution channel or types of expenses attached (Securities and Exchange Commission 2014). For example, mutual funds may offer A, B, and C shares to retail investors but these shares contain different fee structures. A shares usually have a front-end sales charge (or load). B shares have a back-end load and a 12b-1 fee that changes over time. C shares may have multiple fees but they are lower than the other retail classes. The final share class (Class "I") is reserved for mutual funds bought by institutions. An investor willing to purchase shares of a mutual fund can do so in several ways. For example, Table 22.1 shows the Wells Fargo Advantage Growth Fund (ticker SGROX):

According to Morningstar (2014a) as illustrated in Table 22.2, SGROX has been closed to new investors since January 2012, but existing fund investors and accountholders can continue to buy shares in the mutual fund. A minimum initial investment of $2,500 is required and investors can make additional investments as long as they meet the minimum level of $100. Share classes differ according to minimum initial purchase amounts, expenses that apply, and type of access. Finally, the fund is available through various brokers and not just to those with a Wells Fargo account. As Table 22.2 shows, the fund is available through 82 different avenues.

This wide array of distribution channels for mutual funds did not exist a decade or so ago. Historically, a mutual fund complex sold only its own funds and did not allow others to sell its funds. Similar to other industries, funds now provide investors with more choice and selection while promoting funds through other broker networks. This change has affected the competitive nature of the funds making them less expensive to own resulting in higher achievement benchmarks and a more crystallized strategy for fund companies. Specifically, fund families and complexes now offer a broader array of products, services, and fund features at lower costs. Combined with regulation of horizon and risk funds and new approaches to quantitative research and behavioral science, product innovation in the sphere of mutual funds has never been greater.

BOARD OF DIRECTORS

Each fund has a board consisting of officers and directors or trustees, depending on whether the fund is set up as a corporation or as a trust. The board has a combination of

Table 22.1 **Wells Fargo Advantage Growth Fund Structural Characteristics**

SGROX	
Minimum initial investment	$2,500
Additional investments	$100
Closed to all investors	No
Closed to new investors as of January 31, 2012	Yes

SGROX

Fund Name	*Front Load (%)*	*Deferred Load (%)*	*Expense (%)*	*Minimum Initial Purchase ($)*	*12b-1 Actual (%)*	*Purchase Constraint*
Wells Fargo Advantage Growth A	5.75	—	1.19	1,000	0.00	C
Wells Fargo Advantage Growth Adm	—	—	0.96	1,000,000	0.00	T/A/C
Wells Fargo Advantage Growth C	—	1.00	1.94	1,000	0.75	C
Wells Fargo Advantage Growth I	—	—	0.75	5,000,000	0.00	T/C
Wells Fargo Advantage Growth Inv	—	—	1.25	2,500	0.00	C

Note: This table illustrates the buy-in minimum, whether the fund is closed to all or new investors, as well as the specific annual, front-end, 12b-1, or deferred load costs of owning the Wells Fargo Advantage Growth Fund (SGROX), depending on the distribution channel. For the "Purchase Constraints" column, C refers to closed to new investments, T refers to institutional access, A refers to qualified access.

Source: Morningstar 2014a.

insider and independent members. It provides oversight of the fund and has the general responsibility to represent the interests of the fund's shareholders. The board has three major directives:

- Review and approve major contracts with service providers including the fees paid to the *investment advisor*, which is the company that decides how to invest the pool of money provided by the fund's shareholders.

Table 22.2 **Brokerage Channel Availability for Wells Fargo Advantage Growth Fund**

ADP Access OFA	JP Morgan INVEST
Ameriprise Brokerage	LPL SAM Eligible
Ameriprise SPS Advantage	Matrix Financial Solutions
Ameritas NTF P	Met Life Resources MFSP Alliance List
Ameritas NTFN	Mid Atlantic Capital Corp
Ausdal Financial Partners, Inc.	Mony Securities Corp
Bear Stearns	Northwestern Mutual Inv Srvc, LLC
Bear Stearns No-Load Transaction Fee	NYLIM 401(k) Complete
Cetera Advisors LLC PAM and PRIME	Pershing FundCenter
Cetera Advisors Networks LLC PAM & PRIME	Pershing FundVest NTF
Cetera Financial Specialists LLC	Principal Advantage
CommonWealth NTF	Protected Investors of America NTF
CommonWealth Universe	PruChoice Investments
DailyAccess Corporation FRIAG	Prudential Retail
DailyAccess Corporation MATC	Raymond James
DailyAccess Corporation Matrix	Raymond James WRAP Eligible
DailyAccess Corporation Mid-Atlantic	RBC Wealth Management-Advisory Eligible
DailyAccess Corporation RTC	RBC Wealth Management-Network Eligible
DATALynx	Robert W. Baird & Co.
DATALynx IMS	Royal Alliance
DATALynx NTF	Schwab All (Retail, Institutional, and Retirement)
Dreyfus NTF	Schwab Existing Shareholders Only
DWS Retirement Sevs Investment Offerings	Schwab OneSource & NTF (No-Load and No Transaction Fee)
E TRADE Financial	Scottrade NTF
ETrade No-Load Fee	Shareholders Services Group
ETrade No-Load NTF	Standard Retirement Services, Inc.
Federated TrustConnect NTF	Sterne, Agee & Leach, Inc.,
Fidelity Institutional FundsNetwork	SunAmerica Securities Premier / Pinnacle

continued

Table 22.2 **(continued)**

Fidelity Institutional FundsNetwork-NTF	SunGard Transaction Network
Fidelity Retail FundsNetwork	T. Rowe Price
Fidelity Retail FundsNetwork-NTF	TD Ameritrade Institutional NTF
Firstrade	TD Ameritrade Retail NTF
H&R Block Financial Advisors Inc	TD Ameritrade Trust Company
HDVest-Wells Fargo	Thrivent – Advisory Eligible
HSBC Brokerage (USA) Inc	TIAA-CREF Brokerage Services
ING Financial Ptnrs PAM and PRIME Approv	TIAA-CREF NTF
Investacorp NTF	Trade PMR Transaction Fee
JP Morgan No-Load NTF	TradeStation Securities
JP Morgan No-load Transaction Fee	UBS Financial Services Inc.
JP Morgan NTF	Vanguard NTF
JP Morgan	WR Hambrecht Co LLC

Note: This table shows the available companies from which investors can access the Wells Fargo Advantage Growth Fund. A total of 82 distinct ways to obtain this fund are available.

- Ensure that the fund complies with the law and establish policies and procedures to ensure compliance including oversight around the fund's share pricing, valuation, and portfolio liquidity.
- Review the fund's performance, which includes adherence to the fund's stated investment objectives.

FUND SPONSOR OR INVESTMENT ADVISOR

Companies acting as fund sponsors determine when to initiate the process to launch a new mutual fund. This process involves navigating regulations, constructing the fund's infrastructure, and putting together the board of directors, which in turn contracts with third-party or related affiliates to help run the fund. According to the Investment Company Institute (2014), there were 68 mutual funds in 1940 and 7,707 at the end of 2013. The proliferation of mutual funds has resulted from several factors: (1) the combination of demographic and societal factors, including moving defined benefit (DB) to DC pension plans, (2) a burgeoning middle and upper-middle class, (3) knowledge and education about investment opportunities, and (4) the low cost of starting and maintaining investment accounts. From a marketing perspective, fund sponsors continue to improve their opportunities to attract new customers and to increase the account size of existing customers.

As customers demand more choices, fund firms have provided them. A proliferation of fund categories has emerged over time as investors have become more in tune to the necessity of global asset allocation. Fund sponsors are adept at removing funds that are not performing well or gaining enough market share. For example, Swedroe (2014) cites a study by Vanguard that only 54 percent of mutual funds survived over a 15-year period ending in December 2011. The rest disappeared mainly through mergers into other funds. Using the same 15-year horizon and combining data from the Investment Company Institute, the results show 6,684 total mutual funds in 1997. By the end of 2011, the number of mutual funds had increased to 7,580. Over the period between 1997 and 2011, 2,364 funds were merged or liquidated indicating that fund sponsors initiated 3,260 mutual funds over that horizon. From a product management perspective, fund sponsors have been pulling about two funds for every three they start. Over time, the death rate of mutual funds hovers around 2 percent per year, whereas the birth rate of mutual funds averages about 3 percent per year. Thus, fund sponsors decide the birth and death of funds as well as control much of the fund's daily operations through other services and contracts.

Besides offering a portfolio of funds to investors, fund sponsors typically serve as the fund's investment advisor. As the name suggests, the mutual fund's board "hires" the fund sponsor to invest the mutual fund's pool of capital in a manner that is consistent with the fund's investment objective in a way that the investment advisor best sees fit to achieve performance objectives within a risk framework. Investment advisors can make investment decisions for a single mutual fund or for more than 100 mutual funds. The fund's board of directors oversees payments from the mutual fund to the investment advisor. As a result of enhanced competition since about 2000, advisor fees have declined substantially.

FUND ADMINISTRATOR

The mutual fund's board also hires the fund administrator who handles the fund's back-office operations. Generally, the administrator operationalizes and oversees the internal controls and compliance procedures by which the fund is regulated including filings to the Securities and Exchange Commission (SEC) and tax authorities. The administrator also oversees the funds internal audit function, produces shareholder reports, and performs fund accounting and clerical support, data processing, and bookkeeping. The administrator works closely with the investment advisor, and often the fund advisor and administrator are the same company.

FUND UNDERWRITER, TRANSFER AGENT, AND CUSTODIAN

The mutual fund's board of directors hires the underwriter (distributor), transfer agent, and custodian to handle transactions with shareholders, oversee the fund's marketing and advertising, and safeguard its assets and securities. For example, when investors seek to buy or sell (redeem) shares of the mutual fund, the fund's underwriter handles the transactions. An *underwriter* is technically a broker-dealer and is the legal entity that stands in between a mutual fund and investors, selling the fund's shares to investors and buying its shares from investors, either directly or indirectly through other distribution channels. In turn, the underwriter buys shares from and sells shares to the mutual fund. The underwriter also provides advertising and fund marketing services.

The *transfer agent* handles shareholder accounts and transaction requests, oversees disbursing funds from transactions including the calculation and distribution of capital gains and dividends. The transfer agent provides a range of shareholder services including preparing and mailing account statements and tax information, other shareholder notices, and fund prospectuses, reports, statements, and other material information of interest to the fund's investors. Not surprisingly, the transfer agent maintains a customer interface and investor service departments.

Finally, the mutual fund contracts with a *custodian* whose primary function is to handle the transactions and warehouse the mutual fund's securities and cash. An average equity mutual fund has an annual turnover rate of 80 to 100 percent (i.e., the fund buys and sells securities equal to between 80 percent and 100 percent of its total size over a year) totaling about $1 billion. Depending on the mutual fund type and at the portfolio manager's discretion, the mutual fund could have millions of dollars in cash at any given time. Thus, in practice, the custodian is tasked with holding the cash in a secure set of accounts, safeguarding hundreds of millions of dollars in securities at a given time, and settling portfolio transactions of additional hundreds of millions of dollars in a given year. The custodian also collects dividends and interest from the securities owned by the portfolio and manages the payment of authorized expenses and shareholder disbursements and redemptions from the standpoint of the fund's portfolio of securities owned.

The fund must pay each of these parties for the functions that they perform. For example, in the most recent annual report for Fidelity's Magellan Fund, the fund paid a management fee of roughly $85 million during fiscal year 2014 (Fidelity Magellan Annual Report 2014). This fee was, by far, the largest fee paid out by the fund. But the fund also paid about $21 million in transfer agent fees, $1.5 million in accounting fees, just under $300,000 in custodian fees and expenses, $78,000 in compensation to the independent trustees, and about $200,000 in audit fees and $63,000 in legal expenses.

Services Provided by Mutual Funds and Fund Firms

Mutual fund firms are essentially financial intermediaries. That is, they invest capital from investors and return it to investors on demand. Like most organizations that operate in a competitive environment, mutual fund firms offer investors incentives to entrust them, enhance brand awareness and image with marketing, partner with other firms to improve their tactical strengths and work with customers to create stronger bonds and loyalty. Historically, mutual funds have offered investors a low-cost way to diversify and access professional money management. Financial institutions are involved because of the amount of capital at stake and the tax incentives and consequences resulting from regulations. This framework results in an industry that is structured in a manner that promotes operational and product innovation while inhibiting corporate risk-taking. In recent years, the worlds of banking, investing, and payment systems have become blurred.

Although mutual fund firms have been at the forefront of financial innovation, the industry has been on the receiving end of disruptive innovations such as ETFs and *crowdfunding*, which is a direct funding tool for smaller companies. These innovations have collectively eroded the economic benefits enjoyed by mutual fund firms since the 1980s. Along with new regulation and a more educated customer base, fund firms have been forced to adapt their product offerings and enhance the services offered to their customers. Based on data obtained from Morningstar Direct (2014), 6,553 mutual fund firms offered a total of 92,208 distinct mutual fund portfolios worldwide as of August 31, 2014. This total compares to 10,555 CEFs, 11,537 ETFs, and 14,733 UITs.

INVESTMENT PRODUCT PORTFOLIO

A mutual fund firm is analogous to a transportation company that provides an array of alternatives to take someone from one place to another. In a transportation company, choices range from a personal limousine to public transport. Those needing transport rely on the transportation company to get them to their destination safely or at least in a manner that allows customers to choose along the trade-off dimensions of both speed and risk and expense and customization.

For portfolio management, the analogous selection criterion is between active management and passive investing. As recently as two decades ago, fund companies offered only five or six categories of funds such as equity, bond, aggressive growth, and money market funds. Funds within each category were mostly actively managed using a fundamental analysis strategy, which matched the informational advantage fund analysts and portfolio managers enjoyed at that time. Since the 1990s, fund firms changed their product and service offerings in response to new regulations and consumer demographics and choices. The following sections describe the drivers of fund and fund company services.

MORE FUND CHOICES

Since the 1990s, the investment and portfolio management community adopted the mantra that the asset allocation framework trumps security selection as a driver of portfolio returns and diversification. The genesis of this framework stems from the seminal work of Brinson, Hood, and Beebower (1986). Although Ibbotson and Kaplan (2000) find that asset allocation contributes less to returns than previously thought, this insight remains a fundamental tenet of product introduction strategies of asset management firms. Fund families now seek to offer an array of fund choices that fall within asset allocation buckets that have been shown to help diversify an investor's portfolio, such as large, mid-, small cap funds and value or growth funds. Also, much of the world's gross domestic product (GDP) growth is now concentrated overseas producing more fund choices focusing on that geography simultaneous to global markets opening to foreign equity investment. Funds categories have emerged based on sector or industry. In sum, the fund categories match the research into asset allocation diversification potential in recent years. Morningstar (2014b) lists 50 overall categories of mutual funds with many of these containing additional subdivisions.

INDEX FUNDS AND ETFS

Besides having more choices, investors recognize that identifying mutual funds that can beat the market is challenging. So investments that seek to match a benchmark, such as index funds and ETFs, are the products that continue to see sizable growth in market share. Fund families that focus and maintain tactical strength in active management also offer index funds or access to others' index funds. They now focus their active management funds in categories that have shown some propensity to achieve market-beating returns on an after-expense basis. A search on http://www.morningstar.com by fund name containing "ind" (representing index funds) returned 859 results and the Morningstar Direct database of worldwide funds lists 6,029 index funds as of mid-2014. According to the Investment Company Institute (2014), 33 percent of equity mutual fund assets are held in index funds. The market share of index funds stands at nearly 20 percent.

Perhaps the most staggering statistic is the most recent annual cash inflow to ETFs and index funds compared to active funds during 2013. Domestic equity index funds and ETFs saw net cash inflows of $800 billion during 2013 but active equity funds experienced net outflows of $600 million in the same year. Actively managed mutual funds and fund families whose strategy has historically focused on active management have had to modify their fund portfolios away from active management in environments where they historically have had a difficult time beating the index. These same firms have retained a focus on active management in environments where they seek to maintain an informational advantage, such as small cap and global equity markets.

Most ETFs are designed to act like less expensive and more flexible versions of an index fund so matching the performance of various markets has become easier for investors. The average expense ratio of ETFs in 2013 was 88 basis points, compared to 250 basis points for mutual funds (Potter 2014). Newer versions of ETFs have increasingly narrower objectives, such as a focus on firms that have a high social responsibility or entrepreneurship score. So ironically, these more narrowly defined ETFs have resulted in higher risk profiles for ETFs, on average, compared with traditional mutual funds even in similar categories. For example, Potter (2014) reports a mean (median) beta of 2.77 (0.94) for ETFs and a mean (median) beta of 1.18 (0.90) for comparable mutual funds.

Figure 22.1 shows comparisons of mutual funds and ETFs in terms of tenure, fund size, expense ratio, and turnover. Expense ratios are greater for mutual funds than for ETFs in more than 90 percent of the 50 matched categories of mutual funds and ETFs. Turnover is also higher for mutual funds in most categories although mutual funds are larger and the fund manager tenure is longer. As mutual funds and ETFs offer the potential for diversification benefits, each fund or ETF may not be well diversified even if they own 80 to 100 securities on average, especially if the fund's mandate specifies a particular focus. For example, Potter (2014) also finds that ETFs exhibit greater *tracking error* (i.e., deviation from a pre-specified benchmark) thus potentially reducing diversification benefits.

Figure 22.2 shows the role tracking error plays in the cross-sectional variation in performance and diversification potential of mutual funds and ETFs. For example, about 10 mutual funds would be needed to reduce the cross-sectional standard deviation of performance equivalent to roughly double the number of ETFs to achieve a commensurate risk reduction. That is, mutual fund performance more closely aligns with category objectives and benchmarks compared to ETFs.

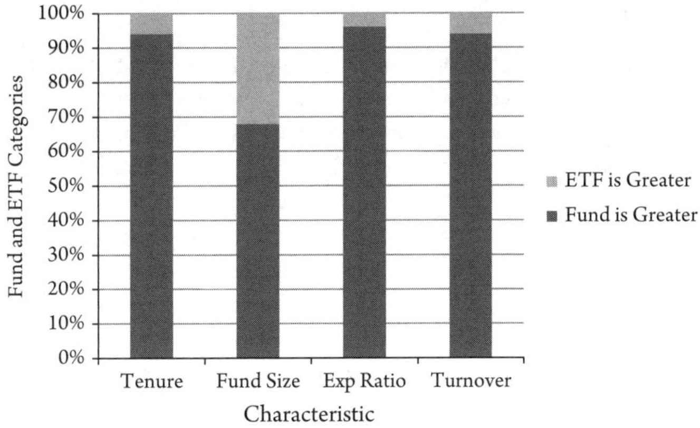

Figure 22.1 Comparison of Other Fund and Exchange-Traded Fund Characteristics during 2013. This figure depicts the relative characteristics comparison of ETFs and mutual funds for the 50 categories that are common between the two groups during 2013. Characteristics for comparison include manager experience (tenure), fund size, expense ratio, and turnover.

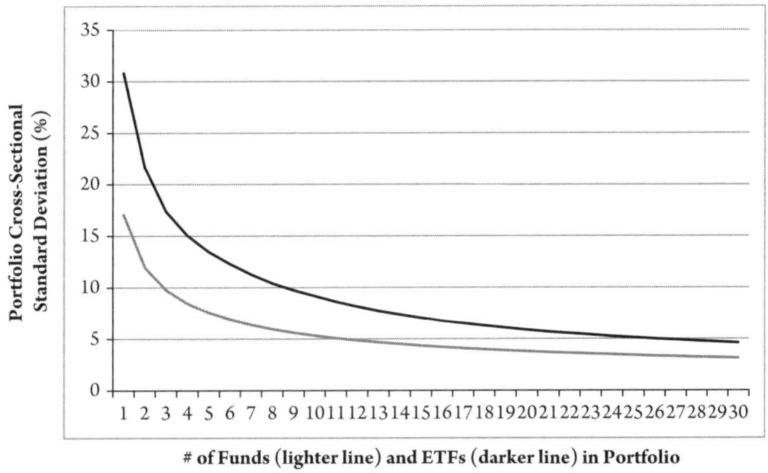

Figure 22.2 Diversification Potential of Mutual Funds and Exchange-Traded Funds during 2013. This figure shows the result of a simulation of randomly created portfolios of mutual funds (lighter line) and ETFs (darker line). For example, 20,000 randomly created three-fund portfolios have a standard deviation of 10 percent and 20,000 randomly created eight-ETF portfolios have a standard deviation of 10 percent.

HYBRID FUNDS

Besides a heightened emphasis on asset allocation, more mutual funds are aligning their portfolio strategy directly to investor objectives. In order to reduce the burden of decision-making on investors, recent reform in pension legislation requires corporations to assist employees in selecting the right mix of mutual funds for their long-term goals. In short, the biggest product proliferation has been in hybrid funds, a type of fund of funds in which the portfolio manager selects several equity mutual funds and bond mutual funds to hold in the portfolio. According to the Investment Company Institute (2014), the number of hybrid funds increased from about 50 in 2008 to nearly 400 by the end of 2013. Morningstar Direct (2014) lists 3,238 lifestyle funds worldwide as of mid-2014. A *lifestyle fund* is a fund that seeks to pre-identify a risk metric that the portfolio manager attempts to match by selecting stocks, bonds, or other funds that fit into the overall fund's objective (e.g., low risk).

Interestingly, most hybrid and lifestyle funds rarely result from newly created mutual funds, but rather involve combinations of existing funds. For example, the T. Rowe Price 2030 target date fund recommends an asset allocation of 80 percent stocks and 20 percent bonds for investors who want to retire in 2030. This allocation adjusts to 60 percent stocks and 40 percent bonds for investors who want to retire five years from today. The hybrid 2030 fund will automatically adjust the asset allocation according to the target retirement goal date of 2030. The top 10 holdings of the T. Rowe Price 2030 fund are: (1) Emerging Markets Stock Fund, (2) Equity Index 500 Fund, (3) Growth Stock Fund, (4) International Growth and Income Fund, (5) International Stock Fund, (6) Mid-Cap Value Fund, (7) New Income Fund, (8) Overseas Stock Funds, (9) Real Assets Fund, and (10) Value Fund. Thus, the 2030 fund is just a combination of other T. Rowe Price mutual funds that are held in a proportion recommended by a quantitative asset allocation optimization program.

The stickiness of flows into and out of mutual funds is an important subject that is very much related to product offerings of fund companies since fund families and portfolio managers want to retain and increase market share, while reducing the volatility of fund flows. Since Sirri and Tufano's (1998) seminal study on the stickiness of mutual fund flows, various studies have followed that seek to address the question about volatility of fund flows depending on asset or product type. For example, according to Sialm, Starks, and Zhang (2014), mutual funds that are part of a DC plan offerings set experience much greater sensitivity of flows related to performance. Both the plan sponsors (employers) and fund participants (employees) appear to be monitoring performance more closely than investors in non-DC fund environments. Whether the more recent target date and lifestyle fund offerings will experience a similar flow-performance relationship remains to be seen especially given the challenges involved in creating and applying transparent benchmarks to these types of mutual funds.

The services offered by the mutual fund company are to recommend a particular asset allocation to an investor with a pre-defined investment goal or objective and to automatically funnel the investor into the funds appropriate to that mix. Expense ratios for target-date funds and hybrid funds are larger and they are a renewed source of profitability for fund complexes. Other hybrid funds seek to match to an investor's risk level instead of the time horizon. For customers who have a determinate and measurable risk tolerance, fund companies match their allocation to a particular hybrid fund designed to target that risk level.

IMPACT OF BIG DATA

The big data revolution is driving the services offered by mutual funds. The availability of information related to potential customers, investor backgrounds, securities, and global markets is steering mutual fund tactics, especially in light of recent regulation around the equitable availability of data. Mutual funds now operate in an environment in which relevant and material information about companies is made available to all investors simultaneously. Tactically, to retain superior service and performance, mutual funds have migrated toward spending resources in order to filter and analyze large amounts of data. For example, fund firms use electronic tracking mechanisms to determine how analysts and portfolio managers seek and absorb information to make buy and sell decisions, then filter the most useful news to specific desktops accordingly.

Mutual funds embed more quantitative research into their portfolio analytics to move the efficient frontier toward a more optimal solution. Smart beta strategies are a recent useful tool in this arsenal because they disentangle risk factors into compartmentalized asset categories solely for enhancing diversification and understanding risk analytics (Jacobs and Levy 2014). The volume of data available has also allowed mutual funds to spend considerable time and resources analyzing tail or downside risk (Chong and Phillips 2011).

INTEGRATED SHAREHOLDER SERVICES AND TAX MANAGEMENT

Perhaps the most valuable service offered by funds and fund companies relates to the enhanced account management opportunity. This development is a way for funds and complexes to help investors with combining investing strategy with tax strategy. A host of retirement plans are available to investors (Individual Retirement Accounts or IRAs, Roth IRAs, 403b, 401k, and others), health care savings accounts, and college savings plans, each having distinct objectives, horizons, and tax rules. To get a sense of the variety of services offered, the Morningstar Direct (2014) database contains 1,518 fund and portfolio management companies as of mid-2014. Of those, 76 percent manage portfolios for other asset management institutions and 59 percent manage portfolios directly for individuals and small businesses. Slightly fewer than 10 percent offer financial planning services and 7 percent provide pension consulting.

Investors are armed with the knowledge to manage many of these investments themselves, but to combine them into a comprehensive after-tax portfolio management strategy is challenging. By merging all investor accounts, the fund company can optimize the appropriate asset allocation. For example, the fund company could analyze information about the investor related to objectives, risk tolerance, horizon or multiple horizons, and any constraints. It could also use a questionnaire to ascertain an investor's psychological or behavioral profile to ensure the overall portfolio strategy is consistent. The fund company could then launch an appropriate asset allocation strategy. The location of the funds and securities is carefully placed so that those with the greatest tax

Table 22.3 **Approximate Tax-Efficiency Ranking for Major Asset Classes**

Place in a Taxable Account or Anywhere	*Generally Most Tax Efficient* • Low-yield money market, cash, and short-term bond funds • Tax-managed stock funds • Large cap and total market stock index funds • Balanced index funds • Small cap or mid-cap index funds • Value index funds
Place in a Taxable Account or Tax-Deferred Account Depending on Specific Investment Characteristics	*Moderately Tax Efficient* • Moderate-yield money market and bond funds • Total market bond funds • Active stock funds
Place in a Tax-Free or Tax-Deferred Account	*Highly Inefficient* • Real estate or REIT funds • High-turnover active funds • High-yield corporate bonds

Note: This table shows the relationship between the types of asset classes typically held by investors, alongside the types of accounts in which they should be held in the general order needed to maximize after-tax returns.

liability or potential future tax liability are moved into the accounts that are non-taxable or non-taxable for the longest amount of time.

Table 22.3 shows that securities and funds that have the lowest tax liability are optimally housed in a representative investor's taxable accounts. Another strategy involves *tax loss harvesting* in which losses in one account can offset gains in another account reducing the investor's near-term tax liability. A fund company managing multiple investor accounts can be set up to recognize this and automatically deploy sell and buy decisions to minimize taxes while not violating wash-sale rules. Mutual funds can employ these tactics independently of investor characteristics to achieve a balance of tax alpha, which emphasizes transactions designed to enhance after-tax returns and minimize tax liability and tracking error, or the deviation of performance against a pre-determined benchmark. Regardless of how this is accomplished, these current techniques require combining data around the investor, optimization, future tax rate predictions, and embedded market risk and return expectations.

Lau (2014) estimates that the impact to a baseline investment strategy that pays attention to tax and financial planning in the allocation and location process can add 320 basis points per year to the overall portfolio's performance. Given this result and that these data are more readily available to mutual funds and fund firms, tax location and efficiency investing has become an important source of new products and services as well as a new tactical tool used by mutual funds to create value. Admittedly, the fees are greater for fund families with a greater array of investor assets under their umbrellas.

Since they are explicitly tied to a tax strategy, investors are less likely to switch to other funds or complexes.

IMPACT OF STRUCTURE AND SERVICES ON FUND PERFORMANCE AND RISK

As noted previously, a mutual fund segregates the contracts between investors and the investment advisor. This structure of separating the investment assets from the management assets is fairly novel among organizational forms. Some contend that investors should contract directly with the fund's investment managers. Morley (2013) argues that although this structure restricts investors' rights to control managers, it offers investors the opportunity to benefit from their success. This structure gives investors the right to easily exit those funds that are not managing funds efficiently. This "ease of exit" creates a de facto control provision that effectively serves as control rights. Haslem (2013) maintains that because of the segregated structure, coupled with a lack of transparency and fund boards that may not be acting in the best interests of fund shareholders, investors experience a lack of control and achieve lower performance while fund firms enjoy a greater profitability. In recent years, fund boards and firms are becoming more active in proxy voting and are voting "with their feet."

Duan and Jiao (2013) find that mutual fund families have improved their governance mechanisms particularly through proxy voting, although funds with shorter horizons or that own smaller share volumes will revert to trading behavior especially in a small company environment. Moreover, Ding and Wermers (2013) report that independent board members are critical in holding portfolio managers accountable for performance, although large fund complexes appear to actively monitor, evaluate, and respond to underperformance.

A fund complex can take on various shapes and sizes. For example, comprehensive fund management firms offer private wealth services, tax strategy advice, and unique and personalized financial planning. By contrast, some fund management firms focus primarily on offering low-cost products and services designed for investors who make their own decisions. Similarly, the thousands of mutual fund choices competing for market share and performance offer an array of structures designed to reduce costs, create value, or enhance the level of service offered to investors. In fact, Del Guercio, Reuter, and Tkac (2011) find that only 3.3 percent of fund families serve multiple target markets. Further, segmentation among funds and how brokers are compensated reinforces dual distribution channels. In a review and analysis of broker benefits and costs in the mutual fund industry, Bergstresser, Chalmers, and Tufano (2009) find that brokers do not deliver sufficient tangible benefits to investors relative to their costs.

The structure of fund management and analysis is poised to have the greatest impact on performance. Nanda, Narayanan, and Warther (2000) explain why mutual funds are set up as either OEFs or CEFs according to fund managers' skills, liquidity needs, and expense set up. Portfolio management teams, normally groups of two to five individuals, now manage 60 percent of mutual funds, whereas funds managed by a single person is down to 40 percent, which is the lowest on record. Evidence shows that teams generally have similar performance to funds managed by individuals but at a lower risk (Bliss, Potter, and Schwarz 2008). Csaszar (2012) finds that a team-managed structure makes fewer errors of commission (i.e., make bad decisions), but more errors of omission (i.e., miss good decisions). Massa and Zhang (2010) analyze the organizational structure of bond fund managers. They find that the more hierarchical the management team is, the less likely it will display local investment bias, but will hold more concentrated portfolios, and exhibit strong performance. A relationship also appears among team fund management, performance, and the fund's board of directors. Adams, Nishikawa, and Rao (2013) find that team-managed funds with highly independent boards exhibit superior performance, especially when compared to their individually managed fund counterparts.

Nanda, Wang, and Zheng (2009) analyze the effects of introducing new share classes on fund flows and performance. They find that fund inflows are significant during the first two years following new share class introductions, but the shareholders are shorter term in focus and are more sensitive to past performance. Fund performance drops after the first two years further eroding fund inflows.

Summary and Conclusions

Mutual funds and the structure of fund complexes follow a logical framework designed to improve efficiency and maintain objectivity and independence. This structure uses a complex contractual design network that the mutual fund's board of directors manages. From this network, the fund complex makes business strategy decisions about which new funds, products, and services to pursue according to the ability to create and maintain an economic moat around potential competitive threats and pressures. Mutual funds and their families have become operationally efficient and innovative in the face of declining margins and product line threats. In response, fund companies have used recent regulation and data analysis techniques to enhance services and products, particularly in hybrid funds and integrated shareholder services. This change has not only allowed fund companies a new or renewed source of profitability but also potentially cemented existing investors into investment products that are difficult to unwind or exit, creating an intentional "loyalty" base.

Just as mutual funds solved the problem of investing for the middle class, they are now solving the problem of tax-efficient financial planning, which has previously been reserved for upper or upper-middle class clients. With increased globalization of markets, enhancements to statistical optimization techniques, lower costs, and improved access to a wider range of potential investors, mutual funds will continue to transform themselves through the structural forms they take and the products and services they offer.

Discussion Questions

1. Describe how a mutual fund is organized, its legal and contractual relationships, and the motivation that drives this structure.
2. Explain the structure of a fund's board including the most important decisions that its members make.

3. Identify the most critical services offered by mutual funds and fund complexes.
4. Discuss the major conclusions of studies that analyze the structure of a fund's board and fund management regarding performance.
5. Identify the most likely future drivers of a mutual fund's structure and services.

REFERENCES

Adams, John C., Takeshi Nishikawa, and Ramesh P. Rao. 2013. "Mutual Fund Performance, Management Teams, and Boards." Working Paper #2251191, Social Science Research Network. Available at papers.ssrn.com/sol3/papers.cfm?abstract_id=2251191.

Bergstresser, Daniel, John M. R. Chalmers, and Peter Tufano. 2009. "Assessing the Costs and Benefits of Brokers in the Mutual Fund Industry." *Review of Financial Studies* 22:10, 4129–4156.

Bliss, Richard T., Mark Potter, and Chris Schwarz. 2008. "Performance Characteristics of Individual vs. Team Managed Mutual Funds." *Journal of Portfolio Management* 34:3, 110–119.

Brinson, Gary P., L. Randolph Hood, and Gilbert L. Beebower. 1986. "Determinants of Portfolio Performance." *Financial Analysts Journal* 42:4, 39–44.

Chong, James, and G. M. Phillips. 2011. "Beta Measures Market Risk Except When It Doesn't: Regime-Switching Alpha and Errors in Beta." *Journal of Wealth Management* 14:3, 67–72.

Csaszar, Felipe A. 2012. "Organizational Structure as a Determinant of Performance: Evidence from Mutual Funds." *Strategic Management Journal* 33:6, 6–11.

Del Guercio, Diane, Jonathan Reuter, and Paula A. Tkac. 2011. "Demand for Financial Advice, Broker Incentives, and Mutual Fund Market Segmentation." Working Paper #1361710, Social Science Research Network Working Paper. Available at papers.ssrn.com/sol3/papers.cfm?abstract_id=1361710.

Ding, Bill, and Russell R. Wermers. 2013. "Mutual Fund Performance and Governance Structure: The Role of Portfolio Managers and Boards of Directors." Working Paper #2207229, Social Science Research Network. Available at papers.ssrn.com/sol3/papers.cfm?abstract_id=2207229.

Duan, Ying, and Yawen Jiao. 2013. "The Role of Mutual Funds in Corporate Governance: Evidence from Mutual Funds' Proxy Voting and Trading Behavior." Working Paper #1894942, Social Science Research Network. Available at papers.ssrn.com/sol3/papers.cfm?abstract_id=1894942.

Fidelity Magellan Annual Report. 2014. Available at https://fundresearch.fidelity.com/mutual-funds/summary/316184100.

Haslem, John A. 2013. "Mutual Fund Markets Are Imperfectly Competitive." Working Paper #2071326, Social Science Research Network. Available at papers.ssrn.com/sol3/papers.cfm?abstract_id=2071326.

Ibbotson, Roger G., and Paul Kaplan. 2000. "Does Asset Allocation Policy Explain 40, 90, or 100 Percent of Performance?" *Financial Analysts Journal* 56:1, 26–33.

Investment Company Institute. 2014. *2014 Factbook*, 54th edition. Washington, DC: Investment Company Institute.

Jacobs, Bruce I., and Kenneth N. Levy. 2014. "Smart Beta versus Smart Alpha." *Journal of Portfolio Management* 40:4, 4–7.

Lau, David. 2014. "Solving the Retirement Income Puzzle: Gamma and the Tax Efficient Frontier." ThinkAdvisor. Available at http://www.thinkadvisor.com/2014/05/28/solving-the-retirement-income-puzzle-gamma-and-the.

Massa, Massimo, and Lei Zhang. 2010. "The Role of Organizational Structure: Between Hierarchy and Speculation." Asia-Pacific Financial Markets 2010 Annual Conference. Available at http://www.apjfs.org/conference/2010/cafm2010/6-3.pdf.

Morley, John D. 2013. "The Separation of IFunds and Managers: A Theory of Investment Fund Structure and Regulation." Working Paper #2240468, Social Science Research Network. Available at papers.ssrn.com/sol3/papers.cfm?abstract_id=2240468.

Morningstar. 2014a. "Wells Fargo Advantage Growth Inv." Available at http://financials.morningstar.com/fund/purchase-info.html?t=SGROX&region=usa&culture=en-US.

Morningstar. 2014b. "Morningstar Category." Available at http://www.morningstar.com/InvGlossary/morningstar_category.aspx.

Morningstar Direct. Web database.

Nanda, Vikram K., M. P. Narayanan, and Vincent A. Warther. 2000. "Liquidity, Investment Ability, and Mutual Fund Structure." *Journal of Financial Economics* 57:3, 417–443.

Nanda, Vikram K., Z. J. Wang, and Lu Zheng. 2009. "The ABCs of Mutual Funds: On the Introduction of Multiple Share Classes." *Journal of Financial Intermediation* 18:3, 324–345.

Potter, Mark. 2014. "Tracking Error and Portfolio Diversification Using Mutual Funds and ETFs." Working Paper #2477364, Social Science Research Network. Available at papers.ssrn.com/sol3/papers.cfm?abstract_id=2477364.

Securities and Exchange Commission. 2014. "Mutual Fund Classes." Available at http://www.sec.gov/answers/mfclass.htm.

Sialm, Clemens, Laura T. Starks, and Hanjiang Zhang. 2014. "Defined Contribution Pension Plans: Sticky or Discerning Money?" Working Paper #2090096, Social Science Research Network. Available at papers.ssrn.com/sol3/papers.cfm?abstract_id=2090096.

Sirri, Erik, and Peter Tufano. 1998. "Costly Search and Mutual Fund Flows." *Journal of Finance* 53:5, 1589–1622.

Swedroe, Larry. 2014. "How the Mutual Fund Graveyard Can Hurt Investors." *Moneywatch*, May 8. Available at http://www.cbsnews.com/news/its-getting-crowded-in-the-mutual-fund-graveyard/.

23

Selected Topics in Mutual Fund Distribution

JOHN A. HASLEM
Professor Emeritus of Finance, University of Maryland

Introduction

This chapter provides a discussion of important issues related to mutual fund distributions. Two major topics are fund distribution channel characteristics and Rule 12b-1 fees and distribution. Distribution channel characteristics discuss the following channels: direct, advice, retirement, institutional, supermarket, and multiple-share classes. A final major topic discusses direct-sold and broker-sold services.

Haslem (2010) discusses mutual fund principal underwriters (distributors)—the fund "marketing machines." The distributor's primary role is to attract new shareholders to grow fund assets. Many funds use direct-sold distribution and sell shares directly to individual investors and institutional investors. Other funds use indirect-sold distribution and engage brokers and other financial intermediaries to sell fund shares to investors. Distribution costs have declined as investors have become more responsive to lower costs in direct-sold distribution, such as no-load and index funds.

Using direct distribution, mutual fund distributors transact directly with shareholders to redeem fund shares. A prime example is Vanguard's no-load funds. Funds provide ongoing shareholder services, including account financial statements, and transaction processing and record-keeping. Shareholders also have access to fund websites and telephone service centers to make trades, get account information, and access various other services. Funds may impose minimum initial account balances, early redemption fees, low balance fees, and other fees.

With indirect distribution, mutual fund distributors with load mutual funds contract with broker/dealers and other financial intermediaries to transact with their shareholders to sell and redeem fund shares and to provide customer account services. Distribution through an advice channel includes full-service brokers, registered investment advisers, financial planners, financial advisors, bank-registered sales representatives, and insurance company agency representatives. Other intermediaries include fund supermarkets and employer-sponsored pension plans.

Services provided by financial intermediaries include mutual fund shareholder account statements, and transaction processing and record-keeping. Services also include coordination in distribution of shareholder fund prospectuses, fund financial reports, and fund proxy statements.

Mutual fund advisers have created funds and share classes designed for direct and indirect distribution channels. Increases in fund distribution channels have been facilitated by fund offerings of multiple fund share classes designed for each channel and the financial intermediaries that distribute fund shares through each channel.

The remainder of the chapter is organized as follows. The next section introduces characteristics associated with distribution channels, followed by a section on SEC Rule 12b-1. The next section discusses broker-sold and direct-sold mutual funds, followed by a summary and conclusions.

Distribution Channel Characteristics

Haslem (2010) states mutual fund shares are sold through five principal types of distribution channels: (1) direct; (2) advice; (3) retirement plan; (4) supermarket; and (5) institutional. The first four channels primarily serve individual investors. In the direct and institutional channels, fund distributors transact directly with investors in the sale and redemption of fund shares. In the other indirect channels, fund shareholders transact with funds through financial intermediaries.

DIRECT CHANNEL

Reid and Rea (2003) and Haslem (2010) discuss distribution channel issues. Direct channel investors rely on telephone and websites to communicate with customers for inquiries and to perform transactions. However, direct-sold funds are not in the primary business of providing investment guidance and advice. The percentage of fund shares sold directly to small investors has declined as new channels have developed.

In traditional direct-sold channels, mutual fund distributors sell fund shares directly to individual investors and institutional investors. For example, the Vanguard 500 Index Admiral Shares is distributed directly and has an expense ratio of 0.05 percent with a minimum initial investment of $10,000.

In more recent direct-sold channels, mutual fund distributors also sell fund shares directly to large institutional investors. These institutions include corporations, nonprofit organizations, financial institutions, endowments, and foundations. Institutional funds also vary in minimum purchase requirements and corresponding expense ratios. For example, Vanguard's direct-sold Institutional Index Fund requires a minimum initial purchase of $5 million.

Vanguard Brokerage executes trades involving other mutual funds and exchange-traded funds, as well as stocks and bonds, which implies shares are "pure" no load and other financial intermediaries are not involved. Brokerage fees are charged for non-Vanguard products.

Direct channel mutual funds directly engage financial intermediaries to sell fund shares to clients. Financial intermediaries include discount brokers, financial advisors, fund supermarkets, employer-sponsored retirement plans, and financial institutions. A sample of financial intermediaries directly engaged by Vanguard include Ameriprise Brokerage, E-Trade Financial, Morgan Stanley Brokerage, Consulting Group Advisor and Portfolio Management, MSSB MassMutual, Northwestern Mutual Investment Services, Pershing Fund Center, Raymond James, Robert W. Baird, Schwab Retail, and Schwab Institutional.

ADVICE CHANNEL

In the advice channel, mutual fund advisers directly engage financial intermediaries to sell fund shares to clients. The intermediaries include full-service brokers, discount brokers, financial advisors, fund supermarkets, employer-sponsored retirement plans, and financial institutions. Financial intermediaries provide investment guidance, planning, and advice at least to some degree for clients. Intermediaries also facilitate shareholder transactions and provide maintenance of account records, and periodic financial statements.

Mutual funds may compensate financial intermediaries with front-end loads or more likely with 12b-1 fees and fees for continuing account servicing. Alternatively, financial professionals may charge clients annual fees of 1 to 2 percent of account assets.

RETIREMENT CHANNEL

The retirement channel primarily includes employee-sponsored defined contribution retirement plans. Employers provide mutual fund choices for employees to purchase through payroll deductions. To manage these plans, company sponsors employ third-party administrators to provide and administer plan services, including websites, plan record-keeping, participant service centers, participant accounts, transactions, and tax records. Administrators typically help employer sponsors select mutual funds to provide investment management and related services. Funds provide specific share classes designed for this channel.

In cases in which employer plan sponsors pay all or portions of plan expenses, participants receive plan services as employee benefits. In other cases, third-party plan services are paid by employer subsidies, direct charges to participants, or by "add-on" participant fees included in mutual fund expense ratios for investment services.

INSTITUTIONAL CHANNEL

Mutual funds use direct distribution to sell designed share classes to institutional investors. The institutional channel includes large investors that directly purchase mutual fund shares for their portfolios. Institutional investors include large individual investors, corporations, nonprofit organizations, financial institutions, endowments, foundations, and state and local government retirement plans. Institutional share classes have lower costs because portfolios are large and fund expenses are relatively fixed.

Institutional investors directly purchase mutual fund shares, but they also use banks and other third parties to manage their portfolios, especially cash holdings. Third parties may offer multiple money market funds to meet institutional requirements for diversification of cash holdings.

SUPERMARKET CHANNEL

The supermarket channel is home to discount brokers. Mutual fund supermarkets are financial intermediaries that directly sell fund shares to investors. Supermarkets sell shares of many funds (thus, "supermarkets") from many fund advisers.

The major mutual fund supermarket promotional feature is the "no-transaction fees" (NTF) program. Discount broker programs may offer thousands of no-load funds to investors at branches or online. Supermarkets provide fund advisers access to national retail distribution channels, which promote competition with comparisons of fund fees, expenses, and performance.

Mutual fund supermarkets normally do not give investors investment guidance or advice, but they do provide investment products, tools, and fund literature. Supermarkets provide funds with omnibus fund accounts and they provide clients with individual accounts of fund holdings, sales, and redemptions and provide related services and reports. Supermarkets also provide investors with fund proxy statements, shareholder reports, prospectuses, and tax reports. Investors maintain their investing relationships with the supermarkets, not the funds.

Mutual funds may use 12b-1 fees (included in expense ratios) to compensate supermarkets for distribution expenses (distribution fees) and ongoing shareholder account services (shareholder service fees). However, fund advisers may also make revenue-sharing payments for other supermarket services. In this case, these payments are purported to be paid from adviser "profits." However, these payments from profits are likely derived from larger fund payments of management fees, which reduce investor fund assets.

Reid and Rea (2003) and Haslem (2010) state that besides offering NTF programs, supermarkets sell shares of mutual funds that do not participate in these programs. In these cases, supermarkets charge commissions on sales of fund shares based on transaction size. Some supermarkets allow financial advisors to buy fund shares for their clients without transaction fees.

Rule 12b-1 Fees and Distribution

This section discusses the history and issues with Rule 12b-1 fees in mutual fund distribution. Haslem (2014) discusses related issues in fund distribution, namely, revenue-sharing payments and soft dollar trades.

ADOPTION OF RULE 12B-1

The Securities and Exchange Commission (SEC) (2010) provides a historically based discussion of "Rule 12b-1" fees. While some investors purchase mutual fund shares directly from no-load funds with no sales charges, most investors purchase fund shares through financial intermediaries, including broker-dealers (brokers), banks, insurance companies, supermarkets, financial advisors, discount brokers, and pension plans. When investors purchase fund shares through financial intermediaries, they typically directly or indirectly pay sales fees or service fees for provided services. Investors may pay sales loads at time of purchase or deferred sales loads when shares are redeemed. Investors may also pay fees deducted from their accounts in separate wrap fee programs. Investor payments depend on fund fee structure and how sales charges are paid depends on the class of shares purchased.

With passage of the Investment Company Act of 1940, investors typically paid high sales charges (loads) when purchasing mutual fund shares. Fund distributors deducted these charges from investor purchases at the time of sale. These charges paid broker commissions, advertising, and sales promotions. In 1975, the National Association of Securities Dealers (NASD), which is now the Financial Industry Regulatory Authority, Inc. (FINRA), limited maximum sales loads to "only" 8.75 percent. Very few funds were sold directly to investors as no-load funds. Today, load funds are relatively fewer and those loads charged have declined substantially due to investor resistance and other sources of revenue to pay distribution costs.

Before adoption of Rule 12b-1, the SEC's traditional position was that it was improper under the 1940 Act for mutual funds to pay direct or indirect costs related to distribution, but it was proper for fund advisers to finance distributions from their profits. The SEC also stated that the term "no-load fund" should not be used for sales of shares without front-end loads when fund assets were used to pay distribution costs (Investment Company Institute 2007). Current shareholders derived little or no benefit from fund sales of shares to new shareholders, and it reflected an inherent conflict of interest between fund advisers and shareholders.

The SEC adopted Rule 12b-1 in 1980 in Section 12(b) of the Investment Company Act of 1940 (1940 Act). The rule emphasizes the role of independent fund directors in monitoring fund use of assets for distribution. The purpose is to protect funds from excessive sales and promotional charges. The rule also addresses conflicts of interest between funds and fund advisers when funds pay distribution fees to "grow" fund assets. These costs include "distribution fees" and "shareholder service fees." When funds make distribution payments, fund advisers and distributors are relieved of paying these expenses. Fund advisers further benefit from fund payments for distribution expenses if they result in growth in fund assets that provide larger dollars of management fees.

Two important developments in the 1970s motivated SEC adoption of Rule 12b-1. Many funds, especially smaller ones, experienced prolonged periods of net share redemptions. The fund industry argued that spending fund assets to promote sales of fund shares could actually benefit shareholders by increasing fund size and providing fund economies of scale and by reducing expenses (expense ratios). These actions would reduce fund problems with net redemptions and small asset size that cause higher expense ratios.

Other important developments at that time included offerings of money market funds, no-load fund groups, and internally managed funds (Vanguard) that did not charge sales loads but required reserves based on revenue to support sales efforts. No-load funds promised to provide greater price competition in the fund marketplace in serving "retail" investors. Vanguard successfully sought to be exempt from the 1940 Act by internalizing marketing and distribution functions and costs in a wholly owned fund subsidiary.

Rule 12b-1 requires that mutual funds adopt written "Rule 12b-1 plans" before using fund assets to pay for distribution expenses. Plans must be approved initially by the fund's boards of directors and separately by independent fund directors. These plans also require annual re-approval. Directors are given primary responsibility for decisions concerning fund spending for distribution. Plans must include all material information concerning financing of fund distribution and provisions similar to those required for board approval of fund investment advisory contracts. The SEC provides nine factors intended to provide guidance to fund directors in deciding whether 12b-1 plans would benefit shareholders.

The original 12b-1 rule lacked uniform disclosure of 12b-1 fees, sales loads, and other expenses in mutual fund prospectuses. No limit existed for the amount of fund fees that could be approved under plans, and payments of non-distribution expenses were not limited.

RULE 12B-1 AFTER ADOPTION

The Securities and Exchange Commission (2010) states that initially some mutual funds adopted limited 12b-1 plans that were used to pay for advertising and sales materials. These first plans provided for maximum 12b-1 fee payments of 0.25 percent of average annual total net assets. Funds generally used these fees to reimburse fund advisers and distributors for advertising expenses, and printing and mailing of fund prospectuses.

In 1985, the SEC granted exemption orders to mutual funds that permitted offerings of multiple share classes, each class attached to the same fund portfolio. Funds began to adopt 12b-1 plans with higher fees as alternatives to front-end sales loads used to pay fund intermediaries for sales efforts, not just defraying promotional costs. Plans often were coupled with fund share classes with contingent deferred sales loads (CDSLs) as part of spread load arrangements. The SEC permitted funds to use share classes with CDSLs in combination with 12b-1 fees, which essentially finance front-end loads.

Unlike traditional front-end loads, shareholders owning share classes with CDSLs pay them when they redeem shares. Amounts of CDSLs are contingent because potential loads decline to zero over several years, often six or seven years. When combined with 12b-1 fees, CDSLs effectively function as deferred payments for upfront sales charges. In contrast to upfront sales loads, CDSLs effectively allow shareholders to invest more of their dollars at purchase. Early shareholder redemptions of share classes with CDSLs reimburse fund distributors for time of purchase payments to sales intermediaries in place of uncollected 12b-1 fee revenues from fund assets.

The SEC expressed concerns about spread load arrangements. The 12b-1 fees were higher than expected and appeared inconsistent with the fund industry's argument that their use would facilitate economies of scale with lower shareholder expenses. The fee arrangements appeared more permanent because they required multi-year underwriter obligations and plan termination would deny them future revenue. In 1988, the SEC proposed amendments to Rule 12b-1 that would have banned spread load arrangements.

Before 1992, the NASD sales charge rule had not been applied to 12b-1 fees when substituted for front-end sales loads. In 1992, the SEC amended the 12b-1 rule to include all types of fund sales fees. The rule caps asset-based sales charges at 75 basis points. Funds with asset-based fees are subject to aggregate caps of 6.25 percent of new gross sales and 7.25 percent with no shareholder service charges on all current and deferred sales charges. The aggregate caps require funds to keep running balances from which all sales charges are deducted. However, this does not limit sales charges paid by individual shareholders. An unlimited cap of 25 basis points on shareholder servicing fees was also placed on the amount of assets that could be deducted to pay intermediaries.

Over time, other steps were taken to improve investor understanding of 12b-1 fees and their impacts on mutual fund expenses and performance. Funds were required to have prospectus fee tables identifying 12b-1 fee payments and other expenses. Registered brokers were prohibited from advertising funds with 12b-1 fees higher than 0.25 percent of average annual total net assets as no-load funds. Fund managers were required to provide shareholders with material facts when requesting approval of and amendments to 12b-1 plans.

The SEC also permitted mutual fund managers to sell shares with multiple share classes, each with its own arrangement of distribution fees and shareholder services. Share classes provide investors with payment options in purchasing and holding particular funds. Share classes are not standardized, but most funds use similarly labeled classes. Class A shares generally have front-end sales loads that may be waived or reduced for large holdings and new purchases (breakpoint discounts) and usually 12b-1 fees of 25 basis points. Class B shares normally do not have front-end loads, but they have 12b-1 fees of 100 basis points, which is the legal maximum including shareholder account servicing fees, and declining CDSLs. Class B shares are typically automatically converted to Class A shares for holdings of six to eight years. In Class B shares, when fund distributors recoup sales commissions advanced to selling brokers, shareholders are considered to have paid their share of distribution costs. If distributors advance commissions they retain 75 of the 100 basis points collected in 12b-1 fees and forward only 25 basis points. Class C shares generally have "level loads" of 12b-1 fees of 100 basis points and perhaps CDSLs of 100 basis points for investor redemptions within one year. Other share classes are offered to large investors, institutional investors, pension plans, financial planners, and other financial intermediaries.

Class B mutual fund shares have been widely criticized and subjected to SEC scrutiny. While Class A shares have front-end loads and often small 12b-1 fees, Class B shares usually have higher 12b-1 fees and CDSLs that decline each year. Investors buying Class B shares may be better served by another share class. Unlike Class A shares, Class B shares do not offer breakpoint discounts for large purchases (Investment Company Institute 2007).

CURRENT 12B-1 FEES

The Securities and Exchange Commission (2010) states that Rule 12b-1 fees continue to play important roles in mutual fund distribution costs. Most funds consist of 12b-1 plans and investors have moved away from funds with the highest sales loads and 12b-1 fees. Funds with no-load share classes have attracted more new investor cash flows than funds with load share classes. Funds with Class B shares have experienced investor net cash outflows, while funds with Class C shares have received the largest amounts of new cash flows.

While more investors are investing in no-load mutual funds and funds with share classes, they have not moved away from funds using financial intermediaries. The Investment Company Institute (2011) reports that 12b-1 fees are now used to provide: (1) fund underwriter compensation (6 percent); (2) fund marketing, advertising, and promotion (2 percent); (3) broker compensation for initial sales of fund shares (40 percent); and (4) broker compensation for continuing customer account service (52 percent). Thus, a major use of 12b-1 fees is to compensate brokers for continual shareholder account servicing and also to compensate them for initial sales of shares, all of which motivate higher sales. Underwriter compensation was a major motivation for original uses of 12b-1 fees, although it is now a minor expense.

A common use of mutual fund 12b-1 fees is to access third-party platforms that sell fund shares, such as employer-sponsored pension plans and fund supermarkets that have become major sources of fund shares. The NASD sales charge rule permits no-load funds to compensate discount brokers and supermarkets up to 25 basis points for servicing shareholder accounts. Discount brokers and supermarkets typically hold omnibus accounts with funds and provide sub-accounting for individual shareholder accounts. Some fund advisers pay supermarkets through revenue-sharing arrangements. Funds sold through employer-sponsored pension plans may pay fees up to 50 basis points or more annually to plan administrators for servicing participant accounts.

Many mutual funds use 12b-1 fees in lieu of traditional sales loads, but others adopt defensive plans to avoid liability from charges fund assets were indirectly used for distribution. Fund advisers could use stated portions of fund advisory fees to finance share distribution, and these payments were not considered to be indirect when paid out of adviser resources. Arguably, defensive plans permit fund directors to consider fees paid by fund advisers when assessing the reasonableness of fund advisory fees (Investment Company Institute 2007). In 2004, the SEC prohibited the mutual fund practice of directing brokerage (directed brokerage) to executing brokers to reward them for sales of fund shares because it provides strong incentives for fund advisers to do so at the expense of shareholders.

ISSUES WITH 12B-1 FEES

The Securities and Exchange Commission (2010) reports findings of the 2007 roundtable on 12b-1 fees, which found many issues needing reform. For example, requirements are outdated in current markets and should be substantially revised or repealed; fees are obscured in fund expense ratios and are less likely to be competitively priced; and investor are confused over what the term "12b-1 fees" means and often equate such feed to paying sales loads over time. Additionally, 12b-1 fees increase expense ratios and decrease investor returns; confuse investors by including many different activities; provide less investor transparency than front-end sales loads; and lack adequate disclosure on individualized investor account statements. The SEC report also notes that 12b-1 fees create difficulties for directors. For instance, directors lack adequate bargaining power with intermediaries to lower fees; legal uncertainties create difficulty for directors to perform their duties under the rule; independent directors do not play active roles in setting distribution fees; and director monitoring factors are inadequate. Finally, fund adviser-shareholder conflicts of interest exist when fund assets are used for distribution.

Not surprisingly, former SEC Chairman Cox notes that 12-b plans need to be re-evaluated. He also states that mutual fund independent directors should further review use of 12b-1 fees (Securities and Exchange Commission 2007).

The Securities and Exchange Commission (2010, p. 39) also discusses past proposed revisions to asset distribution fees along with the most recent proposal to "rescind Rule 12b-1 in its entirety," and to install a new regulatory framework for how fund assets may be distributed. The proposed changes would address concerns about protecting investors from the use of alternatives to sales loads and provide a means to finance other distribution costs.

The SEC proposed a new "Rule 12b-2" permitting mutual funds to deduct fees for all share classes up to the NASD shareholder account servicing limit of 25 basis points on annual average net total assets for fund distribution. Funds would most likely use the fees to pay intermediaries for shareholder account servicing, to pay brokers trailing commissions for sales of fund shares, and to pay for fund supermarket distribution. Payments to supermarkets could also include non-distribution-related administrative expenses.

Under proposed Rule 12b-2, mutual funds could use proceeds of marketing and service fees deducted from fund assets (1) to participate in supermarket platforms; (2) to provide investors with convenient ways of buying shares; (3) to pay trailing broker fees for shareholder account servicing; (4) to compensate pension plan administrators for services to plan participants; (5) to support shareholder call centers; (6) to compensate fund distributors; (7) to pay for advertising and printing and mailing of fund prospectuses; and (8) to pay for traditional distribution activities.

Under proposed Rule 12b-2, mutual funds could pay fees similar to those approved by fund directors following adoption of 12b-1 fee plans. Other attributes of proposed Rule 12b-2 would also include: (1) permitting any type of fund distribution cost; (2) not requiring directors to adopt or renew fund plans; (3) allowing the same director oversight as for fund operating expenses and focusing on conflicts of interest; (4) including marketing and shareholder service fees in prospectus fee tables as types of operating expenses; and (5) making unbundled fess more transparent to shareholders. The Investment Company Institute (2007) offers the fund industry's position on 12b-1 fees,

Numerous studies exist that critique 12b-1 fees. In an early mutual fund study, McLeod and Malhotra (1994, pp. 231, 239) confirm yet an earlier study: "The findings are consistent with previous studies that find charges [12b-1 fees] are a deadweight cost borne by shareholders. . . . Our study confirms . . . that 12b-1 charges resulted in additional costs to shareholders, but the magnitude of these costs has also increased."

Casavecchia and Scotti (2009, pp. 2–3) report that

> [O]n 4 December 2002, in a remark to a roundtable on Investment Company Regulation at the SEC, Joel Goldberg, former Director of the SEC's Division of Investment Management at the time of the controversial approval of Rule 12b-1, stated that if a mistake had been committed by the SEC in

> promulgating this rule, it was that they . . . did not foresee that payments out of fund assets would be used as a substitute for a sales load. . . . [I]t is just astounding that we never thought of it. Since its inception in 1980, Rule 12b-1 has been designed to regulate when and how expenses for share distribution can be made by mutual funds. However, what started as a minor supplemental marketing boost available to mutual funds to garner more new money and support growth has become an industry addiction at the expense of fund shareholders. To give an idea of the economic relevance of the issue, the U.S. mutual fund market . . . generated a staggering all-time high of $13.4 billion [2007] in 12b-1 fees. Furthermore, this figure does not even include the additional proceeds from front- and back-end loads paid by fund shareholders.
>
> The use and abuse of 12b-1 fees and front-end loads remain a controversial topic. Some studies have examined it by asking whether the introduction and adoption of 12b-1 plans have actually conveyed any benefits to shareholders. . . . Another approach has been to investigate the hauling effect of distribution fees on the asset growth of mutual funds. Despite the numerous studies . . . and the increased levels of public scrutiny, we are not aware of any work that has directly addressed the question of how mutual funds determine their distribution fees in the first place.

Haslem (2004, p. 11) states:

> [R]ule 12b-1 fees . . . allow fund managers to use fund assets to pay distribution expenses, including sales fees and commissions, customer servicing fees, administrative expenses, and advertising and promotion. However, fund managers have not used 12b-1 fees to provide shareholders with the promised reductions in expenses due to economies of scale. The irony in this is that it is the fund managers who have reaped the bonanza from larger funds—larger amounts of investment advisory fees, larger amounts of 12b-1 fees, and larger expense savings from scale economies. In fact, stock and bond funds with 12b-1 fees have lower returns, higher expenses, and more risk. Further, the justification for the use of multiple share classes rests on the weak foundation of 12b-1 fees.

Next, Haslem (2008, p. 1) states that "[t]he 'bottom line' for shareholders of mutual funds with 12b-1 fees is whether fund economies of scale are large enough to pay the fees, and, if so, whether cost savings are sufficiently passed on to shareholders." These savings may or may not be large enough, but they certainly have not been sufficiently shared with investors. Further, Haslem (2008, p. 2) states that "[a]ny argument supporting 12b-1 plans must explain why mutual funds that are closed increasingly continue to charge 12b-1 fees. This behavior perhaps more than anything shows the hypocrisy in arguing that 12b-1 plans benefit shareholders. The reality is that fund adviser benefit greatly from this practice."

> Mahoney (2004, p. 5) states:12b-1 fees are controversial. The mutual fund industry argues that these fees are a means by which investors who purchase

> through brokers can spread out the broker's compensation over time rather than bear it all at once in the form of a sales load. Critics of 12b-1 fees note that they, unlike sales loads, are not paid directly by the investor in connection with a transaction, but deducted annually from the fund's assets. Thus, in effect, current shareholders bear the cost of attracting new shareholders. Because the manager has a greater interest in maximizing the size of the fund than do investors, the manager may spend more of the shareholders' money on marketing than the shareholders would prefer.

Freeman (2007, p. 11) critiques "the mutual fund distribution expense mess" and its agency conflicts. When Rule 12b-1 was adopted, some argued that mutual fund shareholders would benefit from scale economies generated by growth in fund assets. Using fund assets to attract new investors would provide the growth. The results have not been in the best interests of fund shareholders: "The idea that sales to new investors financed out of fund assets are beneficial to existing fund shareholders is dubious and not supported by the literature. No credible evidence exists demonstrating shareholders receive a pecuniary benefit from 12b-1 fees."

Cuthbertson, Nitzsche, and O'Sullivan's (2010, p. 102) critique of 12b-1 fees in no-load mutual fund supermarkets finds that "directly marketed funds may use the 12b-1 fee to pay for advertising or shelf space at a fund supermarket. To the extent that the 12b-1 fee is used to advertising this implies that current shareholders bear the cost of attracting new shareholders."

Morningstar's Gogerty (2007, p. 1) finds hypocrisy in mutual fund industry support for 12b-1 fees: "The fact that closed funds continue to charge 12b-1 fees clearly illustrates that the fees are no longer primarily used for their intended purpose—to market and promote a fund. A 2005 survey conducted by the Investment Company Institute revealed that less than 5% of the estimated $10.9 billion collected in 12b-1 fees that year were used for promotion and advertising."

Finally, Bullard (2010, p. 1) attacks the "unbearable meaninglessness of 12b-1 fees" at some length:

> Regarding mutual fund 12b-1 fees, [former] SEC chairman Mary Shapiro recently noted that: "Investors may have no idea these fees are being deducted from their mutual funds, what services they are paying for, or who they are ultimately compensating." Indeed, the meaning of 12b-1 fees, like the meaning of "bipartisan" in the political realm, no longer has any common foundation. When someone is talking about 12b-1 fees, you can't be sure what they are talking about. The term "12b-1 fees" is full of sound and fury, signifying nothing.
>
> Consider the regulatory term "distribution fees" that funds use to describe 12b-1 fees in the fund fee table. 12b-1 fees actually pay for a grab-bag of services—not just distribution. For example, 12b-1 fees may cover record keeping and the tracking of shareholders' purchases and sales of fund shares. Yet the SEC tells funds to label this administrative service as "distribution." The explanation for this is regulatory. Rule 12b-1 says that, if you charge fees that could be viewed as primarily intended to result in the distribution of fund

shares, then they must be treated as a 12b-1fees. Fees paid to a broker who distributes fund shares therefore are 12b-1 fees. But the same broker might also provide administrative services. Lawyers worry that this blurs the separation of fees between distribution and administration. To avoid the risk of leaving what regulators might consider a "distribution" fee out of the 12b-1 fee, funds dump administration and distribution fees in what is known as a "defensive" 12b-1 plan. So a large chunk of 12b-1 "distribution" fees are not for distribution.

The non-distribution aspect of 12b-1 fees is not their only misunderstood feature. For example, many have decried and even sued funds that charge 12b-1 fees while the fund is closed to new investors. If the fund is not distributing new shares, why is it charging a distribution fee? One answer, as noted above, is that the administrative services that a 12b-1 fee may cover continue when a fund is closed. Another answer is that part of 12b-1 fees reflects "service fees" paid to brokers to manage the ongoing relationship with existing shareholders. 12b-1 fees are also paid on new shares sold to those existing shareholders. This still counts as distribution. In addition, closed funds' 12b-1 fees often are attributable to sales to new shareholders. How can that be? When a broker is paid, for example, a one-time, 3% commission for selling shares to a new shareholder, and the fund receives only an annual 1% 12b-1 fee on that sale, someone must front the full 3% commission. Some funds borrow the 3% from a bank and use the stream of 12b-1 fees to repay the loan. So some 12b-1 fees collected by a closed fund are being used to finance earlier sales to new shareholders.

Broker-Sold and Direct-Sold Mutual Funds

Bergstresser, Chalmers, and Tufano (2009) discuss the value of services provided by direct-sold and broker-sold mutual funds, excluding institutional funds and investor characteristics. Potential broker service benefits include (1) assistance in selecting funds that are difficult to find or analyze; (2) access to funds with lower costs and the avoidance of distribution costs; (3) access to high performance funds; (4) access to superior funds; and (5) avoidance of investor behavioral biases.

Mutual fund investors in broker-sold funds pay higher fees for fund selection and advice, but they do not receive substantial tangible benefits. Broker-sold funds provide lower risk-adjusted returns than direct-sold funds, even before subtracting distribution fees. Brokers also have no more skill than direct-sold fund managers in allocating fund assets. Brokers either provide substantial intangible benefits or material conflicts of interest exist with investors.

Deciding which distribution channels to use for mutual funds is central to a successful overall strategy and affects fund and fund adviser revenue, costs, and performance. Distribution channels that increase investor inflows and retain fund assets provide higher returns for fund advisers. Distribution strategies that provide stable asset bases have lower less frequent investor trades, with lower trading costs and transfer agency fees.

Direct-sold mutual funds are distributed directly to investors. Distribution channels include banks, captive brokers, brokerage firms that sell their own funds, and independent brokers. Mutual fund shares are often offered in different share classes for retail and institutional investors that vary by distribution channels.

BROKER-SOLD FUNDS

Bergstresser et al. (2009) find that broker-sold mutual fund managers have numerous attributes and implications relative to direct-sold fund managers including: (1) lower risk-adjusted returns before distribution fees; (2) a lack of superior market-timing advice; (3) fund inflows that are increased by investor-chasing performance; (4) non-distribution expenses that do not offset distribution fees; and (5) more investor services provided including portfolios adjusted for risk tolerance and investor comfort. Additionally, broker-sold mutual fund managers may act out of self-interest and may not provide legal suitable investments. Other characteristics of broker-sold fund managers include more complex financial arrangements between investors and fund advisers, investor distribution fees including front-end loads, back-end loads, and 12b-1 fees, and revenue-sharing payments that are used for marketing and distribution. Broker-sold mutual funds have a larger proportion of share classes with fewer multiple classes; a lower performance gross of 12b-1 fees and more so net of fees lower fund performance, lower performance on equal-weighted asset basis, and equal-weighted fund basis. Sharpe ratios indicate poor asset allocation and brokers lack forecasting ability, both relatively and absolutely. Funds may be more difficult to find or analyze and may be accompanied by higher non-distribution expenses. Broker-sold mutual fund managers may be more likely to offer foreign funds and may not act in investor interests. Finally, 12b-1 fees increase fund outflows of broker-sold mutual funds. On-distribution expenses do not increase outflows and expense ratios have smaller outflows and higher loads and distribution fees.

Investor characteristics in broker-sold mutual funds and relative to direct-sold investors include:

- motivation by professional money management;
- a focus on fund performance;
- increased risk aversion, but an acceptance of higher risk if compensated with returns;
- less wealth, education, and financial assets, but in upper ranks nationally;
- a belief that fund fees and expenses are somewhat or very important although they pay more;
- less experience or confidence in decisions;
- less time or desire to make fund choices;
- a predisposition to broker assistance in explaining lower pre-distribution fee performance;
- ignorance of short-run fund performance;
- inflows that are strongly related to past fund performance;
- redemptions more sensitive to poor performance;
- similar demographics and attitudes; and
- tendency to choose funds with higher loads.

DIRECT-SOLD FUNDS

Bergstresser et al. (2009) find direct-sold mutual funds have several attributes and implications: (1) relative to broker-sold funds, they are more straightforward; (2) there are typically no front-end loads or back-end loads; (3) direct-sold mutual fund managers may charge 12b-1 fees for marketing and distribution; (4) increasingly complex channels include investor payments to fee-based financial advisors, fund supermarkets, and specified contribution plans; and (5) such funds provide higher investor longer term cumulative wealth.

Investor characteristics of direct-sold mutual fund managers are similar to broker-sold investors in many ways: (1) they both state that they desire professional money management; (2) they both focus on fund performance; (3) they both state that they ignore short-run performance; (4) they both chase past performance; (5) the inflows of both direct-sold mutual fund managers and broker-sold investors are strongly related to past fund performance; and (6) similar demographics and attitudes exist for both direct-sold mutual fund managers and broker-sold investors.

Summary and Conclusions

This chapter provides an in-depth discussion of important issues related to mutual fund distribution. Two major topics are fund distribution channel characteristics and Rule 12b-1 fees and distribution. Distribution channel characteristics discussed include direct channel, advice channel, retirement channel, institutional channel, supermarket channel, and multiple-share classes. Rule 12b-1 fees and distribution discuss adoption of Rule 12b-1, Rule 12b-1 after adoption, current 12b-1 fees, and issues with 12b-1 fees. A final major topic discussed direct-sold and broker-sold services.

The 12b-1 fee compensates brokers for initial sales of fund shares, ongoing servicing of fund shareholder accounts, and advertising and promotion expenses. Higher broker sales increase fund adviser assets under management (higher inflows) and adviser profits-primary motivations. Additionally, higher fund share sales increase broker profits, while higher broker fund share sales increase the size and cost of fund portfolio trades, amounts of broker commissions, and execution fees. Higher 12b-1 fees increase fund outflows, but higher share sales increase fund inflows. Rule12b-1 fees are transparent direct line-item costs in fund expense ratios that motivate using multiple share classes in direct and broker (and other intermediary) sold funds, including sales of fund shares to large individual and institutional investors. Payments reduce current fund net asset values (NAVs) and shareholder returns. Lastly, 12b-1 fees provide major agency conflicts with shareholder interests and returns.

Discussion Questions

1. List the five primary channels of distribution and indicate which channels are direct.
2. Discuss the motivation for adopting Rule 12b-1 fees.
3. Identify the two most common uses of 12b-1 fees.
4. Explain the greatest irony in fund use of 12b-1 fees.

References

Bergstresser, Daniel, John M. R. Chalmers, and Peter Tufano. 2009. "Assessing the Costs and Benefits of Brokers in the Mutual Fund Industry." *Review of Financial Studies* 22:10, 4129–4156.

Bullard, Mercer. 2010. "The Unbearable Meaninglessness of 12b-1 Fees." Morningstar. Available at http://news.morningstar.com/articlenet/article.aspx?id=326706.

Casavecchia, Lorenzo, and Massimo Scotti. 2009. "Dynamic Setting of Distribution Fees in the U.S. Mutual Fund Industry." 2009 Annual Meeting of the European Financial Management Association, Milan, Italy. Available at http://papers.ssrn.com/sol3/papers.cfm?abstract_id=1364141.

Cuthbertson, Keith, Dirk Nitzsche, and Niall O'Sullivan. 2010. "Mutual Fund Performance: Measurement and Evidence." *Financial Markets, Institutions, & Instruments* 19:2, 95–187.

Freeman, John P. 2007. "John Freeman's Working Paper Responding to the Advisory Fee Analysis in AEI Working Paper #127, June 2006, 'Competition and Shareholder Fees in the Mutual Fund Industry: Evidence and Implications for Policy' by John C. Coates, IV, and R. Glenn Hubbards." Available at http://ssrn.com/abstract=984507.

Gogerty, Andrew. 2007. "Memo to SEC: 12b-1 Fees Must Go." Morningstar. Available at http://news.morningstar.com/articlenet/article.aspx?id=191307.

Haslem, John A. 2004. "Are Mutual Fund Expenses Too High? A Commentary." *Journal of Investing* 13:2, 8–12.

Haslem, John A. 2008. "An Idea Whose Time Has Come: Should the SEC Rid Mutual Fund Investors of 12b-1 Fees?" *Journal of Indexes* 11:3, 42–45, 47.

Haslem, John A. 2010. "Mutual Funds: Conflicted Distribution and the New Total Expense Ratio Construct." *Journal of Index Investing* 1:3, 65–73.

Haslem, John A. 2014. "Issues in Mutual Fund Distribution." Available at http://ssrn.com/abstract=2070112.

Investment Company Institute. 2007. "Report of the Working Group on Rule 12b-1." Investment Company Institute Board of Governors. Washington, DC: Investment Company Institute.

Investment Company Institute. 2011. *Investment Company Fact Book*, 51st edition. Washington, DC: Investment Company Institute.

Mahoney, Paul G. 2004. "Manager-Investor Conflicts in Mutual Funds." *Journal of Economic Perspectives* 18:2, 161–182.

McLeod, Robert W., and D. K. Malhotra. 1994. "A Re-Examination of the Effect of 12b-1 Plans on Mutual Fund Expense Ratios." *Journal of Financial Research* 17:2, 231–240.

Reid, Bryan K., and John D. Rea. 2003. "Mutual Fund Distribution Channels and Distribution Costs." *Perspective* (Investment Company Institute) 9:3, 1–20.

Securities and Exchange Commission. 2007. Speech by Chairman Christopher Cox: "Address to the Mutual Fund Directors Forum, Seventh Annual Policy Conference," April 13. Washington, DC: Securities and Exchange Commission.

Securities and Exchange Commission. 2010. "Mutual Fund Distribution Fees; Confirmations." Available at http://www.sec.gov/rules/proposed/2010/33-9128.pdf.

24

Mutual Fund Disclosure and Related Fund Investor Protection Features

JOSEPH A. FRANCO
Professor of Law, Suffolk University Law School

Introduction

In the United States, mutual funds are regulated as investment companies. Investment companies are defined, in part, as entities that issue securities to investors to get capital to engage in the business of investing, reinvesting, or trading in securities. The main sources of regulation for investment companies under federal law in the United States are: (1) the Investment Company Act of 1940 (ICA), which regulates the activities of investment companies; (2) the Investment Advisers Act of 1940 (IAA), which regulates the activities of investment advisers, such as money managers who manage investment companies; and (3) rules adopted by the Securities and Exchange Commission (SEC) to implement those statutes. Other securities law statutes—the Securities Act of 1933 and the Securities Exchange Act of 1934—supplement fund disclosure obligations.

This chapter focuses on one aspect of the regulatory scheme: disclosure requirements for mutual funds, including restrictions applicable to advertising and sales materials. While disclosure regulation affects investors, the larger regulatory scheme contains numerous additional features beyond the scope of the chapter that provide additional forms of investor protection. These additional features include provisions relating to the governance of mutual funds, pricing of securities, fund compliance policies and procedures, and various prohibitions relating to fund portfolio transactions and capital structure.

The chapter begins with a discussion of differences between mutual fund disclosure and conventional public company disclosure. It proceeds to describe the chief challenges for policymakers in designing disclosure policy, namely making disclosure rules that are informative for investors and devising an approach that promotes rational investment behavior and fund selection strategies by average retail investors. The remainder of the chapter focuses on basic legal requirements governing: mutual fund offering disclosure, other forms of mutual fund disclosure, selected disclosure topics, and civil and law enforcement sanctions and other investment protection measures. The final section offers a summary and conclusions.

Mutual Fund Disclosure versus Conventional Public Company Disclosure

Mutual fund disclosure requirements adhere to the basic disclosure requirements applicable to conventional public companies such as Apple, Google, or GE. The basic forms of mandated disclosure for funds—registration statements, prospectuses, and periodic shareholder reports—are well-recognized features of disclosure regulation for public companies. While mutual fund disclosure mimics this basic regulatory structure, the SEC has, over time, tailored the disclosure requirements for mutual funds and other investment companies to fit the special needs of mutual fund investors.

The purpose of mutual fund disclosure differs from that of conventional public company disclosure. Mutual funds issue redeemable securities, which entitle an investor to receive the net asset value (NAV) of the investor's shares at the end of the day, or the investor's proportionate ownership stake in the fund's underlying investment portfolio less accrued liabilities. For example, in a fund that has one million shares, each share owned by an investor is worth one one-millionth of the fund's aggregate NAV as determined on any given day. The NAV is also used as the price for each fund share. An investor may purchase fund shares at NAV plus any applicable sales charges.

This aspect of mutual fund pricing has direct implications for understanding the purpose of mutual fund disclosure. Disclosure by conventional public companies, such as Google, Apple, or GE, provides information that markets use in determining the price of the company's securities. Efficient markets incorporate public disclosure in determining securities prices. In this way, securities markets provide a mechanism for determining or "discovering" the trading price for a company's shares and other securities.

By contrast, mutual fund disclosure serves no price discovery function because fund shares are priced at their underlying NAV or intrinsic value. Instead, mutual fund disclosure provides investors or their financial advisors with necessary information to make the most appropriate investment given an investor's financial objectives. It also ensures that investors have ready access to information about basic terms and conditions of ownership, such as tax and redemption policies. Disclosure also enhances competition among funds, and indirectly among sponsors and advisers of funds, by enabling investors to compare funds on a standardized basis in terms of fund performance, expenses, and risk. These features combine to serve a consumer protection function.

Rational Fund Selection Strategies and Retail Investor Behavior

Understanding the circumstances that generate the need for regulation and their likely effects in terms of investor behavior and market conduct is necessary to evaluate regulatory policy. This section addresses two divergent narratives: (1) what financial economics says about rational fund selection strategies and (2) what is known about the factors that are most likely to influence investor behavior (Franco 2009).

RATIONAL FUND SELECTION STRATEGIES

Financial economics offers insight into the factors that should apply to rational investors in making fund selection decisions. A vast literature exists exploring the many factors that determine expected and observed return. These factors include market efficiency, market risk, non-systematic risk, diversification, asset allocation, timing, and individual security selection (or "stock-picking" ability). Actively managed funds are invariably more expensive than funds that are passively managed. Added costs for active management can be justified if the added costs result in risk-adjusted returns that exceed the added costs. A mountain of evidence suggests this is not true in the aggregate (Gruber 1996; Malkiel 2005; French 2008; Fama and French 2010).

Whether retail investors should seek actively managed funds that will consistently offer superior performance seems dubious especially given the empirical evidence. First, managers are unlikely to consistently outperform their benchmarks after adjusting for risk, since such superior performance would imply consistent access to superior information for some managers, a result that would contradict the assumption that securities markets are relatively informationally efficient (Goetzmann and Ibbotson 1994). Second, even if some active managers could consistently deliver superior performance, retail investors are likely unable to differentiate between managers whose superior performance derives from luck and those whose superior returns genuinely reflect superior skill (Sirri and Tufano 1998; Cooper, Gutierrez, and Marcum 2005; Frazzini and Lamont 2008; Mauboussin 2012). Finally, superior performance, even if genuinely attributable to skill, is unlikely to persist for long (Brown and Goetzmann 1995; Carhart 1997; Bollen and Busse 2004). Over time, superior managers would gather additional assets, which progressively increases the difficulty of delivering superior results (Berk and Green 2004). Additionally, as others copy the investment strategies of superior managers, the superior managers' relative advantage should disappear.

If actively managed funds cannot deliver consistently superior performance on a cost and risk-adjusted basis or if retail investors cannot identify such funds, then such investors would be better served by seeking low-cost funds that deliver average performance. This outcome would mean a passive indexing strategy (French 2008). Bogle (2005) illustrates this view through his epigrammatic hypothesis, the "cost matters hypothesis." While the heavy reliance of retail investors on actively managed funds seems difficult to account for in terms of financial rationality, recent trends suggest that retail investor interest in passive investment strategies is growing, as evidenced by the rapid growth in assets managed by indexed mutual funds and passively managed exchange-traded funds (Investment Company Institute 2014). Unresolved issues remain from a social policy perspective. For instance, excessive utilization of passive strategies by the investing public could undermine price discovery in securities markets and could contribute to market volatility.

THE REALITY OF RETAIL FUND INVESTOR BEHAVIOR

The observed behavior of retail fund investors is problematic when tested in light of financial rationality considerations. Retail investor behavior exhibits two characteristics inconsistent with any form of rational fund selection strategy. First, retail investors broadly exhibit a tendency to chase performance results, especially recent fund performance (Harless and Peterson 1998; Sirri and Tufano 1998; Del Guercio and Tkac 2002; Karceski 2002; Swensen 2005; Palmiter and Taha 2012). Chasing performance is problematic because fund performance rarely persists and recent performance is affected by probabilistic factors that cannot serve as a basis for predicting actual future performance.

A second characteristic is the relative stickiness of retail investors in their fund selection decisions (Goetzmann and Peles 1997; Harless and Peterson 1998; Del Guercio and Tkac 2002). Once retail investors make fund selection decisions, they are unlikely to reconsider those decisions as new evidence emerges. This predisposition compounds the problematic nature of performance chasing: investors stick with fund selection decisions that are flawed.

Observed patterns of irrational financial behavior are the product of a combination of factors. For example, retail investors exhibit low financial literacy for funds and devote limited time to their efforts (Alexander, Jones, and Nigro 1997, 1998, 2001; Capon, Fitzsimons, and Prince 1997; Agnew and Szykman 2005; Hu 2005; Palmiter and Taha 2008; Fisch and Wilkinson-Ryan 2014). Investors also underestimate the complexity of the investment decision and their own cognitive limitations (Benartzi and Thaler 2001; Cox and Payne 2005). Finally, empirical studies show that investors are subject to a host of behavioral biases in their investment behaviors, which causes them to deviate from rational fund selection strategies (Wilcox 2003; Elton 2004; Cooper Gulen, and Rau 2005; Choi, Laibson, and Madrian 2010). Chief among these biases is overconfidence about likely investment outcomes and an investor's own ability to make rational decisions, the tendency to take responsibility for successful investment decisions while blaming others for unsuccessful ones (self-attribution), the unwillingness to confront the disparity between expected and realized performance, and trend chasing itself.

To be effective, disclosure policy needs to take into account the limitations of retail investors when making investment decisions. Disclosure policy designed to assist retail investors in finding actively managed funds that consistently deliver superior returns does not appear to be sound for the reasons previously discussed. Instead, disclosure policy more closely aligned with consumer protection objectives seems more appropriate, providing retail investors with information likely to encourage rational investment behavior (Cox and Payne 2005; Franco 2009).

Mutual Funds and Offering Disclosure

As noted previously, fund offering disclosure is modeled after the regulatory approach used for securities offerings of conventional public companies. The disclosure requirements, however, have been tailored and supplemented to address the unique character of investment companies and needs of investment company investors. This section focuses on requirements relating to mutual fund offering disclosure because of the pervasive importance of mutual funds among the several types of registered investment companies. Kirsch (2014) is an excellent two-volume secondary legal reference that explores these requirements in greater detail. A later section describes how some of these requirements are modified for other types of funds such as closed-end funds (CEFs), exchange-traded funds (ETFs), and unit investment trusts (UITs).

INVESTMENT COMPANY REGISTRATION AND MUTUAL FUND OFFERINGS

Mutual funds register as entities under the ICA. Like conventional public companies, they also register their securities under the Securities Act. Congress and the SEC permit mutual funds to file an integrated (i.e., company and securities) registration statement called Form N-1A that serves both purposes.

Offerings by conventional public companies are discrete capital-raising events that continue only until all of the securities being offered are sold. In most public offerings, a company proceeds through a well-established cycle of activities: (1) drafting and filing disclosure relating to the offering; (2) disseminating preliminary disclosure materials to the public and engaging in oral marketing efforts; and then (3) selling the registered securities as soon as possible after going effective (i.e., after the SEC has authorized actual sales pursuant to the filed registration statement). The company may issue additional securities in subsequent offerings.

In contrast, mutual fund offerings are typically continuous (i.e., the offering continues in time unless the fund closes itself to new investments). Mutual fund offerings remain open to enable funds to grow assets under management (AUM) by selling more shares. The pressure for funds to remain open to new investments is intensified because existing shareholders are free to redeem their shares upon request.

MANDATED OFFERING DISCLOSURE

Four interrelated disclosure documents are used in mutual fund offerings. First, a *registration statement*, which is a comprehensive disclosure document that must be approved by the SEC before public sales of a security, must be filed with the SEC. The SEC makes registration statements available to the public, but the fund offering the securities does not circulate the document to investors. Because mutual funds make continuous offerings, their filed registration statement must be amended annually to update information including pertinent financial results.

The other three documents constitute parts of the registration statement and are circulated directly to investors or are at least accessible to investors from funds: the statutory (or final) prospectus, the statement of additional information, and the summary prospectus. The *statutory prospectus* is the principal, legally mandated disclosure document used to solicit investors. The current form of statutory prospectus has evolved over time. The original purpose of the document was to convey all material information relating to the fund to investors. The prospectus from earlier times was long, somewhat turgid, and not user-friendly. In 1981, the SEC adopted a new approach. For the first time, the SEC explicitly acknowledged a tension between two different disclosure policy goals: *comprehensiveness* (i.e., disclosure of all material information) and *understandability* (i.e., usefulness of information to the likely end-user such as the average retail investor). The SEC bifurcated the old-style prospectus into two different documents: (1) a new statutory prospectus, which was designed to provide the material information most relevant to ordinary retail investors and (2) a statement of additional information.

The statutory prospectus contains information that is directly useful to investors in understanding the fund's investment objectives and its historical performance in terms of risk, return, and fees or expenses. It also describes matters relating to incidence of ownership such as redemption rights, taxes, and contact information. Traditionally, the SEC required that investors receive a copy of the statutory prospectus at the time of sale, but that is no longer required if a summary prospectus is delivered to investors and a copy of the statutory prospectus is accessible on an Internet site sponsored by the fund or the seller. The next section discusses selected disclosure items some of which appear in the statutory prospectus.

The *statement of additional information* (SAI) contains supplemental material information that might apply to some investors, but would not necessarily apply to the average retail investor. This additional information may elaborate on the disclosure found in the statutory prospectus and provide disclosure regarding matters whose effect on investors is less direct, such as fund brokerage arrangements. While the statutory prospectus must be sent to investors at the time of their initial investment, the SAI was initially only available to investors upon request. However, the Internet now provides a low-cost means to afford continuous accessibility to both the statutory prospectus and the SAI.

The *summary prospectus* is a relatively recent regulatory addition to fund disclosure. In 2009, the SEC permitted use of a new form of streamlined disclosure. The summary prospectus must appear in the forepart of the statutory prospectus but also can be circulated independently of the statutory prospectus as an offering document provided certain conditions are met. The summary disclosure template requires succinct summary statements as to seven items mandated in the statutory prospectus. The SEC deemed these disclosure items to be the most important for average retail investors, such as investment objectives and strategies, a fee table, and a risk/return summary.

The approval of simplified summary prospectuses embodied a new SEC disclosure philosophy regarding funds referred to as "layered disclosure." The layered disclosure approach embraces the view that disclosure should be offered to investors in several formats of increasing complexity, allowing investors to choose the appropriate level of disclosure for their own needs. As noted, the summary prospectus must appear at the beginning of the statutory prospectus, but it can also be used as its own document to solicit investors provided that the fund or its distributor maintains a website containing the additional layers of disclosure comprising the statutory prospectus, the SAI, and the most recent annual or semi-annual shareholder report. Whether simplified summary prospectuses are likely to lead to improved decision-making by investors has been questioned in empirical studies (Beshears, Choi, Laubson, and Madrian 2009; Fisch and Wilkinson-Ryan 2014).

ADVERTISING AND SALES LITERATURE REGULATION

An integral aspect of the disclosure regulation scheme in the United States entails express restrictions governing funds' written marketing materials. By virtue of certain statutory requirements in the Securities Act, an issuer such as a mutual fund faces severe limitations regarding the publicly disseminated written documents that may be used in soliciting prospective investors while conducting an offering. For mutual funds engaged in continuous offerings, the restriction applies at all times. In effect, mutual funds cannot use forms of written communication, such as advertising or sales literature, other than a prospectus unless the communication (1) is accompanied with delivery of a statutory prospectus, or (2) comes within an excepted category of communication authorized by SEC regulation. Funds have considerable latitude, however, in the use and design of web-based platforms because the platforms routinely carry links to the statutory prospectus and therefore fit within the first exception.

The SEC allows funds to use two forms of offering materials independent of a statutory final prospectus or summary prospectus. One form of communication is the so-called "Rule 482" advertisement, which funds use widely to advertise fund shares. These advertisements offer fund shares to the investing public, provided that the advertisement complies with the conditions of Rule 482 under the Securities Act. Rule 482 advertisements may, but are not required to, include fund performance figures.

Fund sponsors use fund performance results if investors are likely to view such information positively. The performance figures must at least contain standardized performance periods such as 1-, 5-, and 10-year benchmarks and must follow a prescribed method in calculating total return or yield. Rule 482 also contains various formatting requirements, including mandating use of certain cautionary legends. For example, advertisements must contain legends stating that investors can lose money and when using performance figures, that past returns do not guarantee future performance. The effectiveness of such boilerplate cautionary statements for investors is subject to question (Mercer, Palmiter, and Taha 2010).

Another widely used form of advertising by funds is a so-called "generic advertisement." Under Securities Act Rule 135a, investment companies may use advertisements in print or the Internet that contain generic types of information about a family of funds or a fund manager without mentioning specific funds by name. The advertisements may invite requests for additional information and describe and explain in generic terms the purpose of mutual funds and the importance of investment objectives.

Other Mutual Fund Disclosure Documents

This section discusses two other disclosure documents. *Shareholder reports* are distributed semi-annually by funds and provide investors with current information about the funds operations and finances. *Proxy statements* are distributed when funds seek a vote of the fund's shareholders.

SHAREHOLDER REPORTS

The SEC currently requires mutual funds to provide shareholder reports to their shareholders semi-annually (usually referred to as the semi-annual and annual shareholder reports), which are also filed with the SEC. This requirement is in lieu of the periodic annual and quarterly reporting requirements applicable to conventional public companies. While the requirements for fund annual reports are greater than for the semi-annual reports, both require varying degrees of updated financial information. In 2015, the SEC issued a significant proposal on Investment Company Reporting Modernization[1] to replace the existing scheme of semi-annual reporting to shareholders with one of annual reporting that will be accessible to shareholders on fund websites. The new regime, however, will maintain key disclosure features of the semi-annual reporting scheme.

Shareholder reports currently contain concrete illustrations of fund performance and fees. First, the annual report must illustrate fund performance relative to a broad-based market index for a hypothetical investor investing $10,000 in the fund over the last 10 fiscal years. Second, funds must provide a tabular rendering of actual fund expenses incurred semi-annually in dollars for an investor investing $1,000, and also an analogous hypothetical calculation based on the firm's expense ratio, assuming a 5 percent annual return.

Shareholder reports also contain two additional items of disclosure that are of special importance: (1) Management's Discussion of Fund Performance (MFDP), which is narrative disclosure about the fund's performance and the factors that materially affected the fund's performance; and (2) a detailed discussion of the basis for the trustees' approval of the investment advisory contract.

PROXY STATEMENTS

Registered funds are subject to proxy disclosure requirements in connection with shareholder votes, but as a practical matter, these requirements are less relevant for registered investment companies than for conventional public companies. Public companies are required to prepare proxy statements annually to solicit proxies from their shareholders about directors and the appointment of an independent auditor. In contrast, annual votes by the shareholders of registered investment companies are relatively rare because business entity laws frequently permit fund directors to remain in office for many years without a shareholder vote. In practice, shareholder votes and proxy statements are triggered in only three circumstances for funds: (1) conducting an election of directors; (2) getting approval of an investment advisory contract if a new investment advisor has been retained or if a change of control has occurred for the existing investment adviser; and (3) getting approval of a merger of the fund into another fund.

Specific Content Requirements

SEC disclosure regulations contain specific requirements regarding certain types of disclosure content. This section discusses the most notable disclosure content topics including disclosure relating to investment objectives, policies, and risks. The section then addresses two important areas of disclosure content: performance disclosure and disclosure relating to expenses incurred by investors. Two other areas of disclosure

[1] Investment Company Reporting Modernization, Investment Company Act Release No. 31610 (May 20, 2015).

are also noted: disclosure relating to proxy voting by funds and disclosure about the fund's use of derivatives.

DISCLOSURE OF INVESTMENT OBJECTIVES, INVESTMENT STRATEGIES, AND RISKS

Among the most fundamental features of SEC-mandated offering disclosure is information about the fund's investment objectives and goals as well as its principal investment strategies and risks. These items along with the fee table and standardized performance figures are commonly referred to as the *risk/return summary*. The risk/return summary must appear at the beginning of both the summary prospectus and the statutory prospectus. The fund's investment objectives and goals, such as long-term capital appreciation or current income, should assist investors in identifying funds that meet their general investment needs. *Investment strategy,* as defined in Form N-1A, refers to "any policy, practice, or technique used by the fund to achieve its investment objectives." Common investment strategies regularly contained within the risk/return summary include items such as: (1) the type of securities in which the fund invests or will invest, or (2) any policy that dictates the fund will invest mostly in a certain industry or group of industries.

The prospectus seeks to convey risk in easily understood narrative and quantitative terms. It describes the principal risks affecting the fund with a bar chart and table that (1) show the variability of returns from year-to-year and for 1-, 5-, and 10-year benchmarks relative to a broad measure of market performance, and (2) present the annual return for each of the last 10 calendar years. The information must also disclose the fund's highest and lowest quarterly return during the 10-year period. In 1998, the SEC considered requiring a more sophisticated approach to risk disclosure based on financial economic concepts such as beta, Sharpe ratios, and Treynor ratios, but opted instead for a disclosure approach based on a demonstrative illustration of the fund's historical variability in returns. In its more recent 2015 Investment Company Reporting Modernization initiative, the SEC has signaled a willingness to adopt new requirements obligating funds to provide the SEC with specified risk metrics relating to debt portfolio risk exposure (specifically for duration and spread duration) in a new scheme of monthly portfolio disclosure.

STANDARDIZED, NON-STANDARDIZED, AND AFTER-TAX PERFORMANCE DISCLOSURE

No form of disclosure is arguably more controversial and important for retail investors than performance disclosure. As previously discussed, a clear risk exists that retail investors may be misled by such disclosure because of a propensity to chase performance. Although some have suggested that the SEC should ban such disclosure because of its potential to mislead, whether such a proposal would keep this information out of the media and out of the hands of retail investors is doubtful. Instead, the SEC has sought to elevate the quality and reliability of performance disclosure.

The SEC established an affirmative regime that prescribes standardized methodologies when calculating performance results and creates standardized periodic benchmarks that funds must disclose in their prospectus for the 1-, 5-, and 10-year periods, which are current to the last completed quarter. Both features facilitate comparison among funds based on performance disclosure. The same requirements also apply to performance-based advertising.

SEC requirements permit using performance results based on non-standardized time periods such as year-to-date or 3-year returns provided they are accompanied no less prominently with standardized performance results and funds must make more recent results readily available to investors by telephone or the Internet. The prospectus also requires disclosure of after-tax returns or yields because tax costs are among the most substantial faced by investors when investing in mutual funds and can vary dramatically among funds with similar fund objectives and investment strategies. Finally, in using performance advertising, funds must ensure that performance disclosure, if used, is not misleading in terms of facts and circumstances of which investors are unaware.

POTENTIAL PROBLEMS IN PERFORMANCE DISCLOSURE

Notwithstanding requirements relating to the calculation and presentation of standardized performance results, fund sponsors have enormous discretion over when such information is voluntarily disclosed through advertising. For example, the investment adviser, who is often also the sponsor for the fund, may choose which funds to advertise. While this kind of bias may seem driven by sound and practical business considerations from a sponsor's perspective, the sponsor's control over how funds are marketed introduces a selection or screening bias that distorts the information that investors receive (Jain and Wu 2000; Cooper, Gulen, and Rau 2005; Cronqvist 2006). Consider the difference between a fund family touting the fact it has "two high performing funds" versus an assertion by the same fund family that it has "two high performing funds, five mediocre funds, and 20 funds that are terrible compared to peer funds." The latter statement puts prospective investors on notice in a way that the former statement does not.

Another source of distortion arises from the fact that fund sponsors directly control elimination of funds with poor performance records. This process can occur through liquidation or merger into a more successful fund, thereby eliminating the performance record of the poorly performing fund. The problem of so-called *survivorship bias* is well known in the finance literature and leads to a systematic upward bias in aggregate performance figures for funds over time. Because poor performing funds are gradually pruned from the data, surviving funds will be disproportionately represented by firms that are more successful. Aggregate fund performance figures when viewed in hindsight actually appear better than they are (Elton, Gruber, and Blake 1996; Swensen 2005).

Even though investors may receive information that is accurate, retail investors may not correct for the sponsor's selection bias in presenting information. Historically, some sponsors offered highly selective performance results about individual funds, but this problem has been addressed through standardization of performance calculations and relevant reporting periods, and through application of anti-fraud principles that proscribe communication of performance results that mislead investors. However, a host of opportunistic practices remain available to sponsors. For example, a fund family with a wide selection of fund choices will market those funds that at the time are doing comparatively well relative to other funds. In this form of cyclical bias, investors see only funds that are doing well in terms of their potential marketing story, which might be bond funds one year and stock funds another year (Swensen 2005; Koehler and Mercer 2009; Palmiter and Taha 2012). A variant of this practice is known as *incubation*, which occurs when a fund sponsor seeds several funds that have different investment strategies, and some outperform the market while others underperform under the existing market conditions (Palmiter and Taha 2009). The sponsor then markets the fund with the best track record.

Fund sponsors also have strong incentives to give the appearance that their funds should be compared with a less attractive, non-comparable peer group (Brown and Goetzmann 1997; Chevalier and Ellison 1997; diBartolomeo and Witkowski 1997; Kim, Skukla, and Tomas 2000). Information intermediaries, such as Morningstar and Lipper, know of this propensity and consistently reevaluate peer group classifications. Finally, funds use marketing arrangements, especially through broker-sold distribution channels, to promote their own fund offerings that are in vogue. Marketing arrangements such as shelf-space fees also have the potential to influence brokerage fund recommendations, especially where potential conflicts of interest remain undisclosed to investors.

EXPENSES

As previously discussed, many financial economists regard investor expenses as the most important determinant of investor performance when selecting among funds with similar asset class exposure, rather than the stock-picking ability of a particular investment manager. This conclusion is particularly compelling if active managers cannot significantly and consistently outperform passive managers. These considerations underscore the importance of expense disclosure for ordinary investors. The SEC requires that mutual funds disclose the expenses borne by its investors.

A mutual fund must disclose fees and expenses in several ways. First, a fund's prospectus must disclose its *expense ratio*, which is the ratio of its operating costs divided by the average dollar value of its assets. A fund's shareholder reports must also show in tabular form the actual dollar operating costs that an investor would have incurred associated with investing $1,000 over the last six months and the hypothetical costs that would have been incurred based on the fund's expense ratio, assuming a 5 percent annual return. Finally, the financial information in the shareholder reports must provide a breakdown of the fund's actual expenses.

PORTFOLIO DISCLOSURE

Mutual funds are currently required to disclose their portfolio holdings data to shareholders quarterly in the annual and semi-annual report and supplementary quarterly reports in the first and third quarters. The quarterly portfolio holding disclosure must include: (1) a complete schedule of investments, or alternatively, an abbreviated schedule of investments as long as the complete schedule is available upon request; and (2) a graphic presentation of its portfolio holdings. In its 2015 Investment Company Reporting Modernization initiative, the SEC has proposed to replace the existing scheme of quarterly portfolio disclosure with a new portfolio disclosure scheme that will require monthly portfolio disclosure to the SEC, while retaining the key features of quarterly public portfolio disclosure to the public on a sixty-day lag.

Frequent disclosure may have negative effects on fund performance. The more often a fund releases its holdings, the more frequently other market participants can accurately anticipate the funds' trading and strategies. Funds exhibiting relative superior performance when disclosure of portfolio holdings was less frequent suffered after the mandate for more frequent disclosure (Parida and Teo 2011). Recent evidence by Choi and Chhabria (2013) and Schwarz and Potter (2014) shows that more frequent disclosures may have increased the frequency of *window dressing*, which is a practice of selling underperforming positions before quarterly disclosure deadlines to mask how those investment decisions may have contributed to the fund's reported performance.

PROXY VOTING BY FUNDS

Most registered investment companies are required to disclose how they voted proxies relating to portfolio securities and the fund's proxy voting policies and procedures. The policies and procedures typically address practices related to delegating voting power to the investment adviser who frequently relies on recommendations from outside proxy advisory firms. The fund must also disclose its actual voting records annually on Form N-PX, which is available to investors from the SEC and either upon request to the fund or through the fund's website.

USE OF DERIVATIVES

As noted previously, mutual funds make various disclosures about their principal investment strategies, major risks associated with those strategies, and material factors that affected the fund's performance during the preceding fiscal year. These disclosures may contain information about the fund's use of derivatives. In the past, the staff of the SEC has criticized the quality of fund disclosure relating to use of derivatives and has urged funds to adhere to disclosure policies that describe the strategies that the fund is actively using or likely will use in its investments. In its 2015 Investment Company Reporting Modernization initiative, the SEC proposed enhanced derivatives disclosure in fund financial statements and fund portfolio disclosure. The specific enhancements will promote standardization in how fund derivatives holdings are disclosed and require greater transparency regarding use of derivatives by funds.

Civil Liability and Law Enforcement Sanctions

While SEC rules prescribe affirmative disclosure obligations for funds, this prescriptive authority is supplemented by a legislatively mandated scheme of civil liability remedies for investors and civil and administrative enforcement powers assigned to the SEC. Under the Securities Act, shareholders purchasing mutual fund shares may seek recovery for injury arising from a material misstatement in the registration statement, including the statutory prospectus. With liability under Securities Act Section 11, the fund and (absent an affirmative defense) trustees may be liable for the material misstatements.

Under Section 12, the fund or its selling agents may be liable for material misstatements in any prospectus disseminated to investors in connection with a sale of securities. Under these civil liability provisions, no requirement exists to show either fraud or reliance.

Recovery may also be obtained for fraudulent misstatements found in any fund disclosure. The Supreme Court's decision in *Janus Capital Group v. First Derivative Traders* (2011)[2] greatly limits the liability of investment advisers for materially misleading fund disclosure, even though routinely the fund sponsor or investment adviser prepares such disclosure. For the Court, the critical requirement for liability was the actor's ultimate control over disclosure (ultimately, the fund's trustees) rather than who prepared it. The securities laws also contain law enforcement provisions under the ICA, IAA, Securities Act, and Securities Exchange Act that enable the SEC to seek administrative or civil sanctions for a broad array of misconduct by funds, trustees, investment advisers, and other service providers.

Investor Protection and Fund Advisory Fees

The assets of almost every registered investment company are externally managed by non-employees rather than managed internally by the fund's employees. External management arrangements require written advisory contracts between the fund and the investment adviser. Although originally approved by the fund's shareholders, the advisory agreement is, as a practical matter, subject to annual review by the fund's board and more importantly, by the board's independent trustees. Some criticize the effectiveness of this process in protecting investors (Freeman and Brown 2001; Freeman, Brown, and Pomeratz 2008). Others suggest that competition mitigates most aspects of the problem (Coates and Hubbard 2007).

Separately, Section 36(b) of the ICA imposes a fiduciary duty on investment advisers regarding receipt of fees from funds, notwithstanding the contractual nature of the relationship. In adopting this provision, Congress recognized that contracting in this situation was unlikely to mirror arm's-length bargaining between the fund's board and the investment adviser, which may have been the fund sponsor. The section authorizes shareholders to bring actions against the investment adviser for any fiduciary breaches regarding compensation or payments paid by the fund to its adviser.

The U.S. Supreme Court's decision in *Jones v. Harris Associates, L.P.* (2010)[3] endorsed a general legal standard, known as the *Gartenberg* test, used to evaluate advisers' fees. The Supreme Court noted that courts should explore all relevant factors typically applied in a *Gartenberg* analysis including: (1) the nature and quality of the adviser's services; (2) the expertise and conscientiousness of the independent trustees in reviewing the advisory fees; (3) the profitability of managing the fund for the adviser; (4) the presence of economies of scales in managing the fund; and (5) fall-out benefits to other parts of the adviser's business from managing the fund and even discrepancies in fees between captive mutual fund clients and independent clients.

[2] *Janus Capital Group v. First Derivative Traders*, 131 S. Ct. 2296 (2011).

[3] *Jones v. Harris Associates, L.P.*, 559 U.S. 335 (2010).

ICA Section 36(b) has spawned much litigation (Curtis and Morley 2014). The resulting case law has been influential in shaping the procedures used by independent trustees in reviewing and approving investment advisory fees and agreements. As a result, independent trustees invariably consider the various *Gartenberg* factors in connection with their review of the advisory agreement and obtain written information from the adviser in connection with their review. These materials typically include industry or peer group fund information to inform the trustees' deliberations.

Disclosure Involving Other Registered Vehicles

While preceding sections of the chapter focus on the disclosure regime applicable to mutual funds, there are other forms of registered investment companies, such as CEFs, ETFs, UITs, and variable annuities, where analogous disclosure requirements operate. ETFs can be organized either as a mutual fund or a UIT and must adhere to the applicable disclosure requirements. These requirements function differently when applied to ETFs because of their unique two-level structure: the ETFs' creation units are the redeemable security and the purchaser-investor of the creation units is limited to institutional authorized participants (APs). The APs fractionalize the creation unit for trading on listed markets. Thus, the ETFs disclosure delivery obligations relate to the AP and only indirectly to the eventual shareholders. Most ETFs make their disclosure documents readily available to the eventual shareholders by means of the Internet. Unlike ETFs, exchange-traded products such as exchange-traded commodity pools must comply with the registration and periodic reporting requirements applicable to conventional public companies.

CEFs file a slightly different registration statement than mutual funds. Because their shares trade as listed securities and are not redeemable, CEFs do not need to engage in continuous offerings. As a result, CEFs face fewer regulatory restrictions in communicating directly with investors because they are seldom engaged in offering activity.

Summary and Conclusions

When mutual funds sell their shares to the public, they are essentially selling the investment management services of an investment adviser with which the fund has contracted for management of the fund's assets. No price discovery exists in the price of mutual fund shares because its shares are priced at the NAV. Nonetheless, investors still need information relating to how their assets will be managed, including risks, expenses, and past performance. This information can make investors more informed in their fund selection decisions.

The SEC has helped to standardize disclosure practices to promote greater comparability. Although the requirements for actual offering documents and other shareholder communications are detailed and compel disclosure of some practices that funds might otherwise be reluctant to share, many shareholders are likely to rely on fund-affiliated websites that have considerable latitude in framing the presentation of information provided the funds also provide ready access to SEC-mandated disclosure documents.

Shareholders have remedies for materially false or misleading disclosure. They also have remedies to seek recovery of excessive advisory fees. Shareholder remedies do not yield large recoveries, but they have a deterrent effect and arguably promote better practices at funds. The same can be said of SEC enforcement oversight that results in imposing administrative and civil sanctions. Like shareholders remedies, the principal importance of SEC enforcement authority is its ability to influence practices among funds on an industry-wide basis.

Considerable empirical evidence exists that retail investors' decisions on average are not rational from a financial perspective, notwithstanding robust fund disclosure. Retail investors exhibit tendencies to chase performance and stick with fund selection decisions once making them. Many investors overlook or give too little weight to portfolio risk and fund expenses. Shareholder remedies enhance the potential for investor protection, but such measures do not guarantee it.

Discussion Questions

1. Compare and contrast disclosure regulation for mutual funds versus conventional public companies.
2. Explain whether mutual fund investors ever pay an unfair price for their shares in the fund. If not, discuss why disclosure regulation is necessary.
3. Describe how ordinary retail investor behavior may depart from rational investment decision-making in choosing among funds to invest.
4. Explain whether an equity fund is likely to use performance figures in a print advertisement if marketing an equity fund with a high relative 1-year total return, but with low or negative 5- and 10-year total return figures.
5. Discuss differences between prescriptive regulation (e.g., disclosure requirements) and remedial regulation (e.g., prohibitions on fraud).

References

Agnew, Julie R., and Lisa R. Szykman. 2005. "Asset Allocation and Information Overload: The Influence of Information Display, Asset Choice, and Investor Experience." *Journal of Behavioral Finance* 6:2, 57–70.

Alexander, Gordon J., Jonathan D. Jones, and Peter J. Nigro. 1997. "Mutual Fund Investing Through Employer Sponsored Pension Plans: Investor Knowledge and Policy Implications." *Managerial Finance* 23:7, 5–29.

Alexander, Gordon J., Jonathan D. Jones, and Peter J. Nigro. 1998. "Mutual Fund Shareholders: Characteristics, Investor Knowledge, and Sources of Information." *Financial Services Review* 7:4, 301–316.

Alexander, Gordon J., Jonathan D. Jones, and Peter J. Nigro. 2001. "Does Mutual Fund Disclosure at Banks Matter? Evidence from a Survey of Investors." *Quarterly Review of Economics and Finance* 41:3, 387–403.

Benartzi, Shlomo, and Richard H. Thaler. 2001. "Naïve Diversification Strategies in Defined Contribution Saving Plans." *American Economic Review* 91:1, 79–98.

Berk, Jonathan B., and Richard C. Green. 2004. "Mutual Fund Flows and Performance in Rational Markets." *Journal of Political Economy* 112:6, 1269–1295.

Beshears, John, James J. Choi, David Laubson, and Brigitte C. Madrian. 2009. "How Does Simplified Disclosure Affect Individuals' Mutual Fund Choices?" Working Paper, National Bureau of Economic Research.

Bogle, John C. 2005. "The Relentless Rules of Humble Arithmetic." *Financial Analysts Journal* 61:6, 22–35.

Bollen, Nicolas P. B., and Jeffrey A. Busse. 2004. "Short-Term Persistence in Mutual Fund Performance." *Review of Financial Studies* 18:2, 569–597.

Brown, Stephen J., and William Goetzmann. 1995. "Performance Persistence." *Journal of Finance* 50:2, 679–697.

Brown, Stephen J., and William Goetzmann. 1997. "Mutual Fund Styles." *Journal of Financial Economics* 43:3, 373–399.

Capon, Notel, Gavan J. Fitzsimons, and Russ Alan Prince. 1997. "An Individual Level Analysis of the Mutual Fund Investment Decision." *Journal of Financial Services Research* 10:1, 59–82.

Carhart, Mark M. 1997. "On the Persistence in Mutual Fund Performance." *Journal of Finance* 52:1, 57–82.

Chevalier, Judith, and Glenn Ellison. 1997. "Risk Taking by Mutual Funds as a Response to Incentives." *Journal of Political Economy* 105:5, 1167–1200.

Choi, Seun Hee, and Maneesh Chhabria. 2013. "Window Dressing in Mutual Fund Portfolios: Fact or Fiction." *Journal of Financial Regulation and Compliance* 21:2, 136–149.

Choi, James J., David Laibson, and Brigitte C. Madrian. 2010. "Why Does the Law of One Price Fail? An Experiment on Index Mutual Funds." *Review of Financial Studies* 23:4, 1405–1432.

Coates, John C., and Glenn Hubbard. 2007. "Competition in the Mutual Fund Industry: Evidence and Implications for Policy." *Journal of Corporate Law* 33:1, 151–222.

Cooper, Michael J., Huseyin Gulen, and P. Raghavendra Rau. 2005. "Changing Names with Style: Mutual Fund Name Changes and Their Effects on Fund Flows." *Journal of Finance* 60:6, 2825–2858.

Cooper, Michael J., Roberto C. Gutierrez, and Mill Marcum. 2005. "On the Predictability of Stock Returns in Real Time." *Journal of Business* 78:5, 469–499.

Cox, James D., and John W. Payne. 2005. "Mutual Fund Expense Disclosures: A Behavioral Perspective." *Washington University Law Quarterly* 83:5, 907–938.

Cronqvist, Henrik. 2006. "Advertising and Portfolio Choice." Working Paper, Social Science Research Network, China Europe International Business School.

Curtis, Quinn, and John Morley. 2014. "An Empirical Study of Mutual Fund Excessive Fee Litigation, Do the Merits Matter?" *Journal of Law and Economic Organization* 30:2, 275–305.

Del Guercio, Diane, and Paula A. Tkac. 2002. "The Determinants of the Flow of Funds of Managed Portfolios: Mutual Funds vs. Pension Funds." *Journal of Financial and Quantitative Analysis* 37:4, 523–557.

diBartolomeo, Dan, and Erick Witkowski. 1997. "Mutual Fund Misclassification: Evidence Based on Style Analysis." *Financial Analysts Journal* 53:5, 32–43.

Elton, Edwin J. 2004. "Are Investors Rational? Choices among Index Funds." *Journal of Finance* 59:1, 261–268.

Elton, Edwin J., Martin J. Gruber, and Christopher R. Blake. 1996. "Survivorship Bias and Mutual Fund Performance." *Review of Financial Studies* 9:4, 1097–1120.

Fama, Eugene F., and Kenneth R. French. 2010. "Luck versus Skill in the Cross-Section of Mutual Fund Returns." *Journal of Finance* 65:5, 1915–1947.

Fisch, Jill E., and Tess Wilkinson-Ryan. 2014. "Why Do Retail Investors Make Costly Mistakes? An Experiment on Mutual Fund Choice." *University of Pennsylvania Law Review* 162:3, 605–647.

Franco, Joseph A. 2009. "A Consumer Protection Approach to Mutual Fund Disclosure and the Limits of Simplification." *Stanford University Journal of Law, Business & Finance* 15:1, 1–85.

Frazzini, Andrea, and Owen A. Lamont. 2008. "Dumb Money: Mutual Fund Flow and the Cross-Section of Stock Returns." *Journal of Financial Economics* 88:2, 299–322.

Freeman, John P., and Stewart Brown. 2001. "Mutual Fund Advisory Feeds: The Cost of Conflicts of Interest." *Journal of Corporate Law* 26:3, 610–673.

Freeman, John P., Stewart L. Brown, and Steve Pomeratz. 2008. "Mutual Fund Advisory Fees: New Evidence and a Fair Fiduciary Test." *Oklahoma Law Review* 61:1, 83–151.

French, Kenneth R. 2008. "Presidential Address: The Cost of Active Investing." *Journal of Finance* 63:4, 1537–1573.

Goetzmann, William N., and Roger G. Ibbotson. 1994. "Do Winners Repeat? Patterns in Mutual Fund Behavior." *Journal of Portfolio Management* 20:2, 9–18.

Goetzmann, William N., and Nadav Peles. 1997. "Cognitive Dissonance and Mutual Fund Investors." *Journal of Financial Research* 20:2, 145–158.

Gruber, Martin J. 1996. "Another Puzzle: The Growth in Actively Managed Mutual Funds." *Journal of Finance* 51:3, 783–810.

Harless, David W., and Steven P. Peterson. 1998. "Investor Behavior and the Persistence of Poorly-Performing Mutual Funds." *Journal of Economic Behavior and Organization* 37:3, 257–276.

Hu, Henry T. C. 2005. "The New Portfolio Society, SEC Mutual Fund Disclosure and the Public Corporation Model." *Business Lawyer* 60:4, 1303–1367.

Investment Company Institute. 2014. *Investment Company Fact Book: A Review of Trends and Activities in the U.S. Investment Company Industry*, 54th Edition. Washington, DC: Investment Company Institute. Available at http://www.ici.org/pdf/2014_factbook.pdf.

Jain, Prem C., and Joanna Shuang Wu. 2000. "Truth in Mutual Fund Advertising: Evidence on Future Performance and Fund Flows." *Journal of Finance* 55:2, 937–958.

Karceski, Jason. 2002. "Return-Chasing Behavior, Mutual Funds and Beta's Death." *Journal of Financial and Quantitative Analysis* 37:4, 559–594.

Kim, Moon, Ravi Shukla, and Michael Tomas. 2000. "Mutual Fund Objective Misclassification." *Journal of Economics and Business* 52:4, 309–323.

Kirsch, Clifford E., ed. 2014. *Mutual Funds and Exchange Traded Funds Regulation*. New York: Practicing Law Institute.

Koehler, Jonathan J., and Molly Mercer. 2009. "Selection Neglect in Mutual Fund Advertisements." *Management Science* 55:7, 1107–1121.

Malkiel, Burton G. 2005. "Reflections on the Efficient Market Hypothesis: 30 Years Later." *Financial Review* 40:1, 1–9.

Mauboussin, Michael J. 2012. *The Success Equation: Untangling Skill and Luck in Business, Sports and Investing*. Boston, MA: Harvard Business Review Press.

Mercer, Molly, Alan R. Palmiter, and Ahmed Taha. 2010. "Worthless Warnings? Testing the Effectiveness of Disclaimers in Mutual Fund Advertisements." *Journal of Empirical Legal Studies* 7:3, 429–459.

Palmiter, Alan R., and Ahmed E. Taha. 2008. "Mutual Fund Investors: Divergent Profiles." *Columbia Business Law Review* 2008:3, 934–1020.

Palmiter, Alan R., and Ahmed E. Taha. 2009. "Star Creation: The Incubation of Mutual Funds." *Vanderbilt Law Review* 62:5, 1487–1503.

Palmiter, Alan R., and Ahmed E. Taha. 2012. "Mutual Fund Performance Advertising: Inherently and Materially Misleading?" *Georgia Law Review* 46:2, 289–353.

Parida, Sitikantha, and Terence Teo. 2011. "The Impact of More Frequent Portfolio Disclosure on Mutual Fund Performance." Working Paper, Social Science Research Network. Available at http://ssrn.com/abstract=2097883.

Schwarz, Christopher, and Mark E. Potter. 2014. "Revisiting Mutual Fund Portfolio Disclosure." Working Paper, Social Sciences Research Network. Available at http://ssrn.com/abstract=2093688.

Sirri, Erik R., and Peter Tufano. 1998. "Costly Search and Mutual Fund Flows." *Journal of Finance* 53:5, 1589–1622.

Swensen, David F. 2005. *Unconventional Success: A Fundamental Approach to Personal Investment*. New York: Free Press.

Wilcox, Ronald T. 2003. "Bargain Hunting or Stargazing? Investors' Preferences for Stock Mutual Funds." *Journal of Business* 76:4, 645–663.

25

New Developments in Exchange-Traded Funds

OJWANG' GEORGE OMONDI
Lecturer, Department of Business Studies, Siaya Institute of Technology

Introduction

Financial institutions are constantly designing and marketing innovative financial products that promise to meet investors' return expectations as market conditions and global risk appetites change. In the low global interest rate environment of 2002 and 2003, qualified banks, dealers, and special purpose vehicles (SPVs) packaged and sold structured credit products to institutional investors to gear up investment returns as the value of their liabilities increased. Banks were also willing buyers because these products offered higher returns to comparably rated plain vanilla assets. Rising investor demand for these products later helped banks to fund the rapid growth in credit demand between 2004 and 2006 through the securitization structures that these products supported.

Interest in structured credit products decreased as a result of the financial crisis of 2007–2008. Yet, the low global interest rates that supported growth in structured credit products returned in 2010 with institutional investors facing similar problems to those in 2002 and 2003. This time, however, financial intermediaries responded by adding some innovative features to existing plain vanilla investment funds, marketed under the name exchange-traded funds (ETFs). These funds emerged in the early 1990s as a cost- and tax-efficient alternative to mutual funds. ETFs essentially replicated the underlying index exposure gained by buying the physical stocks or securities in the index. Investors looking for alternative investment vehicles to structured products turned to ETFs as flexible and transparent investment products that can be traded as stocks on an exchange.

Financial intermediaries typically respond to informed investors by packaging innovative products to satisfy their risk appetites. The dealer incentives to seek alternative funding sources to comply with the liquidity coverage ratio (LCR) standard under the Basel III Accord may drive some product innovation for better assessment of liquidity risk across all on and off balance sheet items. Liquidity coverage ratio limits overreliance on short-term wholesale funding during times of vibrant market liquidity. Certain product structures might facilitate run-off rates on liabilities short, which decreases their notional value from prepayments to arbitrageurs. As a result, ETFs have evolved from being plain vanilla, cost- and tax-efficient alternatives to mutual funds to become a more complex and diverse array of products with varying replication schemes (Cano, Feldman, and Smith 2009).

The purpose of this chapter is to examine these investment vehicles from inception to the present and their prospects for the global investment scene. The remainder of the chapter is organized as follows. The next section explores the evolution and structure of ETFs followed by a discussion of the positive features of these instruments including flexibility, intraday trading, and efficiency. Next, the chapter explores their limitations such as encouraging short-term speculation and targeting niche markets without a track record. The next section examines ETF growth prospects and strategies of product launches such as partnering with an established issuer. ETF performance is then discussed based on empirical data on ETF trading within America, Europe, Asia-Pacific, and other regions through January 2014. The final section concludes and presents directions for further research.

Evolution and Structure of Exchange-Traded Funds

An *ETF* is a type of fund structure that issues shares tradable on a stock exchange at a market determined price throughout the day in the same manner as common stocks. Each ETF pool contains the assets of multiple investors and invests the funds according to its investment objective. ETFs offer investors a diversified exposure to financial assets across geographical regions, sectors, or asset classes. ETFs are traded through brokers on a commission basis through market, limit or stop orders. Their shares can be purchased on margin and also can be shorted (Agapova 2011).

EARLY DEVELOPMENT OF EXCHANGE-TRADED FUNDs

The first ETF originated in Canada in 1989 and launched in March 1990. It traded as the Toronto Index Participation Fund (TIP 35). On Friday, January 22, 1993, the first ETF in the United States started operating by issuing 150,000 shares to be traded on the American Stock Exchange (AMEX). These shares, known as Standard &Poor's Depository Receipts (SPDRs, which is pronounced "spiders") represented ownership interests in an investment trust that held a portfolio of shares of common stock comprising all companies in the S&P 500 index in substantially the same proportion as the index. The fund had no affiliation with Standard & Poor's but acknowledging the importance of the S&P 500 index in the broader stock market, licensed the right to use the index's name and composition. Any investor who purchased SPDRs would, in a single share, be invested in the entire S&P 500 index, and the value of SPDRs would fluctuate with the rise and fall of the S&P 500 index (Birdthistle 2011).

In 1924, Massachusetts Financial Services (MFS) created the first mutual fund, Massachusetts Investors Trust (MIT), to provide similar opportunity for individuals to invest in a broad swath of diverse securities through a single vehicle. MIT solicited investments from shareholders for shares in the fund. Using those investment proceeds, MFS, the fund's adviser, purchased a portfolio of underlying securities for the fund.

As with shares of ETFs, the price of shares in MIT increases (decreases) as the aggregate value of the fund's underlying portfolio rises (falls). The critical difference between an ETF and a mutual fund involves how they price their fund shares. Mutual funds are priced just once daily after the close of business. The fund's investment adviser calculates the value of the fund's portfolio by multiplying the number of shares of each of the securities it owns by the respective closing prices of those shares. This aggregate product of the portfolio is then added to any cash or other assets owned by the fund, while liabilities such as fees owed to the adviser or other service providers are subtracted.

The resulting sum is then divided by the total number of shares issued by the mutual fund to calculate the net asset value (NAV) of a single fund share. Waiting until the price of each portfolio security has ceased to fluctuate for the day makes this computation much easier. Although mutual fund advisers find this method administratively easy, fund investors have some reservations because it encourages market timing and fair valuation for illiquid assets to the advantage of fund advisers keen on improving their expense ratios.

Recognizing both the appeal of mutual funds as pools of diversified investments and their pricing limitations, Nathan Most, an AMEX employee, developed the mechanisms used by the first ETF (Laurent 2008). When developing SPDRs, Most sought to provide investors with an opportunity to invest in a diversified investment vehicle via shares that traded at accurate prices throughout the business day. To do so, he introduced *creation units*, which are large blocks of ETF shares denominated in groups of 50,000 shares or greater that an ETF issues and redeems to investors. Only large institutional investors and brokerage houses can buy and sell such wholesale bundles of investments worth millions of dollars. An investor must enter an agreement to become an authorized participant (AP) in the fund to gain eligibility to trade directly with an ETF.

Unlike mutual funds, ETFs do not sell and buy their creation units for cash. Instead, they require that these large institutional APs barter in-kind baskets of portfolio securities for the creation units. Any AP wanting to acquire a creation unit must therefore provide a portfolio deposit equal in value to the NAV of all the ETF shares in the creation unit. For example, to buy a creation unit of SPDRs, an AP would need to provide a portfolio deposit comprising a representative collection of investments in the S&P 500 index. The transaction is reversed when an AP wants to redeem ETF shares.

The AP must assemble the ETF shares into creation units and then present them, bundled accordingly, to the fund for a redemption basket of the fund's underlying securities. Thus, cash rarely changes hands directly in the purchase and sale of ETF shares between the fund and its largest investors (i.e., the APs). Once institutional APs buy blocks of ETF shares in these initial transactions with ETFs, they may then resell them on a securities exchange in a secondary transaction to retail investors at a transaction fee (Kosev and Williams 2011). For the retail investor, shares in an ETF may operationally behave in ways similar to shares of an operating company.

REPLICATION METHODS

Not every ETF replicates the exact composition of its benchmark index. Instead a fund sponsor may try to track the index using only a representative sample of the securities in that index. Such sampling strategy comes with greater flexibility and cost-effectiveness but at a compromised perfect accuracy. If an AP can pay less for 50,000 SPDRs trading on a stock exchange to assemble a creation unit than to acquire all the underlying S&P 500 index stocks required in a portfolio deposit, then the AP can make quick profit by buying the 50,000 SPDRs and redeeming them with the fund for redemption basket of S&P 500 index securities on a stock exchange for cash. Conversely, if the S&P 500 index stocks are trading at prices lower than the SPDRs, the AP can make a quick profit by purchasing the S&P 500 index stocks required for a portfolio deposit and trading them to the ETF for a creation unit, and then selling the 50,000 ETF shares in that creation unit on a stock exchange for a higher price.

ETFs indexed to equity and fixed-income benchmarks are registered under the Investment Company Act of 1940 and classified under open-end funds (OEFs) or as unit investment trusts (UITs). This U.S. legislation permits only physical index replication techniques but does not permit synthetic replication. ETF sponsors do not sell shares directly to investors but issue them in large blocks called creation units to APs who effectively act as market makers (Kosev and Williams 2011). Investors then buy or sell individual shares in the secondary market on an exchange based on the fund's NAV without attracting subscription or redemption charges.

In the primary market, ETFs redeem creation units to APs through securities that comprise the ETF rather than through cash. The limited ability of ETFs to redeem shares in the United States distinguishes them from mutual funds. This feature differs from ETFs issued in Europe where they can be established under the Undertakings for Collective Investment in Transferable Securities (UCITS). The UCITS are a set of European Union (EU) directives that aim to allow collective investment schemes to operate freely throughout the EU on the basis of a single authorization from one member state. Both physical and synthetic index replication is permissible by UCITS and funds.

In the early phase of the development of the ETF industry, index replication was done through plain vanilla structures involving buying all the underlying securities comprising the index. Subsequent changes involved replicating the index by holding an optimized basket of the underlying securities in the index and generating additional income by lending out the securities. In the United States, this process involved organizing ETFs as OEFs rather than as UITs because UITs do not permit securities lending. Almost all ETFs benchmarked against fixed-income or equity indexes in the United States are plain vanilla structures involving physical replication of the underlying index. In Europe about 50 percent of ETFs are plain vanilla types and the rest are replicated using synthetic structures.

REGULATORY REQUIREMENTS

Regulatory structures that stipulate how ETFs are managed in the United States encourage adopting plain vanilla structures. One requirement, which became operational in July 2002, requires that investment companies registered under the Investment Company Act 1940; including ETFs, hold at least 80 percent of their assets in securities matching the fund's name. Another requirement is the notification by the U.S. Securities and Exchange Commission (SEC) in March 2010 to review the use of derivatives to achieve their investment objectives (Securities and Exchange Commission 2010).

UCITS regulation applying in Europe permits exchange-traded and over-the-counter (OTC) derivatives to be held in a fund to meet investment objectives. This UCITS framework has also been adopted in Asia and other emerging markets with more than 70 percent of authorized funds in Hong Kong and Singapore now being UCITS compliant. But a substantial share of ETFs benchmarked to emerging markets assets are domiciled in Luxembourg and Dublin and are UCITS III compliant. UCITS III, adopted in 2001, is a version of EU regulations governing the creation and distribution of pooled investment funds including mutual funds and ETFs. It extended eligible assets to include money market instruments, derivatives, units of other funds and financial indexes. This arrangement may be related to greater European institutional demand for exposure to these asset classes.

Synthetic and Exotic Structures

Synthetic ETFs allow replication of the index using derivatives as opposed to owning the physical assets to reduce costs. If the index has a narrow regional or sector focus and is widely traded, replicating the ETF benchmark can be cost-efficient. However, physical replication can be an expensive method for tracking broad market indexes such as emerging market equity or fixed-income indexes, or other less liquid market indexes. In less liquid markets, the wider bid-ask spreads increase replication costs, particularly when the fund has high turnover.

These considerations led to using synthetic structures to replicate the ETF benchmark. One popular structure involves using total return swaps, which ETF sponsors refer to as the *unfunded swap*. In a total return swap, the swap counterparty exchanges index returns for a basket of collateral returns with the ETF sponsor who exchanges cash for a basket of stock from the counterparty as depicted in Table 25.1. Under the synthetic replication scheme, the APs receive the creation units from the ETF sponsor against cash rather than a basket of the index securities as in physical replication scheme. The ETF sponsor separately enters a total return swap with a financial intermediary, often its parent bank, to receive the total return of the ETF index for a nominal exposure.

For example, assume an Australian company has AU$200 million in revenues, which translates to about $100 million in U.S. dollars. It has $50 million of costs denominated in U.S. dollars. The nominal exposure to the Australian/U.S. exchange rate is $100 million less $50 million, which is $50 million. This exposure makes up the first leg of the swap. Cash is then transferred by the ETF sponsor through a custodian to the swap counterparty equal to the notional exposure, equal in value to the payoff required to counter risk of financial loss. Such counterparty risk could lead to broad industry run thereby threatening financial stability (Baba, McCauley, and Ramaswamy 2009; Bank of England 2010; Financial Stability Board 2011). In return, the swap counterparty transfers a basket of collateral assets like shares representing a collateral pledge to the ETF sponsor. The assets in the collateral basket could differ completely from those in the benchmark index, which the ETF replicates. The total return on this collateral basket is then transferred from the ETF sponsor to the swap counterparty, which constitutes the second leg of the total return swap. Table 25.1 depicts a *total return swap*,

Table 25.1 **Total Return Swap**

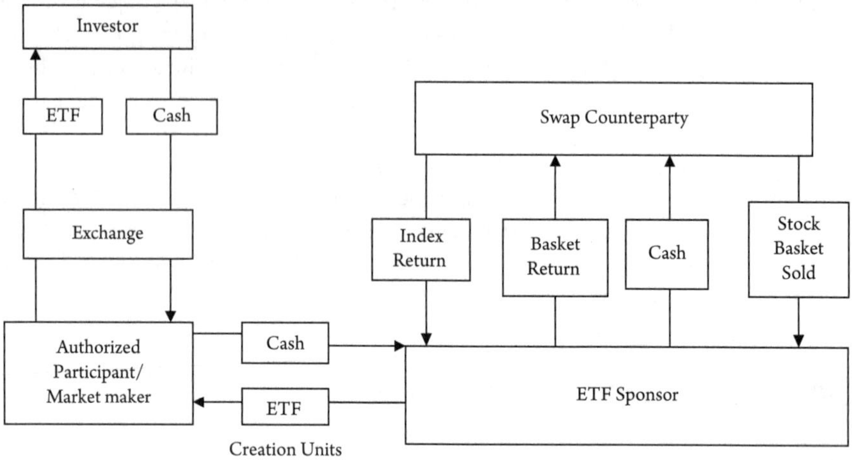

Note: This table depicts a total return swap, which is a bilateral financial transaction in which the counterparties swap total return of a single asset or basket of assets for periodic cash flows typically a floating rate such as the London Interbank Offered Rate (LIBOR). From the table index return and basket return comprise the total return swap.

Source: Table adapted from Srichander 2011.

which is a bilateral financial transaction in which the counterparties swap the total return of a single asset or basket of assets for periodic cash flows at a floating rate such as London Interbank Offered Rate (LIBOR).

Some structures use multiple swap counterparties for the transaction. The composition of the assets in the collateral basket can change daily as the swap counterparty recycles its inventory. Being the beneficial owner of the collateral basket, the ETF sponsor can sell the collateral assets if the swap counterparty defaults and repays the investors. Under UCITS regulation, the daily NAV of the collateral basket, which can include cash or equities and bonds of the Organization for Economic Cooperation and Development (OECD) countries including the United States, the United Kingdom, Germany, and Switzerland, should cover at least 90 percent of the ETF's NAV. This limits the swap counterparty risk to a maximum of 10 percent of the ETF's market value. Assets in the collateral basket are eligible for securities lending. Secured lending is usually done through a custodian who is responsible for the safekeeping of assets, trade processing, and settlement and clearance.

Funded Swap Structure

An alternative replication strategy used by ETF sponsors is to employ a *funded swap structure*. Under this format, the ETF sponsor transfers cash to the swap counterparty that then provides the total return of the replicated ETF index. This transaction is collateralized, with the swap counterparty posting the eligible collateral into a ring-fenced custodian account to which the ETF sponsor has legal claims. *Ring fencing* involves keeping a client's account with a custodian, usually an AAA-rated financial institution, separately from the ETF sponsor's other assets for enhanced protection of client funds. But unlike in the unfunded swap structure, the sponsor is not the beneficial owner of the collateral assets. *Beneficial owners* are investors engaged in lending their portfolio assets on a short-term basis to generate incremental revenues collateralized at 102 or 105 percent thereby reducing the lenders credit exposure to the borrower. This structure might lead to delays in realizing the value of collateral assets if the swap counterparty fails. A bankruptcy administrator can freeze these assets even when they are held in client accounts (Fender, Frankel, and Gyntelberg 2008).The collateral composition and the extent of minimum collateralization must comply with the UCITS regulation. Usually this transaction is over collateralized by 10 to 20 percent leaving the counterparties with adequate protection in case of security price fluctuations. Securities lending is permitted. This structure is less commonly used by sponsors for synthetic replication of ETF indexes.

The transaction can be separated into buying a credit or equity linked note from a financial intermediary and then mitigating the counterparty risk by requesting collateral posting that is UCITS compliant. A *credit linked note* is a security with an embedded credit default swap allowing the issuer to transfer a specific credit risk to the credit investor who buys securities from a trust collateralized with securities paying a fixed or floating coupon during the life of the note. The ETF sponsor buys a structured note secured by a collateral pledge. Synthetic replication is common with commodity ETFs. But in these markets, a lack of sufficient diversification of assets in the index prohibits using the mutual fund structure. As a result, exchange-traded products that provide exposure to commodities use other trust structures and are marketed as exchange-traded commodities (ETCs). While some sponsors use physical replication of some commodity indexes, such as gold and copper, synthetic replication using futures or forward contracts is common.

The increased demand for ETF products has brought with it product complexity and aggressive risk profiles. More exotic products known as leveraged ETFs delivering returns in multiples of the daily performance of the index have been introduced into the market. Conversely, leveraged inverse ETFs deliver a return in multiples of the inverse performance of the underlying index.

ETF sponsors usually emphasize the swap-based replication schemes to deliver the investment performance of mimicked exposures. Investor's exposure is more similar to buying or selling an Asian option where the payoff is determined by the average underlying price over a pre-set time period rather than a European option in which the payoff on the underlying index is determined on a single predetermined date.

Motivation for Synthetic Replication

Synthetic replication schemes transfer the risk of any deviation in the ETF's return from its benchmark to the swap provider, which is affected by entering a derivatives contract to receive the total return of the benchmark (Committee on the Global Financial System 2005, 2008). This structure protects investors from the tracking error risk, arising whenever a disparity exists between the returns of the underlying index and the returns of ETF shares. The lower tracking error risk comes at the cost of increased counterparty risk to the swap provider. The increased popularity of ETF products among investors has led to greater competition among ETF sponsors, forcing them to seek alternative replication techniques to optimize their fee structures.

One outcome of this fee structure review has been to explore the scope for possible synergies that might exist between the investment banking activities of the parent bank and its asset management subsidiary. These synergies arise from the market-making activities of investment banking that require maintaining a large inventory of stocks and bonds that has to be provided. By transferring these stocks and bonds as collateral assets to the ETF provider sponsored by the parent bank, the investment banking activities may benefit from reduced warehousing costs for these assets. Part of this cost-savings may then be passed onto the ETF investors through a lower total expense ratio for the fund holding. Table 25.2 compares two synthetic replication schemes: a funded swap

Table 25.2 **Exchange-Traded Fund Synthetic Replication Schemes**

Attribute	*Unfunded Swap Structure*	*Funded Swap Structure*
Type of transaction	Total return swap	Credit or equity linked note
Counterparty risk	Mitigated through ownership of collateral assets effected through true sale	Mitigated through the pledge of collateral assets through counterparty agreement
Overcollateralization	Typically small, if any	Typically up to 120 percent of the ETF's NAV
Haircuts(margin on collateral assets)	Usually none, but under UCITS, some jurisdiction can impose haircuts for certain assets	Usually none, but some jurisdictions can impose haircuts for certain assets under UCITS
Composition of collateral assets	Can change daily	Can change daily
Balance sheet implication for swap counterparty	True sale of collateral assets can alter risk-weighted capital charges	Pledge of collateral assets unlikely to alter risk-weighted capital charges

Note: This table compares two ETF synthetic replication schemes (i.e., a funded swap structure and an unfunded swap structure) under various attributes such as the type of transaction, counterparty risk, and collateralization.

Source: Adapted from Srichander 2011.

structure and an unfunded swap structure under various attributes such as the type of transaction, counterparty risk, and collateralization.

Positive Attributes of Exchange-Traded Funds

Financial innovation is mostly driven by inadequacies of current instruments' failure to satisfy investor requirements. ETFs are a market response to inadequacies of mutual funds' forward pricing, market timing, fair valuation, and hidden management fees. They offer investors flexibility in their transactions as discussed in this section.

FLEXIBILITY AND EXCHANGE TRADING

ETFs are attractive to traders because of their ability to trade in the same manner as a security throughout the business day at real time prices on a stock exchange. The limits of mutual funds' system of forward pricing means investors cannot react to negative news occurring during a trading day. In contrast, ETF investors can react immediately to positive or negative news by buying or selling their ETF shares. They can exert control over the purchase and disposition of the holdings in their portfolios by placing market, stop, or limit orders on their ETF shares. ETF benefits include the ability to short against movements of broad market indexes, hedge against the performance of other holdings in their portfolio, and purchase shares on margin.

INVESTMENT OPTIONS

The intraday pricing feature allows investors to time market movements to bet on upward or downward swings in stock exchanges. Similarly, institutional investors holding uninvested cash during periods between investment activities may choose to equitize that cash by using ETF shares to invest the funds in broad market indexes for short periods of time. ETFs provide exposure to derivatives, futures, commodities, currencies, and preferred stock. This allows investors to construct a core and satellite portfolio, purchasing passive and broad-based ETFs in a diverse pattern of asset allocation as the portfolio's core, while choosing more specialized niche ETFs as a satellite to boost portfolio performance.

EFFICIENCY AND COSTS

Unlike mutual funds, especially actively managed funds, ETFs suffer few of the transaction costs associated with the turnover of portfolio securities. Mutual funds must process all the purchases and redemptions of every single investor in their fund, large or small. Those transactions generate substantial costs associated with shareholder record-keeping and managing accounts. Conversely, ETFs conduct far fewer large-scale transactions, with investors wealthy and sophisticated enough to traffic in creation units, portfolio deposits, and redemption baskets. All other transactions involving ETF shares take place on secondary stock exchanges and therefore do not generate expenses that the fund must bear. ETFs can operate with far lower cash reserves on hand compared to mutual funds because ETFs do not redeem their shareholders in cash but rather in kind through redemption baskets of portfolio securities.

TAX ADVANTAGES

An ETF grows primarily through the accretion of in-kind portfolio deposits of underlying securities from investing shareholders and then redeems those shareholders by returning securities in redemption baskets. Unlike mutual funds, ETFs rarely, if ever, alter investment strategies and therefore seldom require direct purchases or sales of portfolio securities. If any of the securities contributed by investors to an ETF experience substantial appreciation while owned by the fund, the fund can redeem its securities to rid itself of those with the highest potential unrealized capital gains first. So ETFs incur comparatively few taxable purchases and sales of securities and pass fewer capital gains liabilities to their shareholders (Huang and Guedj 2009).

Limitations of Exchange-Traded Funds

The rapid development of ETFs starting in 1993 has been both a blessing to investors and a curse to short-term speculative traders. The speculators constantly watch the dynamic market and want to gain from price changes. Such regular daily transactions are costly as discussed in this section.

SHORT-TERM SPECULATION

Bogle (2004), the founder of Vanguard, concludes that if long-term investing was the paradigm for mutual funds, trading ETFs can only be described as short-term speculation allowing intraday trading, which attracts brokerage fees and financial transaction tax on every transaction. Emotions encourage performance-chasing investors to become their own worst enemies as they interpret public information (Spence 2007). Mutual funds suffer from their architectural weaknesses, which permit market timing, late trading, unfair valuation, and hidden fees and expenses. ETFs have potential risks because the ability to trade ETFs continuously may tempt rapid and unsuccessful day trading by overly optimistic retail investors (Benz 2011).

SATURATION AND NICHE VOLATILITY

When only a few companies operate in a particular investment sector, ETFs and other investment funds attempting to invest in that sector may drive the price of those companies artificially higher. This dynamic occurs not because of faith in the value of any particular company, but because of the need to hold those shares in the fund. Also, creating ETFs to track the value of commodities such as silver and gold has driven up the price of the underlying commodities (Costa 2011). The securities of esoteric investment niches, such as foreign issuers or micro-cap companies, are likely to be traded with thin volumes and therefore susceptible to the volatility of dramatic price swings.

LACK OF A TRACK RECORD

Any ETF sponsor incapable of providing a concrete record of results over a long operational period is offering a promise of its ability to deliver returns to the investor without a demonstrable business model over time. Morningstar rates funds that have operated over three years. Only after viewing several years of results will an investor have a realistic sense of a particular fund's management expertise and appreciate the difference between theoretical indexes and actual investment results.

TRACKING ERROR

ETFs fail to adhere reliably to the index to which they are supposedly benchmarked for various reasons. First, a fund may replicate the entire composition of its underlying index or use a representative sample of index securities in its portfolio. Second, currency fluctuations may create a disparity in returns for a benchmark comprising foreign stocks if the fund itself is denominated in U.S. dollars. Third, the costs that a fund incurs create a differential drag on its performance. Thus, transaction costs, custody costs, foreign exchange impact of investing in overseas securities, and differences in the timing of dividend payments affect tracking error.

Retail Distribution and Growth Prospects

ETFs need to be promoted and sold without negatively affecting its investors. Market makers in the United States and Europe are focusing their promotional efforts on asset managers and private wealth managers. Promoters with in-house wealth managers have an upper hand in terms of identifying a specific index to track, composition of creation units, approval of creation orders, dividend payments as well as trade execution of the underlying securities through this valuable distribution channel because their expense ratio includes management fees instead of reporting them separately. Thus, they act as a one-stop shop for ETF transactions. In turn, this translates into lower fees to their clients. Education alone will not create a culture of ETF investment. Independent advisers and investment platforms will be crucial to unlocking retail growth because the advisers are no longer only engaged in stock selection for the client but are offering tactical asset allocation advice in which they charge an asset-based management fee for access to low-cost vehicles.

TAX IMPLICATIONS OF TRADING

ETF participants must consider tax-related issues with their investments. In Europe, the financial transactions tax, which became effective in early 2015, alarms some investors more than any other regulatory initiative as it assumes that the pass through of the tax from traders to investors is close to 100 percent including any intermediate transaction (Oxera 2011). The financial transaction proposes to impose a levy on every financial transaction undertaken by market participants, which directly hurts speculators keen on betting on price changes through intraday trading. Trader-oriented investors fail to correctly time the market leading to poor investment outcomes thereby destabilizing capital markets (Barber and Odean 2000; Zweig 2011).

SERVICE PROVIDERS

Service providers supply the infrastructure that promoters and traders need to uphold their promises to investors. Asset providers are expected to act as enablers for the further development of ETF markets, which should lower costs, improve liquidity, and help meet complex tax and regulatory reporting requirements. The liquidity of ETFs and the degree of automated trading in the market contribute to the complexity of ETF support. Cross-listing is a complication in the fragmented European market, while local regulations in Asia-Pacific often require service providers to develop separate systems in every market (Amihud 2002). Promoters and market makers need to recognize that developing a new fund is often quicker and easier than developing the administrative platforms required to function effectively.

THE FUTURE OF THE EXCHANGE-TRADED FUNDs INDUSTRY

For this financial innovation to achieve growth potential, the ETF industry should focus on the following variables:

- *Education.* A need exists for public–private partnerships among regulators, service providers, and academic institutions to implement financial literacy programs to the investing public to ensure that more informed choices are made and to help decision-making by distinguishing between noise and information in the capital markets. *Noise trading* occurs when short-term speculators trade irrationally based on herd behavior of buying and selling what others are doing. Trading on information involves purchasing material data to be analyzed before a transaction occurs. Noise keeps security prices in check, whereas buying pertinent information can yield superior returns. Both noise and information co-exist to make capital markets functional. Success in educational efforts will better ensure that trading volumes will be commensurate with the level of economic activity. The Asia-Pacific region is a huge market with an ever-expanding middle class in China, India, Singapore, and Hong Kong that needs to bring on board institutional investors to enjoy their trading volumes in order to boost its position in the emerging markets category.
- *Communication and distribution.* The ETF industry needs to speak with one voice when communicating with regulators, legislators, tax authorities, and other stakeholders. To achieve effective and efficient distribution, formal engagements are needed with a range of partners to develop infrastructure conducive to both retail and institutional channels.
- *Innovation.* A need exists to put in place ceilings on financial innovations that could be sold to potential investors. Finance houses on the sell side want to develop new products that circumvent regulatory barriers to satisfy unsuspecting potential investors. These ceilings could curb systemic and reputational risks so that fund strategies and structure vulnerability can be mitigated at short notice to check on contagion and industry runs. For this change to be effective, industry regulators

need to monitor the activities of industry players and to curb the sale of inadequate products to noise traders. This monitoring is particularly important because product growth leads to complexity calling for advanced management of regulatory and tax issues. Cross-border listing requires establishing a professional body dedicated to devising shared approaches to common ETF issues in a collaborative manner.

- *Collaboration and cooperation.* A need exists for a centralized clearing system to enable cross-border settlements particularly in the fragmented European market. This change will harmonize regulatory requirements and boost growth. Additionally, creating a professional industry body dedicated to devising shared approaches to common ETF issues is essential.

Table 25.3 depicts product launches in ETF market in 2013 based on geographical regions. From the table, the United States has the highest number of product launches with 16 followed by Europe, the Rest of the World, and the Asia-Pacific.

Table 25.3 **New Exchange-Traded Fund Products**

Region	*ETF Provider*	*Assets ($ millions)*	*Cash Flow ($ millions)*	*Turnover ($ millions)*	*Products*
United States	Velocity Shares	62.5	59.7	67.8	6
	Cambria Funds	208.6	189.6	413.6	2
	Horizons	30.8	28.5	69.0	2
	KraneShares	24.8	21.9	49.2	2
	Renaissance Capital	30.6	28.4	69.7	1
	Franklin Templeton Investments	27.7	27.7	3.8	1
	LocalShares	6.8	6.3	8.3	1
	Recon Capital	2.6	2.5	1.1	1
Europe	First Trust	12.3	11.3	7.6	3
	FinEx Fund Plc	59.4	62.3	34.4	2
	Nordea Investment Funds	0.0	0.0	0.5	2
	Commerzbank AG	42.1	37.7	0.9	1
	Avana Investment AG	7.5	7.5	0.0	1
	Landsbankinn	0.0	0.0	1.0	1
Asia Pacific	Changsheng Fund	19.0	0.0	134.4	1
	First Metro Asset Management	16.8	17.9	2.7	1
	China International Fund Management	8.1	0.0	100.2	1

continued

Table 25.3 **(continued)**

Region	*ETF Provider*	*Assets ($ millions)*	*Cash Flow ($ millions)*	*Turnover ($ millions)*	*Products*
	Wanjia Asset Management	0.0	0.0	57.6	1
Rest of the World	Purpose Investments	120.9	115.1	200.2	6
	First Trust	54.6	40.2	426.8	1

Note: This table depicts product launches in the ETF market in 2013 for different geographical regions. The order of product launches from highest to lowest is the United States (16), Europe (10), Rest of the World (7), and Asia-Pacific (4).

Source: Table adapted from Lan et al. 2014.

Evaluating Exchange-Traded Funds

Various metrics are available to investors to evaluate an ETF. Depending on the type of investor, the importance of these metrics may vary.

PERFORMANCE

Various studies find little or no evidence of predictive power of past performance on future performances (Sharpe 1966; Jensen 1968). However, investors may want to evaluate an ETF's performance against its stated objective or benchmark. A simulation of risk-adjusted returns from 1994 to 2009 shows that the Research Affiliates Fundamental Indexation (RAFI) Composite index would have returned a 12.9 percent annually with a volatility of 15 percent, whereas the Morgan Stanley Capital International (MSCI) index would have returned only 9.9 percent with a higher volatility of 15.5 percent(Costa 2011). Rational investors are guided by the risk-return trade-off and are risk-averse. With almost the same risk level, a rational investor would select the RAFI Composite return of 12.9 percent, which is higher than the MSCI return of 9.9 percent. For an index based ETF, an ETF's tracking error serves as a performance measure. When evaluating an actively managed ETF, investors might look at how the ETF has performed relative to its stated benchmark. Any deviation from the two returns could be because of fund manager portfolio rebalancing, management fees, and industrial stability.

COST

Investing in an ETF involves various costs such as fees charged by the ETF sponsor, brokerage commissions, and account fees associated with receiving financial advice. But ETFs suffer few of the transaction costs associated with the turnover of portfolio securities common with actively managed mutual funds because large institutional APs buy their shares in substantial amounts of creation units. Few purchases are enough for portfolio construction thereby attracting low management fees compared to mutual funds. For example, Lyxor ETF World Water, which is tradable in Switzerland, Italy, the United Kingdom, France and Germany, had assets under management (AUM) of Euros 81.5 million but a total expense ratio of 0.6 percent in 2011. By contrast, Swisscanto (LU) Equity Fund Water Invest, which is tradable in Switzerland, Germany, Australia, and Luxembourg, had AUM of Euros 117.83 million but a total expense ratio of 2 percent in 2011. This large difference exists despite both ETFs investing in water treatment and technologies.

PREMIUMS AND DISCOUNTS

Although ETF shares trade on the secondary market at a price that approximates the market value of their underlying assets, their market price may sell at a premium (higher) or a discount (lower) to the estimated market value of their underlying assets. Although the prices of commodities such as gold do not fluctuate like bonds and equities, such products are prone to be traded at premium prices further increasing their prices in the secondary markets. By contrast, energy products are volatile and might be sold at a discount when their prices are falling to induce investors to trade them. By tracking which asset classes attract premiums and discounts, investors could potentially forecast potential gains in the market.

LIQUIDITY

Liquidity refers to how easily shares can be bought or sold without moving the market price. Securities with high trading volumes tend to be more liquid. ETF liquidity should be evaluated relative to both the ETF shares and the underlying securities the ETF holds. Liquidity helps determine the price of ETF shares given that liquid shares have their prices displayed every 15 seconds compared to illiquid shares whose pricing is prone to fair valuation due to their thin markets. Liquidity is crucial for the efficiency of ETFs as hedging tools and for arbitraging that makes capital markets vibrant (Ben-David, Franzoni, and Moussawi 2012).

BID-ASK SPREAD

When buying or selling ETF shares on the secondary market, a difference occurs between the highest price a buyer is willing to pay for an ETF share (the *bid*) and the lowest price a seller will accept to sell an ETF share (the *ask*). As a result, an investor will buy ETF shares for slightly over market price and sell for slightly less. Bid-ask spreads are smaller for larger ETFs in which the market has many buyers and sellers, resulting in less volatility and greater liquidity compared to smaller ETFs tracking niche markets.

Exchange-Traded Funds Performance Outlook

Global ETF assets grew to $1.76 trillion during 2012 registering close to 30 percent growth. About 18 percent of the growth came from new cash flows ($249 billion), while the remaining 11 percent came from asset price increases. The U.S. ETF market led global growth with record inflows of $174 billion in 2012. The United States, Europe,

Asia-Pacific, and Rest of the World regional ETF asset and respective growth rates ended 2012 with $1.21 trillion (+29 percent), $333 billion (+24 percent), $136 billion (+50 percent), and $72 billion (+29 percent), respectively. In the United States, ETFs continue to take market share away from mutual funds, especially in equities. Since 2006, mutual funds have seen more than $400 billion in outflows while ETFs have seen more than $500 billion in inflows in the equity space (Deutsche Bank 2013). ETFs appear to be a panacea to mutual fund drawbacks involving market timing, late trading, fair valuation, and hidden fees and expenses because ETFs offer flexibility, efficiency, lower cost, a tax advantage, and an array of investment options.

Among ETF providers, fierce competition has ignited a price war with multiple remedial actions. Trading activity picked up in 2013 with ETF turnover levels registering a rise of 9.5 percent over 2012. Overall, annual ETF turnover in 2013 and 2012 has been $15.7 trillion and $14.3 trillion, respectively. In 2013, Asia-Pacific region ETFs recorded the highest increase of 103 percent in trading volumes at $601 billion, a rise of 9.5 percent compared to the other three geographical regions. U.S. ETFs continue to dominate the global ETF trading activity at $14 trillion, representing a rise of 7.7 percent over the previous year (Deutsche Bank 2013).

Table 25.4 lists the 10 largest ETF providers and their family composition. BlackRock tops the list with 741 ETFs followed by Deutsche Bank with 371 ETFs, State Street Global Advisors and Vanguard come in next at 196 and 100, respectively. Vanguard's positioning occurs despite the resistance to the ETFs offered by John C. Bogle, Vanguard's founder.

In the United States, ETFs outperformed mutual funds in the race for assets in their home turf. In a year with low volatility levels and lower pair-wise correlations among equities supposed to benefit active management, ETFs grew faster and gathered more new assets than mutual funds for both equity and fixed-income products. For many years, some viewed ETFs as disruptors of the traditional asset management industry. However, recent developments suggest that the perception of these products is changing and the industry participants have begun to appreciate the evolution of the fund industry rather than disruptors of the same.

The U.S. ETF market experienced remarkable asset growth of 30 percent during 2013 with strong inflows of $190.6 billion, representing a 15.7 percent rise over 2012. In contrast, the mutual fund industry assets grew by 17.3 percent experiencing positive flows of $174 billion, a rise of 1.7 percent over 2012. The fact that ETFs grew at a faster rate and gathered more new assets than mutual funds is even more notable considering that 2013 was one of the biggest equity bull markets in 25 years with the S&P 500 index increasing by 32 percent. Furthermore, lower pair-wise correlation and volatility should have benefited mutual-fund-related practices such as stock picking and active management. Within the fixed-income space, ETFs recorded the first major win over mutual funds. ETFs had received $10.5 billion of new assets as of the end of November2013, while mutual funds had recorded outflows of $57.9 billion in the same period (Lan, Mercado, and Rajendra 2014).This difference shows the level of acceptance ETF products are gathering within investors' fixed-income portfolios.

As a result many traditional asset managers are implementing or fine-tuning their entry strategies into the ETF industry. The following are some of those strategies.

Table 25.4 **Top 10 Exchange-Traded Fund Families in 2013 by Assets Under Management**

Family	*Number of ETFs*	*AUM*	*YTD Asset Flows*
BlackRock	741	$911,445,020,315	$57,693,603,692
State Street Global Advisors	196	403,033,049,654	11,307,219,287
Vanguard	100	333,105,550,542	53,544,295,199
PowerShares	196	97,905,717,498	12,423,745,837
Deutsche Bank	371	52,857,528,032	−4,881,730,358
Société Générale	255	42,069,114,403	−1,141,314,815
Nomura Asset Management	52	36,395,379,879	5,014,696,578
WisdomTree	56	34,485,590,353	13,989,237,851
ProShares	144	26,418,641,383	4,848,972,809
Van ECK Securities Corporation	61	22,565,514,948	1,633,377,419
Top 10 total	2,172	1,960,281,107,006	154,432,103,500

Note: This table lists the 10 largest ETF providers including the number of ETFs. BlackRock has the highest AUM followed by State Street Global Advisors and Vanguard.

Source: Table adapted from Lan et al. 2014.

1. *Launch an ETF suite.* This process requires setting up operations including legal, portfolio management, marketing, sales, and capital markets. This alternative represents a major commitment of resources and may be appropriate for those companies that see ETFs as a core area of their future strategy. Examples of those adopting this strategy include PIMCO in 2009 and Franklin Templeton and Fidelity both in 2013(Lan et al. 2014).
2. *Acquire an ETF issuer.* Because adopting this strategy involves a substantial business commitment to the new entrant, it is suitable to fund companies seeking ETFs as a core part of their future business strategy. BlackRock used this strategy to buy iShares in 2009 as did INVESCO with the purchase of PowerShares in 2006 and Guggenheim with the purchase of Claymore in 2009 and Rydex in 2010(Lan et al. 2014).
3. *Partner with an existing ETF Issuer.* This strategy takes the form of a co-branded ETF issued under one of the ETF issuer's fund families with the asset manager specialist as a sub-adviser to the ETF. The new ETF sponsor links up with an existing fund

issuer investing in various markets tracking different indexes with a track record of more than three years. This enables potential investors to capitalize on the track record as material information to their asset allocation. An asset manager specialist helps pick the underlying securities either by direct replication or synthetically until the new ETF gains clients' confidence after a minimum of three years when most rating bodies such as Morningstar could rate the ETF's performance. The ETF provider addresses all of the capital markets requirements such as identifying the fund's target benchmark, the number of shares to equate to a creation unit, and dissemination of daily fund NAV as well as marketing activities while the asset manager oversees the portfolio management of the fund. This strategy involves less commitment than acquiring a whole business, but it still provides a foothold in the ETF market. The strategy is appropriate for firms looking for additional distribution channels for their already successful strategies especially with new asset classes. Blackstone/GSO implemented this strategy when it partnered with State Street in 2013. Other examples include Legg Mason's Western Asset Management partnering with Wisdom Tree in 2012, TCW Group partnering with Emerging Global Advisors in 2014, and MFS Investment Management partnered with State Street Global Advisors in 2014.

4. *Non-transparent active ETF*. This strategy is still in its exploratory phase with pending regulatory hurdles to cross. It offers a venue to fund managers to evaluate a transition/replacement strategy without full commitment to ETFs. Examples of firms exploring this path at the time of this writing include BlackRock, Eaton Vance, and T. Rowe Price.

The global investment arena is geographically divided into four regions: the United States, Europe, Asia, and Rest of the World. Asia had the largest number of new ETF launches of the four regions with 14, followed by the United States with five, the Rest of the world with four, and Europe with three launches. In 2012, three new providers—Alpcot Capital Management, Swedbank Robur, and Vanguard—made their debut in the European market with one, three, and five products, respectively. Vanguard entered the European market offering low-cost products to investors translating into higher competition to the existing providers.

During 2012, five new providers entered the U.S. market, each offering one to three products. Horizon Management entered the Asian ETF industry because of its acquisition by Mirae Asset MAPS Global Investments in 2012. Also, 13 new providers launched 19 products in the ETF markets across Asia in 2012. All 13 providers launched one product each except Enhanced Investment Products Ltd., which entered the market with seven launches. Four new ETF providers—Caixa, Grindrod Bank, IMTrust, and Royal Canadian Mint—entered the rest of the world market with one product each during 2012.

At a global level, five providers left the ETF industry in 2012. In the United States, FocusShares delisted its ETF range of 15 products and exited the industry. Russell Investments shut down all but one of its ETFs in 2012. JP Morgan and Marshall Wace LLP left the European ETF markets with delisting their complete range of products. In Asia, AMP and China International Capital were among the providers who left the industry in 2012 (Deutsche Bank 2013).

Low-Cost Indexes

An important development in the cost-cutting race has been the trend to move to lower cost indexes as product underlying implying that the value of the index chosen determines the value of the basket of securities transacted. Such a move leans more toward core allocations with no front loads charges than satellite allocations with front loads charges. Multiple ways are available to move away from branded and relatively more expensive benchmarks including self-indexing, boutique index providers, and partnerships.

SELF-INDEXING

Some ETF providers such as WisdomTree, Market Vectors, and Index IQ have opted to develop their own benchmarks for their products. With internal development, all functions are performed in-house. The index division of the ETF provider manages the methodology, construction, calculations, index maintenance, and reconstruction.

BOUTIQUE INDEX PROVIDERS

Other providers such as EGShares and Global X Funds use smaller index providers such as Indxx. Indxx Super Dividend U.S. Low Volatility Index is a 50 stock equal-weighted index designed to follow the market performance of companies in the United States that have a high dividend yield and low beta and structured solutions. In this case, most of the index-related tasks are outsourced to the index provider, although the genesis of the benchmark can often involve the ETF provider.

PARTNERSHIPS

Partnerships are structured in a similar manner as boutique index providers, with the only difference being that partnerships involve larger index institutions and in most cases a tailored index. The ETF provider usually initiates the index generation process by approaching the index provider with a methodology that needs to be turned into an index. Beyond this point, the index provider handles all other index-related tasks. Examples of partnerships include those between Vanguard and CRSP and First Trust and NYSE Euronext.

Low-cost indexing offers lower costs to investors. A less known benchmark would usually have a lower pool of passive assets tracking it. Therefore, any rebalancing activity would have less impact on the underlying securities, which benefits investors in the passive product by reducing the number of active players that could be tempted to front run the passive fund.

Summary and Conclusions

An ETF is a pooled investment vehicle with shares tradable throughout the day on a stock exchange at a market-determined price. These funds follow a wide range of strategies including equities, fixed-income, and commodities with most of them being index-based through either physical or synthetic replication. Physical replication uses security weighting through market capitalization or dividends. In the United States, ETFs are regulated under the Investment Company Act of 1940, which allows oversight by an independent board of directors and requires that fund assets be held separately from the assets of the fund adviser.

ETFs allow large broker dealers called APs to create and redeem their shares in large blocks of 50,000 to 100,000 (creation units) in exchange for cash or a basket of securities along with transaction charges and subsequently sell the shares in secondary markets. These actions of buying and selling of shares between APs and ETFs create arbitrage opportunities in the market thereby harmonizing market-determined ETF share prices and the market value of their underlying securities.

Trading ETF shares occurs through market orders and/or limit orders with the evaluation of which ETF to purchase being multi-functional on performance, tracking difference, costs, premiums and discounts, liquidity, and the bid-ask spread. The three largest ETF families in 2013 based on AUM are BlackRock, State Street Global Advisors, and Vanguard.

The future of ETFs appears bright as more retail investors join their institutional counterparts in embracing these vehicles due to the enhanced transparency, tax efficiency, and diversified market exposure that they offer investors. The SEC has eased the process of launching new ETFs even as it allows ETFs to access the 401(k) funds, which previously were the preserve of mutual funds. Mutual funds are also joining these innovations by targeting the actively managed ETF market for liquidity, low costs, and flexibility purposes as less exotic indexes reduce tracking error.

Discussion Questions

1. Discuss the costs associated with investing in ETFs.
2. Explain four factors that investors should consider when selecting ETFs.
3. Discuss various investment roles played by ETFs.
4. Discuss the most popular forms of ETF investment strategies.

References

Agapova, Anna. 2011. "Conventional Mutual Index Funds versus Exchange Traded Funds." *Journal of Financial Markets* 14:2, 323–343.

Amihud, Yakov. 2002. "Illiquidity and Stock Returns: Cross-Section and Time-Series Effects." *Journal of Financial Markets* 5:1, 31–56.

Baba, Naohiko, Robert, N. McCauley, and Srichander Ramaswamy. 2009. "US Dollar Money Market Funds and Non-US Banks." *BIS Quarterly Review*, March, 65–81.

Bank of England. 2010. "Financial Stability Report, Box 5: Exchange Traded Funds." 27:June, 1–79. Available at http://www.bankofengland.co.uk/publications/documents/fsr/2010/fsrfull1006.pdf.

Barber, Brad M., and Terrance Odean. 2000. "Trading Is Hazardous to Your Wealth: The Common Stock Investment Performance of Individual Investors." *Journal of Finance* 55:2, 773–806.

Ben-David, Itzhak, Francesco Franzoni, and Rabih Moussawi. 2012. "ETFs, Arbitrage and Shock Propagation." Working Paper, Fisher College of Business, The Ohio State University.

Benz, Christine. 2011. "Bogle: Investors Have Tough Time with ETFs." Morningstar, October 11. Available at http://www.morningstar.com/cover/videocenter.aspx?id=397704.

Birdthistle, William A.2011. "The Fortunes and Foibles of Exchange Traded Funds: A Positive Market Response to the Problems of Mutual Funds." *Delaware Journal of Corporate Law* 33:1, 69–111.

Bogle, John C. 2004. "Convergence: The Great Paradox." Remarks Made before "The Art of Indexing" Conference, September 30, Washington, DC. Available at http://www.vanguard.com/bogle_site/sp20040930.htm.

Cano, Guillermo, Barry Feldman, and Joseph Smith. 2009. "ETFs, Swaps and Futures: Trade at Index Close and the Co-evolution of Financial Markets." *ETFs and Indexing* 1:Fall, 50–58.

Committee on the Global Financial System. 2005. "The Role of Ratings in Structured Finance: Issues and implications." *CGFS Papers*, Number 23, January. Available at http://www.bis.org/publ/cgfs23.pdf.

Committee on the Global Financial System. 2008. "Ratings in Structured Finance: What Went Wrong and What Can Be Done to Address Shortcomings?" *CGFS Papers*, Number 32, July. Available at http://www.bis.org/publ/cgfs32.pdf.

Costa, David.2011. *The Portable Private Banker: Investing Efficiently through Funds and ETFs*, 1st Edition. Zurich: Robert Kennedy College.

Deutsche Bank. 2013. "Synthetic Equity and Index Strategy 2012, ETF Review and 2013 Outlook." *Deutsche Bank Markets Research*, January. Available at http://www.exchangetradedfunds.com/helpmedothenews11gn.php?helpmedothenews11gn=24910.

Fender, Ingo, Allen Frankel, and Jacob Gyntelberg. 2008. "Three Market Implications of the Lehman Bankruptcy." *BIS Quarterly Review*, December, 6–7. Available at http://www.bis.org/publ/qtrpdf/r_qt0812x.htm.

Financial Stability Board. 2011. "Potential Financial Stability Issues Arising from Recent Trends in Exchange Traded Funds (ETFs)." April. Available at http://www.financialstabilityboard.org/wp-content/uploads/r_110412b.pdf.

Huang, Jennifer C., and Ilan Guedj. 2009. "Are ETFs Replacing Index Mutual Funds?" Available at http://papers.ssrn.com/sol3/papers.cfm?%20Abstract-id=1108728.

Jensen, Michael.1968. "The Performance of Mutual Funds in the Period 1945–1964." *Journal of Finance* 23:2, 389–416.

Kosev, Mitch, and Thomas Williams. 2011. "Exchange-Traded Funds." *Reserve Bank of Australia Quarterly Bulletin*, March, 50–61. Available at http://www.rba.gov.au/publications/bulletin/2011/mar/bu-03113–8a.html.

Lan, Shan, Sebastian Mercado, and Ari Rajendra. 2014. "Synthetic Equity and Index Strategy ETF Annual Review and Outlook." Deutsche Bank Markets Research, January. Available at http://www.fullertreacymoney.com/system/data/files/pdfs/2014/january/20th/etfreport.pdf.

Laurent, Deville. 2008. "Exchange Traded Funds: History, Trading and Research." In Doumpos, Michael, Constantin Zopounidis, and Panos M. Pardalos, eds., *Handbook of Financial Engineering*, 1–37. Paris: Springer.

Oxera.2011. "What Would Be the Economic Impact on the EU of the Proposed Financial Transaction Tax? Review of the European Commission's Latest Commentary." Available at file:///C:/Users/Greg/Downloads/Oxera%20review%20of%20latest%20FTT%20commentary.pdf.

Securities and Exchange Commission. 2010. "SEC Staff Evaluating the Use of Derivatives by Funds." Available at http://www.sec.gov/news/press/2010/2010–2045.htm.

Sharpe, William. F.1966. "Mutual Fund Performance." *Journal of Business* 39:1, 119–138.

Spence, John. 2007. "Buffett Gives Nod to Index Funds over ETFs." *Market Watch*, May 7. Available at http://www.marketwatch.com/story/warren-buffett-backs-index-mutual-funds-over-etfs.

Srichander, Ramaswamy. 2011. "Market Structures and Systemic Risks of Exchange Traded Funds." Working Paper 343, Monetary and Economic Department, Bank for International Settlements.

Zweig, Jason. 2011. "Why a Legendary Market Skeptic Is Upbeat about Stocks." *Wall Street Journal*, September 10. Available at http://www.wsj.com/news/articles/SB10001424053111904103404576560913892680574?mod=personal_fin_newsreel&mg=reno64-wsj.

26

Ethical Standards in Mutual Funds

ROSA ADAMO

Professor of Banking and Finance, University of Calabria, Italy

Introduction

The development of financial markets has led to increased investor attention to ethical standards and practices. This interest is especially evident in the investment industry because fund advisors must maintain public trust (Baker and Veit 1998). This chapter discusses ethical standards for mutual funds. Failure to comply with established standards can lead to inefficient allocation of resources within financial markets.

The chapter develops three ethical guidelines in finance. The first guideline stems from research intended to explain ethical principles underlying financial trading and discusses how ethics can lead to improved financial behavior. The second guideline identifies ethical standards of mutual funds and explains why transparency, trust, and social responsibility are important criteria to safeguard financial relationships. The third guideline examines the importance of adopting ethical standards for mutual funds and focuses on actions needed to mitigate conflicts of interest through public interventions and knowledge of ethical standards. The chapter concludes by discussing why adopting ethical standards is the best way for mutual funds to achieve allocative efficiency in financial markets. *Allocative efficiency*, sometimes called social efficiency, means that scarce resources are used in a way that meets the needs of people in a Pareto-optimal way.

Ethics in Financial Trading

The globalization of markets and information, technology development, and deregulation has resulted in contradictory scenarios around the world. Developed countries offer mixed results in their ability to enhance living standards exhibiting improvement in some countries but stagnation in others. Under such circumstances, the need for ethics in finance has increased to improve the capacity of financial markets and to diminish the gap among countries. Incorporating ethical criteria in finance enables the maximization of economic results subject to simultaneously safeguarding resources, human dignity, and solidarity. Researchers view ethics in finance as a "moral tension" that drives implementing criteria to improve the propriety of behavior in financial trading. Ethics in financial trading spurs respect for the transparency of financial assets, helps to maintain public trust, and contributes to the development of a process of social responsibility among all the parties interested in financial assets.

Ethics in Finance

The term "ethics" is derived from the Greek "ethos," meaning habit, usage, manner of being, traditions, and customs. More generally, ethics concerns the sum of principles and rules that distinguish good from bad and allows individuals to act in a rational and objective manner in conformance to an ideal. Ethics is a component of human consciousness and represents a set of principles and components shared by civil society. Moore (1903) defined these principles at the beginning of the twentieth century. Russ-Eft (2001) maintains that these principles require a greater revival in relation to the profound changes in the sociocultural horizon.

Ethics cannot exist without responsibility toward others. Under these conditions, character disintegrates. A society that fails to provide the individual with compelling arguments for compassion will not remain sound for long. The deterioration of relations comes from the following:

- *The absence of a values framework that is binding to all.* The result is a shift that encroaches upon interpersonal relationships and shatters trust, which is an essential factor of economic and human life.
- *The focus on quantitative and material aspects.* An individual no longer feels like a person but rather like a cog in a machine.
- *The constraint of the immediate future.* An individual is likely to be guided by the attainment of immediate results and not by value prospects that sustain long-term investments.
- *The decline in competition in absorbing and/or eliminating the other (rival/foe).* In this case, competition is no longer the mainspring of innovation or success.

Some of the greatest philosophers in Western civilization explore moral behavior based on duty and respect for the liberty of others. In particular, Irwin (2007) presents a study of the development of moral philosophy starting with the seminal ideas of Socrates, Plato, and Aristotle and examines the history of ethics in the Socratic tradition. Broadie (1991) provides an overview of the main topics of Aristotle's ethics: happiness, virtue, voluntary agency, practical reason, weakness of will, pleasure, and the ethical status of theory.

The cultural melting pot that underpins the rapport between ethics and economics is rooted in the history of humanity. Specifically, from the time of Calvinism beginning in the sixteenth century, the notion of individuals working conscientiously with money was restored. Calvin was among the first to accept that money could be used as a universal commodity, producing more money. With Calvin, the canonical prohibition of lending at interest, which was proscribed by the Council of Nicaea in 775 and defined as usury was finally overcome (Le Van Baumer 1978).

Around the eighteenth century, the science of economics was born from the beginning of the Industrial Revolution and the development of capitalism. Resulting advancements in economic studies by Hutcheson (1728), Hume (1752), and Smith (1776) consider economics and scientific fields such as finance as "technical." In all technical fields, dispositions, values, and beliefs influence human actions. Smith (1759) maintains that neglecting this framework could lead to serious errors. Moreover, starting in the nineteenth century, a more utilitarian vision of human behavior takes form.

In financial trading, the availability of money for the benefit it creates becomes increasingly important and the maximization of this advantage serves as a guiding principle for individual behavior. According to Mandeville (1714) and Dumont (1977), utilitarianism drives away both the tradition of moral philosophy and religion. Material advantage and well-being are elevated from a means of survival—and, hence, useful for realizing goals—to an end in themselves.

Stimuli for reuniting economics and finance with moral values returned during the twentieth century with Arendt (1963), Gorz (1988), and Bauman (2001). At this point in history, moral responsibility had become sovereign in all sciences. Specifically, Bauman (2001, p. 108) states that decisions should be made to "measure the quality of a society on the quality of its ethical standards."

In the contemporary era, restoring ethics in economics is due to Sen (1983), who inserted the "human factor" in classical welfare economics. Sen identifies welfare research, the right to act, and individual liberty as factors that impact choice and inevitably the economy.

Ethics in Financial Instruments

The essential element in financial products and services containing ethical standards considers the non-economic consequences of economic choices (i.e., the social repercussions). This process entails a careful evaluation of the consequences brought about through financial management. Assessing against the widest possible horizon is necessary because in finance, as in an economy, the consequences are not only those immediately perceived but also the ones achieved later in life (Sen 1991). Specifically, discussing ethical standards in financial products and services suggests the need to verify three features present in financial assets: transparency, trust, and social responsibility.

TRANSPARENCY

Transparency in financial assets aims to make customers aware of the essential elements of the contractual relationship, as well as their variations, while respecting the autonomy of negotiations. Furthermore, transparency of financial assets entails transparency in the use of financial resources. In turn, the use of financial resources spurs on responsible investing and saving. This framework allows individuals to choose to invest their money in a manner most consistent with their objectives and values. Knowing the true use of one's savings allows the selection of one financial product over another. More so than with real physical assets, financial products must be defined to be traded. This defining process implies acquiring information about the services to which one is entitled, as well as the conditions for their use. Chan (1983) clarifies the role of intermediaries acting as informed investors, allowing for the allocation of financial resources to the best investments. Chan (1983, p. 1543) "develops a theory of financial intermediation that highlights the contribution of intermediaries as informed agents in a market with imperfect information." Thus, transparency becomes a moral virtue of the people working in financial management.

TRUST

Trust between the individuals interested in financial assets must also be considered. Trust breaks down barriers associated with guarantees and knowledge. The starting point is the perception of derived benefits at both the individual and social levels. The joint action enables better results to be obtained with more involved individuals than could have been obtained by acting alone. This possibility is due to diverse forms of coordination and cooperation based primarily on interpersonal trust. Empirical studies recognize such perception by illustrating the so-called virtues of trust. That is, greater trust results in "virtues" in the following sectors: (1) economic, (2) financial, and (3) social. In the economic sector, greater trust implies higher rates of economic growth and higher incomes distributed in a more egalitarian manner. In the financial sector, greater trust implies more developed financial markets. In the social sector, greater trust implies more just and efficient institutions and higher levels of subjective well-being and happiness than of those living in communities where mistrust and opportunism prevail. Knack and Keepfer (1997, p. 1252) demonstrate that "trust and civic cooperation are associated with stronger economic performance," while Guiso, Sapienza, and Zingales (2004, p. 526) maintain that "one of the mechanisms through which social capital impacts economic efficiency is by enhancing the prevailing level of trust."

SOCIAL RESPONSIBILITY

Social responsibility argues for the necessity of assessing the management of financial assets in order to guarantee a minimum return to all interested parties (i.e., the "stakeholders" such as shareholders, customers, employees, and the community within which the business interacts). This role is particularly important because stakeholders would abandon any financial asset not guaranteeing a minimum return, thereby dictating its failure. Freeman (1984) explores methods by which management must respect the interests of stakeholders. His theory of management and business ethics highlights morals and values in managing a company. Additionally, because of the need for social responsibility, Pallavicini (1968) weighs the importance of the other-than-merely-economic consequences of the ethical, moral, social, cultural, and environmental expectations on the value of the activity. Social responsibility stimulates financial managers to behave conscientiously, thereby implementing financial instruments with ethical standards. Social responsibility also maximizes the benefits for the community in which managers operate. Ethical behavior in finance, aside from safeguarding those who consume its products, strives to have a positive impact on its customers' lives. In fact, safeguarding customers is a good example of how to create benefits for them.

Ethical Standards in Mutual Funds

As a result of the problems generated by financial crises, both stakeholders and the public are demanding that financial management adopt ethical behaviors. Baker and Veit (1998, p. 917) maintain that "ethics plays an important role in the investment industry because investment professionals manage other people's money. Investment professionals must live up to high standards of ethical behavior to maintain public trust." Furthermore, following the financial scandals that involved mutual funds between 2001 and 2004, both the Securities and Exchange Commission (SEC) and the U.S. Congress sought to ensure greater protection for investors (Securities and Exchange Commission 2004).

Aside from the cultural and regulatory differences among countries, a fundamental need has arisen to have ethical standards capable of "regulating" finance. This need also applies to protecting consumers of financial products, who are the financial market's weak contracting parties. A better form of protection for consumers translates into creating more transparent financial products that recover elements of trust and social responsibility.

Transparency in Mutual Funds

The principle of transparency provides that mutual funds communicate information, which mainly involves the price, terms, and conditions to investors in a clear, sufficient, and timely manner so that they may understand and make informed decisions (Bauman 1982; General Accounting Office 2003). The norms governing mutual funds are intended to guarantee maximum transparency. Haslem (2010) offers an overview of the normative transparency of mutual funds disclosure. In Europe, the Green Paper European Transparency Initiative (Commission of the European Communities 2006) endorsed several initiatives regarding transparency, which led to the establishment of the European Transparency Register (European Union 2011).

Information on a mutual fund is available to investors both before the investment occurs (generally with the prospectus) and afterwards from updates from the mutual fund's management. The prospectus contains all the information necessary for investors to make well-founded judgments on the investments offered. With regard to transparency in the management process of mutual funds, investors are usually informed about the mutual fund's investment objectives, risks, performance, and expenses. The mainstream media publishes a mutual funds daily value, which is its net asset value (NAV), allowing subscribers to monitor the performance of their investments. Lack of transparency has a negative effect on both investors and the investment advisor. A risk exists that investors may abandon the investment program or be constrained to invest more than what was expected or understood. However, the investment advisor risks creating a bad reputation, which would translate into losses in terms of portfolio quality and damage to the sector's image, thus triggering a vicious circle that could lead to the loss of customers or investments.

Trust in Mutual Funds

Investors in a mutual fund delegate financial management to the investment advisor. The key to the delegation process is an act of trust. Brown, Goetzmann, Liang, and Schwarz (2009, p. 1) maintain that "trust is thus an essential feature of the principal–agent relationship in the investment industry and integrity is an important factor in delegated fund management." As Valsan and Yahya (2013) note, managers of investment portfolios may be subject to fiduciary law's strict requirements in various capacities such as trustees, agents, financial advisors, or corporate directors.

In the fiduciary process, a fundamental component is the reciprocal trust between the delegator and the delegates, who can only build a solid relationship by fielding skills and capabilities tied to their professional profiles and the communications and relational process. Through trust, delegates perform concrete actions to the benefit of investors and within the scope of the common good (i.e., pools of investors and the investment advisor).

The investors boast "a credit right" compared to the investment advisor. In the relationship, the investment advisor assumes the agent's obligations and responsibilities. With collective management, the sums paid by individual investors converge indistinctly in a single mutual fund that represents a true pool wholly managed for the investors. Investors take on all the risk and delegate each investment and disinvestment decision to the investment advisor. Filbeck and Tompkins (2004) point out the positive relationship between management tenure and performance showing that more experienced managers perform better. The investment advisor assumes the agent's obligation to act in the exclusive interest of the mutual fund's investors. This fiduciary duty serves as the counterpart to the fact that investors assume all risk related to the fluctuations in value of the assets.

Furthermore, the fund manager pools money with other investors' assets to invest in various securities issued by different firms. Mutual fund managers vote on behalf of all of their investors. Therefore, investment companies have a fiduciary responsibility to act in the best interest of their investors and an obligation to vote accordingly.

The investors' trust in the stability and honesty of mutual funds is a crucial factor. Mutual funds cannot guarantee a set yield, but they must fairly treat and fully inform all investors of the risks and associated fees, as well as abide by the policies and rules published in prospectuses. Mutual funds are also required to disclose why and how they vote their proxies.

On January 31, 2003, the SEC established the rules governing disclosure requirements by mutual funds to address investment companies' fiduciary responsibility to their investors (Securities and Exchange Commission 2003). On June 30, 2014, the Division of Investment Management and the Division of Corporation Finance of the SEC provided guidance about investment advisors' responsibilities in voting client proxies and retaining proxy advisory firms, and on the availability and requirements of two exemptions to the federal proxy rules that are often relied upon by proxy advisory firms (Securities and Exchange Commission 2014).

Social Responsibility in Mutual Funds

Mutual funds offer favorable results for pools of investors by distributing the returns to all those purchasing the mutual funds' shares (Haslem 2003; Tompkins and Filbeck 2007). The concept of social responsibility is theorized in this context (i.e., the return offered to the entire pool of the mutual fund's investors). Some mutual funds adopt socially responsible behavior by monitoring and responding to the economic, environmental, and social expectations of their stakeholders. More broadly, because the efficiency of mutual funds and the well-being of the community of investors are mutually dependent, the creation of shared value could be achieved through social responsibility (Porter and Kramer 2011).

In this context, the elements present in a mutual fund's operational model provide for the identification of returns. Investors benefit from investment advisors' safeguarding their assets in a manner consistent with appropriate risk-return trade-offs. In fact, mutual funds set out to satisfy the investment requirements of a pool of investors by identifying their investment needs, designing investment solutions, and jointly setting a profit-yielding structure. Selecting a capable investment advisor is instrumental; yet the presence of a pool of interested and engaged investors makes that advisor's role less dominant.

A mutual fund's investment advisor also selects investments to meet the needs of a group of investors that financial markets might neglect or only partially satisfy. Such underserved needs relate to individual vulnerability, such as a lack of financial knowledge and culture. Specifically, they can relate to the potential of unidentified investments, which offer opportunities for individuals and groups to innovate. In this sense, mutual funds attempt to broaden funding investments to different investors, including those who the financial markets could exclude.

These aspects appear interesting for the identification by mutual funds with social responsibility goals. Often mutual funds satisfy the investment behavior of a very narrow group of investors. These investors have strong and specific targets that require tapping into a highly select group of investment advisors. Many types of mutual funds exist to create and to sell new securities and to accommodate new investors. In other words, different mutual funds are available for various investment objectives. The investment policies or investment strategies of the mutual funds summarize the types of securities that they purchase to achieve investors' objectives and to offer them suitable investments.

With and Without Ethical Standards

A driving principle in a mutual fund's operation is based on a fiduciary relationship between the delegator and the delegate, and the latter's commitment to operate solely for the benefit of the former. In this regard, the fund manager must:

- Work with diligence, fairness, and transparency on behalf of the mutual fund's investors, as well as for the integrity of the financial markets.

- Operate in a manner that both minimizes the risk of conflicts of interest, including among the various financial assets managed, and ensures an impartial handling of the assets contained within mutual funds.
- Adopt measures that safeguard the rights of the mutual fund's investors.
- Have sufficient resources and suitable procedures to ensure efficient management.

Mutual funds play an important part in the development of financial markets for three major reasons. First, mutual funds allow public access to diversified portfolios, which are more efficient than other options available to individual investors. Second, mutual funds perform an essential role in the risk assessment of individual securities and, hence, in verifying cost-effective pricing. Thus, mutual fund managers work for results leading to optimization over the medium-to-long run with a focus on the major qualities of the securities from which the long-term risk-return ratio depends. Although the real world does not always approach the ideal, the investment rationale of these managers is closest to the theoretical model that achieves allocative efficiency in financial markets. Third, mutual funds give investors the right to vote on specific matters affecting the fund.

Even if built upon ethical standards, mutual funds must also comply with them to safeguard their investors. Only in this manner can mutual funds play a vital economic role. Although cost-effective in producing information (i.e., achieving economies of scale and scope), mutual funds can generate potential costs because of conflicts of interest. These conflicts, in turn, raise issues of an ethical nature because incentives exist to hide or distort information, thereby hurting investors. This link is much more obvious when weighing the elements critical to the success of mutual funds. In looking at the relationship among affordability, information, diversification, costs, and liquidity of the investments, theoretical and empirical results confirm the existence of a link among them. This seems evident from various empirical studies of mutual fund performance (Fortune 1997; Fink 2011). ICI Global (2014, p. 1) points out that "around the globe, the mutual fund industry has seen strong growth in assets in the past two decades. Global assets in mutual funds increased from $4.0 trillion in 1993 to $28.9 trillion in September 2013, reflecting increases in each of four broad regions: the United States, Europe, Asia-Pacific, and the rest of the world."

Conflicts of Interest without Ethical Standards

Asset management, even when founded on ethical standards, will have problems of conflicts of interest when it fails to abide by such standards (Crockett, Harris, Mishkin, and White 2003; Mehran and Stulz 2007). Conflicts of interest generally induce financial service providers to assume unethical behavior. The main problem is that investment advisors must struggle daily with completing transactions that benefit their business more than the investors.

Many plausible examples aimed at understanding how numerous and extended conflicts of interest arise out of asset management exist. The following list shows roles in which the need exists to pursue ethical standards of mutual funds to deter unethical behavior.

- *Securities selection.* The investment advisor could be induced to select securities issued by corporate customers of the investment company or to choose newly issued securities placed by the same investment company. This phenomenon is even more glaring when the securities purchased, whether newly issued or not, are of firms that belong to the advisor's own banking group.
- *Portfolio management.* A high and unnecessary portfolio turnover rate generates fees and, hence, costs to investors. Trading costs directly associated with the mutual fund are hidden and complicate the determination of the fund's full costs.
- *Performance distortion.* The general principle of fair treatment applies to funds managed by the same investment advisor. The investment advisor could favor one mutual fund to the detriment of another (e.g., having a more popular product because that particular mutual fund has performance fees that are particularly appealing or for other reasons).
- *Late trading.* The fund manager could be enticed to settle transactions received after 4:00 p.m. at the day's closing price, rather than more properly at the opening price of the following day. In the aftermath of the financial scandals that rocked U.S. markets at the beginning of the current century, this phenomenon has fallen under much more rigorous control and oversight.
- *Market timing.* The fund manager could take advantage of different time zones that allow for arbitraging, particularly with foreign securities. The practice continues despite diverse policies against it such as applying a redemption fee if the shares are sold between 60 and 90 days from the date of purchase.

Generally, investor advisors manage conflicts of interest. Thus, the rules on corporate governance are particularly important because they aim to reduce and properly manage conflicts of interest. To this end, various countries have different types of regulations usually as a form of self-discipline to stimulate ethical standards among mutual funds.

How to Remedy Conflicts of Interest

Distinguishing between two approaches is useful when studying the resolution of conflicts of interest. These approaches are public interventions aimed at their reduction or elimination and knowledge of and education in ethics in finance to lessen the likelihood of inappropriate behavior.

PUBLIC INTERVENTIONS

Opportunities for public intervention as remedies to conflicts of interest have generally considered tightening market rules and regulations with regulatory interventions. This approach entails either penalizing those managers who use conflicts of interest to their own advantage or promoting new organizational models aimed at containing conflicts of interest.

Penalizing managers who use conflicts of interest for their gain may be appropriate in dealing with mutual funds that trade exclusively at the following day's rate to avoid late trading for transactions received after 4:00 p.m. However, this action would penalize those investors whose transactions are not completed due to an accumulation of orders and could not avoid market timing arbitrage between time zones.

Introducing increased and mandatory redemption fees could be a choice. Yet, this alternative could penalize investors who need to make unexpected and emergency withdrawals from the investment. The mutual fund's image could also suffer, making this option less attractive.

Another imposition or form of regulation and oversight would be to increase the transparency of management practices. However, greater transparency could be problematic if it revealed confidential information that prevented the investment advisor from operating profitably. The result could lead to less rather than more informational efficiency. Furthermore, compulsory transparency could be useless if investment advisors were to evade regulations or hide the information about conflicts of interest. At this point, the most radical solution could be the socialization of information. The dissemination of more information to the public leads to more informed investors and lessens the likelihood of deceiving them. The limitation here is that a government entity could be less inclined to share quality information with private institutions so that even if conflicts of interest diminish, informational efficiency could also decrease.

New organizational models of investment companies represent another way to contain conflicts of interest. Such conflicts could be reduced or even completely eliminated through more independent internal roles and separate departments. An imposition would be to increase the number of independent directors of investment companies. In many countries, both the legal system and the companies' best practice are giving a growing role to independent directors. In the United States, the Investment Company Act of 1940 requires the presence of independent directors of the companies that manage mutual funds. With the passage of the Sarbanes-Oxley Act of 2002, the United States strengthened the requirement of independence. This legislation increases supervision over the management of conflicts of interest and compliance with legal obligations in the interest of customers. Another imposition would be to separate the companies' investment departments. In this case, the corporate governance should clearly and rigorously define the concept of separation of activities owned by each department to lessen the onset of conflicts. However, separating the conflicting activities should prevent one internal department from carrying out activities that conflict with the interests of another. Still, an evaluation is needed if the separation results in decreasing synergies derived from the production of information precluding the benefits of economies of scope. The increase in costs could lead to a decrease in informational efficiency. Determining the most advantageous degree of separation would imply a compromise between the advantages derived from the decrease in conflicts of interest and the cost associated with the missing economies of scope.

KNOWLEDGE OF AND EDUCATION IN ETHICS IN FINANCE

The second approach to remedy conflicts of interest entails knowledge of ethics in finance. Restoration of ethical knowledge in finance allows achieving a community's interests. An efficient financial system works in favor of collective rather than individual targets. In fact, it sets out to reach the summation of the financial balances of the economic units present in the system, greater than or equal to zero. Thus, its activity is targeted to satisfy the economic and financial interests of all the economic units present in the system and, therefore, to perform a collective, social goal. This action characterizes the social nature of finance.

Aside from considering the knowledge of ethics in finance, ethics education in finance is also necessary. Conflicts of interest raise questions of an ethical nature for those working in the financial system because incentives exist to hide or distort information to the detriment of investors. One way to repress the problem at the source is the formation of ethical behavior by providing instruction in how to behave. Thus, education in ethics makes improper behavior less likely. Teaching ethics in financial situations leads to knowing, understanding, and sharing those values. As a result, individuals will tend to base their actions on ethical principles and values. Education in ethics helps to develop positive and efficient guidance and directions in the financial sciences. Such education can lead to progressive and profound change that should affect all economic fields. As a result, most leading business schools have introduced ethics in finance into their curriculum.

Success with Ethical Standards

Several studies document the importance of ethical standards for investment professionals (Morley 1987; Casey 1988; Baker, Veit, and Murphy 1995). Ethical standards are successful for mutual funds when regularly pursued. Ethically oriented financial management represents a valid opportunity for mutual funds whose strategies entail a full-scale presence in financial markets. Conduct based on ethical criteria allows mutual funds to gain prominent positions in the asset management market.

Adopting ethical standards allows mutual funds to be successful because their investment logic is the closest to the theoretical model that leads to allocative efficiency in financial markets. This is due to five aspects of the operation of financial markets.

- *Affordability*. Investors distinguish themselves by their risk aversion and the share of savings to be invested.
- *Information availability*. The small investor is in a weak position involving information availability. Investing in securities requires constant updating, a continuous flow of information on the companies in which mutual funds invest to determine or anticipate market fluctuations in securities, eventual shocks, and frequent assessment of whether securities are under or overvalued. This process is especially true given the creativity in the financial world. In recent years, an exponential increase in the number of innovative financial products has occurred, linking their value to variable interest rates, the occurrence or lack of occurrence of probabilistic events, and the possibility of conversion to other financial instruments. Knowing these financial products in depth distinguishes fund managers from each another. Making sound and appropriate investment decisions requires having a flow of information and advanced technical knowledge that is beyond that of the typical small investor. Mutual funds overcome this drawback by delegating these tasks to experts who have a moral obligation to manage the mutual fund professionally and transparently and to assist and advise investors based on their personal needs.

- *Diversification.* The enormous wealth available to mutual funds allows them to invest in many securities that would otherwise be inaccessible to individual investors. Such investors often have only a simple portfolio consisting of a few securities due to the high entry, management, and transaction costs. This scenario implies that having only a single security or a few securities raises exposure to critical volatility levels. Markovitz (1952) shows that adding securities to a portfolio lowers volatility and, therefore, risk, when compared to single securities with the same expected return. Constructing a diversified portfolio enables investors to exploit the diverse correlations and to improve the risk-return relationship.
- *Cost reduction.* Building a diversified portfolio entails incurring various costs. However, a mutual fund can markedly reduce transaction costs, fees, and expenses due to economies of scale.
- *Liquidity.* A fund's liquidity often attracts small investors. Mutual fund investors can easily redeem their shares at any time with a price equal to the current NAV less any redemption fees.

The production process implemented by mutual funds centers on the ability to identify, evaluate, select, implement, verify, and ultimately liquidate securities, with timeliness and competency for the interests of investors. To be concerned with ethical standards in mutual funds partly means to confront issues of socially responsible finance since with transparency, mutual funds are careful to not hurt investors and to act in an ethical manner. With reciprocal trust between the delegator and the delegate, a mutual fund can build a solid social relationship, which is necessary for developing financial markets. With social responsibility, besides guaranteeing the principles of transparency and trust, a mutual fund commits to having a positive impact on the lives of the investors. Responsible financial management is important to guarantee a sustainable financial future based on economic growth and real improvement in living conditions.

Greater satisfaction of investors triggers a virtuous circle that generates a lower propensity to withdraw from investment programs. This, in turn, leads to greater financial well-being, that entails new possibilities of saving as well as new capacities of investment. Ultimately, mutual funds play a critical role in education savings by increasing investment finances.

Summary and Conclusions

Mutual funds should base their management on implementing specific ethical standards: transparency, trust, and social responsibility. Basic to transparency is the need for greater disclosure of the management provided by investment advisors. The opportunity to offer financial instruments capable of diffusing indicators of trust is a winning proposition to restore confidence in securities and financial markets.

The delegating process upon which mutual funds are based is no less than an ultimate expression of trust. In the logic of mutual funds, the traditional causal relationship that leads to trusting someone once their trustworthiness has been verified is reversed because the mutual fund starts to function after the investors have committed their capital.

Mutual funds attempt to allocate capital in a socially responsible manner. Investments should be based not only on the yield to the investment advisor but also on its impact on the community of investors who believe in the mutual fund's quality. Thus, if mutual funds do not pursue ethical standards, conflicts of interest are likely to arise. Such conflicts can be checked by public interventions aimed at their reduction or elimination, or by knowledge and education in ethics in finance.

Ethically oriented financial management permits mutual funds to acquire higher market profiles. Financial instruments with ethical standards trigger a virtuous circle that improves the conditions of markets' stability, as well as the capacity to eliminate tensions and inefficiencies and achieves allocative efficiency in the financial markets.

Proviso and Acknowledgments

This chapter contains the author's current thoughts. The author is responsible for any inaccuracies and/or omissions. The author thanks Domenica Federico and Antonella Notte, lecturers at the University of Calabria, for their generous assistance in preparing this chapter.

Discussion Questions

1. Explain why ethics is important in finance.
2. Discuss the ethical standards of transparency, trust, and social responsibility for mutual funds.
3. Discuss the implications if mutual funds do not adopt ethical standards.
4. Identify two actions to mitigate conflicts of interest from asset management.
5. Explain why mutual funds should adopt ethical standards.

References

Arendt, Hannah. 1963. *Eichmann in Jerusalem: A Report on the Banality of Evil.* New York: Viking Press.

Baker, H. Kent, and E. Theodore Veit. 1998. "A Comparison of Ethics of Investment Professionals: North America versus Pacific Rim Nations." *Journal of Business Ethics* 17:8, 917–937.

Baker, H. Kent, E. Theodore Veit, and Michael R. Murphy. 1995. *Ethics in the Investment Profession: An International Survey.* Charlottesville, VA: Research Foundation of the CFA Institute.

Bauman, W. Scott. 1982. *Guidelines for Communications to Investors: Standards of Disclosures for Investment Managers of Pension Funds, Mutual Funds, Advisory Accounts, and Financial Institutions.* Charlottesville, VA: Financial Analysis Research Foundation.

Bauman, Zygmunt. 2001. *The Individualized Society.* Cambridge: Polity Press. Italian Translation 2002. *La Società Individualizzata,* 108. Bologna: Il Mulino.

Broadie, Sarah. 1991. *Ethics with Aristotle.* Oxford: Oxford University Press.

Brown, Stephen J., William Goetzmann, Bing Liang, and Christopher Schwarz. 2009. "Trust and Delegation." Working Paper, National Bureau of Economic Research, Cambridge.

Casey, John L. 1988. *Ethics in the Financial Market Place.* Scudder, NY: Stevens & Clark, Inc.

Chan, Yuk-Shee. 1983. "On the Positive Role of Financial Intermediation in Allocation of Venture Capital in a Market with Imperfect Information." *Journal of Finance* 35:5, 1543–1568.

Commission of the European Communities. 2006. *Green Paper European Transparency Initiative*. Brussels. Available at http://europa.eu/documents/comm/green_papers/pdf/com2006_194_en.pdf.

Crockett, Andrew, Trevor Harris, Frederic S. Mishkin, and Eugene N. White. 2003. *Conflicts of Interest in the Financial Services Industry: What Should We Do about Them?* Geneva and London: International Center for Monetary and Banking Studies and Centre of Economic Policy Research.

Dumont, Louis. 1977. *Homo Equalis: Genèse et Apanouissement de l'Idéologie Économique*. Paris: Gallimard.

European Union. 2011. *Transparency Register*. Brussels. Available at http://ec.europa.eu/transparencyregister/info/homePage.do?locale=en#en.

Filbeck, Greg, and Daniel L. Tompkins. 2004. "Management Tenure and Risk-Adjusted Performance on Mutual Funds." *Journal of Investing* 13:2, 72–80.

Fink, Matthew P. 2011. *The Rise of Mutual Funds*. Oxford: Oxford University Press.

Fortune, Peter. 1997. "Mutual Funds, Part I: Reshaping the American Financial System." *New England Economic Review*, July/August, 45–72.

Freeman, Robert Edward. 1984. *Strategic Management: A Stakeholder Approach*. London: Pitman.

General Accounting Office. 2003. *Mutual Funds: Greater Transparency Needed in Disclosures to Investors*. Washington, DC: United States General Accounting Office.

Gorz, Andre. 1988. *Métamorphoses du travail: Quête du sens. Critique de la raison économique*. Paris: Éditions Galilée.

Guiso, Luigi, Paola Sapienza, and Luigi Zingales. 2004. "The Role of Social Capital in Financial Development." *American Economic Review* 94:3, 526–556.

Haslem, John A. 2003. *Mutual Funds: Risk and Performance Analysis for Decision Making*. Oxford: Blackwell Publishing.

Haslem, John A. 2010. "Normative Transparency of Mutual Funds Disclosure." In John A. Haslem, ed., *Mutual Funds: Portfolio Structures, Analysis, Management, and Stewardship*, 319–336. Hoboken, NJ: John Wiley and Sons, Inc.

Hume, David. 1752. *Political Discourses*. Edinburgh: Kincaid and Donaldson.

Hutcheson, Francis. 1728. *Illustrations upon the Moral Sense*. Menton: Scolar Press reprint.

ICI Global. 2014. "Globalisation and the Global Growth of Long-Term Mutual Funds." *ICI Global Research Perspective* 1:1, 1–44.

Irwin, Terence. 2007. *The Development of Ethics: A Historical and Critical Study*. Vol. 1: *From Socrates to the Reformation*. Oxford: Oxford University Press.

Knack, Stephen, and Philip Keefer. 1997. "Does Social Capital Have an Economic Payoff? A Cross-Country Investigation." *Quarterly Journal of Economics* 112:4, 1251–1288.

Le Van Baumer, Franklin. 1978. *Main Currents of Western Thought: Readings in Western Europe Intellectual History from the Middle Ages to the Present*. New Haven, CT: Yale University Press.

Mandeville, Bernard. 1714. *The Fable of the Bees; or, Private Vices, Publick Benefits*. London: J. Roberts.

Markowitz, Harry. 1952. "Portfolio Selection." *Journal of Finance* 7:1, 77–91.

Mehran, Hamid, and René M. Stulz. 2007. "The Economics of Conflicts of Interest in Financial Institutions." *Journal of Financial Economics* 85:2, 267–296.

Moore, George E. 1903. *Principia Ethica*. Cambridge: Cambridge University Press.

Morley, Alfred C. 1987. "Ethical Standards for Investment Professionals." *Business Economics* 22:4, 27–34.

Pallavicini, Giancarlo. 1968. *Strutture Integrate nel Sistema Distributivo Italiano*. Milan: Giuffré Editore.

Porter, Michael E., and Mark R. Kramer. 2011. "The Big Idea: Creating Shared Value, Rethinking Capitalism." *Harvard Business Review* 89:1/2, 62–77.

Russ-Eft, Darlene F. 2001. "A Case for Case Studies on HRD Ethics and Integrity." *Human Resource Development Quarterly* 11:2, 101–103.

Securities and Exchange Commission. 2003. 17 CFR Part 275. Proxy Voting by Investment Advisers. Release No. IA-2106, File No. S7–38–02. Available at http://www.sec.gov/rules/final/ia-2106.htm.

Securities and Exchange Commission. 2004. 17 CFR Parts 270, 275 and 279. Investment Adviser Codes of Ethics. Release No. IA-2256, IC-26492; File No. S7–04–04. Available at http://www.sec.gov/rules/final/ia-2256.htm.

Securities and Exchange Commission. 2014. Proxy Voting: Proxy Voting Responsibilities of Investment Advisers and Availability of Exemptions from the Proxy Rules for Proxy Advisory Firms. Staff Legal Bulletin No. 20. Available at http://www.sec.gov/interps/legal/cfslb20.htm.

Sen, Amartya K. 1983. "Liberty and Social Choice." *Journal of Philosophy* 80, 5–28.

Sen, Amartya K. 1991. *Denaro e Valore: Etica ed Economia della Finanza*. Rome: Edizioni dell'Elefante.

Smith, Adam. 1759. *The Theory of Moral Sentiments*. Edinburgh: Kincaid and Bell.

Smith, Adam. 1776. *An Enquiry into the Nature and Causes of the Wealth of Nations*. London: W. Strahan.

Tompkins, Daniel L., and Greg Filbeck. 2007. "Management Age and Mutual Fund Performance." *Journal of Business and Economic Perspectives* 33:2, 229–240.

Valsan, Remus D., and Moin A. Yahya. 2013. "Fiduciary Duties and Responsibilities of Portfolio Managers." In H. Kent Baker and Greg Filbeck, eds., *Portfolio Theory and Management*, 165–181. Oxford: Oxford University Press.

Part Six

MUTUAL FUNDS WORLDWIDE

27

Mutual Funds in Emerging and Developing Markets

PARVEZ AHMED
Professor of Finance, University of North Florida

Introduction

This chapter examines the market and performance of mutual funds investing in emerging markets. The term "emerging markets" was coined by economists at the International Finance Corporation in 1981, but definitions of what makes up an emerging market vary. MSCI classifies markets into three subgroups: (1) developed, (2) emerging, and (3) frontier (Ahmed 2013). In doing so, MSCI uses both objective metrics (e.g., company size, security size, liquidity, and gross national income) and subjective criteria (e.g., openness to foreign ownership, ease of capital flows, and efficiency and stability of market-based institutions). Khanna and Palepu (2010) assert that one of the fundamental characteristic of emerging markets is the inefficiency and higher cost of completing a transaction between buyers and sellers. The quality and quantity of market intermediaries make an enormous difference in how markets are classified as developed, emerging, or frontier. This chapter defines emerging markets according to MSCI criteria.

Both academia and the financial services industry have engaged in substantial research about the nature and efficacy of mutual funds. However, investing in emerging market mutual funds (EMMFs) has received little attention despite evidence showing that such funds often outperform domestic mutual funds. A proper understanding of the history, context, portfolio performance, expenses, investment style, and fund flows can better prepare investors and professional money managers to navigate the uncharted waters of personal investing via mutual funds.

Since the 1980s, the growth of emerging market equity mutual funds is one of the more important developments in the asset management industry. Despite the growing popularity of these funds, research on their efficacy and factors that determine performance is lacking due to limited data. For domestic funds, the literature suggests that fund performance is predicated upon informational advantages. But these results may not have the same impact for EMMFs as informational costs are higher and less reliable in lesser developed economies.

A recent report on the popular business news channel CNBC noted that mutual fund managers are pushing for investments in emerging markets (Delevingne 2014). As people move into a more affluent status in emerging economies, the demand for private investments is likely to grow and follow the same trajectory of growth that fueled the rise of the global mutual fund industry. Based on calculations from MSCI data from January 1988 to September 2014, the MSCI Emerging Market Index has averaged an annualized return of 11.47 percent. In contrast the MSCI USA index has annually averaged 8.96 percent. However, the growth in the emerging market sector came with significant market volatility. The standard deviation of the Emerging Market index was higher (23.42 percent) compared to the U.S. index (14.53 percent). Investing in emerging markets is lucrative as long as investors and fund managers understand the risks associated with such investments. The correlation between MSCI Emerging Market Index and MSCI USA Index is about 0.67 but has increased to 0.84 between 2008 and 2014.

U.S. investors use institutional mechanisms such as open-end funds (OEFs) and closed-end funds (CEFs) to invest in emerging markets. A growing mutual fund market also exists in several emerging countries. EMMFs domiciled in emerging economies are often closed to foreign investments. Even when allowing foreign investments, they are subject to many restrictions when investing directly in mutual funds. For many investors, seeking portfolio diversification via EMMFs, the most common choices are U.S.-based EMMFs, such as those categorized as diversified emerging markets by Morningstar, which defines this category as funds having at least 50 percent invested in emerging markets.

The historically low correlation between emerging markets and U.S. markets often serves as a powerful motivator for harvesting diversification benefits by investing in EMMFs. Lessard (1973), Errunza (1983), Bailey and Stulz (1990), and Bailey and Lim (1992) show the benefits of portfolio diversification from international investing. Eun, Kolodny, and Resnick (1991) assert that international mutual funds offer the best method for most investors to access foreign markets and achieve higher diversification benefits. By the end of the last millennium, markets all across the world, including emerging markets, were liberalizing. Liberalization of emerging markets occurs when the following characteristics are observed: free repatriation of capital, dividends, and capital gains; foreign-owned majority interests in a company; and direct foreign investment in the capital markets (Bekaert, Harvey, and Lundblad 2003). DeSantis and Gerard (1997) show that with increased economic liberalization, international markets are highly correlated with the U.S. markets during periods when new economic data are being released. The increases in international correlations are only evident during periods of large market declines and the effect is not very persistent. Although such contagion led to higher correlations, it was responsible for only small losses in expected gains from international diversification. The average gain from international diversification was 2.51 percent before 1980 and 1.84 percent thereafter. DeSantis and Gerard (1997, p. 1908) conclude "as long as diversification generates positive gains on average and investors are not able to predict bear and bull markets, it is still optimal to hold internationally diversified portfolios."

The chapter begins by discussing the domestic and global growth in the mutual fund industry including in the emerging markets. Following this section is a description of the various models that can be used to measure mutual fund performance. The next section describes the results from the extant research regarding the performance of EM-MFs. The chapter then discusses the factors that can explain mutual fund performance including factors behind the persistence of performance. The next two sections briefly discuss bond funds and hedge funds that invest in emerging markets. Before concluding the chapter, the final section discusses the flow of money into mutual funds, which can often predict future performance.

Growth of Mutual Funds

Since the 1960s, the mutual fund industry has seen impressive global growth. U.S. markets led most of the growth with mutual funds experiencing an annual growth rate of more than 16 percent. In 1940, the United States had only 68 mutual funds with 296,000 shareholder accounts investing $0.45 billion in assets. By 2013, the combined assets of mutual funds in the United States grew to $15.02 trillion with nearly 9,000 funds in existence (Investment Company Institute 2014). Household investing in private portfolios have driven this growth in mutual funds. The Investment Company Institute, an interest group for the mutual fund industry, singles out individual retirement accounts (IRAs) and defined contribution (DC) plans, particularly 401(k) plans as preferred vehicles that channel investments into mutual funds. At year-end 2013, households had 8.8 percent of their financial assets in 401(k) and other DC plans, up from 6.7 percent in 1993. Mutual funds managed 60 percent of the assets in these plans in 2013, triple the 20 percent in 1993 (Investment Company Institute 2014).

According to the Investment Company Institute (2014), worldwide numbers are also impressive. At the end of 2013, worldwide flow of funds into mutual funds stood at $30.05 trillion in 76,200 funds. In 2003, worldwide flow of funds into mutual funds stood at $14.04 trillion in 54,568 funds. Between 2003 and 2013, worldwide investing in mutual funds grew at an annual rate of 7.91 percent. In 2013, the emerging markets of Brazil, Chile, Mexico, Czech Republic, Greece, Hungary, Poland, China, India, South Korea, Philippines, Taiwan, and South Africa accounted for $2.31 trillion in mutual fund investments. However, the annual growth rate in these markets stood at 15.86 percent. In contrast, the United States alone had $15.01 trillion invested in mutual funds but the annual growth rate was slower at 7.33 percent.

Unlike mutual funds, hedge funds lack precise legal definitions. They are a type of pooled investment that provides more flexibility to investors, albeit wealthy ones, by engaging in leveraging (borrowing) and using derivatives in the portfolio. Although hedge funds historically have been exempt from registration with the Securities and Exchange Commission (SEC), the Dodd-Frank Wall Street Reform and Consumer Protection Act became effective in 2011 and eliminated exceptions for registration and increased public disclosures requirements. Thus, these changes require considering emerging market hedge funds as an investment choice.

Contrary to their name, hedge funds are not necessarily fully hedged against market risk. The name "hedge" came from an investment management strategy started in 1949 that used short selling to protect portfolios from losses during down markets. Hedging strategies have now evolved to include exotic uses of derivatives with highly leveraged portfolios. Hedge funds can reduce their market or systematic risk.

Connor, Goldberg, and Korajczyk (2010) find the average beta of a hedge fund relative to the S&P 500 index is about 0.44. According to HedgeFund Intelligence's 2014 report (Hedge Fund Intelligence 2014), hedge funds grew globally from under \$500 billion in 2000 to nearly \$2.632 trillion in 2013, which translates into an annual growth of 12.5 percent. The United States has the bulk of the hedge fund market and accounts for about 72 percent of the global market. Hedge fund markets in emerging countries are small but rapidly developing. While the main focus of this chapter focuses on mutual funds, hedge funds cannot be ignored because of the rapid growth of this market and increasing regulatory scrutiny of them.

The growth of emerging market debt has been explosive increasing from \$969 billion in 1995 to \$10,893 billion in 2010. Emerging debt markets have low correlations with developed bond markets. As Schroder Fund Advisors show, emerging market debt has a correlation of only 0.30 with U.S. equities and 0.54 with emerging market equities (Schroders 2011). The correlation of emerging market debt with U.S. aggregate bonds is –0.60. Thus, emerging market bonds provide a good source of diversification. The market volatility of emerging market debt is lower than that of the world's major equity markets. Besides the debt capacity of emerging markets is often unused. For example, emerging markets collectively produce 38 percent of the world's gross domestic product (GDP), but hold only 10 percent of the world's debt.

Measuring Performance of Emerging Market Mutual Funds

Determining the performance of EMMFs is similar to domestic funds. A main difference is often in the choice of benchmark index. As Equation 27.1 shows, a typical method uses a single index model. Because the expense-adjusted fund return does not account for risk, the model computes Jensen's alpha (α) using an appropriate benchmark index. A statistically significant positive α signifies outperformance by the mutual fund:

$$\left(R_{i,t} - R_{f,t}\right) = \alpha_i + \beta_1\left(R_{index,t} - R_{f,t}\right) + \varepsilon_{i,t}, \tag{27.1}$$

where $R_{i,t}$ is the return for fund i at time t; $R_{f,t}$ is the risk-free rate of return; and $R_{index,t}$ is the return of the benchmark index. Subject to data availability, a variation of Fama and French (1993, 1996) three-factor as Equation 27.2 shows and Carhart (1997) four-factor alphas as Equation 27.3 shows can also be used. The specifications for the Jensen, Fama–French, and Carhart models are:

$$\left(R_{i,t} - R_{f,t}\right) = \alpha_i + \beta_1\left(R_{index,t} - R_{f,t}\right) + \beta_2(SMB_t) + \beta_3(HML_t) + \varepsilon_{i,t} \tag{27.2}$$

$$\left(R_{i,t} - R_{f,t}\right) = \alpha_i + \beta_1\left(R_{index,t} - R_{f,t}\right) + \beta_2(SMB_t) + \beta_3(HML_t) + \beta_4(PR1YR_t) + \varepsilon_{i,t}, \tag{27.3}$$

where R_{index} is the return on the appropriate benchmark index; R_f is the risk-free rate of return; SMB_t (small minus big) is the size factor that captures the stock return performance of small firms relative to large firms; HML_t (high minus low) is the relative return of value and growth stocks; and $PR1YR_t$ is a momentum factor computed as the difference in returns of prior-year high- and low-return portfolios. The three alpha measures are computed using monthly data.

Implementing the Fama and French models may require using diversified portfolios of stocks as a proxy for the market portfolio. The first three models thus focus on stock markets and are useful when evaluating the performance of OEFs and exchange-traded funds (ETFs). However, Fung and Hsieh (1999) contend that hedge funds, which are also akin to mutual funds with less market regulation, use dynamic trading strategies, which may frequently involve short sales, leverage, and derivatives. These three models should be extended to capture alternative asset classes. They define eight standard asset classes useful for analyzing fund performance:

- three equity indices—MSCI North American (MSUSAM), MSCI non-US (MSWXUS), IFC Emerging Markets (IFCOMP)
- two bond indices—JP Morgan U.S. Government Bonds (USMGUSRI), JP Morgan non-U.S. Government Bonds (USMGEXRI),
- currencies—Federal Reserve Traded Weighted Index of the U.S. dollar (USD), the one-month Eurodollar Deposit Return of the previous month (ECUSD1M), and London gold (GOLDBLN).

These variables yield an eight-factor model shown in Equation 27.4:

$$\begin{aligned}\left(R_{i,t}-R_{f,t}\right) &= \alpha_i + \beta_1(\text{MSUSAM}) + \beta_2(\text{MSWXUS}) + \beta_3(\text{IFCOMP}) + \beta_4(\text{USMGUSRI}) \\ &\quad + \beta_5(\text{USMGEXRI}) + \beta_6(\text{USD}) + \beta_7(\text{ECUSD1M}) + \beta_8(\text{GOLDBLN}) + \varepsilon_{i,t}.\end{aligned} \tag{27.4}$$

Equation 27.4 anticipates the frequent switching of assets in a hedge fund. However, hedge funds also invest in options. Fung and Hsieh (2001, 2004, 2009) use the S&P 500 index excess returns (SNPMRF), and a size spread factor, the Russell 2000 index minus the S&P 500 (SCMLC). They consider two bond-oriented factors—10-year Treasury constant maturity yield as a bond market factor (BD10RET) and the spread of the change of the Moody's Baa yield over the change of the 10-year Treasury constant maturity yield as a credit spread factor (BAAMTSY); three trend-following factors—the Bond Trend-Following Factor (PTFSBD), Currency Trend-Following Factor (PTFSFX), and the Commodity Trend-Following Factor (PTFSCOM); and MSCI Emerging Market Index (MSEMKF) in developing Equation 27.5:

$$\begin{aligned}\left(R_{i,t}-R_{f,t}\right) &= \alpha_i + \beta_1(\text{SNPMRF}) + \beta_2(\text{SCMLC}) + \beta_3(\text{BD10RET}) + \beta_4(\text{BAAMTSY}) \\ &\quad + \beta_5(\text{PTFSBD}) + \beta_6(\text{PTFSFX}) + \beta_7(\text{PTFSCOM}) + \beta_8(\text{MSEMKF}) + \varepsilon_{i,t}.\end{aligned} \tag{27.5}$$

Eling and Faust (2010) extend these models and set up an asset class factor model for EMMFs using various emerging market stock indices provided by MSCI, and emerging market bond indices provided by JP Morgan. They also contend that two ways are available to construct these factor models. The first is to screen many variables through stepwise regression techniques (Liang 1999; Agarwal and Naik 2000; Vrontos, Vrontos, and Giamouridis 2008). This approach leads to a high in-sample R^2, but to a low out-of-sample R^2. The second option is to select a short list of variables assumed to be economically relevant (Amenc, El Bied, and Martellini 2003). Eling and Faust assert that choosing the right approach involves a trade-off between quality of fit (higher with stepwise regression but lower with economic reasoning) and robustness (lower with stepwise regression but higher with economic reasoning).

The Sharpe ratio can also be used to measure fund performance. The return of the fund minus the risk-free rate is the portfolio's risk premium. Dividing the risk premium by the standard deviation provides a measure of reward-to-risk for the portfolio. Higher Sharpe ratios imply that investors realize better relative performance. Equation 27.6 shows the Sharpe ratio (S_p):

$$S_p = \frac{R_i - R_f}{\sigma_p}, \tag{27.6}$$

where R_i is the return on the fund; R_f the risk-free rate; and σ_p is the standard deviation of fund returns. The Sharpe ratio calculates the excess return above the risk-free rate and does not depend on a proxy for the market portfolio. If finding an appropriate benchmark for the market portfolio presents a challenge, then the Sharpe ratio can be attractive for examining the performances of EMMFs. A higher Sharpe ratio implies outperformance of the fund on a risk-adjusted basis.

Performance of emerging market bond funds can be tested using a multifactor model such as the one shown in Equation 27.7:

$$R_{i,t} = \alpha_i + \sum_{j=1}^{K} \beta_{i,j} I_{j,t} + \varepsilon_{i,t}, \tag{27.7}$$

where $R_{i,t}$ is the return of fund i over the three-month Treasury-bill (T-bill) at month t; α_i is Jensen alpha for fund i; $\beta_{i,j}$ is the sensitivity of fund i on index j; $I_{j,t}$ is the return of index j over three-month T-bill at month t; K is the number of benchmark indexes in the model; and $\varepsilon_{i,t}$ is the residual term of fund i at month t. The indexes, I, vary according to the objectives of the study. Polwitoon and Tawatnuntachai (2008) include several indexes for benchmarking bond performance such as Citigroup Global Emerging Market Sovereign–Capped Bond (ESBI), Lehman Brothers (LB) Emerging Market World All Series (Emerging World), CSFB High-yield, LB Credit, LB Government/Credit, and Citigroup World Government (WGI) Bond indexes. When evaluating regional bond funds, their model includes that region's benchmark plus high yield and credit.

Performance of Emerging Market Mutual Funds

As choices proliferate, investors are increasingly interested in more information before making their investments in mutual funds. Many studies try to explain the performance of mutual funds. Ultimately, selecting any fund must be on the basis of its performance. According to Anderson and Ahmed (2005), this straightforward endeavor is deceptively difficult owing to two principal issues in testing fund performance: the choice of benchmark and the choice of model.

Jensen (1968), Grinblatt and Titman (1989), and Malkiel (1995) are among the early papers that comprehensively evaluate fund performance. Results in Table 27.1 show that actively managed funds do not outperform various broad market benchmarks. Lehmann and Modest (1987) is an early paper that stresses the critical importance of benchmarking for determining "normal performance." Given evidence that the usual proxies for the market portfolio are mean-variance inefficient and the existence of several anomalies such as firm size and price/earnings (P/E) ratios, the use of the single-factor capital asset pricing model (CAPM) model is often questionable. Ross (1976) contends that systematic risk need not be represented by a single factor and instead offers that K factors (where $K > 1$) affect the return of securities.

When testing the performance of mutual funds, most studies include fund characteristics such as fund size, age, fees and expenses, loads, turnover, flows, and returns as potential determinants of future fund performance. Although Wermers (2000) shows that mutual funds on average hold stocks that outperform the market index, the amount of the outperformance is subsumed by expenses and transactions costs. High-turnover funds incur substantial transactions costs and higher expense ratios but also hold stocks that have significantly higher average returns than low-turnover funds. A portion of the higher returns for the high-turnover funds comes from the stock-picking skills of the manager. Evidence also shows short-term persistence in performance and money flows to past good performers. Although Hendricks, Patel, and Zeckhauser (1993) find evidence of persistence, other studies report that consistency of performance from one period to the next is elusive. For example, in the 1970s, the top performing funds were more likely to perform well in the next year than they were likely to do so during the 1980s. Some studies also conclude that "poor" performers are far more consistent than "good" performers (Brown and Goetzmann 1995; Carhart 1997).

Table 27.1 **Mutual Fund Performance in Classical Studies**

Study	*Sample Period*	*Sample Size*	*Benchmark Index*	*Alpha (%)*	*t-Ratio*
Jensen (1968)	1945–1964	115	S&P500	–1.10	–0.69
Grinblatt and Titman (1989)	1974–1984	157	CRSP EW	–0.03	–0.99
Malkiel (1995)	1971–1991	239	Wilshire 500	–0.93	–1.78
Gruber (1996)	1974–994	270	Prudential-Bache	–0.13	N/A
Carhart (1997)	1962–1993	1892	CRSP VW	–0.16	–2.90
Wermers (2000)	1975–1994	1788	CRSP VW	–1.15	–2.93

Note: This table shows the results from several major studies often regarded as seminal work in evaluating mutual fund performances.

In summary, some managers can beat the market only some of the time. Investors display some fund selection ability as they invest in funds with subsequent good performance. Evidence also shows that fund performance worsens with fund size (Chen, Hong, Huang, and Kubik 2004) and fees (Gil-Bazo and Ruiz-Verdu 2009).

Ferreira, Keswani, Miguel, and Ramos (2013) study the determinants of the performance of open-end actively managed equity mutual funds in 27 countries including 8 countries included in MSCI's Emerging Market Index. They find important differences in the determinants of mutual fund performance between the United States and the rest of the world. U.S. funds are much larger than elsewhere and the U.S. fund industry is older. Country characteristics such as economic development, financial development, quality of legal institutions and law enforcement, and mutual fund industry structure affect performance. Equity mutual funds around the world underperform on average by 20 basis points per quarter after fees. Chen et al. (2004) find evidence on diseconomies of scale in the United States, which Ferreira et al. (2013) also find in EMMFs. However, this finding is not a universal truth because diminishing returns to scale do not seem to affect non-U.S. funds and international funds.

One factor that distinguishes the impact of size in U.S. versus foreign funds is that U.S. funds, by their style, have to invest in small and illiquid stocks. This is not the case for non-U.S. funds. Scale does not adversely affect the performance of international funds even for those funds located in the United States. Controlling for fund size, Ferreira et al. (2013) find that fund performance improves with the size of its fund family as large fund families benefit from economies in trading commissions and fees.

Table 27.2 shows the number of funds and total net assets (TNA) under management (sum of all share classes in U.S. dollars millions) of the sample of funds by country at the end of 2007. The results are summarized from Ferreira et al. (2013) but are segmented into emerging and developed markets. EMMFs represent a small fraction of the global mutual fund market. Most of the funds in emerging markets are domestic but a substantial percentage of the funds in developed markets are international.

Table 27.3 shows the means of fund characteristics as reported in Ferreira et al. (2013). The sample includes open-end actively managed domestic equity funds. The sample period is from 2000 to 2007. Results show that the average return of 7.38 percent for the EMMFs is larger than the average returns of 3.18 percent for the four largest markets for mutual funds (i.e., the United States, Canada, United Kingdom, and Germany). The reported alpha is based on the Carhart four-factor model shown in Equation 27.3. The average alpha for emerging markets is positive (0.36) while those for developed markets are on average negative (–0.18). The difference in means between the emerging market group and the developed market group is statistically significant at the 5 percent level. Fund TNA, defined as TNA in millions of U.S. dollars of the fund primary share class, is statistically larger for the developed sample compared to the emerging market sample. This is not surprising because the age of the funds in the emerging markets is significantly lower by a factor of almost 2 than those in the developed markets. However, the expense ratios for the emerging markets are higher albeit not statistically significant. Emerging markets charge lower loads, which are statistically insignificant, and their funds are marketed to fewer countries abroad. Thus, a general picture emerges that funds in emerging markets provide better risk-adjusted returns when compared to the developed markets.

Table 27.2 **Number and Size of Mutual Funds by Country**

Country	All Funds		Domestic Funds		International Funds	
	Number of Funds	*TNA ($ million)*	*Number of Funds*	*TNA ($ million)*	*Number of Funds*	*TNA ($ million)*
Panel A Emerging Countries Listed in MSCI Emerging Market Index						
India	145	28,674	145	28,674		
Indonesia	21	2,742	21	2,742		
Malaysia	158	6,177	158	6,177		
Poland	20	10,542	20	10,542		
Singapore	210	17,474	12	1,513	198	15,961
South Korea	205	30,465	205	30,465		
Taiwan	217	16,487	161	11,852	56	4,635
Thailand	125	3,035	125	3,035		
Total Emerging	1,101	115,596	847	95,000	254	20,596
Panel B Developed Countries						
Canada	1,491	410,546	594	237,924	897	172,623
Germany	364	150,438	61	44,037	303	106,401
United Kingdom	934	519,649	384	277,166	550	242,484
United States	2,741	4,533,223	2,216	3,216,470	525	1,316,753
Total Developed	5,530	5,613,856	3,255	3,775,597	2,275	1,838,261

Note: This table summarizes key results from Ferreira et al. (2013) that show the number of funds and their total net assets. The table compares the EMMFs with the mutual funds in developed markets.

Emerging markets are generally perceived to be less efficient than developed markets. Active fund managers may uncover more opportunities to find abnormal returns in such markets. Huij and Post (2011) contend that because emerging markets offer investors a wide range of weakly correlated investment opportunities, funds invested in these markets may have a competitive advantage over funds invested in developed markets. This is because the higher levels of correlation with aggregate market movements can make attaining large excess returns difficult. Kiymaz (2012) reports the performance of 463 U.S.-based emerging equity funds for the period 2000 to 2011. Using a single index model against the MSCI Index, he finds an average alpha of 0.14. The Sharpe ratio calculated using Equation 27.6 is 0.07. The fund Sharpe ratio is lower than the Sharpe ratio for the MSCI Emerging Market Index.

Table 27.3 **Fund Performance in Emerging Markets**

Country	*Number*	*Return (%)*	*Alpha (%)*	*TNA ($ million)*	*Family TNA ($ million)*	*Age in Years*	*Expense Ratio (% year)*	*Total Load (%)*	*Countries Sold*
Panel A Emerging Countries Listed in MSCI Emerging Market Index									
India	2,101	12.24	0.57	38	13,800	6.2	1.24	2.72	1.44
Indonesia	209	10.58	0.01	40	5,710	7.6	1.78	2.86	1.05
Malaysia	2,633	4.72	0.34	40	2,290	9.1	1.53	6.24	1.06
Poland	414	6.74	0.48	135	23,200	5.4	3.25	4.25	1.00
Singapore	270	5.57	0.11	45	6,890	9.1	1.40	3.94	1.19
South Korea	6,011	6.45	0.76	21	8,520	4.5	2.68	0.05	1.00
Taiwan	984	5.38	−0.34	52	22,700	8.8	1.55	2.72	1.00
Thailand	1,989	7.32	0.92	11	968	8.3	1.37	1.20	1.00
Average Emerging	1,826	7.38	0.36	47.75	10,510	7.38	1.85	3.00	1.09
Panel B Developed Countries									
Canada	5,453	4.61	−0.58	265	19,700	10.6	1.52	5.33	1.01
Germany	1,733	3.46	−0.07	418	23,000	17.5	1.24	4.45	1.88
United Kingdom	6,156	2.86	0.23	471	31,000	16.0	1.46	4.21	1.75
United States	58,957	1.80	−0.30	949	44,900	12.6	1.31	2.45	1.04
Average Developed	18,075	3.18	−0.18	525.75	29,650	14.18	1.38	4.11	1.42

Note: This table summarizes the results from Ferreira et al. (2013) and shows the number performance of mutual funds in emerging markets. The table compares the quarterly returns from emerging market versus developed market mutual funds.

Ahmed, Gangopadhyay, and Nanda (2003) address the performance of open-end stock and bond EMMFs conditional on the monetary policy regime in the United States. Results show that emerging market stock funds underperform their corresponding country indices, as evidenced by their lower returns, higher risk, and lower Sharpe ratios. Among the various categories of funds, Latin American funds have the highest Sharpe and Treynor ratios (measures excess return per unit of beta as shown in Equation 27.8), while funds investing in Pacific and Latin American countries have the next highest Sharpe and Treynor ratios and the highest Jensen alpha:

$$T_p = \frac{R_i - R_f}{\beta_p} \tag{27.8}$$

Emerging market stock funds have higher Sharpe ratios than the corresponding indexes during restrictive periods, but have lower Sharpe ratios than their indexes during expansive periods. Similarly, the Jensen alphas of all but the Latin American funds are positive during periods of restrictive U.S. monetary policy. Diversified Emerging Market and Asia Pacific funds exhibit the largest differences in mean returns between the restrictive and expansive policy regimes.

Persistence of Performance for Emerging Market Mutual Funds

Individual investors often pursue a "chasing winners" strategy in which they select funds on the basis of prior quarter performance. However, each time investors alter their portfolio of funds, front-end or deferred loads could reduce their realized return. Thus, persistence of fund performance needs to be tested on an expense and risk-adjusted basis. An additional complication occurs because the holding period return is taxable when investors sell their mutual funds presumably to invest in other mutual funds. Investors could also face redemption fees, which act as levies when redeeming shares after a short holding period.

For domestic funds, Carhart (1997) finds that strong persistence of short-run mutual fund returns is largely explained by common-factor sensitivities, expenses, and transactions costs. Over the longer periods, only top and bottom decile funds maintain their rankings more than would be expected randomly. In contrast, Hendricks et al. (1993) find that recent past performance is a better predictor of future performance. Grinblatt and Titman (1989, 1994) show that smaller size funds tend have better future performance. Wermers (2000) finds funds with high turnover are superior predictors of future performance. Berk and Green (2004) show theoretically that a fund manager's informational advantage will be short-lived when investors direct their capital to recent winners. Bollen and Busse (2005) suggest that mutual fund managers possess certain informational advantages. The authors find that top-performing funds generate a statistically significant abnormal return in the post-ranking quarter. However, Bollen and Busse conclude that the economic significance of persistence in mutual fund abnormal returns is questionable, after taking into account transaction costs and taxes. Even if short-term performance is predictable, investors may generate superior returns by following a naive buy-and-hold strategy.

Table 27.4 **Performance Measures of Mutual Funds across Varying Periods**

Performance Measures	*Number*	*Mean*	*Media*	*Standard Deviation*
	1997–1999			
Mean monthly excess returns (%)	57	0.3976	0.3659	0.4544
Standard deviation of returns (%)	57	8.9226	9.1317	0.9362
Sharpe ratio	57	0.0463	0.0413	0.0554
Jensen's alpha	57	0.1309	0.0945	0.4641
	2000–2002			
Mean monthly excess returns (%)	82	−1.4035	−1.4271	0.3439
Standard deviation of returns (%)	82	6.8274	6.7800	0.6293
Sharpe ratio	82	−0.2048	−0.2105	0.0438
Jensen's alpha	82	−0.2397	−0.2467	0.2939
	2003–2005			
Mean monthly excess returns (%)	73	2.6102	2.5810	0.2928
Standard deviation of returns (%)	73	4.7780	4.7539	0.3518
Sharpe ratio	73	0.5469	0.5467	0.0516
Jensen's alpha	73	0.0394	0.0019	0.2882

Note: This table summarizes the results from Gottesman and Morey (2007) and shows the extent to which funds in emerging markets show persistence in performance.

Gottesman and Morey (2007) are among the first to examine the determinants of performance persistence for EMMFs. Table 27.4 summarizes key results from their study on the performance measures of EMMFs in different segmented periods. Results show poor average performance of an emerging market fund between 2000 and 2002, strong performance between 2003 and 2005, and mixed performance between 1997 and 1999. Gottesman and Morey regress fund performance against the usual list of explanatory variables: beginning-of-the-sample expense ratios, net asset size, the fund's previous 12-month total excess return, turnover, and manager tenure against the out-of-sample fund performance as measured by the Sharpe ratio, the single-index alpha, and mean monthly returns. Their evidence shows that only the expense ratio is a significant predictor of future fund performance. The expense ratio is negatively and significantly related to fund performance similar to Carhart (1997) for domestic funds. Thus, funds with lower expenses perform better than those with higher expenses for both emerging market and U.S. funds.

Huij and Post (2011) introduce a method that allows them to test the economic viability of any statistical persistence in the performance of EMMFs. Using a survivorship-bias free data period spanning January 1993 to December 2006, they present evidence in favor of performance persistence in EMMFs. When ranking the funds by their monthly returns over the past quarter and evaluating their performance in the following

Table 27.5 **Performance of Emerging Market Mutual Funds Ranked by Past Returns**

Tercile	*Return (%)*	*Sharpe*	*Alpha*	*Alpha (t-stat)*	$R_{index} - R_f$	$R_{index} - R_f$ *(t-stat)*	*Adjusted* R^2
1 (top)	10.75	0.48	2.10	1.38	0.94	49.26	0.94
2 (middle)	7.84	0.35	−0.97	−0.93	0.96	73.26	0.97
3 (bottom)	6.26	0.29	−2.34	−2.19	0.94	69.86	0.97

Note: This table summarizes key results from Huij and Post (2011) showing the persistence of mutual fund performance in emerging markets.

month, the return spread between the top and bottom ninth of funds is significant. Huij and Post conclude that differences in market risk exposures, fund expenses, and load fees do not explain persistence in fund performance. For EMMFs, the contribution of winner funds to the return spread in the future is larger than those found for domestic funds.

Table 27.5 uses Equation 27.1 to show the average excess returns, Sharpe ratios, alphas, single factor exposures including *t*-statistics, and adjusted R^2 for terciles (thirds) of EMMFs ranked monthly by their return over the past quarter. Tercile 1 contains the funds with the highest past returns and tercile 3 has the funds with the lowest returns in the past quarters. Funds that display high (low) returns over the past quarter tend to earn higher (lower) returns the following month. The return spread between the top and bottom ninth of funds is 7.26 percent per year (i.e., 11.55 percent for the top third of the first tercile and 4.29 percent for the bottom third of the last tercile). This spread is in the same order of magnitude as those reported for domestic U.S. funds in Carhart (1997) and Hendricks et al. (1993). Investors in EMMFs can exploit a "hot-hands effect" by investing in recent winners. However, only sophisticated investors with sizable financial capacity can take advantage of such market imperfections.

Emerging Market Bond Funds

During the 1990s, emerging market bond funds did not provide an attractive investment opportunity. According to Erb, Harvey, and Viskanta (1999, 2000), the emerging bond market experienced considerable volatility. Recent improvements in the credit ratings of emerging countries and the surge in bond issuance from these countries provide high-yield investors with renewed investment opportunities.

Polwitoon and Tawatnuntachai (2008) analyze U.S.-based emerging market bond funds over the period 1996 to 2005. They show that emerging market bond funds outperform comparable domestic and global bond funds. These funds also provide international diversification benefits to U.S. and international bond and equity portfolios. For example, by including 20 percent emerging funds in their portfolios, U.S. investors can enhance the portfolio returns by 0.81 percent to 1.53 percent a year without increasing risk. Finally, these funds exhibit persistence in performance and seasonality.

The improving economic prospects of emerging countries along with the increased debt capacity of these economies create an opportunity for investors to diversify into high-yield securities. Polwitoon and Tawatnuntachai (2008) conclude that emerging market bond funds offer a good opportunity for international diversification. Consistent with the bond and equity fund literature, emerging funds underperform benchmark indexes. However, the funds outperform not only comparable domestic bond funds but also global bond funds on both total and risk-adjusted returns. On a total return basis, turnover and fund size but not the size of fund family help to increase fund returns. Just as for emerging market equity funds, high expense ratios and fees also negatively affect bond funds for emerging markets. These results are consistent with Dellva and Olson (1998) and Chen et al. (2004).

Adding a low correlation asset to an existing portfolio creates opportunities for diversification benefits. Elton, Gruber, and Rentzler (1987) show that diversification benefits are incurred if the Sharpe ratio of the new asset is greater than the product of the Sharpe ratio of the existing asset and the return correlation between the new and existing assets. To test whether emerging bond funds provide incremental diversification benefits to existing assets, Polwitoon and Tawatnuntachai (2008) calculate the difference between the Sharpe ratio of emerging funds (SHR_{emg}) and the product of the Sharpe ratio of an existing asset and the return correlation between emerging funds and the existing asset ($SHR_p \times \rho_{emg,p}$). Statistically significant positive differences show that emerging funds provide diversification benefits.

Table 27.6 shows the incremental diversification benefits from adding emerging market bond funds to a portfolio of existing assets. The table is ranked in the order of assets that provide the greatest benefit from diversification when adding emerging market bond funds to the portfolio. The correlation ($\rho_{emg,p}$) is the correlation of monthly portfolio returns between emerging bond funds and the existing asset identified in the first column of the table. The last column of Table 27.6 shows the difference in the cross-sectional mean difference between the Sharpe ratio of emerging bond funds and the return correlation between emerging funds and the existing asset ($SHR_p \times \rho_{emg,p}$). All of the differences are statistically significant at the 1 percent level.

Table 27.6 **Diversification Benefits from Adding Emerging Market Bond Funds**

Existing Assets	SHR_p	$\rho_{emg,p}$	SHR_p x $\rho_{emg,p}$	*Difference*
S&P 500 funds	0.0174	0.5643	0.0098	0.1314
Global bond funds	0.0421	0.3938	0.0166	0.1247
Domestic bond funds	0.0648	0.6442	0.0417	0.0995
World equity funds	0.0859	0.5599	0.0481	0.0932
Emerging equity funds	0.1096	0.6965	0.0763	0.0650

Note: This table summarizes the results from Polwitoon and Tawatnuntachai (2008) and shows the incremental diversification benefits from adding emerging market bond funds to a portfolio of existing assets.

Emerging Market Hedge Funds

Hedge funds differ from mutual funds in that hedge funds use dynamic trading strategies while mutual funds use buy-hold trading strategies. As Fung and Hsieh (1999) note, hedge funds typically leverage their bets by margining their positions and using short sales. In contrast, the use of leverage is often limited if not restricted for mutual funds. Unlike mutual funds, hedge funds are not restricted to investing in stocks and bonds but can invest in other assets such as derivatives, commodities, and private equity. Finally, hedge funds are subject to fewer regulations than mutual funds. This allows hedge funds to engage in risky trading strategies such as long-short, leverage, and derivatives to increase returns and reduce systematic risk. Hedge funds also practice market timing to a greater degree than mutual funds (Ackerman, McEnally, and Ravenscraft 1999).

Hedge funds investing in emerging markets are challenged on many fronts. As Abugri and Dutta (2009) note, EMMFs are restricted in practicing dynamic trading strategies because of the trading restrictions that often characterize emerging markets. The lack of liquidity in emerging markets forces hedge funds to primarily use long strategies. Given these constraints, hedge funds in emerging markets are likely to behave differently than hedge funds operating in developed markets. Not surprisingly, hedge funds in emerging markets behaved more like mutual funds before 2007. However, recent data suggest that emerging market hedge funds are behaving more like their counterparts in the developed markets. On a risk-adjusted basis, emerging market hedge fund indices outperform their benchmarks. Yet, such superior performances are not pervasive enough to suggest that emerging market hedge funds consistently outperform their benchmarks.

Cao and Jayasuriya (2012) use emerging market hedge fund data for the period 1983 to 2007 to show that some emerging market hedge funds can generate positive risk-adjusted returns. Still, only a few funds show market-timing ability on a monthly or daily basis. High market volatilities in emerging markets often hurt fund performance. The authors also report that management fees, growth rates of fund, and leverage are all positively related to the manager's ability to generate outperformance. While fees play a negative role in the performance of mutual funds, they are both statistically and economically significant in producing positive alpha for hedge funds.

Caglayan and Ulutas (2014) examine emerging market hedge funds for the period 1999 to 2012 from the Lipper Trading Advisor Selection System. They find consistent results showing a positive and significant relationship between the emerging market equity beta (MSCI beta) and future hedge fund returns, and a positive and significant link between the emerging market currency beta (EMFX beta) and future hedge fund returns. The authors also show that fund managers have superior abilities to time the markets. Their results suggest that hedge funds can earn positive excess returns by timing their exposure to emerging market securities. Dutta (2012) reports the performance of hedge funds segmented by category for the period 2000 to 2007. Emerging market hedge funds registered superior performance against their benchmarks in general particularly the MSCI equity benchmark. However, these funds do not provide good protection for downside risk to investors.

Table 27.7 **Summary Statistics of Emerging Market Hedge Funds**

	Mean Returns	*Standard Deviation*	*Alpha*	*Positive Alpha (%)*	*Mean Excess Returns*	*Sharpe Ratio*
Asia	0.94	5.41	0.43	23.08	0.67	0.047
Eastern Europe and Russia	2.80	6.86	1.85	90.00	2.53	0.395
Latin America	1.57	6.78	1.01	83.33	1.30	0.228
Emerging markets global	1.29	3.54	1.01	81.82	1.03	0.309

Note: This table summarizes the results for hedge funds as provided by Dutta (2012).

Table 27.7 reports the summary statistics for hedge funds. Asian funds have the lowest average returns and have high volatility. The mean return for the Emerging Markets Global category is impressive because this category has the lowest volatility. Funds in the Eastern Europe and Russia have the highest Sharpe ratios, while the Asian region has the lowest Sharpe ratios. The monthly excess fund returns are returns over the monthly returns for the 90-day T-bill. Once again, funds invested in Eastern Europe and Russia exhibit the best performance. Using a multifactor regression, Caglayan and Ulutas (2014) also report alpha for equally weighted portfolios and the percentage of funds with positive alphas. Asian funds have the lowest alphas and the lowest number of funds with positive alphas. Conversely, for Eastern Europe and Russia, Latin America, and Emerging Global funds, a substantial proportion of the alphas are positive and significant. None of the fund alphas for any of the four categories is negative and significant.

Fund Flows into Emerging Market Mutual Funds

Despite an extensive literature on EMMFs, understanding EMMFs requires going beyond performance evaluation and also studying the role of fund flows. Understanding the flow of funds is important because it can often predict future performance. The effect of flows on return may result from momentum trading strategies (i.e., investing in funds that have recently performed well and selling those that have performed poorly). Thus, momentum trading could create a spurious co-movement between past flows and current returns.

Jinjarak and Zheng (2010) compare the dynamics of flow and return between two periods: a low-volatility tranquil period (2003 to 2007) and a high-volatility financial panic (2008 to 2009). Using weekly data for emerging markets, they show that during periods of financial panic, emerging markets face more difficulty in attracting new investments in mutual funds. If contemporaneous flow contains information that can affect asset value, then new investment in funds may push the asset price according to that informational content. Flow contemporaneously affects asset price and thus return and flow precedes return. Jinjarak and Zheng find that both price pressure and information effects drive the predictive power of flow on return in a tranquil period but the information effect dominates during a financial panic.

Using data from U.S.-domiciled EMMFs, Kaushik (2012) finds that investors in EMMFs chase past returns. Both the flow and raw returns in the previous month heavily influence the flow in the current month. Flow of funds in the current month increases by 15 basis points for every 100 basis points increase in flow of funds in the previous month. The flow in the current period increases by 29 basis points for every 100 basis points increase in raw return in the previous month. Their results also show that investors are concerned about a fund's size and diversification but they are not concerned about a fund's loads and fees. Investors dislike investing in large funds but are willing to invest in a well-diversified fund. Hsieh, Yang, Yang, and Lee (2011) find positive stock returns and currency appreciation affect flows of mutual funds into the emerging market in Asia. These markets also exhibit positive feedback effects and herding behaviors. However, the influence of herding or positive feedback depends on market conditions. For example, the positive feedback effect is stronger for countries that are more volatile and positive feedback and herding behavior occurs both during and after times of crisis.

Summary and Conclusions

The rapid growth in emerging economies is fueling the market for EMMFs and investment advisors are pushing for investments in EMMFs. Two main factors fuel investing in emerging markets: the higher returns on stocks in emerging markets and the lower correlation of these stocks with their counterparts in developed markets. Although the benefits from diversification into emerging markets are positive, the magnitude of those gains has slowed in recent years. Besides OEFs, investors in the United States are increasingly using hedge funds and bond funds to invest in emerging markets.

Country characteristics such as economic development, quality of legal institutions, and market microstructure all affect the performance of EMMFs. Although EMMFs perform better than the mutual funds in developed markets, EMMFs tend to underperform a broad emerging market index on a risk-adjusted basis using the Sharpe ratio. The most important determinant of fund performance in emerging markets is the fund's expense ratio, which is negatively related to fund performance. However, the expense ratio does not explain persistence of fund performance. Investors in EMMFs can exploit the "hot-hands effect" by investing in recent winners.

Emerging market bond funds provide an attractive investment option. U.S. investors can gain substantial diversification benefits by adding emerging market bond funds to their portfolio. Emerging market bond funds generally outperform global bond funds on a risk-adjusted basis. The size of the bond fund has a positive impact on bond fund performance but similar to equity funds, expense ratios have a negative impact on performance.

Investing via emerging market hedge funds is gaining popularity among investors. Despite facing many more restrictions in emerging markets than in developed markets, emerging market hedge funds can generate positive risk-adjusted returns but demonstrate no ability to time the market. Management fees, growth rate of funds, and leverage are all positively related to fund performance.

In terms of the flow of cash into EMMFs, evidence shows that positive stock returns and currency appreciation affect such flows. The influence of herding is not as pronounced and is influenced by market conditions. Positive feedback is stronger in markets with higher volatility.

Discussion Questions

1. Contrast the growth of the EMMFs to the market for mutual funds in developed markets.
2. Outline the most effective models for evaluating the performance of EMMFs.
3. Contrast the risk-adjusted performance of EMMFs to those in developed markets such as the United States.
4. Identify the factors that best explain the performance of EMMFs.
5. Discuss why hedge funds in emerging markets gaining popularity and the factors that can best explain their performance.

References

Abugri, Benjamin A., and Sandip Dutta. 2009. "Emerging Market Hedge Funds: Do They Perform Like Regular Hedge Funds?" *Journal of International Financial Markets, Institutions and Money* 19:5, 834–849.

Ackermann, Carl, Richard McEnally, and David Ravenscraft. 1999. "The Performance of Hedge Funds: Risk, Return and Incentives." *Journal of Finance* 54:3, 833–874.

Agarwal, Vikas, and Narayan Y. Naik. 2000. "Multi-Period Performance Persistence Analysis of Hedge Funds." *Journal of Financial and Quantitative* Analysis 35:3, 327–342.

Ahmed, Parvez. 2013. "Stock Market Efficiency and Market Microstructure in Emerging Markets." In H. K. Baker and H. Kiymaz, eds., *Market Microstructure in Emerging and Developed Markets: Price Discovery, Information Flows, and Transaction Costs*, 387–406. Hoboken, NJ: John Wiley & Sons, Inc.

Ahmed, Parvez, Partha Gangopadhyay, and Sudhir Nanda. 2003. "Investing in Emerging Market Mutual Funds." *Journal of Business and Economic Perspectives* 29:1, 5–15.

Amenc, Noël, Sina El Bied, and Lionel Martellini. 2003. "Predictability in Hedge Fund Returns." *Financial Analysts Journal* 59:5, 32–46.

Anderson, Seth C., and Parvez Ahmed. 2005. *Mutual Funds: Fifty Years of Research Findings*. New York: Springer.

Bailey, Warren, and Joseph Lim. 1992. "Evaluating the Diversification Benefits of New Country Funds." *Journal of Portfolio Management* 18:3, 74–80.

Bailey, Warren, and René M. Stulz. 1990. "Benefits of International Diversification: The Case of Pacific Basin Stock Markets." *Journal of Portfolio Management* 16:4, 57–61.

Bekaert, Geert, Campbell R. Harvey, and Christian T. Lundblad. 2003. "Equity Market Liberalization in Emerging Markets." *Journal of Financial Research* 26:3, 275–299.

Berk, Jonathan B., and Richard C. Green. 2004. "Mutual Fund Flows and Performance in Rational Markets." *Journal of Political Economy* 112:6, 1269–1295.

Bollen, Nicolas P. B., and Jeffrey A. Busse. 2005. "Short-Term Persistence in Mutual Fund Performance." *Review of Financial Studies* 18:2, 569–597.

Brown, Stephen J., and William N. Goetzmann. 1995. "Performance Persistence." *Journal of Finance* 50:2, 679–698.

Caglayan, Mustafa O., and Sevan Ulutas. 2014. "Emerging Market Exposures and the Predictability of Hedge Fund Returns." *Financial Management* 43:1, 149–180.

Cao, Bolong, and Shamila A. Jayasuriya. 2012. "Volatility and the Cross-Sectional Performance of Emerging Market Hedge Funds." *Journal of Alternative Investments* 14:4, 40–50.

Carhart, Mark M. 1997. "On Persistence in Mutual Fund Performance." *Journal of Finance* 52:1, 57–82.

Chen, Joseph, Harrison Hong, Ming Huang, and Jeffrey D. Kubik. 2004. "Does Fund Size Erode Mutual Fund Performance? The Role of Liquidity and Organization." *American Economic Review* 94:5, 1276–1302.

Connor, Gregory, Lisa R. Goldberg, and Robert A. Korajczyk. 2010. *Portfolio Risk Analysis*. Princeton, NJ: Princeton University Press.

Delevingne, Lawrence. 2014. "Top Mutual Fund Managers Push These Markets." CNBC. Available at http://www.cnbc.com/id/101776835#.

Dellva, Wilfred L., and Gerard T. Olson. 1998. "The Relationship between Mutual Fund Fees and Expenses and Their Effects on Performance." *Financial Review* 33:1, 85–104.

DeSantis, Giorgio, and Bruno Gerard. 1997. "International Asset Pricing and Portfolio Diversification with Time-Varying Risk." *Journal of Finance* 52:5, 1881–1912.

Dutta, Sandip. 2012. "Emerging Market Hedge Funds: Analysis of Security Selection and Market Timing." *Banking & Finance Review* 4:2, 85–105.

Eling, Martin, and Roger Faust. 2010. "The Performance of Hedge Funds and Mutual Funds in Emerging Markets." *Journal of Banking and Finance* 34:8, 1993–2009.

Elton, Edwin J., Martin J. Gruber, and Joel C. Rentzler. 1987. "Professionally Managed, Publicly Traded Commodity Funds." *Journal of Business* 60:2, 175–199.

Erb, Claude B., Campbell R. Harvey, and Tadas E. Viskanta. 1999. "New Perspectives on Emerging Market Bonds." *Journal of Portfolio Management* 25:2, 83–92.

Erb, Claude B., Campbell R. Harvey, and Tadas E. Viskanta. 2000. "Understanding Emerging Market Bonds." *Emerging Market Quarterly* 4, 17–23.

Errunza, Vihang R. 1983. "Emerging Markets: A New Opportunity for Improving Global Portfolio Performance." *Financial Analysts Journal* 39:5, 51–58.

Eun, Cheol S., Richard Kolodny, and Bruce G. Resnick. 1991. "U.S.-Based International Mutual Funds: A Performance Evaluation." *Journal of Portfolio Management* 19:3, 88–94.

Fama, Eugene F., and Kenneth R. French. 1993. "Common Risk Factors in the Returns on Bonds and Stocks." *Journal of Financial Economics* 33:1, 3–53.

Fama, Eugene F., and Kenneth R. French. 1996. "Multifactor Explanations of Asset Pricing Anomalies." *Journal of Finance* 51:1, 55–84.

Ferreira, Miguel A., Aneel Keswani, António F. Miguel, and Sofia B. Ramos. 2013. "The Determinants of Mutual Fund Performance: A Cross-Country Study." *Review of Finance* 17:2, 483–525.

Fung, William, and David A. Hsieh. 1999. "A Primer on Hedge Funds." *Journal of Empirical Finance* 6:3, 309–331.

Fung, W. William, and David A. Hsieh. 2001. "The Risk in Hedge Fund Strategies: Theory and Evidence from Trend Followers." *Review of Financial Studies* 14:2, 312–341.

Fung, William, and David A. Hsieh. 2004. "Hedge Fund Benchmarks: A Risk-Based Approach." *Financial Analysts Journal* 60:5, 65–80.

Fung, William, and David A. Hsieh. 2009. "Measurement Biases in Hedge Fund Performance Data: An Update." *Financial Analysts Journal* 65:3, 36–38.

Gil-Bazo, Javier, and Pablo Ruiz-Verdu. 2009. "The Relation between Price and Performance in the Mutual Fund Industry." *Journal of Finance* 64:5, 2153–2183.

Gottesman, Aron A., and Matthew R. Morey. 2007. "Predicting Emerging Market Mutual Fund Performance." *Journal of Investing* 16:3, 111–122.

Grinblatt, Mark, and Sheridan Titman. 1989. "Mutual Fund Performance: An Analysis of Quarterly Portfolio Holdings." *Journal of Business* 62:3, 393–416.

Grinblatt, Mark, and Sheridan Titman. 1994. "A Study of Monthly Mutual Fund Returns and Performance Evaluation Techniques." *Journal of Financial and Quantitative Analysis* 29:3, 419–444.

HedgeFund Intelligence. 2014. "Global Review." Autumn. HedgeFund Intelligence, Nestor House, London. Available at http://www.hedgefundintelligence.com.

Hendricks, Darryll, Jayendu Patel, and Richard Zeckhauser. 1993. "Hot Hands in Mutual Funds: Short-Run Relative Persistence of Relative Performance, 1974–1988." *Journal of Finance* 48:1, 93–130

Hsieh, Meng-Fen, Tzu-Yi Yang, Yu-Tai Yang, and Jen-Sin Lee. 2011. "Evidence of Herding and Positive Feedback Trading for Mutual Funds in Emerging Asian Countries." *Quantitative Finance* 11:3, 423–435.

Huij, Joop, and Thierry Post. 2011. "On the Performance of Emerging Market Equity Mutual Funds." *Emerging Markets Review* 12:3, 238–249.

Investment Company Institute. 2014. " Investment Company Fact Book: A Review of Trends and Activities in the U.S Investment Company Industry." Washington, DC: Investment Company Institute. Available at http://www.icifactbook.org/pdf/2014_factbook.pdf.

Jensen, Michael C. 1968. "The Performance of Mutual Funds in the Period 1945–1964." *Journal of Finance* 23:2, 389–416.

Jinjarak, Yothin, and Huanhuan Zheng. 2010. "Financial Panic and Emerging Market Funds." *Applied Financial Economics* 20:23, 1793–1805.

Kaushik, Abhay. 2012. "Flow of Funds and Abnormal Performance of Emerging Market Equity Funds: Is It Simply the Market Attraction or the Real Deal?" *Banking & Finance Review* 4:1, 77–88.

Khanna, Tarun, and Krishna G. Palepu. 2010. *Winning in Emerging Markets: A Road Map for Strategy and Execution.* Boston, MA: Harvard Business School Press.

Kiymaz, Halil. 2012. "An Investigation of Performance of Emerging Market Diversified Equity and Bond Funds." Working Paper, Global Conference on Business & Finance Proceedings 7:12, Institute for Business and Finance Research.

Lehmann, Bruce N., and David M. Modest. 1987. "Mutual Fund Performance Evaluation: A Comparison of Benchmarks and Benchmark Comparisons." *Journal of Finance* 42:2, 233–265.

Lessard, Donald R. 1973. "International Portfolio Diversification: A Multivariate Analysis for a Group of Latin American Countries." *Journal of Finance* 28:3, 619–633.

Liang, Bing. 1999. "On the Performance of Hedge Funds." *Financial Analyst Journal* 55:4, 72–85.

Malkiel, Burton G. 1995. "Returns from Investing in Equity Mutual Funds: 1971–1991." *Journal of Finance* 50:2, 549–572.

Polwitoon, Sirapat, and Oranee Tawatnuntachai. 2008. "Emerging Market Bond Funds: A Comprehensive Analysis." *Financial Review* 43:1, 51–84.

Ross, Stephen A. 1976. "The Arbitrage Theory of Capital Asset Pricing." *Journal of Economic Theory* 13:3, 341–360.

Schroders. 2011. "The Case for Emerging Market Debt." Schroder Fund Advisors. Available at https://www.schroders.com/staticfiles/Schroders/Sites/Americas/usintermediary/pdfs/The-Case-For-Emerging-Market-Debt.pdf.

Vrontos, Spyridon D., Ioannis D. Vrontos, and Daniel Giamouridis. 2008. "Hedge Fund Pricing and Model Uncertainty." *Journal of Banking & Finance* 32:5, 741–753.

Wermers, Russ. 2000. "Mutual Fund Performance: An Empirical Decomposition into Stock-Picking Talent, Style, Transactions Costs, and Expenses." *Journal of Finance* 55:4, 1655–1695.

28

Performance of Global Mutual Funds

TARIK BAZGOUR
Research Assistant and PhD Candidate in Finance, HEC-University of Liège

LAURENT BODSON
Affiliate Professor of Finance, HEC-University of Liège

DANIELLE SOUGNÉ
Professor of Finance, HEC-University of Liège

Introduction

U.S. global and international mutual funds offer U.S. investors a convenient vehicle for gaining exposure to global markets. *International mutual funds* are funds investing only in non-U.S. assets. By contrast, *global mutual funds* are those offering exposure to the United States with foreign markets. In recent years, the total net asset value (NAV) of world (global and international) mutual funds has grown tremendously. For example, according to the Investment Company Institute (2014), between 2004 and 2013, U.S. world equity mutual fund assets attracted total inflows of $626 billion, while U.S. domestic funds recorded cumulative outflows of $487 billion over the same time period. Despite the strong demand for these types of funds, they receive little attention in academia. These funds differ from U.S. domestic funds in the nature of risks they bear as they engage in global investing. Thus, their performance should be assessed using appropriate measures.

This chapter provides a selective review of the methods for evaluating global portfolio performance and the evidence on the performance of global and international mutual funds. The first section discusses potential sources of systematic risk in the performance of global mutual funds. The second section presents appropriate performance measures and reviews the evidence they have produced for these types of funds. In this section, performance measures are divided into three broad groups: (1) stock selection measures based on systematic risk; (2) stock selection measures based on absolute risk; and (3) market-timing measures. The third section discusses empirical findings on whether global funds provide diversification benefits to U.S. investors. In the fourth section, this chapter discusses the traits that help to determine the performance of global mutual funds.

Sources of Systematic Risk in Global Mutual Fund Returns

An accurate performance evaluation requires an in-depth understanding of the sources of systematic risk in the operation of mutual funds. Through an awareness of the sources of systematic risk, investors can accurately assess fund managers' performance on a risk-adjusted basis.

To evaluate the performance of U.S. domestic equity funds, for example, investors rely on multifactor models such as the Carhart (1997) four-factor model that includes a momentum factor in addition to the Fama–French (1993) three factors (market, size, and value). The model is widely accepted among academics and professionals. However, for investors focusing on global mutual funds, the situation is far more complex. Not only do they need to know which markets they should consider, but they also have to consider the relationship between the different markets. Additionally, the effect of exchange rate risk on international asset returns is a cause of disagreement among researchers.

So far, no consensus exists about the set of factors driving global markets. To deal with this complexity, researchers usually rely on broad multifactor models when assessing the performance of global mutual funds. These models come with their own endogenous biases or assumptions about the relative importance of the set of selected factors. The following sections present factors that are widely used by researchers as sources of systematic risk. The aim is not to highlight the importance of each factor but rather to shed light on the debate as a whole and clarify each argument.

GLOBAL VERSUS LOCAL MARKET RISK

Global mutual funds invest in multiple countries around the world. When evaluating these types of funds, investors have three options: (1) to consider the exposure of global fund managers to the global market as a single market, (2) to consider their exposures to each country in which they are investing, or (3) to consider both local and global factors. The favored solution depends on the assumption as to whether international financial markets are integrated, segmented, or partially segmented.

In an integrated market, national markets are assumed to be fully globalized. Thus, investors should consider only the asset's exposure to the world market portfolio (Solnik 1974; Adler and Dumas 1983). Many studies on financial market integration such as Phylaktis and Ravazzolo (2005) show that national markets have become increasingly integrated. Lewis (2011) argues that the financial crisis of 2007–2008 reveals the high degree of connectivity among international financial markets. However, other studies highlight that markets are still segmented and emphasize the importance of assets' exposures to local factors. For example, Harvey (1995) shows that emerging markets' returns display relatively little sensitivity to global risk factors and show strong exposure to local risk factors. Another body of studies such as Karolyi and Stulz (2003) suggests that international markets are partially segmented. These studies highlight that both local and global risk factors drive returns in international markets. These differences in attitudes to market integration have led to disagreements about the right way to evaluate the performance of global mutual funds. Some researchers assume that markets are fully integrated and consider only the sensitivity of fund returns to global risk factors, while other researchers consider the effect of local factors.

GLOBAL VERSUS LOCAL STYLE FACTORS

U.S. style factors such as size, value, and momentum have become common practice in the performance evaluation of U.S. portfolio managers. The key success of these factors lies in their ability to account for some anomalous patterns in U.S. stock returns. However, using U.S. style factors to assess the performance of global mutual funds poses problems. These types of funds invest in markets worldwide and are not limited to the U.S. markets. Motivated by their success in the U.S. market, many researchers use broad style factors that span the global markets. Still their ability to explain anomalous patterns in international stock returns is questionable.

Fama and French (2012), for example, examine the ability of both local and global style factors to explain anomalous patterns in the global and regional stock markets. Although global style factors perform well with global portfolios based on size, value, and momentum characteristics, these global factors fail to explain expected returns of micro-cap stocks and regional portfolios. Conversely, local style factors perform well in Europe, Japan, and North America, but they fail to explain average returns in Asia Pacific. In another notable work, Hou, Karolyi, and Kho (2011) use a large set of firm characteristics and examine which set of global factors can better explain expected returns in the global stock market. The authors propose, instead, a three-factor model that includes momentum and cash flow/price in addition to the world market portfolio.

CURRENCY RISK

Another question that arises in the performance evaluation of global mutual funds is whether to consider currency risk. Global fund managers hold assets denominated in foreign currencies. Besides ordinary market risk, the dollar value of their holdings is also exposed to the overall fluctuations of foreign currencies relative to the U.S. dollar. If the dollar rises, the dollar value of foreign holdings falls. Conversely, if the dollar declines, the dollar value of foreign holdings rises. Thus, the dollar return earned by global fund managers is highly sensitive to changes in the value of foreign currencies against the U.S. dollar. The question of whether currency risk is a source of systematic risk in international assets is still controversial.

The theory of purchasing power parity (PPP), which is based on the law of one price, states that all changes in exchange rates merely reflect changes in inflation rates between countries. Consequently, in a world in which PPP holds, currency risk is not priced. Conversely, Solnik (1974) shows that, in a world in which PPP fails to hold, currency risk should be priced in international asset returns. To test whether currency risk is priced as an additional risk factor, several theoretical and empirical models test unconditional and conditional international asset pricing models that include both the world market portfolio and currency risk. The results from empirical tests yield conflicting conclusions. Jorion (1991) finds that currency risk is not priced. In contrast, Dumas and Solnik (1995), De Santis and Gerard (1998), and Lustig and Verdelhan (2007) among others find supporting evidence that currency risk is priced.

Performance of Global Mutual Funds

Mutual fund managers are generally evaluated by their ability to provide superior performance on a risk-adjusted basis. Sharpe (1966) is the first author to propose a measure to evaluate the risk-adjusted performance of portfolio managers. Since his seminal work, researchers have proposed many other measures. Cogneau and Hübner (2009a, b) identify more than 100 measures based on survey results. Furthermore, the authors divide the measures into multi-level homogeneous categories. Based on their classification methodology, Figure 28.1 presents a summary of the different categories as well as the traditional measures of performance in the literature.

Active managers can produce superior performance through either superior stock selection or market-timing skills. Therefore, performance metrics can be divided initially into two broad groups based on the skills they measure: stock selection measures and market-timing metrics. Performance measures reflecting stock selection skills are further divided into three subsections based on the way the measure adjusts for risk: return-based ratios, return-based differences, and preference-based measures.

The category of return-based ratios contains all measures computed by dividing a fund manager's return by some risk measure. Within this category, risk is measured in several ways. Some measures consider risk in absolute terms such as the Sharpe's (1966) ratio and all its modified versions. Other measures are based on systematic risk such as the Treynor ratio (Treynor 1965) or the modified Jensen's alpha (Jensen 1968). A third

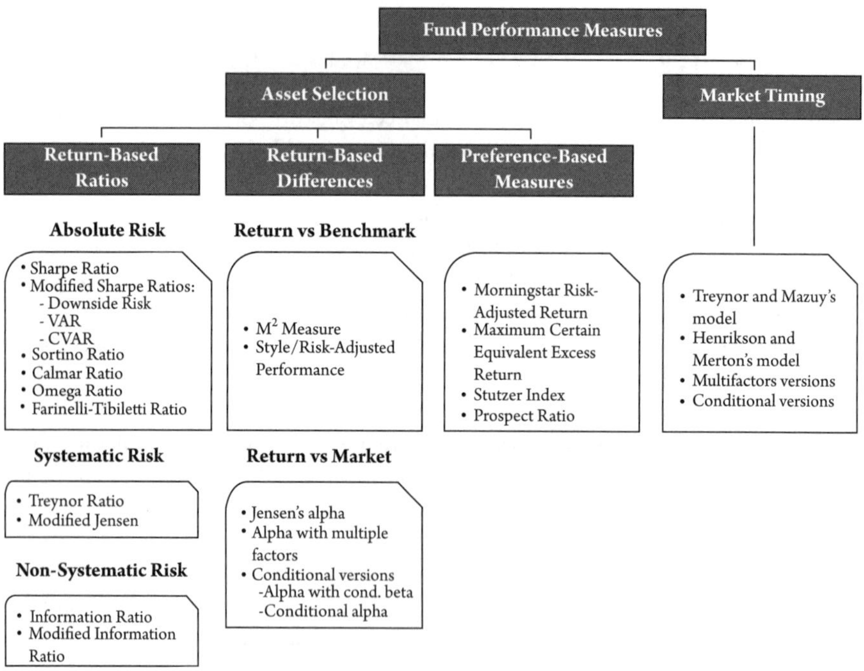

Figure 28.1 Classification Tree of Performance Measures.

set of measures is based on the non-systematic risk term such as the information ratio (Treynor and Black 1973).

The category of return-based differences covers measures that adjust for risk by subtracting a penalty from the absolute fund return. This category can be, in turn, subdivided into two main subsections. Measures that subtract a penalty from the absolute return using a benchmark index include the M squared measure of Modigliani and Modigliani (1997) or the style/risk-adjusted measure. Other measures such as the Jensen's alpha (Jensen 1968) rely on an asset pricing model.

Finally, the category of preference-based measures uses some utility function to account for the investors' risk preferences. Within this subsection, for instance, the Stutzer's index (Stutzer 2000) and the Morningstar risk-adjusted return (Morningstar 2007) are widely used in practice.

STOCK SELECTION MEASURES BASED ON SYSTEMATIC RISK

Risk-adjusted performance measures based on systematic risk are among the metrics commonly used to evaluate U.S. domestic funds. The advantage of this class of metrics, called *alpha measures*, is that they allow quantification of the abnormal return generated by a portfolio manager relative to a passive benchmark portfolio with similar exposures to a set of systematic risk factors. A significant positive alpha suggests that the fund manager has stock selection skills. These alpha measures rely mainly on standard asset pricing models that explain the dynamics of U.S. stock returns. The Jensen's (1968) alpha, based on the domestic capital asset pricing model (CAPM), considers only the domestic market portfolio as a source of systematic risk. An alpha based on the Fama–French three-factor model considers size and value factors as sources of risks (Fama and French 1993), while alpha based on the four-factor Carhart model adds the momentum factor as an additional source of risk (Carhart 1997).

An outstanding issue is whether these metrics based on domestic asset pricing models can accurately evaluate the performance of international and global fund managers. These types of funds hold foreign assets that are exposed to other global market risks not considered by domestic factor models. Furthermore, foreign assets are exposed to currency risk. Since these assets are denominated in foreign currency, any change in the exchange rate will affect their dollar value. The success of the risk-adjusted performance measures based on systematic risk, in evaluating U.S. domestic fund managers' skills, has motivated researchers to extend their use to an international context. To this end, several international asset pricing models have been proposed in literature on the subject. So far, all the proposed models suffer from several critical issues, and none is fully able to model the dynamics of stock returns in international markets.

The next section presents the well-known international factor models used by researchers to measure the stock-picking ability of global fund managers. This section also discusses specific issues with each model and presents evidence on the performance of global mutual funds.

Alpha Based on the World Capital Asset Pricing Model

Unlike domestic mutual funds, global funds can invest in both domestic and foreign assets. They provide investors with a large opportunity set with international

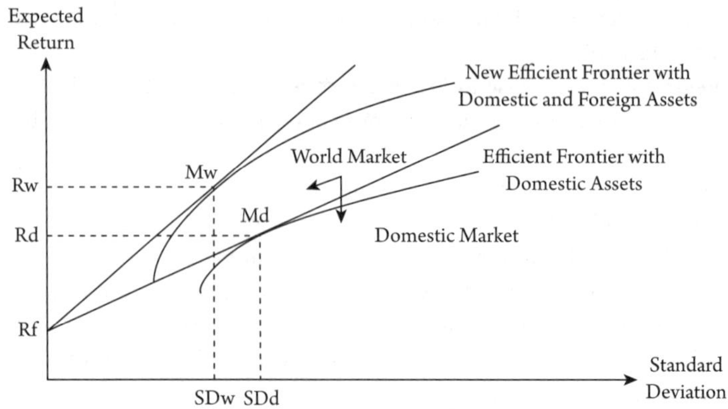

Figure 28.2 EFFICIENT FRONTIER FOR INTERNATIONALLY DIVERSIFIED PORTFOLIOS.

diversification benefits. To explain the benefits of global funds, Figure 28.2 displays the efficient frontier with only domestic assets, as well as the new efficient frontier when foreign assets are added to the investment opportunity set. The new efficient frontier provides lower risk for each expected return level as compared to the domestic efficient frontier.

As global funds hold both domestic and foreign assets in their portfolios, their returns are expected to correlate with the world market rather than the domestic market. Thus, using the standard Jensen's alpha (Jensen 1968) for performance evaluation may yield incorrect conclusions. Jensen's alpha is based on the domestic CAPM model, which is not well suited to model the dynamics of international asset returns. As a result, computing the fund's alpha measure based on the domestic portfolio may not capture all its systematic risk, and therefore may misprice the manager's stock selection ability.

Stulz (1981) and Adler and Dumas (1983) provide conditions under which the domestic CAPM can be extended to a single-factor model based on the global market portfolio. Theoretically, a world CAPM could explain the cross-section of international asset returns if national markets are perfectly integrated and PPP holds. This model assumes that national markets are perfectly open to foreign investors and implies that assets with the same risk level will have the same price regardless of where they are traded. PPP implies no currency risk because any fluctuation in the exchange rate will simply mirror inflation differentials.

Despite its unrealistic assumptions, many researchers build on the world CAPM model when evaluating the performance of global fund managers. It is usually used in combination with other risk-adjusted measures (Cumby and Glen 1990; Detzler 1999; Arugaslan, Edwards, and Samant 2007; Breloer, Scholz, and Wilkens 2014). Professional organizations such as Morningstar also use alpha based on the world CAPM and can be estimated by regression analysis using Equation 28.1:

$$R_{p,t} = \alpha_p + \beta_p R_{w,t} + \varepsilon_{p,t}, \tag{28.1}$$

where $R_{p,t}$ denotes the excess return on the global equity fund p; $R_{w,t}$ is the excess return on the world market portfolio; and α_p measures the fund p's stock selection ability. A significant and positive α_p indicates the fund manager has captured excess risk-adjusted returns by a particular strategy such as having superior stock selection skills. However, no consensus exists among researchers about the empirical proxy for the world market portfolio. Overall, researchers focusing on global equity funds use either the MSCI World index that measures the equity performance of the 23 developed countries (Cumby and Glen 1990), the MSCI ACWI that includes securities from both emerging and developed markets (Breloer et al. 2014), or the MSCI EAFE index that only contains securities from the 21 developed markets excluding the United States and Canada (Arugaslan et al. 2007). For global bond funds, researchers also use global bond indices such as Salomon Brothers World Government Bond Index (Detzler 1999).

Alpha Based on the World Capital Asset Pricing Model with Currency Risk

Solnik (1974) shows that in a world in which PPP fails to hold, currency risk should be priced in international asset returns. Several authors including Dumas and Solnik (1995) and De Santis and Gerard (1998) have subsequently reviewed the PPP hypothesis in world CAPM models and developed international asset pricing models that include both the world market portfolio and currency risk. Since global fund managers invest in international assets, many researchers consider currency risk in the performance evaluation of these types of funds. To this end, they adopt the index model shown in Equation 28.2 to detect abnormal performance:

$$R_{p,t} = \alpha_p + \beta_p R_{w,t} + \gamma_p R_{x,t} + \varepsilon_{p,t}, \tag{28.2}$$

where $R_{p,t}$ is the excess return on the global equity fund p; $R_{w,t}$ is the excess return on the world market portfolio; and $R_{x,t}$ is the excess return on a currency risk factor. In Equation 28.2, α_p measures the fund p's stock selection ability after controlling for the currency effect.

Cumby and Glen (1990) are the first to use the world CAPM with currency risk to evaluate the performance of 15 U.S. global equity funds between 1982 and 1988. Their two-factor model includes the MSCI World index and a currency risk factor. To proxy for the currency risk factor, the authors construct an equally weighted portfolio of Eurocurrency deposits in seven currencies. The performance evaluation shows no evidence of a superior performance by fund managers.

Gallo and Swanson (1996) also consider currency risk when evaluating the performance of 37 U.S.-based international equity funds during the period 1985 to 1993. They adopt two models: (1) the world CAPM with currency risk and (2) the international arbitrage pricing theory (IAPT) model. In their first model, the authors include the MSCI World index and the D131 Dollar index, a trade-weighted currency index of 131 countries. In the IAPT model, Gallo and Swanson assume the model shown in Equation 28.3:

$$R_{p,t} = \alpha'_p + \beta_p f_{1,t} + \gamma_p f_{2,t} + \varepsilon_{p,t}, \tag{28.3}$$

where $R_{p,t}$ is the excess return on the global equity fund p; and $f_{1,t}$ and $f_{2,t}$ are factor scores of two common factors as obtained by performing principal factor analysis. The two common factors are extracted from a set of factors that include the excess returns of indices of 17 countries, the U.S.-based Wilshire 5000 index, in addition to the excess currency return of 17 countries. The values α_p and α'_p in Equations 28.1 and 28.2 measure the risk-adjusted performance of fund p after controlling for the effect of currency risk.

Using the two models, Gallo and Swanson (1996) obtain conflicting conclusions. The world CAPM with currency risk model shows no evidence of stock selection ability among fund managers. Conversely, the IAPT two-factor model shows that fund managers generate significant abnormal returns. The authors also test which model performs well for international funds. The results show that the two-factor IAPT model presents superior explanatory power in comparison to the world CAPM with currency risk model.

The use of the world CAPM with currency risk can also be found in the work of Turtle and Zhang (2012), who examine the conditional performance of the U.S., developed, and emerging markets funds between 1989 and 2009. The authors focus on the conditional performance of funds during bull and bear times. To this end, they use various Markov switching regime models with one and two factors. The factors are the world market portfolio as proxied by the MSCI All Country World Index (ACWI) and a currency risk factor. Turtle and Zhang use excess returns on the trade-weighted exchange index as the currency risk factor. They conduct out-of-sample tests to evaluate the ability of the various models to forecast fund performance. The tests show that the world CAPM with the exchange rate factor has superior forecasting power. The outputs from this model reveal that emerging market funds outperform during bull markets.

Alpha Based on Global Multi-Style Factors

Evidence shows that size, value, and momentum factors, commonly known as *style factors*, significantly improve the ability of the CAPM model in explaining expected returns in the U.S. stock market. Their use has become common practice in the performance evaluation of U.S. domestic funds (Carhart 1997; Fama and French 2010). According to Fama and French (2010, p. 1918), style factors can be seen as “diversified passive benchmark returns that capture patterns in average returns”. When added to the market factor, they allow a better measure of stock selection skills. The success of multi-style factor models in the performance evaluation of U.S. domestic fund managers has pushed researchers to use their international versions to assess the performance of global and international equity funds. More formally, researchers adopt the multi-style factor model shown in Equation 28.4:

$$R_{p,t} = \alpha_p + \beta_{1,p}R_{w,t} + \beta_{2,p}SMB_{w,t} + \beta_{3,p}HML_{w,t} + \left(\beta_{4,p}MOM_{w,t}\right) + \varepsilon_{p,t}, \qquad (28.4)$$

where $R_{p,t}$ is the excess return on the global equity fund p; $R_{w,t}$ is the excess return on the world market portfolio; and $SMB_{w,t}$, $HML_{w,t}$, and $MOM_{w,t}$ denote the excess return on global size, value, and momentum factors, respectively. In this model, α_p measures the fund p's stock selection ability after controlling for the global style effects. The model can be implemented as either a stock-based model (Ferreira, Keswani, Miguel, and Ramos 2013; Busse, Goyal, and Wahal 2014) or an index-based model (Breloer et al. 2014). Users of stock-based models construct style factors considering the whole universe of stocks, while users of index-based models construct their factors based on global style indices such as MSCI style indices.

Busse et al. (2014) use both the global three-factor and four-factor models to analyze the performance of global equity funds between 1991 and 2009. They find that, on average, the studied funds show no evidence of superior performance. Breloer et al. argue that the global four-factor model does not control for index momentum strategies based on country and sector indices. As a result, the model may overestimate the stock selection ability of fund managers, especially those managers who take advantage of these passive strategies. To test their claim, the authors study the performance of 287 global and 704 international U.S.-based equity funds, using monthly returns between 1996 and 2009. They assess the funds' performance by using a five-factor model that includes country and sector momentum factors in addition to the international version of the Fama–French (1993) three-factor model. The authors construct the country momentum factor using MSCI indices of 23 countries from developed markets and MSCI indices of 22 countries from emerging markets. Breloer et al. form the sector momentum strategy from 10 MSCI sector indices. Their evidence shows that more than 50 percent of the studied funds load significantly on at least one of their index-based momentum factors. Furthermore, the results show that Fama and French's three-factor model overprices the risk-adjusted performance of fund managers who exhibit high exposure to index momentum. A risk-adjusted performance based on the three-factor model may show fund managers as stock picking simply because they take advantage of index momentum strategies. Overall, the authors find no evidence of stock selection skills among both international and global mutual funds.

Larrymore and Rodriguez (2007) also propose a global multifactor model to assess the performance of *global asset allocation mutual funds*, which are hybrid funds that dynamically shift their exposures between equity, bonds, and cash to take advantage of changes in the world market conditions. The authors argue that classical risk-adjusted performance measures based on fixed benchmark models may fail to correctly assess the performance of this type of fund. Instead, they propose a methodology to assess the funds using the funds' own dynamic benchmarks. To this end, Larrymore and Rodriguez rely on the Sharpe analysis to dynamically construct monthly benchmarks from daily data. The benchmarks are a mix of a world equity index, world bond index, and cash index. They also examine whether the fund outperformed its benchmark as computed from data on the past month. The authors find strong evidence that global asset allocation funds outperform the market.

Alpha Based on Local Multi-Style Factors

The main drawback of measures based on global multi-style factor models is that they may fail to correctly explain expected returns of some international assets. As a result, their use in performance evaluation of global mutual funds may yield incorrect judgments about the fund manager's skill. Fama and French (2012), for example, report that their global four-factor model fails to explain expected returns of micro-cap stocks and regional portfolios. The reason for this finding is that markets are not fully integrated. Thus, markets still depend on local factors.

To address this issue for global equity funds, Comer and Rodriguez (2012) examine how the choice of the benchmark model may influence the risk-adjusted performance of international and global equity funds between 1999 and 2010. Based on an analysis of funds' regional data holdings, the authors find that the one-factor and the international version of the Fama–French three-factor model tend to overestimate risk-adjusted performance of some funds. Indeed, global funds tilting their portfolios toward emerging and Pacific funds are rewarded mistakenly as good stock pickers. The authors divide international stock markets into four regions—the United States, Europe, Pacific, and emerging market—and advocate using a local multi-style factor model. Equation 28.5 shows their 12-factor model:

$$R_{p,t} = \alpha_p + \sum_{reg=1}^{4} \beta_{p,reg} R_{reg,t} + \sum_{reg=1}^{4} \gamma_{p,reg} SMB_{reg,t} + \sum_{reg=1}^{4} \theta_{p,reg} HML_{reg,t} + \varepsilon_p, \qquad (28.5)$$

where $R_{p,t}$ is the excess return on the global equity fund p; and $R_{reg,t}$, $SMB_{reg,t}$, $HML_{reg,t}$ denote the excess return on the regional market portfolio, size, and value factors, respectively. In this model, α_p measures fund p's stock selection ability using regional factors instead of global factors. Comer and Rodriguez claim the 12-factor model shows a superior ability to assess fund managers' skills as compared to various global factor models. The R^2 of their model ranges between 0.89 and 0.99. Overall, results based on the local 12-factor model show no evidence of fund managers' selection skills among both international and global equity funds.

Detzler (1999) also uses local multifactor models to evaluate the performance of U.S. global bond funds. In her analysis, she adopts three local multifactor models. The first one is a 10-factor model that includes a U.S. corporate bond factor, a U.S. government bond factor, and government bond indices of four countries, including the excess returns of their corresponding exchange rates. The government bond indices are in local currencies and include Canada, the United Kingdom, Germany, and Japan. The second one is six-factor model that contains the U.S. government and corporate bond factors in addition to the dollar-denominated excess returns on the four government indices. The third local model includes the same factors as the second model but with currency-hedged indices instead of unhedged indices.

Detzler (1999) contends that these model specifications can capture the funds' exposures to the different countries from different perspectives. The first model can separately describe the funds' exposure to the major market participants as well as to their corresponding exchange rate movements. The model with unhedged indices assumes that global bond funds do not hedge their positions against currency risk. Finally, the third model supposes that the funds' positions are fully hedged against currency risk.

Overall, three main conclusions can be drawn from Detzler's study. First, global bond funds do not show superior performance after expenses relative to the various benchmarks. Second, results from the 10-factor model reveal that the funds exhibit significant exposure to the exchange rate factors suggesting that currency risk is priced in global bond fund returns. Finally, the poor explanatory power of the model with hedged indices suggests that global mutual funds use hedging strategies superior to the full-hedging strategy.

STOCK SELECTION MEASURES BASED ON ABSOLUTE RISK

Alpha measures based on international factor models are the metrics most commonly used by researchers focusing on the performance evaluation of international and global mutual funds. On the whole, researchers use a broad set of factors that cover international markets. Yet, owing to the complexity of these markets, no consensus exists to date on the most appropriate international factor model to use. So, these alpha measures may fail to accurately assess the performance of these kinds of funds.

Alternatively, some researchers rely also on the Sharpe (1966) ratio to assess the performance of international and global mutual funds. The Sharpe ratio is a risk-adjusted performance measure based on total risk and is computed as shown in Equation 28.6:

$$SR_p = \frac{E(R_{p,t})}{\sigma(R_{p,t})}, \tag{28.6}$$

where $R_{p,t}$ is the excess return on the global mutual fund p; $E(R_{p,t})$ is the fund's expected excess return; and $\sigma(R_{p,t})$ is the standard deviation of the fund's excess returns. According to Gallo and Swanson (1996), the advantage of this measure in the performance evaluation of global mutual funds is that it does not depend directly on a benchmark market portfolio. The authors use the measure to compare the performance of 15 international equity funds to that of the MSCI World index. Overall, as measured by absolute risk, no difference exists in the performance of international equity funds and the MSCI World index.

Polwitoon and Tawatnuntachai (2006) also use the Sharpe ratio to assess the performance of 188 U.S. global bond funds during the period 1993 to 2004. The authors examine the performance of global bond funds relative to three world bond indices as well as in comparison to a comparable set of domestic bond funds. The selected bond indices are: (1) the Salomon Smith Barney World Government Bond (SBWG) index, (2) the SBWG ex. U.S. index, and (3) the currency-hedged SBWG index. The results reveal that, on average, global bond funds underperform all three world bond indices based on both absolute return and the Sharpe ratio. Furthermore, the authors document that the currency-hedged index has the highest Sharpe ratio, highlighting the importance of hedging with international bonds. When compared to U.S. domestic funds, global funds produce higher returns and comparable risk-adjusted returns to those of U.S. domestic funds. Additionally, exchange rate risk negatively and significantly affects the difference in the returns between global and domestic funds.

In a similar work, Polwitoon and Tawatnuntachai (2008) use the Sharpe ratio to evaluate the performance of U.S.-based emerging market funds relative to the performance of their comparable global and domestic bond funds between 1996 and 2005. The authors find that emerging market funds underperform against their benchmark indices but they outperform U.S. domestic and global funds. The difference in returns between emerging bond funds and comparable bond funds is weakly related to exchange rate changes and is driven rather by liquidity and country-specific risks. The authors argue that the weak effect of exchange rate changes is justified by the fact that more than 50 percent of emerging bonds in the funds are denominated in U.S. dollars.

MARKET-TIMING MEASURES

Active fund managers can outperform the market through either stock selection or market timing. The previous section only covered measures that assess stock selection skills of global mutual funds. In this section, the focus is on market-timing measures. According to Aragon and Ferson (2006, p. 86), *market timing* refers to the ability of fund managers to "use superior information about the future realizations of common factors that affect overall market returns." To study the timing skills of global mutual funds, researchers typically built on the Treynor and Mazuy (1966) model as expressed in Equation 28.7:

$$R_{p,t} = \alpha_p + \beta_p R_{w,t} + \gamma_p R_{w,t}^2 + \varepsilon_{p,t}, \tag{28.7}$$

where $R_{p,t}$ is the excess return on the global equity fund p; and $R_{w,t}$ is the excess return on the world market portfolio.

Based on the Treynor and Mazuy (TM) model, Cumby and Glen (1990), Gallo and Swanson (1996), and Glassman and Riddick (2006) examine the market-timing ability of U.S. international and global equity funds at the fund level. Each study documents negative market timing among equity fund managers. Rodriguez (2008) uses the TM measure to assess market-timing ability of 27 U.S. global asset allocation funds over the period 2001 to 2005. This type of fund dynamically shifts its exposures among equity, bonds, and cash to take advantage of changes in the world market conditions. The classical TM measure shows that most global allocation fund managers exhibit a significant negative market-timing ability. However, Rodriguez argues that the measure is not well suited for U.S. global asset allocation funds. Instead, he uses two multi-factor extensions of the measure similar to those introduced in Comer (2006): (1) a stock-extended model and (2) a stock- and bond-extended model. The first model is expressed in Equation 28.8:

$$R_{p,t} = \alpha_p + \beta_{p,1} R_{small,t} + \gamma_p R_{small,t}^2 + \beta_{p,2} R_{growth,t} + \beta_{p,3} R_{value,t} + \varepsilon_{p,t}, \tag{28.8}$$

where $R_{p,t}$ is the excess return on the fund p; and $R_{small,t}$, $R_{growth,t}$, and $R_{value,t}$ are MSCI global indices for small, value, and growth stocks, respectively. In Equation 28.8, γ_p measures the fund manager's stock-timing skill. For the second model, the author adopts the settings shown in Equation 28.9:

$$R_{p,t} = \alpha_p + \beta_{p,1} R_{small,t} + \gamma_{p,1} R_{small,t}^2 + \beta_{p,2} R_{treasury,t} + \gamma_{p,2} R_{treasury,t}^2 + \sum_{j=1}^{6} \theta_j R_{j,t} + \varepsilon_{p,t}, \tag{28.9}$$

where $R_{p,t}$ is the excess return on the fund p; $R_{small,t}$ and $R_{treasury,t}$ are the excess returns on global indices of small cap stock and treasury; $R_{j,t}$ is the excess return on two global stock indices (value and growth stocks) and four global bond indices (long and short maturity bonds, and high and low quality bonds). In Equation 28.9, $\gamma_{p,1}$ measures the fund manager's stock-timing skill.

Based on the two extended models, Rodriguez (2008) finds no evidence of a positive stock-timing skill. The results do not suggest a significant negative stock timing as indicated by the TM model. An examination of the explanatory power of the three models suggests that the stock- and bond-extended model has a higher average adjusted R^2 than the two other models. Therefore, Rodriguez advocates using multifactor models that control for both stock and bond factors when measuring market timing of global asset allocation funds.

Glassman and Riddick (2006) also examine another type of timing ability among U.S. global equity funds. The authors consider the national market-timing skill, which reflects the ability of fund managers to successfully shift their portfolios across national markets when any national market is expected to rise or to fall. Glassman and Riddick consider four national markets—Germany, Japan, the United Kingdom, and the United States—as well as an index for the "rest of world." Furthermore, to assess this type of timing skill, they extend the TM model to a multi-index model that includes the five national indices. Overall, global fund managers show no evidence of world market-timing skill, but they do exhibit strong evidence of national market-timing skills. The authors highlight that any assessment of global fund manager's timing ability should consider national market timing as fund managers are simultaneously shifting their investments from country to country while cash is considered only when they want to flee to safety.

Rodriguez (2014) investigates the timing ability of 94 global equity fund managers working between the U.S. market and international markets. The study explores whether fund managers successfully adjust their exposures between the two markets. To this end, Rodriguez partitions the monthly observations over the sample period 2001 to 2007 into two groups. The first group contains observations from months when the S&P 500 index outperformed the MSCI ex. U.S. index. The second group includes observations from months when the MSCI ex. U.S. index outperformed the S&P 500 index. For each group, the author performs a Sharpe style analysis to estimate the funds' exposure to the two benchmark indices and cash. Analyzing the difference in exposures between the two groups of months, Rodriguez finds no evidence of timing ability for the studied funds.

Global Mutual Funds and International Diversification

Global mutual funds provide a convenient vehicle for investors to access large and worldwide markets. Thus, global mutual funds can achieve low systematic risks using their capacity to benefit from many diversification opportunities. For instance, Cumby and Glen (1990) find that the outperformance of U.S. international equity funds over a representative U.S. index is a consequence of diversification benefits rather than superior performance created by the fund managers.

Other studies examine the impact of investing in global mutual funds for a domestic portfolio. For instance, Polwitoon and Tawatnuntachai (2006) consider the diversification benefits from adding global bond funds to a domicile portfolio from the perspective of U.S. investor holding either a domestic bond or a domestic equity fund. In both cases, a U.S. investor can gain from global investing by buying global bond funds. For example, the authors determine that a U.S. investor who holds U.S. domestic bond funds can enhance their annualized return by 0.5 to 1.0 percent without increasing risk. Polwitoon and Tawatnuntachai (2008) conclude that emerging markets create a renewed investment opportunity for U.S. investors who seek high-yield and international exposure. Other authors such as Gallo and Swanson (1996) and Detzler (1999) maintain that the benefits from diversifying globally may be offset by excessive charges and management fees.

Global Mutual Fund Characteristics and Performance

Several studies try to identify relationships between global mutual fund characteristics (e.g., expenses, size, and future fund flows) and their performance. For instance, Detzler (1999) and Polwitoon and Tawatnuntachai (2006) demonstrate that expense ratios negatively affect the risk-adjusted performance of global mutual funds. Their results are consistent with findings from domestic fund studies. Polwitoon and Tawatnuntachai also perform a regression analysis of performance on a larger set of global bond fund characteristics. The authors document that performance is negatively related to age and positively related to the average maturity of bonds in the fund.

Regarding the relationship between the fund size and its performance, Ferreira et al. (2013) find a negative correlation between fund size and performance among U.S. domestic funds. They do not find the same results in U.S. international mutual funds. To explain this relationship between performance and size, the authors perform further analyses and find that U.S. domestic funds tend to invest in small and illiquid stocks more than U.S. international funds. Therefore, the authors argue that when U.S. domestic funds become large, fund managers face liquidity constraints as they are limited to the U.S. market. As a result, fund size erodes performance because of liquidity constraints. In contrast, U.S. international funds do not suffer from liquidity constraints when they are getting larger because they have more investment opportunities available as they invest worldwide. Consequently, U.S. international fund size does not seem to have adverse effects on performance.

Comer and Rodriguez (2012) consider the relationship between risk-adjusted performance and future flows of international and global equity funds. Their results show little evidence about the effect of past performance on future flows. Conversely, Busse et al. (2014) study how future fund flows are related to past performance in a sample of international and global equity funds. Consistent with the existing results for domestic funds, they find a strong positive relationship between fund flows and past performance.

Summary and Conclusions

Global and international mutual funds invest in international assets and therefore give investors opportunities to access international markets. Unlike domestic funds that are exposed to domestic market movements, these types of funds are exposed to world market movements. Consequently, their performance must be assessed using appropriate performance measures.

This chapter outlines several measures that academic researchers propose to assess the performance of global and international mutual funds. It starts by discussing controversies associated with identifying sources of systematic risk in global fund returns.

The central questions considered are whether international markets are integrated or segmented and whether currency risk is a priced risk factor. Following this, several performance measures are presented and discussed. The chapter includes both stock selection and market-timing measures and reviews the evidence these measures have produced on the performance of global and international actively managed funds.

Overall, global fund managers do not seem to have stock-picking or market-timing skills. This finding contradicts the claims of proponents of global active management, who argue that international markets are less efficient than the U.S. market and can therefore be exploited by skilled portfolio managers.

The question of whether global funds provide diversification benefits to U.S. investors is also discussed. The empirical findings are mixed. While some authors document diversification benefits from investing in these types of funds, others find that international diversification is offset by excessive charges and management fees.

Discussion Questions

1. Explain why an alpha measure based on the domestic CAPM model is inappropriate for assessing the stock selection ability of a global mutual fund manager. Indicate in which situations an alpha measure based on the world CAPM can give accurate estimates.
2. U.S. global mutual funds hold assets denominated in foreign currencies. Thus, their dollar returns are exposed to changes in the value of foreign currencies against the U.S. dollar. Identify a situation in which currency risk becomes a priced risk factor.
3. Identify two ways to consider currency risk in an alpha measure based on an international asset pricing model.
4. Describe the difference between the world CAPM with a currency risk factor model and a two-factor IAPT model.
5. Indicate two situations in which an alpha measure based on the global three-factor model, which includes the world market portfolio, global size, and value factors, may fail to correctly estimate the stock selection ability of a global equity fund manager.
6. Discuss three types of global equity fund managers' timing skills.

References

Adler, Michael, and Bernard Dumas. 1983. "International Portfolio Choice and Corporation Finance: A Synthesis." *Journal of Finance* 38:3, 925–984.

Aragon, George O., and Wayne E. Ferson. 2006. "Portfolio Performance Evaluation." *Foundations and Trends in Finance* 2:2, 83–190.

Arugaslan, Onur, Ed Edwards, and Ajay Samant. 2007. "Risk-Adjusted Performance of International Mutual Funds." *Managerial Finance* 34:1, 5–22.

Breloer, Bernhard, Hendrik Scholz, and Marco Wilkens. 2014. "Performance of International and Global Equity Mutual Funds: Do Country Momentum and Sector Momentum Matter?" *Journal of Banking and Finance* 43:1, 58–77.

Busse, Jeffrey A., Amit Goyal, and Sunil Wahal. 2014. "Investing in a Global World." *Review of Finance* 18:2, 561–590.

Carhart, Mark M. 1997. "On Persistence in Mutual Fund Performance." *Journal of Finance* 52:1, 57–82.

Cogneau, Philippe, and Georges Hübner. 2009a. "The (More Than) 100 Ways to Measure Portfolio Performance. Part 1: Standardized Risk-Adjusted Measures." *Journal of Performance Measurement* 13:4, 56–71.

Cogneau, Philippe, and Georges Hübner. 2009b. "The (More Than) 100 Ways to Measure Portfolio Performance. Part 2: Special Measures and Comparison." *Journal of Performance Measurement* 14:1, 56–69.

Comer, George. 2006. "Hybrid Mutual Funds and Market Timing Performance." *Journal of Business* 79:2, 771–797.

Comer, George, and Javier Rodriguez. 2012. "International Mutual Funds: MSCI Benchmarks and Portfolio Evaluation." Working Paper, Georgetown University and University of Puerto Rico.

Cumby, Robert E., and Jack D. Glen. 1990. "Evaluating the Performance of International Mutual Funds." *Journal of Finance* 45:2, 497–521.

De Santis, Giorgio, and Bruno Gerard. 1998. "How Big Is the Premium for Currency Risk?" *Journal of Financial Economics* 49:3, 375–412.

Detzler, Miranda Lam. 1999. "The Performance of Global Bond Mutual Funds." *Journal of Banking and Finance* 23:8, 1195–1217.

Dumas, Bernard, and Bruno Solnik. 1995. "The World Price of Foreign Exchange Risk." *Journal of Finance* 50:2, 445–479.

Fama, Eugene F., and Kenneth R. French. 1993. "Common Risk Factors in the Returns on Stocks and Bonds." *Journal of Financial Economics* 33:1, 3–56.

Fama, Eugene F., and Kenneth R. French. 2010 "Luck Versus Skill in the Cross-Section of Mutual Fund Returns." *Journal of Finance* 65:5, 1915–1947.

Fama, Eugene F., and Kenneth R. French. 2012. "Size, Value, and Momentum in International Stock Returns." *Journal of Financial Economics* 105:3, 457–472.

Ferreira, Miguel A., Aneel Keswani, António F. Miguel, and Sofia B. Ramos. 2013. "The Determinants of Mutual Fund Performance: A Cross-Country Study." *Review of Finance* 17:2, 483–525.

Gallo, John G., and Peggy E. Swanson. 1996. "Comparative Measures of Performance for U.S. Based International Equity Mutual Funds." *Journal of Banking and Finance* 20:10, 1635–1650.

Glassman, Debra A., and Leigh A. Riddick. 2006. "Market Timing by Global Fund Managers." *Journal of International Money and Finance* 25:7, 1029–1050.

Harvey, Campbell R. 1995. "Predictable Risk and Returns in Emerging Markets." *Review of Financial Studies* 8:3, 773–816.

Hou, Kewei, G. Andrew Karolyi, and Bong-Chan Kho. 2011. "What Factors Drive Global Stock Returns?" *Review of Financial Studies* 24:8, 2527–2574.

Investment Company Institute. 2014. *2014 Investment Company Fact Book: A Review of Trends and Activities in the U.S. Investment Company Industry*, 54th edition. Washington, DC: Investment Company Institute. Available at http://www.ici.org.

Jensen, Michael C. 1968. "The Performance of Mutual Funds in the Period 1945–1964." *Journal of Finance* 23:2, 389–416.

Jorion, Philippe. 1991. "The Pricing of Exchange Rate Risk in the Stock Market." *Journal of Financial and Quantitative Analysis* 26:3, 363–376.

Karolyi, Andrew, and René M. Stulz. 2003. "Are Financial Assets Priced Locally or Globally?" In George M. Constantinides, Milton Harris, René M. Stulz, eds., *The Handbook of the Economics of Finance*, 975–1020. New York: North-Holland Publishers.

Larrymore, Norris L., and Javier Rodriguez. 2007. "Active Fund Management: Global Asset Allocation Funds." *Journal of Multinational Financial Management* 17:3, 244–256.

Lewis, Karen K. 2011. "Global Asset Pricing." Working Paper, National Bureau of Economic Research.

Lustig, Hanno, and Adrien Verdelhan. 2007. "The Cross Section of Foreign Currency Risk Premia and Consumption Growth Risk." *American Economic Review* 97:1, 89–117.

Modigliani, Franco, and Leah Modigliani. 1997. "Risk-Adjusted Performance." *Journal of Portfolio Management* 23:2, 45–54.

Morningstar. 2007. "The Morningstar Rating™ Methodology." Morningstar Methodology Paper.

Phylaktis, Kate, and Fabiola Ravazzolo. 2005. "Stock Market Linkages in Emerging Markets: Implications for International Portfolio Diversification." *Journal of International Financial Markets, Institutions and Money* 15:2, 91–106.

Polwitoon, Sirapat, and Oranee Tawatnuntachai. 2006. "Diversification Benefits and Persistence of U.S.-Based Global Bond Funds." *Journal of Banking and Finance* 30:10, 2767–2786.

Polwitoon, Sirapat, and Oranee Tawatnuntachai. 2008. "Emerging Market Bond Funds: A Comprehensive Analysis." *Financial Review* 43:1, 51–84.

Rodríguez, Javier. 2008. "Market Timing: A Global Endeavor." *Journal of International Financial Markets, Institutions and Money* 18:5, 545–556.

Rodriguez, Javier. 2014. "The Forecasting Ability of World Mutual Funds." *Studies in Economics and Finance* 31:2, 130–140.

Sharpe, William F. 1966. "Mutual Fund Performance." *Journal of Business* 39:1, 119–138.

Solnik, Bruno H. 1974. "An Equilibrium Model of the International Capital Market." *Journal of Economic Theory* 8:4, 500–524.

Stulz, René M. 1981. "A Model of International Asset Pricing." *Journal of Financial Economics* 9:4, 383–406.

Stutzer, Michael. 2000. "A Portfolio Performance Index." *Financial Analysts Journal* 56:3, 52–61.

Treynor, Jack L. 1965. "How to Rate Management of Invested Funds." *Harvard Business Review* 43:1, 63–75.

Treynor, Jack L., and Fischer Black. 1973. "How to Use Security Analysis to Improve Portfolio Selection." *Journal of Business* 46:1, 66–86.

Treynor, Jack L., and Kay Mazuy. 1966. "Can Mutual Funds Outguess the Market?" *Harvard Business Review* 44:4, 131–136.

Turtle, Harry J., and Chengping Zhang. 2012. "Time-Varying Performance of International Mutual Funds." *Journal of Empirical Finance* 19:3, 334–348.

29

Performance of Exchange-Traded Funds

PANAGIOTIS SCHIZAS

Institute Banking and Finance, University of Zurich and Advisor at the Greek Ministry of Finance

Introduction

The first exchange-traded fund (ETF) was issued in 1993 on the American Stock Exchange with the name SPDRs, which stands for Standard & Poor's Depository Receipts or "Spiders," and tracks the S&P 500 index. ETFs have evolved considerably over time. According to Stone (2014), as of January 2014, more than 1,500 ETFs traded in the United States with over $1.7 trillion in assets.

ETFs are organized as regulated investment companies similar to mutual funds and closed-end funds (CEFs). Some refer to ETFs as "hybrid" mutual funds because they capture the dynamics of index-tracking unit trusts with the merits and tradability of listed investment companies. Compared to mutual funds and CEFs, ETFs have lower operating expenses, greater trading liquidity, and more efficient tax structures. ETFs also have the features of ordinary stock transactions.

ETFs can be acquired, held, and disposed either as short- or long-term market-timing investment strategies. They provide an economical way to rebalance portfolio allocations to achieve higher return, to "equitize" cash by investing it quickly, and to get an optimal yield through a diversified strategy. ETFs offer exposure to different markets, including broad-based domestic and international indices, country-specific indices, industry sector-specific indices, bond indices, commodities, and currencies. Most ETFs are index funds that attempt to replicate the performance of a specific index. They accomplish this goal by investing 100 percent of their assets proportionately in the securities underlying an index or 80 to 95 percent of their assets in the securities of an underlying index with the remainder in other holdings, such as futures, options, and swap contracts. Conventional mutual funds are bought or sold at the end of a day's trading, whereas ETFs can be traded whenever the market is open. As Gastineau (2002) points out, ETF investors can carry out the same types of trades as stocks including selling securities short, executing limit or stop-loss orders, and buying on margin.

The great expansion of ETFs has resulted in the emergence of new structures that allow investors and traders to potentially increase their returns. For example, as already discussed in previous chapters, two special types of ETFs—actively managed and leveraged ETFs—increase flexibility and allow market-timing strategies. Schizas (2014) provides information on actively managed versus passive ETFs, mutual funds, and hedge funds. Actively managed ETFs, which exhibit complete transparency in trading activities, are at risk from arbitrage activities by market participants who might front run its trades based as daily reports of the ETF's holdings. *Front running* is a practice in which traders execute orders taking advantage of advance knowledge of pending orders. In terms of performance, Bogle (2014) argues that higher hidden fees coming from trading opportunities requiring cash holdings reduce annual returns for investors by around 2.66 percentage points. These fees produce a huge differential considering that real returns from U.S. equities have averaged 6.45 percent since the 1970s. Even without considering hidden costs, higher fees negatively affect long-term performance.

The second special ETF type is the leveraged and inverse ETFs. Gallagher and Segara (2006), Svetina and Wahal (2008), Avellaneda and Zhang (2013), and Hassine and Roncalli (2013) provide a more detailed analysis of leveraged and inverse ETFs. Leverage ETFs use derivatives to achieve daily returns that could double or triple the gain or loss of the underlying market. A 2.5 percent increase in the index will reduce a –2x bear fund (i.e., a fund that provides a return twice the negative value of the underlying) by 5 percent.

Differences between the structure of ETFs and conventional mutual funds, also called open-end funds (OEFs) have raised many questions. A major question concerns performance. This chapter investigates the relative performance of ETFs to the market and the ability of achieving alpha or excess risk-adjusted returns using ETFs. The chapter also explores benchmark selection and considers alternatives to conventional index funds. The remainder of the chapter is organized as follows. The next section discusses factors affecting ETF performance. This presentation is followed by factors affecting performance. Methodology and empirical results are reported next followed by a summary and conclusions.

Factors Affecting Performance

Besides making fee comparisons, technical issues, tracking error, and liquidity considerations are important to examine when comparing an ETF to its underlying index. To understand each factor, this section analyses and presents specific characteristics that affect performance of the entire universe of ETFs. The absolute differences in return between how an ETF behaves in relation to the index it tracks is very important for a potential investor. An example of how these return differences occur in practice is given by differences in dividend reinvestment assumptions between index and fund. And differences in return between competing funds can easily outweigh differences, so, a potential investor is able to scrutinize these differences in performance versus the alternative options of a portfolio (i.e., mutual funds).

TRACKING ERROR

Tracking error is the difference between the returns of an ETF and its reference index or asset. It is computed based on the prevailing price of an ETF and its reference. Tracking error can affect performance forecasts. A nonzero tracking error represents a failure to replicate the reference index as stated in the ETF prospectus. Tracking error differs from a *premium* or *discount*, which is the difference between the ETF's market price and its net asset value (NAV). For buy-and-hold ETF investors, the performance difference between a fund and its index is likely to be the most important measure of the fund's performance.

Tracking errors are more relevant when the ETF provider uses strategies other than full replication of the underlying index. By definition, an ETF can invest 100 percent of its assets proportionately in the securities underlying an index (full replication) or 80 percent to 95 percent of its assets in the securities of an underlying index with the remainder in other holdings such as futures, options, and swaps. Thus, in the latter case, tracking error increases due to the deviation. Some of the most liquid equity ETFs tend to have better tracking error performance because the underlying asset is also sufficiently liquid, allowing for full replication. In contrast, ETFs such as commodities ETFs or leveraged ETFs do not necessarily use full replication because the physical assets cannot be stored easily, or used to create a leveraged exposure, or the reference asset or index is illiquid. Deductions from the NAV are one cause of the tracking difference between a fund and its index. As expenses accrue across time, they do not create tracking error or performance volatility.

Futures-based ETFs may also suffer from negative roll yields. A *negative roll yield* occurs when futures prices decrease toward an expected spot price as contracts near expiration. The volatility of an ETF's performance relative to its index is also an important type of tracking error. This ETF characteristic is highly relevant for anyone seeking to use it for short-term hedging purposes. ETFs tracking the same index may have comparable figures for tracking difference but very different tracking errors. The driving factors in the volatility in an ETF's return regarding its index include the following: (1) differences in optimization and sampling techniques; (2) rebalancing costs of an ETF including financial transaction costs and taxes; (3) differences in dividend reinvestment assumptions between the index and the fund; (4) corporate actions by the ETF firm; (5) *cash drag* (i.e., the loss in return from cash holdings in the ETF); (6) differences in the tax treatment of dividends between the index and the fund; and (7) and inefficient fund management.

LIQUIDITY

Besides technical issues and tracking error, market liquidity is a third performance measure of ETFs. Liquidity differences exist based on the flexibility and valuation transparency affecting an ETF's degree of tradability. ETFs are commonly listed on multiple exchanges, which sometimes results in sizable variations in exchange-based turnover and spreads. The most active ETFs such as S&P5000 (SPY), Russell 2000 (IWM), and NASDAQ 100 (QQQQ) are highly liquid because of their high volume resulting in tight spreads. As a result, Hegde and McDermott (2004) note that investors expect to get a "reasonable" price even during volatile market conditions. However, in contrast to mutual funds, same day trades in less liquid ETFs do not result in the same price for everyone because of the lack of a uniform market-pricing mechanism. So even during the same business day, an ETF's price depends on either the market maker's or the stock exchange's price.

A large proportion of institutional ETF trading still takes place in the over-the-counter (OTC) market and goes unrecorded. This means that reported turnover figures often give an unnecessarily pessimistic impression of liquidity. ETFs provide the best liquidity to investors when a virtuous circle develops involving the fund and its market makers. That is, the final price depends on the market makers and the market price depends on the market value. More precisely, the liquidity of an ETF depends on the number of market makers involved, but market makers are attracted by ETFs with large on-exchange trading volumes. The duty of an ETF issuer is therefore to incentivize the largest possible number of secondary market participants in its funds. The way to increase liquidity is by contracting as much as possible with *authorized participants* (APs) to create and redeem units at the market price. Such actions provide APs with the flexibility of deal size.

The true secondary market liquidity of an ETF is measured by more than the fund's bid-ask spread, as recorded in an exchange's trading statistics. The *bid-ask* spread is the difference in price between the highest price that a buyer is willing to pay for an asset and the lowest price for which a seller is willing to sell it. In larger trade sizes, the *interquartile range* (i.e., the 50 percent of the distribution of the results falling between the 25th and 75th percentile) of bid-ask spreads for Euro STOXX 50 ETFs widens significantly, and market liquidity is highly correlated (Hassine and Roncalli 2013). In Figure 29.1, the notional trade size is given by the *x*-axis and varies from €100,000 to €2,000,000 for each fund. For each box plot, the shaded box shows the interquartile range, minimum value,

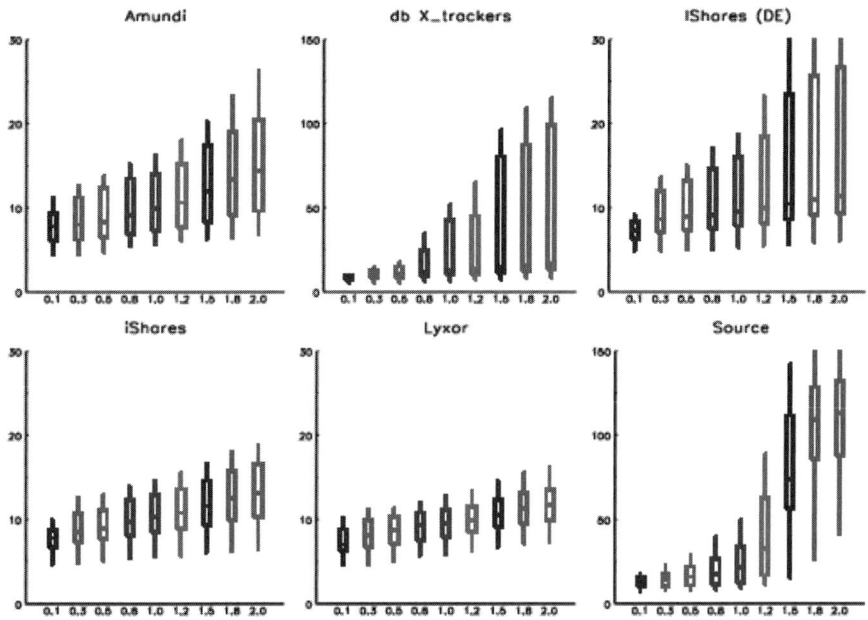

Figure 29.1 The Box Plot of Euro Stoxx 50 ETF. This figure shows the box plot of EuroStoxx 50 ETF bid-offer spreads of the basic ETF providers. The bid-offer spread is shown on the *y*-axis in percent. The analysis uses data from the NYSE Euronext Paris and German stock exchanges for 2012.

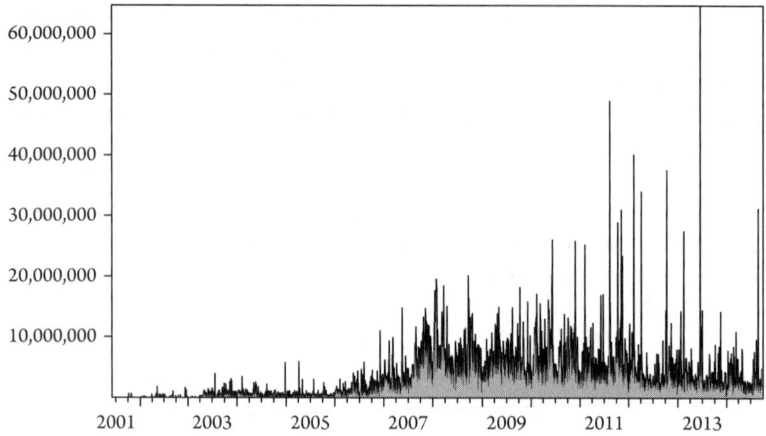

Figure 29.2 DAILY TRADING VOLUME EXCHANGE-TRADED FUND MSCI HONG-KONG. This figure plots the daily trading volume of iShares MSCI Hong-Kong (EWH), as shown on the *y*-axis, between June 2001 and April 2014.

quartile range, median spread, and last decile. Part of the tracking error is attributed to the proliferation of ETFs targeting exotic investments or areas where trading is less frequent, such as emerging-market stocks, future-contracts-based commodity indices, and junk bonds.

Liquidity by definition is based on daily volume. Figure 29.2 presents the trading volume of iShares MSCI Hong-Kong between 2001 and 2014. The figure shows that market liquidity in terms of trading volume has increased since 2005. The increase in the trading volume during the period of analysis is observed in the majority of the class signaling that ETFs have become more popular and thus more liquid among investors. Variations in secondary market liquidity will ultimately reflect the robustness of the secondary market infrastructure put in place by an issuer to support trading in its funds. Beyond this, any representative measure of ETF efficiency must account for variations in the depth of an exchange's secondary market order book.

Measuring Exchange-Traded Fund Performance

Four factors primarily affect ETF performance: (1) tracking cost efficiency, (2) management fees and transaction costs, (3) tax attribution, and (4) differences between the closing price and the NAV. This section explains the impact of each factor on the final performance of ETFs.

TRACKING COST EFFICIENCY

Kostovetsky (2003) points out the role that costs play in determining ETF performance. He assumes that over a one-year holding period an investor should have at least $60,000 invested in an ETF for the management fee and taxation savings to offset the transaction costs. This amount reduces to $13,000 for a long-term holding period of 10 years. From a cost perspective, ETFs have both advantages and disadvantages compared to traditional index funds. Directly comparing how ETFs handle these costs helps in making an informed decision when choosing between the two investment vehicles. The daily rebalancing occurring with index funds due to daily net redemptions results in explicit costs as commissions and implicit costs in the form of bid-ask spreads. Moreover, ETFs have the unique process of in-kind creation/redemption that avoids these transaction costs. *In-kind creation/redemption* means that the authorized participant borrows stock shares and places those shares in a trust using them to form ETF creation units. Then, the trust provides shares of the ETF. Because this transaction is an in-kind trade, securities are traded for securities. Because ETFs trade on an exchange, each transaction is generally subject to a brokerage fee. Boehmer and Boehmer (2003) discuss the segmentation of trading places. That is, brokerage or general transaction costs, varies among different trading venues. Such discrepancies may affect daily performance, which sometimes undercover potential losses/gains over the long-run period.

Sharpe (2013) brings a renewed focus on the impact of investment expenses on investors' financial well-being by offering methods for calculating relative terminal wealth levels for those investing in funds with different expense ratios. According to Sharpe, someone who saved by using a low-cost fund would have a standard of living in retirement considerably higher than someone who saved using a high-cost fund.

ETFs have an advantage over traditional index funds because cash drag affects the later. That is, traditional index funds need to hold cash to deal with potential daily net redemptions. ETFs do not incur this cash drag because of their aforementioned creation/redemption in-kind process. However, dividend policy is a drawback of ETFs compared to index funds. Index funds invest their dividends immediately, whereas the trust nature of ETFs requires them to accumulate this cash during the quarter until fund managers distribute it to shareholders at the end of each quarter.

MANAGEMENT FEES AND TRANSACTION COSTS

Non-tracking costs comprise three categories: (1) management fees, (2) shareholder transaction costs, and (3) taxes. Management fees are generally lower for ETFs than for mutual funds. Index funds involve two types of fees: transaction fees and the fees included in the fund's expense ratio. In mutual funds, transaction fees include sales loads (or sales charges) or redemption fees that investors pay directly. In comparison, ETF transactions include brokerage commissions, which investors pay directly.

The *expense ratio* represents a fund's operating costs divided by the average dollar value under management annually. The fund's prospectus reports the expense ratio. The largest and most variable part of the operating costs is usually the fee paid to the fund managers—the *management fee*. Operating costs can also include custodial services, recordkeeping, legal expenses, acquired fund fees and expenses (if the fund invests in other funds), accounting and auditing fees, and a marketing fee. Operating expenses are excluded, which lowers the return to the investors (Edelen, Evans, and Kadlec 2007). Since fees vary across funds, investors should understand all the fees associated with a fund they might purchase.

Table 29.1 **Annual Operating Expenses**

Sector	*Mutual Funds (%)*	*ETFs (%)*	*D (MF-ETFS) (%)*
U.S. large cap stocks	1.31	0.47	0.84
U.S. mid-cap stocks	1.45	0.56	0.89
U.S. small cap stocks	1.53	0.52	1.01
International stocks	1.57	0.56	1.01
Taxable bonds	1.07	0.30	0.77
Municipal bonds	1.06	0.23	0.83

Note: This table represents the annual total operating expenses in percent of several sectors of the existing peer group of mutual funds and ETFs. The expense ratio is for the fiscal year of 2013.

Table 29.1 shows the annual total operating expenses of the universe of the mutual funds and ETFs. At the start of 1985, only three S&P 500 index funds were available along with two small stock funds. This universe did not contain growth, value, or bond funds. The average expense ratio of the S&P 500 index funds was 1.24 percent a year compared to small stock funds at 0.875 percent a year. In 2014, the relative comparison between mutual funds and ETFs reveals substantially lower operating expenses for the ETFs. This difference is higher for U.S. small cap stocks and international stocks but less for taxable bonds and municipal bonds. As Table 29.1 shows for taxable and municipal ETFs versus mutual funds, the difference in expenses is high at 77 and 83 basis points, respectively. In general, traditional mutual funds have difficulty achieving the low expense ratios attained by ETFs, which helps to explain the growing popularity of ETFs.

TAX ATTRIBUTION

ETFs are structured to shield investors from capital gains taxes. Because most ETFs are index funds, they typically trade less often than actively managed funds and generate fewer taxable capital gains. A key difference between ETFs (active and index) is that investors buy and sell ETF shares with other investors on an exchange. As a result, the ETF manager does not have to sell holdings, potentially triggering capital gains, to meet investor redemptions. Mutual fund shareholders redeem shares directly from the fund. The fund manager must sell fund securities to honor redemptions, potentially triggering capital gains that affect all fund shareholders. ETF shareholders can incur tax consequences when they sell shares on the exchange, but that tax consequence is not passed on to other ETF shareholders (Pennathur, Delcoure, and Anderson 2002; Poterba and Shoven 2002).

ETFs are structured for tax efficiency and can be more attractive and profitable than mutual funds. In the United States, whenever a mutual fund realizes a capital gain that is not balanced by a realized loss, it must distribute the capital gains to its shareholders. This distribution occurs whenever the mutual fund sells portfolio securities, whether to reallocate its investments or to fund shareholder redemptions. These gains are taxable to all shareholders, even those who reinvest their gains in more fund shares. In contrast, ETFs are not redeemed by holders, but sell their ETF shares on the stock market, an action that affects non-taxable investors. Thus, investors typically realize capital gains only when they sell their shares or when the ETF trades to reflect changes in the underlying index. Furthermore, the tax-efficient structure of ETFs helps to increase investor performance compared to mutual funds. Although investors do not get all the tax advantages, they get an additional advantage from tax loss harvesting any capital losses from net redemptions.

CLOSING PRICE VERSUS NET ASSET VALUE

Investors buy and sell ETFs from a stock exchange throughout the day or at the NAV calculated, once per day, at the end of the day. Tucker and Laipply (2010) discuss the importance of premiums or discounts in the terminal performance in a portfolio. They contend that four factors account for the performance discrepancies: (1) the value of the underlying securities, (2) the level of ETF supply and demand in the secondary market, (3) the cost of share creation through the underlying fixed income markets, and (4) the level of fixed income market volatility and liquidity. Cherry (2004) emphasizes the importance of premiums or discounts in arbitrage opportunities. Returns to strategies that incorporate information in the variation of discounts outperform buy-and-hold strategies by 15 percent on an annualized basis, net of transaction costs, but only expose the investor to about one-fifth of the risk.

Figure 29.3, plots the monthly ratio of the closing market price including dividends versus the NAV. As Figure 29.3 shows, eliminating periods of turbulence, the closing price/NAV ratio ranges between a discount of 0.8 to a premium of 1.2 during the entire time horizon, During the financial crisis of 2007–2008, the ratio for ETFs remained at or below one, but by April 2009, the ratio started rising above one almost monotonically. After August 2013, the ratio exhibits extreme values in both sides. According to Salisbury (2008), during a period of market turbulence, some lightly traded ETFs exhibited divergence between the closing price and NAV of 5 percent or more, exceeding 10 percent in a few cases. However, even for these ETFs, the average deviation was only slightly more than 1 percent. In traditional index funds or in specific sectors such as fixed-income funds, higher fluctuations may substantially diminish portfolio performance.

EXCHANGE-TRADED FUND PERFORMANCE

The literature contains various studies about ETFs performance. Elton, Gruber, Comer, and Li (2002) examine Spiders tracking the S&P 500 index and find that they underperform the market by 28 basis points annually, as well as competing index funds by 18 basis points annually.

Jares and Lavin (2004) examine the pricing efficiency of ETFs compared to the value of the underlying stocks. They find that for foreign ETFs the asynchronous nature

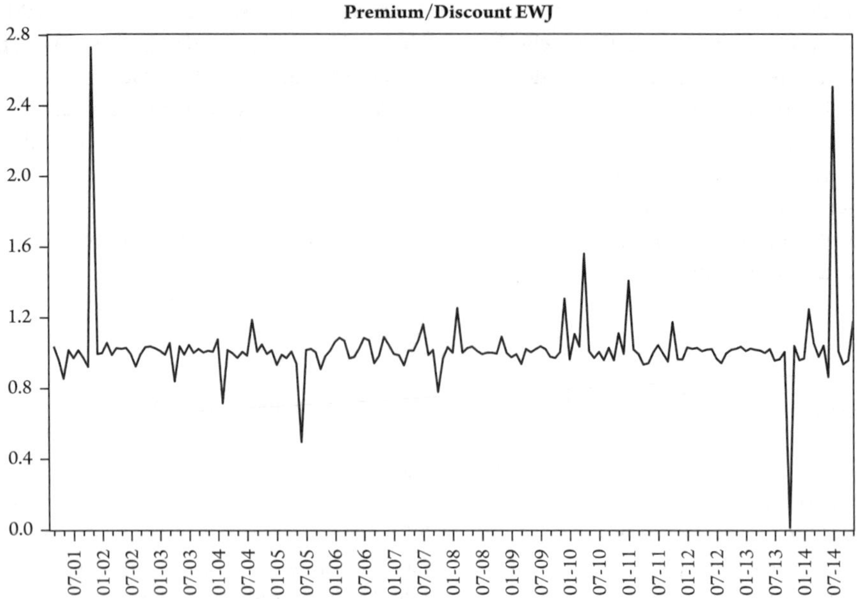

Figure 29.3 CLOSING MARKET PRICE/NET ASSET VALUE. This figure shows the monthly closing price/NAV ratio for the EWJ (MSCI Japan) international ETF, as shown on the *y*-axis, between June 1, 2001, and April 29, 2014.

of trading and the information flow across markets lead to frequent premiums and discounts in ETF valuation.

Rompotis (2005) compares ETF and index funds performance between April 3, 2001, and November 20, 2002. He uses 16 ETFs and a matched set of index funds to track the same indices and to estimate their average return and mean risk level. His evidence shows that both produce similar results. The author does not find any excess returns for the ETFs using a regression-based analysis of ETF and index funds returns on the return of the underlying indices. His evidence also shows no differences in tracking error between ETFs and index funds.

Harper, Madura, and Schnusenberg (2006) study 29 closed-end country funds (CEFs) for 14 countries between April 1996 and December 2001. Their performance proxies are mean returns and risk-adjusted returns. The results show that ETFs exhibit higher mean returns and higher Sharpe ratios than foreign closed-end funds, while CEFs exhibit negative alphas. This finding shows that a passive investment strategy using ETFs may be superior to an active investment strategy using CEFs. Specifically, some potential exists for additional types of ETFs that offer higher risk-adjusted returns than CEFs. Such ETFs may be able to offer higher risk-adjusted returns as part of an internationally diversified portfolio.

Miffre (2007) shows that country-specific ETFs enhance global asset allocation strategies. Because investors can sell ETFs short even on a downtick, global strategies that diversify risk across country-specific ETFs generate efficiency gains that cannot be achieved by simply investing in a global index OEF or CEF. Besides, the benefits of international diversification can be achieved with country-specific ETFs at a low cost, with a low tracking error and in a tax-efficient way.

Hassine and Roncalli (2013) propose a performance measure based on a value-at-risk (VaR) framework, which is perfectly adapted to passive management and ETFs. Depending on three parameters (i.e., performance difference, tracking error volatility, and liquidity spread), this efficiency measure is easy to compute and may help investors in selecting funds.

An Empirical Study

The following empirical analysis focuses on 21 international passive ETFs from both developed and developing economies. The ETFs are primary listed at the American Stock Exchange (AMEX) and are provided by Barclays Global Investors (iShares). The list includes the following countries accompanied by their ticker: MSCI Australia (EWA), MSCI Belgium (EWK), MSCI Austria (EWO), MSCI Canada (EWC), MSCI France (EWQ), MSCI Germany (EWG), MSCI Hong–Kong (EWH), MSCI Italy (EWI), MSCI Japan (EWJ), MSCI Malaysia (EWM), MSCI Mexico (EWW), MSCI Netherlands (EWN), MSCI Singapore (EWS), MSCI Spain (EWP), MSCI Sweden (EWD), MSCI Switzerland (EWL), MSCI Japan (EWJ), MSCI S. Korea (EWY), MSCI European Monetary Union EMU (EZU), MSCI United Kingdom (EWU), MSCI BRAZIL (EWZ), and MSCI TAIWAN (EWT). These ETFs include all international ETFs launched before May 5, 2001, and represent a subsample of a broader group of international ETFs. They are popular ETFs with high trading volumes and large market capitalization.

The study period is between June 1, 2001, and April 29, 2014. The analysis is based on daily observations including closing prices (dividend adjusted due to the possibility of price divergences) for each ETF series. All ETFs used have futures contracts and some also have options including MSCI Australia, MSCI Brazil, MSCI Canada, MSCI Germany, MSCI Hong-Kong, MSCI Japan, MSCI United Kingdom, MSCI Taiwan, and S&P 500. Options increase the liquidity of the respective ETFs. Almost all can be traded on the OTC and to electronic platforms (ECN) during AMEX trading hours. The MSCI indices are suitable for the chosen data set because they are free of survivorship bias and are a robust proxy of market performance for each country (Delcoure and Zhong 2007).

Figure 29.4 plots the quantile-to-quantile distribution of the returns of 21 international ETFs between June 2001 and April 2014. The figure is a *probability plot,* which is a graphical method for comparing two probability distributions by plotting their quantiles against each other. If the two distributions being compared are similar, the points in the quartile-to-quartile plot will approximately lie on the line $y = x$. The figure shows the abnormalities in the performance of the ETFs versus a normal distribution. The greater diversions from normality occur with three indices: MSCI in the United Kingdom (EWU), MSCI in Taiwan (EWT), and MSCI in Japan (EWJ). The distribution in these ETFs does not match up consistently the normal distribution.

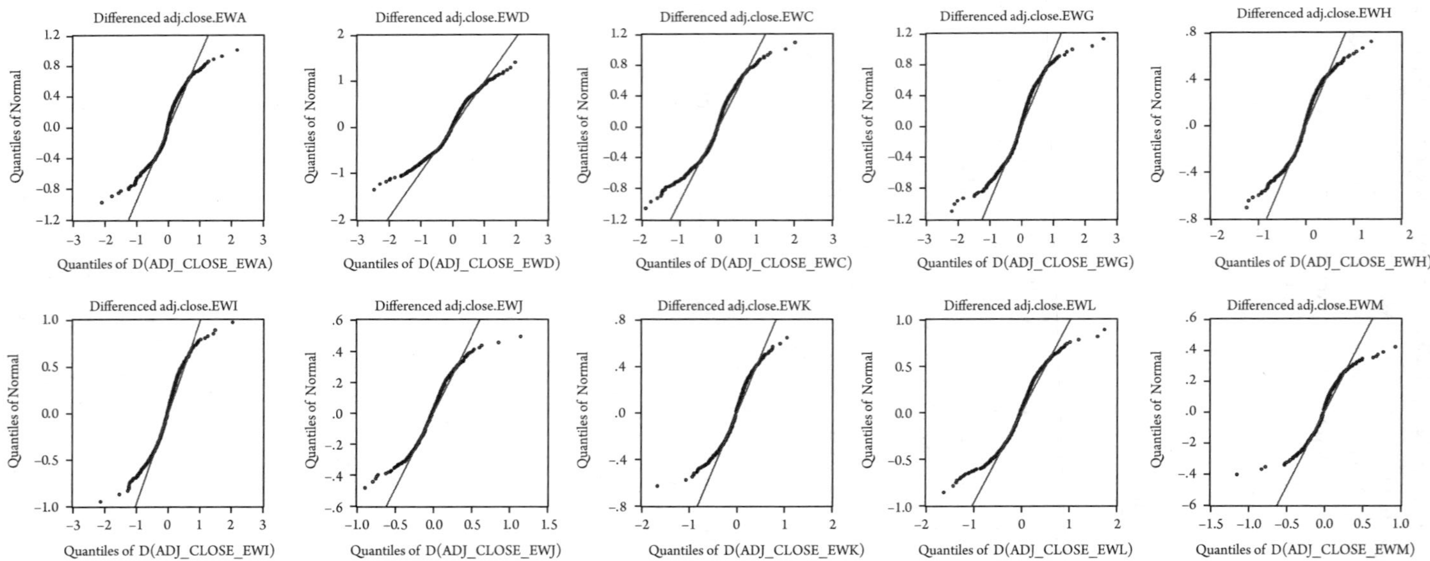

Figure 29.4 QUANTILE-TO-QUANTILE DISTRIBUTION. This figure plots the quantile-to-quantile distribution of international ETFs, as shown on the *y*-axis, between June 2001 and April 2014.

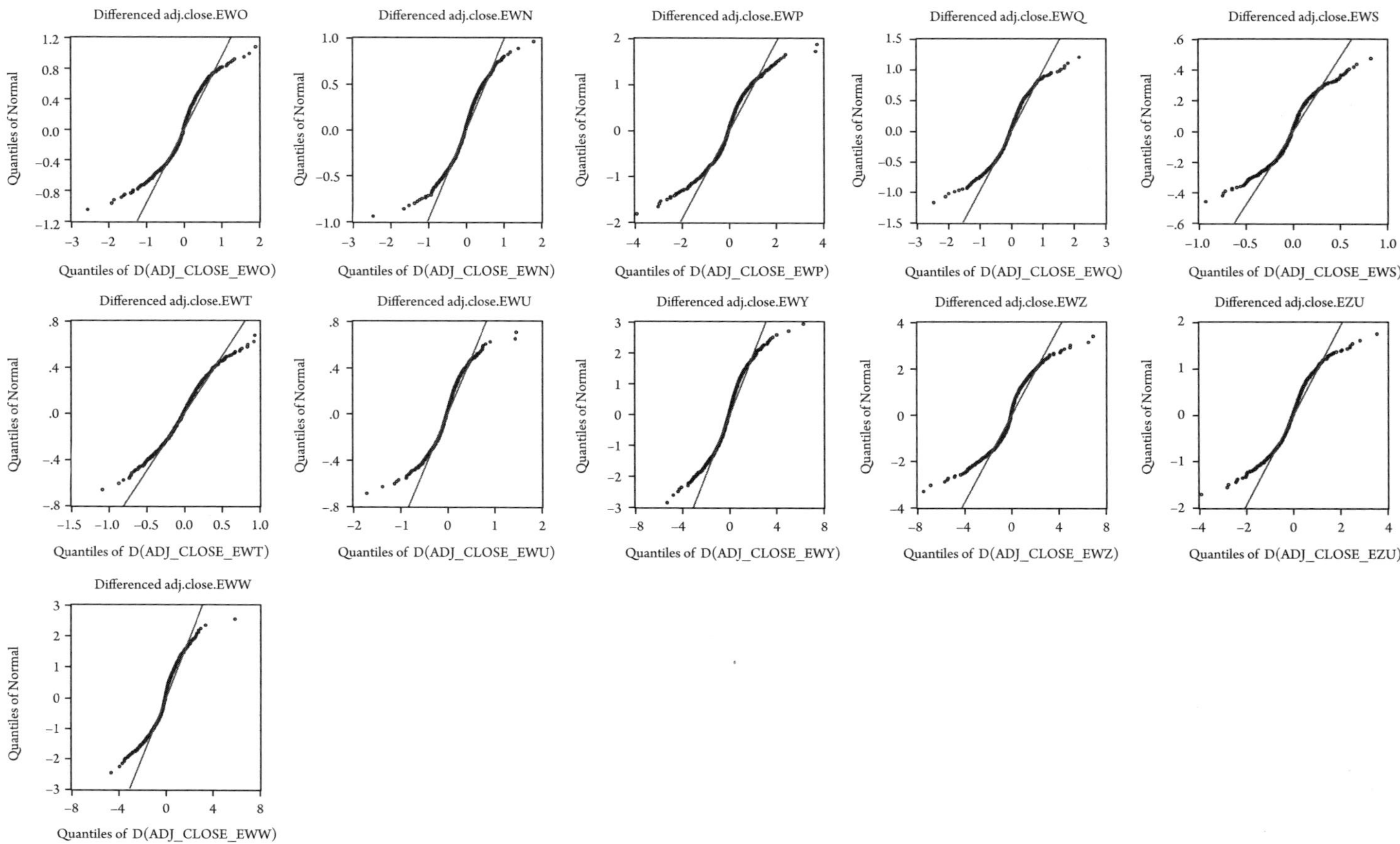

Figure 29.4 (continued)

Methodology and Empirical Estimations

This section presents three performance measures: (1) a measure of return relative to the market, (2) the excess return from a single index, and (3) the Sortino and Omega ratios.

Equation 29.1 presents the relative return of each ETF versus the market:

$$R_{it} - R_{mt}. \tag{29.1}$$

Equation 29.2 represents the excess return from a single index model:

$$R_{it} - R_{ft} = a_i^1 + \beta_{mi}^1 (R_{mt}\text{-}R_{ft}) + e_i, \tag{29.2}$$

where R_{it} is the return on fund i in month t; R_{ft} is the return on a 30-day Treasury-bill in month t; and R_{mt} is the return on the S&P 500 index in month t.

All indices in Equation 29.2 are computed as zero investment portfolios. This assumption implies that the intercept (a) of a time-series regression of a random portfolio against the indexes should be zero. Table 29.3 presents the daily performance of the average between 2001 and 2014. Besides providing the full sample results, the sample is divided into two different sub-periods: June 1, 2001, to December 31, 2007, and January 1, 2008, to April 29, 2014. The rationale behind these sample splits is to examine if any patterns exist across different periods and to check any identified relationship for different capital market conditions. The first sub-period (June 2001 to December 2007) corresponds to the pre-crisis period to a bull market, while the second sub-period corresponds to a bear market in the first half of the recovery and the rally in more recent years.

The results in Table 29.2 show the findings of ETF performance relative to market returns. ETFs performance differs between the two sub-periods. During the first period, the daily relative percentage returns outperform the market from 0.02 to 0.13 percent, and a daily volatility from 0.85 to 1.72 percent. The highest yield comes from MSCI Brazil (EWZ) at 0.13 percent and followed by MSCI Mexico (EWW) at 0.09 percent. Examining the results in Figure 29.2 shows that ETFs during the first period do not reveal any pattern between ETFs investing in developed or emerging markets. The distribution for the entire data set exhibits a positive median, slightly negative skewness, and slightly positive kurtosis confirming the positive excess returns for the period before the financial crisis of 2007–2008.

During the second sub-period, the behavior of returns relative to the market changes dramatically as shown by the wide range of excess returns. Specifically, daily excess performance ranges from –0.017 to 0.022 percent, while the volatility is not reduced compared with the first sub-period, compressing the risk-adjusted returns. Moreover, the median is negative in many ETFs signaling a further deterioration of performance.

During the first sub-period, ETFs in the eurozone achieve the highest mean return and during the second time period, as illustrated in Panel B, ETFs in Swedish capital market achieve an even higher mean return. In contrast, ETFs in South Korea (EWW) achieve among the higher daily mean excess return. In summary, over time

Table 29.2 **Realized Excess Returns**

Panel A Sub-period: June 1, 2001, to December 31, 2007

	EWA	*EWC*	*EWD*	*EWG*	*EWH*	*EWI*	*EWJ*	*EWK*	*EWL*	*EWM*	*EWN*
Mean	0.074	0.053	0.039	0.041	0.038	0.036	0.021	0.038	0.026	0.054	0.020
Median	0.110	0.100	0.025	0.030	0.015	0.030	0.030	0.070	0.050	0.050	0.030
Maximum	5.620	6.830	8.940	3.960	7.060	4.750	6.610	5.870	6.010	5.580	5.350
Minimum	–4.850	–5.190	–6.730	–4.380	–6.230	–5.460	–5.210	–8.090	–4.750	–7.210	–5.480
Std. Dev.	1.251	1.110	1.522	1.003	1.211	1.089	1.142	1.302	1.153	1.362	1.144
Skewness	–0.100	–0.048	0.098	–0.056	–0.064	–0.272	0.105	–0.280	0.108	–0.163	–0.172
Kurtosis	4.555	4.878	5.562	4.458	5.282	5.316	4.927	6.763	4.719	5.007	5.702
	EWO	*EWP*	*EWQ*	*EWS*	*EWT*	*EWU*	*EWW*	*EWY*	*EWZ*	*EZU*	
Mean	0.081	0.059	0.035	0.056	0.022	0.029	0.088	0.097	0.133	0.036	
Median	0.110	0.090	0.055	0.100	0.030	0.040	0.130	0.075	0.225	0.040	
Maximum	5.650	8.800	4.260	6.160	8.410	5.380	6.820	7.560	8.800	3.310	
Minimum	–6.060	–5.620	–4.470	–9.410	–9.790	–3.920	–5.370	–6.470	–13.420	–4.580	
Std. dev.	1.395	1.127	1.011	1.398	1.719	0.922	1.300	1.660	2.042	0.851	
Skewness	–0.351	–0.129	–0.096	–0.307	–0.052	0.182	0.029	0.011	–0.220	–0.196	
Kurtosis	5.086	7.115	4.805	5.826	5.567	5.609	4.524	4.314	5.314	4.587	

continued

Table 29.2 **(continued)**

Panel B Sub-period: January 1, 2008, to April 29, 2014

	EWA	*EWC*	*EWD*	*EWG*	*EWH*	*EWI*	*EWJ*	*EWK*	*EWL*	*EWM*	*EWN*
Mean	0.015	–0.005	0.030	0.002	–0.008	–0.014	0.018	–0.010	0.015	0.018	–0.004
Median	0.000	–0.010	0.060	0.020	–0.030	0.060	–0.025	0.030	0.030	0.000	0.035
Maximum	9.150	6.590	7.450	8.980	7.130	7.310	4.200	5.690	5.180	8.820	4.930
Minimum	–8.290	–5.860	–5.210	–4.040	–6.120	–5.770	–6.370	–7.780	–3.580	–10.130	–4.960
Std. dev.	1.237	0.977	1.437	1.046	1.059	1.394	1.006	1.079	0.858	1.089	0.975
Skewness	0.360	–0.021	0.276	0.342	0.414	0.002	–0.011	–0.149	0.185	–0.073	–0.025
Kurtosis	8.957	8.123	5.370	7.779	8.072	4.843	5.377	7.276	5.478	14.413	5.588
	EWO	*EWP*	*EWQ*	*EWS*	*EWT*	*EWU*	*EWW*	*EWY*	*EWZ*	*EZU*	
Mean	–0.017	0.012	–0.002	0.008	0.006	–0.003	0.012	0.022	0.000	–0.004	
Median	0.040	0.040	0.020	0.000	–0.010	0.000	–0.010	0.040	–0.040	0.030	
Maximum	9.230	10.140	4.830	7.080	10.070	6.300	9.910	19.480	13.990	5.920	
Minimum	–8.100	–5.780	–4.430	–6.080	–7.120	–3.750	–6.830	–7.860	–10.600	–4.070	
Std. dev.	1.413	1.411	1.045	1.076	1.231	0.853	1.086	1.569	1.609	1.026	
Skewness	0.169	0.340	0.157	0.334	0.409	0.260	0.279	1.734	0.483	0.169	
Kurtosis	7.439	6.417	4.987	8.968	9.530	7.214	10.708	25.723	11.397	5.291	

Note: This table shows the average realized daily percentage returns net of the S&P 500 index between two sub-periods: (1) June 1, 2001, to December 31, 2007 (2) January 1, 2008, to April 29, 2014. The sample consists of 21 international ETFs.

the performance of ETFs comes closer to the characteristics of the market because the outperformance in returns diminishes. Moreover, the maximum and minimum performance increased during the second sub-period, while the volatility does not diminish linearly with the reduction of the returns.

Table 29.3 shows the results of the single index model explaining ETF return behavior. The performance of international ETFs relative to the market is positive. Table 29.3 shows that the excess returns for the first period is important for a fund manager or retail investor as shown by the β_{it} coefficient for the factor $R_{mt} - R_{ft}$. In the majority of the ETFs, the β_{it} coefficient is statistically significant at 1 percent level and close to one. Furthermore, MSCI in Brazil (EWZ) and MSCI in South Korea (EWY) show the highest β_{it} coefficient, while the MSCI in Austria (EWO) shows the lowest β_{it} coefficient. The coefficient measures the sensitivity of the return relative to changes in the market return. Thus, a higher β_{it} coefficient would imply the ability to outperform the market more frequently in a rising market relative to a lower β_{it} coefficient. A particularly important finding is that ETFs with the lowest β_{it} coefficient exhibit a lower R^2 signaling the decoupling from the market results in lower returns.

Based on the R^2, the model explains from 30 to 71 percent of the variability of the return for the average fund in the sample during the first period and increases to around 80 percent for the second period. These results confirm that ETFs have moved closer to the market. The β_{it} coefficient of the factor $R_{mt}–R_{ft}$, which overall is higher in the second period than in the first period, confirms this finding.

During the second period, the β_{it} coefficient outperforms the market yields since in the entire sample β_{it} is statistically significant and surpasses one. Furthermore, R^2 is high and ranges from 0.77 to 0.89. The combination of the aforementioned two factors means that ETFs outperform the market and become more related to the performance of the market performance. In other words, market slack leads to higher returns. MSCI in Italy (EWI) is the only international ETF with a statistically significant negative intercept.

A relative comparison between the two periods reveals that ETFs have higher mean returns during the first period. During the second period, mean returns diminish and in some markets are negative. The mean returns during the first period imply that ETFs could not beat the market, even though this becomes the base case scenario as time passes. ETFs performance has become closer to the properties of the market as evidenced by the R^2. For the entire dataset, the β_{it} value for factor $R_{mt} - R_{ft}$ is higher (i.e., greater than one) implying that ETFs outperform the market.

THE SORTINO AND OMEGA RATIOS

This section presents a performance assessment and concentrates on evaluating alpha. The Sortino ratio is a modification of the Sharpe ratio that considers downside deviation. Downside deviation differentiates the harmful volatility from general volatility by taking into account the standard deviation of negative asset returns. As Equation 29.4 shows, the Sortino ratio subtracts the risk-free rate of return from the portfolio's return, and then divides that by the downside deviation. In this case, a specific threshold

Table 29.3 **Single Index Model**

Panel A Sub-period: June 1, 2001, to December 31, 2007											
	EWA	*EWC*	*EWD*	*EWG*	*EWH*	*EWI*	*EWJ*	*EWK*	*EWL*	*EWM*	*EWN*
Intercept	0.0006	0.0005	0.0004	0.0005	0.0005	0.0003	0.0002	0.0003	0.0003	0.0006	0.0002
	(0.0393)	(0.053)	(0.2434)	(0.0608)	(0.0879)	(0.2094)	(0.5868)	(0.2977)	(0.3497)	(0.0818)	(0.4129)
$R_{mt} - R_{ft}$	0.8118	0.7880	1.0427	1.0822	0.9805	0.8366	0.8450	0.8324	0.8285	0.7149	0.9509
	(0,000)	(0,000)	(0,000)	(0,000)	(0,000)	(0,000)	(0,000)	(0,000)	(0,000)	(0,000)	(0,000)
R^2	0.4328	0.4681	0.4674	0.6613	0.5154	0.5288	0.4814	0.4235	0.4729	0.3442	0.5473
	EWO	*EWP*	*EWQ*	*EWS*	*EWT*	*EWU*	*EWW*	*EWY*	*EWZ*	*EZU*	
Intercept	0.0008	0.0006	0.0003	0.0007	0.0004	0.0003	0.0009	0.0009	0.0016	0.0004	
	(0.0124)	(0.0426)	(0.1791)	(0.0454)	(0.2953)	(0.2094)	(0.0042)	(0.0336)	(0.0029)	(0.0807)	
$R_{mt} - R_{ft}$	0.6745	0.8454	0.9887	0.9144	1.0900	0.8949	0.9877	1.1593	1.2193	1.0368	
	(0,000)	(0,000)	(0,000)	(0,000)	(0,000)	(0,000)	(0,000)	(0,000)	(0,000)	(0,000)	
R^2	0.3030	0.4924	0.6128	0.4139	0.4045	0.6250	0.4925	0.4485	0.3596	0.7109	

continued

Table 29.3 **(continued)**

Panel B Sub-period: January 1, 2008, to April 29, 2014											
	EWA	*EWC*	*EWD*	*EWG*	*EWH*	*EWI*	*EWJ*	*EWK*	*EWL*	*EWM*	*EWN*
Intercept	0.000	0.000	0.000	0.000	0.000	—0.000	0.000	0.000	0.000	0.000	0.000
	(0.6686)	(0.6635)	(0.5915)	(0.363)	(0.3821)	(0.1243)	(0.5821)	(0.2691)	(0.1942)	(0.2007)	(0.2403)
$R_{mt} - R_{ft}$	1.122	1.005	1.188	1.096	1.035	1.142	0.967	1.062	0.966	0.894	1.089
	(0.000)	(0.000)	(0.000)	(0.000)	(0.000)	(0.000)	(0.000)	(0.000)	(0.000)	(0.000)	(0,000)
R^2	0.828	0.855	0.807	0.865	0.843	0.799	0.837	0.846	0.878	0.802	0.879
	EWO	*EWP*	*EWQ*	*EWS*	*EWT*	*EWU*	*EWW*	*EWY*	*EWZ*	*EZU*	
Intercept	-0.000	0.000	0.000	0.000	0.000	0.000	0.000	0.000	0.000	0.000	
	(0.1244)	(0.6058)	(0.2184)	(0.7171)	(0.8556)	(0.4692)	(0.9169)	(0.5743)	(0.2642)	(0.2006)	
$R_{mt} - R_{ft}$	1.115	1.128	1.107	1.037	1.009	1.045	1.080	1.164	1.187	1.116	
	(0,000)	(0.000)	(0,000)	(0,000)	(0,000)	(0,000)	(0,000)	(0,000)	(0,000)	(0,000)	
R^2	0.782	0.790	0.869	0.842	0.792	0.894	0.853	0.764	0.766	0.876	

Note: This table shows the average realized daily percentage returns net of the S&P 500 index and the average coefficients from a time-series regression of excess percentage returns against the single index model between two sub-periods: (1) June 1, 2001, to December 31, 2007 and (2) January 1, 2008, to April 29, 2014. The sample consists of 21 international ETFs. The *p*-values are in parentheses.

replaces the risk-free rate as the minimum required return. A large Sortino ratio indicates a low probability of a large loss.

$$Sortino\ Ratio_i = \frac{R_i - Threshold}{\sigma_d} \tag{29.3}$$

where R_i is the expected asset return; *Threshold* is the rate above the risk-free rate; and σ_d is the standard deviation of negative asset returns.

Some consider the Omega ratio developed by Keating and Shadwick (2002) as a more sophisticated ratio than alpha. As Equation 29.5 shows, the Omega ratio incorporates all the moments of the distribution (i.e., mean, standard deviation, skewness, and kurtosis) for a given targeted return level (r). The *Omega ratio* is the weighted gain/loss ratio relative to the threshold r. It splits the return universe into two subparts according to a threshold, where the "good" returns are above this threshold and the "bad" returns are below.

The importance of the Omega ratio is greater when considering that the distributions of the profits of the trading strategies are non-normal.

$$\Omega(L) = \frac{\int_L^b [1 - F(r)]dr}{\int_a^L [F(r)]dr} \tag{29.4}$$

where $F(r)$ is the distribution of the asset return and the numerator is the integral of $1 - F(r)$.

Table 29.4 shows the results of the Sortino and Omega ratios under a competitive daily threshold of 0.025. As a robustness check, the results show the ETFs exhibit positive alpha performance. Compared to the Omega measure, the Sortino ratio has a more diversified range of daily alpha performance. The Sortino ratio is positive for all

Table 29.4 **Sortino and Omega Ratios**

ETF	*EWA*	*EWD*	*EWC*	*EWG*	*EWH*	*EWI*	*EWJ*	*EWK*	*EWL*	*EWM*	*EWO*
Sortino	0.019	0.011	0.012	0.006	0.006	0.000	-0.003	0.004	0.008	0.022	0.014
Omega	1.058	1.033	1.034	1.019	1.019	0.999	0.991	1.013	1.022	1.065	1.041
	EWN	*EWP*	*EWQ*	*EWS*	*EWT*	*EWU*	*EWY*	*EWZ*	*EZU*	*EWW*	
Sortino	0.001	0.016	0.003	0.015	0.006	0.004	0.025	0.025	0.003	0.027	
Omega	1.002	1.049	1.010	1.046	1.016	1.011	1.075	1.075	1.010	1.080	

Note: This table presents the results for the daily Sortino and Omega ratios of international ETFs. The threshold for both ratios is 2.5 percent. The estimations are between June 1, 2001, and April 29, 2014. The sample consists of 21 international ETFs.

international ETFs except EWJ with a daily Sortino ratio of –0.003. The results show that downside performance risk is limited.

The Omega ratio shows that daily returns belong to the universe with "good" returns. The Omega ratio for the sample is above one compared to the 0.025 threshold indicating a positive alpha return. The Omega ratio shows that the upside mean is not limited for international ETFs. By contrast, the Sortino ratio confirms that the downside risk is limited. These results confirm an alpha return and show the superior structure of ETFs in building portfolios.

Summary and Conclusions

Index-linked products, whether open-end managed funds or ETFs, attempt to replicate the returns and risk of an underlying market index. Index management, at face value, appears to be a simple type of investment management but in practice its implementation is not necessarily straightforward. Due to the existence of an inverse relationship between tracking error accuracy and cost, investors using a passive investment vehicle will not ultimately achieve the return of the underlying index.

Research on ETF performance is limited. However, some studies examine the pricing mechanism of ETFs and the relative performance of market investment vehicles relative to an underlying benchmark and index fund alternatives. Elton et al. (2002), Harper et al. (2006), and Hassine and Roncalli (2013) provide evidence of the superior performance of ETFs and contend that ETFs enhance global asset allocation strategies.

According to Bogle (2014), ETFs represent short-term speculation, experience trading expenses that decrease returns to investors, and often provide insufficient diversification. He concedes that a broadly diversified ETF that is held over time can be a good investment. ETFs are dependent on the efficacy of the arbitrage mechanism in order for their share price to track the NAV. Although the average deviation between the daily closing price and the daily NAV of ETFs that tracks domestic indices is generally less than 2 percent, the deviations may be greater for ETFs (Morgan Stanley 2009).

Evidence provided in this chapter is consistent with previous research that ETFs create arbitrage opportunities and can outperform well-defined and accepted benchmarks. Such factors as tracking error, liquidity, and the difference between the closing price and the NAV may influence the choice of a performance measure. International ETFs, due to different time zones, offer the suitable benchmark to confirm that ETFs achieve alpha returns. A ranking based on the Sortino and Omega ratios displays a sufficiently high level of positive returns even when the threshold is higher than the risk-free rate. The excess return according to the single index model is positive. The outcome considers if any patterns exist only during specific periods and checks the relationship to different capital market conditions. Under such circumstances, based on the research presented in this chapter, ETF investors between 2001 and 2014 achieved superior performance compared with the market.

Discussion Questions

1. Discuss two factors that affect the performance of ETFs.
2. Discuss two factors used to measure the efficiency of ETFs.
3. Define the Sortino and Omega ratios and discuss their value in assessing ETF performance.
4. Define the single index model and discuss its effectiveness in assessing performance of international ETFs.

References

Avellaneda, Marco, and Stanley Zhang. 2013. "Path-Dependence of Leveraged ETF Returns." *SIAM Journal of Financial Mathematics* 1:1, 586–603.

Boehmer, Beatrice, and Ekkehart Boehmer. 2003. "Trading Your Neighbor's ETFs: Competition or Fragmentation." *Journal of Banking and Finance* 27:9, 1667–1703.

Bogle, John C. 2014. "The Arithmetic of 'All-In' Investment Expenses." *Financial Analysts Journal* 70:1, 31–51.

Cherry, Joshua. 2004. "The Limits of Arbitrage: Evidence from Exchange Traded Funds." Working Paper, University of California–Berkeley.

Delcoure, Natalya, and Maosen Zhong. 2007. "On the Premiums of iShares." *Journal of Empirical Finance* 14:2, 168–195.

Edelen, Roger M., Richard B. Evans, and Gregory B. Kadlec. 2007. "Scale Effects in Mutual Funds Performance: The Role of Trading Costs." Working Paper, University of California, University of Virginia, and Virginia Polytechnic Institute and State University.

Elton, Edwin, Martin Gruber, George Comer, and Kai Li. 2002. "Spiders: Where Are the Bugs?" *Journal of Business* 75:3, 453-472.

Gallagher, David, R., and Reuben Segara. 2006. "The Performance and Trading Characteristics of Exchange Traded Funds." *Journal of Investment Management* 1:2, 50–60.

Gastineau, Gary. 2002. *The Exchange-Traded Funds Manual.* Hoboken, NJ: John Wiley and Sons, Inc.

Harper, T. Joel, Jeff Madura, and Oliver Schnusenberg. 2006. "Performance Comparison between Exchange-Traded Funds and Closed-End Country Funds." *Journal of International Financial Markets Institutions and Money* 16:2, 104–122.

Hassine, Marlène, and Thierry Roncalli. 2013. "Measuring Performance of Exchange Traded Funds." Working Paper, Lyxor Asset Management.

Hegde, Shantaram P., and John B. McDermott. 2004. "The Market Liquidity of Diamonds, Q's, and Their Underlying Stocks." *Journal of Banking and Finance* 28:5, 1043–1067.

Jares, Timothy E., and Angeline M. Lavin. 2004. "Japan and Hong-Kong Exchange Traded Funds (ETFs): Discounts, Returns and Trading Strategies." *Journal of Financial Services Research* 25:1, 759–776.

Keating, Con, and William F. Shadwick. 2002. "An Introduction to Omega." Working Paper, Finance Development Centre, Duke University.

Kostovetsky, Leonard. 2003. "Index Mutual Funds and Exchange Traded Funds." *Journal of Portfolio Management* 29:4, 80–92.

Miffre, Joelle. 2007. "Country-Specific ETFs: An Efficient Approach to Global Asset Allocation." *Journal of Asset Management* 8:2, 112–122.

Pennathur, Anita K., Natalya Delcoure, and Dwight Anderson. 2002. "Diversification Benefits of iShares and Closed-End Country Funds." *Journal of Financial Research* 25:1, 541–557.

Poterba, James M., and John B. Shoven. 2002. "Exchange Traded Funds: A New Investment Option for Taxable Investors." *American Economic Review* 92:2, 422–427.

Rompotis, Gerasimos. 2005. "An Empirical Comparing Investigation on Exchange-Traded Funds and Index Funds Performance." Working Paper, University of Athens.

Salisbury, Ian. 2008. "Some ETFs Fall Short on Pricing Certain Trades Slip Below Value of Holdings." Wall Street Journal. Available at http://www.wsj.com/articles/SB122723379809546887.

Schizas, Panagiotis. 2014. "Active ETFs and Their Performance vis-à-vis Passive ETFs, Mutual Funds and Hedge Funds." *Journal of Wealth Management* 17:3, 84–98.

Sharpe, William F. 2013. "The Arithmetic of Investment Expenses." *Financial Analysts Journal* 69:2, 34–41.

Morgan Stanley. 2009. "Morgan Stanley Exchange-Traded Funds Average Tracking Error Rose Meaningfully in 2009." Available at http://www.morganstanley.com/institutional/research/pdf/Tracking_Error2009.pdf.

Stone, Gary. 2014. "The Gary Stone Journal." Available at http://blog.sharewealthsystems.com/?m=20140923.

Svetina, Marko, and Sunil Wahal. 2008. "Exchange-Traded Funds: Performance and Competition." Working Paper, University of San Diego and WP Carey School of Business.

Tucker, Matthew, and Stephen Laipply. 2010. "Understanding Bond ETF Premiums and Discounts: A Conceptual Framework." *Journal of Indexes* 39:2, 40–48.

30

Issues, Trends, and Future Developments in the Mutual Fund Industry

HUNTER M. HOLZHAUER
Assistant Professor of Finance, University of Tennessee–Chattanooga

Introduction

John C. Bogle, founder of The Vanguard Group, Inc., notes (Haslem, 2010, p. 34):

> Broadly stated, my goal is an industry that is focused on stewardship, the prudent handling of other people's money solely in the interests of our investors—an industry that is of the shareholder, by the shareholder, and for the shareholder. An industry that has both vision and values—a vision of fiduciary duty and shareholder service, and values rooted in the principles of long-term investing and of trusteeship that demands fair management costs and integrity in serving our shareholders.

Bogle's view is appropriate considering the enormous opportunity that mutual funds have to become more investor-driven. However, the current mutual fund industry is massive and size creates inertia, which makes creating momentum for change difficult. The mutual fund industry will need to become more nimble to meet rapid changes in investor demand. History teaches that demand will be met with supply. When one fund no longer meets that demand, another fund will take its place. The future is not yet written, but mutual funds should be wary of the adage that "history repeats itself."

This chapter highlights the changing demands of investors and how these changes will likely impact the mutual fund industry. The chapter aims to identify both potential threats and opportunities that await the mutual fund industry in the near future. To accomplish this task, the chapter begins with two sections analyzing the mutual fund industry over time and among its competitors. For example, this introductory section includes both a historical and a global perspective on the mutual fund industry while the subsequent section discusses three major competitors in relation to mutual funds. This latter section ends by exploring a few possibilities for turning competitive threats into profitable opportunities. The second half of the chapter continues with two sections that analyze current developments within the mutual fund industry and within specific mutual fund types, respectively. The first of these two sections focuses on changes in investor demand in the mutual fund industry and how those changes have affected the firms that sponsor mutual funds. The second of these two sections explores recent trends and important issues for specific types of mutual funds including: bond funds, target-date funds, hybrid funds, index funds, and money market mutual funds (MMMFs). The chapter concludes with a brief synopsis suggesting that the future of the mutual fund industry relies heavily on sponsoring firms' willingness to adapt to the evolving demands of their investors.

Historical Perspective of Mutual Funds

The origin of the mutual fund industry dates back to the formation of investment trusts over two centuries ago formed on the basic premise of diversification. Specifically, investors were motivated to pool their funds to achieve a more diversified portfolio than they could individually achieve by investing their own resources in specific securities. During the 1890s, investment trusts were established in the United States as closed-end funds (CEFs) issuing a fixed number of shares. However, CEFs garnered formidable competition in 1924 with the introduction of the first open-end fund (OEF) with redeemable shares, the Massachusetts Investors Trust (Rouwenhorst 2004). Although OEFs only accounted for 5 percent of the $27 billion mutual fund industry in 1929, they quickly became more popular than their closed-end counterparts after the market crashed later that year (Fink 2008). CEFs fell out of favor primarily because of their lack of disclosure about leverage and their lack of liquidity without easily redeemable shares (Haslem 2010). The demand for OEFs is now more than 50 times larger than the demand for CEFs (Investment Company Institute 2014). The market implosion in 1929 also created demand for change in the industry regarding both regulation and transparency. Similarly, the financial crisis of 2007–2008 brought back to the forefront many of the same issues, trends, and behaviors displayed by investors after the Crash of 1929 and following the Great Depression (Haslem 2010). For example, both time periods created substantial demand for increased transparency and regulation to restore investor confidence. The long-term effects of the recent financial crisis on the mutual fund industry are still unfolding at the time of this writing. Whether the industry will respond in a similar fashion as it has historically is unclear.

From a historical perspective, the mutual fund industry did not fully recover from the Crash of 1929 and the Great Depression until after the end of World War II. Two primary reasons help to explain the increased demand in mutual funds at the turn of the twentieth century: (1) the industry received massive fund inflows from the rapid growth in income and wealth in developed economies; and (2) the value of the industry increased rapidly with the steady increase in stock prices. In fact, the U.S. mutual fund industry grew approximately 2,000 times in value from roughly $50.0 billion in assets in the late 1960s to nearly $10.4 trillion at the end of 2006 (Fuchita and Litan 2008). Although that number dropped drastically after the financial crisis of 2007–2008, by the end of 2013, the market recovery brought mutual fund assets to a new high of $15.0 trillion (Investment Company Institute 2014).

Global Perspective of Mutual Funds

From a global perspective, the worldwide mutual fund industry is about double the size of the U.S. industry with assets exceeding $21.0 trillion by the end of 2006 (Fuchita and Litan 2008). These assets also suffered after the financial crisis of 2007–2008, but rose to $30.0 trillion by the end of 2013 (Investment Company Institute 2014). During 2012 and 2013, the mutual fund industry realized substantial growth in both domestic and worldwide mutual fund assets compared to three preceding years, 2009 to 2011. Specifically, at the year-end of 2009 to 2013, the U.S. mutual fund industry had net assets of $11.1 trillion, $11.8 trillion, $11.6 trillion, $13.0 trillion, and $15.0 trillion, respectively. For the same years, the global mutual fund industry had assets of $23 trillion, $24.7 trillion, $23.8 trillion, and $26.8 trillion, and $30.0 trillion, respectively (Investment Company institute 2010, 2011, 2012, 2013, 2014).

Looking more closely at the U.S. mutual fund industry from 1995 to 2013, the net asset values (NAVs) rose steadily from $2.8 trillion to $15 trillion. *NAV* is the total market value of all securities in a fund based on prices from the preceding trading day. In fact, over that period, only three recorded drops occurred in year-end NAVs. The first downturn was $592 billion in 2002 after the 2001 recession. Similarly, the second and most substantial decline was approximately $2.4 trillion in 2008 following the financial crisis of 2007–2008. The last and most recent dip was relatively small at around $200 billion in 2011. Although no recession occurred in 2011, the stock market experienced a steep decline during the third quarter—particularly during late July and early August—and high volatility for the remainder of the year (Investment Company Institute 2010, 2011, 2012, 2013, 2014).

Competition in the Investment Fund Industry

At the end of 2013, net investment assets in the United States totaled $17.1 trillion. Most of those assets, approximately $15 trillion (87.7 percent), are classified within the mutual fund industry as open-end mutual funds (Investment Company Institute 2014). However, in reality, two basic types of mutual funds exist: CEFs and OEFs. Two other common fund types are grouped with mutual funds: a hybrid investment fund type called unit investment trusts (UITs), and a relatively newer fund type called exchange-traded funds (ETFs). This section explores how these three fund types compete with the mutual fund industry.

CLOSED-END FUNDS

CEFs hold a fixed number of securities with a fixed number of outstanding shares. These outstanding shares are bought and sold in the open market similar to equities. Since the market determines the value of the outstanding shares, they often trade at prices below the fund's liquidation per share. In contrast, OEFs continuously accept or redeem shares and reinvest the proceeds into a changing portfolio of securities. These shares are traded based on the fund's NAV (Fuchita and Litan 2008).

Due to the popularity of OEFs over CEFs, most mutual funds statistics only include OEFs. A comparison of OEFs and CEFs shows that OEFs dominate the mutual fund industry. For example, as of 2013, CEFs represent only $279 billion (1.6 percent) of the $17.1 trillion of investment assets. In other words, OEFs with $15 trillion in assets are more than 50 times larger (Investment Company Industry 2014). The total value of CEF versus OEF assets has decreased substantially over time. For example, in 1959, OEFs with $15.8 billion in assets were less than three times the size of CEFs with $5.5 billion in assets. Using even more recent figures, in 1995, OEFs with $2.8 trillion in assets were only about 20 times larger than CEFs with $143 billion (Investment Company Institute 2010). This steady decline has occurred for decades. In fact, both OEFs and CEFs display similar growth patterns from 1995 to 2013 (i.e., growing and declining in the same years), but the growth rate for CEFs was clearly smaller. Additionally, the financial crisis of 2007–2008 proved far more costly to CEFs. In fact, CEFs lost roughly 40 percent of their net assets in 2008 compared to a 20 percent decline for OEFs (Investment Company institute 2010, 2011, 2012, 2013, 2014).

UNIT INVESTMENT TRUSTS

Besides CEFs, a few other investment classes exist that should be compared to mutual funds. Note that the term "mutual funds" refers only to OEFs for the remainder of this chapter. As for other investment classes, one of the least understood investment vehicles are unit investment trusts (UITs). *UITs* are a hybrid investment that combines characteristics of both OEFs and CEFs. Similar to CEFs, UITs issue a set number of shares or "units." However, the difference is that these units cannot be actively traded like CEFs and OEFs. In other words, UITs establish portfolios at an inception date and hold the original securities until the termination date. UITs are similar to mutual funds in that an investor can redeem shares instead of trading on a stock exchange. However, unlike mutual funds, UITs have a termination date, a set number of shares at issuance, and are passively managed (McGowan 2009). The four leading investment companies sponsoring UITs are First Trust Portfolios, Advisor's Asset Management, Guggenheim Funds, and Invesco. Most large brokerage companies such as Morgan Stanley, A. G. Edwards, and Merrill Lynch sell UITs backed by these sponsors (Morgan Stanley 2014).

UITs, like CEFs, amount to only a small portion of total investment fund assets. As of 2013, the UIT industry represented only $87 billion (0.5 percent) of the $17.1 trillion of investment assets. The mutual fund industry with $15 trillion in assets is more than 172 times larger (Investment Company Institute 2014). However, unlike CEFs, UITs have not displayed similar growth patterns between 1995 and 2013. For example, in 1995, mutual funds with $2.8 trillion in assets were about 38.5 times larger than UITs with $73 billion (Investment Company Institute 2010). UITs grew to $94 billion in 1998, and then declined for four years before leveling off at $36 billion in 2002 and 2003. UIT assets again rose to $53 billion dollars in 2007 before the financial crisis of 2007–2008 and then declined to $29 billion in 2008. Like other investment funds, UITs experienced impressive growth from 2009 to 2013 with their assets tripling in value to $87 billion in 2013. Still, UITs represent a small piece of the investment asset pie (Investment Company Institute 2010, 2011, 2012, 2013, 2014).

EXCHANGE-TRADED FUNDS

Still, the mutual fund industry has some serious competition. The fund type starting to seriously challenge mutual funds is the ETF. ETFs are primarily passively managed index funds designed to track and mimic the performance of a particular index. ETFs also combine features of UITs, OEFs, and CEFs. For example, ETF valuation is based on a NAV similar to OEFs and UITs. However, OEFs and UITs can only be traded at the end of each trading session ETFs, like CEFs, trade throughout the trading day at prices that may be at a premium or discount to their NAVs (Investment Company Institute 2014).

ETFs are also a newer investment asset and have enjoyed a higher asset growth rate than OEFs over the past 20 years. OEFs have been around since 1924 and CEFs long before that. Yet, even primitive ETFs have only existed for about 25 years with the first major ETF—Standard & Poor's Depository Receipts (SPDR with the ticker symbol SPY) being introduced in 1993. SPDR is simply a domestic equity fund that tracks the S&P 500 index (Gastineau 2002).

The U.S. ETF industry has grown quickly since its inception. In only two years after spawning SPDRs, the domestic ETF industry approached $1 billion in assets. Over the next five years from 1996 to 2000, the U.S. ETF industry nearly doubled annually with values totaling $2 billion, $7 billion, $16 billion, $34 billion, and $66 billion, respectively. During the early 2000s, the U.S. ETF industry continued to grow despite the 2001 recession. Specifically, from 2001 to 2003, the U.S. ETF industry grew its assets under management (AUM) to $83 billion, $102 billion, and $151 billion, respectively. These values clearly show the popularity of ETFs during the early 2000s. Recall, that mutual funds lost nearly $600 billion after the 2001 recession. The fund inflows for ETFs were greater than any performance losses suffered in the early 2000s, suggesting a growing popularity for passive index funds. Over the next decade, the U.S. ETF industry grew more than 10 times to $1.7 trillion and represented nearly 10.0 percent of the investment asset market. Those growth numbers are even more impressive when considering that domestic ETF assets have only dipped one year since inception. That year was 2008 when U.S. ETF assets dropped $77 billion from $608 billion to $531 billion following the financial crisis of 2007–2008. Thus, U.S. ETF assets only dropped 12.7 percent in 2008 compared to far more drastic declines in mutual funds (–19.9 percent), CEFs (–39.9 percent), and UITs (–45.2 percent) (Investment Company Institute 2010, 2011, 2012, 2013, 2014).

In summary, until the 1920s, CEFs were the major investment fund type. However, OEFs quickly replaced CEFs after the Crash of 1929 for both transparency and liquidity reasons. After the Great Depression and World War II, OEFs rapidly grew to own the giant share of the current investment fund industry, especially compared to the other three major fund types: CEFs, UITs, and ETFs. This comparison does not mean that OEFs have no real competition. Unlike CEFs and UITs, ETFs have considerable momentum. If current trends persist, ETFs are the most likely candidate for eventually dethroning OEFs. If the future holds a figurative "David" worthy of knocking down the "Goliath" mutual fund industry, ETFs are the most likely challenger to cast the fatal stone.

A Potential Survivor Story

Mutual funds are currently the primary vehicle for investors. However, the future of the mutual fund industry no longer exhibits the transparency it once did. Although mutual funds will probably be an option for investors for a very long time, these funds may not always have the largest market share among fund types (Emspak 2014). The mutual fund industry is headed in a direction that will most likely be determined by how this industry responds to the rapid rise of challengers such as ETFs. ETF assets are expected to top $2 trillion by 2015 (BNY Mellon Asset Servicing 2011), and fund firms are realizing investors' change in appetite.

Mutual fund firms seem to employ one of three strategies. First, to remain relevant, some mutual fund families are entering the ETF market as a growth play. These fund firms cite several more favorable attributes of ETFs including tax efficiencies, lower expense ratios, lower 12b-1 marketing fees, exposure to different asset classes, and the added flexibility to liquidate a position before the end of the trading day (Deloitte Center for Financial Services 2013).

Other fund families such as Pacific Investment Management Co. (PIMCO) have taken a different route and developed actively managed ETFs that track mutual funds. For example, in March 2012, PIMCO established the PIMCO Total Return Exchange-Traded Fund (using the current ticker BOND), which is simply an ETF that track's PIMCO's biggest mutual fund, its Total Return Fund. Tracking future fund flows for PIMCO's BOND ETF and similar ETFs developed by other fund families will indicate whether this new fund presents a popular hybrid investment that successfully combines favorable features of both mutual funds and ETFs (Brown 2012).

The third mutual fund strategy for competing with ETFs is to become more nimble. In other words, mutual funds will need to shift back to focusing on operational excellence. To use this strategy, several funds will need to make tough decisions about the importance of cost, risk, scale, and flexibility (Deloitte Center for Financial Services 2013). From a cost perspective, investors are increasingly choosing lower cost firms with more transparent fee structures. A strong argument exists that a change in fee structure is needed. Despite the growing AUM, most funds have not passed on any economies of scale to investors. In fact, average expense ratios have actually increased over the last few decades. From 1977 to 1987, expense ratios grew 44 percent from 0.96 percent to 1.38 percent while assets grew nearly 15 times in value from $37 billion to $588 billion. By 1998, the average expense ratio still managed a small rise to 1.43 percent even though assets increased to a staggering $3.5 trillion. As of 2014, expense ratios flattened, but are still more than 50 percent higher than they were in the 1970s even though today's mutual fund industry has grown to $15 trillion. Thus, one likely trend is that fees will have to decrease for mutual funds to remain competitive (Haslem 2010).

Besides fees, three key areas for improving operational efficiency will be in technological innovation, product offerings, and risk management. Technological innovation has allowed fund firms to consider outsourcing several traditional functions such as accounting and newer roles including foreign exchange, securities lending, and collateral management. In the same manner, technological innovation has also allowed fund firms to consider consolidating many services and products to increase control, especially over costs. In particular, many fund firms have responded to past growth and market swings by adding different technology platforms, which are now being evaluated for consolidation to optimize costs, scale, and flexibility. To eliminate redundancy, fund firms are also rationalizing their approach to product offerings with overlapping fund types, classes, or brands. If a firm can manage the same volume of assets through fewer products, it can limit operational complexities and, therefore, costs. Finally, consolidation is being considered for improving reporting on risk management. Two chief goals include better single-sourced data and more fluid processes allowing managers to increase their focus on outliers instead of standard tasks. Thus, the future will likely produce a variety of hybrid fund firms that have opted to leverage the advantages of both outsourcing and consolidation (Deloitte Center for Financial Resources 2013).

Current Trends in the Mutual Fund Industry

Although the mutual fund industry is large and slower to change than some of its competitors, several noticeable developments are emerging. Some of these changes include increasing reliance on mutual funds by investors. This improved reliance has led to increasing cash inflows for the industry, especially from an international standpoint. Changes in investor demand have had a profound effect on the firms sponsoring mutual funds. Thus, this section ends with a brief discussion on recent changes to the types of firms sponsoring mutual funds.

RENEWED RELIANCE ON MUTUAL FUNDS

Although businesses and other institutions invest in mutual funds, households hold the greatest share of mutual funds. The percentage of household financial assets held in investment companies has increased steadily from 2 percent in 1980 to 22 percent in 2013. The only temporary downturn was directly after the financial crisis of 2007–2008. One primary reason for increasing reliance on investment companies is the growth of individual retirement accounts (IRAs) and defined contribution (DC) plans such as 401(k) plans. For example, over the 20-year period from 1993 to 2013, the share of household financial assets in 401(k) plans increased from 6.7 percent to 8.8 percent. This proportion is even more relevant when considering that mutual funds managed 60 percent of these assets in 2013, which is three times the 20 percent they managed in 1993 (Investment Company Institute 2014).

In 2013 alone, registered investment companies reported cash inflows of $430 billion. However, over this same period, demand for directly held investments, especially stocks, fell dramatically. From 2003 to 2013, directly held equities experienced net outflows every year totaling more than $4.6 trillion with an average annual outflow of $420 billion. Directly held bonds have fared better from 2003 to 2013 with total net inflows of nearly $1.1 trillion with an average annual inflow over $97 billion. Yet, demand for directly held bonds has been weak following the financial crisis of 2007–2008. Between 2009 and 2013, bonds experienced net outflows of $269 billion with a record outflow of $239 billion in 2013 (Investment Company Institute 2014).

Mutual funds play a large role in several types of investment accounts. For example, similar to patterns with 401(k) plans, IRAs have also increased their share of household financial assets. IRAs represented 9.8 percent of household financial assets for 2013 with mutual funds managing 45 percent of IRA assets. Besides retirement accounts, mutual funds also manage $1.2 trillion of assets in variable annuities and $5.1 trillion of assets in taxable household accounts (Investment Company Institute 2014).

STEADY RISE OF INFLOWS

During 2013, total net assets for the mutual fund industry increased by almost $2 trillion. Equity funds with their high returns represented the majority of this growth. However, inflows have also played a role. The mutual fund industry received cash inflows for 2013 in the amount of $167 billion, which is approaching the average cash inflow of $201.5 billion from 2000 to 2013. This change was also the second year of consecutive cash inflows following $196 trillion of inflows during 2012. Several factors explain this increased demand for mutual funds including improving economic data in the United States and Europe, strong stock market returns, actions by the Federal Reserve, strong preferences for index funds, and ongoing demographic trends (Investment Company Institute 2014).

The recent switch to inflows after three years of outflows from 2009 to 2011 is also a signal that U.S. households are increasing their reliance on mutual funds to meet both their long-term investment objectives including equity, bond, and hybrid funds and short-term cash management objectives with MMMFs. Of the four major fund types, only bond mutual funds experienced outflows ($80 billion) during 2013. However, the higher demand for equity, hybrid, and MMMFs more than offset the lower demand for bond funds. Long-term funds had inflows of $152 billion ($80 billion for equity funds and $72 billion for hybrid funds) and short-term funds had inflows of $15 billion. As of 2013, the assets for the U.S. mutual fund industry include $5.7 trillion (38 percent) in domestic equity funds, $2.1 trillion (14 percent) for world equity funds, $3.3 trillion (22 percent) for bond funds, $1.2 trillion (8 percent) for hybrid funds, and $2.7 trillion (18 percent) for MMMFs (Investment Company Institute 2014).

INCREASED DEMAND FOR GLOBAL MUTUAL FUNDS

As previously mentioned, half ($15 trillion) of all global mutual fund assets ($30 trillion) are domiciled outside of the United States. Europe holds roughly $9.3 trillion (31 percent) of mutual fund assets. The remaining 19 percent is held by Africa and Asia-Pacific with $3.6 trillion (12 percent) and by the other Americas with $2.1 trillion (7 percent) (Investment Company Institute 2014). As the demand for mutual funds grows outside of the United States, many mutual fund firms are considering changing their location strategy. Fund firms may transition soon from single low-cost processing centers to multiple international locations. Several prime popular offshore locations include India, Europe, South America, and Asia Pacific. India, in particular, is a major migration destination for fund families seeking to increase their international presence, primarily because India offers cost-savings, a growing talent pool, and important time zone considerations (Deloitte Center for Financial Services 2013).

CHANGES IN MUTUAL FUND SPONSORS

As of 2013, 801 financial firms competed in the U.S. investment funds market. Independent fund advisors represented the largest category at 79 percent, and these firms managed 64 percent of investment fund assets. International fund advisors made up 8 percent of the firms. The remaining firms were insurance companies (5 percent), banks or thrifts (5 percent), and brokerage firms (2 percent).

Currently, no single firm or group of firms dominates the market. In fact, the mutual fund industry received a Herfindahl-Hirschman Index (HHI) score of 481. The HHI measures market concentration by weighing both the number and relative size of firms in a particular industry. Any number below 1,000 is an indication that an industry shows a lack of market concentration (Investment Company Institute 2014).

The industry has seen competitive forces both increase and decrease the concentration of the largest fund complexes. Market concentration has decreased in that only 13 of the largest 25 fund complexes in 2000 remain in the top 25 grouping of fund complexes in 2013. Thus, the top 25 includes several fresh faces. Additionally, the largest 25 complexes have seen their market share increase only slightly from 68 percent in 2000 to 72 percent in 2013. However, market concentration has increased showing substantial consolidation. For example, from 2000 to 2013, both the largest 10 complexes and largest five complexes saw their market share percentages rise by 9 percent (to 53 percent) and 8 percent (to 40 percent), respectively. Thus, the biggest complexes have made most of the market share gains (Investment Company Institute 2014).

One likely culprit for the recent consolidation of market share is the acquisition of smaller fund complexes by larger ones. Another important factor includes changes in demand for different mutual fund types. For example, from 2006 to 2013, consistent outflows from actively managed equity funds combined with consistent inflows into passively managed equity index funds have radically altered the mutual fund industry. The top 10 fund complexes manage most of the assets of index mutual funds. Further evidence of changing investor demand includes the substantial inflows from 2004 to 2013 into fixed-income funds. These inflows into bond funds are directly correlated with the rise in market share for those fund complexes that offer fixed-income products (Investment Company Institute 2014).

Recent Trends for Different Types of Mutual Funds

The changing demographics and tastes of investors have had a direct effect on several different types of mutual funds. For example, an aging population has increased demand for bond funds, target-date funds, and hybrid fund products. Investors are also more interested in passively managed funds such as index funds that offer lower costs and more liquidity. Finally, the 2001 recession and the financial crisis of 2007–2008 have also changed the regulatory environment for MMMFs. Each of these mutual fund types are discussed in relation to the future of the mutual fund industry.

BOOMING DEMAND IN BOND FUNDS FOR BABY BOOMERS

Inflows into fixed-income funds are a strong indicator of the demand for bond funds and other funds that have fixed-income components. These funds are popular because they allow investors to reduce risk and mitigate concerns about volatile equity markets and future recessions (Deloitte Center for Financial Services 2013). Two factors that have had a large impact on domestic bond flows since the 2001 recession and the financial crisis of 2007–2008 include the quantitative easing administered by the Federal Reserve and the gradual shift in U.S. age demographics. More specifically, bond fund flows show a direct correlation to monetary policy because net new cash flow is directly tied to the current interest rate environment (Investment Company Institute 2014).

An aging population also directly affects bond fund flows. Only 14 percent of those households with the head of household aged 65 or older are willing to take above-average or substantial investment risk. However, more than 20 percent of households with the head of household aged 64 or younger are willing to take above-average or substantial investment risk Thus, the direct correlation between age and risk aversion has likely increased or moderated bond inflows as the baby boomers have entered retirement (Investment Company Institute 2014).

In many ways, the retirement of the baby-boomer generation has created a new market for mutual funds, especially with the shift from defined benefit (DB) to defined contribution (DC) retirement plans. One likely development for the mutual fund industry as a whole will be an increased focus on serving investors for a lifetime. A key component to this design is creating funds specifically for retirement planning (Haslem 2010). Retirement-focused funds are particularly attractive to aging investors who want better options for investing in their golden years.

Increased fund options are also a major reason older investors have increased their share of all mutual funds. In 2000, households in which the head is aged 65 or older held only 10 percent of all mutual fund assets. By 2013, that number had increased to 21 percent. As for the remaining 79 percent, households in which the head is either aged 55 to 64 (32 percent) or aged 45 to 54 (28 percent) hold most of these assets. Of the final 19 percent, households in which the head is aged 35 to 44 hold 15 percent. Thus, households headed by someone younger than 35 hold only 4 percent of mutual fund assets (Investment Company Institute 2014).

LONGER HORIZONS AND THE RISE OF TARGET-DATE FUNDS

One likely catalyst for the boost in mutual fund ownership among older investors is the growing number of funds with long-term investment horizons. The change in investment horizons can be directly measured by turnover rates. For example, the average equity fund portfolio might turn over its assets at an annual rate of 100 percent, which shows that the average stock is held for only one year. Funds with turnover rates this high focus more on short-term speculation plays than on long-term investment strategies (Haslem 2010). However, as of 2013, the turnover rate for the mutual fund industry was 43 percent. This rate is not only low compared to the industry average of 61 percent from 1980, but it also is the lowest turnover rate in 34 years. The highest was around 80 percent in 1987 (Investment Company institute 2014). Thus, mutual funds are currently trending toward longer term horizons.

With longer term horizons has come an increased popularity of target-date funds, also called life-cycle funds, especially as an investment option within DC plans (Investment Company institute 2014). *Target-date funds* have a combination of investments that automatically rebalance to more conservative assets as the fund approaches its target date. Mostly, target-date funds reallocate away from equity mutual funds and toward bond mutual funds over time. Target-date funds grew more than 28 percent or $137 billion in 2013 to amass a total asset value of $618 billion. Their growth came from both impressive inflows ($53 billion) and performance returns ($84 billion). Strong sentiment exists that this number will continue to grow due to tightening regulations. For example, since the Pension Protection Act of 2006, target-date funds have become the default option for allocating new DC plans (Investment Company Institute 2014).

INCREASING DEMAND FOR HYBRID FUNDS

Another rising mutual fund class is hybrid mutual funds. *Hybrid mutual funds,* also called *balanced funds,* invest in a combination of stocks and bonds but without the reallocation feature of target-date funds. Thus, hybrid funds maintain a specific percentage of the fund's assets in stocks and in bonds. These bonds are popular because they offer both capital appreciation on the equity assets and income and stability within the fixed-income assets (Deloitte Center for Financial Services 2013). Hybrid funds have had positive inflows every year over the past decade except for 2008 following the financial crisis of 2007–2008. Inflows for 2013 totaled $73 billion, which is well above the annual average of $52 billion in inflows for the previous six years and $26 billion more than inflows for 2012 (Investment Company Institute 2014).

THE SHIFTING TIDE TOWARD INDEX FUNDS

Investors are also gravitating toward the heavily weighted world of index funds. *Index funds* are a more passive form of management for mutual funds in that these funds are constructed to match or track components of a market index. Similar to ETFs, these funds are popular because they offer broad market exposure and typically have lower operating expenses than more actively managed mutual funds. For example, the largest index mutual fund, Vanguard Total Stock Market Index (VTSMX), has an annual expense ratio of only 0.17 percent. This expense ratio is substantially cheaper than the 1.32 percent average expense ratio for actively managed U.S. equity funds. Thus, ETFs are usually even cheaper than their index fund counterparts. For example, the expense ratio for the ETF version of VTSMX, Vanguard Total Stock Market ETF (VTI), has an average annual expense ratio of just 0.06 percent (Huang 2013).

Like ETFs, index funds have benefited from the investor trend toward more index-focused products. As of 2013, the index mutual fund industry included 372 funds with a combined value of $1.7 trillion. Almost one-third (30 percent) of all households that invested in mutual funds own at least one index mutual fund (Investment Company Institute 2014). However, contrary to ETFs, index funds have been around much longer. Vanguard introduced the first index mutual fund, Vanguard 500 Index, in 1976

(Huang 2013). In other words, the substantial growth in index funds is a more recent phenomenon. Clearly index-focused products in general are in demand. However, one likely contributor to this current rise in demand for index funds is their frequent association—or clever rebranding—with popular ETF products.

Looking at recent cash inflows, investors added $114 billion to index funds in 2013. These inflows almost doubled the $59 billion from the previous year and almost tripled the annual average of $41 billion between 2000 and 2012. Moreover, investors placed almost half (46 percent) of the 2013 inflows in funds tied to domestic stock indexes. This $52 billion of inflows represents over three times the demand for domestic equity index funds compared to inflows from the previous year ($15 billion). Besides domestic equity index funds, investors allocated another quarter (about $28 billion) of the 2013 inflows to funds tied to global stock indexes, and the remaining 30 percent (about $34 billion) of inflows to funds tied to bond or hybrid indexes. These two index fund categories also experienced strong increases in cash inflows from the prior year in the amount of $12 billion and $5 billion, respectively (Investment Company Institute 2014).

Not surprisingly, equity index funds capture a much larger share (82 percent) of the index fund market while the remaining 18 percent is attributed to bond or hybrid index funds. Although index funds track a wide range of domestic and international indexes, the S&P 500 index is by far the most popular. In fact, one-third (33 percent) of all index funds and more than 40 percent of all equity index funds track the S&P 500 index. This number is even more impressive when considering that domestic equity funds not tied to the S&P 500 represent only 37 percent of index funds. Global equity index funds represent a much smaller portion (12 percent) of all index funds. In total, equity index funds are also gaining a larger share of the equity mutual fund market. The $1.4 trillion invested in index equity funds now accounts for roughly 18 percent of all assets managed within equity mutual funds. This percentage has risen consistently by about 1 percentage point a year since 2007.

The only downside to the index market may be stiff competition from ETFs. Since 2007, the domestic equity ETF market has attracted almost twice the inflows as the domestic equity index mutual funds. However, index mutual funds are faring much better than actively managed mutual funds. From 2007 to 2013, the combined inflows for passively managed domestic equity ETFs and domestic index mutual funds totaled $795 billion. Yet, over that same period, investors redeemed a total of $575 billion from actively managed domestic equity mutual funds. In fact, from 2007 to 2013, the annual amount of inflows for the former versus outflows for the latter have produced an almost mirror image. Thus, cash appears to be flowing directly from actively managed domestic equity funds into index-oriented products (Investment Company Institute 2014).

THE ROLE AND REGULATION OF MONEY MARKET FUNDS

In 2013, MMMFs received their first annual inflow ($15 billion) since 2008. However, cash flows for MMMFs experienced considerable volatility in 2013 due to various factors including tax issues, decisions about long-term interest rates, and uncertainty surrounding the U.S. debt ceiling. For example, tax payments by corporations and individuals likely contributed to net outflows of $125 billion for the first four months of

2013. Whereas, most of the inflows for the year, especially after April, can be attributed to increased demand due to rising long-term interest rates. The only real interruption during the second half of the year was a net outflow of $12 billion in October due to the standoff over the U.S. fiscal debt ceiling.

Traditionally, the two largest classes of MMMFs are retail MMMFs and institutional MMMFs. The major difference between the two fund types is that individual investors primarily use retail MMMFs, whereas pension funds, businesses, and governments at the state and local level typically buy institutional MMMFs. From an individual investor perspective, retail MMMF cash flows were minimal for 2011 (–$1 billion), 2012 (–$1 billion), and 2013 (–$12 billion) compared to the massive cash outflows in 2009 (–$308 billion) and 2010 (–$124 billion). This period of outflows logically coincides with monetary policy decreasing interest rates and maintaining short-term interest rates near zero. With the recent end of the third round of quantitative easing (QE3) since the financial crisis of 2007–2008, short-term interest rates may soon rise, which should increase inflows into retail MMMFs.

Institutional MMMFs also had high outflows for 2009 (–$231 billion) and 2010 (–$401 billion). However, these funds may have already turned the corner. Institutional MMMFs reported cash inflows for 2012 ($1 billion) and 2013 ($27 billion), which are most likely the result of increased corporate profits, especially in 2013. From a corporate perspective, institutional MMMFs remain an important aspect of short-term cash management strategies for domestic nonfinancial businesses. Even with the recent increase of inflows from these firms, the percentage of their cash balances held in MMMFs has steadily decreased to 20 percent in 2013 from a high of 37 percent in 2008. Looking back even further, the portion of cash held in MMMFs for domestic nonfinancial businesses averaged 25 percent from 2000 to 2013. In fact, the 20 percent recorded for 2013 is the lowest percentage for MMMFs over the entire 14-year period (Investment Company Institute 2014).

Finally, from a regulatory standpoint Dodd-Frank Wall Street Reform and Consumer Protection Act (Dodd-Frank) did not affect mutual funds to the same degree as hedge funds. However, Dodd-Frank highlighted one group of mutual funds for additional oversight—MMMFs (Deloitte Center for Financial Services 2013). In June 2014, the U.S. Securities and Exchange Commission (SEC) issued additional regulations for MMMFs that will be implemented by October 2016 (Fidelity Investments 2014). In particular, these new rules addressed concerns from the Financial Stability Oversight Council (FSOC) that investor-led runs on MMMFs could collapse or substantially damage the financial system (Deloitte Center for Financial Services 2013).

The SEC's new 2014 rules addressed systemic risk concerns for money MMMFs by making three major changes. First, the new rules require certain institutional MMMFs to transact at a floating NAV. Second, the rules allow for changes in shareholder liquidity fees during periods of extreme market stress. Third, if a fund experiences a drop of 30 percent or more in its liquid assets, the new rules permit the use of a *redemption gate,* which would halt all withdrawals for up to 10 days (Fidelity Investments 2014).

An example of the effect of regulations on MMMFs can be seen in *prime MMMFs,* also called *general purpose funds* (Investment Company Institute 2014). Prime MMMFs can hold any eligible money market product as defined by SEC Rule 2a-7 under the

Investment Company Act of 1940, including commercial paper, certificates of deposit, corporate debt, and other debt products (Fidelity Investments 2014). However, prime MMMFs are becoming more conservative and increasingly resemble government MMMFs due to tighter regulations such as the SEC's 2010 amendment to Rule 2a-7. This amendment imposed stricter liquidity and maturity guidelines for holdings. As a result, prime MMMFs have substantially increased their holdings of liquid assets with shorter maturities such as Treasury and agency securities and also guaranteed repurchase agreements (repos). Prime MMMFs were only 12 percent invested in these assets in May 2007 but these funds increased their positions to a peak of 36 percent in November 2012. This number decreased in 2012 but in December 2013, prime MMMFs reported that Treasury and agency securities and repos account for 28 percent of their total assets, which is still much higher than before the financial crisis of 2007–2008 (Investment Company Institute 2014).

Summary and Conclusions

The persistence of the trends outlined in this chapter will depend largely on investor demand. The more that investors drive the industry instead of fund managers, the quicker the industry will see many of its problems resolved. Some of the more pressing needs for the mutual fund industry include improving the operational efficiency of funds, reducing costs for investors, and increasing long-term horizon fund options. These areas are critical for selling active-management funds as a better long-term strategy for retirement planning.

Regardless, the current trajectory for the industry looks promising in the short term. Mutual fund values should increase assuming inflows remain constant and the market grows at historical averages. OEFs easily remain the largest player among the four broad types of investment funds (i.e., OEFs, CEFs, UITs, and ETFs) but ETFs are gaining ground. In the long term, actively managed mutual funds will need to conform toward demands for lower costs, better transparency, and increased efficiency similar to most index funds and ETFs. Opportunity exists for substantial growth if mutual funds rise to the challenge, especially with the increase in DC plans. Thus, the mutual fund industry will likely be more efficient and better serve the needs of investors in the future. If not, investors will find other investment funds and products that meet their demands.

Discussion Questions

1. Define both OEFs and CEFs.
2. Identify two major reasons for the shift from CEFs to OEFs after the Crash of 1929.
3. Identify the investment fund type that presents the most competition to the mutual fund industry and explain the survival strategies for mutual fund firms.
4. Differentiate between a traditional bond fund, target-date fund, and hybrid fund and discuss the role that an aging population is likely to play in the growth of these funds.
5. Identify the type of mutual fund that has the highest regulatory risk and explain why.

References

BNY Mellon Asset Servicing. 2011. "ETFs 2.0: The Next Wave of Growth and Opportunity in the U.S. ETF Market." Available at http://www.propertyfundsworld.com/sites/default/files/ETFs2.0TheNextWave2011.pdf.

Brown, Joshua. 2012. "The End of Mutual Funds Is Coming." Available at http://fortune.com/2012/01/24/the-end-of-mutual-funds-is-coming/.

Deloitte Center for Financial Services. 2013. "2013 Mutual Fund Outlook: Shifting Gears for Future Growth." Available at http://www.deloitte.com/assets/Dcom-UnitedStates/Local%20Assets/Documents/FSI/US_FSI_2013MFOutlook_121912.pdf.

Emspak, Jesse. 2014. "Will ETFs Eventually Replace Mutual Funds?" Investopedia. Available at http://www.investopedia.com/articles/investing/102014/will-etfs-eventually-replace-mutual-funds.asp?view=print.

Fidelity Investments. 2014. "Money Market Mutual Fund Reform 2014: Key Changes Ahead." Money Market Reform Communication Series. Available at https://www.fidelity.com/bin-public/060_www_fidelity_com/documents/fidelity/money-market-reform-communication-august-2014.pdf.

Fink, Matthew P. 2008. *The Rise of Mutual Funds*. New York: Oxford University Press.

Fuchita, Yasuyuki, and Robert E. Litan. 2008. *Pooling Money: The Future of Mutual Funds*. Baltimore, MD: Brookings Institution Press.

Gastineau, Gary L. 2002. *The Exchange-Traded Funds Manual*. Hoboken, NJ: John Wiley & Sons, Inc.

Haslem, John. 2010. *Mutual Funds*. Hoboken, NJ: John Wiley & Sons, Inc.

Huang, Nellie. 2013. "How to Pick the Best Index Funds." Kiplinger's Personal Finance. Available at http://www.kiplinger.com/article/investing/T041-C000-S002-how-to-pick-the-best-index-funds.html.

Investment Company Institute. 2010. *2010 Investment Company Fact Book: A Review of Trends and Activities in the U.S. Investment Company Industry*, 50th Edition. Available at http://www.ici.org/pdf/2010_factbook.pdf.

Investment Company Institute. 2011. *2011 Investment Company Fact Book: A Review of Trends and Activities in the U.S. Investment Company Industry*, 51st Edition. Available at http://www.ici.org/pdf/2011_factbook.pdf.

Investment Company Institute. 2012. *2012 Investment Company Fact Book: A Review of Trends and Activities in the U.S. Investment Company Industry*, 52nd Edition. Available at http://www.ici.org/pdf/2012_factbook.pdf.

Investment Company Institute. 2013. *2013 Investment Company Fact Book: A Review of Trends and Activities in the U.S. Investment Company Industry*, 53rd Edition. Available at: http://www.ici.org/pdf/2013_factbook.pdf.

Investment Company Institute. 2014. *2014 Investment Company Fact Book: A Review of Trends and Activities in the U.S. Investment Company Industry*, 54th Edition. Available at http://www.ici.org/pdf/2014_factbook.pdf.

McGowan, Lee. 2009. "UITs: The Neglected Cousin of Mutual Funds." Available at http://mutualfunds.about.com/od/typesoffunds/a/UITS.htm.

Rouwenhorst, K. Geert. 2004. "The Origins of Mutual Funds." Working Paper, Yale University. Available at http://www.akatcr.cz/download/349–225-the_origins_of_mutual_funds.pdf.

Morgan Stanley. 2014. "Unit Investment Trusts: Features, Costs and Compensation." Available at http://www.morganstanley.com/wealth/investmentsolutions/pdfs/uit_features.pdf.

Discussion Questions and Answers

Chapter 2 The Economics of Mutual Funds: Rewards and Risks

1. Discuss the advantages that mutual funds provide to investors.

   Mutual funds provide investors with advantages such as efficient diversification, low transaction costs, timely portfolio rebalancing, index tracking, and accurate record-keeping. Financial advisors and brokers who distribute mutual funds also offer attendant services that investors consider to be valuable, such as financial planning and portfolio monitoring.

2. Describe the structure of the U.S. mutual fund industry.

   Mutual funds come in at least four types: open-end funds (OEFs), closed-end funds (CEFs), exchange-traded funds (ETFs), and unit investment trusts (UITs). Mutual funds are managed by fund sponsors. Market share among fund sponsors is moderately concentrated, with the top two holding one-quarter of the assets under management (AUM) and the top nine holding half of AUM. Based on concentration indexes, the industry is becoming increasingly concentrated.

3. Describe the various types of fees and loads that mutual fund investors must pay.

   Some funds charge a front-end load reflecting a percent of the purchase amount. Others charge a deferred load upon redemption of fund shares. All funds require that shareholders compensate them for expenses through payment of an expense ratio, whose average value is just over 1 percent a year. Expenses covered by this ratio include a portfolio management fee contributing more than 50 percent to the expense ratio, a 12b-1 distribution fee, a transfer and custodian fee, and various other fees including accounting and legal expenses. One type of cost that shareholders bear but that does not appear in the expense ratio is trading costs. These costs take the form of brokerage fees and the market impact cost of the fund's trades and they can total more than 1 percent.

4. Explain why mutual fund managers face an inherent conflict in their roles as fiduciaries.

   Under the Investment Company Act of 1940, mutual fund managers and boards have a fiduciary duty to act in the interests of fund shareholders. However, managers are compensated principally based on the level of AUM. In the short run, expending effort gathering investment flows from new investors is likely to be more profitable to managers than generating alpha on behalf of existing investors.

5. Discuss the relationship among fund performance, fees, size, and investor flows.

   Fund performance has a significantly negative relationship to the level of the expense ratio. With loads, the mere existence of a load as opposed to its magnitude is negatively related to performance. Institutional investor flows are closely related to risk-adjusted performance and fees. For retail investors, flows are more responsive to the level of raw return and the amount the fund sponsor spends on marketing. As for association between fees and size, funds show evidence of economies of scale only up to a certain level of AUM.

Chapter 3 The Role of Mutual Funds in Retirement and Education Savings

1. Explain how the composition of U.S. retirement assets has changed over time and identify the factors that drove that change.

   U.S. retirement assets have risen over time from $0.5 trillion at the time Congress passed ERISA to $23.3 trillion at year-end 2013. The composition of those accumulations has shifted toward individual account-based retirement savings in the form of defined contribution (DC) plan assets and individual retirement accounts (IRAs). DC plan assets rose concurrently with the rising stock market in the 1990s, recognition of the mobility of U.S. workers, increasing costs of maintaining defined benefit (DB) plans, and an increasing number of companies and their workers for which a DC structure made sense. IRAs have grown mainly as workers rolled over retirement accumulations at job change or retirement.

2. Explain how the asset allocations of 401(k) and IRA investors vary with age.

   Investors saving for retirement tend to focus on equity investing with younger investors having higher allocations to equities than older investors. For example, at year-end 2012, 64 percent of 401(k) plan participants in their twenties held more than 80 percent of their account in equities, and only 10 percent of these participants held 20 percent or less. Of 401(k) plan participants in their sixties, 20 percent held more than 80 percent of their account in equities, and 23 percent held 20 percent or less. Similarly, traditional IRA investors in their thirties had, on average, more than 50 percent of their assets in equities and equity funds and another 17 percent in target-date funds (TDFs). Investors in their sixties held nearly 46 percent of their traditional IRA assets in equities and equity funds, and 5 percent of their traditional IRA assets in TDFs. Traditional IRA investors in their sixties had nearly one-quarter of their assets in bonds and bond funds, while investors in their thirties held less than 10 percent of their assets in that category. Equity mutual fund assets make up 57 percent of the nearly $6.9 trillion in mutual funds held in DC plans and IRAs at year-end 2013.

3. Identify the role of mutual funds in the U.S. retirement market.

   About half of DC plan and IRA assets are invested in mutual funds and mutual fund investors tend to concentrate their assets in lower cost funds. At year-end 2013, investors held $3.5 trillion (56 percent) of DC plan assets in mutual funds and $3.3 trillion (48 percent) of IRA assets in mutual funds.

4. Discuss whether target-date fund investing provides diversification and rebalancing over time, and whether retirement savers are increasingly relying on these funds to manage their retirement funds.

   TDF investing offers a diversified portfolio that follows a predetermined reallocation of assets over time based on a specified target retirement date. The fund typically rebalances its portfolio to become less focused on growth and more focused on income as it approaches and passes the target date, which is usually stated in the fund's name. Analysis of data from the EBRI/ICI 401(k) database indicates that the role of TDFs in 401(k) plan investing has grown over time: the share of 401(k) plan assets invested in TDFs, the share of 401(k) plans that offer TDFs, the share of 401(k) plan participants offered TDFs, and the share of 401(k) plan participants holding target-date funds all have increased. At year-end 2012, TDFs accounted for 15 percent of 401(k) assets, up from 5 percent at year-end 2006. In 2012, 72 percent of 401(k) plans offered TDFs, up from 57 percent at year-end 2006; and 41 percent of 401(k) plan participants held at least some plan assets in TDFs, up from 19 percent at year-end 2006.

Chapter 4 The Structure and Regulation of Mutual Funds

1. Discuss factors contributing to the substantial growth in the assets in mutual funds since 1990.

   Several factors account for the rapid growth in the assets of mutual funds since 1990. First, the growth in part reflects appreciation in the value of the securities that mutual funds hold. Between 1990 and 2013, the S&P 500 index rose 423 percent and the return on bonds, as measured by the Citigroup Broad Investment Grade Bond index, has totaled 363 percent. These kinds of gains are reflected in capital appreciation of the underlying securities that long-term mutual funds hold. Second, since 1990 mutual funds experienced substantial inflows of new money, reflecting strong demand for the product. The strong demand in turn reflects the product's structure: mutual funds offer investor access to market returns via a professionally managed pooled product that is highly transparent and heavily regulated to protect the interests of fund shareholders. Research indicates that mutual funds are "income elastic" in that investor demand increases more than in proportion to income. As countries have grown wealthier over time, investor demand for mutual funds has increased. Finally, demographics have played a role. As baby boomers move toward retirement, they have saved, often through mutual funds, to fund their retirements.
2. Discuss the core principles of the Investment Company Act of 1940 including how these principles help protect mutual fund shareholders.

   The core principles of the Investment Company Act of 1940, the primary law governing mutual funds, relate to transparency, daily valuation, liquidity of fund assets, limits on leverage, diversification, custody, and the prohibition of transactions that raise conflicts of interest. Mutual funds are among the most transparent financial products in the marketplace, with comprehensive disclosure through fund documents and other disclosures required by the Securities and Exchange Commission (SEC). Funds must price their shares at least once a day, must not hold more than 15 percent of their portfolio assets in "illiquid securities," must abide by strict limits on leverage, and must place the fund's asset in custody. Also, the Investment Company Act contains strong and detailed prohibitions on transactions between a mutual fund and affiliated organizations such as the fund's advisor, a corporate parent of the fund's advisor, or an entity under common control with the fund's advisor. All of these core principles help protect fund shareholders. For example, the limits on fund leverage greatly minimize the possibility that a fund's liabilities will exceed the value of its assets, or, in other words, that a fund would ever go bankrupt.

3. Discuss how the Investment Company Act of 1940 limits leverage in mutual funds.

   The Investment Company Act and related guidance from the SEC and its staff strictly limit mutual funds' ability to take on leverage. These limitations stem from Section 18(f) of the Investment Company Act, which prohibits a mutual fund from selling any "senior security," but permits borrowing from a bank provided asset coverage is at least 300 percent for all such borrowings. The SEC also takes the view that these requirements prohibit a fund from creating any future obligation to pay unless it "covers" the obligation with sufficient liquid assets. As a result, the maximum ratio of debt-to-assets allowed by law is 1 to 3, which translates into a maximum allowable leverage ratio of 1.5 to 1.0. In practice, leverage ratios at most mutual funds are much lower. These limitations greatly minimize the possibility that a fund's liabilities will exceed the value of its assets.

4. Explain several reasons that mutual funds have much lower leverage ratios especially compared to most commercial banks.

   Under the Investment Company Act of 1940, the maximum ratio of debt-to-assets allowed by law for a mutual fund is 1 to 3, which translates into a maximum allowable leverage ratio of 1.5 to 1.0. This greatly limits the borrowing that mutual funds might undertake. Many funds voluntarily go beyond the prohibitions in the Investment Company Act, adopting policies that further restrict their ability to issue senior securities or borrow. Given these restrictions on borrowing, the SEC's requirement to "cover any senior security with liquid assets," most mutual funds operate with little or no leverage. By comparison, the average leverage ratio for U.S. commercial banks is 8.87 to 1.

Chapter 5 Open-End Funds

1. Identify three distinctive characteristics of OEFs and discuss how they position the structure within the range of alternatives.

   OEFs, commonly referred to as mutual funds, have three distinctive characteristics. First, OEFs provide daily liquidity at the NAV with the fund acting as the counterparty to the trade. Second, OEFs can be actively managed, meaning that a portfolio manager tries to identify mispriced securities and trade them to earn the fund a positive risk-adjusted return. Third, OEFs are often part of a larger family of funds. The fund family allows an investor to build a diversified portfolio across a range of asset classes, investment objectives, and global regions. None of the other investment structures combines these three attributes. Daily liquidity at the NAV with the fund as counterparty is perhaps the most unique aspect of OEFs. It is unavailable in CEFs and only available to certain investors in ETFs. Daily liquidity could be limited in hedge funds or separately managed accounts.

2. Explain how the timing of inflows and outflows can affect OEF performance.

   When inflows and outflows to the OEF are especially well-timed, they can dilute a fund's returns. *Well-timed* means that new money enters or leaves the fund just before increases (decreases) in the value of the fund's risky assets such as stocks. Good timing can be a result of a *stale NAV*, which is one that does not reflect up-to-date information. Dilution can be amplified if well-timed inflows and outflows occur frequently. In contrast, poor timing of flows can hurt an investor's actual performance when compared to the fund's performance. The return an investor actually earns (dollar-weighted) is often less than the return that the fund earns (time-weighted) suggesting that investor flows are often poorly timed.

3. Discuss the advantages and disadvantages of using OEFs as investment options in a DC retirement plan.

   OEFs have been the mainstay of DC retirement plans for several reasons. First, OEFs can be part of a family of funds, which allows plan participants to build a portfolio of funds to suit individual needs. Second, target-date OEFs have become a popular default option in many plans. Target-date OEFs adjust their asset allocation (glide slope) as the participant nears retirement. This means that the participant does not need to rebalance the portfolio. OEFs also permit daily trading at the NAV for participants. Recently, however, ETFs are growing in popularity in retirement plans because they offer two attributes attractive to some participants: (1) some ETFs have ultra-low costs even compared to index OEFs and (2) ETFs allow intraday trading.

4. Evaluate how changes in the nature of stock exchanges and the number of firms that have listed securities on them could impact OEFs in the future.

   Over the past two decades, the number of publicly traded stocks has declined while the number of equity OEFs has grown. Thus, more OEFs are focusing their analysis and trading strategy on a smaller number of public stocks. Arguably, these trends increase the competition in active management. Also, the growth in high-frequency trading (HFT) is changing the nature of markets. Even if actively managed OEFs have superior information about a stock, those funds must still trade successfully to capture that information benefit. Both the growth in HFT and the "basket trading" of ETFs could obscure the benefits of active management. Since a large percentage of OEFs are actively managed, the competitive environment for them is likely to grow more challenging should these trends continue.

Chapter 6 Target-Date Funds and Other Funds-of-Funds

1. Define a TDF.

   A *target-date fund* (TDF) is an investment strategy in which the asset allocation evolves through time to meet the changing risk and return needs of a cohort of individuals saving for retirement. It provides a "one-stop shop" for investors. With minimal effort, an investor can benefit from a lifecycle investment approach where the asset allocation is mainly in risky assets such as equities when the investor is young and moves to less volatile assets such as bonds as the investor nears retirement.

2. Explain the difference between a "to" and a "through" target-date glidepath.

   The glidepath of a TDF switches from risky assets to more stable assets through time. In a "to" glidepath that evolution stops on the target retirement date and the asset allocation is stable thereafter. In a "through" approach, the asset allocation continues to evolve after retirement for several years. A "to" glidepath is typically predicated on the notion that investors exhaust their human capital at the point of retirement. By contrast, the basis of the "through" approach reflects the idea that investors still have some human capital left in the early years of retirement.

3. Discuss the meaning of the Qualified Default Investment Alternative (QDIA) in the U.S. DC market.

   The Pension Protection Act 2006 provides "safe harbor" provisions for the fiduciary of a pension plan that protect the fiduciary from legal action based on the performance of the plan's default fund provided that fund meets the criteria to be a QDIA. To qualify as a QDIA, the investment strategy must be:

   - A product with a mix of investments that takes into account the individual's age or retirement date (e.g., a TDF);
   - An investment service that allocates to provide an asset mix that takes into account the individual's age or retirement date (e.g., a managed account);
   - A product with a mix of investments that takes into account the characteristics of a group of individuals (e.g., a balanced fund), or
   - A capital preservation product (e.g., cash fund) only in the first 120 days of membership.

4. Explain how the TDF implemented by NEST is unusual.

   The NEST TDF begins with a "foundation" phase of moderate risk, increases investment risk as the member moves into the middle stages of their membership of the plan, before reducing risk again as retirement approaches. This framework contrasts to typical TDF approaches that begin with higher levels of investment risk and only begin to reduce risk as retirement approaches. The motivation of the NEST approach focuses on the concern that members who realize losses in their accounts in the early years of their membership might withdraw from the plan and cease saving for retirement. The foundation phase seeks to limit the scope of losses at this stage.

5. Identify four major factors contributing to the desire for custom TDFs.

   Four major factors contributing to the desire for customized TDFs are:

   - *Investment preferences.* Where the plan sponsor has a preference for certain investment funds or managers and wants to use them in the TDF.
   - *Demographics.* Where employees in the sponsoring company have characteristics that set them apart from the wider population. For example, they start work later in life or retire earlier.
   - *Benefit programs.* Where the risk level of the TDF is adjusted to take account of the extent to which the employees have other benefits such as rights to a DB pension or large investments in the company's stock.
   - *Risk preferences.* Where the fiduciary has a strong preference about the amount of risk to which members should be exposed in the TDF.

Chapter 7 Closed-End Funds

1. Compare the organizational structure of CEFs with OEFs and discuss the main advantages of a closed-end structure.

   The main distinction between the organization structure of CEFs and OEFs lies in the liquidity provision. OEFs must meet the investors' liquidity needs on a daily basis at the closing NAV. The fund must not only honor any redemption requests by using its cash reserves or liquidating its investments but also accept any new capital inflows even if no obvious investment opportunities are available to absorb the additional capital. By contrast, organizational design protects a CEF's capital base from investors' liquidity demands. CEF investors can liquidate or expand their existing investments in a CEF only by trading the CEF shares with other investors in the secondary market. This "closed" structure provides CEFs a unique advantage of investing in less liquid securities. At the end of 2013, CEFs allocated the majority of their assets to less liquid asset classes including municipal bonds, domestic and international taxable bonds, and international equities.
2. Describe the empirical patterns for the CEF discount and discuss the behavioral and rational explanations.

   There are four major empirical patterns for the CEF discount. First, new CEFs are initially sold in initial public offerings (IPOs) at a premium, whereas within 100 days the premium typically disappears and turns into a discount. Second, discounts vary considerably across both funds and over time. Third, discounts exhibit mean reversion and positive correlation among CEFs. Fourth, discounts disappear immediately upon fund termination through open-ending, liquidation, or merger. Evidence shows that, regardless of whether the CEFs invest in small-cap stocks or not, discounts narrow when small-cap stocks are performing well.

   Both behavioral and rational theories have emerged in the literature to explain the CEF discount puzzle. Investor sentiment theory builds on the empirical fact that small investors, sometimes called *noise traders*, are the major investors in CEF shares. The theory assumes that irrational sentiment drives the trading behavior of these small investors, leading to greater share price volatility that cannot be diversified. Arbitrageurs therefore require an additional risk premium known as the *noise trader risk premium* to compensate for the investor sentiment risk. This relationship explains why CEF shares have to trade at a discount. Investor sentiment theory can also explain other pieces of the CEF discount puzzle. Fluctuations in investor sentiment explain the co-movement and reversion to the mean. Investor optimism raises the prices of existing CEFs and creates demand for new CEFs.

   Studies also offer a rational explanation based on the dynamic trade-off between managerial contribution and managerial rent extraction. The fund can trade at a discount or a premium depending on whether the valuable services provided by fund managers outweigh the rent they extract as management fees. The capitalized value of management fees is therefore the source of the discount. The theories, however, differ in the source of value added by fund managers. Some suggest managerial ability as a source of value added, whereas others build on value added by liquidity transformation.

3. Discuss the impact of the 1992 proxy reform by the SEC on shareholder activism in the CEF industry.

   The SEC regulates shareholder communication during proxy contests. The early rules enacted by the SEC imposed severe restrictions on any public communication between activists and shareholders. The 1992 proxy reform relaxed the communication restrictions and essentially allowed independent shareholders to freely engage in communication without being monitored by the SEC.

   Evidence shows that the frequency of activist attacks increased dramatically after the 1992 proxy reform. The proportion of CEFs subject to activist attacks increased from only 3 to 4 percent in the early 1990s to around 30 percent in the peak years of 1999 and 2002. The smaller costs of communication (proxied by turnover of CEF shares, average trade size of CEF shares, and the percentage of institutional holdings) enhance activist attacks and these effects are present only after the 1992 proxy reform. This provides convincing evidence that the 1992 proxy reform reduced the costs borne by activist shareholders during the proxy contests and dramatically increased the intensity of activism activities.

4. Discuss the effectiveness of the MDP on reducing the fund discount and fending off activist attack.

   A managed distribution policy (MDP) is a payout policy that the fund management company commits to a minimum annual payout ratio, typically 10 percent of the NAV, regardless of the underlying portfolio performance. If the fund's earnings fall short of the MDP commitment, then partial asset liquidation could fund the shortfall. The MDPs, especially the ones with high payout targets, have had remarkable success in reducing the long-run discounts. Since managers can no longer charge advisory fees on assets paid out to shareholders, adopting MDPs can induce a direct wealth transfer from fund managers to shareholders. This development leads to an increase (a decrease) in shareholders' (managerial) claim on fund assets and thus a decline in discounts.

   The MDP has become a frequently used policy among CEFs to deter activist attacks. More than 40 percent of closed-end equity funds in the United States adopted MDPs by the end of 2006. Depending on the fund characteristics and the expected likelihood of activist attacks, managers might choose to adopt an MDP either preemptively (before an activist emerges) or reactively (in response to the emergence of an activist). Preemptive MDPs are effective in reducing the likelihood of being attacked by activists and subsequently being terminated through open-ending, liquidation, or merger. Conditional on being attacked by activists, funds reacting with MDPs are also much less likely to be terminated.

Chapter 8 Non-U.S. Closed-End Funds

1. Identify similarities and differences between U.S. and non-U.S. CEFs.

   Various similarities exist between U.K and U.S. CEFs. For example, owners of CEFs in both countries must pay income taxes on the dividends and capital gains from their CEFs. However, U.K. and U.S. CEFs differ in that U.S. CEFs have to distribute almost all of their income and capital gains to shareholders, whereas U.K.

CEFs may retain up to 15 percent of their income from securities. Another difference is that bond CEFs dominate the U.S. CEF sector, whereas equity CEFs dominate the U.K. CEF sector. A further difference is that U.S. CEFs currently tend to use more leverage than U.K CEFs whereas in the past U.K. CEFs used more leverage than U.S. CEFs. Finally, U.K. and U.S. CEFs differ markedly in their ownership. U.K. CEFs are primarily owned by institutions, whereas U.S. CEFs are mainly owned by retail investors.

2. Discuss the U.S. and U.K. research evidence involving the rationale for the CEF discount. CEFs have both a publicly available share price, which is the price at which the share trades on the stock market, and a NAV. The premium or discount is the difference between the fund share price and the NAV, divided by the NAV. This calculation is usually expressed as a percentage. Using U.S. data, some studies suggest that initial premiums can arise and fall into discount because of investor evaluation of managerial performance. Also, investors are prepared to pay for the liquidity benefits of CEFs, whereas they might not want to invest in illiquid sectors. However, while U.K. research supports the role of liquidity and managerial factors in discount fluctuations, the evidence generally supports investor sentiment, proxied by various measures, as the pervasive factor in the U.K. CEF discount.
3. Discuss whether investors obtain superior performance when investing in CEFs and, if not, the rationale for investing in CEFs.

   Studies typically show that U.K. CEFs do not outperform market benchmarks. Although empirical evidence generally shows underperformance, a few studies document outperformance. The difficulty in drawing comparisons in this sector is due to the different samples, benchmarks, and performance measures used. Despite the lack of superior performance, investors could still buy CEFs for rational reasons such as the diversification benefits such funds provide. Investors could also purchase CEFs because they are swayed by the marketing or by sentiment toward a particular market sector.
4. Examine potentially effective trading strategies for CEFs.

   In theory, an arbitrage trading strategy could work with CEFs, which are typically at a discount. Studies examine the profitability of buying high discount shares and selling low discount shares. The difficulty with implementing this strategy in the United Kingdom is that trading can be very thin in some shares, resulting in high bid-ask spreads, which reduce the profitability of such strategies. The lack of liquidity within the sector is a key barrier to executing profitable arbitrage strategies within the United Kingdom.

Chapter 9 Exchange-Traded Funds

1. Identify four main differences between mutual funds and ETFs.

   Compared to mutual funds, ETFs provide superior intraday liquidity, tax efficiency, cost-savings, and transparency. ETFs allow investors to determine their own holding period because they can buy ETFs intraday. By contrast, mutual funds trade after market hours at their respective NAVs.

2. Discuss why ETFs are considered tax-efficient vehicles and how their tax treatment differs from mutual funds.

   Compared to mutual funds, ETFs are considered more tax-efficient because investors only realize capital gains/losses when they sell the ETF due to the creation/redemption process. With mutual funds, taxable events can occur without investors selling shares. This process is unique because of the structure of the Investment Company Act of 1940.

3. Explain how passive, active, and smart beta ETFs differ.

   Passive ETFs track an index but active ETFs do not. Smart beta ETFs are a new type of indexing that differs from the typical market capitalization index, which some have criticized for delivering sub-optimal returns by overweighting overvalued stocks and, conversely, underweighting undervalued ones. Smart beta emphasizes capturing investment factors or market inefficiencies in a rules-based and transparent way. Smart beta strategies attempt to deliver a better risk and return trade-off than conventional market cap weighted indices by using alternative weighting schemes based on measures such as volatility or dividends.

4. Explain how individual investors, institutional investors, and financial advisors are using ETFs.

   Individual investors use ETFs in their personal brokerage accounts. ETFs provide them with the same access to certain geographic regions or asset classes as institutions. Institutional investors use ETFs in a more robust fashion allowing them to establish a hedge for an existing position, express a certain view on a specific country with a large notional amount, and execute a large position throughout a single trading day. Financial advisors use ETFs to create global asset allocation models for their clients. These types of models can include ETFs from each asset class such as U.S. equities, international equities, commodities, and currency.

5. Discuss whether a need exists for a hybrid ETF such as an ETMF.

   An exchange-traded managed fund (ETMF) is a form of diversification across strategies for passive and active investors. Given the rise of volatility and uncertainty over time, some believe that investors could be uncomfortable investing only in a passive portfolio such as the SPY, which mainly replicates the S&P 500 index. Hence, a hybrid ETF such as the ETMF might accommodate those who want to mix their strategies.

Chapter 10 Leveraged and Inverse Exchange-Traded Funds

1. Identify several potential benefits of using LIETFs.

   LIETFs could serve a purpose in some portfolios. Although individual investors who have long time horizons should likely avoid allocating a large portion of their portfolios to LIETFs, more sophisticated investors who use short-term strategies might find appropriate uses for LIETFs. Sophisticated investors sometimes use LIETFs as part of a hedging strategy or to complement another position to which the fund is related rather than being stand-alone investments. Investors who find the best uses for LIETFs understand the short-term nature of these funds' return objectives.

2. Discuss the most important risks that individual investors should know about LIETFs before investing.

   Individual investors should understand the implications of volatility drag and that LIETFs aim to mirror the daily returns or inverse daily returns of their benchmarks, which differs from taking a longer-term perspective on return objectives. Individual investors should also familiarize themselves with the holdings of any fund under consideration for investment and understand the exposure to high-risk investments in derivative securities that accompanies owning LIETF shares. Finally, investors should consider their exposure to market risk. A downturn in equity markets could cause their LIETF holding to lose more value than if they held a traditional ETF tracking the same underlying assets.
3. Discuss why the market for LIETFs has grown so rapidly despite the risks associated with them.

   The universe of available LIETFs has increased dramatically since being introduced in 2006. Firms continued to expand their product offerings to meet growing demand. The growth in demand stemmed largely from retail investors who likely did not fully understand the risks of investing in LIETFs. Thus, growth primarily occurred to meet the demand of a largely undereducated group of individual investors who found the leverage and exposure available increasingly attractive.
4. Explain why the performance of a LIETF could differ substantially from its stated return objective.

   Several factors contribute to what can lead to substantial tracking error. The cost of maintaining and rolling derivative positions, the threat of taking losses on relatively illiquid derivative securities, and the possibility of failing to gain the proper exposure required to generate the desired return all can reduce the actual return the fund earns. Further, losses from counterparty defaults in forward and swap agreements can cause a loss of value and pressure the return on a fund's shares.

Chapter 11 Money Market Mutual Funds

1. Discuss why MMMFs developed.

   MMMFs developed for several reasons. First, MMMFs provided interest rates above the Regulation Q limits on bank deposit interest rates in the early 1970s. Second, a need existed for an intermediary specializing only in short-term assets and liabilities. Advantages that MMMFs offer to the investors through the pooling of large amounts of short-term funds include economies of scale, liquidity, divisibility, and diversification.
2. Explain how MMMFs maintain a constant $1 a share NAV.

   The Investment Company Act (ICA) of 1940, Rule 2a-7 allows MMMFs to value shares based on the amortized cost or the book value of assets, which is an accounting-based rather than a market-based principle. The cost of a security is established on the purchase date at its fair value. In contrast to the mark-to-market method, amortized cost valuation does not allow changes in market interest rates to affect the value of the MMMF's portfolio. The amortized cost valuation method leads to a constant share price. Each security's value is fixed on the purchase date. The straight-line increase in its value (i.e., income earned on the security net of expenses) is credited in a form of dividends to shareholders on a daily basis. This ICA provision allows MMMFs to maintain a constant $1 a share NAV.

3. Discuss why money fund managers sometimes waive fees.

   Historical data show that MMMF managers often waive fees, beginning in the late 1970s. Investors face both upfront costs and ongoing costs. The upfront costs include any kind of load fees (front or back). MMMFs automatically deduct ongoing fees such as contractual management fees from gross returns. MMMF managers often adjust ongoing expenses to change the net returns. To avoid a fixed structure of nominally flat fees, managers charge higher contractual fees and then selectively waive these fees throughout the year. MMMF managers rely on partial fee waiving to increase net returns to shareholders.

4. Discuss how the current MMMF structure can create runs on funds.

   If shareholders expect the fund to "break the buck" (i.e., if they suspect that the NAV will be below $1), then they have an incentive to withdraw their money before other investors do. Generally, funds do not hold large cash positions to meet massive redemptions. If an unusually high demand for redemptions arises, MMMFs could be forced to sell some of their assets at a fire sale. Shocks to the liquidity of the secondary market would suppress asset prices. High demand for redemptions could result in the NAV falling farther below $1. Thus, similar to commercial banks, MMMFs are susceptible to runs. Unlike commercial banks, MMMFs do not benefit from deposit insurance or a lender of last resort. Until September 2008, MMMFs relied on implicit guarantees from their sponsoring financial institutions to prevent runs.

Chapter 12 Bond Mutual Funds

1. Identify four vehicles for investors to acquire exposure to the fixed-income market and describe advantages and disadvantages of each.

   Four vehicles available to gain exposure to the fixed-income asset class are (1) self-directed portfolios, (2) mutual funds, (3) CEFs, and (4) ETFs or UITs.

   - *Self-directed portfolios.* An advantage of this method includes tailoring the portfolio to an investor's goals such as the opportunity to match future liabilities. An example would be a defined benefit plan seeking to meet retirement liabilities. A disadvantage is that a self-managed portfolio of individual bonds makes sense only beyond a specific asset size and only if the investor makes a limited number of transactions in managing the portfolio.
   - *Mutual funds.* Advantages of this approach include gaining professional management and portfolio diversification. For these benefits, investors incur fees and expenses. Another disadvantage is that using mutual funds requires investors to identify an appropriate fund to meet their investment objectives and to determine how to measure a fund manager's performance against a benchmark.
   - *CEFs.* With a CEF, investors can trade their shares in the secondary market but the price might be at a discount or premium from the fund's NAV. Previously, managers seeking to leverage their investments could use CEFs for margin borrowing but the advent of ETFs also diminishes this benefit.

- *ETFs and UITs.* Investors can trade ETFs anytime during the trading day and ETFs do not trade at a wide premium or discount from the NAV. They can be sold short or purchased on margin. Most ETFs provide investors with indexing opportunities. Currently, an investor seeking active management has limited opportunities available through ETFs but this is changing. A UIT is a hybrid security with characteristics of mutual funds and CEFs. Two advantages of UITs are that they trade on the secondary market and can meet specific investment objectives like matching the cash flow of a future liability. A disadvantage is that UITs have finite lives and eventually must be liquidated. This possibly creates reinvestment risk. UITs also are often more expensive as compared to mutual funds and ETFs.

2. Discuss the challenges faced by bond index mutual fund managers compared with equity indexing.

   Passive bond mutual fund managers face the challenge of matching the performance of an index. This challenge results from the bond market being less liquid than the stock market. Unlike a large proportion of stocks in a stock index, not all bonds in the index trade frequently. This makes full replication difficult. Therefore, fund managers often resort to cell matching or statistical optimization techniques. Anything short of full replication can result in substantial tracking errors.

   In the absence of a timely trade between two independent parties, the pricing of bonds in any broad-based index is to some extent subjective. When a bond does not trade on a trading day, it is *matrix priced,* which means making an estimate of the trade price. During periods of market stress, estimating the trade price becomes quite important because the matrix price might not be the price at which the trade would eventually occur. This distorts index performance and leads to inaccurate benchmarking.

   Bonds are time-decaying securities because they have finite lives and thus mature. Call provisions and refunding further compromise the stability of a bond portfolio. These factors require the portfolio manager to replace such bonds frequently. Compared to equity indexes in which the constituent securities are largely perpetual, the bond index fund manager faces a unique challenge of creating a perpetual security (e.g., mutual fund) from a set of securities with finite lives.
3. Define window dressing and discuss its occurrences in bond mutual funds.

   Window dressing occurs when an actively managed bond mutual fund manager includes well-performing securities and removes poorly performing securities from the portfolio to make the portfolio look better. This process usually happens close to the end of the reporting period. Window dressing gives the false impression that the fund manager is holding securities that have performed well, showing superior selection skill. The limited evidence available shows no pervasive practice of window dressing in bond mutual funds. When it does occur, larger funds are more prone to such practices.
4. Describe the dimensions available for analyzing the bond mutual fund market.

   The bond mutual fund market is segregated on three broad dimensions: credit risk, interest rate risk, and issuers. The spectrum of credit risk starts with Treasury securities that are regarded as virtually default free to high yield bonds, which sometimes default. Interest rate risk is largely a function of three factors: time to maturity, coupon rate of the bond, and market interest rate (yield). These are jointly measured using duration. Longer duration bond mutual funds carry higher interest rate risk. A bond mutual fund's objective is often to specify the characteristics of the bond portfolio that the fund primarily holds. Each type or segment of the bond market based on the issuer has unique characteristics and therefore requires a different set of skills for analysis. For example, Treasury securities carry the explicit guarantee of the U.S. government while the guarantee for agency bonds is only implicit.

5. Describe the universe of securities available to municipal bond mutual fund managers.

   Gaining an understanding of the municipal bond market involves looking at various dimensions on which this bond segment can be analyzed. First, coupon payments from most municipal bonds are exempt from federal tax. These are referred to as single tax-free bonds if the coupon payment is only exempt from federal tax. Coupon payments from a municipal bond could be exempt from both federal and state income taxes. Such a municipal bond is called a double tax-free bond. A triple tax-free municipal bond is one in which coupon income is exempt from federal, state, and local (county, town or city) income taxes.

   Municipal bonds are also classified based on the collateral/guarantee accompanying them. General obligations (GOs) municipal bonds are backed by the full faith and credit of the municipality, whereas revenue bonds are backed by the cash flows of a particular project such as a sewer project. Most municipal bonds carry a rating and the market covers the entire range of risk from investment grade to high yield.

   Some municipal bond issues carry additional *monocline* insurance. Here, the insurer promises to compensate investors in the event the issuer cannot make coupon payments or defaults on the repayment of principal. Evidence shows that the issuer typically captures the benefit from this additional guarantee. However, the ability of the insurers to pay all claims in the face of a systemic event has not been fully tested.

Chapter 13 Stock Mutual Funds

1. Define alpha.

   Alpha is a measure of risk-adjusted performance relative to a benchmark. One measure of alpha is the return on a portfolio minus the return estimated from the capital asset pricing model (CAPM). A positive alpha represents a risk-adjusted return above that of the benchmark, possibly implying superior performance or simply luck. A negative alpha shows inferior performance. An alpha of zero shows that the portfolio performed exactly as it should have.

2. Discuss issues with measuring alpha.

   One issue in measuring alpha is that different measurement techniques produce different results. For example, a single index model and a four-factor model produce different alphas for the same portfolio. Even when using the same approach, different benchmarks result in dissimilar alphas. Research also finds that some benchmarks have negative alphas, further complicating the meaning of a portfolio outperforming such an index.

3. Define performance attribution.

   Performance attribution is an effort to understand what factors contribute to the performance of an investment or fund. Although many factors can contribute to fund performance, the two major factors are asset allocation decisions including sector allocations and individual security selections. With a true equity mutual fund, the manager does not have major asset allocation decisions and might even have sector allocation restrictions. In such a case, the manager might be able to add value through security selection decisions. Performance attribution helps the ownership of the fund determine how the manager's security selection decisions contribute (positively or negatively) to overall fund performance.

4. Explain how trading distorts risk analysis.

   Managers often change risk levels during the year in response to how their portfolios perform relative to their benchmarks. These changes can involve shifts based on the market capitalization of companies held in the portfolio to investing in more or less volatile investments. Evidence also shows that due to trading, the same portfolio can have different betas and alphas depending on whether they are calculated from assets in the portfolio or overall portfolio returns.

5. Explain closet indexing.

   Some active managers follow a portfolio management strategy called *closet indexing*. In closet indexing, the portfolio manager allocates a portion of the portfolio to the benchmark index and actively manages the remaining funds. Investors pay a higher active management fee despite only a portion of the funds being actively managed. On the indexed portion of the portfolio, the manager can earn benchmark returns at the benchmark level of risk, and do so without research or brokerage costs beyond the initial allocation. The higher active management fee and the lower index-like operating expenses result in larger profits for the management company. Closet indexing has the long-run effect of reducing the likelihood that the portfolio will substantially outperform or underperform the benchmark.

Chapter 14 Socially Responsible Mutual Funds

1. Friedman contends that a necessary trade-off exists between corporate "social responsibilities" and corporate profits. Provide an argument against this view.

   Friedman argues that a company should have no social responsibility to the public or society because its only concern is to increase profits for itself and for its shareholders, and shareholders in their private capacity are the ones with the social responsibility. However, financial management has shifted its focus from a traditional to a modern approach. The modern approach focuses on value maximization, not profit maximization. This shift gives a longer term horizon for assessment, making way for sustainable performance by businesses. A myopic person or business is mostly concerned about short-term benefits. A shorter term horizon might fulfill the objective of earning profit but might not help in creating wealth. This relationship emerges because value creation needs a longer term horizon. Therefore, financial management emphasizes value maximization rather than profit maximization. Management and stakeholders of modern corporations make business decisions with real ethical and social consequences. Ignoring social responsibility and externalities, a company could face a greater risk in the long run, which might reduce its ability to generate value.

2. Explain whether a best strategy exists for constructing SRMF portfolios.

No single best strategy exists for constructing SRMF portfolios because each strategy has its strengths and weaknesses. For instance, many consider environmental, social, and governance (ESG) integration a more complex and robust strategy, but it can be harder to implement. By contrast, a screening strategy is the easiest and most popular strategy, but the portfolio results might not be better compared to other more active investment strategies such as best-in-class or ESG integration strategies. The best way for constructing SRMF portfolios is to match a client's profile to the applied strategy. Screening, best-in-class, and ESG integration strategies attract "feel good" investors, and thematic and engagement strategies appeal to "activist" investors.

3. Discuss several hypotheses to explain why the performance between SRMFs and conventional funds may differ significantly on a risk-adjusted basis.

Several hypotheses help to explain why the performance between SRMFs and conventional funds might differ. First, modern portfolio theory indicates that removing stocks limits portfolio construction and diversification. However, an efficient portfolio can still be constructed when excluding some stock. In this case, the SRMF portfolio could contain stocks as in a conventional portfolio that appeal to investors with a specific risk preference. On a risk-adjusted basis, no difference exists. Second, "sin stocks" tend to have higher betas and consequently higher expected returns. Removing sin stocks leads to a lower portfolio beta and thus a lower expected return. When the market is rising, a portfolio with a higher beta should outperform one with a lower beta. When the market is falling, a portfolio with a lower beta should outperform one with a higher beta. This relationship might explain why some results support the SRMFs while others favor conventional funds.

4. Discuss whether SRMFs are likely to remain a niche financial product in the future.

According to the Global Sustainable Investment Alliance (2012), at least \$13.6 trillion worth of professionally managed assets incorporated ESG concerns into their investment selection and management. This figure accounted for 21.8 percent of the total assets managed in the regions covered by the report. From this figure, ESG assets represent 49 percent of the total European managed portfolios, which means that SRMFs are no longer a niche in Europe, Africa, and Canada. Despite SRMFS still being a niche in many other countries, they are likely to grow in the future.

Chapter 15 Mutual Funds: Management Styles, Social Responsibility, Performance, and Efficiency

1. Distinguish between active and passive mutual funds.

Active managers form portfolios with the goal of attaining higher returns than their benchmarks. Managers of actively managed mutual funds select securities that they forecast to outperform the market. Active management strategies are diverse. For example, some funds focus on momentum, others on growth stocks, and still others on specific industries. Passive management or indexed investing is the simplest form of fund management. In this case, a fund's holdings are intended to mirror the composition of a benchmark, usually a market index. For example, the Vanguard 500 fund invests in stocks of the S&P 500 index and the portfolio weights reflect the market capitalization of the individual stocks.

2. Discuss the types of active investing and screening for socially responsible funds.

   Four types of active investing and screening for socially responsible funds are available. First, negative screening is the most basic type with origins in religion. Negative screens eliminate stocks that are involved in "sin" industries such as alcohol, tobacco, military, weaponry, abortion, and pornography. Second, positive screens select companies that meet above average standards in areas such as protecting the environment, promoting of human rights, or fostering the sustainability of investments. A branch of positive screens is the best-in-class approach: all companies are ranked within an industry based on sustainability criteria, then stocks that meet the fund's SRI requirement serve as the investment universe. Third, negative and positive screens are often combined to yield the so-called "transversal," "sustainable," or "triple bottom line" (i.e., people, planet, and profit) screens. Finally, the fourth generation of ethical funds combines the sustainable investing approach (third generation) with shareholder activism. In this case, portfolio managers or the companies specialized in granting ethical labels try to influence the company's policies through direct dialogue with management or by using voting rights at annual general meetings.

3. Identify the potential benefits and concerns of indexed investing.

   The main benefit of indexed or passive investing lies in its simplicity. That is, indexed investing attempts to replicate a market index such as the S&P 500. It can also result in lower costs to investors. By investing in ETFs, investors can combine the convenience of stock trading while still holding a diversified portfolio. However, indexed investing can have negative effects on the aggregate economy. Market inefficiencies, such as the index exclusion effect, can have a negative impact as a company's value might become disconnected from its fundamental value, potentially leading to underinvestment in the stock. Index investing can amplify the effects of booming and crisis periods, creating strong cyclicality in the market.

4. Discuss several measures of active management.

   Several measures are available to assess the performance of active management. One measure is *active share*, which is the proportion of mutual fund holdings that differs from the benchmark index. Another measure that captures unobserved managerial actions is the *return gap*, which is the difference between the reported fund return and the return on a portfolio with previously disclosed holdings. In case of SRI funds, the level of active management can be associated with the complexity of the screening process.

Chapter 16 Strategic Asset Allocation and Rebalancing

1. Define SAA and TAA.

   Strategic asset allocation (SAA) is the allocation of investments to various asset classes that integrate an investor's return objectives, risk tolerance, and investment constraints with long-term capital market expectations. *Tactical asset allocation* (TAA) involves making short-term adjustments to asset class weights based on short-term predictions of relative performance among asset classes.

2. Explain the steps needed to determine a portfolio's SAA.

   The first step in determining a portfolio's SAA is to specify what percentage of the portfolio should be invested in each of the primary asset classes such as equity, fixed-income, and cash and cash equivalents according to an investor's risk tolerance and investment horizon. Next, the portfolio manager selects the specific stocks, bonds, or other assets to include in the portfolio.
3. Identify the three characteristics of an effective benchmark for a SAA analysis.

   An effective benchmark must be exclusive (i.e., it must not contain any securities that already form part of any other benchmark being considered), exhaustive (i.e., it must include as many strategic assets as possible), and independent (i.e., it must have a low correlation with other benchmarks).
4. Discuss the importance of rebalancing a portfolio.

   Rebalancing refers to adjusting the actual portfolio to the current SAA due to price changes in portfolio holdings. Rebalancing is necessary to account for the dynamism of financial markets, changes in the investment horizon, and possible deviations from the SAA. For instance, managers could increase (decrease) the portfolio weight invested in equity assets in expected bullish (bearish) markets. Rebalancing also occurs in an investor's target asset class weights due to changes in the investor's investment objectives, constraints, or changes in capital market expectations.

Chapter 17 Building and Monitoring Mutual Fund Portfolios

1. Discuss the fees and expenses of mutual funds and their impact on returns.

   Mutual fund investors are expected to pay fees such as front-end loads, back-end loads, 12b-1 fees, management expenses, and other expenses. *Front-end loads* are fees charged to an investor when buying shares in a mutual fund and *back-end loads* are fees paid when an investor redeems fund shares. *12b-1 fees,* also known as distribution fees, are expenses charged to mutual fund investors to pay for marketing and advertising expenses such as commissions paid to brokers who sell funds to investors. 12b-1 fees are deducted from the fund's assets. *Management fees* are expenses paid out of the fund assets to the fund's investment advisor for managing the fund's investment portfolio. *Other expenses* not included in the categories of management fees or 12b-1 fees include custodial, legal, accounting, transfer agent, and other administrative expenses. Studies find that load fees, expense ratios, and 12b-1 fees have a significantly negative impact on performance and investors cannot recoup high fees. Therefore, choosing a fund with no-load and a low expense ratio could prove to be a good strategy.
2. Identify mistakes that investors should avoid when selecting mutual funds.

   The following are mistakes that investors should avoid when selecting mutual funds:

   - *Not having an investment plan.* Investors should establish investment goals before investing and select funds that meet their needs for liquidity, time horizon, return expectation, risk tolerance, and tax efficiency.

- *Not knowing the fund.* Investors should study information from multiple sources including the fund's investment objective, risks, performance, fund manager experience, and expenses.
- *Chasing performance.* Investors should not rely exclusively on past performance or a single rating system to select funds because such information does not guarantee future returns.
- *Over-diversification.* Investors should not overemphasize diversification because having too many mutual funds in a portfolio can be costly and time-consuming to monitor.
- *Underestimating scale effects in fund performance.* Investors should recognize that large funds do not necessarily produce superior returns. Instead, performance of funds declines with size, especially for small cap funds because of illiquidity and organizational diseconomies.
- *Ignoring the corrosive impact of compounding costs on returns over time.* Investors should know the expenses and fees that funds charge because a small difference in costs can have a substantial impact on a fund's long-term returns.

3. Discuss the evidence on whether actively managed funds outperform the market.

   Most empirical research on the performance of actively managed mutual funds suggests that they fail to consistently outperform the market. Studies also fail to find evidence of market-timing ability. However, a particular fund might have superior performance in any given year or even a sustained number of years.
4. Explain how to compute turnover and its importance when screening funds.

   Turnover is computed by dividing the dollar value of assets sold and replaced by the average total assets. Funds with high turnover could have high realized capital gains, which makes them tax inefficient. If the portfolio is tax-sheltered, tax efficiency might not be a concern. However, if the portfolio is not in a tax shelter, investors might want to consider the tax efficiency of the funds. Turnover is reported in the annual report, prospectus, and semi-annual report as well as in many mutual fund information sources.

Chapter 18 Analyzing Mutual Funds

1. Calculate the total return, standard deviation of returns, CV, Sharpe ratio, and M^2 for OARMX. Compare the answers for OARMX to those found in the chapter for FMAGX and the market benchmark index ^SP500TR.

   The following are risk and return measures for OARMX:

   Total period return = 68.57 percent. To calculate total return with the data in Table 18.1 use the array formula = $PRODUCT(1 + C2{:}C37) - 1$ in Excel.

   Standard Deviation of returns = 3.79 percent. Use = $STDEV.S(C2{:}C37)$.

   $CV = \sigma_p/r_p = 0.0379/0.6857 = 0.0553.$

   Sharpe ratio = $(r_p - r_f)/\sigma_p = (0.6857 - 0.0007)/0.0379 = 18.0739$ to calculate r_f with the data in Table 18.1 use the array formula = $PRODUCT(1 + E2{:}E37) - 1$ in Excel.

   $M^2 = \sigma_m(S_p - S_m) = 0.0365(18.075 - 16.503) = M^2 = 5.56$ percent.

OARMX has a higher total return than FMAGX and SP500TR. OARMX's standard deviation is less than FMAGX and greater than the standard deviation of SP500TR. OARMX has the lowest (best) CV ratio and highest (best) Sharpe ratio. OARMX also has a positive M^2, which is much better than the negative M^2 for FMAGX.

2. Use a single factor CAPM regression analysis to calculate Jensen's alpha and beta for OARMX.

Regression Statistics

Multiple R	0.982913152
R Square	0.966118264
Adjusted R Square	0.965121743
Standard Error	0.007080195
Observations	36

ANOVA

	df	*SS*	*MS*	*F*	*Significance F*
Regression	1	0.048599748	0.048599748	969.490501	1.41087E-26
Residual	34	0.001704392	5.01292E-05		
Total	35	0.05030414			

	Coefficients	*Standard Error*	*t Stat*	*P-value*	*Lower 95%*	*Upper 95%*	*Lower 95.0%*	*Upper 95.0%*
Intercept	0.001727108	0.001257826	1.373089368	0.178713042	−0.000829103	0.004283319	−0.000829103	0.004283319
Mkt-RF	1.00194485	0.032178963	31.13664242	1.41087E-26	0.93654933	1.06734037	0.93654933	1.06734037

OARMX Alpha: 0.001727108
OARMX Beta: 1.00194485

3. Use the beta from the CAPM regression analysis to calculate the Treynor ratio for OARMX. Compare this Treynor ratio to those in the chapter found for FMAGX and the market index ^SP500TR.

The Treynor ratio for OARMX is $(0.68572 - 0.00070)/1.00194 = 0.6850$. Thus, OARMX has a higher (better) Treynor ratio than FMAGX and SP500TR.

4. Discuss the meaning and significance of the Jensen's alpha for OARMX and whether OARMX's management team added value.

The alpha of the regression model is Jensen's alpha, which measures abnormal performance above and beyond the market proxy. In this case, the alpha is positive but insignificant suggesting that OARMX does not underperform or outperform the market on a risk-adjusted basis over the 36-month holding period.

5. Use the four-factor regression approach for OARMX to calculate the Carhart alpha and factor loadings for *Mkt – RF, SMB, HML,* and momentum.

The following table contains the Carhart four-factor regression output from Excel for OARMX. Alpha is the coefficient labeled *Intercept*. Alpha represents the risk-adjusted abnormal return. The factor loadings or coefficients on each of the Carhart factors show the level of the fund's different risk characteristics.

Regression Statistics

Multiple R	0.989421135
R Square	0.978954182
Adjusted R Square	0.976238592
Standard Error	0.005843915
Observations	36

ANOVA

	df	*SS*	*MS*	*F*	*Significance F*
Regression	4	0.049245448	0.012311362	360.4941724	1.65151E-25
Residual	31	0.001058692	3.41513E-05		
Total	35	0.05030414			

	Coefficients	*Standard Error*	*t Stat*	*P-value*	*Lower 95%*	*Upper 95%*	*Lower 95.0%*	*Upper 95.0%*
Intercept	0.001956158	0.00109284	1.789977635	0.083230457	−0.000272703	0.004185019	−0.000272703	0.004185019
Mkt-RF	0.97778965	0.033612403	29.09014435	4.54869E-24	0.909236702	1.046342597	0.909236702	1.046342597
SMB	−0.000832131	0.065992148	−0.012609552	0.990020103	−0.135424004	0.133759741	−0.135424004	0.133759741
HML	0.157322807	0.066244005	2.374898799	0.02392385	0.022217269	0.292428346	0.022217269	0.292428346
Mom	−0.123176981	0.039447836	−3.122528193	0.003867159	−0.203631374	−0.042722588	−0.203631374	−0.042722588

OARMX Carhart Alpha: 0.001956158

6. Discuss the direction and significance of the Carhart alpha and factor loadings and whether OARMX's management team added value.

   Using the Carhart model, the alpha is now both positive and significant. This result suggests that OARMX management outperformed the market on a risk-adjusted basis. The coefficient on *Mkt – RF* is close to one and significant, which suggests that OARMX held a portfolio of similar market risk relative to the overall market. The *SMB* coefficient is very close to zero and only slightly negative and statistically insignificant. The positive and significant loading on *HML* is consistent with a more value-oriented portfolio. Finally, the negative and significant coefficient on the momentum factor suggests the portfolio tends to hold non-momentum stocks.

Chapter 19 Predicting Mutual Fund Performance

1. Identify the factors that are most likely to predict fund outperformance.

   Evidence shows that several factors are likely to predict fund outperformance. First, when investing in small cap mutual funds (i.e., funds that hold small company stocks), the smaller the fund size, the better is the performance. The reason is that a small-sized fund can invest all of its money in its best ideas because the fund's positions will not influence the price of those stocks. The fund's small size allows the fund to take the optimal amount of the stock. Conversely, a large-sized fund cannot invest in small company stocks without taking very large positions that might affect the stock's price and thus hurt fund performance. Large funds also might have to take bigger positions in the stock than optimal.

   Second, funds with redemption fees seem to have better performance. The main reason for this positive relationship is that the redemption fee allows funds to hold lower amounts of cash. Rather than holding cash, the fund puts more money into investments that outperform cash over the long run.

   Third, the very short-term past (i.e., the past six months) of performance appears to predict better future short-term performance (i.e., about six months into the future). The reason for this is that some momentum in stock returns occurs. Hence, strong recent past performance seems to carry forward for short period of time.
2. Explain the term *active share* and why it might predict future performance.

   Active share shows the difference in a fund's portfolio from its underlying index. It might predict performance because actively managed funds need to differ from their benchmark index to outperform. However, a Vanguard study shows that active share did not predict future outperformance between 2001 and 2011.
3. Discuss how the Regulation Fair Disclosure Act of 2000 affected fund family size and mutual fund performance.

   Using samples with data ending before 2000, some research finds that funds in large fund families have better performance. However, more recent evidence shows that after implementing the Regulation Fair Disclosure Act of 2000, fund family size is no longer significantly related to fund performance. This research suggests that a larger fund family's ability to outperform resulted from selective disclosures of information. After implementing the Act, large fund families do not have an informational advantage over other funds and thus this ability to outperform diminished.
4. Discuss whether some mutual fund managers exhibit skill or luck when they outperform.

   Whether some mutual fund managers exhibit skill or luck when they outperform is unclear. Kosowski, Timmermann, White, and Wermers (2006) and Fama and French (2010) illustrate this frustration. These authors examine the question of the degree to which mutual fund outperformance is due to manager skill as opposed to luck. Kosowski et al. examine 25 years of mutual fund data and find outperformance is not solely due to luck. That is, sampling variability cannot explain outperformance. Instead, they find that some mutual fund managers truly have skill. If investors can identify and invest in these managers, their portfolios are likely to outperform. The results also imply that some managers are worth paying higher fees for their skills. Conversely, using somewhat different techniques and time periods than Kosowski et al., Fama and French find that few funds show evidence of manager skill. Instead, outperformance, if it exists at all, is based more on luck than skill. If fund performance rarely reflects managerial skill, then the search to find a winning fund is much harder, if not impossible.

Chapter 20 Evaluating Mutual Fund Performance within the Stochastic Discount Factor Approach

1. Describe the stochastic discount factor approach to evaluating mutual fund performance.

   The stochastic discount factor approach to fund performance stems from the fundamental pricing equation $p_{it} = E(m_{t+1}x_{it+1}|Z_t)$. Chen and Knez (1996) develop the relevant framework. Consider an uninformed investor who trades in the N assets using Z_t and a fund manager who trades in the N primitive assets using information set Ω_t, which includes Z_t. Where the uninformed investor does not use any public information, Z_t is a constant and Chen and Knez show that the unconditional performance of the fund is given by $\alpha_p = E(m_{t+1}R_{pt+1}) - 1$. Where α_p is zero, the fund has neutral performance. When α_p is positive (negative), the fund is interpreted as having superior (inferior) performance. When uninformed investors use public information, the fund's conditional performance is given by $\alpha_{pt} = E(m_{t+1}R_{pt+1}|Z_t) - 1$. Ferson, Henry, and Kisgen (2006a) and DeSouza and Lynch (2012) provide alternative approaches to model a fund's conditional performance as a function of Z_t.
2. Evaluate the alternative approaches used to estimate stochastic discount factors to evaluate fund performance.

   Two main approaches use stochastic discount factor models to evaluate fund performance. The first approach is to use a stochastic discount factor from a specific asset pricing model such as the CAPM or consumption CAPM. The main downside of this approach is that the model might be inadmissible, which means it assigns non-zero performance to passive trading strategies involving no skill. The second approach is to use a stochastic discount factor based on weaker economic restrictions than a full parametric asset pricing model such as the LOP and NA restrictions as in Chen and Knez (1996), or the good-deal bounds in Chretien and Kammoun (2013). The downside of this approach is that the resulting admissible stochastic discount factor used in one set of primitive assets might be inadmissible in a different set of primitive assets.
3. Discuss the weight-based performance measures of Ferson and Mo (2013).

   Ferson (2013a) shows that when having access to the portfolio weights of the fund, then $\alpha_{pt} = cov(m_{t+1}\, R_t'x(\Omega_t)|Z_t)$. If Z_t is a constant, then $\alpha_p = cov(m_{t+1}\, R_{t+1}'x(\Omega_t))$. Ferson and Mo (2013) develop the first weight-based performance measures using the stochastic discount factor approach to provide a decomposition of overall fund performance into different components. The authors assume a linear factor model for the stochastic discount factor and show that $\alpha_p = aCov(w'r_B) - b'E[(r_B r_B' - E(r_B r_B))w] + E[(a - b'r_B)x'v]$. The first term captures the fund's level timing ability for the K factors (α_m). The second term captures the fund's volatility timing ability for the K factors (α_σ). The last term captures the fund's stock selection ability (α_s).

4. Discuss empirical results from mutual fund performance studies using the stochastic discount factor approach.

   The empirical findings of studies using the stochastic discount factor suggest that the average fund does not provide significant value added to investors and the number of funds with significant superior performance is small. These results are similar to regression-based studies but with some differences. First, fund performance appears less sensitive to the stochastic discount factor model used compared to regression-based studies. Second, even for linear factor models, important differences can occur in performance between the two approaches.

   Using the stochastic discount factor approach to evaluate fund performance shows that fund performance is more favorable when accounting for investor heterogeneity or using performance measures based on weaker economic restrictions. These studies suggest that funds add value for at least one clientele of investors.

Chapter 21 Mutual Fund Risk

1. Describe the main points of financial due diligence for a mutual fund.

   Financial due diligence reports market-based mutual fund risks. The mutual fund risk quantification is assessed based on ex post and ex ante returns, which aid in understanding the risk-return drivers (risk factors), how mutual funds behave over time conditional on market dynamics (risk dynamics), and the performance in both negative and positive market scenarios (market-timing ability). Financial due diligence analytically examines mutual funds from various risk perspectives to provide sufficient information needed by actual and potential clients to correctly evaluate past performance and thus form expectation on future risk-return dynamics.

2. Discuss how to quantitatively decompose mutual fund risks.

   Mutual fund risks are quantitatively decomposed using two main approaches: portfolio returns (*return-based analysis*) and portfolio weights (*portfolio weight-based analysis*). The main objective of the return-based analysis is to decompose the *total risk* of mutual fund, expressed in terms of return volatility, through a benchmark-based analysis. Mutual fund performance is evaluated relative to style investing benchmarks and in turn permits computing *active risk* (or *tracking error*), which is the volatility of the excess performance relative to the benchmark's returns. Through portfolio weight-based analysis, mutual fund risks are decomposed by conducting performance attribution analysis. Such analysis attributes the excess return of the mutual fund to three main components for each main asset class: (1) allocation, which is computed based on different portfolio allocation of mutual fund compared to the benchmark; (2) selection, which is based on different returns received by the same asset class of mutual fund and the benchmark; and

(3) interaction between allocation and selection, which cannot be attributed to the sole allocation or selection effects.

3. Identify the elements of an effective risk-mapping strategy for mutual funds.

   An effective risk-mapping strategy for mutual funds should show a hierarchical structure with the following levels (dimensions) of risk: (1) fund-specific risk dimensions including equity-based mutual funds (e.g., geographic market location and industry sectors), fixed-income-based mutual funds (e.g., geographic market location, government bonds, and corporate bonds, which are also known as *spread bonds*); (2) curve risks; (3) swap spread risk; and (4) overall risk dimensions including currency risk and investment style.

4. Discuss the rationale behind the methodology called "swing pricing."

   Swing pricing is a common practice used in mutual funds to treat equally subscribing/redeeming investors and continuing investors. Swing price is a temporary adjustment in the NAV applying only to subscribing or redeeming investors who are the only ones who bear the portfolio unwinding costs. The adjustment process protects investors who remain invested in the fund.

Chapter 22 Organization, Structure, and Services of Mutual Funds

1. Describe how a mutual fund is organized, its legal and contractual relationships, and the motivation that drives this structure.

   Because a mutual fund is an independent legal entity, it creates and maintains contracts with many parties. Shareholders provide capital to the fund. The fund has a board of directors or trustees that acts and serves to protect the interests of the shareholders. The board hires the investment management company, which has the responsibility to invest the shareholders' capital in a manner consistent with the mutual fund's stated objectives, in an efficient and productive way. The mutual fund hires other organizations to provide services for its shareholders or related to the securities and assets held by the fund. These organizations provide services related to job roles including the fund administrator, underwriter, transfer agent, and custodian. This structure has historically been optimal because it segregates the relationships so that the fund maintains its independence from those hired to support the fund, including the investment advisor. This structure works well when the fund's board of directors follows the legal guidelines and takes its responsibilities seriously.

2. Explain how a fund's board is structured including the most important decisions that its members make.

   Depending on how the fund is structured, the fund's board of directors or trustees legally contains a set of independent directors and a set of "insider" directors. The board's decisions having the greatest impact involve hiring and monitoring the performance and cost of the fund's investment advisors. The board also approves other contracts and ensures the fund complies with the law. The board uses subcommittees to create and maintain controls, supervise, monitor, and evaluate the fund's contractual obligations.

3. Identify the most critical services offered by mutual funds and fund complexes.

   Historically, mutual funds offered middle-class investors the opportunity to invest in securities and markets they could not access themselves, using a method that is both low-cost and effective from the standpoint of access and diversification. More recently, mutual funds and fund families have enhanced product offerings to provide more choices to investors and to improve diversification. These products include OEF opportunities with various load structures and ETFs. Mutual funds and their research analysts use quantitative research strategies to meld portfolio strategy with investor optimization, particularly in horizon or risk-based mutual funds. They also use behavioral questionnaires to identify investor risk tolerances and objective structures. Finally, mutual funds use an integrated account management framework to improve customer service, create and maintain customer loyalty, and optimize performance on an after-tax basis.

4. Discuss the major conclusions of studies that analyze the structure of a fund's board and fund management with respect to performance.

   Regarding the legal structure of the mutual fund vis-à-vis its contractual counterparts, the research evidence is mixed. The theory is sound as long as the parties operate in an independent and objective manner, but the evidence reveals that this assumption is not always the case and performance of the shareholders might suffer. Boards that are more independent and boards of larger fund families more quickly respond to underperformance. Fund complexes tend to focus either on low-cost or high-service target investor segments, but not both. Brokers might not provide a level of benefits to match their costs. Fund management structured as teams seems to produce superior performance or risk characteristics, especially for team-managed funds that also have a more independent board structure. The structure of their management teams, especially if they are more hierarchical, could also affect bond fund performance.

5. Identify the most likely key drivers of a mutual fund's structure and services in the future.

   Mutual fund families operate in a constrained market environment. Regulation and tax strategy will continue to push fund companies to provide information-technology-driven solutions to match specific client needs and provide a more improved tax alpha strategy. As the understanding of behavioral investing increases, funds will deploy more psychology-based approaches to stress test investors' appetites for risk. Although not a primary focus of this chapter, mutual fund firms will need to maintain the trust of investors whose patience has been strained by the financial market difficulties that stoked the recent recession, especially if they are to be considered in the same category as banks, mortgage companies, or insurance firms.

   The availability and analysis of quality data, especially when measuring and assessing portfolio metrics such as tail risk and downside deviation will be accompanied by the need to quantify event risk, political risk, and macroeconomic uncertainty. The mutual fund structure will likely become more democratized and advances in crowdfunding, which has until now focused on new ventures, migrates into broader financial markets and infrastructure. Administrative back-office operations will become leaner as electronic warehousing, transactions, and shareholder reporting and tracking are more seamless, and this will be replaced by more information technology security administration. Globalization of funds will be driven by the openness of foreign markets and the degree to which overseas middle-class growth occurs coupled with societal acceptance of equity market risk and foreign governments' willingness to move long-term savings onto the marketplace through corporate pension plans and tax incentives.

Chapter 23 Selected Topics in Mutual Fund Distribution

1. List the five primary channels of distribution and indicate which channels are direct.
   The five primary channels of distribution are (1) direct, (2) advice, (3) retirement plan, (4) supermarket, and (5) institutional. Direct and institutional channels are considered to be direct.
2. Discuss the motivation for adopting Rule 12b-1 fees.
   Many funds, especially smaller ones, experienced prolonged periods of net share redemptions. The fund industry argued that spending fund assets to promote fund share sales could benefit shareholders by increasing fund size, providing fund economies of scale, and reducing expenses (expense ratios).
3. Identity the two most common uses of 12b-1 fees.
   The two most common uses of 12b-1 fees are broker compensation for continual customer account service and broker compensation for initial fund share sales.
4. Explain the greatest irony in fund use of 12b-1 fees.
   Fund managers continue to charge 12b-1 fees even when their funds are closed to new investors. If new shares of these funds are not being distributed, why do fund managers charge distribution fees?

Chapter 24 Mutual Fund Disclosure and Related Fund Investor Protection Features

1. Compare and contrast disclosure regulation for mutual funds versus conventional public companies.
   Mutual fund disclosure entails similar offering disclosure and periodic reporting requirements to those required for conventional public companies. Mutual funds file registration statements, provide investors with prospectuses, and disseminate annual and semi-annual reports. However, the purpose of disclosure differs between conventional public companies and mutual funds. Disclosure for conventional public companies causes information to be disseminated into public markets, aiding markets in finding appropriate prices for securities. In contrast, mutual fund disclosure has no effect on the market price of fund shares because they are sold and redeemed at the NAV per share. The SEC has changed fund

disclosure requirements to make fund disclosure more relevant to the needs of average retail investors by helping them to make informed choices about funds, compare competing funds based on standardized quantitative and qualitative information, and evaluate fund investments on a continuing basis. In this sense, mutual fund disclosure serves as an investor protection function analogous to consumer protection.

2. Explain whether mutual fund investors ever pay an unfair price for their shares in the fund. If not, discuss why disclosure regulation is necessary.

    Mutual fund investors never pay an unfair price for their shares because they are sold and redeemed at the NAV per share. Mutual fund disclosure enables average retail investors to make more informed choices relating to funds based on objectives and investment strategies, risk, costs, past performance, and other attributes of ownership.

3. Describe how ordinary retail investor behavior may depart from rational investment decision-making in choosing among funds to invest.

    Retail investors suffer from bounded rationality and behavioral biases. They also lack sufficient financial knowledge to meaningfully or reliably differentiate among actively managed funds. Retail investors chase short-term performance despite a lack of empirical assurance of continued or superior performance in the future. They frequently stick with their original selection decisions, even in the face of information that calls into question the basis of their original decision. Finally, retail investors appear to underappreciate the importance of fund expenses as a determinant of long-term fund performance relative to peer funds.

4. Explain whether an equity fund is likely to use performance figures in a print advertisement if marketing an equity fund with a high relative 1-year total return, but with low or negative 5- and 10-year total return figures.

    Under these circumstances, the equity fund would likely not use performance figures in a print advertisement. Because the fund would have to reveal the 1-, 5-, and 10-year performance figures, the negative 5- and 10-year figures would likely discourage prospective investors and especially any rational investor. Accordingly, a fund in these circumstances is unlikely to use performance figures in its marketing.

5. Discuss differences between prescriptive regulation (e.g., disclosure requirements) and remedial regulation (e.g., prohibitions on fraud).

    Prescriptive regulation, such as disclosure requirements, is mandated regulation intended to work prospectively in ensuring that investors receive certain types of information before investing. Ideally, such regulation would reduce the ability of funds to make sales on less than complete information and equip investors to make more informed investment selection decisions. In contrast, *remedial regulation* provides investors with recourse retroactively when funds have engaged in improper conduct. Such regulation might afford investors who have been deceived with a remedy. The prospect of damage liability could act as a deterrent for funds. Liability and the possibility of law enforcement sanctions incentivize funds to engage in precautionary behavior to prevent false or misleading disclosure.

Chapter 25 New Developments in Exchange-Traded Funds

1. Discuss the costs associated with investing in ETFs.

   Three costs are typically associated with investing in ETFs: fund operating expenses, brokerage commissions, and the bid-ask spread.

   - *Fund operating expenses.* ETFs charge annual fees to cover operating expenses such as advisory services, administration, and record-keeping. These expenses are expressed as a percentage of fund assets, called the *expense ratio*. ETFs have lower total expense ratios than retail share classes of comparable mutual funds.
   - *Brokerage commissions.* ETF investors must buy and sell ETF shares through a broker who is typically compensated for this service. Some brokers charge a flat fee for each transaction while others could assess a fee based on the total assets in the investor's account.
   - *Bid-ask spread.* When buying and selling ETF shares on the secondary market, a difference exists between the highest price a buyer will pay for an ETF shares (the *bid*) and the lowest price a seller will accept to sell an ETF share (the *ask*). Bid-ask spreads are typically lower for larger ETFs and those that are heavily traded and or highly liquid.

2. Explain four factors that investors should consider when selecting ETFs.

   Investors should consider the following four factors when selecting ETFs: performance, liquidity, size, and tracking error.

   - *Performance.* Although past performance does not show how an ETF might perform in the future, it shows how effectively a fund manager has performed relative to his or her benchmark index. A potential investor may want to evaluate an ETF's performance against its stated objective or benchmark.
   - *Liquidity.* Liquidity refers to how easily investors can buy and sell shares without changing the price for those shares. Securities with high trading volumes are generally more liquid. Highly liquid ETFs with highly liquid underlying securities typically have narrower bid-ask spreads than ETFs that trade less or hold less liquid securities.
   - *Size.* Small ETFs target niche markets such as emerging market economies or precious metal commodities. Due to the difficulty of entering such sectors, these ETFs charge front-end load fees and their total expense ratios are usually higher than other ETFs. Conversely, large established ETFs are diversified in their index composition and usually have lower total expense ratios due to managing a large asset base.
   - *Tracking error.* Tracking error shows the difference between the ETF performance from the index performance. ETF operators choose three different options through which they replicate an index. Most ETFs use direct replication in which exact weighting of all the index components forms the ETF portfolio. Sampling involves selecting a representative portfolio composition from the index

components. Synthetic replication is swap based and the ETF shares do not have to correspond to the index. The deviations could emanate from index rebalancing. The larger the negative tracking error, the less appealing an ETF is to potential investors.

3. Discuss various investment roles played by ETFs.

   Some ETFs could be cross-listed on several stock exchanges allowing investors to access geographically protected markets without physical presence. Institutional investors could invest in an ETF as a way to gain interim exposure to a market while gradually investing directly in that market. Core portfolio composition allows investors to gain long-term or short-term exposure to reputable firms at low costs. By contrast, satellite composition allows investors to gain access to niche or restricted sectors, such as precious metals, at premium rates. Investors gauge their risk-return trade-off based on their risk profiles.
4. Discuss the most popular forms of ETF investment strategies.

   ETFs are broadly categorized on the basis of their investment strategies. Most invest in equities, bonds, and commodities. Certain commodities such as coffee depend on the forces of supply and demand for price determination, whereas the price of gold does not. Investing in an ETF offering a substantial weighting to oil products could be pro-cyclical as the prices of energy products are determined through demand and supply parameters. A negative correlation exists between the returns from equities and commodities making these commodities portfolio stabilizers. While most ETFs are passively managed based on mathematical formulas, some are actively managed involving human intervention. ETFs are also categorized by geographical location.

Chapter 26 Ethical Standards in Mutual Funds

1. Explain why ethics is important in finance.

   Ethics must be present in finance because it represents a "moral tension" that spurs the adoption of behavioral criteria to improve the propriety of behavior in financial trading. Ethics is considered a component of human consciousness and represents a set of principles and components shared by civil society. The cultural melting pot that underpins the rapport between ethics and economics is rooted in the history of humanity. The moral behavior of man, the necessity for ethics disengaged from any external finality, formulated on a rigorous sense of duty and respect for the liberty of others, has been the object of reference for the greatest philosophers of Western civilization. Ethics in financial trading leads to using financial resources responsibly. Efficient financial management can be viewed in terms of social responsibility. This framework is important in assessing the management of financial assets that has to guarantee a minimum return to all stakeholders. Ethics in financial trading spurs development of a responsibility process among all the parties interested in financial assets. Furthermore, ethics in financial trading spurs respect of transparency of financial assets while maintaining public trust. Ethical behavior in finance, aside from safeguarding those who consume its products, strives to have a positive impact on its customers' lives. Ethics in finance guarantees a sustainable financial future based on economic growth and real improvement in living conditions.

2. Discuss the ethical standards of transparency, trust, and social responsibility for mutual funds.

   In adopting principles of transparency, mutual funds are concerned with acting ethically and not harming investors. Transparency allows customers to choose to invest their money in the manner most consistent with their personal objectives and values. Transparency enables the development of efficient financial markets. This process explains why the norms governing mutual funds are intended to guarantee maximum transparency. Investing in mutual funds involves trust because managers of the mutual funds have a fiduciary responsibility to act in the best interest of their clients. The fiduciary relationship entails the investment advisor's assuming the agent's obligations and responsibilities. The investment advisor has to invest and vote in the exclusive interest of the mutual fund's investors. This duty explains why U.S. norms establish the rules governing disclosure requirements by mutual funds to address investment companies' fiduciary responsibility to their investors. Some mutual funds follow the ethical standard of social responsibility. In seeking to satisfy the investment goals of a pool of investors, they also seek to affect the financial well-being of the community. In fact, mutual funds should adopt socially responsible behavior, monitoring, and responding to the economic, environmental, and social expectations of all stakeholders. Consequently, the financial well-being of the community generates credibility in mutual funds.

3. Discuss the implications if mutual funds do not adopt ethical standards.

   Asset management poses problems of conflicts of interest that should be reduced and managed appropriately. A fundamental problem is that fund managers are tempted to perform operations that are more beneficial to their business than to their investors. Conflicts of interest generally induce fund managers to assume unethical behaviors (e.g., in securities selecting or in portfolio management). This relationship explains why various countries have different forms of self-discipline to stimulate the recovery of ethical standards in mutual funds.

4. Identify two actions to mitigate conflicts of interest from asset management.

   Two main actions are available to mitigate conflicts of interest: (1) public interventions aimed at reducing or eliminating conflicts of interest and (2) dissemination of knowledge on ethics and the education of financial managers on ethics. The first action usually involves tightening financial market's rules and regulations with supervisory interventions. The rules can either penalize those managers who exploit the conflicts of interest to their own advantage or promote new internal organizational models of investment companies (independence of roles and separation of departments) to contain the conflicts. The second action involves teaching mutual fund managers about ethics. The knowledge of ethics in finance re-establishes a practice of evaluating interest in a collective rather than individual context. Ethics in finance recovers and reasserts the social nature of finance. Education in ethics makes improper behavior less likely. An efficient financial system will be possible with the rigorous development of an ethical framework in finance.

5. Explain why mutual funds should adopt ethical standards.

   Adopting ethical standards allows mutual funds to be successful because their investment logic is the closest to the theoretical model that leads to the allocative efficiency of financial markets and social responsibility in finance. Five reasons for mutual funds to adopt ethical standards are:

- *Affordability*. Mutual funds are available to investors with limited initial capital, which allows them to take advantage of financial investments from which they would normally be precluded.
- *Information availability*. Mutual funds provide information that is often unavailable to ordinary investors.
- *Diversification*. Mutual funds manage a pool of financial resources that allows investment in securities that would otherwise be inaccessible to individual investors.
- *Cost reduction*. Through economies of scale, mutual funds can reduce transaction costs, fees, and expenses.
- *Liquidity*. Liquidity is a specific condition for protecting investors. Mutual fund investors can easily redeem their shares at any time, for the current NAV plus any redemption fees.

Chapter 27 Mutual Funds in Emerging and Developing Markets

1. Contrast the growth of the EMMFs to the market for mutual funds in developed markets.

   Since 2003, the U.S. mutual fund market has grown at an annual growth rate of 7.33 percent. Likewise, worldwide growth between 2003 and 2013 has been around 7 percent. In contrast, EMMFs have grown at an annual growth rate of 15.86 percent. The faster growth rate in emerging markets is partly because these markets continue to be a relatively smaller segment of the global mutual fund industry. The U.S. mutual fund market is nearly seven times the size of the all EMMFs combined. In 2013, the combined assets of mutual funds in the United States grew to $15.02 trillion with nearly 9,000 funds available to investors. In contrast, the emerging markets of Brazil, Chile, Mexico, Czech Republic, Greece, Hungary, Poland, China, India, South Korea, Philippines, Taiwan, and South Africa attracted $2.31 trillion in mutual fund investments.
2. Outline the most effective models for evaluating the performance of emerging market funds.

   Evaluating the performance of EMMFs is similar to that for domestic funds. However, the choice of benchmark index differs for EMMFs compared to domestic funds. The most common method is to use a single index model where the model computes Jensen's alpha using the most appropriate benchmark index. Such a model regresses the excess return (i.e., the difference between fund return and risk-free rate) of the funds with the excess return of the index. If the intercept or alpha is statistically significant, the fund outperformed its benchmark index:

$$\left(R_{i,t} - R_{f,t}\right) = \alpha_i + \beta_1 \left(R_{index,t} - R_{f,t}\right) + \varepsilon_{i,t}.$$

Multifactor modes are more appropriate, such as the one below:

$$\left(R_{i,t} - R_{f,t}\right) = \alpha_i + \beta_1 \left(R_{index,t} - R_{f,t}\right) + \beta_2 \left(SMB_t\right) + \beta_3 \left(HML_t\right) + \beta_4 \left(PR1YR_t\right) + \varepsilon_{i,t},$$

where SMB_t captures the stock return performance of small firms relative to large firms; HML_t is the relative return of value and growth stocks; and $PR1YR_t$ is a momentum factor computed as the difference in returns of prior-year high- and low-return portfolios. Similar to the single index model, the alpha in this model also measures the extent of outperformance. However, evaluating a hedge fund using a multifactor model requires further tweaking to add factors that affect hedge funds such as size spread factor, the spread between large cap and small cap index, bond-oriented factors, and factors that track market trends in currencies and commodities. Performance can also be determined using the *Sharpe ratio*, which is the ratio of the excess fund return divided by standard deviation of the fund returns.

3. Contrast the risk-adjusted performance of EMMFs to those in developed markets such as the United States.

   Results from a 2013 study of open-ended mutual funds in 27 countries, including eight that are part of MSCI's Emerging Market Index, show important differences between factors explaining mutual fund performance. U.S. funds are much larger than those in emerging markets given the difference that exists in the maturity of the industry between locations. Country characteristics, such as economic development, financial development, quality of legal institutions and law enforcement, and mutual fund industry structure, affect the performance of EMMFs. Globally, equity mutual funds underperform, on average, by 20 basis points per quarter after fees. The diseconomies of scale that are present in the United States are also reinforced in EMMFs. However, this finding is not universal because diminishing returns to scale do not seem to affect non-U.S. funds and international funds. U.S. funds generally invest in small and illiquid stocks. This observation is not the case for non-U.S. funds. Scale does not adversely affect the performance of international funds even for those funds located in the United States.

   The average return for EMMFs is 7.38 percent, which is larger than the average returns of 3.18 percent for the four largest markets for mutual funds (i.e., the United States, Canada, United Kingdom, and Germany). Alpha is computed on the basis of the Carhart four-factor model and shows that the average alpha for emerging markets is 0.36 implying EMMFs outperform their benchmarks, while the alpha for developed markets is –0.18, implying that developed market funds underperform their benchmarks.

4. Identify the factors that best explain the performance of EMMFs.

   For EMMFs, the expense ratio is the only significant predictor of future fund performance. The expense ratio is negatively and significantly related to fund performance. This result is similar to that found for domestic funds. Funds with lower expenses tend to perform better than those with higher expenses. Other factors such as turnover, manager tenure, and net asset size do not predict fund performance. Evidence for persistence in fund performance also exists. Funds that are winners in a particular period tend to do well in the near future. Investors in EMMFs can take advantage of this persistence in fund performance, also termed as the "hot hands effect."

5. Discuss why hedge funds in emerging markets are gaining popularity and the factors that can best explain their performance.

   Unlike open-ended mutual funds, hedge funds use dynamic trading strategies. They often leverage their portfolios by using margin trading, short sales, or derivatives. In other words, hedge funds engage in far more risky strategies, partly because they are subject to less regulation. Increasing systematic risk allows hedge funds to generate higher returns. This ability to generate higher returns attracts investors into hedge funds in general. Emerging market hedge funds exhibit superior abilities to time the market, partly due to the inherent market efficiencies that characterize emerging markets. Studies show that emerging market hedge funds have superior performance against their benchmarks, particularly the MSCI equity index.

Chapter 28 Performance of Global Mutual Funds

1. Explain why an alpha measure based on the domestic CAPM model is inappropriate for assessing the stock selection ability of a global mutual fund manager. Indicate in which situations an alpha measure based on the world CAPM can give accurate estimates.

   Since global mutual funds invest in assets around the world, their returns are expected to correlate with the broad market rather than the domestic market. Thus, computing the fund's alpha measure based on the domestic portfolio might not capture all its systematic risk, and therefore could misprice the manager's stock selection ability. Alpha measures based on the world CAPM can correctly assess the performance of global mutual funds under two conditions: (1) international financial markets are fully integrated and (2) purchasing power parity (PPP) holds.
2. U.S. global mutual funds hold assets denominated in foreign currencies. Thus, their dollar returns are exposed to changes in the value of foreign currencies against the U.S. dollar. Identify a situation in which currency risk becomes a priced risk factor.

   When PPP collapses, currency risk should be priced into international asset returns. In this case, to assess the performance of a global fund manager, the alpha measure should be computed based on an international asset pricing model that includes both the market portfolio and currency risk factors.
3. Identify two ways to consider currency risk in an alpha measure based on an international asset pricing model.

   Two ways are available to include currency risk in an alpha measure based on an international asset pricing model: (1) currency risk can be broken down into a separate factor for each foreign currency and (2) it can be approximated by a single factor that proxies for the overall change in the foreign exchange rates against the domestic currency.
4. Describe the difference between the world CAPM with a currency risk factor model and a two-factor IAPT model.

   The world CAPM with a currency risk model is an international asset pricing model that includes both the market portfolio and currency risk factors. A two-factor IAPT model also contains two factors but these factors are extracted from a wider set by performing principal component analysis.

5. Indicate two situations in which an alpha measure based on the global three-factor model, which includes the world market portfolio, global size, and value factors, may fail to correctly estimate the stock selection ability of a global equity fund manager.

   An alpha measure based on the global three-factor model might misprice the stock selection skill of a global equity fund manager if:

   - A fund manager tilts the portfolio toward emerging markets stocks. These stocks display exposures to local factors rather than global factors. In this case, the performance of the fund manager will be more accurately assessed by using local factors instead of global factors.
   - A fund manager takes advantage of passive index momentum strategies such as country and sector index momentum strategies. The global three-factor model does not capture these passive strategies. In this case, the fund manager's performance should be assessed using a five-factor model that includes country and sector index momentum factors in addition to the three global factors.

6. Discuss three types of global equity fund managers' timing skills.

   Global equity fund managers have three types of timing skills. First, traditional world market timing concerns the ability of fund managers to anticipate global equity market movements and to adjust their portfolios' exposures to global equities accordingly. Second, national market-timing skill reflects the ability of fund managers to successfully shift their portfolios from national markets with low expected returns to those with high expected returns. Third, global fund managers might be able to successfully shift their portfolios between the domestic equity market and foreign equity markets.

Chapter 29 Performance of Exchange-Traded Funds

1. Discuss two factors that affect the performance of ETFs.

   Two factors affecting the performance of ETFs are tracking error and market liquidity. *Tracking error* is the difference between the returns of the ETF and its reference index or asset. A nonzero tracking error represents a failure to replicate the reference as stated in the ETF prospectus. *Market liquidity* is the degree to which an asset or security can be bought or sold in the market without affecting the asset's price. Liquidity is characterized by a high level of trading activity. Inventors combine the stock exchange that matches up the best features of the liquidity of securities markets and the flexibility and valuation transparency.
2. Discuss two factors used to measure the efficiency of ETFs.

   Two factors used to measure the efficiency of ETFs are directly comparing how ETFs handle costs and on-tracking costs. The daily rebalancing that occurs with index funds due to net redemptions results in explicit costs in the form of commissions and implicit costs in the form of bid-ask spreads. Moreover, ETFs have the unique process of in-kind creation/redemption that avoids these transaction costs. Because ETFs trade on an exchange, each transaction is generally subject to brokerage costs.

   On-tracking costs can be divided into management fees and shareholder and transaction costs. Management fees are generally lower for ETFs than mutual funds because ETFs are not responsible for the fund accounting. For index funds, the two major types of fees are transaction fees and the fees included in the fund's expense ratio.

3. Define the Sortino and Omega ratios and discuss their value in assessing ETF performance.

   The *Sortino ratio* is a performance ratio that replaces standard deviation in the Sharpe ratio with downside deviation. The *Omega ratio* is the weighted gain/loss ratio relative to the threshold *r*. It splits the returns into two subparts according to a threshold, where the "good" returns are above the threshold and the "bad" returns are below it.

4. Define the single index model and discuss its effectiveness in assessing performance of international ETFs.

   The single index model written in excess returns form is:

$$R_{it} - R_{ft} = a_i^1 + \beta_{mi}^1 \left(R_{mt} - R_{ft}\right) + e_i,$$

   where R_{it} is the return on fund *i* the month *t*; R_{ft} is the return on a risk-free asset in month *t*; and R_{mt} is the market return in month *t*. Here, the expected excess return (i.e., the return above the risk-free rate) is the product of the factor weight or factor sensitivity, beta (β_{mi}), and the risk factor, which in this model is the excess return on the market portfolio or market index. The single index model results reveal that between 2001 and 2007, ETFs exhibit higher mean returns, while between the 2008 and 2014, mean returns diminished significantly and in some markets turn negative. The mean returns during the first period imply that ETFs could not outperform the market. ETFs performance has become closer to the properties of the market as evidenced by the R^2 noted in the model results. Between 2008 and 2014, the β_{it} coefficient of factor $R_m - R_{ft}$ rate exceeds a value of one, which confirms the hypothesis that ETFs outperformed the market. The coefficient measures the sensitivity of the return relative to changes in the market return. Thus, a higher β_{it} coefficient might outperform the market more times than a lower β_{it} coefficient.

Chapter 30 Issues, Trends, and Future Developments in the Mutual Fund Industry

1. Define both OEFs and CEFs.

   OEFs are standard mutual funds that maintain a changing portfolio of securities. These funds reinvest all proceeds back into the fund and they can both continuously accept and continuously redeem shares. Investors buy and sell shares for these funds at the fund's NAV. In contrast, CEFs are created based on a fixed number of securities and a fixed number of outstanding shares. CEFs also do not have easily redeemed shares. Instead, their shares are traded in the open market at prices frequently below the fund's liquidation per share.

2. Identify two major reasons for the shift from CEFs to OEFs after the Crash of 1929.

   Two major reasons for the shift in investor demand from CEFs to OEFs after the Crash of 1929 are liquidity and transparency. Investors desired funds with more easily redeemable shares. Many CEFs did not fully disclose how they were levered. Both of these issues caused investors to panic during the crash leaving a bad impression with investors. Although CEFs still exist today, liquidity and transparency continue to curb investor appetites for these funds.

3. Identify the investment fund type that presents the most competition to the mutual fund industry and explain three survival strategies for mutual fund firms.

   ETFs are by far the most formidable competition for mutual funds among the four broad types of investment funds: mutual funds or OEFs, CEFs, UITs, and ETFs. Compared to mutual funds, ETFs offer more tax efficiencies, lower expense ratios, lower 12b-1 marketing fees, exposure to different asset classes, and the added flexibility to liquidate a position before the end of the trading day.

   Mutual fund firms can use three basic strategies to compete with ETFs: joining the ETF market, creating new hybrid products, and increasing operational efficiency. The first strategy follows the mentality "if you can't beat them, join them." In other words, some traditional mutual fund firms accept that ETFs have several favorable features and these firms have decided to create their own ETFs. The second strategy is to form a hybrid product that combines the favorable features of both ETFs and mutual funds. For example, some firms have created ETFs that track their largest mutual funds. The third strategy is to become a leaner more nimble firm, primarily to lower costs. Possible methods for improving efficiency include taking advantage of technological innovations, consolidating overlapping products, and improving risk management practices.

4. Differentiate between a traditional bond fund, target-date fund, and hybrid fund and discuss the role that an aging population is likely to play in the growth of these funds.

   Bond mutual funds are allocated entirely to fixed-income securities. TDFs are allocated based on a combination of securities that automatically rebalance to more conservative assets such as bond funds as the fund approaches and passes the target date. Thus, target funds usually resemble bonds funds over time. Hybrid funds do not have the reallocation feature of TDFs. Instead, a hybrid fund maintains specific percentages of the fund's assets in different securities such as stocks and bonds.

   As a result of an aging population, the cash flow for these funds will most likely increase considering that all three funds have a fixed-income component. Fixed-income funds are traditionally popular with older investors seeking an alternative to volatile equity markets. As U.S. age demographics change, investors are become increasingly interested in retirement-focused funds. TDFs could be the real winners due to the rise of defined contribution plans, which frequently use TDFs as the default option for new investors.

5. Identify the type of mutual fund that has the highest regulatory risk and explain why.

   The 2001 recession and the financial crisis of 2007–2008 have created a sharp increase in regulations for many participants in financial markets such as hedge funds. However, most types of mutual funds escaped jurisdiction from the bulk of these regulations including the Dodd-Frank Wall Street Reform and Consumer Protection Act. The one exception is MMMFs. In 2014, the SEC announced new regulations for MMMFs to mitigate systemic risk in three specific ways. First, the new rules mandate that certain institutional MMMFs make all transactions using a floating NAV. Second, the rules provide flexibility for modifying liquidity fees for shareholders during recessions and other periods of extreme market volatility. Third, the new rules permit using a redemption gate for funds with substantial declines in value.

Although the new regulations for MMMFs will not be implemented until 2016, recent evidence shows that regulations can impact these funds. Prime MMMFs are a good example. Due to the SEC's 2010 amendment to Rule 2a-7, prime MMMFs have operated under stricter liquidity and maturity guidelines for their holdings. As a result, prime MMMFs use more conservative investment practices similar to government MMMFs. Thus, the new rules for MMMFs have increased their regulatory risk.

Index

(Please note: "*t*" designation represents tables; "*f*" designation represents figures)

E

F

M

S

U